HISTORY OF THE GREAT WAR

BASED ON OFFICIAL DOCUMENTS

PRINCIPAL EVENTS
1914—1918

COMPILED BY

THE HISTORICAL SECTION OF THE
COMMITTEE OF IMPERIAL DEFENCE

LONDON:
PRINTED & PUBLISHED BY HIS MAJESTY'S STATIONERY OFFICE
To be purchased through any Bookseller or directly from H.M. STATIONERY OFFICE
at the following addresses: Imperial House, Kingsway, London, W.C. 2, and
28 Abingdon Street, London, S.W. 1; 37 Peter Street, Manchester;
1 St. Andrew's Crescent, Cardiff; and
23 Forth Street, Edinburgh.

1922

Price 10s. 6d. net.

First published by His Majesty's Stationery Office 1922

This edition published 1987 by The London Stamp Exchange Ltd.,
5 Buckingham Street, London WC2

ISBN 0 948 13031 8

Printed & bound by Antony Rowe Ltd, Eastbourne

PREFATORY NOTE.

This record of the events of the Great War is arranged in three Parts.

Part I is a general chronological list, in which all events of political, military or naval importance are entered. The bare facts only have been noted, and no attempt has been made to record the results, except in particular cases.

Part II consists in the main of the same entries as Part I, divided into four sections: "Political," "Military," "Naval" and "Air." The sub-divisions of each section have been printed in parallel columns in order to show the synchronisation of events.

The Military section has been sub-divided into two parts, dealing with the main and subsidiary theatres of war respectively.

Part III contains in general the same entries as Parts I and II, arranged alphabetically, and is designed to enable the date of any known event to be ascertained at once.

Though the entries in the three different Parts are to a great extent the same, each Part serves a different purpose, and need for economy in space has compelled the exclusion of certain of the less important events from one or other of the Parts.

This is particularly the case with regard to the battles and actions in the Eastern Theatre; where, owing to the lack of any Russian official record of events, the German official designations have been adopted. These battle-names are often so unfamiliar, that only the most important are shown in all three Parts; an exhaustive list is, however, contained in Part II.

All the belligerent States engaged in the Western Theatre have produced their own official lists of battles, but these vary so radically, both in regard to dates and nomenclature, that it has been found impossible to combine them in one list. In Part II, therefore, only the main operations of the fighting in this theatre have been included. In Parts I and III a somewhat greater elaboration has been permitted, and all the British and most of the French battle-names have been entered. In order to show the relation between the various official lists, a comparative table, including the German battle-names, has been prepared and appears as an Appendix.

Again, in certain of the minor theatres of war, Part II contains a number of entries which were considered useful in order to complete the record of the sequence of events, but were not considered of sufficient importance for inclusion in Parts I and III.

In Part II certain entries will be found repeated in more than one section—*e.g.*, "Political" entries are often included in the "Military" or "Naval" lists, in order to emphasise the co-relation of events. In these cases events entered in lists other than that to which they normally belong have been, as a rule, printed in italics.

The Permanent Committee on Geographical Names have been consulted with regard to the spelling of names, and their ruling has been accepted. The only exceptions are names which, by common usage, have become familiar in other forms.

In cross references against entries in Parts I and II the date refers to the same month if no month is mentioned, and to the same year if no year is mentioned.

All dates are in the New Style.

In all operations in theatres of war where British troops were engaged the names and dates officially approved by the War Office have been adopted.

The authorities on which these lists are based have been, whenever possible, official documents or records, but in some instances (notably the Russo-Turkish operations in the Caucasus and Armenia) an absence of official information has compelled recourse to unofficial sources. Every endeavour has been made to avoid mistakes, but the Committee of Imperial Defence, under whose authority this book is issued, cannot guarantee the accuracy of each entry.

This work has been compiled mainly by Major H. T. Skinner, D.S.O., 29th Punjabis, and Captain H. FitzM. Stacke, M.C., The Worcestershire Regiment, who have been assisted from time to time by other officers employed in the Historical Section.

With regard to "Political" events, thanks are due to Mr. E. Parkes, O.B.E., of the Foreign Office Library, for the valuable assistance he has rendered in furnishing information and verifying entries.

E. Y. DANIEL, *Secretary,*
Historical Section, Committee of Imperial Defence.

2, *Whitehall Gardens, London, S.W.*1.
  December 1921.

CONTENTS.

	Page
Part I.	
GENERAL CHRONOLOGICAL LIST	5
Part II.	
SECTION I.—Political	85
" II (A).—Military Operations: Main Theatres of War	163
" II (B).—Military Operations: Subsidiary Theatres of War	205
" III.—Naval	219
" IV.—Air	249
Part III.	
ALPHABETICAL LIST	255
Appendix TO PART II, SECTION II (A)	*At end*

PART I.

GENERAL CHRONOLOGICAL LIST.

JUNE 1914.

28th ... **The Archduke Franz Ferdinand assassinated at Sarajevo.**

JULY 1914.

5th ... The Kaiser receives at Potsdam special nvoy from Austrian Emperor and promises " the full support of Germany " in the event of Austrian action against Serbia. He consults his military and naval advisers before leaving for a cruise in northern waters.

14th ... Council of Austro-Hungarian Ministers finally determine on action against Serbia.

19th ... Council of Austro-Hungarian Ministers approve of draft ultimatum to Serbia.

23rd ... **Austro-Hungarian Government send ultimatum to Serbia** (see 25th).

24th ... German Government submit note to Entente Governments approving Austrian ultimatum to Serbia (see 23rd).
British Foreign Minister (Sir E. Grey) initiates proposals for an international conference in order to avert war (see 27th and 28th).
Belgian Government declare that, in the event of war, Belgium will uphold her neutrality " whatever the consequences " (see 31st).

25th ... **Serbian Government order Mobilisation** (see 23rd).
Austria-Hungary severs diplomatic relations with Serbia. Austro-Hungarian Minister leaves Belgrade (see 26th).
Serbian Government transferred from Belgrade to Nish (see November 3rd, 1915).

26th .. **Austro-Hungarian Government order Partial Mobilisation as against Serbia** (see 28th and 31st).
Montenegrin Government order Mobilisation (see August 5th).
British Admiralty countermand orders for dispersal of Fleets (see 28th).
The Kaiser returns from the Baltic to Berlin (see 5th).

27th ... French and Italian Governments accept British proposals for an international conference (see 24th).
German High Seas Fleet recalled from Norway to war bases.

28th ... **Austria-Hungary declares war on Serbia** (see 25th and 26th).
German Government reject British proposals for an international conference (see 24th and 27th).
British Fleets ordered to war bases (see 26th).

29th ... **Russian Government order Partial Mobilisation as against Austria.**
(Evening) Russian Minister for War orders General Mobilisation without the knowledge of the Tsar (see 30th and 31st).
Hostilities commence between Austria-Hungary and Serbia: Belgrade bombarded by Austrian artillery (see 25th, and December 2nd).
German Government make proposals to secure British neutrality (see 30th).
British Admiralty send " Warning Telegram " to the Fleets.
British War Office send out telegrams ordering " Precautionary Period " (2.10 P.M.).

30th ... The Tsar signs order at 4 P.M. for mobilisation of Russian army (see 29th and 31st).
British Government reject German proposals for British neutrality (see 29th).
Australian Government place Australian Navy at disposal of British Admiralty.

July–Aug. 1914

31st ... **Belgian Government order Mobilisation** (see 24th).
Russian Government order General Mobilisation (see 29th and 30th).
Austro-Hungarian Government order General Mobilisation (see 26th and 28th).
German Government send ultimatum to Russia (presented at midnight, 31st-1st) (see August 1st).
State of "Kriegsgefahr" proclaimed in Germany (see August 1st).
Turkish Government order Mobilisation (to commence August 3rd) (see October 29th).
London Stock Exchange closed (see January 4th, 1915).

AUGUST 1914.

1st ... **British Government order Naval Mobilisation.**
German Government order General Mobilisation and declare war on Russia (see July 31st).
Hostilities commence on Polish frontier.
French Government order General Mobilisation.

2nd ... **German Government send ultimatum to Belgium demanding passage through Belgian territory** (see 3rd, and July 24th).
German troops cross frontier of Luxembourg (see November 20th, 1918).
Hostilities commence on French frontier.
Libau bombarded by German cruiser "Augsburg" (see November 17th).
British Government guarantee naval protection of French coasts against German aggression by way of the North Sea or English Channel.
Moratorium proclaimed in Great Britain (see November 4).
General von Moltke* appointed Chief of the General Staff of the German Field Armies (see September 14th).

3rd ... **Belgian Government refuse German demands** (see 2nd and 4th).
British Government guarantee armed support to Belgium should Germany violate Belgian neutrality.
Germany declares war on France.
British Government order General Mobilisation.
British Government issue Proclamation authorising requisition of shipping.
Italy declares neutrality.
The Grand Duke Nicholas appointed Commander-in-Chief Russian armies (see 14th).

4th ... **British Government send ultimatum to Germany.**
Great Britain declares war on Germany at 11 p.m. (midnight 4th-5th by Central European time).
Belgium severs diplomatic relations with Germany (see 2nd and 3rd).
Germany declares war on Belgium.
German troops cross Belgian frontier and attack Liége (see 3rd and 7th, and November 26th, 1918).
Two German airships pass over Brussels by night (first hostile act in the air).
German warships "Goeben" and "Breslau" bombard Philippeville and Bona respectively (see 7th and 11th).
Secret Alliance between Germany and Turkey signed at Berlin.
British Grand Fleet constituted under Admiral Sir John Jellicoe (see November 29th and December 4th, 1916).
Staff of British Expeditionary Force appointed:—
  Commander-in-Chief: Field-Marshal Sir John French (see December 15th, 1915).
  Chief of General Staff: Lieut.-General Sir Archibald Murray (see January 24th, 1915).
  Adjutant-General: Lieut.-General Sir Nevil Macready (see February 21st, 1916).
  Quartermaster-General: Lieut.-General Sir William Robertson (see January 24th, 1915).
British Government issue Proclamation specifying articles to be treated as contraband (see 20th, and September 21st).
German armed merchant cruiser "Kaiser Wilhelm der Grosse" leaves Bremen (see 26th).

* Chief of the Great General Staff since 1906.

August 1914

5th ... **Montenegro declares war on Austria-Hungary** (see July 26th).
Minelaying in the open sea commenced by the Germans (east of Southwold) (see October 3rd). German minelayer "Königin Luise" sunk.
First meeting of British War Council (see May 14th, 1915).*

6th ... **Austria-Hungary declares war on Russia. (Declaration presented at St. Petersburg).**
Serbia declares war on Germany (see July 28th).
"**Battle of the Frontiers**"† **begins in France.**
Field-Marshal Earl Kitchener succeeds Mr. Asquith as Secretary of State for War, Great Britain. (Mr. Asquith held the appointment from March 31st, 1914.) (See June 5th, 1916.)
H.M.S. "Amphion" sunk by mine off Yarmouth.
Naval Convention between France and Great Britain concluded in London. French Admiral to command Allied Naval Forces in the Mediterranean. (See November 9th.)
Action between H.M.S. "Bristol" and German cruiser "Karlsruhe" in the West Indies (see November 4th).
German armed merchant cruiser "Prinz Eitel Friedrich" leaves Tsingtau (see January 28th and April 8th, 1915).
Admiral von Spee's squadron‡ leaves Ponape (Caroline islands) (see September 22nd).

7th ... City of Liége occupied by German forces (see 4th and 16th).
First units of British Expeditionary Force land in France (see 16th).
French troops cross the frontier of Alsace (see 2nd).
Action between H.M.S. "Gloucester" and the "Goeben" and "Breslau" off the coast of Greece (see 4th and 11th).

8th ... Montenegro severs diplomatic relations with Germany.
"**State of War**" **commences between Montenegro and Germany** (see 5th).
Mulhouse (Alsace) occupied by French forces (see 7th and 11th).
British forces cross frontier of Togoland and occupy Lome (see 13th and 26th).
Swiss Government order Mobilisation.
Hostilities commence in East Africa (see 15th). H.M.S. "Astræa" bombards Dar es Salaam (see September 4th, 1916).

9th ... British aerial cross-Channel patrol for the protection of transports instituted.
Belgian Government proposal for neutralisation of African free trade zone formulated (see 22nd).
H.M.S. "Birmingham" sinks German submarine "U.-15" in the North Sea. (First submarine destroyed.)

10th ... British aerial coast patrol established.
France severs diplomatic relations with Austria-Hungary (see 12th).

11th ... German warships "Goeben" and "Breslau" enter the Dardenelles (see 4th and 7th).
Mulhouse retaken by German forces (see 8th and 19th).
French Government issue first list of contraband (see 25th and November 6th).

12th ... **Great Britain and France declare war on Austria-Hungary** (see 10th).
Austrian forces cross the Save and seize Shabatz (see 25th).

13th ... **Austrian forces cross River Drina and begin first invasion of Serbia** (see 25th).
Four squadrons Royal Flying Corps fly from Dover to France. (First units to cross by air.)
Allied advance on Kamina (Togoland) from Lome begins (see 8th and 26th).

14th ... Proclamation issued by Russian Commander-in-Chief (The Grand Duke Nicholas) promising autonomy to Poland (see April 3rd, 1915).
Battles of Morhange and Sarrebourg begin (see 20th).

15th ... **Japanese Government send ultimatum to Germany demanding evacuation of Tsingtau** (see 23rd, and September 2nd).
German troops cross frontier of British East Africa and occupy Taveta (see 8th, November 2nd, and March 10th, 1916).
Junction of British and French squadrons effected at entrance to the Adriatic.

---

* Formed to exercise the functions of the Committee of Imperial Defence, but with additional executive powers.
† General name covering all operations of the French armies up to the Battle of the Marne.
‡ "Scharnhorst" (flag), "Gneisenau," "Nürnberg." "Dresden" and "Leipzig" joined on October 12th and 14th respectively.

August 1914

16th ... **Landing of original British Expeditionary Force* in France completed** (announced August 18th) (see 7th).
Last forts of Liège captured by German forces (16th/17th) (see 4th and 7th).
Naval action in the Southern Adriatic: Austrian light cruiser " Zenta " sunk by Allied squadron.

17th ... **Battle of the Tser and the Jadar (Serbia) begins** (see 13th and 21st).
Belgian Government transferred from Brussels to Antwerp (see October 7th).

18th ... Battle of the Gette (18th/19th).
Vossuq ed Douleh, Persian Foreign Minister, resigns. (Appointed January 11th, 1913.) (See 19th, and August 29th, 1916.)

19th ... Belgian Army retreats from the Gette on Antwerp.
Mulhouse again taken by French forces (see 11th and 25th).
First unit of Indian Expeditionary Force " C "† leaves India for East Africa (see September 1st).
Ala es Sultaneh, Persian Prime Minister, resigns (appointed January 11th, 1913) and is appointed Foreign Minister (see 18th, and February 20th, 1915).
Mustaufi ul Mamalek appointed Persian Prime Minister (see March 14th, 1915).

20th ... **Brussels occupied by German forces** (see November 18th, 1918).
Battles of Morhange and Sarrebourg end (see 14th).
Longwy invested by German forces (see 26th).
Battle of Gawaiten-Gumbinnen (East Prussia) (19th/20th).
Death of Pope Pius X (see September 3rd).
First British Order in Council revising " Declaration of London " issued (see October 29th).

21st ... **German forces begin attack on Namur** (see 25th).
Battle of Charleroi begins (see 24th).
Battle of the Tser and the Jadar ends. Austrian Armies in Serbia retreat (see 17th).
German forces from German South-West Africa cross frontier of British South Africa (see September 19th).
British Government issue orders for the raising of the first New Army of six Divisions (see May 9th, 1915).

22nd ... **Austria-Hungary declares war on Belgium** (see 28th).
Battle of the Ardennes begins (see 24th).
German Government agree to Belgian proposal, made through Spanish Government, re African free trade zone (see 9th, and November 20th).

23rd ... **Battle of Mons** (see 24th).
German airship " Z.-8 " shot down in the Vosges.
Battle of Tannenberg begins (see 31st).
First Battle of Krasnik (Poland) begins (see 25th).
Germany severs diplomatic relations with Japan (see 15th).
Japan declares war on Germany (see 15th).
General C. M. Dobell appointed to command Allied land forces operating in the Cameroons.
General von Hindenburg takes over command of German Eighth Army (see September 18th).

24th ... British army retreats from Mons (see 23rd, and September 5th).
Battle of Charleroi ends (see 21st).
Battle of the Ardennes ends (see 22nd).
Austria-Hungary severs diplomatic relations with Japan (see 25th).
First units of Indian Expeditionary Force " A " leave India for France (in first place for Egypt) (see September 26th).

25th ... **Namur captured by German forces** (see 21st, and November 21st, 1918.)
Battle of the Meuse begins (see 28th).
Battle of Malines begins (see 27th).
Valenciennes taken by German forces (see November 3rd, 1918).
Maubeuge invested by German forces (see September 7th).
Battle of the Mortagne (Vosges) begins (see September 3rd).
Mulhouse again retaken by German forces (see 19th, and November 17th, 1918).

* 4 Divisions and 1 Cavalry Division.
† This unit, the 29th Punjabis, was the first to leave India for any theatre of war.

25th (contd.)	First use of aircraft for patrol purposes (over retreating British forces in France). First Battle of Krasnik (Poland) ends (see 23rd). Shabatz (see 12th) retaken by Serbian forces. Last Austrian forces recross the Drina (see 13th). **End of First Austrian invasion of Serbia** (see September 8th). Japan severs diplomatic relations with Austria-Hungary (see 24th). **Japan declares "State of War" with Austria-Hungary.** Nigerian frontier of the Cameroons crossed by British forces. Affair of Tepe. Chad frontier crossed by French forces. French Government issue new decree defining contraband (see 11th, and November 6th).
26th	Louvain sacked by German troops. **Battle of Le Cateau.** Noyon taken by German forces (see September 21st). **Longwy capitulates to German forces** (see 20th). Cambrai occupied by German forces (see November 20th, 1917, and October 9th, 1918). Douai occupied by German forces (see October 17th, 1918). **First Battle of Lemberg (Galicia) begins** (see 30th). **Battle of Zamosc-Komarow begins** (see September 2nd). Naval action off the Aaland Islands. German cruiser "Magdeburg" destroyed by Russian squadron. **German forces in Togoland capitulate to the Allied forces** (see 8th, 13th and 31st). Action between H.M.S. "Highflyer" and German armed merchant cruiser "Kaiser Wilhelm der Grosse" off the Rio de Oro: latter sunk (see August 4). General Galliéni appointed Governor of Paris (see October 30th, 1915). M. Messimy, French Minister for War,* resigns (see 27th). M. Delcassé succeeds M. Doumergue† as French Foreign Minister.
27th	Battle of Malines ends (see 25th). British Marines landed at Ostend, accompanied by R.N.A.S. unit. Lille occupied by German cavalry (see September 5th). Mezières occupied by German forces (see November 10th, 1918). M. Millerand appointed French Minister for War (see 26th, and October 29th, 1915). First attack on Mora (Cameroons) (see September 8th, 1915).
28th	Battle of the Meuse ends (see 25th). **Austro-Hungarian declaration of war received by Belgian Government** (see 22nd). **Naval action off Heligoland** (German light cruisers "Köln," "Mainz," and "Ariadne" sunk by British squadron).
29th	Arras evacuated by the French forces (see September 30th). **First Battle of Guise begins** (see 30th). Sedan taken by German forces (see November 6th, 1918). German airship "Z.-5" brought down by gunfire at Mlawa (Poland).
30th	Laon, La Fère, and Roye occupied by German forces (see March 17th, 1917, and October 13th, 1918). **First Battle of Guise ends** (see 29th, and November 4th, 1918). First German aeroplane raid on Paris (see September 16th, 1918). **First Battle of Lemberg (Galicia) ends** (see 26th, and September 3rd). First attack on Garua (Cameroons) (see April 18th, 1915). Samoa occupied by New Zealand Expeditionary Force.
31st	Amiens entered by German forces (see September 13th). **Battle of Tannenberg ends** (see 23rd). Franco-British Agreement defining provisional zones in Togoland concluded (see 26th, and December 27th, 1916).

SEPTEMBER 1914.

1st	Lord Kitchener visits France to confer with the British Commander-in-Chief. Craonne taken by German forces (see May 4th, 1917). Soissons taken by German forces (see 13th). First unit of Indian Expeditionary Force "C" arrives at Mombasa (see August 19th and December 31st). General J. Stewart takes over command of British forces in East Africa (see October 31st).

* Appointed June 14th, 1914.
† Appointed August 3rd, 1914.

Sept. 1914

2nd ... **Battle of Zamosc-Komarow ends** (see August 26th).
    Japanese forces land in Shantung to attack Tsingtau (see August 15th, September 23rd and November 7th).
    French Government transferred from Paris to Bordeaux (see November 18th).

3rd ... Battle of the Mortagne ends (see August 25th).
    Lemberg captured by Russian forces (see August 30th, 1914, and June 22nd, 1915).
    H.M.S. "Speedy" sunk by mine off the Humber.
    Benedict XV elected Pope (see August 20th and November 5th).
    Prince William of Wied leaves Albania (see October 4th).
    French Government inform United States Government that they will observe "Declaration of London" subject to certain modifications.

4th ... **Battle of the Grand Couronné (Nancy) begins** (see 12th).
    German Government agree to observe "Declaration of London" if other belligerents conform thereto, and issue their list of contraband.

5th ... End of the Retreat from Mons (see August 24th, 1914, and November 11th, 1918).
    Battle of the Ourcq begins.
    German forces reach Claye, 10 miles from Paris (nearest point reached during the war).
    Reims taken by German forces (see 14th).
    Lille evacuated by German forces (see August 27th and October 12th).
    H.M.S. "Pathfinder" sunk by submarine in the North Sea (first British warship so destroyed).
    Battle of the Masurian Lakes begins (see 15th).
    German forces cross frontier of North Rhodesia. Defence of Abercorn begins (see 9th).
    British, French, and Russian Governments sign the "Pact of London." Decision not to make separate peace (see April 26th, October 19th, and November 30th, 1915).

6th ... **Battle of the Marne begins*** (see 9th and 10th).
    Serbian passage of the Save. Serbian operations in Syrmia begin (see 11th).
    Affair of Tsavo (East Africa).

7th ... Maubeuge capitulates to German forces (see August 25th, 1914, and November 8th, 1918).
    Battle of Tarnavka (Galicia) begins (see 9th).
    Naval operations off Duala (Cameroons) begin, in preparation for attack by Allied military forces (see 27th).

8th ... **Austrian forces begin second invasion of Serbia** (see August 25th and December 15th). **Battle of the Drina begins** (see 17th).
    Second Battle of Lemberg begins (see 11th).
    General Sir John Maxwell takes over command of British forces in Egypt (see March 19th, 1916).

9th ... German retreat from the Marne begins (see 6th).
    Battle of Tarnavka ends (see 7th).
    Turkish Government announce abolition of "The Capitulations."
    Affairs near Karonga (Nyassaland). First important fighting.
    Defence of Abercorn (Rhodesia) ends. German force retreats (see 5th).
    First units of Indian Expeditionary Force "A" arrive at Suez (see 19th).

10th ... **Battle of the Marne ends†** (see 6th).
    Semlin (Syrmia) occupied by Serbian forces (see 17th).
    German light cruiser "Emden" makes her first capture in the Indian Ocean (Greek collier "Pontoporos") (see 22nd, and October 28th).
    German and Austrian representatives expelled from Egypt (see November 1st).

11th ... **Second Battle of Lemberg ends** (see 8th). **Austrian forces in Galicia retreat** (see October 3rd).
    Serbian advance in Syrmia abandoned (see 6th and 17th).
    British Government issue orders for the raising of the second New Army of six divisions (see August 21st and September 13th).
    Australian Expeditionary Force lands on the Bismarck Archipelago (German New Guinea).

---

* French date } for dates of this battle adopted by the respective belligerents see Appendix.
† British date }

Sept. 1914

12th ... **Battle of the Grand Couronné** (Nancy) **ends** (see 4th).
Battle of the Aisne, 1914, begins (see 15th).
Affair of Herbertshöhe (German New Guinea) (see 11th and 17th).

13th ... Soissons (see 1st, and January 8th, 1915) and Amiens (see August 31st) reoccupied by French forces.
British Government issue orders raising third New Army of six divisions (see 11th).

14th ... Reims evacuated by German forces (see 5th and 19th).
Action between British armed merchant cruiser " Carmania " and German armed merchant cruiser " Cap Trafalgar " in the South Atlantic: latter sunk.
General von Moltke resigns as Chief of the General Staff of the German Field Armies, and is succeeded by General von Falkenhayn (see August 2nd, 1914, and August 29th, 1916).

15th ... **Battle of the Aisne, 1914, ends** (see 12th).
Battle of the Masurian Lakes ends (see 5th).
Czernowitz (Bukovina) taken by Russian forces (see October 22nd).
Rebellion in South Africa begins (see December 1st and 28th)

17th ... **German New Guinea and surrounding Colonies capitulate to Australian Expeditionary Force** (see 21st, and October 11th).
Serbian forces in Syrmia withdrawn. Semlin evacuated (see 10th).
Battle of the Drina ends (see 8th)*.
British Naval Mission leaves Turkey.
Admiral Souchon (Imperial German navy) assumes control of Turkish navy.

18th ... General von Hindenburg appointed Commander-in-Chief of German Armies in Eastern Theatre (see August 23rd and November 27th).

19th ... First units of Indian Expeditionary Force " A " leave Egypt for Marseilles (see 9th).
First bombardment of Reims Cathedral by German artillery (see 14th).
Cattaro bombarded by French squadron.
Lüderitzbucht (German South-West Africa) occupied by South African forces.†
British and French Governments guarantee to Belgium the integrity of her colonies.
Secret agreement for mutual support concluded between Russian and Rumanian Governments.

20th ... H.M.S. " Pegasus " sunk by German light cruiser " Königsberg " at Zanzibar (see October 31st, 1914, and July 11th, 1915).

21st ... Noyon retaken by French forces (see 25th, and August 26th).
Jaroslaw (Galicia) taken by Russian forces (see May 14th, 1915).
German armed forces in New Guinea surrender to the Australian Expeditionary Force (see 17th, and October 11th).
British Proclamation issued adding to list of contraband (see August 4th and December 23rd).

22nd ... **First Battle of Picardy begins** (see 26th).
H.M.S. " Aboukir," " Hogue," and " Cressy " sunk by German submarine " U.-9."
Admiral von Spee's squadron bombards Papeete in Tahiti (see August 6th and November 1st).
German light cruiser " Emden " bombards Madras (see 10th, and October 28th).
First British air raid on Germany (Düsseldorf and Cologne airship sheds attacked) (see October 8th).
First use of wireless telegraphy from aeroplane to artillery (by **British Royal Flying Corps**).

23rd ... British force joins Japanese army before Tsingtau‡ (see 2nd, and November 7th).

---
* See footnote in Part II.
† First German territory to be entered by Union troops.
‡ Force landed September 22nd; in action September 24th.

[8369]

Sept.-Oct. 1914

24th ... Péronne taken by German forces (see March 18th, 1917).
Przemysl isolated by Russian forces. First siege begins (see October 9th).
Russian forces begin first invasion of North Hungary (see October 8th).

25th ... Noyon retaken by German forces (see 21st, and March 18th, 1917).
Actions on the Niemen begin (see 29th).

26th ... **First Battle of Picardy ends** (see 22nd).
Bapaume occupied by German forces (see March 17th, 1917).
First units of Indian Expeditionary Force " A " land at Marseilles (see 19th, and October 19th).

27th ... Siege of Antwerp begins (see October 10th).
First Battle of Artois begins (see October 12th).
Duala (Cameroons) captured by Allied forces (26th/27th) (see 7th).

28th ... Malines taken by German forces.
Distinctive markings on German aircraft first reported (see November 12th).
Lieut.-General Sir A. Barrett appointed Commander-designate of Indian Expeditionary Force " D " for Mesopotamia (see November 13th).

29th ... German offensive on the Niemen abandoned (see 25th).

30th ... Arras reoccupied by French forces (see August 29th).

OCTOBER 1914.

2nd ... Termonde (Belgium) taken by German forces.
Indian Expeditionary Force " E " formed in Egypt from details of Indian Expeditionary Force " A " (see August 24th, 1914, and March 25th, 1915).

3rd ... Ypres occupied by German cavalry (see 13th).
British army begins to leave the Aisne and to move northwards (see 19th).
First units of British Royal Naval Division (Marine Brigade) arrive at Antwerp (3rd/4th).
First contingents of Canadian and Newfoundland Expeditionary Forces leave for England (see 15th).
Retreat of Austro-Hungarian forces in Galicia ends (see September 11th).
Maramaros-Sziget taken by Russian forces (see 7th).
Minelaying in the open sea (between the Goodwins and Ostend) commenced by British (see August 5th).

4th ... Lens and Bailleul occupied by German forces (see 14th, and September 3rd, 1918, and August 30th, 1918).
Austro-Hungarian counter-offensive in Galicia begins (see 3rd).
Provisional Government under Essad Pasha set up in Albania at Durazzo (see February 24th, 1916).

6th ... Units of British 7th Division disembark at Ostend and Zeebrugge to co-operate with Belgian army (see 12th).

7th ... Maramaros-Sziget retaken by Austrian forces (see 3rd).
Belgian Government transferred from Antwerp to Ostend (see August 17th and October 12th and 13th). Evacuation of Antwerp begun.
Japanese naval forces occupy Yap Island (Pacific).

8th ... General Foch appointed to command Allied forces (less Belgians) defending the Flanders coast (see May 15th, 1917).
Second British air raid on Germany (Düsseldorf and Cologne airship sheds attacked) (see September 22nd).
First Russian invasion of North Hungary ends (see September 24th and November 15th).

October 1914

9th ... Merville, Estaires, Armentières, and Hazebrouck taken by German forces (see 10th, 11th and 17th).
*Menin occupied by German forces (see October 15th, 1918).
Last forts of Antwerp taken by German forces (see 10th, and September 27th).
First German offensive against Warsaw. Battles of Warsaw and Ivangorod begin (see 19th and 20th).
Przemysl relieved by advancing Austrian forces (see 4th). **End of First siege** (see September 24th and November 10th).

10th ... **Antwerp capitulates to German forces** (see 9th, and September 27th, 1914, and November 19th, 1918).
Hazebrouck and Estaires captured by British forces (see 9th).
Battle of La Bassée begins (see November 2nd).
Protocol signed by United States of America and Panama as to use of Panama Canal by ships of belligerent Powers.
King Charles of Rumania dies, and is succeeded by his son Ferdinand.

11th ... Merville retaken by British forces (see 9th, and April 11th, 1918).
Russian cruiser "Pallada" sunk by German submarine off Hangö.
German gunboat "Komet" captured by H.M.A.S. "Nusa" near Talassia (Neu Pommern).†

12th ... Battle of Messines, 1914, begins (see November 2nd).
First Battle of Artois ends (see September 27th).
Ostend and Zeebrugge evacuated by Belgian forces (see 6th and 15th).
Lille capitulates to German forces (see September 5th, 1914, and October 17th, 1918).
Ghent evacuated by Belgian forces and occupied by German forces (see November 10th, 1918).

13th ... Battle of Armentières begins (see November 2nd).
Ypres reoccupied by Allied forces retreating from Ghent (see 3rd and 19th).
First appearance of a German submarine on the Southampton-Havre troop-transport route reported.
Battle of Chyrow (Galicia) **begins** (see November 2nd).
Belgian Government set up at Havre (see 7th, and November 21st, 1918).

14th ... Bailleul occupied by British forces (see 4th, and April 15th, 1918).
Bruges occupied by German forces (see October 19th, 1918).
Yabasi (Cameroons) captured by Allied forces.

15th ... Belgian coast-line reached by German forces (see October 20th, 1918).
Zeebrugge and Ostend occupied by German forces (see 12th, and October 17th and 19th, 1918).
First units of Canadian and Newfoundland Expeditionary Forces land in England (see 3rd, and February 9th, 1915).
H.M.S. "Hawke" sunk by German submarine in North Sea.

16th ... **Battle of the Yser begins**‡ (see November 10th).
New Zealand Expeditionary Force leaves New Zealand for France (see December 1st).
Indian Expeditionary Force "B" leaves India for East Africa (see 31st).
First units of Indian Expeditionary Force "D" leave India for the Persian Gulf (see 23rd).
Marquis di San Giuliano, Italian Foreign Minister,§ dies (see November 3rd).

17th ... Armentières recaptured by Allied forces (see 9th, and April 11th, 1918).
Action by H.M.S. "Undaunted" and destroyers with four German destroyers off Dutch coast; latter all sunk.
First British submarines ("E.-1" and "E.-9") enter the Baltic.
German submarines attempt raid on Scapa Flow (see 18th).
First units of Australian Imperial Force embark for France (see December 1st).

* Approximate date.
† Last act of hostilities in Australasian waters.
‡ Belgian date.
§ Appointed March 24th, 1914.

October 1914

18th ... First bombardment of Ostend by British warships (see 15th).
Roulers taken by German forces (see October 14th, 1918).
Grand Fleet withdraws from Scapa Flow to West of Scotland (see 17th, and November 3rd).
Japanese light cruiser "Takachiho" sunk by German destroyer off Tsingtau.

19th ... **Battles of Ypres, 1914, begin** (see 31st, and November 22nd).
Transfer of British army from the Aisne to Flanders completed (see 3rd).
First Indian units reach the Flanders front (see September 26th, and November 10th, 1915).
Battle of Warsaw ends (see 9th).

20th ... **Battle of Ivangorod ends** (see 9th).
First merchant vessel sunk by German submarine (British S.S. "Glitra") (see February 19th and March 13th and 28th, 1915).

21st ... Battle of Langemarck, 1914 (Ypres) begins (see 24th).

22nd ... Czernowitz (Bukovina) reoccupied by Austrian forces (see 28th, and September 15th).
United States Government issue Circular Note to belligerent Governments stating that they will insist on existing rules of International Law (see July 28th, 1916).

23rd ... Advanced troops of Indian Expeditionary Force "D" arrive at the Bahrein Islands (Persian Gulf) (see 16th, and November 6th).

24th ... Battle of Langemarck, 1914 (Ypres), ends (see 21st).

25th ... General Sir C. Douglas, Chief of the Imperial General Staff, Great Britain, dies* (see 26th).

26th ... German forces begin an unprovoked invasion of Angola (Portuguese West Africa) (see December 4th).
Edea (Cameroons) occupied by French forces.
General Sir J. Wolfe Murray appointed Chief of the Imperial General Staff, Great Britain (see 25th, and September 25th, 1915).

27th ... H.M.S. "Audacious" sunk by mine off coast of Donegal.

28th ... Czernowitz (Bukovina) reoccupied by Russian forces (see 22nd, and February 17th, 1915).
German cruiser "Emden" raids Penang Roads and sinks Russian cruiser "Zhemchug" (see September 10th and November 9th).

29th ... Battle of Gheluvelt (Ypres) begins (see 31st).
Turkey commences hostilities against Russia (see July 31st, and November 2nd and 5th). **Turkish warships bombard Odessa, Sevastopol, and Theodosia.**
New British Order in Council revises list of contraband and modifies "Declaration of London" of 1909 (see August 20th, 1914, and July 7th, 1916).
Prince Louis of Battenberg, First Sea Lord, Great Britain, resigns† (see 30th).

30th Stanislau (Galicia) taken by Russian forces (see February 19th, 1915).
Serbian forces begin retreat from the line of the Drina (see November 30th).
Allied Governments present ultimatum to Turkey (see 29th).
Great Britain and France sever diplomatic relations with Turkey. British and French Ambassadors demand passports (see 31st, and November 5th).
Italian Cabinet resign. New Cabinet formed. Signor Salandra remains Premier (previously appointed March 24th, 1914) (see May 13th, 1915).
British hospital ship "Rohilla" wrecked off Whitby.
Lord Fisher appointed First Sea Lord, Great Britain (see 29th, and May 15th, 1915).

* Appointed April 6, 1914.
† Appointed December 9th, 1912.

31st ...	**Critical day of Battles of Ypres, 1914: British line broken and restored** (see 19th, and November 11th). Battle of Gheluvelt ends (see 29th). H.M.S. "Hermes" sunk by German submarine in Straits of Dover. British Government issue orders for hostilities to commence against Turkey (see 30th, and November 1st and 5th). First units of Indian Expeditionary Force "B" arrive at Mombasa (see 16th, and December 31st). General Stewart succeeded in command of British forces in East Africa by General Aitken (see September 1st and December 4th). German light cruiser "Königsberg" located in Rufiji River (see July 11, 1915). Lord Kitchener sends to Sherif of Mecca conditional guarantee of Arabian independence (see July 14th, 1915).

NOVEMBER 1914.

1st ...	Messines taken by German forces (see June 7th, 1917). **Great Britain and Turkey commence hostilities** (see 5th, and October 30th and 31st). **Naval action off Coronel. H.M.S. "Good Hope" and "Monmouth" sunk by Admiral von Spee's Squadron** (see September 22nd and December 8th). Martial law proclaimed in Egypt (see September 10th and December 18th).
2nd ...	Battles of Messines and Armentières end (see October 12th and 13th). **Battle of La Bassée ends** (see October 10th). **Battle of Chyrow ends** (see October 13th). Austrian cruiser "Kaiserin Elizabeth" sunk in Tsingtau harbour. First units of Indian Expeditionary Force "F" leave India for Egypt (see 16th). Government of India announce immunity of the Mussulman Holy Places during hostilities with Turkey. **Russia declares war on Turkey** (see October 29th). **"State of War" commences between Serbia and Turkey.** **British Admiralty declare the North Sea a military zone.** **British force begins attack on Tanga (German East Africa)** (see 5th).
3rd ...	First German naval raid on British coast near Gorleston and Yarmouth. Grand Fleet ordered back to Scapa Flow (see October 18th, 1914, and November 21st, 1918). Northern frontier of German East Africa first crossed by British troops. (Affair of Longido.) (See August 15th.) Allied squadrons bombard forts at entrance of the Dardanelles (see December 13th). Baron Sonnino appointed Italian Foreign Minister (see October 16th and 30th, 1914, and May 13th, 1915).
4th ...	German cruiser "Karlsruhe" sunk in the Atlantic by internal explosion (see August 6th). German cruiser "Yorck" sunk by mine off the German coast. Russian forces cross frontier of Turkey-in-Asia and seize Azap. Moratorium in Great Britain ends (see August 2nd).
5th ...	**Great Britain and France formally declare war on Turkey** (see 1st and 11th, and October 31st). Great Britain annexes Cyprus. **Attack on Tanga ends. British force repulsed** (see 2nd, and July 7th, 1916). Belgian Government reject Papal mediation (see July 30th, 1915).
6th ...	**Advanced troops of Indian Expeditionary Force "D" effect landing in Mesopotamia at Fao** (see 22nd, and October 23rd). Turkey severs diplomatic relations with Belgium. British submarine "B.-11" proceeds two miles up the Dardanelles. (First warship to enter Straits.) (See December 13th). Keupri-Keui (Armenia) taken by Russian forces (see 14th). French Government issue declaration modifying list of contraband (see August 25th, 1914, and January 3rd, 1915).
7th ...	**Tsingtau capitulates to Japanese forces** (see September 2nd and 23rd, 1914, and August 6th, 1915).

Nov. 1914

9th ... German cruiser "Emden" destroyed by H.M.A.S. "Sydney" at the Cocos Islands (see October 28th).
German gunboat "Geier" interned at Honolulu.
British and French Governments conclude convention as to naval "prizes" (see August 6th, 1914, and January 15th, 1917).

10th ... **Battle of the Yser ends*** (see October 16th).
Dixmude stormed by German forces (see September 29th, 1918).
Przemysl again isolated by Russian forces (see October 9th).
Second Siege begins (see March 22nd, 1915).
British force storms Sheikh Saïd (Southern Arabia) and destroys the defences (10th/11th).

11th ... Battle of Nonneboschen (Ypres). Attack by German Guard repulsed (see 22nd, and October 19th and 31st).
Memel (East Prussia) occupied by Russian forces (see February 17th, 1915).†
The Sheikh ul Islam issues Fatwa declaring Jehad (Holy War) against all the Allies (see 2nd, 5th, and 14th).
H.M.S. "Niger" sunk by German submarine off Deal.

12th ... Orders issued for all British aeroplanes on Western front to bear distinguishing marks (see September 28th).

13th ... Dutch Government protest against modifications of the Declaration of London (see October 29th).
Lieut.-General Sir A. Barrett takes over command of Indian Expeditionary Force "D" in Mesopotamia (see September 28th, 1914, and April 9th, 1915).

14th ... Keupri-Keui (Armenia) retaken by Turkish forces (see 6th).
Field-Marshal Earl Roberts dies in France.
Sultan of Turkey as Khalif proclaims Jehad against those making war on Turkey or her allies (see 11th).
Japanese Cabinet decide against despatch of troops or warships to Europe (see February 8th, 1916, and April 17th, 1917).

15th ... **Battle of Cracow begins** (see December 2nd).
Second Russian invasion of North Hungary begins (see October 8th and December 12th).
Affair of Saihan (Mesopotamia).

16th ... First units of Indian Expeditionary Force "F" land in Egypt (see 2nd, and March 25th, 1915).
Second German offensive against Warsaw. Battle of Lodz begins (see December 15th).

17th ... Libau (Baltic) bombarded by German squadron (see August 2nd).
German cruiser "Friedrich Karl" sunk by mine in the Baltic.
Trebizond (Black Sea) bombarded by Russian squadron (see April 6th, 1916).
Affair of Sahil (Mesopotamia).

18th ... Re-transfer of French Government from Bordeaux to Paris begins (see September 2nd).

20th ... British, Belgian, and French Governments withdraw proposal for neutralisation of African free trade zone in view of altered situation (see August 22nd).

21st ... British naval air raid on Friedrichshaven.

22nd ... **Battles of Ypres, 1914, end** (see October 19th, 31st, and November 11th, 1914, and April 22nd, 1915).
War Office assume control of the British operations in East Africa.
Basra (Mesopotamia) occupied by British forces (see 6th).‡
Keupri-Keui (Armenia) again taken by Russian forces (see 14th, and December 17th).

23rd ... Netherlands Overseas Trust formed (see June 3rd, 1915).
Portuguese Government announce prospective co-operation of Portugal with Great Britain (see August 8th, 1916).

26th ... H.M.S. "Bulwark" destroyed by internal explosion in Sheerness harbour.

* French date.
† Approximate date.
‡ Formal occupation took place on the 23rd.

27th	...	General von Hindenburg promoted Field-Marshal (see September 18th, 1914, and August 29th, 1916).
28th	...	Affair of Miranshah (North-West Frontier of India) (28th/29th).*
30th	...	**Battle of Lowicz-Sanniki begins** (see December 17th). Belgrade evacuated by retreating Serbian forces (see October 30th).

DECEMBER 1914.

1st	...	**Battle of Limanova-Lapanov begins** (see 17th). First units of Australian and New Zealand Expeditionary Forces arrive at Suez (see October 16th and 17th, 1914, and February 20th and April 25th, 1915). General de Wet, the leader of South African rebellion, captured by Union troops (see 28th, and September 15th).
2nd	...	Austrian forces cross the Danube and occupy Belgrade (see 15th, and November 30th). **Battle of Cracow ends** (see November 15th).
3rd	...	**Battle of the Kolubara (Serbia) begins** (see 6th). British Government agree to Japanese request that Australia should not occupy German islands north of the Equator (see 16th).
4th	...	First action of Qurna (Mesopotamia) begins (see 8th). General Wapshare succeeds General Aitken in command of the British forces in East Africa: latter recalled (see October 31st and November 5th, 1914, and April 16th, 1915). Portuguese Expeditionary Force leaves Lisbon for Angola (see October 26th, 1914, and August 8th, 1916).
5th	...	Entente *démarche* in Athens, Sofia, and Bukharest to secure help for Serbia (see 6th, and January 24th, 1915). Serbian Government declare that Serbia will never make peace without Allied consent.
6th	...	**Battle of the Kolubara ends.** Austrian forces routed by the Serbians and driven northwards (see 3rd). Rumanian Government decline to guarantee Greece against German attack (see 5th).
7th	...	British Envoy (Sir H. Howard) appointed to the Vatican.
8th	...	First action of Qurna ends (see 4th). **Battle of the Falklands. Admiral von Spee's squadron destroyed. "Scharnhorst," "Gneisenau," "Leipzig," and "Nürnberg" sunk.** Admiral von Spee killed (see November 1st). "Dresden" escapes (see March 14th, 1915).
9th	...	Qurna occupied by British forces (see 8th).
10th	...	Field-Marshal von der Goltz leaves Germany to take over control of the Turkish Army (see November 24th, 1915, and April 19th, 1916). Batum (Georgia) bombarded by the "Goeben" and "Breslau."
11th	...	Dr. B. L. Machado Guimarães, Portuguese Premier, resigns (appointed June 23rd, 1914) (see 12th).
12th	...	Second Russian invasion of North Hungary ends (see November 15th). Senhor V. H. d'Azevedo Coutinho appointed Portuguese Premier (see 11th, and January 25th, 1915).
13th	...	Turkish battleship "Messoudieh" sunk by British submarine "B 11" in the Dardanelles (see November 6th).
14th	...	Allied demonstrations on Flanders front begin. Attack on Wytschaete. German armed merchant cruiser "Cormoran" (ex-Russian S.S. "Ryasan") interned at Guam.
15th	...	**Battle of Lodz ends** (see November 16th). Belgrade occupied by Serbian forces (see 2nd). **End of Second Austrian invasion of Serbia** (see October 6th and 9th, 1915). German airship sighted off East Coast of England (first appearance of hostile aircraft in vicinity of British Isles (see 21st).

* First outbreak on North-West Frontier of India caused by German intrigues.

Dec. 1914—Jan. 1915

16th ... Scarborough and Hartlepool (East coast of England) bombarded by German battle cruiser squadron.
Japanese Foreign Minister declares Japan will not give up German islands occupied north of the Equator (see 3rd, and February 14th, 1917).

17th ... **Battle of Lowicz-Sanniki ends** (see November 30th).
Battle of Limanova-Lapanov ends (see 1st).
Turkish Offensive in the Caucasus begins. Keupri-Keui retaken (see 29th, November 22nd, 1914, and January 17th, 1916).

18th ... British Protectorate over Egypt proclaimed.
Meeting of Scandinavian Kings at Malmö.
Battle of the Rawka-Bzura begins.*

19th ... British Government declare Khedive Abbas Hilmi deposed, and proclaim Prince Hussein Kamel Pasha as Sultan of Egypt (see October 9th, 1917).
Great Britain declares adherence to Franco-Moorish Treaty of 1912.

20th ... **First Battle of Champagne begins** (see March 17th, 1915).
British defence of Givenchy, 1914 (20th/21st).

21st ... First German air raid on England. Aeroplane drops bombs in sea near Dover (see 24th, January 19th, 1915, and July 20th and August 5th, 1918).
Jasin (East Africa) occupied by British forces (see January 18th and 19th, 1915).

23rd ... British Proclamation issued containing revised list of contraband (see September 21st, 1914, and March 11th, 1915).

24th .. Second air raid on England (see 21st). First bomb dropped on English soil (near Dover).

25th ... British seaplane raid on Cuxhaven.

26th ... Italian force lands at Valona; Italy notifies Austria of provisional occupation (see May 29th, 1915).
Garibaldi's Italian Foreign Legion in action for first time on French front.

28th ... End of organised rebellion in South Africa (see September 15th, 1914, and January 11th, 1915).

29th ... **Battle of Sarikamish (Caucasus) begins** (see 17th, and January 2nd, 1915).
British Government send memorandum to United States Government in defence of British blockade policy.

30th ... Russian Commander-in-Chief (Grand Duke Nicholas) suggests a British expedition against the Turks to ease Russian situation in the Caucasus (see January 13th, 1915).

31st ... Indian Expeditionary Force "C" (East Africa) absorbed into Indian Expeditionary Force "B" (see September 1st and October 31st).

JANUARY 1915.

1st ... H.M.S. "Formidable" sunk by German submarine in the English Channel.

2nd ... **Battle of Sarikamish ends** (see December 29th, 1914, and April 4th, 1918).
Urmia (North Persia) evacuated by Russian forces† (see April 16th).

3rd ... French Government issue further revised list of contraband (see November 6th, 1914).

4th ... London Stock Exchange reopens (see July 31st, 1914).

5th ... German attack on Edea (Cameroons) repulsed by French garrison.
Tabriz (North Persia) evacuated by Russian forces† (see 8th and 30th).

* This battle had no definite end; operations subsided into trench warfare.
† This city was occupied by Russian forces before the outbreak of the War.

January 1915

6th ... German S.S. "Dacia" (interned in the United States) sold to Mr. Breitung, an American citizen (see February 11th).

8th ... **Battle of Soissons begins** (see 14th).
Tabriz (North Persia) occupied by Turkish forces (see 5th and 30th).
Battle of Kara Urgan (Caucasus) begins (see 13th).

10th ... British defence of Muscat (Eastern Arabia) (10th/11th).

11th ... Rumanian Government negotiate loan of £5,000,000 in Great Britain.
Last rebels in the Transvaal captured (see December 28th, 1914).

12th ... Mafia Island (German East Africa) seized by a British force.

13th ... Battle of Kara Urgan ends (see 8th).
British War Council resolve that the Admiralty should prepare for a naval expedition in February against the Dardanelles (see 28th, and December 30th, 1914).
Baron Burian succeeds Count Berchtold* as Austro-Hungarian Minister for Foreign Affairs (see December 22nd, 1916).

14th ... **Battle of Soissons ends** (see 8th).
Swakopmund (German South-West Africa) occupied by South African forces.

15th ... Existence of secret agreement for mutual support between Italy and Rumania announced by respective Governments.

18th ... German attack on Jasin (East Africa) begins (see 19th).

19th ... First airship raid on England (see December 21st, 1914, and August 5th, 1918).
Jasin (East Africa) captured by German forces (see 18th, and December 21st, 1914).

21st ... Lieut.-General von Falkenhayn† succeeded as German Minister for War by Lieut.-General Wild von Hohenborn (see October 30th, 1916). General von Falkenhayn remains Chief of the General Staff (see August 29th, 1916).

23rd ... Defence of Upington (South Africa) (23rd/24th).

24th ... **Action of the Dogger Bank.** German cruiser "Blücher" sunk.
German airship "P.L.-19" brought down near Libau.
Lieut.-General Sir A. J. Murray resigns as Chief of the General Staff, British Expeditionary Force, France (see 25th, and August 4th, 1914).
Lieut.-General Sir W. Robertson resigns as Quartermaster-General, British Expeditionary Force, France (see 25th and 27th, and August 4th, 1914).
British Government offer Greek Government concessions in Asia Minor in return for help to Serbia (see 25th and 29th, April 12th, 1915, and December 5th, 1914).

25th ... Lieut.-General Sir W. Robertson appointed Chief of the General Staff, British Expeditionary Force, France (see 24th, and December 22nd).
Rumania refuses Entente suggestion that she should join Greece in support of Serbia (see 24th and 29th, October 15th, 1915, and December 6th, 1914).
General Pimenta da Castro succeeds Senhor Coutinho as Portuguese Premier (see December 12th, 1914, and May 14th, 1915).

26th ... Turkish advance on Egypt through Sinai begins (see February 2nd).
Entente Governments agree to hold "Pact of London" applicable to war with Turkey (see September 5th, 1914).

27th ... Lieut.-General Sir R. C. Maxwell appointed Quartermaster-General, British Expeditionary Force, France (see 24th, and December 22nd, 1917).

28th ... **British Government definitely decide to make naval attack on the Dardanelles** (see 13th).
United States S.V. "William P. Frye" sunk by German armed merchant cruiser "Prinz Eitel Friedrich" (see August 6th, 1914, and April 8th, 1915).

* Appointed February 19th, 1912.
† Appointed in 1906.

29th ... Walney Island battery (Barrow-in-Furness) shelled by German submarine (first operation of German submarines in the Irish Sea).
Greek Government decline to intervene on behalf of Serbia (see 24th and 25th, and February 15th).

30th ... Tabriz (North Persia) reoccupied by Russian forces (see 8th, and June 14th, 1918).
British Admiralty warn British merchant vessels to fly neutral or no ensigns in vicinity of British Isles (see February 6th, 7th and 11th).

31st ... Arab forces (Idrisi) occupy Farasan Islands in the Red Sea (see April 28th).

FEBRUARY 1915.

1st ... British Admiralty issue orders forbidding neutral fishing vessels to use British ports.

2nd ... Turkish advance-guards reach the Suez Canal (see 3rd, and January 26th).
Aden Protectorate invaded by Turkish forces.
Entente communication to Greek, Serbian, and Montenegrin Governments deprecating their intervention in Albania (see June 26th).

3rd ... **Actions on the Suez Canal begin** (see 4th).
Bulgarian Government negotiate loan of £3,000,000 in Germany (see August 6th).
Agreement concluded between Great Britain and Belgium concerning delimitation of Uganda-Congo boundary.

4th ... **The Winter Battle in Masuria (East Prussia) begins** (see 22nd).
Actions on the Suez Canal end (see 3rd). Turkish forces retreat into Sinai.
German Government announce that submarine blockade of Great Britain will begin on the 18th February.

5th ... **British, French and Russian Governments agree to pool their financial resources** (see June 3rd).

6th ... British S.S. "Lusitania" arrives at Liverpool flying United States flag (see 7th, January 30th and May 7th).

7th ... British Foreign Office issue statement justifying use of neutral flag at sea (see 6th, 11th, and January 30th).

9th ... 1st Canadian Division crosses from England to France (9th/11th) (see October 15th, 1914).

11th ... United States Government send Note to British Government deprecating use of neutral flag (see 7th).
S.S. "Dacia" sails from United States for Bremen (Germany) with cargo of cotton (see 27th, and January 6th).

15th ... Entente Governments suggest to Greek Government that Greece should intervene in support of Serbia, and promise military support at Salonika (see January 29th and March 5th).
Mutiny of the 5th Light Infantry (Indian Army) at Singapore.
Agreement concluded between Great Britain and France supplementing "prize" convention of November 9th, 1914.

16th ... Oyem (Cameroons) occupied by French forces.
British Government decide to send a division (the 29th) to the Dardanelles (see 20th, and April 25th).
British Government extend prohibition of "trading with the enemy" to territories in British, enemy, or friendly occupation.

17th ... Czernowitz (Bukovina) retaken by Austrian forces (see October 28th, 1914, and June 17th, 1916).
Memel reoccupied by German forces (see November 11th, 1914, and March 18th, 1915).
German airship "L.-3" stranded and destroyed off Fanö, and "L.-4" destroyed near Blaavands Huk (Denmark).

18th	...	**German submarine blockade of Great Britain begins** (see 4th).
19th	...	**Allied naval attack on the Dardanelles forts commences** (see March 18th). Stanislau (Galicia) captured by Austrian forces (see October 30th, 1914, and March 4th, 1915). Norwegian S.S. "Belridge" torpedoed, but reaches port. First ship torpedoed by German submarine without warning* (see October 20th, 1914, and March 13th, 1915).
20th	...	Orders issued for employment at the Dardanelles of the Australian and New Zealand troops in Egypt (see 16th, and December 1st, 1914). Muavin ed Douleh succeeds Ala es Sultaneh as Persian Foreign Minister (see August 19th, 1914, and April 26th, 1915).
22nd	...	**The Winter Battle in Masuria ends** (see 4th). **First Battle of Przasnysz begins** (see 27th). Net barrage across North Channel (between Ireland and Scotland) established. South African Northern Force begins advance from Swakopmund on Windhuk (see January 14th).
23rd	...	Lemnos (Ægean) occupied by British marines (see March 7th).
24th	...	†The first British Territorial division (the North Midland) leaves England for France.
26th	...	Liquid fire first used by the Germans on the Western front.
27th	...	**First Battle of Przasnysz ends** (see 22nd). S.S. "Dacia" intercepted and seized by French naval forces (see 11th, and March 22nd).

MARCH 1915.

1st	...	British blockade of German East Africa commences. Antivari bombarded by Austrian squadron (see January 22nd, 1916). Joint declaration signed by Great Britain and France to prevent trade by or with Germany (see April 17th, 1916).
4th	...	Stanislau (Galicia) recaptured by Russian forces (see February 19th and June 8th). French Government decide to send Expeditionary Force to the Dardanelles (see February 16th and 20th, and April 25th). First case of "indicator" nets aiding in the destruction of a German submarine ("U.-8," in Straits of Dover).‡ Russian Government send circular telegram to Entente Governments laying claim to Constantinople (see 12th).
5th	...	Greek Premier (M. Venizelos) proffers Greek fleet and troops to Entente for operations at the Dardanelles (see 6th, and February 15th and September 21st). Bombardment of Smyrna by British squadron under Admiral Peirse begins (see 9th).
6th	...	King of Greece refuses assent to policy of M. Venizelos (see 5th). M. Venizelos resigns office as Premier (see 9th, and August 22nd) (date of appointment October 19th, 1910).
7th	...	Greek Government request explanation of British occupation of Lemnos (see 9th, and February 23rd).
9th	...	British bombardment of Smyrna ends (see 5th and 15th). M. Gounaris appointed Premier of Greece (see 6th, and August 22nd). British Government reply to Greek Government as to occupation of Lemnos, pleading military necessity (see 7th and 20th).

* German Government subsequently asserted that this ship was attacked in error.
† Not to be confused with first division of the New Armies, for which see May 9th.
‡ First experimented with in January 1915.

March 1915

10th ... **Battle of Neuve Chapelle begins** (see 13th).

11th ... British "Retaliatory Order in Council" relating to detention of enemy goods and Proclamation extending list of "absolute" contraband issued (see 12th, and December 23rd, 1914).

12th ... Dutch Government issue warning that foreign merchant ships using Dutch flag will be detained (see January 30th and February 11th).
British Government notify Russian Government of their acceptance of Russian claims to Constantinople (see 4th, April 12th, 1915, and December 2nd, 1916).
French Government issue decrees similar to British Order in Council and Proclamation of the 11th March.
General Sir Ian Hamilton appointed Commander-in-Chief, Mediterranean (Dardanelles) Expeditionary Force (see 17th).

13th ... **Battle of Neuve Chapelle ends** (see 10th).
Agreement signed by French and Belgian Governments suspending Franco-Belgian Convention of July 30th, 1891, regarding military service laws.
Swedish S.S. "Hanna" torpedoed without warning. First neutral ship actually sunk by German submarine (see 25th and 28th, and February 19th).

14th ... Light cruiser "Dresden," the last German cruiser left at sea, sunk by British warships in Chilean waters off Juan Fernandez (see December 8th, 1914, and April 26th, 1915).
Mushir ed Dowleh succeeds Mustaufi ul Mamalek as Persian Prime Minister (see August 19th, 1914, and April 26th, 1915).

15th ... British Squadron blockading Smyrna withdrawn (see 5th and 9th).
First merchant ship (S.S. "Blonde") attacked by aircraft.

17th ... French Government lodge claim with British Government to Syria and Cilicia (see April 26th, 1916).
General Sir Ian Hamilton takes over command of Dardanelles Expeditionary Force (see 12th, and October 15th).
First Battle of Champagne ends (see December 20th, 1914).

18th ... **Allied Naval attack on the Dardanelles forts repulsed** (see February 19th). French battleship "Bouvet" and British battleships "Irresistible" and "Ocean" sunk.
Memel (East Prussia) again captured by Russian forces (see 21st, and February 17th).
General Sir John Nixon appointed Commander-in-Chief British Forces in Mesopotamia (see April 9th).
British Government conclude agreement with American cotton interests that cotton should be contraband.

19th ... Dutch Government lodge protest against blockade policy of the Entente (see 11th and 12th).

20th ... Action of Jakalswater (German South-West Africa).
British Government guarantee Greece eventual cession of Lemnos by Turkey (see 9th and July 25th).

21st ... Memel (East Prussia) reoccupied by German forces (see 18th).
First German airship raid on Paris takes place (see August 30th, 1914, and January 29th, 1916).

22nd ... **Przemysl capitulates to Russian forces** (see November 10th, 1914, and June 3rd, 1915).
French Prize Court declare seizure of S.S. "Dacia" valid (see February 27th).

23rd ... First kite-balloon ship, H.M.S. "Manica," commissioned.
Chinese and Japanese Governments conclude secret agreement as to future policy in Manchuria.

25th ... Indian Expeditionary Force "F" (in Egypt) absorbed into Indian Expeditionary Force "E" (see October 2nd, 1914, and November 2nd and 16th, 1914).
General Liman von Sanders appointed to command Turco-German Forces, Dardanelles.
Dutch S.S. "Medea" captured by German submarine and sunk. (First neutral ship sunk after visit and search) (see 13th).

27th ...	Bosporus forts bombarded by Russian Black Sea Fleet (see April 25th).
28th ...	The first passenger ship (British S.S. "Falaba") sunk by a German submarine (see 13th, and October 20th, 1914).
29th ...	British Government conclude agreement with American rubber interests that rubber should not be exported except to Great Britain.
30th ...	Aus (German South-West Africa) occupied by South African forces.

APRIL 1915.

3rd ...	Russian Imperial ukase issued granting municipal self-government to Russian Poland (see August 14th, 1914, and November 5th, 1916).
	Indecisive action in Black Sea between the "Goeben" and part of the Russian Fleet. Turkish cruiser "Medjidieh" sunk by mine off Odessa.
	Dover Straits barrage completed.
7th ...	First Indian units of Indian Expeditionary Force "G" (formed from Force "E") sail from Egypt for the Dardanelles (see December 31st).
8th ...	Deportations and massacres of Armenians by order of the Turkish Government commence* (see May 24th).
	German armed merchant cruiser "Prinz Eitel Friedrich" interned at Newport News, Va. (see January 28th).
9th ...	General Sir John Nixon relieves General Sir Arthur Barrett as Commander-in-Chief Indian Expeditionary Force "D," Mesopotamia (see November 13th, 1914, March 18th, 1915, and January 19th, 1916).
12th ...	**Battle of Shaiba (Mesopotamia) begins** (see 14th).
	First Allied advance on Yaunde (Cameroons) begins (see June 7th and 28th).
	Entente Governments make offer to Greece of Smyrna and hinterland in return for immediate action against Turkey (see 14th, and January 24th).
	French Government notify Russian Government of their acceptance of Russian claims to Constantinople (see March 12th).
14th ...	Germans accuse French of using poison gas near Verdun (see 22nd).
	Battle of Shaiba (Mesopotamia) ends (see 12th).
	Greek Government reject Entente offer of Smyrna (see 12th).
	British Secretary for the Colonies (Mr. Harcourt) states that Dominions will be consulted as to peace terms (see July 14th).
	Japanese Government inform British Government of German overtures for separate peace.
16th ...	Urmia (North Persia) occupied by Turkish regular forces (see January 2nd and May 24th).
	General Tighe succeeds General Wapshare in command of British Forces in East Africa (see December 4th, 1914, and February 19th, 1916).
17th ...	Capture of Hill 60 (Ypres) (17th/22nd).
18th ...	Operations of Allied Force for capture of Garua (Cameroons) begin (see May 31st).
	First Affair of Hafiz Kor (North-West Frontier of India).
20th ...	Armenian revolt at Van: Armenian defence of Van begins (see May 19th).
22nd ...	**Battles of Ypres, 1915, begin** (see November 22nd, 1914, and May 25th, 1915). **First German gas attack** (see 14th).
23rd ...	Battle of Gravenstafel Ridge (Ypres) (22nd/23rd).
	British blockade of the Cameroons commences (see February 29th, 1916).
24th ...	Battle of St. Julien (Ypres) begins (see May 4th).

* Approximate date.

April–May 1915

25th	**Allied Forces effect landing at the Dardanelles** (25th/26th). Bosporus forts shelled by Russian Black Sea Fleet (see March 27th). Action of Gibeon (25th/26th) (German South-West Africa).
26th	**Secret agreement signed in London between Italian Government and the Entente for Italian co-operation in the war and declarations by which Italy adheres to the Pact of London** (see September 5th, 1914, and May 4th, November 30th, and December 1st, 1915). **The last German raider overseas** (armed merchant cruiser "Kronprinz Wilhelm") **interned at Newport News (United States of America)** (see March 14th). French cruiser "Léon Gambetta" sunk by Austrian submarine in Straits of Otranto. Mushir ed Douleh, Persian Prime Minister, resigns (see March 14th and April 27th). Muavin ed Douleh, Persian Foreign Minister, resigns (see February 20th and April 27th).
27th	Ain ed Douleh appointed Persian Prime Minister (see 26th, and August 17th). Mohtashem ed Douleh appointed Persian Foreign Minister (see 26th, and March 5th, 1916).
28th	**First Battle of Krithia (Dardanelles)** (see May 6th). British Government conclude a treaty with the Idrisi for co-operation against the Turks (see January 31st).
30th	Shavli (Baltic Provinces) occupied by German forces (see May 11th).

MAY 1915.

1st	**Austro-German Spring Offensive in Galicia: Battle of Gorlice-Tarnow begins** (see 5th). Battle of Dilman (North Persia). S.S. "Gulflight" torpedoed without warning: damaged, but reaches port. First United States ship attacked by German submarine (see February 19th and March 13th).
4th	**Italy denounces the Triple Alliance** (see April 26th). Battle of St. Julien (Ypres) ends (see April 24th).
5th	**Battle of Gorlice-Tarnow ends** (see 1st).
6th	**Second Battle of Krithia (Dardanelles) begins** (see 8th, and April 28th).
7th	Libau (Baltic Provinces) taken by German forces (see April 30th). **S.S. "Lusitania" sunk by German submarine "U.-20" off Queenstown** (see February 6th). British Foreign Minister (Sir E. Grey) gives conditional guarantee to Serbian Minister of eventual cession of Bosnia and Herzegovina with "wide access to the Adriatic" (see August 15th and 30th). Japan presents ultimatum to China demanding territorial concessions (see 9th).
8th	Battle of Frezenberg Ridge (Ypres) begins (see 13th). **Second Battle of Krithia ends** (see 6th, and June 4th).
9th	**Allied Spring Offensive begins:—** **Battle of Aubers Ridge.** **Second Battle of Artois begins** (see June 18th). The leading division of the British New Armies leaves England for France (see August 21st, 1914, and February 24th, 1915). President Wilson, in a speech, defines United States policy in regard to the "Lusitania" outrage (see 7th). Chinese Government yield to Japanese demands (see 7th and 25th).
10th	Naval Convention signed between Great Britain, France, and Italy.
11th	Shavli evacuated by German forces (see April 30th).
13th	Battle of Frezenberg Ridge (Ypres) ends (see 8th). Windhuk (German South-West Africa) occupied by South African Northern Force.

May 1915

13th ... H.M.S. "Goliath" sunk by Turkish destroyer in the Dardanelles.
(contd.) Signor Salandra, Italian Premier, tenders his resignation (see 16th, and October 30th, 1914).
Baron Sonnino, Italian Foreign Minister, tenders his resignation (see 16th, and November 3rd, 1914).

14th ... Jaroslaw taken by Austro-German forces (see September 21st, 1914).
Last meeting of British War Council (see August 5th, 1914, and June 7th, 1915).
General da Castro, Portuguese Premier, resigns (see 15th, and January 25th).

15th ... **Battle of Festubert begins** (see 25th).
Senhor J. Pinheiro Chagas appointed Portuguese Premier (see 14th, and June 19th).
Lord Fisher, First Sea Lord, Great Britain, tenders his resignation (see 28th, and October 30th, 1914).

16th ... Battle of the San (Galicia) begins (see 23rd).
Signor Salandra reappointed Italian Premier on reconstruction of Cabinet, with Baron Sonnino as Foreign Minister (see 13th, and June 11th, 1916).

19th ... Van (Armenia) taken by Russian forces. Armenian garrison relieved (see April 20th and August 3rd, 1915, and April 5th, 1918).

21st ... Russian Expeditionary Force to West Persia lands at Enzeli (see February 17th, 1918).

23rd ... Battle of the San ends (see 16th).
Italian Government order Mobilisation and declare war against Austria.
General Cadorna appointed Commander-in-Chief* of Italian Armies in the Field (see November 7th, 1917).

24th ... Battle of Bellewaerde Ridge (Ypres) (24th/25th).
Battle of Przemysl begins (see June 3rd and 11th).
Battle of the Stryj (Galicia) begins (see June 11th).
Italian forces cross Austrian frontier (midnight 24th/25th).
†Germany severs diplomatic relations with Italy (see August 28th, 1916).
Urmia (North Persia) retaken by Russian forces (see April 16th).
Entente Governments declare that they will hold Turkish Ministers personally responsible for the Armenian massacres (see April 8th).

25th ... **Battles of Ypres, 1915, end** (see April 22nd, 1915, and July 31st, 1917).
Battle of Festubert ends (see 15th).
H.M.S. "Triumph" sunk by submarine off the Dardanelles.
Italian fleet commences operations in the Adriatic (see 26th).
Coalition Ministry formed in Great Britain by Mr. Asquith (see December 11th, 1916).
Treaty signed between China and Japan concerning Shantung Province (see 7th and 9th).
Treaty signed between China and Japan concerning South Manchuria and Inner Mongolia (see 7th and 9th).

26th ... Italian Government announce blockade of Austro-Hungarian coast.
British battle squadron concentrates at Malta prior to joining Italian fleet in Adriatic (see 27th).

27th ... British squadron joins Italian fleet in the Adriatic (see 26th).
H.M.S. "Majestic" sunk by submarine at the Dardanelles.
Mr. Winston Churchill, First Lord of the Admiralty, Great Britain, resigns (appointed October 24th, 1911) (see 28th).
British minelayer "Princess Irene" destroyed by internal explosion in Sheerness harbour.

* Officially designated "Chief of Staff," the King being the nominal Commander-in-Chief.
† For the purposes of the Treaty of Versailles it was subsequently assumed that this rupture took place on the 27th, which date was accepted as that of the commencement of Italy's belligerence against Germany.

28th ... Mr. Arthur Balfour appointed First Lord of the Admiralty, Great Britain (see 27th, and December 11th, 1916).
Sir Henry Jackson appointed First Sea Lord, Great Britain (see 15th, and December 3rd, 1916).
Dr. Joaquim T. Braga elected President of Portugal (see 29th, and October 5th).

29th ... Valona formally occupied by Italian forces (see December 26th, 1914).
Dr. Manoel Arriaga, Portuguese President, resigns (appointed August 24th, 1911) (see 28th).

30th ... Affair of Sphinxhaven (Lake Nyassa). British command of the lake secured.

31st ... Siege of Garua (Cameroons) begins (see April 18th and June 10th).
First German airship raid on London area (see January 19th 1915, October 19th, 1917, and August 5th, 1918).
Second action of Qurna (Mesopotamia).

JUNE 1915.

2nd ... Blockade of coast of Asia Minor announced by British Government.

3rd ... **Przemysl retaken by Austro-German forces** (see March 22nd and May 24th).
Amara (Mesopotamia) captured by British forces.
First meeting in Paris of Allied Conference on Economic War (see February 5th, 1915, and June 14th, 1916).
Act passed in British Parliament empowering Customs to compel all exports to Holland to be consigned to the Netherlands Oversea Trust (see November 23rd, 1914, and December 7th, 1915).
San Marino declares war on Austria-Hungary.

4th ... **Third Battle of Krithia (Dardanelles).**

5th ... **First Conference of British and French Ministers to co-ordinate war policy and strategy held at Calais.**

7th ... German airship "L.Z.-37" destroyed in mid-air by Lieut. Warneford, R.N.A.S., near Ghent (first occasion of airship successfully attacked by aeroplane).
Russian and Chinese Governments conclude agreement respecting Mongolia (see May 25).
First meeting of Dardanelles Committee* of the British Cabinet (see May 14th and October 30th).
Allied Commander-in-Chief in the Cameroons decides to abandon the advance on Yaunde (see 28th, and April 12th).

8th ... Stanislau recaptured by Austrian forces (see March 4th, 1915, and August 10th, 1916).

9th ... Monfalcone (Isonzo) taken by Italian forces.

10th ... Garua (Cameroons) capitulates to the Anglo-French force under General Cunliffe (see May 31st).

11th ... **Battle of Przemysl ends** (see 3rd, and May 24th).
Battle of the Stryj ends (see May 24th).

14th ... Turkish Attack on Perim (14th/15th).

17th ... **Third Battle of Lemberg begins** (see 22nd).

18th ... **Second Battle of Artois ends** (see May 9th and September 25th).

19th ... South African forces begin advance on Otavifontein (see July 1st).
Dr. José de Castro succeeds Senhor J. P. Chagas as Portuguese Premier (see May 15th and November 29th).

22nd ... **Third Battle of Lemberg ends: city retaken by the Austrian forces** (see 17th, and September 3rd, 1914, and November 23rd, 1918).

---

* Under this title the War Council (see August 5th, 1914, and May 14th, 1915) exercised its functions during the critical period of the Dardanelles campaign.

24th ... Mr. Lansing succeeds Mr. Bryan as United States Secretary of State.

26th ... San Giovanni de Medua (Albania) occupied by Montenegrin forces (see July 29th).
General Sukhomlinov, Russian Minister for War, removed from office (appointed in 1909); succeeded by General Polivanov (see March 29th, 1916).

27th ... British advance up the Euphrates begins (see July 25th).

28th ... Action of Gully Ravine (Dardanelles) begins (see July 2nd).
Operations of the first advance on Yaunde (Cameroons) end (see 7th).
Ngaundere (Cameroons) captured by the Allied Northern Force.

29th ... **First Battle of the Isonzo begins** (see July 7th).

JULY 1915.

1st ... Second Battle of Krasnik begins (see 19th).
Otavifontein (German South-West Africa) captured by South African forces (see June 19th).

2nd ... Action of Gully Ravine ends (see June 28th).
Naval action in the Baltic between Russian and German squadrons off Gottland. German minelayer "Albatross" driven ashore.
Munitions of War Act, 1915, becomes law in Great Britain.
Ministry of Munitions formed in Great Britain.

4th ... Lahej (South Arabia) taken by Turkish forces (4th/5th).
Durazzo occupied by Serbian forces (see 17th, and October 4th, 1914).

7th ... **First Battle of the Isonzo ends** (see June 29th).
Italian cruiser "Amalfi" sunk by Austrian submarine in the Adriatic.

9th ... **German South-West Africa capitulates to General Botha** (see September 19th, 1914).

11th ... German light cruiser "Königsberg" destroyed in Rufiji River, German East Africa, by British monitors (see September 20th and October 31st, 1914).

12th ... British residency at Bushire (South Persia) attacked by Tangistani tribesmen (see August 8th).

13th ... **Great Austro-German Offensive on Eastern front begins.***

14th ... A Dominion Premier (Sir R. Borden, Canada) for the first time attends meeting of the British Cabinet (see April 14th).
Sherif of Mecca opens direct negotiations with British Government for co-operation against the Turks (see October 31st, 1914, and October 24th, 1915).

15th ... National Registration Act becomes law in Great Britain (see August 15th).

17th ... Durazzo evacuated by the Serbian forces at request of Italian Government (see 4th, and August 31st).
Treaty of alliance signed at Sofia between Austria-Hungary, Bulgaria, Germany, and Turkey. Albania to be ceded to Bulgaria in return for Bulgarian participation in war.

18th ... **Second Battle of the Isonzo begins** (see August 10th).
Italian cruiser "Giuseppe Garibaldi" sunk by Austrian submarine in the Adriatic.

19th ... Second Battle of Krasnik ends (see 1st).

21st ... Ivangorod (Poland) invested by Austro-German forces (see August 5th).

* For details of the individual battles in this offensive, see Part II.

July–Aug. 1915

22nd ... Bukoba, on Victoria Nyanza (German East Africa), captured by British forces (22nd/23rd).

24th ... Rozan and Pultusk (North Poland) stormed by German forces.

25th ... Nasiriya (Mesopotamia) taken by British forces (see June 27th).
British Government guarantee to Greece eventual cession of Mitylene by Turkey (see March 20th).

26th ... Pelagosa Island, in Adriatic, occupied by Italian forces.

29th ... Entente Governments warn Montenegro that they will not recognise her occupation of Albanian territory (see June 26th).
Establishment of the East Persia Cordon (Anglo-Russian) begins (see October 7th).

30th ... The Pope sends appeal for peace to belligerent Governments (see November 5th, 1914, and August 1st, 1917).

AUGUST 1915.

1st ... Constantinople harbour raided by British submarine.

3rd ... Van (Armenia) evacuated by the Russian forces (see 5th, and May 19th).

5th ... **Warsaw occupied by German forces** (see July 13th).
Ivangorod taken by Austro-German forces (see July 21st).
Van occupied by Turkish forces (see 3rd).

6th ... **Operations of the landing at Suvla (Dardanelles) begin** (see 15th).
Battle of Sari Bair (Dardanelles) begins (see 9th and 10th).
Dr. Machado Guimarães elected Portuguese President (see October 5th, 1915, and December 11th, 1917).
Bulgarian Government negotiate fresh loan for 400,000,000 francs with Austro-German banks (see February 3rd).
Agreement concluded between Japan and China substituting Japanese authority for German in Tsingtau customs (see November 7th, 1914).

8th ... Bushire (South Persia) occupied by British forces (see July 12th and September 9th).
Turkish battleship "Barbarousse-Hairedine" sunk by British submarine "E.-11" in the Dardanelles.
German naval attack on Riga begins (see 21st).

9th ... **Decisive day of Battle of Sari Bair** (see 6th and 10th).
Viscount Kato, Japanese Minister for Foreign Affairs, resigns (previously appointed April 16th, 1914) (see 10th).

10th ... **Battle of Sari Bair ends** (see 6th and 9th).
Second Battle of the Isonzo ends (see July 18th).
German airship "L.-12" extensively damaged by British aircraft off Ostend.
Marquis Okuma appointed Japanese Minister for Foreign Affairs (ad interim) (see 9th, and September 21st).

12th ... First ship sunk by torpedo from British seaplane (Dardanelles).

13th ... H.M.T. "Royal Edward" sunk in the Ægean by German submarine.*

15th ... **Operations of the landing at Suvla end** (see 6th and 21st).
Entente Governments make conditional offer of territorial acquisitions to Serbia (see 30th, and May 7th).
National Register taken in Great Britain (see July 15th).

16th ... Lowca and Harrington, near Whitehaven (Cumberland), shelled by German submarine.

17th ... **Kowno stormed by German forces** (17th/18th).
Ain ed Douleh, Persian Prime Minister, resigns (see 18th, and April 27th).

18th ... Mustaufi ul Mamalek again appointed Persian Prime Minister (see 17th, and December 24th).

---

* First transport so lost.

19th ...	German battle cruiser "Moltke" torpedoed by British submarine "E.-1" in Gulf of Riga. British submarine "E.-13" attacked by German warships while aground in Danish waters. British S.S. "Arabic" sunk by German submarine. H.M.S. "Baralong" (special service ship) destroys German submarine "U.-27."
20th ...	Novo-Georgievsk (Poland) stormed by German forces.
21st ...	Battle of Scimitar Hill (Suvla) (see 15th). **Italy declares war on Turkey.** First authenticated case of German submarine firing on a ship's crew in open boats (British S.S. "Ruel"). German naval attack on Riga discontinued (see 8th).
22nd ...	Osovets (North Poland) stormed by German forces. M. Venizelos again appointed Premier of Greece in succession to M. Gounaris (see March 6th and 9th and October 5th).
25th ...	Brest-Litovsk (Poland) taken by German forces (25th/26th).
26th ...	Byelostok (Poland) taken by German forces.
30th ...	British Foreign Minister (Sir E. Grey) informs M. Supilo that, provided Serbia agreed, the Allies could guarantee the eventual freedom and self-determination of Bosnia, Herzegovina, South Dalmatia, Slavonia, and Croatia (see 15th, and May 7th).
31st ...	Durazzo reoccupied by Serbian forces (see July 17th and December 6th).

SEPTEMBER 1915.

1st ...	German Government inform United States Government that United States demands for limitation of submarine activity are accepted. Ruad Island, off Syrian coast, occupied by French forces.
3rd ...	Grodno captured by German forces (2nd/3rd).
5th ...	The Tsar supersedes the Grand Duke Nicholas in supreme command of the Russian Armies with General Alexeiev as Chief of Staff* (see 8th, August 3rd, 1914, and March 15th and June 4th, 1917). Action of Hafiz Kor (North-West Frontier of India).
7th ...	Russian counter-offensive in Galicia. Battle of Tarnopol begins (see 16th).
8th ...	The Grand Duke Nicholas appointed Viceroy of the Caucasus (see 5th). Second Allied Attack on Mora (Cameroons) (8th/9th).
9th ...	**Battle of Dvinsk begins** (see November 1st). **Battle of Vilna begins** (see October 2nd). Bushire (South Persia) again attacked by tribesmen (see August 8th). Turco-Bulgarian Frontier Convention signed at Dimotika. United States Government request recall of Austro-Hungarian Ambassador, Dr. Dumba (appointed to United States, March 1913) (see 28th).
16th ...	Pinsk taken by German forces. Battle of Tarnopol ends (see 7th).
18th ...	**Vilna taken by German forces** (see 9th).

* Though nominally Chief of Staff, General Alexeiev was virtually Commander-in-Chief and performed the duties of that office till the Tsar's abdication on March 15th, 1917, and continued as Commander-in-Chief thereafter without further appointment.

Sept.-Oct. 1915

21st ... Bulgarian Government order partial mobilisation (see 22nd).
    Greek Premier (M. Venizelos) asks for guarantee of 150,000 British and French troops as condition for Greek intervention (see 24th, and March 5th).
    Viscount Ishii succeeds Marquis Okuma as Japanese Minister for Foreign Affairs (see August 10th, 1915, and October 9th, 1916).

22nd ... **"Dede Agatch Agreement" concluded between Turkey and Bulgaria rectifying Turkish frontier in favour of Bulgaria.**
Bulgarian Government order general mobilisation for 25th.
    Second Advance on Yaunde (Cameroons) begins (see January 1st, 1916).

23rd ... Greek Government order precautionary mobilisation.

24th   French and British Governments inform Greek Government that they are prepared to send troops requested (see 21st, 27th, and 28th).

25th ... **Allied Autumn Offensive begins:—**
Battle of Loos begins (see October 8th).
Third Battle of Artois begins (see June 18th and October 15th).
Second Battle of Champagne begins (see March 17th and November 6th).
    General Sir J. Wolfe Murray, Chief of the Imperial General Staff, Great Britain, resigns (see 26th, and October 26th, 1914).
    Bulgarian mobilisation begins (see 22nd).
    Serbian Government give undertaking to Greek Government to cede Doiran and Gevgeli eventually to Greece, and not to claim Strumitsa.

26th ... Lieut.-General Sir A. J. Murray appointed Chief of the Imperial General Staff, Great Britain (see 25th, and January 24th and December 22nd).

27th ... Greek Premier (M. Venizelos) obtains secret consent of King Constantine to proposed Entente expedition to Salonika (see 24th and 28th).
    Italian battleship "Benedetto Brin" destroyed by internal explosion in harbour at Brindisi.

28th ... Battle of Kut, 1915 (Mesopotamia).
    Dr. Dumba, Austro-Hungarian Ambassador, recalled from United States of America (see 9th).
    Greek Government formally refuse French and British "offer" of the 24th (see 27th, and October 2nd).
    British and Russian Governments agree to request of Persian Government for a monthly subvention.

30th ... Lord Derby assumes control of recruiting in Great Britain (see December 11th, 1916).

OCTOBER 1915.

1st ... *Beginning of period in which the Germans obtained mastery in the air on the Western front (due to the Fokker machine) (see April 1st, 1916).

2nd ... **Battle of Vilna ends** (see September 9th).
    Greek Premier (M. Venizelos) asks British and French Governments to land troops at Salonika as soon as possible (see 3rd and 5th, and September 28th).

3rd ... **Allied troops arrive at Salonika: Greek Government protest against a landing** (see 2nd, 5th and 6th).
    First German merchant vessel (S.S. "Livonia") sunk by British submarine in the Baltic.

4th ... **Entente Powers send ultimatum to Bulgaria** (see 5th and 13th).

5th ... **French and British forces land at Salonika** (see 3rd).
    King of Greece refuses to support policy of Premier (M. Venizelos) (see 2nd, and September 27th).
    M. Venizelos again resigns (see 6th, and August 22nd, 1915, and June 26th, 1917).

* Approximate date.

October 1915

5th (contd.)   Russia severs diplomatic relations with Bulgaria (see 4th and 19th).
Dr. Machado Guimarães succeeds Dr. J. Braga as Portuguese President (see May 28th, and August 6th, 1915, and December 11th, 1917).

6th   **Final Austro-German invasion of Serbia begins** (see December 15th, 1914).
M. Zaimis appointed Greek Premier (see 5th, and November 5th).
King of Greece gives assurance to British Minister that Greece will maintain neutrality, but Greek mobilisation (see September 23rd) and Allied disembarkation at Salonika will proceed (see 3rd, 5th and 8th).

7th   **Austro-German forces effect passage of the Save and Danube** (see 6th).
Birjand (East Persia) occupied by British forces (see July 29th).

8th   **Battle of Loos ends** (see September 25th).
New Greek Government (see 6th) announce policy of armed neutrality.

9th   **Belgrade taken by Austrian forces** (see December 15th, 1914, and November 1st, 1918).
Second Affair of Hafiz Kor (North-West Frontier of India).

10th   **Greek Government reject Serbian claim for help under Serbo-Greek Treaty of 1912.**

11th   **Hostilities commence between Bulgarian and Serbian forces** (see 14th).
Semendria (Serbia) taken by Austrian forces (see 6th).

12th   Miss Edith Cavell shot in Brussels by order of a German court-martial.

13th   Most severe airship raid on East Coast of England and London; casualties 200 (see January 19th and May 31st, 1915, October 19th, 1917, and August 5th, 1918).
Great Britain severs diplomatic relations with Bulgaria (see 4th and 15th).
Hostilities commence between French and Bulgarian forces in Macedonia.
M. Delcassé, French Foreign Minister, resigns; M. Viviani succeeds temporarily (see 29th and 30th).

14th   **Bulgaria and Serbia declare war on one another** (see 4th and 11th).

15th   **Third Battle of Artois ends** (see September 25th).
Great Britain declares " state of war " with Bulgaria (see 13th).
Montenegro declares " state of war " with Bulgaria.
Rumanian Government refuse to aid Serbia (see January 25th).
Vranje (Serbia) taken by Bulgarian forces (see October 5th, 1918).
General Sir Charles Monro appointed to succeed Sir Ian Hamilton as Commander-in-Chief, Mediterranean Expeditionary Force (see 17th and 28th, and March 17th).

16th   **France declares " state of war " with Bulgaria** (see 4th and 15th).
British Government offer Cyprus to Greece if she will support Serbia (see 20th, and January 24th).
Entente Governments proclaim blockade of Ægean coast of Bulgaria.

17th   General Sir William Birdwood takes over temporary command of Mediterranean Expeditionary Force from Sir Ian Hamilton (see 15th and 28th).

18th   **Third Battle of the Isonzo begins** (see November 3rd).

19th   Ishtip (Serbia) taken by Bulgarian forces (see September 25th, 1918).
Russia and Italy declare war on Bulgaria (see 4th and 5th).
Japan declares adherence to the Pact of London (see September 5th, 1914, and November 30th, 1915).

20th   Greek Government reject British offer of Cyprus (see 16th).

21st   Dede Agatch (Bulgaria) bombarded by Allied squadron.
Veles taken by Bulgarian forces (see Septemer 25th, 1918).

Oct.-Nov. 1915

22nd ... **Kumanovo and Üsküb (Skoplje) taken by Bulgarian forces.**
Shabatz taken by Austrian forces.

23rd ... German cruiser "Prinz Adalbert" sunk by British submarine "E.-8" in the Baltic.

24th ... Negotin, on River Vardar, taken by Bulgarian forces.
First Action of Krivolak (Macedonia).
British Government in letter to Sherif of Mecca define territorial limits of proposed Arab State (see July 14th, 1915, and June 5th, 1916).

28th ... H.M.S. "Argyll" wrecked on east coast of Scotland.
Lieut.-General Sir Bryan Mahon appointed General Officer Commanding British Forces, Balkans (see May 9th, 1916).
General Sir Charles Monro assumes command of Mediterranean Expeditionary Force (see 15th, 17th, and November 4th).

29th ... M. Viviani, French Premier and Foreign Minister, resigns (date of appointment as Premier June 14th, 1914) (see 13th and 30th).
M. Millerand, French Minister for War, resigns (see 30th, and August 27th, 1914).

30th ... Third Allied attack on Mora (Cameroons) begins (see November 4th).
Second Action of Krivolak (Macedonia).
M. Briand succeeds M. Viviani as French Premier and Foreign Minister (see 29th, and March 17th, 1917).
General Galliéni appointed French Minister for War (see 29th, and March 16th, 1916).
Last meeting of Dardanelles Committee of the British Cabinet (see June 7th and November 3rd).

NOVEMBER 1915.

1st   Kragujevatz (North Serbia) taken by Austro-German forces (30th/1st).
Battle of Dvinsk ends (see September 9th).

2nd ... British Premier (Mr. Asquith) declares Serbian independence to be an essential object of the war.
Kasvin (West Persia) occupied by a Russian force.

3rd ... **Third Battle of the Isonzo ends** (see October 18th).
Serbian Government leave Nish (see 23rd, and July 25th, 1914).
First meeting of newly-constituted War Committee of British Cabinet to replace the Dardanelles Committee (see October 30th, 1915, and December 1st, 1916).
Port and Transit Executive Committee formed in Great Britain (see 10th).

4th ... Third Allied attack on Mora abandoned (see October 30th).
Banyo (Cameroons) attacked by General Cunliffe's Allied force (see 6th).
Lord Kitchener leaves England for the Dardanelles (see 10th).
General Sir Charles Monro appointed to command Salonika Force.
Sir William Birdwood to command Mediterranean Expeditionary Force (see 25th, and October 15th, 17th, and 28th).

5th ... **Nish taken by Bulgarian forces** (see 3rd, and October 11th, 1918).
Battle of Kachanik (Serbia) begins (see 8th).
M. Zaimis, Greek Prime Minister, resigns (see 6th, and October 6th).
German airship "L.Z.-39" destroyed near Grodno.

6th ... **Second Battle of Champagne ends** (see September 25th).
Sollum (Western Egypt) attacked by German submarine (see 14th).*
Banyo captured by Allied force (see 4th).
M. Skouloudhis appointed Greek Premier (see 5th, and June 21st, 1916).

7th ... German cruiser "Undine" sunk by British submarine "E.-19."
Italian S.S. "Ancona" sunk by Austrian submarine.

8th ... **Battle of Kachanik ends** (see 5th).
Entente loan (£1,600,000) to Greece concluded (see July 20th, 1916).

---

* Egyptian coastguard cruiser "Abbas" sunk and "Nur el Bahr" disabled.

Nov. 1915

10th	**Fourth Battle of the Isonzo begins** (see December 10th).
	Indian Corps begins to leave France for Mesopotamia (see October 19th, 1914).
	Lord Kitchener arrives at the Dardanelles (see 4th).
	Ship Licensing Committee formed in Great Britain: Order in Council prohibits voyages between foreign ports except under licence (see February 15th, 1916).
	Requisitioning (Carriage of Foodstuffs) Committee formed in Great Britain: Order in Council authorises requisition of ships for carriage of foodstuffs (see November 3rd, 1917).
11th	First British advance on Baghdad begins (see 22nd).
14th	Senussi commence hostilities against British by attacking Egyptian post at Sollum (see 6th and 23rd).
15th	Representatives of Central Powers leave Teheran (Persia) on approach of Russian forces.
16th	Babuna Pass and Prilep (South Serbia) taken by Bulgarian forces (see September 23rd, 1918).
17th	Anglo-French Conference held in Paris to discuss aid to Serbia and Dardanelles expeditions. Project approved in principle to appoint Council of War to co-ordinate Allied action (see December 29th).
	British hospital ship "Anglia" sunk by mine off Dover.
20th	Novi Bazar taken by Austrian forces (see October 14th, 1918).
22nd	**Battle of Ctesiphon (Mesopotamia) begins** (see 25th).
	*General Sir H. Smith-Dorrien appointed Commander-in-Chief of British forces in East Africa (see January 31st, 1916).
23rd	Rovereto (Trentino) taken by Italian forces.
	Mitrovitza and Pristina (Serbia) taken by Austro-German forces (see October 10th, 1918).
	Serbian Government leave Prizren for Scutari (Shkodra) (see 3rd, and December 3rd).
	British military operations against the Senussi commence (see December 13th, 1915, and February 8th, 1917): Sollum post evacuated (see 14th).
	Entente Powers send Note to Greek Government demanding non-interference with Allied troops, and guaranteeing eventual restoration of occupied Greek territory (see 24th, and October 3rd).
	British Government conclude preliminary agreement with the Netherlands Overseas Trust for rationing of Holland (see June 3rd, 1915, and June 30th, 1916).
24th	Greek Government accept Entente demands of the 23rd.
	Field-Marshal von der Goltz (see December 10th, 1914, and April 19th, 1916) takes command of Turkish forces in Mesopotamia.
	Danish merchants and manufacturers conclude agreement with the British Government to restrict supplies to Germany.
25th	**British retreat from Ctesiphon to Kut al Amara begins** (see 22nd, and December 3rd).
	M. Albert Thomas announces arrangements completed for inter-Allied organisation of munitions.
	General Sir Charles Monro appointed Commander-in-Chief reconstituted Mediterranean Expeditionary Force with Sir William Birdwood General Officer Commanding Dardanelles Army (see 4th, and January 9th, 1916).
29th	Dr. A. Augusto da Costa succeeds Dr. J. de Castro as Portuguese Premier (see June 19th, 1915, and March 15th, 1916).
30th	**Serbian retreat through Albania begins** (see January 15th, 1916).
	Formal signature of the Pact of London by Great Britain, France, Russia, Japan, and Italy (see September 5th, 1914; April 26th, 1915; and October 19th, 1915).

* Did not take over command owing to illness.

DECEMBER 1915.

1st ... Prizren (Serbia) taken by Bulgarian forces (see October 11th, 1918)
Italy announces her adherence to the Pact of London (see November 30th).

2nd ... **Monastir (Serbia) taken by Bulgarian forces** (see November 19th, 1916).
French retreat from Serbia to Salonika begins: Krivolak evacuated.

3rd ... British forces, retreating from Ctesiphon, reach Kut (see 7th, and November 25th).
General Joffre, Chief of French General Staff from July 28th, 1911, appointed Commander-in-Chief French Armies. Appointment of Chief of General Staff lapses (see April 29th, 1917).
Serbian Government and military headquarters set up at Scutari (Shkodra) (see November 23rd, 1915, and January 15th, 1916).

4th ... United States Government request recall of German attachés Captains Boy-Ed and Von Papen (see 10th).

5th ... Action of Demir Kapu (5th/6th) in French retreat from Serbia.
Kut placed in state of defence (see 3rd and 7th).

6th ... Durazzo bombarded by Austrian squadron (see 20th, and August 31st).
Ipek (Montenegro) taken by Austro-German forces (see October 14th, 1918).
British Government put economic pressure on Greece by making the " export restrictions " apply to that country **(see 13th).**

7th ... **Siege of Kut begins** (see 3rd, and January 4th and April 29th, 1916).
Actions of Kosturino (7th/8th). British retreat from Macedonia begins.
Agreement concluded between French Government and Netherlands Oversea Trust (see November 23rd, 1914, and November 23rd, 1915).

8th ... **Evacuation of Suvla and Anzac ordered** (see 19th and 20th).
Debra and Okhrida (Serbia) taken by Bulgarian forces.

9th ... General Castelnau appointed Chief of Staff to General Joffre (see 3rd).
General Sarrail demands withdrawal of Greek troops from Salonika (see 11th).

10th ... **Fourth Battle of the Isonzo ends** (see November 10th).
German Government recall from United States attachés Von Papen and Boy-Ed (see 4th, and January 15th, 1916).

11th ... Doiran and Gevgeli (South Serbia) taken by Bulgarian forces (see September 22nd, 1918).
Greek Government refuse Entente demand for withdrawal of Greek troops from Salonika (see 9th).
Yuan-Shih-Kai accepts throne of China (see March 22nd, 1916, and June 6th, 1916).

13th ... Affair of the Wadi Senab (11th/13th) (see November 23rd, 1915, and February 26th, 1916).
British Government order partial relaxation of economic pressure on Greece (see 6th).

14th ... Hamadan (Western Persia) occupied by Russian forces (see August 10th, 1916).
Bulgarian and Greek General Staffs conclude agreement establishing temporary neutral zone along Greek frontier.

15th ... The last Allied forces in Macedonia withdrawn into Greek territory (see 7th, and September 19th, 1916).
Qasr-i-Shirin (Western Persia) occupied by Turkish forces (see May 7th, 1916).
Field-Marshal Sir John French resigns as Commander-in-Chief of British armies in France (see 19th, and August 4th, 1914, and May 5th, 1918).

17th ... German light cruiser " Bremen " sunk by British submarine in the Baltic.

19th ...	Evacuation of Suvla and Anzac begun (see 8th and 20th). General Sir Douglas Haig succeeds Sir John French as Commander-in-Chief of the British Armies in France (see 15th, and January 1st, 1917). Bulgarian and Greek General Staffs conclude agreement establishing temporary neutral zone along Greek frontier.
20th ...	**Evacuation of Suvla and Anzac completed** (see 8th, 19th and 28th). Durazzo occupied by Italian forces (see 6th, and February 27th, 1916).
22nd ...	Lieut.-General Sir W. Robertson resigns as Chief of the General Staff, British Expeditionary Force, France (see 23rd, and January 25th), and is succeeded by Lieut.-General L. E. Kiggell (see January 27th, 1918). Lieut.-General Sir A. J. Murray, Chief of the Imperial General Staff, resigns (see 23rd, and September 26th, 1915, and March 19th, 1916).
23rd ...	British naval operations on Lake Tanganyika begin (see 26th). General Sir W. Robertson appointed Chief of the Imperial General Staff (see 22nd, and February 18th, 1918). "Trading with the Enemy (Extension of Powers) Act, 1915" (beginning of "Black List" policy), comes into force in Great Britain (see January 26th and July 28th, 1916).
24th ...	Mustaufi ul Mamalek (Persian Prime Minister) resigns (see 25th, and August 18th).
25th ...	Turkish Christmas Eve Attack on Kut (24th/25th). Affair of the Wadi Majid (Western Egypt). Kangavar (Western Persia) occupied by a Russian force. Prince Firman Firma appointed Prime Minister of Persia (see 24th, and March 5th, 1916).
26th ...	German raider "Moewe" sails from Bremen on first cruise (see February 1st, 1916). Naval action on Lake Tanganyika: German gunboat "Kingani" captured by H.M.S. "Mimi" and "Toutou" (see 23rd, and February 9th, 1916). Treaty concluded between British Government and Ibn Sa'ud, Emir of Nejd (see July 18th, 1916).
28th ...	Evacuation of remainder of Gallipoli Peninsula ordered (see 20th, and January 8th, 1916).
29th ...	Durazzo raided by Austrian naval light forces: latter brought to action in Southern Adriatic. Draft rules approved for Inter-Allied Council of War (see November 17th).
30th ...	Consuls of Central Powers at Salonika arrested and deported by order of General Sarrail, Commanding French troops. H.M.S. "Natal" destroyed by internal explosion in Cromarty harbour.
31st ...	Last units of Indian Expeditionary Force "G" leave the Dardanelles to amalgamate with Indian Expeditionary Force "E" in Egypt (see April 7th).

JANUARY 1916.

1st ...	Yaunde (Cameroons) taken by General Dobell's forces (see September 22nd, 1915). King of Serbia arrives at Salonika (see 15th).
4th ...	**First Attempt to relieve Kut begins:** relieving force begins advance from 'Ali Gharbi (see 21st, and December 7th, 1915).
6th ...	H.M.S. "King Edward VII" sunk by mine off North of Scotland. Action of Sheikh Sa'ad (Mesopotamia) begins (see 4th and 8th).
7th ...	Evacuation of Helles (Gallipoli Peninsula) begins (see 8th, and December 28th, 1915).
8th ...	**Evacuation of the Gallipoli Peninsula completed** (see 7th, and December 28th, 1915). Action of Sheikh Sa'ad ends (see 6th).

January 1916

9th ... General Sir Charles Monro vacates command of the Mediterranean Expeditionary Force and General Sir William Birdwood vacates command of the Dardanelles army (see November 25th, 1915).*

10th ... Entente Governments inform Greek Government of proposed transport of Serbian Army to Corfu (see 11th and 15th).
Mount Lovchen (Montenegro) taken by Austrian forces.
General Sir A. J. Murray takes over command of the Mediterranean Expeditionary Force (see 9th).

11th ... **Corfu occupied by French forces** (see 10th, 13th and 15th).
Russian offensive towards Erzerum begins (see February 12th).

12th ... Armistice concluded between Montenegro and Austria (see 20th).

13th ... **Cetinje (Montenegro) occupied by Austrian forces.**
Kirmanshah (West Persia) occupied by Turkish forces (see February 26th).
Greek Government refuse consent to the occupation of Corfu (see 11th).

14th ... Action of the Wadi (Mesopotamia) (13th/14th).
Lieut.-General Sir Percy Lake appointed Commander-in-Chief, Mesopotamia (see 19th, and August 28th).

15th ... British S.S. "Appam" captured by German raider "Moewe" (see December 26th, 1915, and February 1st, 1916).
Von Papen papers published in U.S.A. (see December 10th, 1915).
First Serbian troops land at Corfu (see 10th, November 30th, 1915, and February 10th, 1916).
Serbian Government transferred to Brindisi (see December 3rd, 1915, and February 9th, 1916).
King of Serbia leaves Salonika (see 1st and 17th).

16th ... General Sarrail assumes command of all Allied forces at Salonika (see December 14th, 1917).

17th ... Keupri-Keui (Armenia) again captured by Russian forces (see December 17, 1914).
King of Serbia arrives at Edypsos (see 15th, and November 6th, 1918).

18th ... †Baron Beyens succeeds M. J. Davignon as Belgian Minister for Foreign Affairs (M. Davignon was appointed on February 28th, 1914) (see August 4th, 1917).

19th ... Lieut.-General Sir Percy Lake takes over command of British forces in Mesopotamia from General Nixon (see 14th, and August 28th).

20th ... Negotiations between Austria and Montenegro broken off. Armistice ceases (see 12th).

21st ... First British Attack on Hanna (Mesopotamia): **First Attempt to relieve Kut fails** (see 4th, and March 8th).

22nd ... Antivari (Montenegro) occupied by Austrian forces (see March 1st, 1915, and November 4th, 1918).
Rumanian Government open negotiations with Russian Government with a view to military assistance (see August 17th).

23rd ... Scutari (Albania) occupied by Austrian forces (see October 31st, 1918).
Podgoritza (Montenegro) occupied by Austrian forces.

24th ... **First Military Service Bill passed by British House of Commons** (see February 10th).

25th ... San Giovanni di Medua (Albania) captured by Austrian forces (see June 26th, 1915, and October 29th, 1918).

26th ... United States Government make informal protest to British Government regarding their "Black List" policy (see December 23rd, 1915, and July 28th, 1916).

* Sir Charles Monro was appointed later Commander-in-Chief in India. Sir William Birdwood later temporarily commanded the Fourth Army in France and then the Australian Corps, till eventually appointed to command the Fifth Army on May 23rd, 1918.
† Baron Beyens officiated in the appointment from July 26th, 1915, till January 18th, 1916, during which period M. Davignon was absent, owing to ill-health.

27th	...	Shipping Control Committee formed in Great Britain (see November 3rd and 10th, 1915, and December 22nd, 1916).
29th	...	Last German airship raid on Paris (see March 21st, 1915, and September 16th, 1918).
31st	...	*General Sir H. Smith-Dorrien resigns appointment as Commander-in-Chief British Forces, East Africa (see November 22nd, 1915, and February 19th, 1916). Airship raid on England; furthest penetration westwards; casualties 183 (see January 19th, 1915, and August 5th, 1918).

FEBRUARY 1916.

1st	...	British S.S. "Appam" brought to Norfolk, Va., U.S.A., by German prize crew from raider "Moewe" (see January 15th and March 4th). M. Goremikin, Russian Premier, resigns (date of appointment January 30th, 1914). M. Stürmer appointed successor (see July 22nd and November 24th).
2nd	...	Elbasan (Albania) taken by Bulgarian forces (see October 7th, 1918). German airship "L.-19" founders in the North Sea.
8th	...	British Government request naval assistance from Japan (see November 14th, 1914, and April 17th, 1917). French cruiser "Amiral Charner" sunk by submarine off Syrian coast.
9th	...	**Serbian Government set up at Corfu** (see January 15th and May 7th). German gunboat "Hedwig von Wissman" sunk by H.M.S. "Mimi" and "Fifi."† British command of Lake Tanganyika secured (see December 26th, 1915).
10th	...	**Military Service Act comes into operation in Great Britain** (see January 24th and May 16th). **Remnant of Serbian Army concentrated at Corfu** (see January 15th and April 3rd). German Government send Note to United States Government stating that defensively armed merchantmen will be treated as belligerents from March 1st onwards (see 21st).
11th	...	H.M.S. "Arethusa" sunk by mine in North Sea. Italian detachment reaches Corfu (see January 11th and 15th).
12th	...	Russian attack on Erzerum begins (see 16th, and January 11th).
13th	...	Entente Governments notify Greece of forthcoming transfer of Montenegrin Army to Corfu (see 16th).
14th	...	Entente Powers make declaration guaranteeing to Belgium eventual independence and indemnification.
15th	...	**Fifth Battle of the Isonzo begins** (see March 17th). Agreement concluded between British Government and chieftains of the Bakhtiari (Persia) for co-operation in protection of Persian oilfields. British Order in Council extends powers of Ship Licensing Committee to all voyages (see November 10th, 1915).
16th	...	**Erzerum taken by the Russian forces** (see 12th, and March 12th, 1918). Remnants of Montenegrin army land at Corfu (see 13th). War Office take over anti-aircraft defence of London from the Admiralty, and become responsible for anti-aircraft defence generally throughout the kingdom. War Office take over from the India Office control of operations in Mesopotamia.
17th	...	Chios (Ægean) occupied by British forces. Berat (Albania) occupied by Austrian forces (see July 10th, 1918). Last German forces in South Cameroons cross border into Spanish territory for internment (see 18th).

* Did not take over command owing to illness.
† Ex-German Gunboat "Kingani."

Feb.–Mar. 1916

18th ... Mush (Armenia) taken by Russian forces (see August 15th).
Mora, the last German post in the Cameroons, surrenders to the British. **Conquest of the Cameroons by Entente forces completed** (see March 3rd).

19th ... Major-General Tighe succeeded by Lieut.-General Smuts in command of British forces in East Africa (see April 16th, 1915, January 31st, 1916, and January 20th, 1917).

21st ... **Battle of Verdun begins** (see 25th, and August 31st).
German airship "L.Z.-77" brought down by French gunfire at Revigny (night 21st/22nd).
German Government inform United States Government that defensively armed merchantmen will henceforth be regarded as cruisers (see 10th, 29th, and February 26th, 1917).
Lieut.-General Sir H. C. Sclater, Adjutant-General, Home Forces, Great Britain, resigns (appointed April 9th, 1914) (see 22nd).
Lieut.-General Sir C. F. N. Macready, Adjutant-General, British Expeditionary Force, France, resigns (see 22nd, and August 4th, 1914).

22nd ... Lieut.-General Sir G. H. Fowke appointed Adjutant-General, British Expeditionary Force, France (see 21st).
Lieut.-General Sir C. F. N. Macready appointed Adjutant-General, Home Forces, Great Britain (see 21st, and August 30th, 1918).

23rd ... Portugal seizes German steamers in the Tagus (see March 9th).
Ministry of Blockade formed in Great Britain. Lord Robert Cecil appointed Minister of Blockade (see July 18th, 1918).

24th ... Provisional Government of Essad Pasha leaves Durazzo (see 28th, and October 4th, 1914).

25th ... **Fort Douaumont (Verdun) stormed by German forces** (25th/26th) (see 21st).

26th ... Senussi defeated by British forces in Action of Agagiya (Western Egypt) (see December 13th, 1915, and February 5th, 1917).
Kirmanshah (Western Persia) occupied by Russian forces (see January 13th and July 1st).

27th ... **Durazzo captured by Austrian forces** (see December 20th, 1915, and October 2nd, 1918).

28th ... The nucleus of a British air squadron formed to bomb German industrial centres (see June 5th, 1918).
Albanian Provisional Government of Essad Pasha set up at Naples (see 24th, and September 20th).

29th ... Action in North Sea between German raider "Greif" and British auxiliary cruiser "Alcantara": both sunk.
Blockade of the Cameroons raised (see 18th, and April 23rd, 1915).
German Government send note to United States Government stating that it is not intended to postpone the extended submarine campaign (see 10th, 21st, and March 1st).

MARCH 1916.

1st ... **German extended submarine campaign begins** (see February 29th).
Hostilities between Sudan Government and Sultan of Darfur begin (see 16th, and December 31st).

2nd ... Bitlis (Armenia) taken by Russian forces (see August 15th).

3rd ... Agreement as to provisional administration of the Cameroons concluded between French and British Governments (see February 18th).

4th ... German raider "Moewe" returns to Bremen (Germany) (see December 26th, 1915, and November 26th, 1916).
Russian force landed at Atna for attack on Trebizond (see April 17th).

March 1916

5th ... British advance on Kilimanjaro (East Africa) begins (see 10th and 21st).
Prince Firman Firma, Persian Prime Minister, resigns (see 6th, and December 25th, 1915).
Mohtashim ed Douleh, Persian Foreign Minister, resigns (see 6th, and April 27th, 1915).

6th ... Mr. Baker appointed United States Secretary for War.
Sipahsalar A'zam appointed Persian Prime Minister (see 5th, and August 29th).
Sarim ed Douleh appointed Persian Foreign Minister (see 5th, and August 29th).

8th ... **Second attempt to relieve Kut:** British relieving force repulsed at Dujaila Redoubt (see January 21st and April 1st).

9th ... **Germany declares war on Portugal** (see February 23rd).

10th ... Taveta (East Africa) taken by British forces (see 5th, and August 15th, 1914).

11th ... Action of Latema Nek (East Africa) begins (see 5th, 10th, and 12th).

12th ... Action of Latema Nek (East Africa) ends (see 11th).
Karind (West Persia) occupied by a Russian force (later withdrawn).
Allied Military Conference held at Chantilly regarding a general summer offensive.

13th ... New Moshi (East Africa) taken by British forces (see 5th and 12th).

14th ... Sollum (Western Egypt) reoccupied by British forces (see November 23rd, 1915).
Admiral von Tirpitz, German Minister of Marine, resigns (appointed in 1897) (see 15th).

15th ... Austria-Hungary severs diplomatic relations with Portugal.
Austria-Hungary declares war on Portugal.
Admiral von Capelle appointed German Minister of Marine (see 14th, and August 13th, 1918).
Dr. A. José d'Almeida succeeds Dr. A. A. da Costa as Portuguese Premier (see November 29th, 1915, and April 25th, 1917).

16th ... Sudan force advances from Nahud into Darfur (see 1st, and May 22nd).
General Roques succeeds General Galliéni as French Minister for War (see October 30th, 1915, and March 17th, 1917).

17th ... **Fifth Battle of the Isonzo ends** (see February 15th).

18th ... Battle of Lake Naroch (White Russia) begins (see April 30th).

19th ... General Sir A. J. Murray takes over command of the Force in Egypt from General Sir John Maxwell.

20th ... M. Denys Cochin appointed French Under-Secretary of State for Blockade (see August 17th, 1917).

21st ... Action of Kahe (East Africa) brings the Kilimanjaro operations to and end (see 5th). German forces retreat from Kilimanjaro area.

22nd .. Yuan-Shih-Kai relinquishes the throne of China (see December 11th, 1915, and June 6th, 1916).

24th ... S.S. "Sussex" (British) torpedoed by submarine in the English Channel (see April 18th).

28th ... Inter-Allied Conference in Paris (26th/28th). Declaration of Unity between Belgium, France, Great Britain, Italy, Japan, Portugal, Russia, and Serbia regarding military, economic, and diplomatic affairs, drawn up.

29th ... General Polivanov, Russian Minister for War, resigns, and is succeeded by General Shuvaev (see June 26th, 1915, and January 17th, 1917).
Lieut.-General Oka, Japanese Minister for War, resigns (appointed April 16th, 1914) (see 30th).

Mar.–April 1916.

30th ... Russian hospital ship "Portugal" sunk by submarine in the Black Sea.
Lieut.-General Kenichi Oshima appointed Japanese Minister for War (see 29th, and September 29th, 1918).

31st ... German airship raid on England (east coast). Airship "L.15" brought down by gunfire near mouth of the Thames.

APRIL 1916.

1st ... *End of period of German mastery of the air on the Western front (see October 1st, 1915).
Third Attempt to relieve Kut begins (see 5th, and March 8th).

3rd .. Greek Government refuse overland route for transport of Serbian army from Corfu to Salonika (see 15th, and February 10th).

4th .. General Brusilov appointed to command Russian Southern Armies (see June 4th).

5th ... Action of Falahiya (Mesopotamia) (see 1st and 6th).

6th ... Russian attack on Trebizond begins (see 17th, and March 4th).
First attack on Sanna-i-Yat (see 5th and 9th).

9th ... Second attack on Sanna-i-Yat (see 6th and 22nd).

11th ... Kionga (German East Africa) occupied by Portuguese forces.

14th ... Constantinople and Adrianople attacked by aeroplanes of the Royal Naval Air Service from Mudros.

15th ... Serbian Army Headquarters land at Salonika from Corfu (see 3rd).

17th ... British attack on Kondoa Irangi (German East Africa) begins (see 19th).
Trebizond (Asia Minor) taken by Russian forces (see 6th, and February 24th, 1918).
Italian Government issue decrees prohibiting trading with Germany (see March 1st, 1915).

18th ... Action of Bait Aissa (Mesopotamia) (17th/18th).
United States Government send note to German Government on "Sussex" case (see March 24th) and submarine policy in general (see February 10th).

19th ... Kondoa Irangi (German East Africa) taken by British forces (see 17th, and June 9th).
Field-Marshal von der Goltz (see December 10th, 1914, and November 24th, 1915) assassinated by an Albanian officer.

20th ... Russian troops from the Far East arrive at Marseilles (see July 30th).
Disguised German transport "Aud" sinks herself after capture while trying to land arms on Irish coast.
Roger Casement lands in Ireland from a German submarine and is arrested (see 24th, and August 3rd).

22nd ... Third attack on Sanna-i-Yat repulsed (see 9th, 24th and 29th).

24th ... **Outbreak of Rebellion in Ireland** (see May 1st).
Final attempt to succour Kut: loss of H.M.S. "Julnar" (see 29th).
Laying of Belgian coast barrage commenced by British navy.

25th ... Lowestoft (Suffolk) and Yarmouth (Norfolk) raided by German battle cruiser squadron (see November 26th).

26th ... French and Russian Governments conclude "Sykes-Picot" agreement for eventual partition of Asia Minor (see May 9th and May 23rd).
Agreement signed at Berlin for transfer of British and German wounded and sick prisoners of war to Switzerland (see May 13th).

* Approximate date.

27th ... Martial law proclaimed in Dublin and the county (see 24th).
H.M.S. "Russell" sunk by mine in the Mediterranean.

29th ... **Capitulation of Kut** (see 22nd, May 19th, 1916, and December 7th, 1915).
"Havre Declaration" signed by France, Great Britain, Italy, Japan, and Russia guaranteeing integrity of Belgian Congo.

30th ... Battle of Lake Naroch ends (see March 18th).

MAY 1916.

1st ... **Collapse of Irish Rebellion—leaders surrender** (see 3rd, and April 24th).

3rd ... German airship "L.-20," returning from raid on Scotland, wrecked at Stavanger (Norway).
Three Irish rebel leaders executed (see 1st).

4th ... German airship "L.-7" destroyed off the Slesvig coast.

5th ... German airship "L.Z.-85" brought down by British gunfire at Salonika.

7th ... Qasr-i-Shirin (Western Persia) occupied by Russian forces (see December 15th, 1915, June 20th, 1916, and March 25th, 1917).
Serbian Government set up at Salonika (see February 9th, 1916, and December 9th, 1918).

9th ... British and French Governments conclude "Sykes-Picot" agreement as to eventual partition of Asia Minor (see April 26th and May 23rd).
Lieut.-General Sir George Milne succeeds Lieut.-General Sir Bryan Mahon as General Officer Commanding British Forces, Salonika (see October 28th, 1915).

10th ... Agreement signed at Berlin re employment of British and German prisoners of war (see 29th).

11th ... Kwash (East Persia) occupied by British forces.

13th ... Agreement signed at London for transfer of British and German wounded and sick prisoners of war to Switzerland (see April 26th, 1916, and July 2nd and September 11th, 1917).

14th ... **Austrian offensive in the Trentino begins** (see June 3rd).

15th ... Allied blockade of the Hejaz coast to assist revolt of Sherif of Mecca commenced (see June 7th).
Rowanduz (Northern Mesopotamia) occupied by Russian forces.
Khanaqin (North-East of Baghdad) taken by Russian forces (see June 5th).

16th ... Second Military Service Bill extending compulsion to married men passes the British House of Commons (see 25th, and February 10th).
Agreement concluded between Great Britain and France regarding respective claims in Turkish territories (see August 18th, 1917).

17th ... Air Board formed in Great Britain (see January 3rd, 1918).

18th ... Detachment of Cossacks from Russian force in West Persia effects junction with British army on the Tigris.

19th ... Turkish Army evacuates the As Sinn position and withdraws to Kut (see April 29th and December 13th).

22nd ... Sultan of Darfur defeated by Sudan force in affair of Beringiya (Darfur) (see 23rd, March 16th and November 6th).

23rd ... El Fasher (capital of Darfur) occupied by Sudan force (see 22nd).
British Government notify Russian Government of their recognition of Franco-Russian "Sykes-Picot" agreement as to eventual partition of Asia Minor (see April 26th, May 9th, and September 1st).

May-June 1916

24th ... Mamakhatun (Armenia) taken by Russian forces (see 31st).

25th ... British advance from Northern Rhodesia and Nyasaland across the frontier into German East Africa begins (see 27th).
Second Military Service Act becomes law in Great Britain (see 16th, and June 8th).

26th ... Fort Rupel (Greek frontier of Macedonia) occupied by Bulgarian and German forces (see 31st).
United States Government send Note to British Government protesting against search of mails.

27th ... Neu Langenburg (German East Africa) occupied by British forces (see 25th).

29th ... Agreement signed at London re the employment of British and German prisoners of war (see 10th).

31st ... **Battle of Jutland begins** (see June 1st: see Part II for ships sunk).
First British aerial co-operation with fleet in action.
Mamakhatun retaken by Turkish forces (see 24th).
Entente Governments protest to Greece against Bulgarian occupation of Fort Rupel (see 26th).

JUNE 1916.

1st ... **Battle of Jutland ends** (see May 31st).

2nd ... Battle of Mount Sorrel (Ypres) begins (see 13th).
Fort Vaux (Verdun) stormed by German forces* (see November 1st).

3rd ... **End of the main Austrian offensive in the Trentino** (see 16th, and May 14th).
Allied Commander proclaims martial law in city of Salonika (see October 3rd, 1915).

4th ... **Russian offensive ("Brusilov's Offensive") begins**† (see 11th, and August 17th).

5th ... **Sherif of Mecca begins revolt against Turkish rule** (see 7th, 9th, and October 24th, 1915).
H.M.S. "Hampshire" sunk by mine off Scottish coast. Field-Marshal Earl Kitchener and his Staff drowned (see August 6th, 1914).
Turkish offensive into West Persia begins:‡ Khanaqin evacuated by Russian forces (see May 15th).

6th ... Attack on Medina by revolting Arabs repulsed by Turkish garrison (see 5th).
"Pacific blockade" of Greece by Entente Powers begins (see 22nd).
Yuan-Shih-Kai, President of China, dies (date of election October 6th, 1913). Li-Yuan-Hung elected President (see March 22nd, 1916, and July 6th, 1917).

7th ... **Sherif of Mecca issues proclamation denouncing the Committee of Union and Progress and proclaiming the Independence of the Hejaz** (see 5th, and October 29th).

8th ... Bismarckburg (German East Africa) taken by British forces (see May 25th).
Second Compulsory Service Act comes into operation in Great Britain (see May 25th and April 10th, 1918).

9th ... Jidda (Arabia) captured by Arab forces (see 5th).
Action of Mkaramo (on Northern Railway in German East Africa).
German attack on Kondoa Irangi (East Africa) begins (see 10th, and April 19th).

10th ... **Turkish garrison of Mecca surrenders to the Sherif** (see 5th).
German attack on Kondoa Irangi repulsed (see 9th).
Compulsory Service Bill passed in New Zealand (see September 1st).

---
* German date. The French claim a foothold till the 7th.
† The first phase of this offensive is known to the Germans as the "Battle of Wosuzka-Sereth."
‡ Approximate date.

11th	...	"Brusilov's Offensive" continued (see 4th); **Battle of the Strypa begins** (see 30th). Signor Salandra, Italian Premier, resigns (see 15th, and May 16th, 1915).
12th	...	Kirman (Persia) occupied by British forces. Zaleszczyki (Galicia) taken by Russian forces (see July 30th, 1917).
13th	...	Battle of Mount Sorrel (Ypres) ends (see 2nd).
14th	...	Allied Economic Conference reassembles in Paris (see 27th, and June 3rd, 1915).
15th	...	Signor Boselli appointed Italian Prime Minister (see 11th, and October 25th, 1917).
16th	...	**Italian counter-offensive in the Trentino begins** (see 3rd. and July 7th).
17th	...	Czernowitz (Bukovina) reoccupied by Russian forces (see February 17th, 1915, and August 3rd, 1917).
19th	...	Handeni (German East Africa) occupied by British forces.
20th	...	Qasr-i-Shirin (West Persia) taken by Turkish forces (see May 7th, 1916, and March 25th, 1917).
21st	...	Radautz (Bukovina) taken by Russian forces. Entente Governments send Note to Greece demanding demobilisation and change of Government. (Accepted.) (See 27th.) Greek Cabinet (Skouloudhis) resign (see November 6th, 1915). M. Zaimis forms new Ministry (see September 11th).
22nd	...	"Pacific blockade" of Greece suspended (see 6th).
23rd	...	Fort Thiaumont (Verdun) finally stormed by German forces* (see 30th).
24th	...	Austrian forces driven out of The Bukovina.
27th	...	Greek Government order general demobilisation (see 21st). Recommendations of Allied Economic Conference ratified (see 14th).
30th	...	Fort Thiaumont (Verdun) retaken by French forces (see 23rd, and July 1st). **Battle of the Strypa ends** (see 11th). British Government conclude further agreement with the Netherlands Overseas Trust for rationing of Holland (see November 23rd, 1915).

JULY 1916.

1st	...	**Battles of the Somme, 1916, begin** with Battle of Albert, 1916 (1st/13th) (see November 18th). Contact patrol, or liaison with infantry, first instituted in the Royal Flying Corps. Kirmanshah (Persia) reoccupied by Turkish forces (see February 26th, 1916, and March 11th, 1917).
2nd	...	**Battle of Baranovichi begins** (see 9th).
3rd	...	Russian and Japanese Governments conclude treaty with regard to future policy in the Far East.
7th	...	**Italian counter-offensive in the Trentino ends** (see June 16th). Tanga (German East Africa) occupied by British forces (see November 5th, 1914). Mr. Lloyd George succeeds Lord Kitchener as Secretary of State for War, Great Britain (see June 5th and December 11th). **British Government issue Order in Council rescinding Declaration of London of 1909.** French Government issue similar order (see October 29th, 1914, and November 6th, 1914).

* Bulk of position was captured on May 23rd, and this date marks the limit of the German advance on Verdun.

July-Aug. 1916

9th ... **Battle of Baranovichi ends** (see 2nd).

10th ... German commercial submarine "Deutschland" arrives at Norfolk (Va.), from Bremen (see August 23rd).
Russian hospital ship "Vpered" sunk by submarine in the Black Sea.

11th ... Seaham harbour (on coast of Durham) shelled by German submarine.

12th ... Mamakhatun (Armenia) again taken by Russian forces (see May 31st).

14th ... Battle of Bazentin Ridge (Somme) begins (see 17th).
Mwanza, on Victoria Nyanza (German East Africa) taken by British forces.
Inter-Allied Conference on finance held in London (14th/15th).

15th ... Battle of Delville Wood (Somme) begins (see September 3rd).

17th ... Battle of Bazentin Ridge (Somme) ends (see 14th).

18th ... Treaty with Ibn Sa'ud, Emir of Nejd, ratified by British Government (see December 26th, 1915).

19th ... Turkish offensive from Oghratina against the Suez Canal begins (see August 4th).

20th ... Greek Government conclude new loan with the Entente (£800,000) (see November 8th, 1915).

22nd ... M. Sazonov, Russian Foreign Minister, resigns* and is succeeded by M. Stürmer (see February 1st and November 24th).

23rd ... Battle of Pozières Ridge (Somme) begins (see September 3rd).

25th ... Reconstituted Serbian army comes into action on Salonika front (see April 15th).
Erzinjan (Armenia) captured by Russian forces.†

27th ... Yenbo, port of Medina, surrenders to Arab forces (see June 5th).
Captain Fryatt, of British S.S. "Brussels," shot by order of a German court-martial in Belgium.

28th ... United States Government formally protest to British Government against "Black List" policy (see October 22nd, 1914, December 23rd, 1915, and January 26th, 1916).

29th ... German Government send Note to United States Government rejecting British offer to permit passage of foodstuffs to Poland from United States of America.

30th ... First aerial operations carried out by combined French and British air services on French Western front.
Russian troops from France land at Salonika and join Allied force (see April 20th).

31st ... Kilimatinde (German East Africa) taken by British forces.

AUGUST 1916.

2nd ... Italian Dreadnought "Leonardo da Vinci" sunk by internal explosion in harbour at Taranto.

3rd ... Ujiji, on Lake Tanganyika (German East Africa), occupied by Belgian forces.
Roger Casement executed (see April 20th).

4th ... **Battle of Rumani (Sinai)** (4th/5th) (see July 19th).

5th ... Advance of main body of British force in East Africa through the Nguru Hills begins (see 11th).

6th ... **Battle of Gorizia (6th Battle of the Isonzo) begins** (see 17th).

* Appointed in 1910.
† This was the furthest point west reached by Russian forces. It was evacuated subsequently without further fighting.

August 1916

8th ... Portuguese Government decide to extend military co-operation to Europe (see November 23rd, 1914, December 4th, 1914, and January 3rd, 1917).

9th ... Gorizia taken by Italian forces (see 6th).

10th ... Stanislau again taken by Russian forces (see June 8th, 1915, and July 24th, 1917).
Hamadan (Western Persia) taken by Turkish forces* (see December 14th, 1915, and March 2nd, 1917).

11th ... Mpwapwa (German East Africa) occupied by British forces (see 5th).

12th ... Italian troops land at Salonika and join Allied force (see October 3rd, 1915, and July 30th, 1916).

15th ... Mush and Bitlis (Armenia) reoccupied by Turkish forces (see 24th, February 18th and March 2nd).
Bagamoyo (German East African coast) occupied by British forces.

17th ... **Battle of Gorizia (6th Battle of the Isonzo) ends** (see 6th).
End of "Brusilov's Offensive"* (see June 4th).
Battle of Florina† (Macedonia) begins (see 19th).
Rumanian Government conclude agreement with Entente Powers regarding intervention (see 27th, and January 22nd).
Military convention signed at Bukharest between Entente Powers and Rumania.

19th ... H.M.S. "Falmouth" and "Nottingham" sunk by submarine.
Battle of Florina† ends (see 17th).

22nd ... Kilosa (German East Africa) taken by British forces.

23rd ... German commercial submarine "Deutschland" returns to Germany (see July 10th).
Battle of Rayat (Armenia).

24th ... Bitlis and Mush again taken by Russian forces (see 15th, and April 30th, 1917).
Anglo-French Conference on finance held at Calais.

25th ... Russian forces cross the Danube into the Dobrudja to assist the Rumanian forces (see 17th, 27th, and September 2nd).

26th ... Morogoro (German East Africa) taken by British forces.

27th ... **Rumanian Government order mobilisation, and declare war on Austria-Hungary** (see 17th and 28th).

28th ... **Rumanian forces cross Hungarian frontier and invade Transylvania** (see 27th).
Germany declares war on Rumania (see 27th).
Italy declares war on Germany (see May 24th, 1915).
General Sir Stanley Maude succeeds Lieut.-General Sir Percy Lake as Commander-in-Chief, Mesopotamia (see January 19th, and November 18th, 1917).

29th ... Brasov (Transylvania) occupied by Rumanian forces (see 28th, and October 7th).
Iringa (German East Africa) taken by British forces.
Field-Marshal von Hindenburg succeeds General von Falkenhayn as Chief of the General Staff of the German Field Armies (see September 14th and November 27th, 1914), with General von Ludendorff as Chief Quartermaster-General (see October 27th, 1918).
Sipahsalar A'zam, Persian Prime Minister, resigns, and is succeeded by Vossuq ed Douleh, who also acts as Foreign Minister (see March 6th, 1916, and May 29th, 1917).

30th ... Rumania severs diplomatic relations with Bulgaria (see September 1st).
Turkey declares war on Rumania (see 28th).
Venizelist revolt in Salonika (see September 25th and October 9th).

31st ... **Battle of Verdun ends.** (see February 21st).

* Approximate date. † German name and dates.
‡ This is the French date for the close of "The Defensive Battle of Verdun." The German list carries the battle up to September 9th.

SEPTEMBER 1916.

1st — **Bulgaria declares war on Rumania** (see August 30th).
Sibiu (Transylvania) taken by Rumanian forces (see 26th).
Russian and British Governments conclude "Sykes-Picot" agreement as to eventual partition of Asia Minor (see April 26th, and May 9th and 23rd).
Compulsory Military Service Bill in New Zealand comes into operation (see June 10th).

2nd — German and Bulgarian forces invade the Dobrudja (see August 25th, 1916, January 6th, 1917, and December 3rd, 1918).
German raid by fourteen airships (greatest number to attack simultaneously) on London and other parts of England. Airship "S.L.-11" destroyed by aeroplane at Cuffley (night 2nd/3rd).
German ships in Piræus harbour seized by the Allies.

3rd — Battle of Guillemont (Somme) begins (see 6th).
Battles of Delville Wood and Pozières (Somme) end (see July 15th and 23rd).

4th — **Dar es Salaam (German East Africa) surrenders to British forces** (see August 8th, 1914).

6th — Battle of Guillemont (Somme) ends (see 3rd).
Tutrakan (Dobrudja) taken by Bulgarian forces (see 2nd).

7th — British pursuit of retreating German force in East Africa checked at Affair of Kisaki.
Kilwa, on East African coast, occupied by British naval forces.

8th — Orsova (Hungary) occupied by Rumanian forces (see August 28th and November 22nd).

9th — Battle of Ginchy (Somme).

10th — **Silistra (Dobrudja) taken by German and Bulgarian forces** (see 2nd).

11th — M. Zaimis, Greek Premier, resigns (see 16th, and June 21st).

14th — **Seventh Battle of the Isonzo begins** (see 18th).

15th — Battle of Flers-Courcelette (Somme) begins (see 22nd). "Tanks" in action for the first time (see July 28th, 1917).
Aeroplane co-operation with tanks instituted by the British Air Force.

16th — M. Kalogeropoulos forms new Greek Ministry (see 11th, and October 3rd).

17th — Lindi, on East African coast, occupied by British naval forces.

18th — Greek IVth Army Corps at Kavala surrenders voluntarily to German forces.
Seventh Battle of the Isonzo ends (see 14th).

19th — Tabora (capital of German East Africa) occupied by Belgian forces.
Allies commence blockade of Greek Macedonian coast from mouth of the Struma to mouth of the Mesta (see December 15th, 1915).

20th — Albanian Government of Essad Pasha set up in Salonika (see February 28th).

22nd — Battle of Flers-Courcelette (Somme) ends (see 15th).
Turkish garrison of Taif (Hejaz) surrenders to Arab forces (see June 5th).

23rd — Airship raid on England (East Coast and London) involving serious casualties (170, mostly civilian); "L.-32" destroyed by aeroplane at Billericay; "L.-33" brought down by gunfire in Essex (night 23rd/24th).

24th — Krupp works at Essen bombed by French aeroplanes.

25th — Battle of Morval (Somme) begins (see 28th).
M. Venizelos withdraws from Athens (see 29th, and August 30th).

26th ...	Battle of Thiepval Ridge (Somme) begins (see 28th)
	Battle of Sibiu (Transylvania) begins (see 29th).
28th ...	Battles of Morval and Thiepval Ridge end (see 25th and 26th).
29th ...	Battle of Sibiu ends: city retaken by Austrian forces (see 1st and 26th).
	M. Venizelos and Admiral Condouriotis announce formation of Greek Provisional Government in Crete in opposition to the Government at Athens (see December 19th).

OCTOBER 1916.

1st ...	Battle of the Transloy Ridges (Somme) begins (see 18th).
	Battle of the Ancre Heights (Somme) begins (see November 11th).
	German airship "L.-31" destroyed by aeroplane at Potter's Bar, near London (night 1st/2nd).
3rd ...	Greek Cabinet (Kalogeropoulos) resign (see 10th, and September 16th).
5th ...	**Battle of the Cerna and Monastir begins** (see November 19th and December 11th).
7th ...	**Battle of Brasov (Transylvania)** (7th/9th): city retaken by Austro-German forces (see August 29th).
8th ...	German submarine "U.-53" captures and destroys five ships outside Newport, Rhode Island, U.S.A.
9th ...	**Eighth Battle of the Isonzo begins** (see 12th).
	M. Venizelos arrives at Salonika (see August 30th, and September 25th and 29th).
	Marshal-Count Masakata Terauchi succeeds Marquis Okuma* as Japanese Prime Minister and Viscount Ishii as Acting Foreign Minister (see September 21st, 1915, November 20th, 1916, and September 29th, 1918).
10th ...	Entente Governments send ultimatum to Greek Government demanding surrender of the Greek fleet (see 11th).
	Professor Lambros forms new Greek Ministry (see 3rd, September 29th, 1916, and May 3rd, 1917).
11th ...	Greek Government accept Entente demands (see 10th).
12th ...	**Eighth Battle of the Isonzo ends** (see 9th).
13th ...	Norwegian Government issue orders prohibiting belligerent submarines from using Norwegian territorial waters (see February 1st, 1917).
14th ...	Transylvanian frontier of Rumania crossed by German forces (see August 28th and September 29th).
17th ...	Affairs in the Dakhla Oasis (West Egypt) begin (see 22nd).
18th ...	Battle of the Transloy Ridges (Somme) ends (see 1st).
20th ...	Russian battleship "Imperatritsa Mariya" destroyed by internal explosion at Sevastopol.
	Anglo-French Conference held at Calais to discuss Greek participation in the war.
21st ...	Count Stürgkh, Austrian Premier, murdered (appointed Premier November 3rd, 1911) (see 28th).
22nd ...	Constanza (Dobrudja) captured by German and Bulgarian forces.
	Affairs in the Dakhla Oasis end (see 17th).
24th ...	**"First Offensive Battle" of Verdun**† begins (see December 18th).
	Fort Douaumont recaptured by French forces (see February 25th, August 31st, and November 1st).
25th ...	Cernavoda (Dobrudja) captured by Bulgarian forces (see 22nd).
26th ...	First German destroyer raid in Dover Straits (night 26th/27th) (see April 20th, 1917).

* Appointed Prime Minister April 16th, 1914. † French name and date.

Oct.-Nov. 1916

28th ... Dr. E. von Körber appointed Austrian Premier (see 21st, and December 14th).
British hospital ship "Galeka" totally wrecked by mine off Havre.

29th ... Sherif of Mecca proclaimed "King of the Arabs" (see June 7th and November 4th).

30th ... Lieut.-General von Stein succeeds Lieut.-General Wild von Hohenborn as German Minister for War (see January 21st, 1915, and October 9th, 1918).

31st ... **Ninth Battle of the Isonzo begins** (see November 4th).

NOVEMBER 1916.

1st ... Fort Vaux (Verdun) recaptured by French forces (see June 2nd).

4th ... **Ninth Battle of the Isonzo ends** (see October 31st).
Coronation of the "King of the Arabs" at Mecca (see October 29th and December 15th).

5th ... **Germany and Austria proclaim an "Independent State of Poland"** (see April 3rd, 1915, and March 30th, 1917).

6th ... Affair of Gyuba (Darfur). Forces of Ali Dinar, ex-Sultan of Darfur, defeated by Sudan force. Ali Dinar killed (see May 22nd).

7th ... Mr. Wilson re-elected President of the United States.

11th ... Battle of the Ancre Heights (Somme) ends (see October 1st).

12th ... Shiraz (South Persia) occupied by British forces.

13th ... Battle of the Ancre, 1916, begins (see 18th): Beaumont-Hamel stormed by British forces.

15th ... Third Affair of Hafiz Kor (North-West Frontier of India).
British advance into Sinai begins (see December 21st).
Inter-Allied Conference held in Paris to discuss: (*a*) the relations between Governments and Staffs; (*b*) policy and strategy; (*c*) Greece; (*d*) Poland. (Conference continued on 16th.)

16th ... Battle of Târga-Jiu, Rumania (16th/17th).

18th ... Battle of the Ancre, 1916, ends (see 13th), and **Battles of the Somme, 1916, end** (see July 1st, 1916, March 14th and April 5th, 1917, and March 21st, 1918).

19th ... **Monastir (Serbia) captured by Allied forces** (see October 5th, 1916, and December 2nd, 1915).
Entente Governments demand dismissal of Ministers of Central Powers at Athens and surrender of Greek military material (see December 1st).

20th ... Herr von Jagow, German Foreign Minister, resigns (appointed January 1913) (see 21st).
Count Terauchi relinquishes temporary appointment as Japanese Minister for Foreign Affairs (see 21st, and October 9th).

21st ... Craiova (Rumania) taken by German forces.
British hospital ship "Britannic" sunk by mine in Ægean Sea.
Dr. Artur Zimmermann appointed German Foreign Minister (see 20th, and July 15th, 1917).
Emperor Francis Joseph of Austria dies. Archduke Karl succeeds to the throne.
Viscount Motono appointed Japanese Minister for Foreign Affairs (see 20th, and April 21st, 1918).

22nd ... Orsova (Hungary) taken by Austro-German forces (see September 8th).
*German commerce raider "Seeadler" leaves Germany (see August 2nd, 1917).

23rd ... **Greek Provisional Government (M. Venizelos) at Salonika declare war on Germany and Bulgaria** (see September 29th, 1916, and June 27th, 1917).
British hospital ship "Braemar Castle" damaged and beached in Ægean Sea—probably mined.
Mackensen's army effects passage of the Danube at Islaz and Simnitza.

* Approximate date.

24th	...	M. Stürmer, Russian Premier and Foreign Minister, resigns, and is succeeded by M. Trepov as Premier (see February 1st, July 22nd, and December 2nd and 12th, 1916, and January 8th, 1917).
25th	...	The German air forces established as a separate branch of the German army.
26th	...	Second German naval raid on Lowestoft (see April 25th). French battleship "Suffren" sunk by submarine in the Bay of Biscay. German raider "Moewe" sails from Kiel on second cruise (see March 4th, 1916, and March 22nd, 1917).
27th	...	German airship raid on East coast of England: airship "L.-34" destroyed by aeroplane off Hartlepool, and "L.-21" destroyed by aeroplane off Yarmouth (night 27th/28th).
28th	...	First German daylight aeroplane raid on London (by single aeroplane) (see December 21st, 1914, and May 7th, June 13th and July 7th, 1917).
29th	...	Admiral Sir David Beatty appointed to succeed Admiral Sir John Jellicoe as Commander-in-Chief, Grand Fleet (see December 4th).
30th	...	Allied forces landed at the Piræus (see December 1st).

DECEMBER 1916.

1st	...	**Battle of the Arges (Rumania) begins** (see 5th). Rumanian Government removed from Bukharest to Jassy (see November 30th, 1918). **Greek Government refuse Entente demands** (see November 19th). Allied forces withdrawn from Athens and the Piræus after conflicts with Greeks (see November 30th, 1916, and January 24th, 1917). *German commerce raider "Wolff" leaves Germany (see February 24th, 1918). Last meeting of War Committee of British Cabinet (see 9th, and November 3rd, 1915).
2nd	...	Russian Premier (M. Trepov) announces that the Allies have acknowledged Russia's right to Constantinople and the Straits (see March 12th and April 12th, 1915).
3rd	...	Funchal (Madeira) bombarded by German submarine (see December 12th, 1917). Admiral Sir Henry Jackson, First Sea Lord, Great Britain, resigns (see 4th, and May 28th, 1915). British and French Governments conclude agreement (the "Clémentel Agreement"): (1) to unite British ships in French service to those already employed; (2) to co-ordinate Allied tonnage; (3) to create inter-allied bureau to centralise charter of neutral shipping (see January 6th, November 3rd, and December 3rd, 1917).
4th	...	Admiral Sir John Jellicoe appointed First Sea Lord, Great Britain (see 3rd, August 4th, 1914, November 29th, 1916, and December 26th, 1917). Mr. Asquith, British Premier, resigns (appointed April 8th, 1908; see 7th).
5th	...	**Battle of the Arges (Roumania) ends** (see 1st).
6th	...	**Bukharest capitulates to the German forces** (see November 30th, 1918). Massacre of Venizelists in Athens (see 1st, and November 23rd).
7th	...	**Mr. Lloyd George succeeds Mr. Asquith as British Premier** (see 4th). Entente Governments announce forthcoming blockade of Greece from December 8th (see 1st).
8th	...	Murman Railway (from Murmansk to Petrograd) declared open. Entente Powers begin blockade of Greece (see 7th).

*Approximate date.

December 1916

9th ... **War Cabinet formed in Great Britain.* First Meeting held** (see 1st)

11th ... **Battle of the Cerna and Monastir ends** (see October 5th).
Italian battleship "Regina Margherita" sunk on Italian minefield.
Allied Note presented to Greece demanding complete demobilisation (see 1st and 14th).
Mr. Lloyd George's Coalition Ministry formed in Great Britain (see 7th, and May 25th, 1915).
Lord Derby appointed Secretary of State for War, Great Britain, in succession to Mr. Lloyd George (see September 30th, 1915, and July 7th and April 20th, 1918).
Viscount Grey, British Secretary for Foreign Affairs, resigns. (Appointed December 11th, 1905.)
Mr. Arthur Balfour, First Lord of the Admiralty, Great Britain, resigns, and is appointed Secretary for Foreign Affairs (see 12th, and May 28th, 1915).
Ministry of Labour formed in Great Britain.

12th ... Reorganisation of French Government. M. Briand remains Premier. New War Cabinet of five Ministers formed. General Nivelle becomes Commander-in-Chief of French Northern and North-Eastern Groups of Armies (see May 15th, 1917), and General Joffre (see December 3rd, 1915) becomes Technical Military Adviser to the War Cabinet.
Sir Edward Carson succeeds Mr. Balfour as First Lord of the Admiralty, Great Britain (see 11th, and July 19th, 1917).
M. Pokrovski appointed Russian Minister for Foreign Affairs (see November 24th, 1916, and January 27th, 1917).
Identic Notes presented by Austro-Hungarian, Bulgarian, German, and Turkish Governments to United States Ambassadors in their respective countries requesting them to inform the Governments of the Entente Powers that the four Allied Central Powers are ready to negotiate for peace (see 30th).

13th ... British operations for the capture of Kut begin (see May 19th, 1916, and January 9th, 1917).

14th ... **Entente Powers send Ultimatum to Greece; withdrawal of entire Greek Armies from Thessaly demanded** (see 11th and 15th).
Dr. von Körber, Austrian Premier, resigns (see 21st, and October 28th).

15th ... **Greek Government accept Allied Ultimatum** (see 14th).
British Government recognise the "King of the Arabs" as the King of the Hejaz (see November 4th).

17th ... Greek Government issue warrant for arrest of M. Venizelos on charge of high treason (see August 30th and September 29th, 1916, and June 26th, 1917).

18th ... **"First Offensive Battle" of Verdun ends** (see October 24th, 1916, and August 20th, 1917).
President Wilson issues Circular Note suggesting negotiations for peace (see 26th).

19th ... **British Government decide to institute National Service** (see November 1st, 1917).
British Government decide to initiate Imperial Conference (see March 20th, 1917).
British Government decide to recognise Government of M. Venizelos (see September 29th).

21st ... El Arish (Sinai) occupied by British forces (see November 15th).
Count Heinrich Clam-Martinitz appointed Austrian Premier (see 14th, and June 18th, 1917).

22nd ... Ministry of Food formed in Great Britain (see 26th).
Ministry of Pensions formed in Great Britain.
Ministry of Shipping formed in Great Britain (see January 27th).
Count Czernin succeeds Baron Burian as Austro-Hungarian Minister for Foreign Affairs (see January 13th, 1915, and April 15th, 1918).

* The War Committee (see November 3rd, 1915) which held their last meeting on December 1st ceased to function on the formation of the War Cabinet which undertook the duties of the War Committee.

| | | Dec. 1916–Jan. 1917 |

23rd ... Affair of Magdhaba (Sinai).

26th ... German, Austro-Hungarian and Turkish Governments send reply to President Wilson's Note; immediate meeting of delegates suggested (see 18th, and January 10th, 1917).
Anglo-French Conference meets in London to discuss the German and United States "Peace Notes"; also the situation in Greece, the Salonika expedition, and the division of the front in the Western Theatre. (Discussion continued on the 27th and 28th.)
General Joffre created Marshal of France (see 12th).
Lord Devonport appointed Food Controller, Great Britain (see 22nd).

27th ... French battleship "Gaulois" sunk by submarine in the Mediterranean.
British and French Governments conclude agreement regarding temporary administration of Togoland (see August 26th and 31st, 1914).

30th ... Entente Governments reject German peace proposals (see 12th, and January 11th, 1917).
British and Chinese Governments conclude agreement for employment of Chinese labour in France.
Bulgarian Government reply accepting President Wilson's Note (see 18th, and January 10th, 1917).

31st ... Campaign of the Sudan forces in Darfur comes to an end (see March 1st).
Raspútin murdered in Petrograd.

JANUARY 1917.

3rd ... Focsani (Rumania) taken by German forces.
First units of Portuguese Expeditionary Force land in France (see August 8th, 1916, and June 17th, 1917).
Action of Beho-Beho (East Africa) begins (see 4th).
General Sir Douglas Haig promoted Field-Marshal (see December 19th, 1915).

4th ... Russian battleship "Peresvyet" sunk by mine off Port Said.
Action of Beho-Beho ends (see 3rd).

5th ... Braila (Rumania) taken by German forces.
Inter-Allied Conference assembles in Rome to discuss co-operation, and the questions of Macedonia, Greece, the command of the Salonika expedition, and to convene a shipping conference. (Discussions continued on the 6th and 7th.)

6th ... Last Russian and Rumanian forces evacuate the Dobrudja (see August 25th, 1916, and December 3rd, 1918).
"Inter-Allied Chartering Committee" established for chartering shipping (see December 3rd, 1916, and November 3rd, 1917).

8th ... M. Trepov, Russian Premier, resigns and is succeeded by Prince Golitsin (see November 24th, 1916, and March 13th, 1917).

9th ... **Battle of Kut, 1917, begins** (see December 13th, 1916, and February 23rd and 24th, 1917).
Action of Rafah (Sinai). Last Turkish troops in Sinai recross the frontier (see January 26th, 1915).
H.M.S. "Cornwallis" sunk by submarine in Mediterranean.

10th ... Entente Governments send joint reply to President Wilson's Note. Allied war aims outlined (see December 18th, 1916.)
Belgian Government reply to President Wilson's Note placing themselves in hands of Allies (see December 18th, 1916, and September 15th, 1918).

11th ... Settlement Treaty signed at Berlin between Germany and Turkey (see April 10th, 1918).
Austro-Hungarian and German Governments issue Note repudiating responsibility for continuance of war, and declaring that they will prosecute the war to successful end (see December 12th and 30th, 1916, and September 15th, 1918).

Jan.–Feb. 1917

14th	...	Japanese battle cruiser " Tsukuba " sunk by internal explosion in harbour.
15th	...	Italy accedes to Franco-British Convention as to naval " prizes " (see November 9th, 1914).
17th	...	General Shuvaev, Russian Minister for War, resigns and is succeeded by General Byelyaev (see March 29th, 1916, and March 13th, 1917).
		Inter-Allied Conference* (Russia, France, Great Britain and Italy represented) assembles at Petrograd to discuss war policy, finance, supplies and co-operation (see February 20th).
19th	...	German Government send instructions to German Minister in Mexico (von Eckhardt) to negotiate alliance with Mexico and Japan against the United States (see February 28th).
20th	...	General Hoskins succeeds General Smuts in command of British forces, East Africa (see February 19th, 1916, and May 30th, 1917).
23rd	...	Harwich flotilla action with German 6th torpedo boat flotilla in the North Sea: H.M.S. " Simoom " sunk.
24th	...	Wejh (Arabia) captured by Arab forces.
		Greek Government make formal apology to the Allies for the occurrences of December 1st, 1916.
		Allied Naval Conference held in London as to policy in Mediterranean (see November 30th).
25th	...	Southwold and Wangford on the Suffolk coast shelled by German destroyers.
27th	...	M. Pokrovski, Russian Foreign Minister, resigns (see December 12th, 1916, and March 15th, 1917).
31st	..	German Government announce forthcoming " unrestricted " submarine warfare and threaten to sink hospital ships (see February 1st).

FEBRUARY 1917.

1st	...	**German " unrestricted submarine warfare " begins** (see January 31st).
		Norwegian Government forbid all foreign submarines to use Norwegian territorial waters (see October 13th, 1916).
3rd	...	**United States of America sever diplomatic relations with Germany** (see April 6th).
		Affairs in the Siwa Oasis (West Egypt) begin (see 5th).
4th	...	Sa'id Halim, Turkish Grand Vizier, resigns†: succeeded by Talaat Pasha (see October 13th, 1918).
5th	...	Affairs in the Siwa Oasis end (see 3rd and 8th).
8th	...	British operations against the Senussi come to an end (see 5th, and November 23rd, 1915).
13th	...	Scandinavian Governments' joint protest against German submarine warfare published.
14th	...	British Government inform Japanese Government that they will support Japanese claims to German possessions north of the Equator if it is understood that Japan will support similar British claims south of the Equator (see December 16th, 1914).
		British Government give pledge in House of Commons that the restitution of Alsace-Lorraine is an object of the war (see November 15th).
17th	...	Australian War Government formed.
20th	...	Inter-Allied Conference* at Petrograd dissolves (see January 17th).
23rd	...	Kut reoccupied by British forces (see 24th, and January 9th).

* " Commission de Ravitaillement."
† Appointed in 1913.

24th ... **Battle of Kut, 1917, ends.** Turkish Army retreats from Kut (see 23rd, and January 9th).

25th ... German forces withdraw from front line positions on the Ancre (see November 18th, 1916, and March 14th, 1917).
The pursuit to Baghdad begins (see 24th, and March 11th).
German destroyer raid on Margate and Broadstairs (see March 18th).
British S.S. "Laconia" sunk by submarine (see 27th).

26th ... President Wilson in address to Congress asks for power to arm merchant ships (see February 21st, 1916, and March 12th, 1917).
Anglo-French Conference assembles at Calais to discuss operations, the co-operation of the armies and the co-ordination of operations by the French Commander-in-Chief (continued on 27th) (see March 12th).

27th ... President Wilson states that he considers sinking of "Laconia" the "overt act" for which he was waiting (see 25th, and April 6th).

28th ... German proposals to Mexico for alliance against the United States published in the American Press (see January 19th).

MARCH 1917.

1st ... British hospital ship "Glenart Castle" damaged by mine between Havre and Southampton (see February 26th, 1918).

2nd ... Hamadan (Western Persia) recaptured by Russian forces (see August 10th, 1916, and March 16th, 1918).

7th ... Passage of the Diyala (near Baghdad) (7th/10th).

8th ... Count Zeppelin dies.

11th ... **Baghdad occupied by British forces** (see February 25th).
Kirmanshah (Western Persia) again taken by Russian forces (see July 1st, 1916, and February 25th, 1918).
Allied Offensive in Macedonia to free Monastir begins (see 23rd).

12th ... **Russian Revolution begins** (see 13th, 14th and 15th).
United States Government announce arming of all merchant vessels in the war zone (see February 26th).
Anglo-French Conference assembles in London to discuss relations of British and French commanders in the Western Theatre, and employment of prisoners of war in the fighting zone (see February 26th, 1917, and March 26th, 1918).

13th ... Prince Golitsin, Russian Premier, removed from office by Revolutionary party (see 12th, 15th, and January 8th).
General Byelyaev, Russian Minister for War, removed from office by Revolutionary party (see 12th, 15th, and January 17th).

14th ... **German retreat from the Somme to the "Hindenburg Line" begins** (see February 25th and April 5th).
Action of Mushaidiya (Mesopotamia).
New Provisional Government proclaimed in Russia (see 12th, 22nd, and November 8th).
China severs diplomatic relations with Germany (see August 14th).

15th ... **Nicholas II, Tsar of Russia, abdicates** (see 12th, and July 16th, 1918).
Prince Lvov appointed Russian Premier (see 13th, 14th, and July 19th.)
M. Milyukov appointed Russian Foreign Minister (see 14th, January 27th, and May 16th).
General Guchkov appointed Russian Minister for War (see 13th, 14th, and May 16th).

16th ... Action between German raider "Leopard" and H.M.S. "Achilles" and Armed Boarding Steamer "Dundee": "Leopard" sunk.
Mutiny breaks out in Russian Baltic Fleet (see 12th, and June 21st).

17th ... Roye occupied by French forces (see August 30th, 1914, and March 26th, 1918).
Bapaume occupied by British forces (see September 26th, 1914, and March 24th, 1918).

Mar.–April 1917

17th (contd.) — German airship "L.-39" destroyed at Compiègne when returning from raid on England.
Karind (West Persia) occupied by Russian forces.
M. Briand, French Premier, and Minister for Foreign Affairs, resigns (see 20th, and October 30th, 1915).
General Roques, French Minister for War, resigns (see 20th, and March 16th, 1916).

18th — German destroyer raid on Ramsgate and Broadstairs (see April 26th).
Péronne and Noyon occupied by Allied forces (see September 21st, 24th, and 25th, 1914; and March 24th and 25th, 1918).

19th — French battleship "Danton" sunk by submarine in Mediterranean.

20th — M. Ribot succeeds M. Briand as French Premier and Minister for Foreign Affairs (see 17th, December 12th, 1916, and September 9th, 1917).
M. Painlevé appointed French Minister for War (see 17th, September 12th and November 14th).
First meeting of British Imperial War Conference (see December 19th, 1916).

21st — British hospital ship "Asturias" torpedoed off Start Point.

22nd — Provisional Government in Russia recognised by Great Britain, France, Italy, United States of America, Rumania, and Switzerland (see 14th).
German raider "Moewe" returns to Kiel from her second cruise (see November 26th, 1916).

23rd — **Allied Offensive in Macedonia ends** (see 11th).

24th — British offensive into Palestine begins (see 26th).

25th — Qasr-i-Shirin (Western Persia) again taken by Russian forces (see June 20th, 1916, and July 8th, 1917).

26th — **First Battle of Gaza begins** (see 27th).

27th — **First Battle of Gaza ends** (see 26th, and April 17th).

30th — **Russian Provisional Government issue Proclamation acknowledging the Independence of Poland** (see 14th, November 5th, 1916, and April 5th, 1917).
British hospital ship "Gloucester Castle" torpedoed between Havre and Southampton, but towed in.

31st — The Emperor of Austria makes secret proposal, conveyed in a letter to Prince Sixte of Bourbon, to the French President (M. Poincaré) to open conversations with a view to peace (see April 11th, 1918).

APRIL 1917.

3rd — H.M.S. "Jason" (torpedo gunboat) sunk by mine off west coast of Scotland.

4th — Khanaqin (North-East of Baghdad) again occupied by Russian forces.

5th — **German retreat to the "Hindenburg Line" completed** (see March 14th).
British Government inform Russian Provisional Government of their adherence to the principle of an independent and united Poland (see March 30th and September 12th, 1916, and January 10th, 1917).

6th — **United States of America declare war on Germany** (see February 3rd).

7th — Cuba and Panama declare war on Germany.

8th — Austria-Hungary severs diplomatic relations with United States of America (see December 7th).

9th — **Battles of Arras, 1917, begin** with Battle of Vimy Ridge (see 14th) and First Battle of the Scarpe, 1917 (see 23rd, and May 4th).
Admiral Sims, United States Navy, arrives in England (see June 18th).
Russian Provisional Government (see March 14th) **issue Proclamation to Allied Governments declaring in favour of self-determination of peoples and a durable peace.**

10th	...	British hospital ship "Salta" mined off Havre. Bulgaria severs diplomatic relations with the United States of America.
11th	...	Brazil severs diplomatic relations with Germany (see October 26th).
13th	...	Bolivia severs diplomatic relations with Germany.
14th	...	Battle of Vimy Ridge and First Battle of the Scarpe end (see 9th).
16th	...	**French 1917 Offensive begins with the Second Battle of the Aisne** (see 20th).
17th	...	*"**Battle of the Hills**" **(Champagne) begins** (see 20th). **Second Battle of Gaza begins** (see 19th, and March 27th). Japanese flotillas join Allied forces in the Mediterranean (see February 8th, 1916, and November 15th, 1917). British ambulance transports "Lanfranc" and "Donegal" torpedoed and sunk in English Channel.
19th	...	**Second Battle of Gaza ends** (see 17th, and October 27th).
20th	...	**French Offensive stopped** (see 16th): **Battles of the Aisne and of "The Hills" end** (see 16th and 17th). Second German destroyer raid on Straits of Dover (night 20th/21st). Action by the "Swift" and "Broke" (see October 26th, 1916, and February 15th, 1918). Turkey severs diplomatic relations with the United States of America.
22nd	...	Action of Istabulat (Mesopotamia) (21st/22nd).
23rd	...	Second Battle of the Scarpe, 1917 (Arras) (23rd/24th) (see 9th, and May 3rd).
24th	...	Samarra (Mesopotamia) taken by British forces (23rd/24th). First Battle of Doiran begins (first phase 24th/25th) (see May 9th).
25th	...	Dr. A. Augusto da Costa succeeds Dr. A. J. d'Almeida as Portuguese Premier (see March 15th, 1916, and December 10th, 1917).
26th	...	Second German destroyer raid on Ramsgate (night 26th/27th) (see March 18th).
27th	...	Guatemala severs diplomatic relations with Germany (see April 23rd, 1918).
28th	...	United States Congress pass Bill for raising 500,000 men (see 6th, and May 18th). Battle of Arleux (Arras) (28th/29th).
29th	...	General Pétain appointed Chief of French General Staff (see December 3rd, 1915, and May 15th, 1917).
30th	...	Mush (Armenia) occupied by Turkish forces (see August 24th, 1916).

MAY 1917.

2nd	...	First United States destroyer flotilla arrives at Queenstown (see June 18th).
		Third Battle of the Scarpe, 1917 (Arras), begins (see 4th, and April 23rd). Battle of Bullecourt begins (see 17th). Professor Lambros, Greek Premier, resigns and is succeeded by M. Zaimis (see October 10th, 1916, and June 24th, 1917).
4th	...	Craonne (Aisne) retaken by French forces (see September 1st, 1914, April 16th, 1917, and May 27th, 1918). End of Third Battle of the Scarpe, 1917 (see 3rd) brings **Battles of Arras, 1917, to an end** (see April 9th).

* "La Bataille des Monts," otherwise called the Third Battle of Champagne

May 1917

- 5th ... **Battle of the Vardar (Macedonia) begins** (see 22nd).
  Liberia severs diplomatic relations with Germany (see August 4th).

- 7th ... First night air raid on London. Single aeroplane by moonlight (see November 28th, 1916, and September 4th, 1917, and May 19th, 1918).

- 9th ... First Battle of Doiran ends (second phase 8th/9th) (see April 24th, 1917, and September 18th, 1918).

- 10th ... Major-General J. Pershing appointed to command United States Expeditionary Force (see June 8th).

- 12th ... **Tenth Battle of the Isonzo begins** (see June 8th).

- 14th ... German airship "L.-22" destroyed in North Sea by British warships.

- 15th ... Action between Austrian and British naval light forces in the Straits of Otranto: 14 British drifters sunk.
  General Pétain succeeds General Nivelle as Commander-in-Chief of French Northern and North-Eastern Groups of Armies (see April 29th, 1917, and November 19th, 1918).
  General Foch succeeds General Pétain as Chief of the French General Staff of French Ministry of War (see October 8th, 1914, and November 27th, 1917).

- 16th ... M. Kerenski succeeds General Guchkov as Russian Minister for War (see March 15th and November 8th).
  M. Tereshchenko succeeds M. Milyukov as Russian Foreign Minister (see March 15th and November 8th).

- 17th ... Battle of Bullecourt ends (see 3rd).
  Honduras severs diplomatic relations with Germany (see July 19th, 1918).
  The British Admiralty, following on a Cabinet decision, appoint a Committee, in conjunction with the Ministry of Shipping, to draw up a plan to convoy merchant ships (see June 14th and July 2nd).

- 18th ... Compulsory Service Act becomes law in the United States of America (see April 28th).
  Nicaragua severs diplomatic relations with Germany (see May 8th, 1918).

- 19th ... Russian Provisional Government issue declaration repudiating a separate peace.
  United States Government announce decision to send a Division of the United States Army to France at once (see June 25th).

- 20th ... Serbian Government transferred from Corfu to Salonika (see February 9th, 1916, and December 9th, 1918).

- 22nd ... **Battle of the Vardar ends** (see 5th).

- 23rd ... Count Tisza, Hungarian Premier, resigns* (see June 15th, 1917, and October 31st, 1918).

- 25th ... First great aeroplane raid on England (Kent and Folkestone) to cause heavy casualties. Total 290, over half civilians (see December 21st, 1914, and July 20th and August 5th, 1918).

- 26th ... British hospital ship "Dover Castle" sunk by submarine in the Mediterranean.

- 28th ... Anglo-French Conference assembles in London to discuss the deposition of King Constantine of Greece and the occupation of Athens and Thessaly (continued on 29th) (see June 11th).

- 29th ... Vossuq ed Douleh, Persian Prime Minister and Foreign Minister, resigns (see August 29th, 1916, June 6th, 1917, and August 7th, 1918).

- 30th ... General van Deventer succeeds General Hoskins in command of British forces in East Africa (see January 20th).

* Appointed June 10th, 1913.

JUNE 1917.

3rd ... Italy proclaims Protectorate over an independent Albania.

4th ... General Brusilov succeeds General Alexeiev as Russian Commander-in-Chief (see September 5th, 1915, and August 1st, 1917).

5th ... German daylight aeroplane raid on Sheerness and the Naval establishments on the Medway.

6th ... Ala es Sultaneh again appointed Persian Prime Minister and Foreign Minister (see May 29th and November 24th, 1917, and January 19th, 1918).

7th ... **Battle of Messines, 1917, begins** (see 14th; also November 1st, 1914).

8th ... **Tenth Battle of the Isonzo ends** (see May 12th).
Janina (Greece) occupied by Italian forces.
Major-General Pershing arrives in England (see 13th, and May 10th).

9th ... Russian Provisional Government refuse a German proposal for an unlimited armistice.

11th ... **Entente Governments present demand to Greek Government for abdication of King Constantine** (see 12th, and May 28th).
Santo Domingo severs diplomatic relations with Germany.

12th ... **King Constantine of Greece abdicates in favour of his second son, Prince Alexander** (see 11th).
Corinth and Larissa occupied by Entente forces.

13th ... Great German daylight aeroplane raid on London; 157 killed and 432 injured (see November 28th, 1916, and July 7th, 1917).
Major-General Pershing arrives in France (see 8th, and May 10th).

14th ... **Battle of Messines, 1917, ends** (see 7th; also April 10th, 1918).
German airship "L.-43" destroyed in the North Sea.
The British Admiralty formally approve scheme for convoying merchant ships (see May 17th and July 2nd).

15th ... Count Esterhazy appointed Hungarian Premier (see May 23rd and August 9th).

16th ... Haiti severs diplomatic relations with Germany (see July 12th, 1918).

17th ... Portuguese troops in action on Western Front for the first time (see August 8th, 1916, and January 3rd, 1917).
German airship "L.-48" destroyed by aeroplane at Theberton in Suffolk.

18th ... Admiral Sims, United States Navy, hoists his flag at Queenstown as acting C.-in-C. Irish Command (see April 9th and May 2nd).
Count Clam-Martinitz, Austrian Premier, resigns (see 23rd, and December 21st, 1916).

19th ... General Currie appointed to command Canadian troops in France.

21st ... Mutiny breaks out in the Russian Black Sea Fleet at Sevastopol (see March 16th, 1917, and May 1st, 1918).

23rd ... Dr. Ernst Ritter von Seidler appointed Austrian Premier (see 18th, and June 21st, 1918).

24th ... M. Zaimis, Greek Premier, resigns (see May 3rd and June 26th).

25th ... **First contingent of United States troops arrives in France** (see May 19th).

26th ... M. Venizelos appointed Greek Premier (see 24th and 27th, and October 5th, 1915).

June–July 1917

27th ... **M. Venizelos assumes power at Athens. Diplomatic relations severed with Germany, Austria-Hungary and Turkey. Declaration of War by Provisional Government against Germany and Bulgaria of November 23rd, 1916, becomes effective for the whole of Greece. "State of War" also begins between Greece and Austria-Hungary and between Greece and Turkey** (see 26th).
French cruiser " Kléber " sunk by submarine off Brest.

28th ... General Allenby succeeds General Sir A. Murray as General Officer Commanding in Egypt (see March 19th, 1916).

29th ... **Russian Summer Offensive begins*** (see July 18th).

JULY 1917.

1st ... Manchu Emperor (Hsuan-Fung) restored in China (see June 6th, 1916, and July 6th and 7th, 1917).

2nd ... Agreement signed at The Hague for the exchange of combatant and civilian British and German prisoners of war (see May 13th, 1916).
First regular convoy of merchant ships sails from Hampton Roads (Va.)† (see May 17th and June 14th).

4th ... Ponta Delgada (Azores) shelled by a German submarine.
Concerted attack by German submarines on United States transports defeated.

6th ... Aqaba (Arabia) occupied by Arab forces.
Conscription Bill carried in Canadian House of Commons (see October 12th).
Li-Yuan-Hung, President of China, resigns and is succeeded by Feng-Kuo-Chang (see June 6th, 1916, July 7th, 1917, and October 11th, 1918).

7th ... Severe aeroplane raid on England (Margate and London; casualties 250, mostly civilian: last on London by daylight) (see November 28th, and August 22nd, 1916, and May 19th and July 20th, 1918).
Manchu Emperor abdicates (see 1st and 6th).

8th ... Russian forces begin withdrawal from Western Persia: Qasr-i-Shirin evacuated (see May 7th, 1916, March 25th, 1917, and January 8th, 1918).

9th ... H.M.S. " Vanguard " sunk by internal explosion in harbour.

11th ... British attack on Ramadi (Mesopotamia) (11th/14th).

14th ... Herr von Bethmann-Holweg, German Imperial Chancellor, resigns (appointed July 14th, 1909): succeeded by Dr. Michaelis (see October 30th).

15th ... Dr. Artur von Zimmermann, German Foreign Minister, resigns (see November 21st, 1916, and August 5th, 1917).

17th ... Proclamation issued changing name of British Royal House to Windsor.

18th ... **German Counter-Offensive on the Eastern Front: Battle of East Galicia begins** (see 28th, and June 29th).

19th ... Action of Narungombe (East Africa).
Sir Edward Carson, First Lord of the Admiralty, Great Britain, tenders his resignation (see December 12th, 1916, and September 6th, 1917).
The Reichstag passes Resolution as to German War Aims (see January 24th, 1918).
M. Kerenski succeeds Prince Lvov as Premier of Russia temporarily (see March 15th and August 6th).

22nd ... **Battle of Marasesti (Rumania) begins** (see August 1st).
Siam declares war on Germany and Austria-Hungary.

24th ... Stanislau (see August 10th, 1916) and Tarnopol in Galicia retaken by Austro-German forces (see 18th).

---

* For details of the battles of this offensive, see Part II.
† Experimental convoys had been tried in May. Convoys outward from Great Britain did not start till August.

25th ... Full Inter-Allied Conference assembles in Paris to discuss the Balkan situation, with military, naval and political committees to discuss plans in view of a probable collapse of Russia (Conference continued on 26th).

27th ... Agreement concluded between French and Italian Governments defining respective zones of influence in Asia Minor (see August 18th).

28th ... **Battle of East Galicia ends** (see 18th).
Tank Corps formed in British Army (see September 15th, 1916).

30th ... Zaleszczyki (Galicia) recaptured by Austro-German forces (see June 12th, 1916).

31st ... **Battles of Ypres, 1917, begin** with Battle of Pilckem Ridge (see August 2nd and November 10th, 1917, and May 25th, 1915).

AUGUST 1917.

1st ... **End of first phase of Battle of Marasesti** (see July 22nd).
General Kornilov succeeds General Brusilov as Russian Commander-in-Chief (see June 4th and September 8th).
The Pope sends Note to belligerent Governments appealing for peace (see July 30th, 1915).

2nd ... Battle of Pilckem Ridge (Ypres) ends (see July 31st).
German commerce raider "Seeadler" wrecked on Mopelia Island (Pacific) (see November 22nd, 1916).

3rd ... Czernowitz (Bukovina) retaken by Austro-German forces (see June 17th, 1916).
Mutiny breaks out in German Fleet at Wilhelmshaven (see November 3rd, 1918).

4th ... Liberia declares war on Germany (see May 5th, 1917, and April 10th, 1918).
Baron de Broqueville resigns as Belgian Minister for War (appointed February 28th, 1914) and succeeds Baron Beyens as Minister for Foreign Affairs (see January 18th, 1916, and January 1st, 1918). Lieut.-General A. de Ceuninck appointed Minister for War (see November 21st, 1918).

5th ... Herr Richard von Kuhlmann appointed German Foreign Minister (see July 15th, 1917, and July 9th, 1918).

6th ... **Second phase of Battle of Marasesti begins** (see 1st, and September 3rd).
M. Kerenski definitely appointed Prime Minister of Russia (see July 19th, September 10th, and November 8th).

9th ... Count Esterhazy, Hungarian Premier, resigns (see 21st, and June 15th).

10th ... British Labour Party decide to send delegates to a "consultative" Conference at Stockholm (see 13th).

13th ... British Government refuse passports for Stockholm Conference (see 10th).

14th ... **China declares war on Germany and Austria-Hungary** (see March 14th).

15th ... Battle of Hill 70 (Lens) begins (see 25th).

16th ... Battle of Langemarck, 1917 (Ypres), begins (see 18th).

17th ... **Eleventh Battle of the Isonzo begins** (see September 12th).
M. Cochin succeeded by M. Métin as French Under-Secretary for Blockade (see March 20th, 1916, and November 16th, 1917).

18th ... Battle of Langemarck, 1917 (Ypres), ends (see 16th).
British, French, and Italian Governments conclude provisional arrangement with regard to future policy in Asia Minor (see May 16th, 1916, and July 27th, 1917).

Aug.–Sept. 1917

20th ... **"Second Offensive Battle" of Verdun begins*** (see December 15th, 1917, and December 18th, 1916).

21st ... Dr. Wekerle appointed Hungarian Premier (see 9th, and April 17th, 1918).
German airship "L.-23" destroyed in North Sea.
Ministry of Reconstruction formed in Great Britain.

22nd ... **Last German aeroplane raid on England by daylight** (see July 7th and September 2nd).

25th ... Battle of Hill 70 (Lens) ends (see 15th).

SEPTEMBER 1917.

1st ... **Battle of Riga begins** (see 3rd and 5th).

2nd ... First German aeroplane raid on England by moonlight by more than one aeroplane (see 4th, and May 7th).

3rd ... **Battle of Marasesti (Rumania) ends** (see August 6th).
Riga captured by German forces (see 1st and 5th, and October 16th).
Severe aeroplane raid on Kent by moonlight (casualties about 230, mostly military).

4th ... German aeroplanes for the first time raid London by night in force (see 2nd).
German submarine bombards Scarborough (Yorkshire).
Anglo-French Conference assembles in London to discuss the question of military assistance to Italy (see 25th).

5th ... **Battle of Riga ends** (see 1st and 3rd).

6th ... Sir Eric Geddes appointed First Lord of the Admiralty, Great Britain (see July 19th).

8th ... General Kornilov heads revolt against Russian Provisional Government and marches on Petrograd (see 10th and 13th, and August 1st).

9th ... M. Ribot, French Premier and Foreign Minister, resigns (see 12th, and March 20th).

10th ... M. Kerenski assumes Dictatorship of Russia (see August 6th and November 8th) and issues proclamation declaring General Kornilov a traitor (see 8th and 13th).

11th ... First party of repatriated British prisoners reaches England from Switzerland (see May 13th, 1916).

12th ... **Eleventh Battle of the Isonzo ends** (see August 17th).
M. Painlevé succeeds M. Ribot as French Premier (see 9th, and November 14th).
M. Ribot reappointed French Foreign Minister (see 9th, and October 23rd).
Central Powers proclaim grant of temporary Constitution to Poland (see April 5th and October 15th, 1917, and January 10th, 1918).

13th ... General Kornilov's revolt collapses (see 8th, 10th and 14th).

14th ... General Kornilov surrenders to the Provisional Government (see 13th).

15th ... **Russia proclaimed a Republic by the Provisional Government** (see 10th).

20th ... Battle of the Menin Road Ridge (Ypres) begins (see 25th).
Council of Trans-Caucasian peoples, i.e., Armenia, Georgia, Azerbaijan, and Daghestan, proclaim Trans-Caucasia a federal Republic (see April 22nd, 1918).

21st ... Count Bernstorff's correspondence re German intrigues published.
Costa Rica severs diplomatic relations with Germany (see May 23rd, 1918).

22nd ... Jakobstadt (Baltic) stormed by German forces (21st/22nd).

---
* French name and dates.

Sept.-Oct. 1917

25th ... Battle of the Menin Road Ridge (Ypres) ends (see 20th).
Anglo-French Conference assembles in Boulogne to discuss an Italian offensive and the extension of the British front in France (see 4th).

26th ... Battle of Polygon Wood (Ypres) begins (see October 3rd).

28th ... Action of Ramadi (Mesopotamia) (28th/29th).

OCTOBER 1917.

2nd ... H.M.S. "Drake" sunk by submarine in the North Channel.

3rd ... Battle of Polygon Wood (Ypres) ends (see September 26th).

4th ... Battle of Broodseinde (Ypres).

5th ... Peru severs diplomatic relations with Germany.

6th ... Major-General Pershing, Commanding United States Army in France, promoted General (see June 13th).

7th ... Uruguay severs diplomatic relations with Germany.

9th ... Battle of Poelcapelle (Ypres).
Hussein Kamel, Sultan of Egypt, dies. Succeeded by Prince Ahmed Fuad, his youngest brother. (See December 19th, 1914).

10th ... British hospital ship "Goorkha" damaged by mine off Malta.

11th ... German operations against the Baltic Islands begin (see 12th).

12th ... First Battle of Passchendaele (Ypres) (see 26th).
Ösel Island (Baltic) captured by German forces* (see 11th and 18th).
Canadian War Cabinet formed.
Compulsory Service Act comes into operation in Canada (see July 6th).

15th ... Polish Regency Council appointed (see September 12th).

16th ... Action of Nyangao (German East Africa) begins (see 19th).
Naval action in Gulf of Riga. Russian battleship "Slava" sunk (see September 3rd).

17th ... German cruisers raid convoy in North Sea and sink British destroyers "Strongbow" and "Mary Rose" (see December 12th).

18th ... Moon Island and Dagö Island (Baltic) captured by German forces (see 11th and 12th).

19th ... Action of Nyangao (German East Africa) ends (see 16th).
Squadron of 11 German airships attack England.† (Last airship raid on London.) (See May 31st, 1915, and August 5th, 1918.)

20th ... German conquest of the Baltic Islands completed (see 11th, 12th and 18th).

21st ... Turkish attack on Arab stronghold at Petra repulsed.

23rd ... Battle of La Malmaison begins (see November 1st).
M. Barthou succeeds M. Ribot as French Foreign Minister (see September 12th and November 14th).

24th ... **Twelfth Battle of the Isonzo begins: Austro-German offensive** (see December 26th).

25th ... Signor Boselli, Italian Premier, resigns (see 29th, and June 15th, 1916).

26th ... **Brazil declares war on Germany** (see April 11th).
Second Battle of Passchendaele (Ypres) begins (see 12th, and November 6th and 10th).

* Operations not completed until the 16th.
† "L.-44" shot down at St. Clement; "L.-45" shot down at Laragne; "L.-49" shot down at Bourbonne-les-Bains on October 20th; "L.-50" brought down in the Mediterranean on October 21st.

Oct.-Nov. 1917

27th ... **Third Battle of Gaza begins** (see April 19th and November 7th).

28th ... Gorizia retaken by Austro-German forces (see 24th).
Udine (Venetia) captured by Austro-German forces (see 24th).

29th ... Signor Orlando appointed Italian Premier (see 25th).

30th ... Count Hertling succeeds Dr. Michaelis as German Imperial Chancellor (see July 14th, 1917, and September 30th, 1918)

NOVEMBER 1917.

1st ... Battle of La Malmaison ends (see October 23rd).
Ministry of National Service formed in Great Britain (see December 19th, 1916).

2nd ... Raid by British naval light forces on the Kattegat (see April 15th, 1918).

3rd ... Arrival of French troops in Italy announced (see 4th).
Agreement concluded between British, French and Italian Governments for provision of tonnage for the Allied food programme (see November 10th, 1915, January 6th and December 3rd, 1917).

4th ... Arrival of British troops in Italy announced (see 3rd, and June 30th, 1918).

5th ... Action of Tikrit (Mesopotamia) (see 6th).

6th ... Passchendaele captured by British (Canadian) forces (see October 26th, 1917, and April 16th, 1918).
Tikrit (Mesopotamia) occupied by British forces (see 5th).

7th ... **Third Battle of Gaza ends** (see October 27th).
Allied Conference at Rapallo. Inception of Supreme War Council (see 27th).
General Cadorna relieved of the command of the Italian Armies (see May 23rd, 1915, and November 27th, 1917). Succeeded by General Diaz.

8th ... **Bolshevik** *coup d'état* **in Petrograd. M. Lenin and M. Trotski assume power.** Former succeeds M. Kerenski as Premier and latter succeeds M. Tereshchenko as Foreign Minister (see 13th, May 16th, and August 6th).

10th ... Second Battle of Passchendaele ends (see October 26th) and **Battles of Ypres, 1917, end** (see July 31st, 1917, and September 28th, 1918).

11th ... Austro-German forces reach the Piave (see October 24th).

13th ... Kerenski's forces defeated by Bolsheviki near Petrograd (see 8th and 15th).
Action of El Mughar (Palestine).

14th ... M. Painlevé, French Premier and War Minister, resigns (see 16th, and September 12th).
M. Barthou, French Foreign Minister, resigns (see 16th, and October 23rd).

15th ... British Government give further pledge in House of Commons that restitution of Alsace-Lorraine is a War Aim (see February 15th).
Japanese Government unable to comply with request of British Government that two Japanese battle cruisers should join the Grand Fleet in the North Sea (see February 8th, 1916, and April 17th, 1917).
M. Kerenski flees from Petrograd (see 13th).

16th ... Jaffa (Palestine) taken by British forces.
M. Clémenceau appointed French Premier and War Minister (see 14th).
M. Stephen Pichon appointed French Foreign Minister (see 14th).
*M. Jonnart succeeds M. Métin as French Minister for Blockade (see 23rd, and August 17th).

* First Minister: formerly Blockade was under an Under-Secretary.

Nov.–Dec. 1917

17th ... **Battle of Nebi Samwil (Palestine) begins** (see 24th).
Light cruiser action off Heligoland.

18th ... General Sir S. Maude, Commander-in-Chief in Mesopotamia, dies at Baghdad (see August 28th, 1916): succeeded by Lieut.-General Sir W. R. Marshall.

20th ... **Battle of Cambrai, 1917, begins** (see 30th, and December 3rd).
Ukrainian People's Republic proclaimed (see January 3rd, November 15th, and December 26th, 1918).

21st ... Armistice pourparlers begun by Russian Bolshevik Government with Central Powers (see 8th, 27th and 30th).
German airship "L.-59" leaves Yambol (Bulgaria) for East Africa (see 23rd).*

23rd ... M. Lebrun succeeds M. Jonnart as French Minister for Blockade (see 16th).
German airship "L.-59" reaches East Africa, but turns back without alighting (see 21st and 25th).*

24th ... **Battle of Nebi Samwil (Palestine) ends** (see 17th).
Ain ed Douleh succeeds Ala es Sultaneh as Persian Prime Minister (see June 6th, 1917, and January 19th, 1918).

25th ... German airship "L.-59" returns to Yambol from flight to East Africa (see 23rd).*
German force under Colonel von Lettow-Vorbeck effects passage of the Rovuma and defeats Portuguese force at Ngomano. German operations in Portuguese East Africa begin (see December 1st, 1917, and September 29th, 1918).

27th ... Members of Supreme Council appointed—General Sir H. H. Wilson, General F. Foch, General Cadorna, and General Bliss (see 7th).
First meeting of Russian and German delegates behind German lines to arrange for armistice (see 21st and 30th).

28th ... German force under Captain Tafel surrenders to the British in the Mwiti Valley (German East Africa).
Estonia declared independent by the local Diet (see January 13th, 1918).

29th ... First meeting of Great Inter-Allied Conference opens in Paris.
Air Force (Constitution) Act, 1917, comes into operation in Great Britain (see December 21st, 1917, and January 3rd, 1918).

30th ... **The German counter-attacks at Cambrai begin** (see 20th, and December 3rd).
Allied Naval Conference formed in London (see January 24th).
Austro-Hungarian Government accept Bolshevik proposals to negotiate for an armistice and peace (see 21st, and December 3rd).

DECEMBER 1917.

1st ... **Permanent Allied Supreme War Council inaugurated** (see November 7th, 1917, and February 3rd, 1918).
The last German forces driven out of German East Africa into Portuguese territory (approximate date) (see November 25th).

2nd **Suspension of hostilities between the Russian and German Armies begins** (see 8th).†

3rd ... **Battle of Cambrai, 1917, ends** (see November 20th, 1917, and October 8th, 1918).
First session of armistice‡ delegates at Brest-Litovsk—Bolshevik Russia, and Bulgaria, Germany, Austria-Hungary, and Turkey (see 6th, and November 30th).
Allied Conference in Paris resolve to establish an Allied Maritime Transport Council (see January 6th and November 3rd, 1917, and February 15th, 1918).

* Evidence for this event rests on German statements only.
† The actual suspension of hostilities took place on dates fixed by the local Army Commanders (see 8th) in anticipation of truce arranged between the official negotiators (see 6th).
‡ Also known as "Truce Delegates" and "Peace Delegates."

December 1917

6th ... **Finland declares independence** (see January 4th, 1918)
Hostilities between Rumania and Central Powers suspended (see 9th and 10th, and March 5th, May 7th, and November 10th, 1918).
Truce arranged between Russia and Bulgaria, Central Powers and Turkey from 7th to 17th. Negotiations suspended (see 3rd and 13th).
United States Battleship Division, under Rear-Admiral Rodman, joins Grand Fleet at Scapa Flow.

7th ... **United States of America declare war on Austria-Hungary** (see April 8th).
Ecuador severs diplomatic relations with Germany.
Truce between Russia and Central Powers comes into operation officially (see 2nd and 6th).

8th ... **All hostilities on the Eastern front suspended** (see 2nd).

9th ... **Jerusalem surrenders to British forces** (see 11th).
Italian naval raid on Trieste harbour (night 9th/10th). Austrian battleship "Wien" sunk.
Armistice ("Truce of Focsani") signed between Rumania and Central Powers (see 6th, and November 10th, 1918).

10th ... **Hostilities between Rumania and the Central Powers cease** (see 6th).
Panama declares war on Austria-Hungary.
Dr. S. Cardosa da Paes succeeds Dr. A. A. da Costa as Portuguese Prime Minister (see April 25th, 1917, and May 15th, 1918).

11th ... Russian Constituent Assembly meet in Petrograd (see 13th).
General Allenby makes formal entry into Jerusalem (see 9th).
Dr Machado Guimarães, Portuguese President, deposed (see 28th, and August 6th and October 5th, 1915).

12th ... Funchal (Madeira) shelled by German submarine (see December 3rd, 1916).
German destroyers raid British convoy in the North Sea and sink H.M.S. "Partridge" (see October 17th).

13th ... Armistice negotiations on Russian front resumed (see 6th and 15th).
Russian Constituent Assembly dispersed by Bolsheviki (see 11th, and November 8th, 1917, and January 19th, 1918).

14th ... French cruiser "Château Renault" sunk by submarine.
General Sarrail recalled from Salonika (see 22nd, and January 16th, 1916).

15th ... Armistice signed at Brest-Litovsk between Russian Bolshevik Government and Bulgaria, Central Powers and Turkey, to begin at noon December 17th, and terminate January 14th, 1918 (see 13th and 22nd).
"Second Offensive Battle" of Verdun ends (see August 20th).

16th ... Cuba declares war on Austria-Hungary.

17th ... British Government give the King of the Hejaz (see December 15th, 1916, and February 4th, 1918) written assurance of the future independence of the Arab people.
Armistice between Russia and Central Powers begins (see 15th).

21st ... Battle of Jaffa (Palestine) begins (see 22nd).
British Government issue Order in Council instituting the Air Council (see November 29th, 1917, and January 3rd, 1918).

22nd Battle of Jaffa (Palestine) ends (see 21st).
Peace negotiations between Russian Bolshevik Government and Bulgaria, Central Powers and Turkey opened at Brest-Litovsk (see 15th, and January 5th, 1918).
Secret Convention signed at Brest-Litovsk between Germany and Russian Bolshevik Government concerning Poland.
General Guillaumat appointed Allied Commander-in-Chief at Salonika (see 14th, and June 6th, 1918).
Lieut.-General Sir R. C. Maxwell, Quartermaster-General, B.E.F., France, resigns (see 23rd, and January 27th, 1915).

23rd ...	Independent Moldavian Republic (Bessarabia) proclaimed at Kishinev (see April 9th, 1918).
	Lieut.-General Sir T. E. Clarke, appointed Quartermaster-General, B.E.F., France (see 22nd).
26th ...	**Twelfth Battle of the Isonzo ends** (see October 24th).
	British defence of Jerusalem begins (see 30th).
	Admiral Sir John Jellicoe, First Sea Lord, Great Britain, resigns (see 27th, and December 4th, 1916).
27th ...	Admiral Sir Rosslyn Wemyss appointed First Sea Lord, Great Britain (see 26th).
28th ...	French Foreign Minister in speech outlines French War Aims (see January 5th, 1918).
	Dr. da Silva Paes appointed Acting President of Portugal (see December 11th, 1917, and May 9th, 1918).
30th ...	British defence of Jerusalem ends (see 26th).

JANUARY 1918.

1st ...	Arab forces begin Actions for Et Tafile (see 28th).
	M. Hymans succeeds Baron de Broqueville as Belgian Minister for Foreign Affairs (see August 4th, 1917).
2nd ...	Air Ministry formed in Great Britain.
3rd ...	The Air Council takes over functions of Air Board (see May 17th, 1916, and November 29th and December 21st, 1917).
	Ukraine delegation reaches Brest-Litovsk (see November 21st, 1917, and February 1st, 1918).
4th ...	British hospital ship "Rewa" sunk by submarine in Bristol Channel.
	Russian Bolshevik Government and French and Swedish Governments recognise the independence of Finland (see 10th, and December 6th, 1917).
	British Government in message to the King of the Hejaz declare intentions with regard to future status of Palestine (see December 17th, 1917, and February 4th, 1918).
	Allied request for handing over of Dutch ships in Allied ports formulated (see March 7th).
5th ...	British Premier (Mr. Lloyd George) in speech to Trade Union delegates outlines British War Aims (see 24th, and December 28th, 1917).
	Negotiations again suspended on Russian front. Bolshevik demand made for meetings to be held at Stockholm (see 8th, and December 6th, 13th and 22nd, 1917).
8th ...	Qasr-i-Shirin (Western Persia) occupied by British forces (see July 8th, 1917).
	President Wilson delivers Message to Congress laying down the "Fourteen Points" (see February 11th).
	Russian Bolshevik Government withdraw demand for transfer to Stockholm and resume negotiations at Brest-Litovsk (see 5th and 22nd).
10th ...	British Government assure Russian Bolshevik Government of their support in the creation of an independent Poland (see April 5th, 1917, and February 20th, 1918).
	Danish and Norwegian Governments recognise the independence of Finland (see 4th).
12th	**Latvia declares independence** (see November 11th).
13th ...	**Estonian Government issue declaration of independence** (see November 28th, 1917, and February 25th and November 11th, 1918).
14th ...	German destroyers bombard Yarmouth (Norfolk).
18th ...	Russian Constituent Assembly again meet in Petrograd (see 19th, and December 13th, 1917).

Jan.-Feb. 1918

19th ... Russian Constituent Assembly again forcibly dissolved by Bolsheviki (see 18th, and December 13th, 1917).
Mustaufi ul Mamalek succeeds Ain ed Douleh as Persian Prime Minister (see November 24th, 1917, and May 3rd, 1918).
Mushaver ul Mamalek succeeds Ala es Sultaneh as Persian Foreign Minister (see June 6th, 1917, and August 10th, 1918).

20th ... Naval action outside the Dardanelles. German cruiser "Breslau" and British monitor "Raglan" sunk. "Goeben" strikes mine and is beached (see 27th).

22nd ... Russian Bolshevik Government accuse Central Powers of falsification of reports of proceedings (see 8th and 23rd).

23rd ... Negotiations between Russian Bolshevik Government and Central Powers once more suspended (see 8th, 22nd and 30th).

24th ... Count Hertling and Count Czernin (German Imperial Chancellor and Austrian Foreign Minister) make public replies to statements of President Wilson and Mr. Lloyd George on War Aims (see 5th and 8th).
*Lieut.-General The Hon. Sir H. A. Lawrence appointed Chief of the General Staff, British Expeditionary Force, France (see 27th).

27th ... Turkish Dead Sea Flotilla seized by Arab camelry at El Mezraa'.
General Dunsterville's Mission leaves Baghdad for North-West Persia (see February 17th).
The "Goeben" refloated inside the Dardanelles (see 20th).
Lieut.-General Sir L. E. Kiggell, Chief of the General Staff, British Expeditionary Force, France, resigns (see 24th, and December 22nd, 1915).

28th ... Russian Bolshevik Government sever diplomatic relations with Rumania.
Actions for Et Tafile by the Arab forces end (see 1st).

30th ... Negotiations between Russian Bolshevik Government and Central Powers again resumed (see 23rd, and February 10th).

FEBRUARY 1918.

1st ... **Central Powers recognise the Ukraine Republic** (see 9th, and November 20th, 1917).
Extension of the British East Persia Cordon (see July 29th, 1915) into Khorasan begins.†

3rd ... **British Government announce enlargement of powers of Supreme War Council at Versailles** (see November 7th, 1917, and December 1st, 1917).

4th ... General Alexeiev with Don Cossacks moves towards Moscow against the Bolshevik forces (see 13th).
British Government make declaration to King of the Hejaz reaffirming their pledges as to freeing the Arab peoples (see October 24th, 1915, December 15th, 1916, December 17th, 1917, and January 4th, 1918).

5th ... British S.S. "Tuscania," carrying United States troops, sunk by submarine off Irish coast. (The only loss sustained by U.S. transports when under British naval escort.)

6th ... **German Government send ultimatum to Rumania demanding peace negotiations within four days** (see 25th).
M. Bratianu, Rumanian Premier, resigns (appointed January 14th, 1914) (see 9th).

9th ... **Peace signed at Brest-Litovsk between Bulgaria, Central Powers and Turkey and the Ukraine Rada; also supplementary Treaty between Central Powers and The Ukraine;** borders of new Ukrainian State defined (see 1st, and January 3rd).
New Rumanian Cabinet formed, with General Averescu as Premier and Foreign Minister (see 6th, and March 12th).

---

* Did not take up appointment till the 27th.
† In relief of Russian forces withdrawn by Bolshevik Government.

10th ... **M. Trotski announces that state of war between Russia and Central Powers, Bulgaria and Turkey is ended, but that Russia will not sign formal peace treaty** (see 18th, and January 30th).

11th ... **President Wilson delivers Message to Congress laying down four additional Points** (see January 8th and October 6th).

13th ... General Alexeiev defeated by the Bolsheviki (see 4th); General Kaledin commits suicide.

15th ... Third German destroyer raid in Straits of Dover (night 15th/16th) (see April 20th, 1917).
Representatives of Allied Governments arrange establishment of the "Allied Maritime Transport Council" (see December 3rd, 1917, and March 11th, 1918).

16th ... Dover shelled by German submarine.

17th ... General Dunsterville's Mission reaches Enzeli (North-West Persia) (see May 21st, 1915, January 27th and April 1st, 1918).

18th ... Armistice terminates on Russian front. **Hostilities resumed by German armies** (see 10th and 19th). Dvinsk taken by German forces.
General Sir W. Robertson, Chief of the British Imperial General Staff, resigns (see 19th, and December 23rd, 1915).

19th ... Russian Bolshevik Government notify willingness to sign Peace Treaty with Germany (see 18th and 28th).
General Sir H. H. Wilson appointed Chief of the British Imperial General Staff (see 18th).

20th ... British Foreign Minister (Mr. Balfour) informs Polish National Committee that Great Britain does not accept the treaty between The Ukraine and Central Powers (see 9th, January 10th, and June 3rd).

21st ... Jericho taken by British forces (19th/21st).
Ministry of Information formed in Great Britain.

23rd ... Inter-Allied Labour and Socialist Conference in London pass resolution as to War Aims.

24th ... **Trebizond (Asia Minor) retaken by Turkish forces** (see April 17th, 1916).
Dorpat (Estonia) occupied by German forces (see December 26th).
German raider "Wolff" returns to Germany (see December 1st, 1916).

25th ... Pernau, Reval, and Pskov taken by German forces (see 18th).
Kirmanshah (Western Persia) occupied by British forces (see March 11th, 1917).
Peace negotiations begun at Bukharest (see 6th, and March 5th).
Military Convention signed at Bobruisk between Germany and Poland.
British Government inform M. Tonisson that they are prepared provisionally to recognise the independence of Estonia until the future status of Estonia is settled by the Peace Congress (see January 13th and November 11th).

26th ... British hospital ship "Glenart Castle" sunk by submarine in the Bristol Channel (see March 1st, 1917).

28th ... Negotiations again resumed between Russian Bolshevik Government and Central Powers: hostilities nominally cease (see 18th, 19th, and March 3rd).

MARCH 1918.

1st ... Treaty of Peace and Amity signed between the Finnish Social Republic of Workmen and the Russian Federal Soviet Republic.

2nd ... **Kiev (Ukraine) captured by German forces** (see December 20th).
German force landed in the Aaland Islands at request of Finnish Government (see 3rd).

March 1918

3rd ... Meshed (Persia) occupied by troops of British East Persia Cordon.*
Peace signed between Bolshevik Russia and Central Powers, Bulgaria and Turkey at Brest-Litovsk, together with supplementary treaties by the signatories (see 14th and 18th, February 28th and August 27th).
German Government notify Swedish Government of occupation of the Aaland Islands (see 2nd).

4th ... Narva (Estonia) occupied by German forces (see November 28th).

5th ... **Preliminary treaty of peace between Rumania and the Central Powers, Bulgaria and Turkey signed at Buftea** (see December 9th, 1917, and February 25th and May 7th, 1918).

7th ... First German aeroplane raid on England undertaken on moonless night (see July 20th).
Peace signed at Berlin between Germany and Finland.
Final Allied Note presented to Netherlands Government re surrender of Dutch ships in Allied ports (see 18th, and January 4th).

8th ... M. Chichérin appointed Russian Foreign Minister and M. Trotski appointed Minister for War (see November 8th, 1917).

9th ... Hit (on the Euphrates) occupied by British forces.
Treaty of Peace signed between Rumania and Bolshevik Russia (see 5th).

10th ... British hospital ship "Guildford Castle" attacked by German submarine in Bristol Channel, but reaches port.

11th ... First meeting of the Allied Maritime Transport Council (see February 15th).

12th ... **Erzerum retaken by Turkish forces** (see February 16th, 1916).
General Averescu, Rumanian Premier and Foreign Minister, resigns (see 21st, and February 9th).

13th ... **Odessa occupied by German forces** (see December 11th).

14th ... Congress of Soviets meet at Moscow to ratify treaty of peace with Central Powers (see 3rd).

15th ... German Government proclaim protectorate over an independent Kurland.

16th ... Hamadan (West Persia) evacuated by the Russian regular forces (see March 2nd, 1917).

17th ... Nicolaiev (South Russia) captured by German forces (see April 8th).

18th ... Entente Governments issue Note refusing to recognise Russo-German peace treaty (see 3rd and 14th).
Dutch Government accept with reservations the Allied terms for use of Dutch shipping in United States and Entente ports (see 7th and 21st).

20th ... Allied Blockade Committee formed.

21st ... **First Battles of the Somme, 1918, begin** with Battle of St. Quentin (21st/23rd) (see November 18th, 1916, and April 5th, 1918).
Passage of the Jordan by British forces (21st/23rd).
Destroyer action in North Sea between Allied and German flotillas (see October 17th, 1914).
Dutch ships in British ports requisitioned by British Government, and Dutch ships in United States ports requisitioned by United States Government (see 18th).
M. Marghiloman appointed Rumanian Premier (see 12th, and November 8th).
M. Constantine Arian appointed Rumanian Foreign Minister (see 12th, and November 8th).

23rd ... Paris first shelled by long-range gun (from Crépy-en-Valois, 75 miles distant) (see August 15th).

* Approximate date.

24th ...	First Battle of Bapaume (24th/25th): Bapaume and Péronne taken by German forces (see March 17th and 18th, 1917, and August 29th and September 1st, 1918). First action of Es Salt (Palestine) (24th/25th).
25th ...	Noyon taken by German forces (see March 18th, 1917, and August 29th, 1918). German airship raid on Naples from the Dalmatian coast.
26th ...	Albert, Chaulnes, and Roye taken by German forces (see March 17th, 1917, and August 22nd and 27th, 1918). Action of Khan Baghdadi (Mesopotamia) (26th/27th). **"Doullens Agreement" concluded. Decision taken to appoint General Foch to co-ordinate efforts of British and French Armies** (see April 14th).
27th ...	Battle of Rosières (Somme) (26th/27th). Montdidier taken by German forces (see August 10th). First British attack on Amman (Palestine) (27th/30th).
28th ...	First Battle of Arras, 1918 (see August 26th). Ana (Mesopotamia) occupied by British forces.
29th ...	Poltava (South Russia) captured by German forces.

APRIL 1918.

1st ...	Enzeli (Persia) evacuated by the Russian regular forces (see February 17th). German Expeditionary Force for Finland leaves Danzig (see 3rd). Royal Flying Corps and Royal Naval Air Services of Great Britain amalgamated and established a separate service as the Royal Air Force.
3rd ...	German Expeditionary Force lands in South Finland at Hangö (see 1st, 13th, and December 16th). Ekaterinoslav (South Russia) taken by German forces.
4th ...	Battle of the Avre (France). Sarikamish (Russian Caucasus) occupied by Turkish forces (see January 2nd, 1915). British submarines at Helsingfors destroyed to avoid capture (3rd/4th) (see 3rd).
5th ...	Battle of the Ancre, 1918, brings to an **end the First Battles of the Somme, 1918** (see March 21st). Japanese and British marines land at Vladivostok (see August 2nd and 3rd). Van (Armenia) retaken by Turkish forces (see May 19th, 1915).
8th ...	Kharkov (South Russia) captured by German forces.
9th ...	**Battles of the Lys begin** (see 29th): Battle of Estaires (9th/11th): Neuve Chapelle taken by German forces. Count Mirbach appointed German Ambassador at Moscow (see July 6th). National Council of the Moldavian Republic (Bessarabia) pass Act of Union with Rumania, with stipulation for local autonomy (see 16th, December 23rd, 1917, and December 10th, 1918).
10th ...	Battle of Messines, 1918 (10th/11th): Messines taken by German forces (see June 14th, 1917, and September 28th, 1918). Monrovia (Liberia) bombarded by a German submarine (see August 4th, 1917). Third Military Service Act passed in British Parliament. Military age limit raised to 50, and Conscription extended to Ireland (see 18th, and June 8th, 1916). Settlement Treaty between Germany and Turkey ratified at Berlin (see January 11th, 1917). Agreement reached between Italy and the Yugo-Slavs ("Pact of Rome").
11th ...	Armentières and Merville taken by German forces (see October 11th and 17th, 1914, August 19th and October 3rd, 1918). French Government publish text of Emperor of Austria's letter to Prince Sixte of Bourbon proposing peace negotiations (see 15th, and March 31st, 1917).

April 1918

12th ... Battle of Hazebrouck (Lys) begins (see 15th).
    Last airship raid over England in which casualties were inflicted (27) (see January 19th, 1915, and August 5th, 1918).
    Field-Marshal Sir Douglas Haig issues Order of the Day to the British Army in France on the serious situation ("Backs to the Wall" order).

13th ... Battle of Bailleul (Lys) begins (see 15th).
    Helsingfors (Finland) captured by German forces (12th/14th) (see 3rd and 4th).
    Finnish Government announce that all German troops landed in Finland had been despatched at their request.
    United Diets of Baltic Provinces adopt resolution to form themselves into a separate State within the German Empire.

14th ... **General Foch appointed Commander-in-Chief of Allied Armies in France*** (see March 26th, August 6th, and November 5th).

15th ... Battle of Hazebrouck ends (see 12th).
    Battle of Bailleul ends (see 13th).: Bailleul taken by the German forces (see October 14th, 1914, and August 30th, 1918).
    Raid by British naval light forces on the Kattegat (see November 2nd, 1917).
    Batum (Georgia) occupied by Turkish forces (see December 27th).
    Count Czernin, Austro-Hungarian Foreign Minister, resigns (see 17th, and December 22nd, 1916).

16th ... Passchendaele reoccupied by German forces (see November 6th, 1917, and September 29th, 1918).
    The Ukraine Government issue protest against union of Bessarabia and Rumania (see 9th and 23rd).

17th ... First Battle of Kemmel Ridge (Lys) begins (see 19th).
    Baron Burian succeeds Count Czernin as Austro-Hungarian Foreign Minister (see 15th, and October 25th).
    Dr. Wekerle, Hungarian Premier, resigns (see 27th, and August 21st, 1917).

18th ... Battle of Bethune (Lys).
    Third Military Service Act comes into operation in Great Britain (see 10th).

19th ... German forces enter the Crimea.
    First Battle of Kemmel Ridge ends (see 17th and 26th).

20th ... Lord Derby, Secretary of State for War, Great Britain, resigns (see December 11th, 1916).
    Viscount Milner appointed Secretary of State for War, Great Britain

21st ... Viscount Motono, Japanese Minister for Foreign Affairs, resigns (see 22nd, and November 21st, 1916).

22nd ... The Trans-Caucasian Council decide to declare independence (night 22nd/23rd) (see September 20th, 1917, and May 6th and 26th, 1918).
    Baron Goto appointed Japanese Minister for Foreign Affairs (see 21st, and September 28th).

23rd ... **Blocking raid by British naval light forces on Ostend and Zeebrugge** (see May 9th).
    Russian Bolshevik Government issue protest against union of Bessarabia and Rumania (see 9th and 16th, and December 10th).
    Guatemala declares war on Germany (see April 27th, 1917).

24th ... Actions of Villers-Bretonneux (Somme) (24th/25th).

26th ... Second Battle of Kemmel Ridge (25th/26th): Mount Kemmel stormed by German forces (see 19th, and August 31st).

27th ... Kars (Georgia) occupied by Turkish forces.
    First contingent of Italian troops arrive on the French front.†
    Dr. Wekerle again appointed Hungarian Prime Minister (see 17th, and October 24th).

---

* The Belgian forces were not placed under the command of General Foch.
† Approximate date.

29th ... The Battle of the Scherpenberg brings to an **end the Battles of the Lys** (see 9th).
German Government establish a military dictatorship in The Ukraine. General Skoropadski proclaimed Hetman (see May 9th).

30th ... Viborg (Finland) captured by German forces and Finnish White Guards (see 13th).
Second action of Es Salt (Palestine) begins (see May 4th).

MAY 1918.

1st ... **Sevastopol taken by German forces** (April 30th/May 1st).
Part of Russian Black Sea Fleet seized by the Germans (see June 21st, 1917, and June 18th and November 26th, 1918).

2nd ... Agreement concluded regarding export of sand and gravel from The Netherlands for German use (see July 15th).

3rd ... Samsam es Sultaneh succeeds Mustaufi ul Mamalek as Persian Prime Minister (see 31st, and January 19th).

4th ... Second action of Es Salt ends (see April 30th).
Armistice signed at Korenevo between Russia and The Ukraine (German-Ukrainian Command) (see June 12th).

5th ... Field-Marshal Lord French appointed Lord-Lieutenant of Ireland (see December 15th, 1915).

6th ... Turko-German delegates arrive at Batum to negotiate peace with the Georgians and Armenians (see April 22nd, May 26th, and June 8th).

7th ... Kirkuk (Mesopotamia) taken by British forces (see 24th).
Frederickshamn (South Finland) captured by Finnish White Guards: **End of the Finnish Civil War.***
Final Treaty of Peace signed between Rumania and Bulgaria, Central Powers and Turkey (see March 5th), **together with various supplementary treaties between the separate contracting parties** (see November 10th).

8th ... Nicaragua declares war on Germany and on Austria-Hungary (see May 18th, 1917).
Rostov (South Russia) captured by German forces.

9th ... Blocking attack on Ostend. H.M.S. "Vindictive" sunk to block the harbour (see April 23rd).
M. Ustemovich proclaimed President of The Ukraine; General Skoropadski remains Hetman (see April 29th).
Joint Trade Committee of Entente Powers formed in Holland.
Dr. da Silva Paes, elected Portuguese President (see December 28th, 1917, and December 14th, 1918).

11th ... Peace signed in Berlin between Finland and Turkey.

12th ... Military Treaty ("Waffenbund") signed between Germany and Austria-Hungary.

14th ... Italian naval raid on Pola Harbour.

15th ... German submarine bombards St. Kilda (Hebrides).
Agreement between Entente Powers, Japan, and China against German penetration in Far East announced.
Dr. S. B. C. da Paes, Portuguese Premier, resigns (see 16th, and December 10th, 1917).

16th ... Agreement signed at Peking between China and Japan for military co-operation against German and Bolshevik aggression (see 19th).
Senhor J. T. de Souza Barboza, appointed Portuguese Secretary of the Interior† (see 15th, and December 22nd).

17th ... Sinn Fein leaders arrested in Ireland and interned (see 25th).

---
* The civil war may be said to have begun about March 1st, 1918.
† The appointment of Premier lapsed between May 15th and December 23rd. During this period the functions of the office were performed by the Secretary of the Interior.

May–June 1918

18th ... First British retaliatory air raid on German towns. Cologne bombed by day.
Alexandropol (Georgia) occupied by Turkish forces.

19th ... Last German night aeroplane raid on London in which casualties were inflicted; 49 killed and 177 wounded* (see May 7th, July 7th, and October 19th, 1917, and August 5th, 1918).
German air raid on British camps and hospitals at Etaples; heavy casualties.
Agreement signed between China and Japan for naval co-operation (see 16th).

23rd ... Costa Rica declares war on Germany (see September 21st, 1917).

24th ... Kirkuk (Mesopotamia) evacuated by the British forces (see 7th, and October 25th).
General F. C. Poole lands at Murmansk to organise the North Russia Expeditionary Force (see June 4th, 8th and 23rd).

25th ... British Government publish account of Irish-German plots (see 17th).

26th ... **Trans-Caucasian Federal Government** (see September 20th, 1917, and April 22nd, 1918), **dissolved. Georgia declares independence and forms a National Government. Armenian National Council assume charge of Armenian affairs** (see June 8th). **Tatar National Council proclaim establishment of a "Republic of Azerbaijan."**

27th ... **Battle of the Aisne, 1918 ("Third Battle of the Aisne"), begins** (see June 6th).
Craonne again taken by German forces (see May 4th, 1917, and October 12th, 1918).

29th ... Soissons again taken by German forces (see 27th, and August 2nd).
Peace Treaty signed at Vienna between Austria-Hungary and Finland.

30th ... Fère-en-Tardenois taken by German forces (see 27th, and July 28th).

31st ... **German forces reach the Marne.** Château-Thierry and Dormans captured (see July 21st).
Battle of the Skra di Legen (Macedonia).
Samsam es Sultaneh, Persian Prime Minister, resigns (see 3rd, and June 20th).
†M. G. Cooreman succeeds Baron de Broqueville as Belgian Prime Minister (Baron de Broqueville was appointed in 1911) (see November 21st).

JUNE 1918.

3rd ... **British, French, and Italian Governments make declarations supporting national aspirations of Poles, Czecho-Slovaks, and Yugo-Slavs** (see February 20th, June 29th, August 13th, September 25th, and November 16th).

4th ... British Marines land at Pechenga (North Russia) (see May 24th).
The Don Cossacks declare independence.

5th ... British Independent Air Force in France constituted under tactical command of Major-General Sir H. M. Trenchard.

6th ... **Battle of the Aisne, 1918, ends** (see May 27th).
Dutch hospital ship "Koningen Regentes" sunk by mine or torpedo.
General Guillaumat, Allied Commander-in-Chief, Salonika, recalled to Paris (see 15th and 18th, and December 22nd, 1917).

7th ... British force lands at Kem (North Russia) (see May 24th).
Omsk (Siberia) occupied by Czecho-Slovak forces (see November 18th).

---

* There were altogether nineteen aeroplane raids on London during which bombs were dropped, and one air reconnaissance during which no bombs were dropped.

† Baron de Broqueville and M. Cooreman presided over the Cabinet without the title of Prime Minister (see November 21st).

8th ...	German Expeditionary Force to the Caucasus lands at Poti (Georgia). **Russian Bolshevik Government order Entente forces in North Russia to leave the country** (see 30th, and May 24th). **Georgian Government and Armenian National Council sign peace treaties with Turkey** (see May 6th and 26th). **Georgian Government sign peace treaty with Germany** (see May 6th and 26th).
9th ...	**Battle of the Matz begins** (see 14th). First sitting of Anglo-German Conference at The Hague on prisoners of war.
10th ...	Naval action off Premuda Island (Adriatic). Austrian battleship " Szent Istvan " sunk by Italian motor launch.
12th ...	Tiflis (Georgia) occupied by a German force (see 8th, and December 27th). Kurdamir (East Caucasus) occupied by Turkish forces. Armistice concluded at Kiev between the whole State of The Ukraine and Russian Bolshevik Republic (see May 4th).
14th ...	**Battle of the Matz ends** (see 9th). Tabriz (North Persia) again occupied by Turkish forces (see January 30th, 1915).
15th ...	**Battle of the Piave begins** (see 24th). General Guillaumat appointed Governor of Paris (see 6th).
18th ...	Russian battleship " Svobodnaya Rossiya " destroyed in Black Sea to avoid surrender to the Germans (see May 4th). General Franchet d'Esperey appointed Commander-in-Chief Allied Forces, Salonika (see 6th). M. Radoslavov, Bulgarian Premier, resigns (date of appointment July 20th, 1913). M. Malinov appointed Premier and Foreign Minister.
20th ...	Samsam es Sultaneh reappointed Persian Prime Minister (see May 31st and August 3rd).
21st ...	Dr. Ernst Ritter von Seidler, Austrian Premier, resigns (see June 23rd, 1917).
23rd ...	British Expeditionary Forces " Syren " and " Elope " join the North Russian Expeditionary Force at Murmansk (see 4th, May 24th and July 26th).
24th ...	**Battle of the Piave ends** (see 15th).
27th ...	British hospital ship " Llandovery Castle " sunk by submarine off Irish coast.
29th ...	United States Government announce their view that all branches of the Slav races should be completely freed from German and Austrian rule (see 3rd).
30th ...	First contingent of United States troops arrive in Italy (see November 3rd and 4th, 1917). Murman Railway from Murmansk to Soroki seized by Allied forces (29th/30th) (see 23rd). Murman Soviet (Sovdep) decide to support the Entente against the Bolshevik Government (see 8th, and July 7th and November 20th). Treaty signed between the Czecho-Slovaks and Italy, by which Italy recognises Czecho-Slovak Council and their jurisdiction over nationals.

JULY 1918.

1st ...	Affair of Nyamakura (East Africa)* (1st/3rd).
3rd ...	Sultan Mohammed V of Turkey dies. Mohammed VI succeeds to the throne (see November 14th, 1914).
4th ...	Siberian Council declare Independence (see 6th).

* Near Quelimane (Portuguese East Africa). This was the most southerly point reached by Colonel von Lettow-Vorbeck's force.

6th ... French and Italian forces begin offensive in Albania (see 10th and 22nd).
German Ambassador at Moscow (Count Mirbach) murdered (see April 9th).
Declaration of Siberian Independence cancelled (see 4th).

7th ... Agreement signed between France, Great Britain, United States of America, and Murman Sovdep concerning Allied expedition to Murman Coast (see June 30th).

9th ... Admiral von Hintze succeds Herr von Kuhlmann as German Foreign Minister (see August 5th, 1917, and October 4th, 1918).

10th ... Berat (Albania) taken by Italian forces (see 6th, and February 17th, 1916).
New Government formed at Vladivostok under General Horvat (see August 24th).

12th ... Haiti declares war on Germany (see June 16th, 1917).
Japanese battleship "Kawachi" destroyed by internal explosion.

13th ... Irkutsk (Siberia) occupied by Czecho-Slovak forces (see October 14th).

14th ... Kazan (East Russia) captured by Czecho-Slovak forces.

15th ... **Fourth Battle of Champagne begins** (see 18th, and April 17th, 1917).
British Government protest against "Sand and Gravel Agreement" between Germany and The Netherlands (see May 2nd).

16th ... Field-Marhal Conrad von Hötzendorff, Commander-in-Chief, Austro-Hungarian Armies, relieved of his command.
Ex-Tsar Nicholas II, ex-Tsaritsa, and family murdered at Ekaterinburg (see March 15th, 1917).

18th ... **Fourth Battle of Champagne ends** (see 15th).
Second Battle of the Marne begins (see August 7th).
Sir L. Worthington-Evans succeeds Lord Robert Cecil as British Minister for Blockade (see February 23rd, 1916).

19th ... Honduras declares war on Germany (see May 17th, 1917).
British operations in Trans-Caspia begin (see August 26th).
United States cruiser "San Diego" sunk by mine off Fire Island (Atlantic coast).

20th .. German forces retreat across the Marne (see 18th).
*Last attempt to attack the British Isles with aeroplanes (unsuccessful) (see December 21st, 1914, and August 5th, 1918).
British defence of Resht (North-West Persia).

21st ... Château-Thierry retaken by Allied forces (see 18th, 20th, and May 31st).

22nd ... Allied offensive in Albania checked (see 6th, 10th, and August 22nd).

23rd ... Battle of Soissonais and Ourcq begins (see August 2nd).†

26th ... Bulk of French Expeditionary Force troops join the North Russia Expeditionary Force at Murmansk (see June 23rd).
Coup d'état in Baku: Bolshevik Government replaced by Central Caspian Dictatorship.
British Government declare to M. Petrov that they have no intention of infringing the territorial integrity of Russia (see August 6th).

28th .. Fère-en-Tardenois retaken by Allied forces (see May 30th).

30th ... Field-Marshal von Eichhorn, commanding German Army in The Ukraine, assassinated in Kiev (see April 29th).

---

* There were altogether 59 aeroplane raids against the British Isles during which bombs were dropped. There were also 11 reconnaissance flights over parts of Great Britain or in the vicinity of the coast when no bombs were dropped. See also footnotes against entries of May 19th and August 5th.
† British dates.

AUGUST 1918.

1st ... Allied Expeditionary Force attack and capture the defences of Archangel (see 2nd).

2nd ... Battle of Soissonais and Ourcq ends (see July 23rd).
Soissons retaken by Allied forces (see May 29th).
Pro-Entente revolution in Archangel. Entente forces enter the town (see 1st).
Japanese Government decide to land troops at Vladivostok (see 11th, and April 5th).

3rd ... British troops land at Vladivostok (see 2nd, and April 5th).
British ambulance transport "Warilda" sunk by submarine.
Samsam es Sultaneh, Persian Prime Minister, resigns (see 7th, and June 20th).

4th ... British force arrives at Baku (Caspian Sea) (see 26th, and July 19th).
Bolshevik Committee at Enzeli arrested by British military authorities.

5th ... Last attempt to attack England with airships (unsuccessful— "L.-70" destroyed)* (see January 19th, 1915, and April 12th and July 20th, 1918).

6th ... British Government issue Declaration to Russian peoples, stating that they have no intention of interfering in Russian politics (see July 26th).
General Foch created Marshal of France.

7th ... **Second Battle of the Marne ends** (see July 18th).
French cruiser "Dupetit Thouars" sunk by submarine in the Atlantic.
Vossuq ed Douleh appointed Persian Prime Minister (see 3rd, and May 29th, 1917).

8th ... **Battle of Amiens begins** (see 11th).
Battle of Montdidier begins (see 15th).
British Government inform Finnish Government that they are in no way hostile to Finnish aspirations on the Murman Coast and in Karelia.

10th ... Montdidier retaken by French forces (see 8th, and March 27th).
Mushaver ul Mamalek, Persian Foreign Minister, resigns (see 11th, and January 19th).

11th ... **Battle of Amiens ends** (see 8th).
German airship "L.-53" destroyed off Frisian coast. (Last German airship to be destroyed.)
First Japanese contingents arrive at Vladivostok (see 2nd and 24th, and September 5th).
Mushaver ul Mamalek reappointed Persian Foreign Minister (see 10th).

13th ... **The Czecho-Slovaks declare War on Germany.**†
British Government recognise the Czecho-Slovaks as an Allied nation (see June 3rd and September 3rd).
Admiral von Capelle, German Minister of Marine, resigns (see 15th, and March 15th, 1916).

15th ... **Battle of Montdidier ends** (see 8th).
Last bombardment of Paris by German long-range gun (see March 23rd).
Action of Bairam Ali (Trans-Caspia): Trans-Caspian Government defeated by Bolshevik forces.
Vice-Admiral von Behnke appointed German Minister of Marine (see 13th).

17th ... Second Battle of Noyon begins (see 29th).
Slovene National Council meet at Ljubljana (Laibach) (see November 2nd).

---

* There were altogether 51 airship raids against the British Isles during which bombs were dropped. There were also 8 attempted raids which either did not reach the coast, or which, for some other reason, failed in action. There were also 59 aeroplane attacks in which bombs were dropped (see July 20th), and 11 aeroplane reconnaissances. Total number of air raids in which bombs were dropped was 110.

† See footnote in Part III, "War, declarations of."

Aug.–Sept. 1918

18th ... Merv (Trans-Caspia) taken by Bolshevik forces (see November 1st).*
British advance in Flanders begins: Action of Outtersteene Ridge.

19th ... Merville retaken by British forces (see April 11th).

21st ... **Second Battles of the Somme, 1918, begin** with the Battle of Albert, 1918 (21st/23rd) (see September 3rd).

22nd ... Albert recaptured by British forces (see 21st, and March 26th).
Austrian forces begin counter-offensive in Albania (see July 6th and 22nd).

24th ... *Coup d'état* by General Horvat at Vladivostok (see July 10th).
Battle of Dukhovskaya (Eastern Siberia) (23rd/24th). Bolsheviki decisively defeated by Allied forces. †

26th ... **Second Battles of Arras, 1918, begin** with Battle of the Scarpe, 1918 (see 30th, March 28th and September 3rd).
Berat (Albania) retaken by Austrian forces (see 22nd, and July 10th and October 1st).
Defence of Baku (Caspian Sea) against Turkish attack begins (see 4th, July 19th and September 15th).

27th ... Roye recaptured by British forces (see March 26th).
British force occupies Krasnovodsk on Caspian Sea.
German and Russian Bolshevik Governments conclude complementary treaty of peace (see March 3rd).

28th ... Affair near Kaakhka (Trans-Caspia).

29th ... Bapaume retaken by British forces (see March 24th).
Noyon retaken by French forces (see March 25th). Second Battle of Noyon ends (see 17th).

30th ... Battle of the Scarpe, 1918, ends (see 26th)
Bailleul retaken by British forces (see April 15th).
Lieut.-General Sir C. F. N. Macready, Adjutant-General, Home Forces, Great Britain, resigns (see February 22nd, 1916, and September 11th, 1918).

31st ... German forces evacuate Mount Kemmel (see April 26th).
Second Battle of Bapaume begins (see March 24th and September 3rd).
Captain Cromie, R.N., British Naval Attaché, murdered by Bolsheviki in British Embassy, Petrograd.

SEPTEMBER 1918.

1st ... Péronne retaken by British forces (see March 24th).

2nd ... Battle of the Drocourt-Quéant Line (2nd/3rd).
Italian contingent lands at Murmansk to join Allied Expeditionary Force (see July 26th).

3rd ... **Second Battles of the Somme, 1918, end** (see August 21st).
Second Battles of Arras, 1918, end (see August 26th).
Lens occupied by British forces (see October 4th, 1914).
Second Battle of Bapaume ends (see August 31st).
United States Government recognises the Czecho-Slovaks as possessing a *de facto* Government (see August 13th and October 21st).

4th ... Obozerskaya (North Russia) occupied by Allied forces (see August 2nd).
United States contingent lands at Murmansk to join Allied Expeditionary Force (see 2nd).
Hsu-Shih-Chang elected President of China (see October 11th).

5th ... Khabarovsk (Eastern Siberia) taken by Japanese forces (see 18th, and August 11th).

11th ... Ukhtinskaya (Murman front) captured by Allied forces.
Lieut.-General Sir G. M. W. Macdonogh appointed Adjutant-General, Home Forces, Great Britain (see August 30th).

---

* Approximate date.
† Japanese, with one British battalion.

September 1918

12th ... **Battle of St. Mihiel** (12th/13th).
Battles of the Hindenburg Line (see October 9th) **begin** with Battle of Havrincourt.
Actions of Chamova (Archangel front) begin (see 14th).

14th ... Actions of Chamova end (see 12th).
British evacuation of Baku begins (see 15th, and August 26th).

15th ... **Battle of the Dobropolje* (Macedonia) begins** (see 16th).
Baku finally evacuated by the British forces (night 14th/15th) (see August 26th and November 17th).
Austrian Government send Note to President Wilson suggesting an "unofficial" peace conference (see 16th, and January 12th, 1917).
German Government make definite peace offer to Belgium (see January 10th and 12th, 1917).

16th ... **Battle of the Dobropolje ends** (see 15th).
Last German aeroplane raid on Paris (see August 30th, 1914).
President Wilson replies to the Austrian Note rejecting suggestion for a peace conference (see 15th, and October 4th).
H.M.S. "Glatton" sunk by explosion in Dover harbour.

18th ... **Battle of Epéhy.**
Blagovyeschensk (Siberia) occupied by Japanese forces (see 5th)
Battle of Monastir-Doiran (see 24th), including Battle of Doiran, 1918), **begins** (see 19th).

19th ... **Battles of Megiddo (Sharon and Nablus) (Palestine) begin** (see 23rd and 25th).
Battle of Doiran, 1918, ends (see 18th and 22nd).

20th ... Nazareth and Beisan (Palestine) occupied by British cavalry (see 19th).

22nd ... Doiran occupied by British forces (see 19th, and December 11th, 1915).

23rd ... Haifa, Acre, and Es Salt (Palestine) occupied by British forces (see 19th).
Prilep (South Serbia) taken by French forces (see November 16th, 1915).
Ma'an (on Hejaz Railway) evacuated by the Turkish garrison (see 29th).

24th ... **Battle of Monastir-Doiran ends** (see 18th).

25th ... Ishtip (see October 19th, 1915) and Veles (see October 21st, 1915) retaken by Serbian forces.
British cavalry cut Hejaz railway at Amman.
Battles of Megiddo end (see 19th).
Yugo-Slav State recognised as independent by Italy (see June 3rd and October 5th).

26th ... **Battle of Champagne and Argonne begins** (see October 15th).

27th ... **Battle of the Canal du Nord begins** (see October 1st).
Bulgarian Government ask Entente Powers for an armistice (see 30th).

28th ... **Battle of the Flanders Ridges begins** (see October 10th).
Battle of Ypres, 1918, begins (see November 10th, 1917, and October 2nd, 1918).
Messines retaken by British forces (see April 10th).
Baron Goto, Japanese Minister for Foreign Affairs, resigns (see 29th, and April 22nd).

29th ... **Battle of the St. Quentin Canal begins** (see October 2nd).
Passchendaele retaken by Allied forces (see 28th, and April 16th).
Dixmude retaken by Belgian forces (see November 10th, 1914).
Turkish garrison of Ma'an surrenders near Amman (Palestine) (see 23rd).
German force in East Africa recrosses the Rovuma and again enters German territory (see November 25th, 1917, and November 1st, 1918).

* Called by the Serbs "Battle of the Moglenitza."

Sept.–Oct. 1918

29th ... Takashi Hara succeeds Count Terauchi as Japanese Prime Minister
(contd.)   (see October 9th, 1916).
    Count Yasuya Uchida appointed Japanese Minister for Foreign Affairs (see 28th).
    Lieut.-General Kenichi Oshima, Japanese Minister for War, resigns (see 30th, and March 30th, 1916).

30th ... **Armistice between Bulgaria and Entente Powers signed** (see 27th).
Hostilities between Bulgaria and Entente Powers cease at 12 noon.
Canadian contingent lands at Archangel to join Allied Expeditionary Force (see August 2nd).
Count Hertling, German Imperial Chancellor, resigns (see October 30th, 1917, and October 4th, 1918).
Lieut.-General Giichi Tanaka appointed Japanese Minister for War (see 29th).

OCTOBER 1918.

1st ... **Battle of the Canal du Nord ends** (see September 27th).
St. Quentin retaken by French forces (see September 27th).
Berat (Albania) retaken by Italian forces (see August 26th).
Damascus taken by British and Arab forces.
Allies establish net and mine barrage across Straits of Otranto.

2nd ... **Battle of Ypres, 1918, ends** (see September 28th).
Battle of the St. Quentin Canal ends (see September 29th).
Durazzo bombarded by Italian and British warships (see 14th, and February 27th, 1916).

3rd ... Battle of the Beaurevoir Line begins (see 5th).
Armentières retaken by British forces (see April 11th).
Action near Pyavozero Lake (Murman front).

4th ... **Prince Max of Baden appointed German Imperial Chancellor,** and succeeds Admiral von Hintze as Foreign Minister (see September 30th, July 9th, and November 9th).
German and Austro-Hungarian Governments send Notes to President Wilson proposing an armistice (see 8th and 18th).*
Austro-Hungarian Government send Note to President Wilson proposing an armistice (see 27th, and September 16th).
King Ferdinand of Bulgaria abdicates in favour of his son Prince Boris (see September 30th and November 1st).
General Ironside takes over command of Allied forces at Archangel

5th ... Battle of the Beaurevoir Line ends (see 3rd).
Vranje retaken by Serbian forces (see October 15th, 1915).
Yugo-Slav delegates meet at Agram and decide on the formation of a United National Council (see 29th, and September 25th).

6th ... Sidon (Syria) occupied by British forces.

7th ... Beirut (Syria) occupied by French forces.
Elbasan (Albania) taken by Italian forces (see February 2nd, 1916).

8th ... **Battle of Cambrai, 1918, begins** (see 9th).
President Wilson replies to Note of German Government, and demands evacuation of occupied territories as first condition of armistice (see 4th and 12th).

9th ... Cambrai City captured by British forces (see August 26th, 1914).
End of Battle of Cambrai (see 8th) **brings Battles of the Hindenburg Line to a close** (see September 12th).
Major-General Scheuch succeeds Major-General von Stein as German Minister for War (see October 30th, 1916, and December 17th, 1918).

10th ... **Battle of the Flanders Ridges ends** (see September 28th).
Irish mail boat " Leinster " sunk by submarine.
Pristina (Serbia) retaken by French forces (see November 23rd, 1915).

11th ... Prizren (Serbia) retaken by French forces (see December 1st, 1915).
Nish (Serbia) reoccupied by Allied forces (see November 5th, 1915).
Feng-Kuo-Chang, President of China, retires (see July 6th, 1917, and September 4th, 1918).

* The German note was received by President Wilson on October 6th and the Austrian on October 7th.

October 1918

12th ... Craonne again captured by French forces (see May 27th).
Action of Dushak (Trans-Caspia).
German Government reply to President Wilson's Note and accept conditions (see 8th and 14th).
British Government recognise the Polish National Army as autonomous, allied and co-belligerent.

13th ... Laon and La Fère retaken by French forces (see August 30th, 1914).
Tripoli (Syria) occupied by Allied forces.
Izzet Pasha succeeds Talaat Pasha as Turkish Grand Vizier (see February 4th, 1917).

14th ... Battle of Courtrai begins (see 19th).
Roulers recaptured by Allied forces (see October 18th, 1914).
Durazzo (see 2nd), Novi Bazar (see November 20th, 1915), and Ipek (see December 6th, 1915) retaken by Italian forces.
British troops from Vladivostok reach Irkutsk (Siberia) (see 18th, and July 13th and August 3rd).
President Wilson replies to German Government, attaching further military conditions to the terms of armistice, and warning against further breaches of laws of war, and insists on dealing only with a democratic Government (see 12th and 20th).
Turkish Government Note to President Wilson proposing an armistice delivered at Washington.

15th ... **Battle of Champagne and Argonne ends** (see September 26th).
Menin captured by Allied forces (see October 9th, 1914).
Homs (Syria) occupied by British cavalry.

16th ... **Austrian Emperor issues manifesto proclaiming a Federal State on the principle of Nationality** (excluding Hungary) (see 5th and 29th).

17th ... **Ostend** (see October 15th, 1914), **Lille** (see October 12th, 1914), **and Douai** (see August 26th, 1914) **retaken by Allied forces.**
Battle of the Selle begins (see 25th).

18th ... British troops from Vladivostok reach Omsk (see 14th).
President Wilson replies to Austro-Hungarian Note of October 4th (see 27th).

19th ... Battle of Courtrai ends (see 14th).
Zeebrugge and Bruges reoccupied by Belgian forces (see October 12th and 14th, 1914).

20th ... Belgian coast completely reoccupied by Allied forces (see October 15th, 1914).
German Government reply to President Wilson's Note accepting proposals contained therein (see 14th and 23rd).

21st ... The Ban of Croatia refuses offer of Military Governor of Agram to suppress the Yugo-Slav National Council (see 5th and 29th).
The Czecho-Slovaks declare independence (see August 13th, September 3rd, and November 14th).

22nd ... Affair of Imad (Aden).

23rd ... British advance on Mosul (Mesopotamia) begins (see November 4th).
President Wilson replies to German Note of the 20th, and agrees to submit the matter to the Allied and Associated Governments (see 27th, and November 3rd).

24th ... **Battle of Vittorio Veneto begins** (see November 4th).
Dr. Wekerle, Hungarian Premier, resigns (see April 27th and November 1st).

25th ... **Battle of the Selle ends** (see 17th).
Kirkuk (Mesopotamia) again taken by British forces (see May 24th).
Count Andrassy succeeds Baron Burian as Austro-Hungarian Foreign Minister (see April 17th and November 1st).

26th ... **Aleppo (Syria) taken by British forces.**
King of Montenegro issues manifesto in favour of a confederated Yugo-Slavia with autonomous States (see 29th, and November 7th and 23rd).

Oct.–Nov. 1918

27th ... **Austrian Government ask Italy for an armistice** (see 4th, and November 3rd).
German Government acknowledges President Wilson's Note of October 23rd.
Austro-Hungarian Government submit further Note to President Wilson asking for immediate armistice "without awaiting the result of other negotiations") (see 4th and 18th).
General von Ludendorff resigns (see August 29th, 1916).

28th ... Muslimiya Junction, north of Aleppo (Syria), occupied by British cavalry.
Battle of Sharqat (Mesopotamia) begins (see 30th).

29th ... San Giovanni di Medua (Albania) occupied by Italian forces (see January 25th, 1916).
Yugo-Slav National Council at Agram repudiate Imperial policy and declare the independence of the Yugo-Slavs (see 5th, 21st, 26th, and November 7th and 23rd).

30th ... **Armistice between Turkey and Entente Powers signed at Mudros** (see 31st).
Battle of Sharqat ends (see 28th). **Turkish army on the Tigris surrenders.**
Fiume surrendered to the Croats by the Hungarian authorities.
"National Council of Fiume" proclaim the independence of the city and announce desire for union with Italy (see November 5th).
Croation Congress (Sabor) unanimously adhere to Yugo-Slav declaration of independence (see 29th).

31st ... **Hostilities between Entente and Turkey cease at 12 noon** (see 30th).
Scutari (Albania) retaken by Italian forces (see January 23rd, 1916).
Revolutions in Vienna and Budapest (see November 1st, 12th and 16th).
Count Tisza assassinated in Vienna (see May 23rd, 1917).
Austrian Emperor makes over the Austro-Hungarian Fleet to the Yugo-Slav National Council (see 29th).

NOVEMBER 1918.

1st ... **Battle of Valenciennes begins** (see 2nd).
Belgrade retaken by Serbian forces (see October 9th, 1915, and December 9th, 1918).
†Merv retaken by British and Russian forces (see August 18th).
German force in East Africa enters Rhodesia and attacks Fife (see 9th, and September 29th).
Austrian battleship "Viribus Unitis" sunk in Pola harbour.
"State of War" begins between The Ukraine and Poland (see 23rd).
King Boris of Bulgaria abdicates (see October 4th).
Independent Hungarian Government formed. Count Karolyi appointed Premier (see October 24th and 31st).
Baron von Flotow succeeds Count Andrassy (provisionally) as Austro-Hungarian Foreign Minister (see October 25th, and entry next above).

2nd ... **Battle of Valenciennes ends** (see 1st and 3rd).
Last British merchant vessels (S.S. "Surada" and "Murcia") sunk by submarine (in the Mediterranean).
Administration of Carniola taken over from the Austro-Hungarian authorities by Slovene leaders (see August 17th).

3rd ... Valenciennes occupied by British forces (see 2nd, and August 25th, 1914).
Allied Governments agree to Germany's proposal for an armistice and peace on basis of President Wilson's proposals of January 8th (see 5th and October 23rd).
Armistice between Austria-Hungary and the Entente signed (see 4th, 15th, and October 27th).
Trieste occupied by Italian forces.
Mutiny breaks out in the German fleet at Kiel (see August 3rd, 1917).

4th ... **Battle of the Sambre.**
Second Battle of Guise (4th/5th).
Battle of Vittorio Veneto ends (see October 24th).
Hostilities between Austria-Hungary and the Entente cease (see 3rd and 15th).
Antivari (Montenegro) occupied by Italian naval forces (see January 22nd, 1916).
Mosul occupied by British forces (see October 23rd).

*† Approximate date.

November 1918

5th ... Marshal Foch placed in supreme strategical direction of all forces operating against Germany on all fronts (see April 14th).
Fiume occupied by Italian naval forces (see 18th, and October 30th).
H.M.S. "Campania" sunk by collision in the Firth of Forth.
President Wilson sends final Note to the German Government with Allies' acceptance of armistice proposals (see 3rd and 8th).

6th ... Rethel taken by French forces.
Sedan taken by United States forces (see August 29th, 1914).
King Peter of Serbia re-enters Belgrade (see 1st, and January 17th, 1916).

7th ... **Bavaria proclaimed a Republic.**
Yugo-Slav conference at Geneva decide to form a joint Yugo-Slav-Serbian Government to control military and foreign affairs (see 23rd, and October 29th).

8th ... German armistice delegates reach Allied General Headquarters (see 11th, and October 23rd).
Maubeuge retaken by British forces (see September 7th, 1914).
M. Marghiloman, Rumanian Premier, and M. Arian, Rumanian Foreign Minister, resign (see March 21st, and December 1st).

9th ... Alexandretta (Syria) occupied by Entente naval forces.
Kasama (Rhodesia) taken by Colonel von Lettow-Vorbeck's force (see 1st and 13th).
H.M.S. "Britannia" sunk by submarine in the Atlantic (last warship so lost).
Revolution breaks out in Berlin.
German Imperial Chancellor (Prince Max) announces that the Kaiser has decided to abdicate. Prince Max becomes Regent. Herr Ebert becomes Imperial Chancellor (see 10th, 28th, and October 4th).
Joint Declaration by British and French Governments regarding future of Syria and Mesopotamia.
Czech forces at Ekaterinenburg proclaim national independence.

10th ... Mézières retaken by French forces (see August 27th, 1914).
Ghent reoccupied by Belgian forces (see October 12th, 1914).
Allied forces cross the Danube at Ruschuk and enter Rumania.
The Kaiser crosses the frontier into Holland (see 9th and 28th).
King of Rumania announces that the Rumanian nation have taken up arms again on the side of the Allies (see December 6th, 1917).

11th ... Mons retaken by British forces (see August 24th, 1914).
Armistice concluded between the Allied and Associated Powers and Germany.* **Hostilities on the Western front cease at 11 a.m.** (see 8th, and December 14th).
British Government recognise Latvian Provisional Government as independent (see January 12th).
New National Government formed in Estonia (see 16th, and January 13th).

12th ... **Emperor of Austria abdicates** (see October 31st).
Allied fleet passes through the Dardanelles (see 13th, and October 30th).
German-Austrian Republic proclaimed.

13th ... Allied fleet arrives at Constantinople (see 12th and 21st).
German force in East Africa reaches the Chambezi River (Rhodesia). (News of armistice received) (see 9th, 14th and 25th).

14th ... **Hostilities in East Africa cease.**
Professor Masaryk elected First President of the Czecho-Slovak Republic (see October 21st).
H.M.S. "Cochrane" wrecked at entrance to Liverpool.

15th ... German cruiser "Königsberg," with German naval delegates, enters Firth of Forth to arrange surrender of the German fleet (see 20th and 21st).
Hungarian Government (see 1st) **concludes separate armistice with General Officer Commanding Allied Army** (General Henry), **at Belgrade** (see 3rd).
General Petlyura commences revolt against The Ukraine Government (see December 11th).

* Signed in Marshal Foch's special train at Rethondes Station in the Forest of Compiègne.

November 1918

16th ... Allied Armies begin march into Germany.
Polish Government (M. Pilsudski) issue declaration proclaiming Poland an Independent and Sovereign State (see June 3rd).
New National Government in Estonia order general mobilisation (see 11th).
Hungary declares Independence (see 1st, and October 31st).

17th ... Mulhouse again occupied by French forces (see August 25th, 1914).
Baku again occupied by British forces (see September 15th).
M. Moraczewski appointed Polish Prime Minister (see 16th).
Yugo-Slav National Council at Agram protest against the Italian occupation of Fiume (see 5th and 18th).

18th ... Last German troops recross French frontier (see August 2nd, 1914).
Brussels reoccupied by Belgian forces (see 21st, and August 20th, 1914).
Italian troops reinforce naval detachment in Fiume (see 5th and 17th).
Counter-revolutionary *coup d'état* at Omsk. Russian Admiral Kolchak proclaimed "Dictator of all Russia."

19th ... **Metz occupied by French forces.**
Antwerp reoccupied by Belgian forces (see October 10th, 1914).
General Pétain created Marshal of France (see May 15th, 1917).

20th ... Luxembourg frontier crossed by United States forces (see August 2nd, 1914).
First contingent of German submarines surrender to the British Navy at Harwich (see 15th).
General Marushevski appointed Governor-General and Commander-in-Chief of Russian forces in North Russia (Archangel) (see June 30th).

21st ... **German High Seas Fleet arrives at Rosyth, en route for internment in Scapa Flow** (see 15th and 20th).
Belgian Government reinstated at Brussels (see 18th, and August 17th, 1914).
Namur occupied by British forces (see August 25th, 1914).
French troops land in Constantinople (see 13th).
Greek, Serbian, and Rumanian Governments issue circular memorandum announcing their decision to strengthen the union between the three countries by all available means.
*M. L. Delacroix succeeds M. Cooreman as Belgian Prime Minister (see May 31st) and M. Masson succeeds Lieut.-General de Ceuninck as Minister for War (see August 4th, 1917).

23rd ... Lemberg captured by Polish forces (see 1st).
Yugo-Slav National Council vote for union with Serbia and formation of a common State with Serbia and Montenegro (see 7th, 29th, October 29th and December 4th).

24th ... British and United States troops reach German frontier (see December 1st).

25th ... **Strasbourg occupied by French forces.**
German forces in East Africa surrender to Allied forces at Abercorn (Rhodesia) (see 13th and 14th).

26th ... Last German troops recross Belgian frontier (see August 4th, 1914).
French troops cross German frontier.
Allied fleet arrives at Sevastopol and takes over remainder of the Russian Black Sea Fleet from the Germans (see 13th, and May 1st).
United States force enters Fiume (see 17th).

28th ... **Kaiser Wilhelm II signs abdication** (see 9th and 10th).
Narva (Estonia) captured by Bolshevik forces (see March 4th).
The General Congress of The Bukovina decide in favour of complete union with Rumania (see December 7th).

29th ... Montenegrin National Assembly (Skupshtina) meet at Podgoritsa and vote for union with Serbia (see 23rd).

30th ... **Rumanian Government re-established at Bukharest** (see December 1st, 1916).

* M. Delacroix was the first Minister to hold the title of Prime Minister. See note to entry of May 31st.

DECEMBER 1918.

1st ... British and United States troops cross the German frontier (see November 24th). **Trèves occupied by United States troops.**
General Coanda appointed Rumanian Premier and Foreign Minister (see 12th, and November 8th).
National Assembly of the Rumanians of Transylvania, the Banat and other districts of Hungary, assembled at Alba-Julia (Transylvania), decree their union with Rumania (see 7th, 10th, and 27th).

3rd ... Last Bulgarian troops evacuate the Dobrudja (see September 2nd, 1916).

4th ... H.M.S. "Cassandra" sunk by mine in the Baltic (night 4th/5th).
Demobilisation of the British Army begins.
Yugo-Slav National Council at Agram proclaim the union of all Serbs, Croats, and Slovenes in one State (see November 23rd and 29th).

6th ... **Cologne entered by British troops** (see 12th, and November 24th).

7th ... Deputation from the National Council of The Bukovina arrives at Jassy to inform Rumanian Government that National Council has voted for union with Rumania (see 1st, 10th, and November 28th).

8th ... **Coblenz occupied by United States troops** (see 1st).
Naval action in the Caspian between British and Bolshevik vessels.

9th ... Lahej (Southern Arabia) reoccupied by British forces (see July 4th, 1915).
Serbian Government reinstated at Belgrade (see May 7th, 1916, and November 1st and 6th, 1918).

10th ... The Bessarabian National Council abrogate the stipulations for local autonomy and declare the unconditional union of Bessarabia with Rumania (see 1st, and April 9th).

11th ... Odessa occupied by Petlyura's Ukrainian revolutionary forces (see 20th, March 13th, and November 15th).
General Mannerheim elected Regent of Finland (see December 6th. 1917).

12th ... **British troops cross the Rhine at Cologne** (see 6th).
General Coanda, Rumanian Premier and Foreign Minister, resigns (see 1st and 14th).

13th ... Hodeida (Southern Arabia) taken by British forces.

14th ... Armistice on the Western Front prolonged to January 17th, 1919 (see November 11th).
M. Bratianu appointed Rumanian Premier and Foreign Minister (see 12th).
Dr. da Silva Paes, Portuguese President, assassinated (see 16th, and May 9th).

15th ... Poland severs diplomatic relations with Germany (see November 16th).

16th ... Field-Marshal Mackensen and his forces surrender to the Hungarians near Budapest.
Last German troops leave Finland (see April 3rd).
First meeting of "Imperial Conference" of Soldiers and Workmen in Berlin.
Senhor Antunes appointed Acting Portuguese President (see 14th).

17th ... Major-General Scheuch, German Minister for War, resigns (see October 9th).

20th ... Kiev occupied by Petlyura's Ukrainian revolutionary forces (see 11th, and March 2nd).
French troops land at Odessa (see 11th).
M. Pasich, Premier of Serbia, resigns. (Appointed in 1912) (see 29th).

December 1918

22nd ... Senhor J. T. de Sousa Barboza, Portuguese Secretary of the Interior, resigns (see 23rd, and May 16th).

23rd ... Senhor J. T. de Sousa Barboza appointed Portuguese Premier and Minister of Interior (see 22nd).

24th ... Perm (East Russia) taken by Kolchak's forces (see November 18th).

26th ... Formation of West Ukraine Republic announced (see November 20th, 1917).
Dorpat (Estonia) evacuated by the German forces (see February 24th).

27th ... Batum (Georgia) occupied by British forces (see April 15th).*
King of Rumania issues Proclamation annexing the Rumanian provinces of Austria-Hungary (see 1st).

29th ... M. Stoyan Protich appointed Prime Minister of the United Kingdom of the Serbs, Croats and Slovenes (see 4th and 20th).

30th ... Kadish (North Russia) taken by Allied forces.
Birsk (East Russia) taken by Kolchak's forces (see 24th).

31st ... Ufa and Sterlitamak (East Russia) taken by Bolshevik forces.

---

* This force subsequently occupied the whole of Georgia, with headquarters at Tiflis.

POLITICAL
1914.

PART II.

SECTION I.

POLITICAL.

Date.	EVENTS OF OUTSTANDING IMPORTANCE.			OTHER POLITICAL AND ECONOMIC EVENTS.			Date.
	General.	Diplomatic Correspondence.	Declarations, Treaties and Agreements.	Entente and Allies.	Central Powers.	Neutrals and Miscellaneous.	
1914. JUNE 28th	The Archduke Franz Ferdinand assassinated at Sarajevo	.. ..	.. ..	.. ..	.. ..	.. ..	1914. JUNE 28th
JULY 5th	.. ..	.. ..		.. ..	The Kaiser at Potsdam promises to support Austria	.. ..	JULY 5th
14th	.. ..	.. ..	.. ..	.. ..	Austro-Hungarian Council of Ministers determine to act against Serbia	.. ..	14th
19th	.. ..	.. ..	.. ..	.. ..	Austro-Hungarian Council of Ministers approve of draft ultimatum to Serbia	.. ..	19th
23rd	.. ..	Austro-Hungarian Government send ultimatum to Serbia	.. ..	.. ..	.. ..	.. ..	23rd
24th	.. ..	British Foreign Minister (*Sir E. Grey*) initiates proposals for an International Conference. (*See 27th and 28th*) German Government submit note to Entente Governments approving Austrian ultimatum to Serbia	Belgian Government declare that Belgium will uphold her neutrality "whatever the consequences"	.. ..	.. ..	.. ..	24th
25th	Serbian Government order mobilisation Austro-Hungarian Minister leaves Belgrade	.. ..	Austria-Hungary severs diplomatic relations with Serbia	Serbian Government transferred from Belgrade to Nish	.. ..	.. ..	25th
26th	Austro-Hungarian Government order partial mobilisation as against Serbia *British Admiralty countermand orders for dispersal of Fleets* Montenegrin Government order mobilisation	.. ..	.. ..	.. ..	The Kaiser returns from the Baltic to Berlin	.. ..	26th
27th	*German High Seas Fleet recalled from Norway to War Bases*	French and Italian Governments accept British proposals for an International Conference. (*See 24th*)	.. ..	.. ..	.. ..	.. ..	27th
28th	*British Fleets ordered to War Bases*	German Government reject British proposals for an International Conference. (*See 24th*)	Austria-Hungary declares war on Serbia	.. ..	.. ..	.. ..	28th

POLITICAL 1914.

Date.	EVENTS OF OUTSTANDING IMPORTANCE.			OTHER POLITICAL AND ECONOMIC EVENTS.			Date
	General.	Diplomatic Correspondence.	Declarations, Treaties and Agreements.	Entente and Allies.	Central Powers.	Neutrals and Miscellaneous.	
1914. JULY 29th	Hostilities commence between Austria-Hungary and Serbia: Belgrade bombarded by Austrian artillery. Russian Government order partial mobilisation as against Austria. British Admiralty send out the "Warning Telegram" to the fleets. British War Office send out telegrams ordering "Precautionary Period." (*Evening.*) Russian Minister for War orders general mobilisation (*without the knowledge of the Tsar*)	German Government make proposals to secure British neutrality	Bulgaria declares neutrality	..	..	..	1914. JULY 29th
30th	(4 p.m.) The Tsar signs order for mobilisation of Russian army	British Government reject German proposals of 29th	Holland declares neutrality	..	..	..	30th
31st	Austrian Government order general mobilisation. Russian Government order general mobilisation. State of "Kriegsgefahr" proclaimed in Germany. Belgian Government order mobilisation	German Government send ultimatum to Russia. (*Presented midnight 31st/1st*)	..	London Stock Exchange closed	..	Turkish Government order mobilisation	31st
AUG. 1st	German Government order general mobilisation. Hostilities commence between Russia and Central Powers. French Government order general mobilisation	..	Germany declares war on Russia	..	..	..	AUG. 1st
2nd	Hostilities commence on French frontier	German Government send ultimatum to Belgium (*demanding passage through Belgian territory*)	British Government guarantee naval protection of French coasts against German aggression	Moratorium proclaimed in Great Britain. (*See November 4th*)	..	..	2nd
3rd	British Government order general mobilisation	Belgian Government refuse German demands	Germany declares war on France. British Government guarantee armed support to Belgium should Germany violate Belgian neutrality. Italy declares neutrality	British Government issue proclamation authorising requisition of shipping	..	..	3rd

POLITICAL 1914.

Date.	EVENTS OF OUTSTANDING IMPORTANCE.			OTHER POLITICAL AND ECONOMIC EVENTS.			Date
	General.	Diplomatic Correspondence.	Declarations, Treaties and Agreements.	Entente and Allies.	Central Powers.	Neutrals and Miscellaneous.	
1914. AUG. 4th	German troops cross Belgian frontier	British Government send ultimatum to Germany	Belgium severs diplomatic relations with Germany Germany declares war on Belgium Secret alliance between Germany and Turkey signed at Berlin Great Britain declares war on Germany (11 p.m.*)	British Government issue proclamation specifying articles to be treated as contraband	.. ..	.. ..	1914. AUG. 4th
5th	Minelaying in the open sea commenced by the German navy	.. ..	Montenegro declares war on Austria-Hungary	First meeting of British War Council	.. ..	.. ..	5th
6th	Lord Kitchener succeeds Mr. Asquith as Secretary of State for War	.. ..	Austro-Hungarian Declaration of War presented at St. Petersburg Serbia declares war on Germany Naval Convention between France and Great Britain signed in London	.. ..	.. ..	.. ..	6th
7th	*First units of British Expeditionary Force land in France*	.. ..	.. ..	.. ..	.. ..	.. ..	7th
8th	.. ..	.. ..	Montenegro severs diplomatic relations with Germany "State of war" commences between Montenegro and Germany	British forces cross frontier of Togoland	.. ..	Swiss Government order mobilisation	8th
9th	.. ..	Belgian Government formulate proposal for neutralisation of African free trade zone	.. ..	.. ..	.. ..	.. ..	9th
10th	.. ..	.. ..	France severs diplomatic relations with Austria-Hungary	.. ..	.. ..	.. ..	10th
11th	German warships "Goeben" and "Breslau" enter the Dardanelles	.. ..	.. ..	French Government issue first list of contraband	.. ..	.. ..	11th
12th	.. ..	.. ..	Great Britain and France declare war on Austria-Hungary	.. ..	.. ..	.. ..	12th
13th	First Austrian invasion of Serbia begins	.. ..	.. ..	.. ..	.. ..	.. ..	13th

* Midnight 4th/5th by Central European time.

POLITICAL
1914.

Date.	EVENTS OF OUTSTANDING IMPORTANCE.			OTHER POLITICAL AND ECONOMIC EVENTS.			Date.
	General.	Diplomatic Correspondence.	Declarations, Treaties and Agreements.	Entente and Allies.	Central Powers.	Neutrals and Miscellaneous.	
1914. AUG. 14th	..	..	Proclamation issued by Russian Commander-in-Chief (*Grand Duke Nicholas*) promising autonomy to Poland. (*See September 12th*, 1917)	..	..	..	1914. AUG. 14th
15th	..	**Japanese Government send ultimatum to Germany** (*demanding evacuation of Tsingtau*)	..	..	..	..	15th
16th	*Landing of the original British Expeditionary Force in France completed*	..	..	..	..	..	16th
17th	..	..	..	Belgian Government transferred from Brussels to Antwerp	..	..	17th
18th	..	..	..	..	..	Vossuq ed Douleh, Persian Foreign Minister, resigns	18th
19th	..	..	..	..	..	Ala es Sultaneh, Persian Prime Minister, resigns, and is appointed Foreign Minister Mustaufi ul Mamalek appointed Persian Prime Minister	19th
20th	**Brussels occupied by German forces**	..	..	First British Order in Council revising "Declaration of London" issued	..	Death of Pope Pius X	20th
21st	German Forces from South-West Africa cross frontier of South Africa	..	..	*British Government issue orders raising first divisions of New Army*	..	..	21st
22nd	..	German Government agree to Belgian proposal, made through Spanish Government, re African free-trade zone (*See 9th and November 20th*)	Austria-Hungary declares war on Belgium	..	..	..	22nd
23rd	..	..	Germany severs diplomatic relations with Japan Japan declares war on Germany	..	..	..	23rd
24th	..	..	Austria-Hungary severs diplomatic relations with Japan	..	*Massacre of civilians by German troops at Dinant*	..	24th
25th	First Austrian invasion of Serbia ends	..	State of war commences between Japan and Austria-Hungary*	French Government issue new decree defining contraband	..	..	25th

* No formal declaration of war made by either Power.

POLITICAL
1914.

Date.	EVENTS OF OUTSTANDING IMPORTANCE.			OTHER POLITICAL AND ECONOMIC EVENTS.			Date.
	General.	Diplomatic Correspondence.	Declarations, Treaties and Agreements.	Entente and Allies.	Central Powers.	Neutrals and Miscellaneous.	
1914. AUG. 26th	German forces in Togoland capitulate to the Allied forces. (See 8th) *Louvain sacked by German troops*	.. ..	.. ..	M. Delcassé appointed French Foreign Minister General Galliéni appointed Governor of Paris M. Messimy, French Minister for War, resigns	.. .	.. ..	1914. AUG. 26th
27th	.. ..	.. ..	.. ..	M. Millerand appointed French Minister for War	.. ..	.. ..	27th
28th	.. ..	.. ..	Austro-Hungarian declaration of war received by Belgian Government. (See 22nd)	.. ..	.. ..	.. ..	28th
30th	*Samoa occupied by New Zealand Expeditionary Force*	.. ..	.. ..	.. ..	.. ..	.. ..	30th
31st	.. ..	.. ..	Agreement concluded between Great Britain and France defining provisional zones in Togoland. (See *August 26th*, 1914, and *December 27th*, 1916)	.. ..	.. ..	.. ..	31st
SEPT. 2nd	**Hostilities commence between Japan and Germany** *Japanese forces land in Shantung to attack Tsingtau.* (See *November 7th*)	.. ..	.. ..	French Government transferred from Paris to Bordeaux	.. ..	.. ..	SEPT. 2nd
3rd	.. ..	French Government inform United States Government that they will observe "Declaration of London" subject to certain modifications	.. ..	.. ..	.. ..	Prince William of Wied leaves Albania Benedict XV Elected Pope	3rd
4th	.. ..	German Government agree to observe "Declaration of London" if other belligerents conform thereto	.. ..	.. ..	German Government issue list of contraband	.. ..	4th
5th	.. ..	.. ..	British, French, and Russian Governments sign the Pact of London. (See *October 19th*, 1915)	.. ..	.. ..	.. ..	5th
8th	**Second Austrian invasion of Serbia begins**	.. ..	.. ..	.. ..	.. ..	.. ..	8th

POLITICAL 1914.

Date.	EVENTS OF OUTSTANDING IMPORTANCE.			OTHER POLITICAL AND ECONOMIC EVENTS.			Date.
	General.	Diplomatic Correspondence.	Declarations, Treaties and Agreements.	Entente and Allies.	Central Powers.	Neutrals and Miscellaneous.	
1914. SEPT. 9th	.. ..	.. ..	Turkish Government announce abolition of "The Capitulations"	.. ..	.. ..	.. ..	1914. SEPT. 9th
10th	.. ..	.. ..	.. ..	.. ..	German and Austrian representatives expelled from Egypt	.. ..	10th
11th	.. ..	.. ..	.. ..	Australian Expeditionary Force lands in Bismarck Archipelago	.. ..	.. ..	11th
15th	.. ..	.. ..	.. ..	Beginning of the Rebellion in South Africa. (See December 28th)	.. ..	.. ..	15th
17th	British Naval Mission leaves Turkey German New Guinea and surrounding colonies capitulate to Australian Expeditionary Force	.. ..	.. ..	.. ..	.. ..	.. ..	17th
19th	South African forces occupy Luderitzbucht (German South West Africa). First Bombardment of Reims Cathedral by German artillery	.. ..	British and French Governments guarantee to Belgium the integrity of her Colonies Secret agreement for mutual support concluded between Russian and Rumanian Governments	.. ..	.. ..	.. ..	19th
21st	.. ..	.. ..	.. ..	British Government issue Proclamation adding to list of contraband	.. ..	.. ..	21st
23rd	.. ..	.. ..	.. ..	British force joins Japanese army besieging Tsingtau*	.. ..	.. ..	23rd
26th	.. ..	.. ..	.. ..	First units of Indian Expeditionary Force land at Marseilles. (See October 19th)	.. ..	.. ..	26th
OCT. 3rd	Minelaying in the open sea (between the Goodwins and Ostend) commenced by British Navy. (See August 5th)	.. ..	.. ..	First units of Canadian Expeditionary Force leave Canada for England	.. ..	.. ..	OCT. 3rd
4th	.. ..	.. ..	.. ..	.. ..	.. ..	Provisional Government set up in Albania under Essad Pasha at Durazzo. (See September 3rd, 1914, July 17th, 1915, and February 24th, 1916)	4th

* Date of disembarkation.

POLITICAL
1914.

Date.	EVENTS OF OUTSTANDING IMPORTANCE.			OTHER POLITICAL AND ECONOMIC EVENTS.			Date.
	General.	Diplomatic Correspondence.	Declarations, Treaties and Agreements.	Entente and Allies.	Central Powers.	Neutrals and Miscellaneous.	
1914. OCT. 7th	Yap Island (*Pacific*) occupied by Japanese naval forces	.. ..	.. ..	Belgian Government transferred from Antwerp to Ostend	.. ..	.. ..	1914. OCT. 7th
10th	Antwerp capitulates to German forces	.. ..	Protocol signed by United States of America and Panama as to use of Panama Canal by ships of belligerent Powers		.. ..	King Charles of Rumania dies and is succeeded by his son Ferdinand	10th
12th	*Ostend and Zeebrugge evacuated by the Belgian forces* *Lille capitulates to German forces*	.. ..	.. ..	.. ..	.. ..	.. ..	12th
13th	.. ..	.. ..	.. ..	Belgian Government set up at Havre	.. ..	.. ..	13th
15th	*Ostend and Zeebrugge occupied by German forces*	.. ..	.. ..	First units of Canadian and Newfoundland Expeditionary Forces land in England	.. ..	.. ..	15th
16th	.. ..	.. ..	.. ..	New Zealand Expeditionary Force leave New Zealand for France Advanced troops of Indian Expeditionary Force "D" leave Bombay for the Persian Gulf	.. ..	Marquis di San Giuliano, Italian Foreign Minister, dies. (*See November 3rd*)	16th
17th	.. ..	.. ..	.. ..	*First units of Australian Imperial Force leave Australia for France*	.. ..	.. ..	17th
19th	.. ..	.. ..	.. ..	*First Indian units reach the Flanders Front.* (*See September 26th*)	.. ..	.. ..	19th
20th	First merchant-vessel sunk by German submarine (*British s.s. "Glitra."*)	.. ..	.. ..	.. ..	.. ..	.. ..	20th
22nd	.. ..	United States Government issue Circular Note to belligerent Governments stating that they will insist on existing rules of International Law	.. ..	.. ..	.. ..	.. ..	22nd
23rd	.. ..	.. ..	.. ..	*Advanced troops of Indian Expeditionary Force "D" arrive at the Bahrein Islands* (*Persian Gulf*).	.. ..	.. ..	23rd

POLITICAL 1914.

Date.	EVENTS OF OUTSTANDING IMPORTANCE.			OTHER POLITICAL AND ECONOMIC EVENTS.			Date.
	General.	Diplomatic Correspondence.	Declarations, Treaties, and Agreements.	Entente and Allies.	Central Powers.	Neutrals and Miscellaneous.	
1914. OCT. 26th	.. ..	.. ..	.. ..	.. ..	German forces begin an unprovoked invasion of Angola (*Portuguese West Africa*)	.. ..	**1914. OCT.** 26th
29th	Turkey commences hostilities against Russia (*Turkish warships bombard Odessa, Sevastopol, and Theodosia.*) (*See November 2nd and 5th*)	.. ..	British Government issue Order in Council modifying Declaration of London of 1909. (*See July 7th, 1916*)	British Government issue revised list of contraband		.. ..	29th
30th	Entente Ambassadors at Constantinople demand passports	Allies present ultimatum to Turkey	Great Britain and France sever diplomatic relations with Turkey	.. ..	.. ..	Italian Cabinet resign. New Cabinet formed. (*Signor Salandra remains Premier.*) (*See November 3rd*)	30th
31st	British Government issue orders for hostilities against Turkey to begin. (*See November 1st and 5th*)	.. ..	Lord Kitchener sends to Sherif of Mecca conditional guarantee of Arabian independence. (*See July 14th, 1915*)	.. ..	.. ..	.. ..	31st
NOV. 1st	Great Britain and Turkey commence hostilities. (*See 5th*)	.. ..	.. ..	Martial law proclaimed in Egypt	.. ..	.. ..	**NOV.** 1st
2nd	.. ..	.. ..	British Admiralty declare the North Sea a military zone **Russia declares war on Turkey.** (*See October 29th*) **State of war proclaimed between Serbia and Turkey** Government of India announce immunity of the Mussulman Holy Places during hostilities with Turkey	.. ..	.. ..	.. ..	2nd
3rd	.. ..	.. ..	.. ..	Allied squadrons bombard forts at entrance of the Dardanelles	.. ..	Baron Sonnino appointed Italian Foreign Minister. (*See October 30th*)	3rd
4th	.. ..	.. ..	.. ..	Moratorium in Great Britain ends. (*See August 2nd*)	.. ..	.. ..	4th
5th	.. ..	Belgian Government reject Papal mediation	**Great Britain and France formally declare war on Turkey.** (*See October 31st*)	Great Britain annexes Cyprus	.. ..	.. ..	5th
6th	British Forces (*Indian Expeditionary Force "D"*) land in Mesopotamia. (*See October 23rd*)	.. ..	Turkey severs diplomatic relations with Belgium	French Government issue Declaration modifying list of contraband	.. ..	.. ..	6th

POLITICAL 1914.

Date.	EVENTS OF OUTSTANDING IMPORTANCE.			OTHER POLITICAL AND ECONOMIC EVENTS.			Date.
	General.	Diplomatic Correspondence.	Declarations, Treaties and Agreements.	Entente and Allies.	Central Powers.	Neutrals and Miscellaneous.	
1914. NOV. 7th	Tsingtau capitulates to the Japanese forces. (*See September 2nd*)	..	..	..	..	..	1914. NOV. 7th
9th	..	..	British and French Governments conclude Convention as to naval Prizes	..	..	..	9th
11th	..	..	The Sheikh ul Islam issues Fatwa declaring Jehad (*Holy War*) against all the Allies	..	..	..	11th
13th	..	Dutch Government protest against modifications of the Declaration of London. (*See October 29th*)		..	..	..	13th
14th	..	..	Sultan of Turkey as Khalif proclaims Jehad against those making war on Turkey or her Allies	Japanese Cabinet decide against despatch of troops and warships to Europe. (*See April 17th, 1917*)	..	..	14th
18th	..	..	..	Re-transfer of French Government from Bordeaux to Paris begins. (*See September 2nd*)	..	..	18th
20th	..	British, French and Belgian Governments withdraw proposal for neutralisation of African free-trade zone. (*See August 22nd*)	..	..	..	..	20th
22nd	Basra (*Mesopotamia*) occupied by British forces	..	..	..	..	..	22nd
23rd	..	..	Portuguese Government announce prospective co-operation of Portugal with Great Britain. (*See August 8th, 1916*)	..	..	Formation of Netherlands Overseas Trust. (*See June 3rd, 1915*)	23rd
DEC. 1st	..	..	..	De Wet (*the leader of South African Rebellion*) captured by Union troops *First units of Australian and New Zealand Expeditionary Forces arrive in Egypt.* (*See October 16th*)	..	..	DEC. 1st
2nd	Belgrade occupied by Austrian forces	..	..	..	..	..	2nd

POLITICAL 1914.

Date.	Events of Outstanding Importance.			Other Political and Economic Events.			Date.
	General.	Diplomatic Correspondence.	Declarations, Treaties and Agreements.	Entente and Allies.	Central Powers.	Neutrals and Miscellaneous.	
1914. DEC.							**1914. DEC.**
3rd	..	..	British Government agree to Japanese request that Australia should not occupy islands north of the Equator. (*See 16th*)	..	..	..	3rd
4th	..	..	..	..	..	Portuguese Expeditionary Force leaves Lisbon for Angola. (*See October 26th*)	4th
5th	..	..	Serbian Government declare that Serbia will never make peace without Allied consent	..	..	Entente *démarche* in Athens, Sofia, and Bukharest to secure help for Serbia	5th
6th	..	Rumanian Government decline to guarantee Greece against German attack	..	..	..	..	6th
7th	..	..	..	..	..	British Envoy (*Sir H. Howard*) appointed to the Vatican	7th
10th	..	..	..	..	Field-Marshal von der Goltz leaves Germany to take over control of the Turkish Army. (*See November 24th, 1915*)	..	10th
11th	..	..	..	..	..	Dr. B. L. Machado Guimãries, Portuguese Premier, resigns	11th
12th	..	..	..	..	..	Senhor V. H d'Azevedo Coutinho appointed Portuguese Premier	12th
15th	Austrian forces driven out of Serbia: **End of Second Austrian invasion of Serbia**	..	..	..	..	..	15th
16th	..	..	Japanese Foreign Minister declares Japan will not give up German Islands occupied north of the Equator. (*See 3rd*)	..	..	..	16th
18th	..	..	**British Protectorate over Egypt proclaimed**	..	..	Meeting of Scandinavian Kings at Malmö	18th
19th	..	..	Great Britain declares adherence to Franco-Moorish Treaty of 1912	British Government declare Khedive Abbas Hilmi deposed and proclaim Prince Hussein Kamel Pasha as Sultan of Egypt	..	..	19th

POLITICAL
1914-15.

Date.	EVENTS OF OUTSTANDING IMPORTANCE.			OTHER POLITICAL AND ECONOMIC EVENTS.			Date.
	General.	Diplomatic Correspondence.	Declarations, Treaties and Agreements.	Entente and Allies.	Central Powers.	Neutrals and Miscellaneous.	
1914. DEC. 23rd	.. ..	.. ..	.. ..	British Government issue revised list of contraband	.. ..	.. ..	**1914. DEC.** 23rd
26th	*Italian force landed at Valona*	Italy notifies Austria of provisional occupation of Valona. (*See May 29th*, 1915)	. .	.. ..	.. ..	*Garibaldi's Italian Foreign Legion in action for first time on French Front*	26th
28th	.. ..		.. ..	End of organised Rebellion in South Africa. (*See September 15th*)	.. ..	.. ..	28th
29th	.. ..	British Government send memorandum to United States Government in defence of British blockade policy	.. ..	.. ..	.. ..	.. ..	29th
30th	.. ..	Russian Commander-in-Chief (*Grand Duke Nicholas*) suggests a British expedition against the Turks to ease Russian situation in the Caucasus. (*See January 13th*, 1915)	.. ..	.. ..	.. ..	.. ..	30th
1915. JAN. 3rd	.. ..	.. ..	.. ..	French Government issue further revised list of contraband	.. ..	.. ..	**1915. JAN.** 3rd
4th	.. ..	.. ..	.. ..	London Stock Exchange reopens. (*See July 31st*, 1914)	.. ..	.. ..	4th
5th	.. ..	.. ..	.. ..	*Tabriz (North Persia) evacuated by Russian forces**	.. ..	.. ..	5th
6th	.. ..	.. ..	.. ..	.. ..	.. ..	German s.s. "Dacia" (*interned in United States*) sold to Mr. Breitung, an American citizen. (*See February 11th*)	6th
11th	.. ..	.. ..	.. ..	Last rebels in the Transvaal captured. (*See December 28th*, 1914)	. .	Rumanian Government negotiate loan of £5,000,000 in Great Britain	11th

* This city was occupied by Russian forces before the outbreak of war.

POLITICAL 1915.

Date.	EVENTS OF OUTSTANDING IMPORTANCE.			OTHER POLITICAL AND ECONOMIC EVENTS.			Date.
	General.	Diplomatic Correspondence.	Declarations, Treaties and Agreements.	Entente and Allies.	Central Powers.	Neutrals and Miscellaneous.	
1915. JAN. 13th	.. ..	.. ..	.. ..	British War Council resolve that Admiralty should prepare for a naval expedition in February against the Dardanelles. (*See December 30th, 1914, and January 28th, 1915*)	Baron Burian succeeds Count Berchtold as Austro-Hungarian Minister for Foreign Affairs	.. ..	1915. JAN. 13th
15th	.. ..	.. ..	Italian and Rumanian Governments announce existence of secret agreement for mutual support	.. ..	.. ..	.. ..	15th
21st	.. ..	.. ..	.. ..	.. ..	General von Falkenhayn succeeded as German Minister for War by General Wild von Hohenborn	.. ..	21st
24th	.. ..	British Government offer Greek Government concessions in Asia Minor in return for help to Serbia. (*See 29th, and April 12th*)	.. ..	.. ..	.. ..	.. ..	24th
25th	.. ..	Rumania refuses Entente suggestion that she should join Greece in support of Serbia	.. ..	.. ..	.. ..	General Pimenta da Castro succeeds Senhor Coutinho as Portuguese Premier	25th
26th	.. ..	.. ..	Entente Governments agree to hold "Pact of London" applicable to war with Turkey. (*See September 5th, 1914*)	.. ..	.. ..	.. ..	26th
28th	British Government definitely decide to make naval attack on the Dardanelles. (*See 13th*)	.. ..	.. ..	.. ..	.. ..	United States s.v. "William P. Frye" sunk by German armed merchant cruiser "Prinz Eitel Friedrich"*	28th
29th	.. ..	Greek Government decline to intervene on behalf of Serbia	.. ..	.. ..	.. ..	.. ..	29th
30th	.. ..	.. ..	.. ..	British Admiralty warn British merchant vessels to fly neutral or no ensigns in vicinity of British Isles. (*See February 6th*) Tabriz (*North Persia*) reoccupied by Russian forces. (*See 5th*)	.. ..	.. ..	30th
31st	.. ..	.. ..	.. ..	.. ..	.. ..	Arab forces (*Idrisi*) occupy Farasan Islands (*Red Sea*). (*See April 28th*)	31st
FEB. 1st	.. ..	.. ..	.. ..	British Admiralty issue orders forbidding neutral fishing vessels to use British ports	.. ..	.. ..	FEB. 1st

* First United States vessel sunk by belligerent warship.

POLITICAL 1915.

Date.	EVENTS OF OUTSTANDING IMPORTANCE			OTHER POLITICAL AND ECONOMIC EVENTS.			Date.
	General.	Diplomatic Correspondence.	Declarations, Treaties and Agreements.	Entente and Allies.	Central Powers.	Neutrals and Miscellaneous.	
1915. FEB. 2nd	.. ..	Entente communication to Greek, Serbian, and Montenegrin Governments deprecating their intervention in Albania	.. ..	.. ..	.. ..	.. ..	1915. FEB. 2nd
3rd	.. ..	.. ..	Agreement concluded between Great Britain and Belgium concerning delimitation of Uganda - Congo boundary	.. ..	.. ..	Bulgarian Government negotiate loan of £3,000,000 in Germany	3rd
4th	*German Government announce that submarine blockade of Great Britain will begin on the 18th February*	.. ..	.. ..	.. ..	.. ..	.. ..	4th
5th	.. ..	.. ..	British, French and Russian Governments agree to pool their financial resources. (*See June 3rd*)	.. ..	.. ..	.. ..	5th
6th	.. ..	.. ..	.. ..	British s.s. "Lusitania" arrives at Liverpool flying United States flag. (*See January 30th*)	.. ..	.. ..	6th
7th	.. ..	British Foreign Office issue statement justifying use of neutral flag at sea. (*See 6th and January 30th*)	.. ..	.. ..	.. ..	.. ..	7th
9th	.. ..	.. ..	.. ..	*First Canadian Division leaves England for France.* (*See October 15th, 1914*)	.. ..	.. ..	9th
11th	.. ..	United States Government send Note to British Government deprecating use of neutral flag by the ships of belligerents	.. ..	.. ..	.. ..	s.s. "Dacia" sails from United States for Bremen (*Germany*) with cargo of cotton. (*See 27th, and January 6th*)	11th
15th	.. ..	Entente Governments suggest to Greek Government that Greece should intervene in support of Serbia and promise military support at Salonika	Agreement concluded between Great Britain and France supplementing "prize" convention. (*See November 9th, 1914*)	Mutiny of the 5th Light Infantry (*Indian Army*) at Singapore	.. ..	.. ..	15th
16th	British Government decide to send a division (the 29th) to the Dardanelles	.. ..	.. ..	British Government extend prohibition of "Trading with the Enemy" to territories in British, enemy, or friendly occupation	.. ..	.. ..	16th

POLITICAL
1915.

Date.	Events of Outstanding Importance.			Other Political and Economic Events.			Date.
	General.	Diplomatic Correspondence.	Declarations, Treaties and Agreements.	Entente and Allies.	Central Powers.	Neutrals and Miscellaneous.	
1915. FEB. 18th	German submarine blockade of Great Britain begins. (See 4th)	..	..	..	..	..	1915. FEB. 18th
19th	Allied Naval attack on the Dardanelles forts commenced. (See January 13th and March 18th)	..	..	..	..	..	19th
20th	..	..	..	Orders issued for employment of Australian and New Zealand troops in Egypt at the Dardanelles	..	Muavin ed Douleh succeeds Ala es Sultaneh as Persian Foreign Minister	20th
23rd	..	..	..	Lemnos (Ægean) occupied by British marines	..	..	23rd
24th	..	..	..	First British Territorial Division leaves England for France	..	..	24th
26th	First use of liquid fire by the Germans (against the French in the Argonne)	..	..	..	..	..	26th
27th	..	..	..	..	..	s.s. "Dacia" (See 11th) intercepted and seized by French naval forces. (See March 22nd)	27th
MAR. 1st	British blockade of German East Africa commences	..	Joint declaration signed by Great Britain and France to prevent trade by or with Germany	..	..	..	MAR. 1st
4th	French Government decide to send Expeditionary Force to the Dardanelles	Russian Government send circular telegram to Entente Governments laying claim to Constantinople. (See 12th)	..	..	..	..	4th
5th	..	Greek Premier (M. Venizelos) proffers Greek fleet and troops to Entente for operations at the Dardanelles	..	..	..	..	5th
6th	King of Greece refuses assent to policy of M. Venizelos. M. Venizelos resigns office as Premier. (See August 23rd)	..	..	..	..	..	6th
7th	..	Greek Government request explanation of the occupation of Lemnos. (See February 23rd)	..	..	..	..	7th

POLITICAL
1915.

Date.	EVENTS OF OUTSTANDING IMPORTANCE.			OTHER POLITICAL AND ECONOMIC EVENTS.			Date.
	General.	Diplomatic Correspondence.	Declarations, Treaties and Agreements.	Entente and Allies.	Central Powers.	Neutrals and Miscellaneous.	
1915. MAR. 9th	.. ..	British Government send reply as to occupation of Lemnos, pleading military necessity. (*See 20th*)	.. ..	.. ..	.. ..	M. Gounaris appointed Premier of Greece. (*See 6th*)	1915. MAR. 9th
11th	.. ..	.. ..	.. ..	British Government issue the "Retaliatory" Order in Council (*relating to detention of enemy goods*) and Proclamation extending list of "Absolute Contraband"	.. ..	.. ..	11th
12th	.. ..	.. ..	British Government notify Russian Government of their acceptance of Russian claims to Constantinople. (*See 4th, April 12th, 1915, and December 2nd, 1916*)	French Government issue decrees similar to British Order in Council and Proclamation of the 11th March	.. ..	Dutch Government issue warning that foreign merchant ships using Dutch flag will be detained. (*See January 30th*)	12th
13th	First neutral ship sunk without warning by German submarine (Swedish s.s. "Hanna")	.. ..	Agreement signed by France and Belgium suspending Franco-Belgian Convention of July 30th, 1891, regarding military service laws	.. ..	.. ..	.. ..	13th
14th	German light cruiser "Dresden" (*the last German cruiser left at sea*) sunk by British warships in Chilean waters (*Juan Fernandez*). (*See April 26th*)	.. ..	.. ..	.. ..	.. ..	Mushir ed Douleh succeeds Mustaufi ul Mamalek as Persian Prime Minister	14th
17th	.. ..	French Government lodge claim with British Government to Syria and Cilicia	.. ..	.. ..	.. ..	.. ..	17th
18th	*Allied Naval attack on the Dardanelles forts repulsed.* (*See February 19th*)	.. ..	British Government conclude agreement with American cotton interests that cotton should be contraband	.. ..	.. ..	.. ..	18th

[8369]

POLITICAL 1915.

Date.	Events of Outstanding Importance.			Other Political and Economic Events.			Date.
	General.	Diplomatic Correspondence.	Declarations, Treaties and Agreements.	Entente and Allies.	Central Powers.	Neutrals and Miscellaneous.	
1915. MAR. 19th	..	Dutch Government lodge protest against blockade policy of the Entente. (See 11th and 12th)	..	..	..	..	**1915. MAR.** 19th
20th	..	..	British Government give Greek Government secret guarantee of eventual cession of Lemnos by Turkey. (See 9th, and July 25th)	..	..	..	20th
22nd	..	..	..	..	..	French Prize Court declare seizure of s.s. "Dacia" valid. (See February 27th)	22nd
23rd	..	..	Chinese and Japanese Governments conclude secret agreement as to future policy in Manchuria	..	..	..	23rd
25th	First neutral ship sunk by German submarine after visit and search (Dutch s.s. "Medea")	..	..	..	General Liman von Sanders appointed to command Turkish forces at the Dardanelles	..	25th
28th	First passenger ship sunk by German submarine (s.s. "Falaba")	..	..	..	..	..	28th
29th	..	..	British Government conclude agreement with American rubber interests that rubber should not be exported except to Great Britain	..	..	..	29th
APRIL 3rd	..	..	..	Imperial Ukase issued granting municipal self-government to Russian Poland. (See August 14th, 1914)	..	..	**APRIL** 3rd
8th	..	..	..	..	Deportations and massacres of Armenians, by order of the Turkish Government, commenced*	..	8th
12th	..	Entente Governments make offer to Greece of Smyrna and hinterland in return for immediate action against Turkey. (See January 24th)	French Government notify Russian Government of their acceptance of Russian claims to Constantinople. (See March 12th)	..	..	..	12th
14th	Germans accuse French of using poison gas (near Verdun). (See 22nd)	Greek Government reject Entente offer of Smyrna Japanese Government inform British Government of German overtures for separate peace	..	British Secretary for the Colonies (Mr. Harcourt) states that the Dominions will be consulted as to peace terms	..	..	14th

* Approximate date.

POLITICAL
1915.

Date.	EVENTS OF OUTSTANDING IMPORTANCE.			OTHER POLITICAL AND ECONOMIC EVENTS.			Date.
	General.	Diplomatic Correspondence.	Declarations, Treaties and Agreements.	Entente and Allies.	Central Powers.	Neutrals and Miscellaneous.	
1915. APRIL 22nd	*Germans use poison gas for the first time (Battles of Ypres, 1915). (See 14th)*	.. ..	.. ..	.. ..	.. ..	.. ..	1915. APRIL 22nd
23rd	British blockade of the Cameroons begins. (See February 29th, 1916)	.. ..	.. ..	.. ..	.. ..	.. ..	23rd
25th	*Allied forces effect landing at the Dardanelles*	.. ..	.. ..	.. ..	.. ..	.. ..	25th
26th	The last German raider overseas (armed merchant cruiser "Kronprinz Wilhelm") interned at Newport News, U.S.A. (See March 14th)	.. ..	Secret Agreement signed in London between Italian Government and the Entente for Italian co-operation in the war and declaration by which Italy adheres to the Pact of London. (See September 5th, 1914, and December 1st, 1915)	.. ..	.. ..	Mushir ed Douleh, Persian Prime Minister, resigns Muavin ed Douleh, Persian Foreign Minister, resigns	26th
27th	.. ..	.. ..	.. ..	.. ..	.. ..	Ain ed Douleh appointed Persian Prime Minister Motashem ed Douleh appointed Persian Foreign Minister	27th
28th	.. ..	.. ..	British Government conclude a treaty with the Idrisi for co-operation against the Turks. (See January 31st)	.. ..	.. ..	.. ..	28th
MAY 1st	First United States ship torpedoed without warning by German submarine (s.s. "Gulflight")	.. ..	.. ..	.. ..	.. ..	.. ..	MAY 1st
4th	.. ..	.. ..	Italy denounces the Triple Alliance	.. ..	.. ..	.. ..	4th
7th	s.s. "Lusitania" sunk by German submarine	Japan presents ultimatum to China demanding territorial concessions	British Foreign Minister (Sir E. Grey) gives conditional guarantee to Serbian Minister of eventual cession of Bosnia and Herzegovina with "wide access to the Adriatic." (See August 15th and 30th)	.. ..	.. ..	.. ..	7th
9th	President Wilson in speech on "Lusitania" outrage defines United States policy	Chinese Government yield to Japanese demands. (See 7th and 25th)	.. ..	The leading division of the British New Armies leaves England for France. (See August 21st, 1914)	.. ..	.. ..	9th

POLITICAL 1915.

Date.	Events of Outstanding Importance.			Other Political and Economic Events.			Date.
	General.	Diplomatic Correspondence.	Declarations, Treaties and Agreements.	Entente and Allies.	Central Powers.	Neutrals and Miscellaneous.	
1915. MAY 10th	..	..	Naval Convention signed between Great Britain, France and Italy	..	..	..	**1915. MAY** 10th
13th	..	..	..	..	..	Signor Salandra, Italian Premier, tenders his resignation. Baron Sonnino, Italian Foreign Minister, tenders his resignation	13th
14th	..	..	..	Last meeting of British War Council. (*See June 7th*)	..	General de Castro, Portuguese Premier, resigns	14th
15th	..	..	..	Lord Fisher, First Sea Lord, tenders resignation. (*See 28th.*)	..	Senhor J. Pinheiro Chagas appointed Portuguese Premier	15th
16th	..	..	..	..	..	Signor Salandra remains Italian Premier on reconstruction of Cabinet, with Baron Soninno as Foreign Minister	16th
21st	..	..	..	Russian Expeditionary Force to West Persia lands at Enzeli	..	..	21st
23rd	Italian Government order general mobilization	..	Italy declares war against Austria	..	..	..	23rd
24th	Italian forces cross Austrian frontier (*midnight 24th/25th*)	..	Germany severs diplomatic relations with Italy* Entente Governments declare that they will hold Turkish Ministers personally responsible for the Armenian massacres. (*See April 8th*)	..	..	..	24th
25th	..	..	Treaties between China and Japan signed concerning Shantung Province, South Manchuria and Inner Mongolia	Coalition Ministry formed in Great Britain by Mr. Asquith	..	..	25th
26th	..	..	..	Italian Government announce blockade of the Austro-Hungarian coast	..	..	26th
27th	*British squadron joins Italian Fleet in the Adriatic*	..	..	Mr. Winston Churchill, First Lord of the Admiralty, resigns	..	..	27th
	..	..	..	New Admiralty Chiefs appointed (*Mr. Balfour and Sir H. Jackson*)	..	Dr. Joachim T. Braga elected President of Portugal	28th

* See Note in Part I.

POLITICAL 1915.

Date.	EVENTS OF OUTSTANDING IMPORTANCE.			OTHER POLITICAL AND ECONOMIC EVENTS.			Date.
	General.	Diplomatic Correspondence.	Declarations, Treaties and Agreements.	Entente and Allies.	Central Powers.	Neutrals and Miscellaneous.	
1915. MAY. 29th	Valona formally occupied by Italian forces. (*See December 26th*, 1914)	..	..	..	..	Dr. Manoel Arriago, Portuguese President, resigns	1915. MAY. 29th
JUNE 2nd	Blockade of coast of Asia Minor announced by British Government	..	..	..	..	..	JUNE 2nd
3rd	..	..	San Marino declares war on Austria-Hungary	First meeting of Allied Conference on Economic War (*in Paris*). (*See February 5th*) Act passed in British Parliament empowering Customs to compel all exports to Holland to be consigned to the Netherlands Overseas Trust. (*See November 23rd*, 1914)	..	..	3rd
5th	First Conference of British and French Ministers to co-ordinate war policy and strategy (*at Calais*)	..	..	..	..	..	5th
7th	..	..	Russian and Chinese Governments conclude agreement respecting Mongolia	First meeting of the Dardanelles Committee of the British Cabinet*	..	..	7th
19th	..	..	..	..	..	Dr. José de Castro succeeds Senhor J. P. Chagas as Portuguese Premier	19th
24th	..	..	..	..	..	Mr. Lansing appointed United States Secretary of State in succession to Mr. Bryan	24th
26th	San Giovanni di Medua (*Albania*) occupied by Montenegrin force. (*See July 29th*)	..	..	General Sukhomlinov, Russian Minister for War, removed from office	..	..	26th
JULY 2nd	..	..	..	Munitions of War Act, 1915, becomes law in Great Britain. Ministry of Munitions formed in Great Britain	..	..	JULY 2nd
4th	..	..	..	Durazzo occupied by Serbian forces	..	..	4th
9th	Capitulation of German South-West Africa to General Botha	..	..	..	..	..	9th
12th	..	..	..	British Residency at Bushire (*South Persia*) attacked by Tangistani tribesmen. (*See August 8th*)	..	..	12th

* Under this title the War Council exercised its functions during the critical period of the Dardanelles campaign.

POLITICAL 1915.

Date.	Events of Outstanding Importance.			Other Political and Economic Events.			Date.
	General.	Diplomatic Correspondence.	Declarations, Treaties and Agreements.	Entente and Allies.	Central Powers.	Neutrals and Miscellaneous.	
1915. JULY.							**1915. JULY.**
13th	Great Austro-German offensive on Eastern Front begins	..	..	..	..	..	13th
14th	..	Sherif of Mecca opens direct negotiations with British Government for co-operation against the Turks. (*See October 31st, 1914, and June 7th, 1916*)	..	A Dominion Premier (*Sir R. Borden*) for the first time attends meeting of the British Cabinet	..	..	14th
15th	..	..	..	National Registration Act becomes law in Great Britain. (*See August 15th*)	..	..	15th
17th	..	..	Treaty of Alliance signed at Sofia between Austria-Hungary, Bulgaria, Germany and Turkey (*Albania to be ceded to Bulgaria in return for Bulgarian participation in war*).	Durazzo evacuated by the Serbians at request of Italian Government. (*See 4th, and August 31st*)	..	..	17th
25th	..	..	British Government guarantee to Greece eventual cession of Mitylene by Turkey. (*See March 20th*)	..	..	..	25th
29th	..	Montenegro warned by Entente to respect Albanian territory. (*See June 26th*)	..	..	..	Establishment of East Persia cordon begun	29th
30th	..	Pope sends appeal for peace to belligerent Governments. (*See August 1st, 1917*)	..	..	..	..	30th
AUG. 5th	Warsaw occupied by German forces	..	..	..	..	..	**AUG. 5th**
6th	..	..	Agreement concluded between Japan and China substituting Japanese authority for German in Tsingtau customs. (*See November 7th, 1914*)	..	..	Dr. Machado Guimarães elected Portuguese President. Bulgarian Government negotiate fresh loan of 400,000,000 francs with Austro-German banks. (*See February 3rd*)	6th
8th	..	..	..	Bushire (*Persia*) occupied by a British force. (*See July 12th*)	..	..	8th
9th	..	..	..	Viscount Kato, Japanese Minister for Foreign Affairs, resigns	..	..	9th
10th	..	..	..	Marquis Okuma appointed Japanese Minister for Foreign Affairs (*ad interim*)	..	..	10th

POLITICAL 1915.

Date.	EVENTS OF OUTSTANDING IMPORTANCE.			OTHER POLITICAL AND ECONOMIC EVENTS.			Date.
	General.	Diplomatic Correspondence.	Declarations, Treaties and Agreements.	Entente and Allies.	Central Powers.	Neutrals and Miscellaneous.	
1915. AUG. 15th	.. ..	Entente Governments make conditional offer of territorial acquisitions to Serbia. (*See May 7th*)	.. ..	National Register taken in Great Britain. (*See July 15th*)	.. ..	.. ..	1915. AUG. 15th
17th	.. ..	.. ..	.. ..	.. ..	.. ..	Ain ed Douleh, Persian Prime Minister, resigns	17th
18th	.. ..	.. ..	.. ..	.. ..	.. ..	Mustaufi ul Mamalek again appointed Persian Prime Minister	18th
19th	.. ..	.. ..	.. ..	British Submarine "E 13" attacked by German warships whilst aground in Danish waters *s.s. "Arabic" sunk by German submarine* *H.M.S. "Baralong" (special service ship) destroys German submarine "U 27"*	.. ..	.. ..	19th
21st	First authenticated case of German submarine firing on a crew in boats (*s.s. "Ruel"*)	.. ..	Italy declares war on Turkey	.. ..	.. ..	.. ..	21st
22nd	.. ..	.. ..	.. ..	.. ..	.. ..	M. Venizelos again appointed Premier of Greece in succession to M. Gounaris. (*See March 6th and October 5th*)	22nd
30th	.. ..	British Foreign Minister, Sir E. Grey, informs M. Supilo that, provided Serbia agreed, the Allies could guarantee the eventual freedom and self-determination of Bosnia, Herzegovina, South Dalmatia, Slavonia, and Croatia. (*See 15th and May 7th*)	.. ..	.. ..	.. ..	.. ..	30th
31st	.. ..	.. ..	.. ..	Durazzo (*see July 17th*) reoccupied by Serbian forces. (*See December 20th*)	.. ..	.. ..	31st
SEPT. 1st	.. ..	German Government inform United States Government that American demands for limitation of submarine activity are accepted.	.. ..	Ruad Island (*off Syrian coast*) *occupied by French forces*	.. ..	.. ..	SEPT. 1st

[8369]

POLITICAL
1915.

	EVENTS OF OUTSTANDING IMPORTANCE.			OTHER POLITICAL AND ECONOMIC EVENTS.			
Date.	General.	Diplomatic Correspondence.	Declarations, Treaties and Agreements.	Entente and Allies.	Central Powers.	Neutrals and Miscellaneous.	Date.
1915. SEPT. 5th	.. ..	.. ..	.. ..	The Tsar assumes supreme command of the Russian armies (with General Alexeiev as Chief of Staff)	.. ..	.. ..	1915. SEPT. 5th
8th	.. ..	.. ..	.. ..	Grand Duke Nicholas appointed Viceroy of the Caucasus	.. ..	.. ..	8th
9th	.. ..	United States Government request recall of Austro-Hungarian Ambassador, Dr. Dumba. (See 28th)	Turco - Bulgarian frontier Convention signed at Dimotika. (See 22nd)	Bushire (South Persia) again attacked by tribesmen. (See July 12th)	.. ..	.. ..	9th
17th	Vilna (Lithuania) taken by German forces	.. ..	.. ..	.. ..	.. ..	.. ..	17th
21st	.. ..	Greek Premier (M. Venizelos) asks for guarantee of 150,000 British and French troops as condition for Greek intervention	.. ..	Viscount Ishii succeeds Marquis Okuma as Japanese Minister for Foreign Affairs	.. ..	Bulgarian Government order partial mobilisation	21st
22nd	Bulgarian Government order general mobilisation for 25th	.. ..	"Dede Agatch Agreement" concluded between Turkey and Bulgaria (rectifying Turkish frontier in favour of Bulgaria). (See 9th)	.. ..	.. ..	.. ..	22nd
23rd	Greek Government order precautionary mobilisation	.. ..	.. ..	.. ..	.. ..	.. ..	23rd
24th	.. ..	French and British Governments inform Greek Government that they are prepared to send troops requested. (See 21st, 27th and 28th)	.. ..	.. ..	.. ..	.. ..	24th
25th	Bulgarian mobilisation begins	.. ..	Serbian Government give undertaking to Greek Government to cede Doiran and Gevgeli eventually to Greece and not to claim Strumitza	.. ..	.. ..	.. ..	25th
27th	.. ..	.. ..	.. ..	.. ..	.. ..	Greek Premier (M. Venizelos) obtains secret consent of King Constantine to proposed Entente expedition to Salonika. (See 24th)	27th

POLITICAL
1915.

Date.	EVENTS OF OUTSTANDING IMPORTANCE.			OTHER POLITICAL AND ECONOMIC EVENTS.			Date.
	General.	Diplomatic Correspondence.	Declarations, Treaties and Agreements.	Entente and Allies.	Central Powers.	Neutrals and Miscellaneous.	
1915. SEPT. 28th	.. ..	Greek Government formally refuse French and British " offer " of 24th	British and Russian Governments agree to request of Persian Government for a monthly subvention	.. ..	Dr. Dumba, Austrian Ambassador, recalled from United States of America. (See 9th)	.. ..	1915. SEPT. 28th
30th	..	.. ..	.. ..	Lord Derby assumes control of recruiting in Great Britain	..	..	30th
OCT. 2nd	.. ..	Greek Premier (M. Venizelos) asks British and French Governments to land troops at Salonika as soon as possible. (See 5th)	.. ..	.. ..	.. ..	.. ..	OCT. 2nd
3rd	Allied forces arrive at Salonika	Greek Government protest against proposed Allied landing at Salonika	..	.. ..	.. ..	.. ..	3rd
4th	.. ..	**Entente Powers send Ultimatum to Bulgaria**	.. .	.. ..	.. ..	.. ..	4th
5th	Allied forces land at Salonika	.. ..	Russia severs diplomatic relations with Bulgaria	.. ..	.. ..	King of Greece refuses to support policy of Premier (M. Venizelos). (See 2nd) M. Venizelos resigns Dr. Machado Guimarães succeeds Dr. J. Braza as Portuguese President	5th
6th	Austro-German armies begin the final invasion of Serbia	King of Greece gives assurance to British Minister that Greek mobilisation and Allied disembarkation at Salonika will proceed	.. .	.. .	..	M. Zaimis appointed Greek Premier	6th
7th	..	.. ..	.. ..	.. ..	..	..	7th
8th	.. ..	.. ..	New Greek Government announce policy of armed neutrality	.. ..	..	..	8th
9th	*Belgrade taken by the Austrian forces*	.. ..	.. ..	.. ..	.. ..	.. ..	9th
10th	.. ..	Greek Government reject Serbian claim for help under Serbo-Greek Treaty of 1912	.. ..	.. ..	.. ..	.. ..	10th
11th	Bulgarian forces cross Serbian frontier. (See 14th)	.. ..	.. ..	.. ..	.. ..	.. ..	11th
12th	.. ..	.. ..	.. ..	Miss Edith Cavell shot in Brussels by order of a German court-martial	.. ..	.. ..	12th

POLITICAL
1915.

Date.	EVENTS OF OUTSTANDING IMPORTANCE.			OTHER POLITICAL AND ECONOMIC EVENTS.			Date.
	General.	Diplomatic Correspondence.	Declarations, Treaties and Agreements.	Entente and Allies.	Central Powers.	Neutrals and Miscellaneous.	
1915. OCT. 13th	Hostilities commence between French and Bulgarian forces in Macedonia	.. ..	Great Britain severs diplomatic relations with Bulgaria	M. Delcassé, French Foreign Minister, resigns and is succeeded temporarily by M. Viviani. (See 29th)	.. ..	.. ..	1915. OCT. 13th
14th	.. ..	.. ..	Bulgaria and Serbia declare war on one another. (See 11th)	.. ..	.. ..	.. ..	14th
15th	.. ..	Rumanian Government refuse to aid Serbia	Great Britain declares "state of war" with Bulgaria Montenegro declares "state of war" with Bulgaria	.. ..	.. ..	.. ..	15th
16th	Entente Governments proclaim blockade of Ægean coast of Bulgaria	British Government offer Cyprus to Greece if she will support Serbia	France declares "state of war" with Bulgaria	.. ..	.. ..	.. ..	16th
19th	.. ..	.. ..	Russia and Italy declare war on Bulgaria Japan declares adherence to the Pact of London. (See September 5th, 1914, and November 30th, 1915)	.. ..	.. ..	.. ..	19th
20th	.. ..	Greek Government reject British offer of Cyprus	.. ..	.. ..	.. ..	.. ..	20th
24th	.. ..	British Government, in letter to Sherif of Mecca (see July 14th, 1915, and June 5th, 1916), define territorial limits of proposed Arab State	.. ..	.. ..	.. ..	.. ..	24th
28th	.. ..	.. ..	.. ..	.. ..	.. ..	.. ..	28th
29th	.. ..	.. ..	.. ..	M. Viviani, French Premier and Foreign Minister, resigns M. Millerand, French Minister for War, resigns	.. ..	.. ..	29th
30th	.. ..	.. ..	.. ..	M. Briand appointed Premier and Foreign Minister of France Last meeting of Dardanelles Committee of the British Cabinet. (See November 3rd) General Galliéni appointed French Minister for War	.. ..	.. ..	30th

POLITICAL
1915.

Date.	EVENTS OF OUTSTANDING IMPORTANCE.			OTHER POLITICAL AND ECONOMIC EVENTS.			Date.
	General.	Diplomatic Correspondence.	Declarations, Treaties and Agreements.	Entente and Allies.	Central Powers.	Neutrals and Miscellaneous.	
1915. NOV. 2nd	.. ..	.. ..	British Premier (*Mr. Asquith*) declares Serbian independence to be an essential object of the war	.. ..	.. ..	.. ..	1915. NOV. 2nd
3rd	Serbian Government leave Nish	.. ..	.. ..	First meeting of newly-constituted War Committee of British Cabinet to replace the Dardanelles Committee. (*See October 30th*) Port and Transit Executive Committee formed in Great Britain	.. ..	.. ..	3rd
4th	.. ..	.. ..	.. ..	*Lord Kitchener leaves England for the Dardanelles*	.. ..	.. ..	4th
5th	**Nish taken by the Bulgarian forces**	.. ..	.. ..	.. ..	.. ..	M. Zaimis Greek Premier, resigns	5th
6th	.. ..	.. ..	.. ..	.. ..	.. ..	M. Skouloudhis appointed Premier of Greece	6th
7th	.. ..	.. ..	.. ..	Italian s.s. "Ancona" sunk by Austrian submarine	.. ..	.. ..	7th
8th	.. ..	.. ..	.. ..	.. ..	.. ..	Entente Loan (£1,600,000) to Greece concluded	8th
10th	.. ..	.. ..	.. ..	*Lord Kitchener arrives at the Dardanelles* Ship Licensing Committee formed in Great Britain: Order in Council prohibits voyages between foreign ports except under licence Requisitioning (Carriage of Foodstuffs) Committee formed in Great Britain: Order in Council authorises requisition of ships for carriage of foodstuffs	.. ..	.. ..	10th
14th	Senussi commence hostilities against British by attacking Egyptian post at Sollum	.. ..	.. ..	.. ..	.. ..	.. ..	14th
15th	.. ..	.. ..	.. ..	.. ..	Representatives of Central Powers leave Teheran on approach of Russian forces	.. ..	15th

POLITICAL 1915.

Date.	Events of Outstanding Importance.			Other Political and Economic Events.			Date.
	General.	Diplomatic Correspondence.	Declarations, Treaties and Agreements.	Entente and Allies.	Central Powers.	Neutrals and Miscellaneous.	
1915. NOV. 17th	..	..	..	Anglo-French Conference approve project of Council of War to co-ordinate Allied action	..	..	1915. NOV. 17th
23rd	British military operations against the Senussi commence: Sollum post evacuated	Entente Powers send note to Greek Government demanding non-interference with Allied troops, and guaranteeing eventual restoration of occupied Greek territory	British Government conclude preliminary agreement with the Netherlands Overseas Trust for rationing of Holland. (See June 30th, 1916)	Serbian Government leave Prizren for Scutari	..	..	23rd
24th	..	Greek Government accept Entente demands of the 23rd	Danish merchants and manufacturers conclude agreement with British Government to restrict supplies to Germany	..	Field-Marshal von der Goltz (see December 10th, 1914) takes command of Turkish forces in Mesopotamia	..	24th
25th	..	..	..	M. Albert Thomas announces arrangements completed for inter-Allied organisation of munitions	..	..	25th
29th	..	..	..	..	..	Dr. A. Augusto da Costa succeeds Dr. J. de Castro as Portuguese Premier	29th
30th	Serbian retreat through Albania begins. (See February 10th, 1916)	..	Formal signature of the Pact of London by Great Britain, France, Russia, Japan, and Italy. (See September 5th, 1914, April 26th, and October 19th, 1915)	..	..	..	30th
DEC. 1st	..	..	Italy announces her adherence to the Pact of London. (See November 30th)	..	Prizren (Serbia) taken by Bulgarian forces	..	DEC. 1st
2nd	Allied forces in Macedonia begin retreat into Greek territory	..	..	..	Monastir (Serbia) taken by Bulgarian forces	..	2nd
3rd	British Army, retreating from Ctesiphon, reaches Kut al Amara	..	..	Serbian Government and military headquarters set up at Scutari. General Joffre, hitherto Chief of French General Staff, appointed Commander-in-Chief French Armies. Appointment of Chief of General Staff lapses. (See December 12th, 1916, and April 29th, 1917)	..	..	3rd

POLITICAL 1915.

| Date. | EVENTS OF OUTSTANDING IMPORTANCE. ||| OTHER POLITICAL AND ECONOMIC EVENTS. ||| Date. |
	General.	Diplomatic Correspondence.	Declarations, Treaties and Agreements.	Entente and Allies.	Central Powers.	Neutrals and Miscellaneous.	
1915. DEC. 4th	.. ..	United States Government request recall of German Attachés, Captains Boy-Ed and von Papen	.. ..	.. ..	.. ..	.. ..	1915. DEC. 4th
6th	British Government put economic pressure on Greece by making the "Export Restrictions" apply to that country. (*See* 13*th*)	.. ..	.. ..	.. ..	.. ..	.. ..	6th
7th	*Siege of Kut begins*	.. ..	Agreement concluded between French Government and Netherlands Overseas Trust	.. ..	.. ..	.. ..	7th
8th	*Evacuation of the Gallipoli Peninsula ordered.* (*See* 20*th*)	.. ..	.. ..	.. ..	.. ..	.. ..	8th
9th	.. ..	General Sarrail demands withdrawal of Greek troops from Salonika	.. ..	General Castelnau appointed Chief of Staff to General Joffre	.. ..	.. ..	9th
10th	.. ..	.. ..	.. ..	.. ..	German Government recall from United States Attachés von Papen and Boy-Ed. (*See* 4*th*)	.. ..	10th
11th	.. ..	Greek Government refuse Entente demand for withdrawal of Greek troops from Salonika	.. ..	.. ..	.. ..	Yuan-Shih-Kai accepts throne of China. (*See June* 6*th*, 1916)	11th
13th	British Government order partial relaxation of economic pressure on Greece. (*See* 6*th*)	.. ..	.. ..	.. ..	.. ..	.. ..	13th
14th	.. ..	.. ..	Bulgarian and Greek General Staffs conclude agreement establishing temporary neutral zone along Greek frontier	.. ..	.. ..	.. ..	14th
15th	*The last Allied forces in Macedonia withdrawn into Greek territory.* (*See* 2*nd*)	.. ..	.. ..	Field-Marshal Sir John French, Commander-in-Chief of British Armies in France, resigns	.. ..	.. ..	15th
19th	.. ..	.. ..	.. ..	Sir Douglas Haig succeeds Sir John French as Commander-in-Chief of British Armies in France	.. ..	.. ..	19th

POLITICAL
1915-16.

| Date. | EVENTS OF OUTSTANDING IMPORTANCE. ||| OTHER POLITICAL AND ECONOMIC EVENTS. ||| Date. |
	General.	Diplomatic Correspondence.	Declarations, Treaties and Agreements.	Entente and Allies.	Central Powers.	Neutrals and Miscellaneous.	
1915. DEC. 20th	Evacuation of Suvla and Anzac completed. (See 8th)	..	..	Durazzo occupied by Italian forces. (See August 31st, 1915, and February 27th, 1916)	..	..	1915. DEC. 20th
23rd	..	..	..	"Trading with the Enemy (Extension of Powers) Act, 1915" (beginning of "Black List" policy) comes into force in Great Britain	..	..	23rd
24th	..	..	..	..	..	Mustaufi ul Mamalek, Persian Prime Minister, resigns	24th
25th	..	..	..	..	..	Prince Firman Firma appointed Premier of Persia	25th
26th	..	..	Treaty concluded between British Government and Ibn Sa'ud, Emir of Nejd. (See July 18th, 1916)	..	German raider "Moewe" sails from Bremen on first cruise	..	26th
28th	**Evacuation of remainder of Gallipoli Peninsula ordered.** (See 20th)	..	..	..	..	..	28th
30th	..	..	..	..	Consuls of Central Powers at Salonika arrested and deported by order of General Sarrail, commanding French troops	..	30th
1916. JAN. 1st	..	..	..	King of Serbia arrives at Salonika	..	..	1916. JAN. 1st
7th	Evacuation of Helles (Gallipoli Peninsula) begins	..	..	..	..	..	7th
8th	Evacuation of the Gallipoli Peninsula completed	..	..	..	..	..	8th
10th	..	Entente Governments inform Greek Government of proposed transport of Serbian Army to Corfu. (See 15th)	..	..	..	..	10th
11th	..	..	..	Corfu occupied by French forces	..	..	11th
12th	..	..	Armistice concluded between Montenegro and Austria. (See 20th)	..	..	..	12th
13th	**Cetigne (Montenegro) occupied by Austrian forces**	Greek Government refuse consent to the occupation of Corfu	..	..	..	..	13th

POLITICAL
1916.

Date.	EVENTS OF OUTSTANDING IMPORTANCE.			OTHER POLITICAL AND ECONOMIC EVENTS.			Date.
	General.	Diplomatic Correspondence.	Declarations, Treaties and Agreements.	Entente and Allies.	Central Powers.	Neutrals and Miscellaneous.	
1916. JAN. 15th	.. ..	.. ..	.. ..	*First Serbian troops land at Corfu* Serbian Government transferred to Brindisi. (*See December 3rd, 1915*) King of Serbia leaves Salonika	.. ..	Von Papen papers published in United States of America	1916. JAN. 15th
16th	*General Sarrail assumes command of all Allied forces at Salonika.* (*See December 22nd, 1917*)	.. ..	.. ..	.. ..	.. ..	.. ..	16th
17th	.. ..	.. ..	.. ..	King of Serbia arrives at Edypsos	.. ..	.. ..	17th
18th	.. ..	.. ..	.. ..	Baron Beyens succeeds M. Davignon as Belgian Minister for Foreign Affairs	.. ..	.. ..	18th
20th	.. ..	.. ..	Negotiations between Austria and Montenegro broken off. Armistice ceases. (*See 12th*)	.. ..	.. ..	.. ..	20th
22nd	.. ..	Rumanian Government open negotiations with Russian Government with a view to military assistance	.. ..	.. ..	.. ..	.. ..	22nd
23rd	.. ..	.. ..	.. ..	.. ..	*Scutari (Albania) occupied by Austrian forces* *Podgoritza (Montenegro) occupied by Austrian forces*	.. ..	23rd
24th	.. ..	.. ..	.. ..	First Military Service Bill passed by British House of Commons	.. ..	.. ..	24th
25th	.. ..	.. ..	.. ..	.. ..	*San Giovanni di Medua (Albania) captured by Austrian forces.* (*See June 26th, 1915*)	.. ..	25th
26th	.. ..	United States Government make informal protest to British Government regarding their "Black List" policy (*See December 23rd, 1915*)	.. ..	.. ..	.. ..	.. ..	26th
27th	.. ..	.. ..	.. ..	Shipping Control Committee formed by British Government	.. ..	.. ..	27th
FEB. 1st	.. ..	.. ..	.. ..	M. Goremikin, Russian Premier, resigns; M. Stürmer appointed	British s.s. "Appam" brought to Norfolk, Virginia, by German prize crew from raider "Moewe"	.. ..	FEB. 1st

POLITICAL 1916.

Date.	EVENTS OF OUTSTANDING IMPORTANCE.			OTHER POLITICAL AND ECONOMIC EVENTS.			Date.
	General.	Diplomatic Correspondence.	Declarations, Treaties and Agreements.	Entente and Allies.	Central Powers.	Neutrals and Miscellaneous.	
1916. FEB. 8th	.. ..	British Government request naval assistance from Japan. (See November 14th, 1914, and April 17th, 1917)	.. ..	.. ..	.. ..	.. ..	1916. FEB. 8th
9th	.. ..	.. ..	.. ..	Serbian Government set up at Corfu. (See January 15th)	.. ..	.. ..	9th
10th	*Remnant of Serbian army concentrated at Corfu. (See November 30th, 1915)*	German Government send note to United States of America stating that defensively armed merchantmen will be treated as belligerents from March 1st onwards	.. ..	**Military Service Act comes into operation in Great Britain.** (See January 24th)	.. ..	.. ..	10th
13th	.. ..	Entente Governments notify Greece of forthcoming transfer of Montenegrin army to Corfu. (See 16th)	.. ..		.. ..	.. ..	13th
14th	.. ..	.. ..	Entente Powers make declaration guaranteeing to Belgium eventual independence and indemnification	.. ..	.. ..	.. ..	14th
15th	.. ..	.. ..	Agreement concluded between British Government and Chieftains of the Bakhtiari (Persia) for co-operation in protection of Persian oilfields	British Order in Council extending powers of Ship Licensing Committee to all voyages issued	.. ..	.. ..	15th
16th	*Erzerum taken by Russian forces* *Remnants of Montenegrin army land at Corfu*	.. ..	.. ..	.. ..	.. ..	.. ..	16th
17th	.. ..	.. ..	.. ..	*Chios (Ægean) occupied by British forces*	.. ..	.. ..	17th
18th	*Conquest of the Cameroons by Entente forces completed*	.. ..	.. ..	.. ..	.. ..	.. ..	18th
19th	.. ..	.. ..	.. ..	*General Smuts takes command of British forces in East Africa*	.. ..	.. ..	19th
21st	.. ..	German Government inform United States Government that defensively armed merchantmen will henceforth be regarded as cruisers	.. ..	.. ..	.. ..	.. ..	21st

POLITICAL 1916.

Date.	EVENTS OF OUTSTANDING IMPORTANCE.			OTHER POLITICAL AND ECONOMIC EVENTS.			Date.
	General.	Diplomatic Correspondence.	Declarations, Treaties and Agreements.	Entente and Allies.	Central Powers.	Neutrals and Miscellaneous	
1916. FEB. 23rd	Portugal seizes German steamers in the Tagus	..	..	Ministry of Blockade formed in Great Britain	..	..	1916. FEB. 23rd
24th	..	..	..	..	..	Albanian Provisional Government of Essad Pasha leaves Durazzo	24th
26th	..	..	..	*Kirmanshah (Persia) occupied by Russian forces*	..	..	26th
27th	..	..	..	..	*Durazzo captured by Austrian forces. (See 24th, and December 20th, 1915)*	..	27th
28th	..	..	..	..	..	Albanian Provisional Government of Essad Pasha set up at Naples	28th
29th	British blockade of the Cameroons raised. (*See April 23rd, 1915*)	German Government send Note to United States Government stating that it is not intended to postpone the extended submarine campaign. (*See March 1st*)	..	..	..	..	29th
MARCH 1st	German extended submarine campaign begins. (*See February 10th*)	..	..	..	..	..	MARCH 1st
3rd	..	..	French and British Governments conclude agreement as to provisional administration of the Cameroons	..	..	..	3rd
4th	..	..	..	..	*German raider "Moewe" returns to Germany. (See December 26th, 1915)*	..	4th
5th	..	..	..	..	..	Prince Firman Firma, Persian Prime Minister, resigns. Motashim ed Douleh, Persian Foreign Minister, resigns	5th

[8369]

POLITICAL
1916.

Date.	Events of Outstanding Importance.			Other Political and Economic Events.			Date.
	General.	Diplomatic Correspondence.	Declarations, Treaties and Agreements.	Entente and Allies.	Central Powers.	Neutrals and Miscellaneous.	
1916. MARCH 6th	..	..	..	..	..	Sipahsalar A'Zam appointed Persian Prime Minister	1916. MARCH 6th
						Sarim ed Douleh appointed Persian Foreign Minister	
9th	..	..	Germany declares war on Portugal. (See February 23rd)	..	..	..	9th
12th	..	..	..	Allied Military Conference at Chantilly	..	..	12th
14th	..	..	..	..	Admiral von Tirpitz, German Minister of Marine, resigns	..	14th
15th	..	..	Austria-Hungary severs diplomatic relations with and declares war on Portugal	Dr. A. José d'Almeida succeeds Dr. A. A. da Costa as Portuguese Premier	Admiral von Capelle succeeds Admiral von Tirpitz as German Minister of Marine	..	15th
16th	..	..	..	General Roques succeeds General Galliéni as French Minister for War	..	..	16th
20th	..	..	..	French Minister of Blockade appointed*	..	..	20th
22nd	..	..	..	..	..	Yuan-Shih-Kai relinquishes the throne of China	22nd
24th	s.s. "Sussex" torpedoed by submarine in the English Channel	..	..	..	..	..	24th
28th	..	..	..	Inter-Allied Conference in Paris (26th/28th). Declaration of unity between Belgium, France, Great Britain, Italy, Japan, Portugal, Russia and Serbia (regarding military, economic and diplomatic affairs) drawn up	..	..	28th
29th	..	..	..	General Polivanov, Russian Minister for War, resigns: succeeded by General Shuvaev	..	..	29th
				Lieutenant-General Oka, Japanese Minister for War, resigns			
30th	Russian hospital ship "Portugal" sunk by submarine in the Black Sea	..	..	Lieutenant-General Kenichi Oshima appointed Japanese Minister for War	..	..	30th
APRIL 3rd	..	..	Greek Government refuse overland route for transport of Serbian Army from Corfu to Salonika	..	..	..	APRIL 3rd
15th	..	..	..	Serbian A.H.Q. land at Salonika	..	..	15th

* At this period this appointment was termed Under-Secretary of State for Blockade. (See November 16th, 1917.)

POLITICAL
1916.

Date.	EVENTS OF OUTSTANDING IMPORTANCE.			OTHER POLITICAL AND ECONOMIC EVENTS.			Date.
	General.	Diplomatic Correspondence.	Declarations, Treaties and Agreements.	Entente and Allies.	Central Powers.	Neutrals and Miscellaneous.	
1916. APRIL 17th	*Trebizond (Asia Minor) taken by Russian forces*	..	..	Italian Government issue decree prohibiting trading with Germany	..	..	1916. APRIL 17th
18th	..	United States Government send Note to German Government on "Sussex" case (*See March 24th*) and submarine policy in general. (*See February 10th*)	..	..	..	..	18th
19th	..	..	..	..	Field-Marshal von der Goltz assassinated by an Albanian officer (*See November 24th*, 1915)	..	19th
20th	*Russian troops from Far East arrive at Marseilles. (See July 30th)*	..	..	Disguised German transport "Aud" sinks herself after capture while trying to land arms on Irish coast Roger Casement lands in Ireland from a German submarine and is arrested	..	..	20th
24th	..	..	..	**Outbreak of Rebellion in Ireland**	..	..	24th
26th	..	..	French and Russian Governments conclude "Sykes-Picot" Agreement as to eventual partition of Asia Minor. (*See May 9th and 23rd*) Agreement signed at Berlin for transfer of British and German wounded and sick prisoners of war to Switzerland. (*See May 13th*)	..	..	..	26th
27th	..	..	..	Martial law proclaimed in Dublin and the county	..	..	27th
29th	*Capitulation of Kut*	..	"Havre Declaration" signed by France, Great Britain, Italy, Japan and Russia guaranteeing integrity of Belgian Congo	..	..	..	29th
MAY 1st	..	..	..	**Collapse of Irish Rebellion.** (*Surrender of leaders.*) (*See April 24th*)	..	..	MAY 1st

POLITICAL 1916.

Date.	Events of Outstanding Importance.			Other Political and Economic Events.			Date.
	General.	Diplomatic Correspondence.	Declarations, Treaties and Agreements.	Entente and Allies.	Central Powers.	Neutrals and Miscellaneous.	
1916. MAY 3rd	..	..	..	Three leaders of Irish Rebellion executed	..	..	**1916. MAY** 3rd
7th	..	..	..	Serbian Government set up at Salonika	..	..	7th
9th	..	..	British and French Governments conclude "Sykes-Picot" Agreement as to eventual partition of Asia Minor. (*See 23rd, and April 26th*)	..	..	..	9th
10th	..	..	Agreement signed at Berlin *re* employment of British and German prisoners of war. (*See 29th*)	..	..	..	10th
13th	..	..	Agreement signed at London for transfer of British and German wounded and sick prisoners of war to Switzerland (*See April 26th*)	..	..	..	13th
15th	Entente blockade of the Hejaz coast to assist revolt of Sherif of Mecca commenced. (*See June 5th*)	..	..	..	..	..	15th
16th	..	..	Agreement concluded between Great Britain and France regarding respective claims in Turkish territories	Second Military Service Bill extending compulsion to married men passes the British House of Commons	..	..	16th
17th	..	..	..	Air Board formed in Great Britain	..	..	17th
18th	..	..	..	*Detachment of Cossacks from Russian force in West Persia effects junction with British Army on the Tigris*	..	..	18th
23rd	..	..	British Government notify Russian Government of their recognition of Franco-Russian "Sykes-Picot" Agreement as to eventual partition of Asia Minor. (*See 9th, April 26th, and September 1st*)	..	..	..	23rd

POLITICAL
1916.

Date.	EVENTS OF OUTSTANDING IMPORTANCE.			OTHER POLITICAL AND ECONOMIC EVENTS.			Date.
	General.	Diplomatic Correspondence.	Declarations, Treaties and Agreements.	Entente and Allies.	Central Powers.	Neutrals and Miscellaneous.	
1916. MAY 25th	.. ..	.. ..	.. ..	Second Military Service Act becomes law in Great Britain. (See 16th, and June 8th)	.. ..	.. ..	1916. MAY. 25th
26th	Fort Rupel (Greek Macedonia) occupied by Bulgarian and German forces	United States Government send Note to British Government respecting search of mails					26th
29th			Agreement signed at London re the employment of British and German prisoners of war. (See 10th)				29th
31st	.. ..	Entente Governments protest to Greece against Bulgarian occupation of Fort Rupel. (See 26th)	.. ..			.. ..	31st
JUNE 3rd	Allied commander proclaims martial law in city of Salonika	.. ..	.. ..	.. ..	.. ..	.. ..	JUNE 3rd
4th	"Brusilov's Offensive" begins		.. ..				4th
5th	Sherif of Mecca begins revolt against Turkish rule	.. ..	.. ..	Field-Marshal Earl Kitchener drowned in sinking of H.M.S. "Hampshire"	.. ..	.. ..	5th
6th	"Pacific blockade" of Greece by Entente Powers begins	.. ..	.. ..	.. ..	.. ..	Yuan-Shih-Kai (President of China) dies and is succeeded by Li-Yuan-Hung	6th
7th	.. ..	.. ..	Sherif of Mecca issues proclamation denouncing the Committee of Union and Progress, and proclaiming the independence of the Hejaz	.. ..	.. ..	.. ..	7th
8th	.. ..	.. ..	.. ..	Second Compulsory Service Act comes into operation in Great Britain. (See May 25th)	.. ..	.. ..	8th
10th	Turkish garrison of Mecca surrenders to the Sherif		.. ..	Compulsory Service Bill passed in New Zealand. (See September 1st)	.. ..	.. ..	10th
11th	.. ..	.. ..	.. ..	Signor Salandra, Italian Premier, resigns	.. ..	.. ..	11th
12th	.. ..	.. ..	.. ..	Kerman (East Persia) occupied by British forces	.. ..	.. ..	12th

POLITICAL
1916.

Date.	EVENTS OF OUTSTANDING IMPORTANCE.			OTHER POLITICAL AND ECONOMIC EVENTS.			Date.
	General.	Diplomatic Correspondence.	Declarations, Treaties and Agreements.	Entente and Allies.	Central Powers.	Neutrals and Miscellaneous.	
1916. JUNE 14th	..	..	..	Allied Economic Conference re-assembles in Paris	..	..	1916. JUNE 14th
16th	..	..	..	Signor Boselli appointed Italian Prime Minister	..	..	16th
21st	..	Entente Governments send Note to Greece demanding demobilisation and change of Government	..	..	..	Greek Cabinet (*M. Skouloudhis*) resign. M. Zaimis forms new Greek Ministry	21st
22nd	"Pacific blockade" of Greece suspended	..	..	..	..	..	22nd
27th	..	..	..	Recommendations of Allied Economic Conference ratified (*See 14th*)	..	Greek Government order general demobilisation	27th
30th	..	..	British Government conclude further agreement with Netherlands Overseas Trust for rationing of Holland. (*See November 23rd, 1915*)	..	..	..	30th
JULY 1st	..	..	..	..	*Kirmanshah (Persia) reoccupied by the Turkish forces. (See February 26th)*	..	JULY 1st
3rd	..	..	Russian and Japanese Governments conclude Treaty with regard to future policy in the Far East	..	..	..	3rd
7th	..	..	**British Government* issue Order in Council rescinding Declaration of London of 1909.** (*See October 29th and November 6th, 1914*)	Mr. Lloyd George succeeds Lord Kitchener as Secretary of State for War	..	..	7th
10th	*Russian hospital ship "Vpered" sunk by submarine in the Black Sea*	..	..	..	German commercial submarine "Deutschland" arrives at Norfolk (Va.) from Bremen	..	10th
14th	..	..	..	Inter-Allied Conference on Finance in London (14th/15th)	..	..	14th
18th	..	..	Treaty with Ibn Sa'ud, Emir of Nejd, ratified by British Government. (*See December 26th, 1915*)	..	..	..	18th

* French Government issued similar decree on the same date.

POLITICAL
1916.

121

Date.	EVENTS OF OUTSTANDING IMPORTANCE.			OTHER POLITICAL AND ECONOMIC EVENTS.			Date.
	General.	Diplomatic Correspondence.	Declarations, Treaties and Agreements.	Entente and Allies.	Central Powers.	Neutrals and Miscellaneous.	
1916. JULY 20th	.. ..	.. ..	.. ..	.. ..	.. ..	Greek Government conclude new loan with the Entente (£800,000)	1916. JULY 20th
22nd	.. ..	.. ..	.. ..	M. Sazonov, Russian Foreign Minister, resigns; succeeded by M. Stürmer	.. ..	.. ..	22nd
25th	Reconstituted Serbian Army comes into action on Salonika front	.. ..	.. ..	.. ..	.. ..	.. ..	25th
27th	Yenbo (port of Medina) surrenders to the Sherif of Mecca	.. ..	.. ..	Captain C. Fryatt shot by order of a German court-martial in Belgium	.. ..	.. ..	27th
28th	.. ..	United States Government send to British Government formal protest against "Black List" policy. (See January 26th)	.. ..	.. ..	.. ..	.. ..	28th
29th	.. ..	German Government send Note to United States Government rejecting British offer to permit passage of foodstuffs to Poland from United States of America	.. ..	.. ..	.. ..	.. ..	29th
30th	Russian troops from France land at Salonika and join Allied force. (See April 20th)	.. ..	.. ..	.. ..	.. ..	.. ..	30th
AUG. 3rd	.. ..	.. ..	.. ..	Roger Casement executed	.. ..	.. ..	AUG. 3rd
8th	.. ..	.. ..	Portuguese Government decide to extend military co-operation to Europe	.. ..	.. ..	.. ..	8th
11th	Italian troops land at Salonika and join Allied force	.. ..	.. ..	.. ..	.. ..	.. ..	11th
17th	.. ..	.. ..	Rumanian Government conclude Agreement with Entente Powers regarding intervention Military Convention signed at Bukharest between Entente Powers and Rumania	.. ..	.. ..	.. ..	17th

POLITICAL
1916.

Date.	Events of Outstanding Importance.			Other Political and Economic Events.			Date.
	General.	Diplomatic Correspondence.	Declarations, Treaties and Agreements.	Entente and Allies.	Central Powers.	Neutrals and Miscellaneous.	
1916. AUG. 23rd	.. ..	.. ..	.. ..	.. ..	German commercial submarine "Deutschland" returns to Germany. (See July 10th)	.. ..	1916. AUG. 23rd
24th	.. ..	.. ..	.. ..	Anglo-French Conference on finance at Calais	.. ..	.. ..	24th
27th	Rumanian Government order mobilisation. (See 17th)	.. ..	Rumania declares war on Austria-Hungary	.. ..	.. ..	.. ..	27th
28th	Rumanian forces cross Hungarian frontier and invade Transylvania	.. ..	Germany declares war on Rumania Italy declares war on Germany	.. ..	.. ..	.. ..	28th
29th	.. ..	.. ..	.. ..	.. ..	Field-Marshal von Hindenburg succeeds General von Falkenhayn as Chief of General Staff of the German Field Armies (with General von Ludendorff as Chief Quartermaster-General)	Sipahsalar A'zam, Persian Prime Minister, resigns; succeeded by Vossuq ed Douleh, who also acts as Foreign Minister	29th
30th	.. ..	.. ..	Turkey declares war on Rumania Rumania severs diplomatic relations with Bulgaria	.. ..	.. ..	Venizelist revolt in Salonika	30th
SEPT. 1st	.. ..	.. ..	Bulgaria declares war on Rumania Russian and British Governments conclude "Sykes-Picot" agreement as to eventual partition of Asia Minor. (See May 23rd)	Compulsory military service comes into operation in New Zealand. (See June 10th)	.. ..	.. ..	SEPT. 1st
2nd	German ships in Piræus Harbour seized by the Allies	.. ..	.. ..	.. ..	.. ..	.. ..	2nd
4th	Dar es Salaam (East Africa) surrenders to British forces	.. ..	.. ..	.. ..	.. ..	.. ..	4th
6th	.. ..	.. ..	.. ..	.. ..	.. ..	.. ..	6th
11th	.. ..	.. ..	.. ..	.. ..	.. ..	M. Zaimis, Greek Premier, resigns	11th
16th	.. ..	.. ..	.. ..	.. ..	.. ..	M. Kalogeropoulos forms new Greek Ministry	16th

POLITICAL 1916.

Date.	EVENTS OF OUTSTANDING IMPORTANCE.			OTHER POLITICAL AND ECONOMIC EVENTS.			Date.
	General.	Diplomatic Correspondence.	Declarations, Treaties and Agreements.	Entente and Allies.	Central Powers.	Neutrals and Miscellaneous.	
1916. SEPT. 18th	Greek IVth Army Corps at Kavala surrenders voluntarily to the German forces	..	..	..	..	..	1916. SEPT. 18th
19th	Allies commence blockade of Greek Macedonian coast from mouth of the Struma to mouth of the Mesto	..	..	..	..	..	19th
20th	..	..	..	..	..	Albanian Government of Essad Pasha set up in Salonika	20th
25th	..	..	..	..	..	M. Venizelos withdraws from Athens	25th
29th	..	..	..	..	..	M. Venizelos and Admiral Condouriotis announce formation of Greek Provisional Government in Crete (*in opposition to the Government at Athens*)	29th
OCT. 3rd	..	..	..	..	..	Greek Cabinet (*M. Kalogeropoulos*) resign	OCT. 3rd
8th	..	..	..	..	German submarine "*U 53*" *captures and destroys five ships outside Newport* (*Rhode Island*)	..	8th
9th	..	..	..	Marshal Count Masakata Terauchi succeeds Marquis Okuma as Japanese Prime Minister and Viscount Ishii as Acting Foreign Minister	..	M. Venizelos arrives at Salonika	9th
10th	..	Entente Governments send ultimatum to Greek Government demanding surrender of the Greek Fleet	..	..	..	Professor Lambros forms new Greek Ministry	10th
11th	..	Greek Government accept Entente demands	..	..	..	..	11th
13th	..	Norwegian Government issue orders prohibiting belligerent submarines from using Norwegian territorial waters	..	..	..	..	13th
20th	..	..	..	Anglo-French Conference at Calais to discuss Greek participation in the war	..	..	20th
21st	..	..	..	..	Count Stürgkh, Austrian Premier, murdered	..	21st

[8369]

POLITICAL
1916.

EVENTS OF OUTSTANDING IMPORTANCE. | OTHER POLITICAL AND ECONOMIC EVENTS.

Date.	General.	Diplomatic Correspondence.	Declarations, Treaties and Agreements.	Entente and Allies.	Central Powers.	Neutrals and Miscellaneous.	Date.
1916. OCT. 28th	..	..	..	..	Dr. E. von Körber appointed Austrian Premier	..	1916. OCT. 28th
29th	Sherif of Mecca proclaimed "King of the Arabs"	..	..	..	..	..	29th
30th	..	..	..	..	Lieutenant-General von Stein succeeds Lieutenant-General Wild von Hohenborn as German Minister for War	..	30th
NOV. 4th	..	..	..	Coronation of "The King of the Arabs" at Mecca	..	..	NOV. 4th
5th	..	..	Germany and Austria proclaim an "Independent State of Poland"	..	..	..	5th
7th	President Wilson re-elected	..	..	..	..	..	7th
15th	..	..	..	Inter-Allied Conference in Paris	..	..	15th
19th	..	Entente Governments demand dismissal of Ministers of Central Powers at Athens and surrender of Greek military material	..	Monastir (Serbia) captured by Allied forces	..	..	19th
20th	..	..	..	Count Terauchi relinquishes temporary appointment as Japanese Minister for Foreign Affairs	Herr von Jagow, German Foreign Minister, resigns	..	20th
21st	British hospital ship "Britannic" sunk by mine in Ægean Sea	..	..	Viscount Motono appointed Japanese Minister for Foreign Affairs	Death of Emperor Francis Joseph of Austria. Archduke Karl succeeds to the throne. Dr. Artur Zimmermann appointed German Foreign Minister	..	21st
22nd	..	..	..	..	German raider "Seeadler" leaves Germany	..	22nd
23rd	British hospital ship "Braemar Castle" damaged and beached in Ægean Sea (probably mined)	..	Greek Provisional Government (M. Venizelos) at Salonika declare war on Germany and Bulgaria	..	..	..	23rd
24th	..	..	..	M. Stürmer, Russian Premier and Foreign Minister, resigns and is succeeded by M. Trepov as Premier	..	..	24th
26th	..	..	..	..	German raider "Moewe" sails from Kiel on second cruise. (See March 22nd, 1917)	..	26th
29th	..	..	..	Admiral Sir David Beatty appointed Commander-in-Chief Grand Fleet	..	..	29th
30th	Allied forces land at the Piræus	..	..	..	..	..	30th

POLITICAL 1916.

Date.	Events of Outstanding Importance.			Other Political and Economic Events.			Date.
	General.	Diplomatic Correspondence.	Declarations, Treaties and Agreements.	Entente and Allies.	Central Powers.	Neutrals and Miscellaneous.	
1916. DEC. 1st	Allied forces withdrawn from the Piræus after conflicts with Greeks	Greek Government refuse Entente demands. (*See November 19th*)	..	Rumanian Government removed from Bukharest to Jassy Last meeting of War Committee of British Cabinet†	*German commerce-raider "Wolff" leaves Germany**		1916. DEC. 1st
2nd	..	..	Russian Premier (*M. Trepov*) announces that the Allies have acknowledged Russia's right to Constantinople and the Straits. (*See March 12th, 1915*)	..	..	..	2nd
3rd	..	..	British and French Governments conclude agreement (the "Clementel Agreement"): (1) to unite British ships in French service to those already employed; (2) to co-ordinate Allied tonnage; (3) to create Inter-Allied Bureau to centralise charter of neutral shipping	Admiral Sir Henry Jackson, First Sea Lord, resigns	..	..	3rd
4th	..	..	..	Mr. Asquith, British Premier, resigns. (*See 7th*) Admiral Sir John Jellicoe appointed First Sea Lord	..	..	4th
6th	**Bukharest capitulates to the German forces**	..	..	..	..	Massacre of Venizelists in Athens	6th
7th	..	..	Entente Governments announce forthcoming blockade of Greece	**Mr. Lloyd George succeeds Mr. Asquith as British Premier**	..	..	7th
8th	Entente Powers begin blockade of Greece	..	..	Murman Railway (*from Murmansk to Petrograd*) declared open	..	..	8th
9th	..	..	..	**War Cabinet formed in Great Britain**†	..	..	9th
11th	..	..	Allied Note presented to Greece demanding complete demobilisation. (*See 14th*)	Mr. Lloyd George's Coalition Ministry formed in Great Britain Mr. Balfour resigns as First Lord of the Admiralty, and succeeds Viscount Grey as Secretary of State for Foreign Affairs Lord Derby appointed Secretary of State for War Ministry of Labour formed in Great Britain	..	..	11th

* Approximate date. † See note in Part I.

POLITICAL 1916.

Date.	Events of Outstanding Importance.			Other Political and Economic Events.			Date.
	General.	Diplomatic Correspondence.	Declarations, Treaties and Agreements.	Entente and Allies.	Central Powers.	Neutrals and Miscellaneous.	
1916. DEC. 12th	..	Identic Notes presented by Austro-Hungarian, Bulgarian, German and Turkish Governments to United States Ambassadors in their respective countries requesting them to inform the Governments of the Entente Powers that the four Allied Central Powers are ready to negotiate for peace.	..	Reorganisation of French Government. (*M. Briand remains Premier.*) New War Cabinet of five ministers formed. *General Nivelle becomes Commander-in-Chief of French Northern and North-Eastern groups of Armies. (See May 15th, 1917) General Joffre (see December 3rd, 1915) becomes technical Military Adviser to the War Cabinet* Sir Edward Carson appointed First Lord of the Admiralty. M. Pokrovski appointed Russian Minister for Foreign Affairs	..	..	**1916. DEC.** 12th
14th	..	Entente Powers send ultimatum to Greece; withdrawal of entire Greek armies from Thessaly demanded	..	..	Dr. von Körber, Austrian Premier, resigns	..	14th
15th	..	Greek Government accept Allied ultimatum of 14th	British Government recognise the "King of the Arabs" as the "King of the Hejaz."	..	..	..	15th
17th	..	..	..	..	..	Greek Government issue warrant for arrest of M. Venizelos on charge of high treason	17th
18th	..	President Wilson issues Circular Note suggesting negotiations for peace	..	..	..	..	18th
19th	..	..	British Government decide to recognise Government of M. Venizelos	British Government decide to institute National Service. British Government decide to initiate Imperial Conference	..	..	19th
21st	..	..	..	..	Count Heinrich Clam-Martinitz appointed Austrian Premier	..	21st
22nd	..	..	..	Ministries of Food, Pensions and Shipping formed in Great Britain.	Count Czernin succeeds Baron Burian as Austro-Hungarian Foreign Minister.	..	22nd
26th	..	German, Austro-Hungarian and Turkish Governments send reply to American Peace Note of 18th. Immediate meeting of delegates suggested	..	..	..	..	26th

POLITICAL 1916-17.

Date.	EVENTS OF OUTSTANDING IMPORTANCE.			OTHER POLITICAL AND ECONOMIC EVENTS.			Date.
	General.	Diplomatic Correspondence.	Declarations, Treaties and Agreements.	Entente and Allies.	Central Powers.	Neutrals and Miscellaneous.	
1916. DEC. 26th (*contd.*)	Anglo-French Conference meets in London*	..	..	General Joffre created Marshal of France Lord Devonport appointed Food Controller of Great Britain	..	..	**1916. DEC.** 26th (*contd.*)
27th	..	..	British and French Governments conclude agreement regarding temporary administration of Togoland	..	..	..	27th
30th	..	Entente Governments reject German Peace proposals Bulgarian Government reply, accepting President Wilson's Note of December 18th	British and Chinese Governments conclude agreement for employment of Chinese labour in France	..	..	..	30th
31st	..	..	..	Rasputin murdered in Petrograd	..	..	31st
1917. JAN. 3rd	First units of Portuguese Expeditionary Force land in France	..	..	..	..	..	**1917. JAN.** 3rd
5th	Inter-Allied Conference at Rome* (5th/7th)	..	..	..	..	..	5th
6th	..	..	..	"Inter-Allied Chartering Committee" established for chartering of shipping	..	..	6th
8th	..	..	..	M. Trepov, Russian Premier, resigns, and is succeeded by Prince Golitsin	..	..	8th
10th	..	Entente Governments send joint reply to President Wilson's Note. (*See December 18th, 1916.*) Allied war aims outlined Belgian Government reply to President Wilson's Note, placing themselves in hands of Allies	..	..	..	..	10th
11th	..	..	Settlement Treaty signed at Berlin between Germany and Turkey. (*See April 10th, 1918*) Austro-Hungarian and German Governments repudiate responsibility for continuance of war and declare that they will prosecute the war to successful end	..	..	..	11th
15th	..	..	Italy accedes to Franco-British Convention as to naval "prizes"	..	..	..	15th

* For subjects discussed, see Part I.

POLITICAL 1917.

Date.	EVENTS OF OUTSTANDING IMPORTANCE.			OTHER POLITICAL AND ECONOMIC EVENTS.			Date.
	General.	Diplomatic Correspondence.	Declarations, Treaties and Agreements.	Entente and Allies.	Central Powers.	Neutrals and Miscellaneous.	
1917. JAN. 17th	Inter-Allied "Commission de Ravitaillement" meets in Petrograd.* (*See February 20th*)	.. ..	.. ..	General Shuvaev, Russian Minister for War, resigns and is succeeded by General Byelyaev	.. ..	.. ..	1917. JAN. 17th
19th	.. ..	German Government send instructions to German Minister in Mexico (*von Eckhardt*) to negotiate alliance with Mexico and Japan against the United States	.. ..	.. ..	.. ..	.. ..	19th
24th	.. ..	Greek Government make formal apology to the Allies for the occurrences of December 1st, 1916	.. ..	.. ..	.. ..	.. ..	24th
27th	.. ..	.. ..	.. ..	M. Pokrovski, Russian Foreign Minister, resigns	.. ..	.. ..	27th
31st	German Government announce forthcoming "unrestricted" submarine warfare and threaten to sink hospital ships	.. ..	.. ..	.. ..	.. ..	.. ..	31st
FEB. 1st	German "unrestricted submarine warfare" begins. (*See January 31st*)	Norwegian Government issue orders forbidding all foreign submarines to use Norwegian territorial waters. (*See October 13th, 1916*)	.. ..	.. ..	.. ..	.. ..	FEB. 1st
3rd	.. ..	.. ..	United States of America sever diplomatic relations with Germany. (*See April 6th*)	.. ..	.. ..	.. ..	3rd
4th	.. ..	.. ..	.. ..	.. ..	Sa'id Halim, Turkish Grand Vizier, resigns, and is succeeded by Talaat Pasha	.. ..	4th
8th	.. ..	.. ..	.. ..	British military operations against the Senussi come to an end	.. ..	.. ..	8th
13th	.. ..	Scandinavian Governments' joint protest against German submarine warfare published	.. ..	.. ..	.. ..	.. ..	13th
14th	.. ..	.. ..	British Government inform Japanese Government that they will support Japanese claims to German possessions north of the Equator if it is understood that Japan will support similar British claims south of the Equator	.. ..	.. ..	.. ..	14th
15th	.. ..	.. ..	British Government give pledge in House of Commons that the restitution of Alsace-Lorraine is an object of the war	.. ..	.. ..	.. ..	15th

* For subjects discussed, see Part I.

POLITICAL
1917.

Date.	EVENTS OF OUTSTANDING IMPORTANCE.			OTHER POLITICAL AND ECONOMIC EVENTS.			Date.
	General.	Diplomatic Correspondence.	Declarations, Treaties and Agreements.	Entente and Allies.	Central Powers.	Neutrals and Miscellaneous.	
1917. FEB. 17th	..	..	..	Australian War Government formed	..	..	1917. FEB. 17th
20th	Inter-Allied "Commission de Ravitaillement" (see January 17th) at Petrograd dissolves	..	..	..	..	..	20th
23rd	Kut reoccupied by British forces	..	..	..	..	..	23rd
24th	End of Battle of Kut, 1917: Turkish army routed	..	..	..	..	..	24th
25th	s.s. "Laconia" sunk by submarine. (See 27th)	..	..	..	..	..	25th
26th	Anglo-French Conference at Calais on military situation*	..	..	..	..	President Wilson, in address to Congress, asks for power to arm merchant ships	26th
27th		..	..	..	..	President Wilson states that he considers the sinking of "Laconia" the overt act for which he was waiting	27th
28th	..	..	..	..	..	German proposals to Mexico for alliance against the United States published in the American press. (See January 19th)	28th
MARCH 11th	Baghdad taken by British forces	..	..	..	..	..	MARCH 11th
12th	Anglo-French Conference in London on military situation*	..	..	Russian Revolution begins.	..	United States Government announce arming of all merchant vessels in the war zone	12th
13th		..	..	Prince Golitsin, Russian Premier, and General Byelyaev, Minister for War, removed from office by Revolutionary Party	..	..	13th
14th	New Provisional Government proclaimed in Russia†	..	China severs diplomatic relations with Germany. (See August 14th)	..	..	..	14th
15th	Nicholas II, Tsar of Russia, abdicates	..	..	..	..	..	15th
16th	..	..	..	Mutiny breaks out in Russian Baltic Fleet	..	..	16th
17th	..	..	..	M. Briand, French Premier,‡ and General Roques, Minister or War, resign	..	..	17th

* For subjects discussed, see Part I. These conferences initiated the idea of co-ordination of operations under French command.
† For changes of Ministry on this day and the next day, see Part I.   ‡ Also Foreign Minister.

POLITICAL 1917.

Date.	EVENTS OF OUTSTANDING IMPORTANCE.			OTHER POLITICAL AND ECONOMIC EVENTS.			Date.
	General.	Diplomatic Correspondence.	Declarations, Treaties and Agreements.	Entente and Allies.	Central Powers.	Neutrals and Miscellaneous.	
1917. MARCH 20th	.. ..	.. ..	.. ..	First Meeting of Imperial War Conference in London. (*See December 19th*, 1916) M. Ribot appointed French Premier and Foreign Minister M. Painlevé succeeds General Roques as French Minister for War	.. ..	.. ..	1917. MARCH 20th
21st	*British hospital ship "Asturias" sunk by submarine off Start Point*	.. ..	.. ..	.. ..	.. ..	.. ..	21st
22nd	.. ..	.. ..	**Provisional Government of Russia recognised by Great Britain, France, Italy, United States of America, Rumania and Switzerland**	.. ..	*German raider "Moewe" returns to Kiel from second cruise.* (*See November 26th*, 1916)	.. ..	22nd
30th	*British hospital ship "Gloucester Castle" torpedoed between Havre and Southampton*	.. ..	**Russian Provisional Government issue proclamation acknowledging the independence of Poland**	.. ..	.. ..	.. ..	30th
31st	Emperor of Austria makes peace overtures to President of France	.. ..	.. ..	.. ..	.. ..	.. ..	31st
APRIL 5th	.. ..	.. ..	**British Government inform Russian Provisional Government of their adherence to the principle of an independent and united Poland**	.. ..	.. ..	.. ..	APRIL 5th
6th	.. ..	.. ..	**United States of America declare war on Germany.**	.. ..	.. ..	.. ..	6th
7th	.. ..	.. ..	**Cuba and Panama declare war on Germany**	.. ..	.. ..	.. ..	7th
8th	.. ..	.. ..	**Austria-Hungary severs diplomatic relations with United States of America**	.. ..	.. ..	.. ..	8th
9th	.. ..	.. ..	**Russian Provisional Government issue proclamation to Allied Governments declaring in favour of self-determination of peoples and a durable peace**	.. ..	.. ..	.. ..	9th
10th	.. ..	.. ..	**Bulgaria severs diplomatic relations with United States of America**	.. ..	.. ..	.. ..	10th

POLITICAL 1917.

Date.	EVENTS OF OUTSTANDING IMPORTANCE.			OTHER POLITICAL AND ECONOMIC EVENTS.			Date.
	General.	Diplomatic Correspondence.	Declarations, Treaties and Agreements.	Entente and Allies.	Central Powers.	Neutrals and Miscellaneous.	
1917. APRIL 11th	..	..	Brazil severs diplomatic relations with Germany	..	..	..	1917. APRIL 11th
13th	..	..	Bolivia severs diplomatic relations with Germany	..	..	..	13th
17th	Japanese destroyer flotillas join Allied forces in the Mediterranean	..	..	..	..	..	17th
20th	..	..	Turkey severs diplomatic relations with United States of America	..	..	..	20th
25th	..	..	..	Dr. A. Augusta da Costa succeeds Dr. A. J. d'Almeida as Portuguese Premier	..	..	25th
27th	..	..	Guatemala severs diplomatic relations with Germany	..	..	..	27th
28th	..	..	..	..	..	United States Congress pass Bill for raising 500,000 men	28th
29th	..	..	..	General Pétain appointed Chief of French General Staff. (See December 3rd, 1915, and May 15th, 1917)	..	..	29th
MAY 2nd	First United States destroyer flotilla arrives at Queenstown	..	..	..	..	..	MAY 2nd
3rd	..	..	..	..	..	Professor Lambros, Greek Premier, resigns, and is succeeded by M. Zaimis	3rd
5th	..	..	Liberia severs diplomatic relations with Germany	..	..	..	5th
15th	..	..	..	General Pétain succeeds General Nivelle as Commander-in Chief of French Northern and North-eastern Groups of Armies General Foch succeeds General Pétain as Chief of the French General Staff at French Ministry of War. (See April 29th)	..	..	15th
16th	..	..	..	M. Kerenski succeeds General Guchkov as Russian War Minister M. Tereshchenko succeeds M. Milyukov as Russian Foreign Minister	..	..	16th

POLITICAL 1917.

Date.	EVENTS OF OUTSTANDING IMPORTANCE.			OTHER POLITICAL AND ECONOMIC EVENTS.			Date.
	General.	Diplomatic Correspondence.	Declarations, Treaties and Agreements.	Entente and Allies.	Central Powers.	Neutrals and Miscellaneous.	
1917. MAY 17th	.. ..	.. ..	Honduras severs diplomatic relations with Germany	British Admiralty and Ministry of Shipping appoint committee to draw up a plan for convoy of merchant ships	.. ..	.. ..	1917. MAY 17th
18th	.. ..	.. ..	Nicaragua severs diplomatic relations with Germany	**Compulsory Service Act becomes law in United States of America**	.. ..	.. ..	18th
19th	United States Government announce decision to send a division of the United States Army to France at once	.. ..	Russian Provisional Government issue declaration repudiating a separate peace	.. ..	.. ..	.. ..	19th
20th	.. ..	.. ..	.. ..	Serbian Government transferred from Corfu to Salonika	.. ..	.. ..	20th
23rd	.. ..	.. ..	.. ..	.. ..	Count Tisza, Hungarian Premier, resigns	.. ..	23rd
26th	*British hospital ship "Dover Castle" sunk by submarine in the Mediterranean*	.. ..	.. ..	.. ..	.. ..	.. ..	26th
28th	.. ..	.. ..	.. ..	Anglo-French conference in London on Greek situation*	.. ..	.. ..	28th
29th	.. ..	.. ..	.. ..	.. ..	.. ..	Vossuq ed Douleh, Persian Prime Minister and Foreign Minister, resigns	29th
JUNE 3rd	.. ..	.. ..	Italy proclaims Protectorate over an independent Albania	.. ..	.. ..	.. ..	JUNE 3rd
4th	.. ..	.. ..	.. ..	General Brusilov succeeds General Alexeiev as Russian Commander-in-chief. (See August 1st)	.. ..	.. ..	4th
6th	.. ..	.. ..	.. ..	.. ..	.. ..	Ala es Sultaneh again appointed Persian Prime Minister and Foreign Minister	6th
8th	.. ..	.. ..	.. ..	Janina (*Greece*) occupied by Italian forces	.. ..	.. ..	8th
9th	.. ..	Russian Provisional Government refuse German proposal for unlimited armistice	.. ..	.. ..	.. ..	.. ..	9th
11th	.. ..	**Entente Governments present demand to Greek Government for abdication of King Constantine**	Santo Domingo severs diplomatic relations with Germany	.. ..	.. ..	.. ..	11th

* On attitude of King Constantine. This conference decided on his deposition.

POLITICAL
1917.

Date.	EVENTS OF OUTSTANDING IMPORTANCE.			OTHER POLITICAL AND ECONOMIC EVENTS.			Date.
	General.	Diplomatic Correspondence.	Declarations, Treaties and Agreements.	Entente and Allies.	Central Powers.	Neutrals and Miscellaneous.	
1917. JUNE 12th	Corinth and Larissa (*Greece*) occupied by Entente forces	.. ..	.. ..	.. ..	.. ..	King Constantine of Greece abdicates (*in favour of his second son Prince Alexander*)	1917 JUNE 12th
14th	.. ..	.. ..	.. ..	British Admiralty approve scheme for convoying merchant ships	.. ..	.. ..	14th
15th	.. ..	.. ..	.. ..	.. ..	Count Esterhazy appointed Hungarian Premier	.. ..	15th
16th	.. ..	.. ..	Haiti severs diplomatic relations with Germany	.. ..	.. ..	.. ..	16th
17th	Portuguese troops in action on Western Front for the first time. (*See January 3rd*)	.. ..	.. ..	.. ..	.. ..	.. ..	17th
18th	.. ..	.. ..	.. ..	.. ..	Count Clam-Martinitz, Austrian Premier, resigns	.. ..	18th
21st	.. ..	.. ..	.. ..	*Mutiny breaks out in the Russian Black Sea Fleet at Sevastopol*	.. ..	.. ..	21st
23rd	.. ..	.. ..	.. ..	.. ..	Dr. Ernst Ritter von Seidler appointed Austrian Premier	.. ..	23rd
24th	.. ..	.. ..	.. ..	.. ..	.. ..	M. Zaimis, Greek Premier, resigns	24th
25th	First United States troops arrive in France	.. ..	.. ..	.. ..	.. ..	.. ..	25th
26th	.. ..	.. ..	.. ..	.. ..	.. ..	M. Venizelos appointed Greek Premier	26th
27th	.. ..	.. ..	Declaration of war by Greek Provisional Government against Germany and Bulgaria (*see November 23rd, 1916*) becomes effective for the whole of Greece State of war begins between Greece and Austria-Hungary and between Greece and Turkey	M. Venizelos assumes power at Athens	.. ..	.. ..	27th
28th	.. ..	.. ..	.. ..	*General Allenby succeeds General Murray as General Officer Commanding in Egypt*	.. ..	.. ..	28th

POLITICAL
1917.

Date.	EVENTS OF OUTSTANDING IMPORTANCE.			OTHER POLITICAL AND ECONOMIC EVENTS			Date.
	General.	Diplomatic Correspondence.	Declarations, Treaties and Agreements.	Entente and Allies.	Central Powers	Neutrals and Miscellaneous.	
1917. JULY 1st	.. ..	.. ..	.. ..	.. ..	.. ..	Manchu Emperor restored in China. (*See 7th*)	1917. JULY 1st
2nd	.. ..	.. ..	Agreement signed at The Hague for the exchange of combatant and civilian British and German prisoners of war	First regular convoy of merchant ships sails from Hampton Roads, Va. (*See May 17th and June 14th*)	.. ..	.. ..	2nd
6th	.. ..	.. ..	.. ..	Conscription Bill carried in Canadian House of Commons	.. ..	Li-Yuan-Hung, President of China, resigns and is succeeded by Feng-Kuo-Chang	6th
7th	.. ..	.. ..	.. ..	.. ..	.. ..	Manchu Emperor abdicates. (*See 1st*)	7th
14th	.. ..	.. ..	.. ..	.. ..	Dr. Michaelis succeeds Herr von Bethmann-Hollweg as German Imperial Chancellor	.. ..	14th
15th	.. ..	.. ..	.. ..	.. ..	Dr. Artur Zimmermann, German Foreign Minister, resigns	.. ..	15th
17th	.. ..	.. ..	.. ..	Proclamation issued changing name of British Royal House to "Windsor"	.. ..	.. ..	17th
19th	.. ..	.. ..	.. ..	Sir E. Carson, First Lord of the Admiralty, resigns. M. Kerenski succeeds Prince Lvov as Premier of Russia temporarily	Reichstag passes resolution as to German war aims	.. ..	19th
22nd	.. ..	.. ..	Siam declares war on Germany and Austria-Hungary	.. ..	.. ..	.. ..	22nd
25th	Inter-Allied Conference on the Balkan and Russian situation*	.. ..	.. ..	.. ..	.. ..	.. ..	25th
26th		.. ..	.. ..	.. ..	.. ..	.. ..	26th
27th	.. ..	.. ..	French and Italian Governments conclude agreement defining respective zones of influence in Asia Minor. (*See August 18th*)	.. ..	.. ..	.. ..	27th
AUG. 1st	.. ..	The Pope sends Note to belligerent Governments appealing for peace. (*See July 30th, 1915*)	.. ..	General Kornilov succeeds General Brusilov as Russian Commander-in-Chief. (*See June 4th*)	.. ..	.. ..	AUG. 1st
2nd	.. ..	.. ..	.. ..	.. ..	German commerce-raider "Seeadler" wrecked on Mopelia Island (*Pacific*). (*See November 22nd, 1916*)	.. ..	2nd
3rd	.. ..	.. ..	.. ..	.. ..	Mutiny breaks out in German Fleet at Wilhelmshaven	.. ..	3rd

* For subjects discussed, see Part I.

POLITICAL
1917.

Date.	EVENTS OF OUTSTANDING IMPORTANCE.			OTHER POLITICAL AND ECONOMIC EVENTS.			Date.
	General.	Diplomatic Correspondence.	Declarations, Treaties and Agreements.	Entente and Allies.	Central Powers.	Neutrals and Miscellaneous.	
1917. AUG. 4th	.. ..	.. ..	Liberia declares war on Germany. (See May 5th)	Baron de Broqueville, Belgian Minister for War, resigns and succeeds Baron Beyens as Minister for Foreign Affairs Lieutenant-General A. de Ceuninck appointed Belgian Minister for War	.. ..	.. ..	1917. AUG. 4th
5th	.. ..	.. ..	.. ..	.. ..	Herr Richard von Kühlmann appointed German Foreign Minister	.. ..	5th
6th	.. ..	.. ..	.. ..	M. Kerenski definitely appointed Prime Minister of Russia. (See July 19th)	.. ..	.. ..	6th
9th	.. ..	.. ..	.. ..	.. ..	Count Esterhazy, Hungarian Premier, resigns	.. ..	9th
10th	.. ..	.. ..	.. ..	British Labour Party decide to send delegates to a "consultative" conference at Stockholm	.. ..	.. ..	10th
13th	.. ..	.. ..	.. ..	British Government refuse passports for Stockholm Conference	.. ..	.. ..	13th
14th	.. ..	.. ..	China declares war on Germany and Austria Hungary. (See March 14th)	.. ..	.. ..	.. ..	14th
17th	.. ..	.. ..	.. ..	M. Cochin succeeded by M. Métin as French Under-Secretary for Blockade	.. ..	.. ..	17th
18th	.. ..	.. ..	British, French, and Italian Governments conclude provisional arrangement with regard to future policy in Asia Minor	.. ..	.. ..	.. ..	18th
21st	.. ..	.. ..	.. ..	Ministry of Reconstruction formed in Great Britain	Dr. Wekerle appointed Hungarian Premier	.. ..	21st
SEPT. 4th	Anglo-French Conference in London regarding assistance to Italy	.. ..	.. ..	.. ..	.. ..	.. ..	SEPT. 4th
6th	.. ..	.. ..	.. ..	Sir Eric Geddes appointed First Lord of the Admiralty	.. ..	.. ..	6th
8th	.. ..	.. ..	.. ..	General Kornilov heads revolt against Russian Provisional Government and marches on Petrograd	.. ..	.. ..	8th
9th	.. ..	.. ..	.. ..	M. Ribot, French Premier and Foreign Minister, resigns	.. ..	.. ..	9th
10th	.. ..	.. ..	.. ..	M. Kerenski assumes Dictatorship of Russia, and proclaims Kornilov a traitor	.. ..	.. ..	10th

POLITICAL 1917.

Date.	EVENTS OF OUTSTANDING IMPORTANCE.			OTHER POLITICAL AND ECONOMIC EVENTS.			Date.
	General.	Diplomatic Correspondence.	Declarations, Treaties and Agreements.	Entente and Allies.	Central Powers.	Neutrals and Miscellaneous.	
1917. SEPT. 12th	.. ..	.. ..	Central Powers proclaim grant of temporary Constitution to Poland	M. Painlevé succeeds M. Ribot as French Premier M. Ribot reappointed French Foreign Minister	.. ..	.. ..	1917. SEPT. 12th
13th	.. ..	.. ..	.. ..	General Kornilov's revolt collapses	.. ..	.. ..	13th
14th	.. ..	.. ..	.. ..	General Kornilov surrenders to the Russian Provisional Government	.. ..	.. ..	14th
15th	.. ..	.. ..	**Russia proclaimed a Republic by the Provisional Government**	.. ..	.. ..	.. ..	15th
20th	.. ..	.. ..	Council of Trans-Caucasian Peoples proclaim Trans-Caucasia a Federal Republic. (See *May 26th*, 1918)	.. ..	.. ..	.. ..	20th
21st	.. ..	.. ..	Costa Rica severs diplomatic relations with Germany	Count Bernstorff's correspondence *re* German intrigues published	.. ..	.. ..	21st
25th	Anglo-French Conference at Boulogne on the military situation*	.. ..	.. ..	.. ..	.. ..	.. ..	25th
OCT. 5th	.. ..	.. ..	Peru severs diplomatic relations with Germany	.. ..	.. ..	.. ..	OCT. 5th
7th	.. ..	.. ..	Uruguay severs diplomatic relations with Germany	.. ..	.. ..	.. ..	7th
9th	.. ..	.. ..	.. ..	.. ..	.. ..	Hussein Kamel, Sultan of Egypt, dies: succeeded by Ahmed Fuad, his youngest brother	9th
12th	.. ..	.. ..	.. ..	Canadian War Cabinet formed **Compulsory Service Act comes into force in Canada**	.. ..	.. ..	12th
15th	**Polish Regency Council appointed**	.. ..	.. ..	.. ..	.. ..	.. ..	15th
23rd	.. ..	.. ..	.. ..	M. Barthou succeeds M. Ribot as French Foreign Minister	.. ..	.. ..	23rd
24th	*12th Battle of the Isonzo begins*	.. ..	.. ..	.. ..	.. ..	.. ..	24th
25th	.. ..	.. ..	.. ..	Signor Boselli, Italian Premier, resigns	.. ..	.. ..	25th
26th	.. ..	.. ..	Brazil declares war on Germany. (See *April 11th*)	.. ..	.. ..	.. ..	26th

* For subjects discussed see Part I.

POLITICAL
1917.

Date.	EVENTS OF OUTSTANDING IMPORTANCE.			OTHER POLITICAL AND ECONOMIC EVENTS.			Date.
	General.	Diplomatic Correspondence.	Declarations, Treaties and Agreements.	Entente and Allies.	Central Powers.	Neutrals and Miscellaneous.	
1917. OCT. 29th	..	..	..	Signor Orlando succeeds Signor Boselli as Italian Premier	..	..	1917. OCT. 29th
30th	..	..	..	..	Count Hertling succeeds Dr. Michaelis as German Imperial Chancellor. (*See July 14th*)	..	30th
NOV. 1st	..	..	..	Ministry of National Service formed in Great Britain	..	..	NOV. 1st
3rd	*Arrival of French troops in Italy announced*	..	Agreement concluded between British, French and Italian Governments for provision of tonnage for the Allied food programme	..	..	..	3rd
4th	*Arrival of British troops in Italy announced*	..	..	..	..	..	4th
7th	**Allied Conference at Rapallo** (*Italy*)*	..	..	*General Diaz succeeds General Cadorna as Italian Commander-in-Chief*	..	..	7th
8th	**Bolshevik coup d'état in Petrograd. M. Lenin and M. Trotski assume power**	..	..	..	..	..	8th
13th	..	..	..	Kerenski's forces defeated by Bolsheviki near Petrograd	..	..	13th
14th	..	..	..	M. Painlevé, French Premier and War Minister, resigns. M. Barthou, French Foreign Minister, resigns	..	..	14th
15th	..	Japanese Government unable to comply with request of British Government that two Japanese battle cruisers should join the Grand Fleet in the North Sea	British Government give pledge in House of Commons that restitution of Alsace - Lorraine is a War Aim. (*See February 15th*)	M. Kerenski flees from Petrograd	..	..	15th
16th	..	..	..	**M. Clemenceau succeeds M. Painlevé as French Premier and War Minister.** (*See September 12th*) M. Stephen Pichon appointed French Foreign Minister. M. Jonnart succeeds M. Métin as French Minister for Blockade. (*See Part I*)	..	..	16th
18th	..	..	..	Death of General Sir S. Maude at Baghdad	..	..	18th

* Inception of Supreme War Council.

POLITICAL 1917.

Date.	Events of Outstanding Importance.			Other Political and Economic Events.			Date.
	General.	Diplomatic Correspondence.	Declarations, Treaties and Agreements.	Entente and Allies.	Central Powers.	Neutrals and Miscellaneous.	
1917. NOV. 20th	..	..	Ukrainian People's Republic proclaimed	..	..	..	**1917. NOV.** 20th
21st	Armistice pourparlers begun by Russian Bolshevik Government with Central Powers	..	..	..	..	..	21st
23rd	..	..	..	M. Lebrun succeeds M. Jonnart as French Minister for Blockade	..	..	23rd
24th	..	..	..	..	..	Ain ed Douleh succeeds Ala es Sultaneh as Persian Prime Minister	24th
25th	..	..	..	Passage of the Rovuma (East Africa) by Colonel von Lettow-Vorbeck's force	..	..	25th
27th	**Members of Supreme Council appointed** (*General Sir Henry Wilson, General Foch, General Cadorna and General Bliss*) First meeting of Russian and German delegates behind German lines to arrange for armistice	..	..	..	..	..	27th
28th	..	..	..	..	..	Estonia declared independent by the local Diet. (*See January 13th*, 1918)	28th
29th	First meeting of Great Inter-Allied Conference opens in Paris	..	..	..	..	..	29th
30th	Austria-Hungarian Government accept Bolshevik proposals to negotiate for an armistice and peace	..	..	Allied Naval Conference formed in London	..	..	30th
DEC. 1st	**Permanent Inter-Allied Supreme War Council inaugurated**	..	..	..	..	..	**DEC.** 1st
2nd	**Suspension of hostilities between Russian* and German armies begins***	..	..	..	..	..	2nd
3rd	First session of armistice delegates at Brest-Litovsk — Bolshevik Russia and Bulgaria, Germany, Austria-Hungary and Turkey	..	..	Allied Conference in Paris resolve to establish an Allied Maritime Transport Council	..	..	3rd

* See note in Part I.

POLITICAL
1917.

Date.	EVENTS OF OUTSTANDING IMPORTANCE.			OTHER POLITICAL AND ECONOMIC EVENTS.			Date.
	General.	Diplomatic Correspondence.	Declarations, Treaties and Agreements.	Entente and Allies.	Central Powers.	Neutrals and Miscellaneous.	
1917. DEC. 6th	Hostilities between Rumania and Central Powers suspended Negotiations at Brest-Litovsk suspended	.. ..	Truce arranged between Russia and Central Powers from 7th to 17th Finland declares independence	.. ..	.. ..	.. ..	1917. DEC. 6th
7th	Truce between Russia and Central Powers comes into operation officially	.. ..	United States of America declare war on Austria-Hungary Ecuador severs diplomatic relations with Germany	.. ..	.. ..	.. ..	7th
9th	Jerusalem surrenders to British forces	.. ..	Armistice ("Truce of Focsani") signed between Rumania and Central Powers	.. ..	.. ..	.. ..	9th
10th	Hostilities between Rumania and the Central Powers cease	.. ..	Panama declares war on Austria-Hungary	Dr. S. Cardosa da Paes succeeds Dr. A. A. da Costa as Portuguese Prime Minister	.. ..	.. ..	10th
11th	General Allenby makes formal entry into Jerusalem	.. ..	.. ..	Russian Constituent Assembly meet in Petrograd. (See 13th) Revolution in Portugal: Dr. Machado Guimarães, Portuguese President, deposed	.. ..	.. ..	11th
13th	Armistice negotiations at Brest-Litovsk resumed	.. ..	.. ..	Constituent Assembly (see 11th) dispersed by Bolsheviki	.. ..	.. ..	13th
15th	.. ..	.. ..	Armistice signed at Brest-Litovsk between Russian Bolshevik Government and Central Powers to begin noon, December 17th, and terminate January 14th, 1918	.. ..	.. ..	.. ..	15th
16th	.. ..	.. ..	Cuba declares war on Austria-Hungary	.. ..	.. ..	.. ..	16th
17th	.. ..	.. ..	British Government give the King of the Hejaz written assurance of the future independence of the Arab people	.. ..	.. ..	.. ..	17th
22nd	Peace negotiations between Russian Bolshevik Government and Bulgaria, Central Powers and Turkey opened at Brest-Litovsk	.. ..	Secret Convention signed at Brest-Litovsk between Germany and Russian Bolshevik Government concerning Poland	General Guillaumat succeeds General Sarrail as Commander-in-Chief at Salonika. (See January 16th, 1916)	.. ..	.. ..	22nd

POLITICAL 1917-18.

Date.	EVENTS OF OUTSTANDING IMPORTANCE.			OTHER POLITICAL AND ECONOMIC EVENTS.			Date.
	General.	Diplomatic Correspondence.	Declarations, Treaties and Agreements.	Entente and Allies.	Central Powers.	Neutrals and Miscellaneous.	
1917. DEC. 23rd	.. ..	.. ..	Independent Moldavian Republic (*Bessarabia*) proclaimed at Kishinev. (*See April 9th*, 1918)	.. ..	.. ..	.. ..	**1917. DEC.** 23rd
26th 27th	.. ..	.. ..	.. ..	Admiral Sir Rosslyn Wemyss succeeds Admiral Sir John Jellicoe as First Sea Lord	.. ..	.. ..	26th 27th
28th	.. ..	.. ..	.. ..	French Foreign Minister in speech outlines French war aims	.. ..	.. ..	28th
				Dr. A. da Silva Paes appointed Acting President of Portugal			
1918. JAN. 1st	.. ..	.. ..	.. ..	M. Hyams succeeds Baron de Broqueville as Belgian Minister for Foreign Affairs	.. ..	.. ..	**1918. JAN.** 1st
2nd	.. ..	.. ..	.. ..	Air Ministry formed in Great Britain	.. ..	.. ..	2nd
3rd	Ukraine delegation reaches Brest-Litovsk	.. ..	.. ..	.. ..	.. ..	.. ..	3rd
4th	*British hospital ship "Rewa" sunk by submarine in Bristol Channel*	British Government in message to the King of the Hejaz declare intentions with regard to future status of Palestine Allied request for surrender of Dutch ships in Allied ports formulated. (*See March 7th*)	Russian Bolshevik Government and French and Swedish Governments recognise the independence of Finland. (*See December 6th*, 1917)	.. ..	.. ..	.. ..	4th
5th	Negotiations suspended on Russian front: Bolshevik demand made for meetings to be held at Stockholm	.. ..	.. ..	British Premier (Mr. Lloyd George) in speech to trade union delegates outlines British war aims. (*See December 28th*, 1917)	.. ..	.. ..	5th
8th	Russian Bolshevik Government withdraw demand of 5th and resume negotiations at Brest-Litovsk **President Wilson delivers message to Congress laying down the "Fourteen Points"**	.. ..	.. ..		.. ..	.. ..	8th
10th	.. ..	British Government assure Russian Bolshevik Government of their support in the creation of an independent Poland	Danish and Norwegian Governments recognise the independence of Finland	.. ..	.. ..	.. ..	10th

POLITICAL 1918.

Date.	EVENTS OF OUTSTANDING IMPORTANCE.			OTHER POLITICAL AND ECONOMIC EVENTS.			Date.
	General.	Diplomatic Correspondence.	Declarations, Treaties and Agreements.	Entente and Allies.	Central Powers.	Neutrals and Miscellaneous.	
1918. JAN. 12th	.. ..	.. ..	Latvia declares independence	.. ..	.. ..	.. ..	1918. JAN. 12th
13th	.. ..	.. ..	Estonian Government declare Independence. (*See November 28th*, 1917)	.. ..	.. ..	.. ..	13th
18th	.. ..	.. ..	.. ..	Russian Constituent Assembly again meet in Petrograd. (*See December 13th*, 1917)	.. ..	.. ..	18th
19th	.. ..	.. ..	.. ..	Russian Constituent Assembly again forcibly dissolved by Bolsheviki	.. ..	Mustaufi ul Mamalek succeeds Ain ed Douleh as Persian Prime Minister Mushaver ul Mamalek succeeds Ala es Sultaneh as Persian Foreign Minister	19th
22nd	Russian Bolshevik Government accuse Central Powers of falsification of reports of proceedings	.. ..	.. ..	.. ..	.. ..	.. ..	22nd
23rd	Negotiations between Russian Bolshevik Government and Central Powers again suspended	.. ..	.. ..	.. ..	.. ..	.. ..	23rd
24th	Count Hertling and Count Czernin (*German Imperial Chancellor and Austrian Foreign Minister*) make public replies to statements of President Wilson and Mr. Lloyd George on War Aims. (*See 5th and 8th*)	.. ..	.. ..	.. ..	.. ..	.. ..	24th
27th	.. ..	.. ..	.. ..	General Dunsterville's Mission leaves Baghdad for North-West Persia	.. ..	.. ..	27th
28th	.. ..	.. ..	Russian Bolshevik Government sever diplomatic relations with Rumania	.. ..	.. ..	.. ..	28th
30th	Negotiations between Russian Bolshevik Government and Central Powers again resumed	.. ..	.. ..	.. ..	.. ..	.. ..	30th
FEB. 1st	.. ..	.. ..	Central Powers recognise The Ukraine Republic. (*See November 20th*, 1917)	Extension of British East Persia cordon into Khorasan begins	.. ..	.. ..	FEB. 1st

POLITICAL
1918.

Date.	Events of Outstanding Importance.			Other Political and Economic Events.			Date.
	General.	Diplomatic Correspondence.	Declarations, Treaties and Agreements.	Entente and Allies.	Central Powers.	Neutrals and Miscellaneous.	
1918. FEB. 3rd	..	..	..	British Government announce enlargement of powers of Supreme War Council at Versailles	..	..	1918. FEB. 3rd
4th	..	..	British Government make declaration to King of the Hejaz reaffirming their pledges as to freeing the Arab peoples	General Alexeiev with Don Cossacks moves towards Moscow against the Bolshevik forces. (See 13th)	..	..	4th
6th	..	German Government send ultimatum to Rumania demanding peace negotiations within four days	..	M. Bratianu, Rumanian Premier, resigns	..	..	6th
9th	..	..	Peace signed at Brest-Litovsk between Bulgaria, Central Powers and Turkey and The Ukraine Rada, also supplementary Treaty between Central Powers and The Ukraine	General Averescu, as Premier and Foreign Minister, forms new Rumanian Cabinet	..	..	9th
10th	..	..	M. Trotski announces that state of war between Russia and Central Powers, Bulgaria and Turkey is ended, but that Russia will not sign formal Peace Treaty	..	..	..	10th
11th	President Wilson delivers message to Congress laying down four additional points. (See January 8th and October 6th)	..	..	..	..	..	11th
13th	..	..	..	General Alexeiev (see 4th) defeated by Bolsheviki; General Kaledin commits suicide	..	..	13th
15th	..	..	..	Representatives of Allied Governments arrange establishment of the "Allied Maritime Transport Council"	..	..	15th
17th	..	..	..	General Dunsterville's Mission arrives at Enzeli (North-West Persia)	..	..	17th

POLITICAL 1918.

Date.	EVENTS OF OUTSTANDING IMPORTANCE.			OTHER POLITICAL AND ECONOMIC EVENTS.			Date.
	General.	Diplomatic Correspondence.	Declarations, Treaties and Agreements.	Entente and Allies.	Central Powers.	Neutrals and Miscellaneous.	
1918. FEB. 18th	Armistice terminates on Russian front: Germany resumes hostilities *Dvinsk taken by German forces*	..	..	..	..	..	1918. FEB. 18th
19th	..	..	Russian Bolshevik Government notify willingness to sign Peace Treaty with Germany	..	..	..	19th
20th	..	British Foreign Minister (*Mr. Balfour*) informs Polish National Committee that Great Britain does not accept the Treaty between The Ukraine and Central Powers. (*See 9th*)	..	..	..	..	20th
21st	..	..	..	Ministry of Information formed in Great Britain	..	..	21st
23rd	..	..	..	Inter-Allied Labour and Socialist Conference in London pass resolution as to War Aims	..	..	23rd
24th	*Dorpat (Estonia) taken by German forces*	..	..	German commerce-raider "*Wolff*" returns to Germany. (*See December 1st, 1916*)	..	..	24th
25th	Peace negotiations begun at Bukharest *Pernau, Reval and Pskoff taken by German forces*	British Government inform M. Tonisson that they are prepared provisionally to recognise independence of Estonia until the future status of Estonia is settled by the Peace Congress	Military Convention signed at Dobruisk between Germany and Poland	..	..	..	25th
26th	*British hospital ship "Glenart Castle" sunk by submarine in Bristol Channel.*	..	..	..	..	..	26th
28th	Negotiations again resumed between Russian Bolshevik Government and Central Powers: hostilities nominally cease	..	..	..	..	..	28th
MARCH 1st	..	..	Treaty of Peace and Amity signed between Finnish Social Republic of Workmen and the Russian Federal Soviet Republic*	..	..	..	MARCH 1st

* From this date the Finnish Civil War may be said to start. (*See May 7th.*)

POLITICAL 1918.

Date.	EVENTS OF OUTSTANDING IMPORTANCE.			OTHER POLITICAL AND ECONOMIC EVENTS.			Date.
	General.	Diplomatic Correspondence.	Declarations, Treaties and Agreements.	Entente and Allies.	Central Powers.	Neutrals and Miscellaneous.	
1918. MARCH 2nd	Kiev (*The Ukraine*) captured by German forces (*1st/3rd*)	..	..	..	German force landed in the Aaland Islands (*at request of Finnish Government*)	..	1918. MARCH 2nd
3rd	..	..	Peace signed between Bolshevik Russia and Central Powers, Bulgaria and Turkey at Brest-Litovsk, together with supplementary Treaties by the Signatories	Meshed (*East Persia*) occupied by troops of the British East Persia Cordon*	German Government officially notify Swedish Government of occupation of the Aaland Islands. (*See 2nd*)	..	3rd
5th	..	..	Preliminary Treaty of Peace between Rumania and Central Powers, Bulgaria and Turkey signed at Buftea. (*See May 7th*)	..	..	..	5th
7th	..	Final Allied Note presented to The Netherlands Government *re* surrender of Dutch ships in Allied ports (*See January 4th*)	Peace signed at Berlin between Germany and Finland	..	..	..	7th
8th	..	..	..	..	..	M. Chichérin appointed Russian Foreign Minister, and M. Trotski appointed Minister for War	8th
9th	..	..	Treaty of Peace signed between Rumania and Bolshevik Russia	..	..	..	9th
10th	British hospital ship "Guildford Castle" torpedoed in Bristol Channel	..	..	..	..	..	10th
11th	..	..	..	First meeting of "Allied Maritime Transport Council."	..	..	11th
12th	Erzerum retaken by Turkish forces. (*See February 16th, 1916*)	..	..	General Averescu, Rumanian Premier and Foreign Minister, resigns	..	..	12th
13th	*Odessa occupied by German forces*	..	..	..	..	..	13th
14th	..	..	..	..	..	Congress of Soviets meet at Moscow and decide to ratify treaty of peace with Central Powers. (*See 3rd*)	14th

* Approximate date.

POLITICAL
1918.

Date.	Events of Outstanding Importance.			Other Political and Economic Events.			Date.
	General.	Diplomatic Correspondence.	Declarations, Treaties and Agreements	Entente and Allies.	Central Powers.	Neutrals and Miscellaneous.	
1918. MARCH 15th	.. ..	.. ..	Germany proclaims protectorate over an independent Kurland	.. ..	.. ..	.. ..	1918. MARCH 15th
17th	.. ..	.. ..	.. ..	.. ..	Nicolaiev (South Russia) taken by German forces	.. ..	17th
18th	.. ..	Entente Governments issue Note refusing to recognise Russo-German Peace Treaty. Dutch Government accept with reservations the Allied terms for use of Dutch shipping in United States and Entente ports. (See 7th and 21st)	.. ..	.. ..	.. ..	.. ..	18th
20th	.. ..	.. ..	.. ..	Allied Blockade Committee formed	.. ..	.. ..	20th
21st	Great German Offensive in France begins	.. ..	.. ..	M. Marghilonian appointed Rumanian Premier. M. Constantine Arian appointed Rumanian Foreign Minister. Dutch ships in British ports requisitioned by British Government, and Dutch ships in United States ports requisitioned by United States Government	.. ..	.. ..	21st
23rd	.. ..	.. ..	.. ..	Paris first shelled by long-range gun (from Crépy-en-Valois, 75 miles distant). (See August 15th)	.. ..	.. ..	23rd
26th	.. ..	.. ..	Doullens Agreement concluded. Decision taken to appoint General Foch to co-ordinate efforts of British and French Armies. (See April 14th)	.. ..	.. ..	.. ..	26th
APRIL 1st	.. ..	.. ..	.. ..	Enzeli (Persia) evacuated by Russian forces*	German Expeditionary Force to Finland leaves Danzig	.. ..	APRIL 1st
3rd	.. ..	.. ..	.. ..	.. ..	German Expeditionary Force landed in South Finland	.. ..	3rd
5th	Japanese and British marines land at Vladivostok	.. ..	.. ..	.. ..	.. ..	.. ..	5th
8th	.. ..	.. ..	.. ..	.. ..	Kharkov (South Russia) taken by German forces	.. ..	8th

* See note in Part II (Military).

POLITICAL
1918.

Date.	EVENTS OF OUTSTANDING IMPORTANCE.			OTHER POLITICAL AND ECONOMIC EVENTS.			Date
	General.	Diplomatic Correspondence.	Declarations, Treaties and Agreements.	Entente and Allies.	Central Powers.	Neutrals and Miscellaneous.	
1918. APRIL 9th	*Battles of the Lys begin*	..	**National Council of the Moldavian Republic** (*Bessarabia*) **pass Act of Union with Rumania, with stipulation for local autonomy**	..	Count Mirbach appointed German Ambassador at Moscow	..	1918. APRIL 9th
10th	..	..	**Agreement reached between Italy and the Yugo-Slavs** Settlement Treaty between Germany and Turkey ratified at Berlin. (*See January 11th, 1917*)	**Third Military Service Act passed in British Parliament.** Military age limit raised to 50 and conscription extended to Ireland	..	..	10th
11th	Emperor of Austria's letter published. (*See March 31st, 1917*)	..	..	..	..	..	11th
13th	..	Finnish Government announce that all German troops landed in Finland had been despatched at their request	United Diets of Baltic Provinces adopt resolution to form themselves into a separate State within the German Empire	..	Helsingfors captured by German forces	..	13th
14th	General Foch appointed Commander-in-Chief of Allied Armies in France*	..	..	..	..	..	14th
15th	*Batum (Georgia) occupied by Turkish forces*	..	..	..	Count Czernin, Austro-Hungarian Foreign Minister, resigns	..	15th
16th	..	..	..	..	..	Ukraine Government issue protest against union of Bessarabia and Rumania. (*See 9th and 23rd*)	16th
17th	..	..	..	..	Baron Burian appointed Austro-Hungarian Foreign Minister Dr. Wekerle, Hungarian Premier, resigns	..	17th
18th	..	..	..	Third Military Service Act comes into operation in Great Britain	..	..	18th
19th	German forces enter the Crimea	..	..	..	..	..	19th
20th	..	..	..	Lord Milner succeeds Lord Derby as Secretary of State for War	..	..	20th
21st	..	..	..	Count Motono, Japanese Minister for Foreign Affairs, resigns	..	..	21st

* The Belgian forces were not placed under the command of General Foch.

POLITICAL
1918.

Date.	EVENTS OF OUTSTANDING IMPORTANCE.			OTHER POLITICAL AND ECONOMIC EVENTS.			Date.
	General.	Diplomatic Correspondence.	Declarations, Treaties and Agreements.	Entente and Allies.	Central Powers.	Neutrals and Miscellaneous.	
1918. APRIL 22nd	..	..	..	Baron Goto appointed Japanese Minister for Foreign Affairs	..	The Trans-Caucasian Council decide to declare independence (*night 22nd/23rd*)	1918. APRIL 22nd
23rd	..	..	Guatemala declares war on Germany	..	..	Russian Bolshevik Government issue protest against union of Bessarabia and Rumania. (*See 9th*)	23rd
27th	*Kars (Georgia) occupied by Turkish forces* First contingent of Italian troops arrive on French front*	..	..	..	Dr. Wekerle again appointed Hungarian Prime Minister	..	27th
29th	**German Government establish a military dictatorship in The Ukraine.** General Skoropadski proclaimed Hetman	..	..	..	..	..	29th
30th	..	..	..	..	Viborg (*Finland*) captured by German and Finnish force	..	30th
MAY 1st	Sevastopol occupied by German forces *Part of Russian Black Sea Fleet seized by the Germans*	..	..	..	..	..	MAY 1st
2nd	..	..	Agreement concluded as to export of sand and gravel from The Netherlands for German use	..	..	..	2nd
3rd	..	..	..	..	..	Samsam es Sultaneh succeeds Mustaufi ul Mamalek as Persian Prime Minister	3rd
4th	..	..	Armistice signed at Korenevo between Russia and The Ukraine (*German-Ukrainian Command*). (*See June 12th*)	..	..	..	4th
6th	..	..	..	..	..	Turco-German delegates arrive at Batum to negotiate peace with the Georgians and Armenians. (*See June 8th*)	6th

* Approximate date.

POLITICAL 1918.

Date.	EVENTS OF OUTSTANDING IMPORTANCE.			OTHER POLITICAL AND ECONOMIC EVENTS.			Date.
	General	Diplomatic Correspondence.	Declarations, Treaties and Agreements.	Entente and Allies.	Central Powers.	Neutrals and Miscellaneous.	
1918. MAY 7th	Frederickshamn (*South Finland*) captured by Finnish White Guards. **End of Finnish Civil War**	..	Final Treaty of Peace signed between Rumania and Bulgaria and Central Powers and Turkey, together with various supplementary Treaties between the separate contracting parties. (*See March 5th*)	..	..	..	1918. MAY 7th
8th	..	..	Nicaragua declares war on Germany and Austria-Hungary	..	Rostov (*South Russia*) *captured by German forces*	..	8th
9th	..	..	..	Joint Trade Committee of Entente Powers formed in Holland Dr. da Silva Paes elected Portuguese President	..	M. Ustemovich proclaimed President of The Ukraine. (*General Skoropadski remains Hetman*)	9th
11th	..	..	Peace signed in Berlin between Finland and Turkey	..	..	..	11th
12th	..	..	**Military Treaty ("*Waffenbund*") signed between Germany and Austria=Hungary**	..	..	..	12th
15th	..	..	Agreement between Entente Powers, Japan and China against German penetration in Far East announced	Dr. S. B. C. da Paes, Portuguese Premier, resigns	..	..	15th
16th	..	..	**Agreement signed at Pekin between China and Japan for military co-operation against German and Bolshevik aggression**	Senhor J. T. de Sousa Barboza appointed Portuguese Secretary of the Interior*	..	..	16th
17th	..	..	..	Sinn Fein leaders arrested in Ireland and interned	..	..	17th
18th	..	..	..	..	*Alexandropol* (*Georgia*) *occupied by Turkish forces*	..	18th
19th	..	..	Agreement signed between China and Japan for naval co-operation	*German air raid on British camps and hospitals at Etaples*	..	..	19th
23rd	..	..	Costa Rica declares war on Germany	..	..	..	23rd

* See footnote in Part I.

POLITICAL
1918.

149

Date.	EVENTS OF OUTSTANDING IMPORTANCE.			OTHER POLITICAL AND ECONOMIC EVENTS.			Date.
	General.	Diplomatic Correspondence.	Declarations, Treaties and Agreements.	Entente and Allies.	Central Powers.	Neutrals and Miscellaneous.	
1918. **MAY** 24th	.. ..	.. ..	.. ..	General Poole lands at Murmansk to organise the North Russia Expeditionary Force	.. ..	.. ..	**1918.** **MAY** 24th
25th	.. ..	.. ..	.. ..	British Government publish account of Irish-German plots	.. ..	.. ..	25th
26th	.. ..	.. ..	Trans-Caucasian Federal Government (see September 20th, 1917) dissolved Georgia declares independence and forms a national government Tatar National Council proclaim establishment of a "Republic of Azerbaijan" Armenian National Council assume charge of Armenian affairs	.. ..	.. ..	.. ..	26th
29th	.. ..	.. ..	Peace Treaty signed at Vienna between Austria-Hungary and Finland	.. ..	.. ..	.. ..	29th
31st	.. ..	.. ..	.. ..	M. G. Cooreman succeeds Baron de Broqueville as Belgian Prime Minister	.. ..	Samsam es Sultaneh, Persian Prime Minister, resigns	31st
JUNE 3rd	.. ..	.. ..	British, French, and Italian Governments make declarations supporting national aspirations of Poles, Czecho-Slovaks, and Yugo-Slavs	.. ..	.. ..	.. ..	**JUNE** 3rd
4th	.. ..	.. ..	The Don Cossacks declare independence	British marines landed at Pechenga (North Russia)	.. ..	.. ..	4th
6th	*Dutch hospital ship "Koningen Regentes" sunk by mine or torpedo*	.. ..	.. ..	.. ..	.. ..	.. ..	6th
7th	.. ..	.. ..	.. ..	*British force landed at Kem (North Russia). (See May 24th)* *Omsk (Siberia) occupied by Czecho-Slovak forces*	.. ..	.. ..	7th
8th	Russian Bolshevik Government order Entente forces in North Russia to leave the country. (See 4th, and May 24th)	.. ..	Georgian Government sign Peace Treaty with Germany Georgian Government and Armenian National Council sign Peace Treaties with Turkey. (See May 6th and 26th)	.. ..	German Expeditionary Force to the Caucasus landed at Poti (Georgia)	.. ..	8th

POLITICAL 1918.

Date.	Events of Outstanding Importance.			Other Political and Economic Events.			Date.
	General.	Diplomatic Correspondence.	Declarations, Treaties and Agreements.	Entente and Allies.	Central Powers.	Neutrals and Miscellaneous.	
1918. JUNE 9th	..	..	..	..	..	First sitting of Anglo-German Conference at The Hague on prisoners of war	**1918. JUNE** 9th
12th	..	..	Armistice concluded at Kiev between whole State of The Ukraine and Russian Bolshevik Republic. (See May 4th)	..	Tiflis (Georgia) occupied by a German force	..	12th
14th	..	..	..	..	Tabriz (North Persia) again occupied by Turkish forces. (See January 30th, 1915)	..	14th
15th	..	..	..	..	..	..	15th
18th	..	..	..	Russian battleship "Svobodnaya Rossiya" destroyed in Black Sea to avoid surrender to the Germans	M. Radoslavov, Bulgarian Premier, resigns. M. Malinov appointed Premier and Foreign Minister	..	18th
20th	..	..	..	..	..	Samsam es Sultaneh reappointed Persian Prime Minister	20th
21st	..	..	..	..	Dr. Ernst Ritter von Seidler, Austrian Premier, resigns	..	21st
23rd	..	..	..	British Expeditionary Forces "Syren" and "Elope" join the North Russia Expeditionary Force at Murmansk. (See May 24th)	..	..	23rd
27th	British hospital ship "Llandovery Castle" torpedoed and sunk off Irish coast	..	..	..	..	..	27th
29th	..	..	United States Government announce their view that all branches of the Slav races should be completely freed from German and Austrian rule	Murman Railway seized by Allied forces as far as Soroki	..	..	29th
30th	First contingent of United States troops arrive in Italy	..	Treaty signed between the Czecho-Slovaks and Italy; Italy recognises Czecho-Slovak Council and their jurisdiction over nationals. Murman Soviet (Sovdep) decide to support the Entente against the Bolshevik Government. (See 8th)		..	..	30th

POLITICAL 1918.

Date.	EVENTS OF OUTSTANDING IMPORTANCE.			OTHER POLITICAL AND ECONOMIC EVENTS.			Date.
	General.	Diplomatic Correspondence.	Declarations, Treaties and Agreements.	Entente and Allies.	Central Powers.	Neutrals and Miscellaneous.	
1918. JULY 3rd	..	..	..	..	Death of Sultan Mohammed V of Turkey. Mohammed VI succeeds to the throne	..	1918. JULY 3rd
4th	..	..	Siberian Council declare independence	..	..	..	4th
6th	..	..	Declaration of Siberian independence cancelled	..	German Ambassador at Moscow (*Count Mirbach*) murdered	..	6th
7th	..	..	**Agreement signed between France, Great Britain, United States of America and Murman Sovdep concerning Allied expedition to Murman coast**	..	..	..	7th
9th	..	..	..	..	Admiral von Hintze succeeds Herr von Kühlmann as German Foreign Minister	..	9th
10th	..	..	..	New Government formed at Vladivostok under General Horvat. (*See August 24th*)	..	..	10th
12th	..	..	Haiti declares war on Germany	..	..	..	12th
13th	..	..	..	*Irkutsk (Siberia) occupied by Czecho-Slovak forces*	..	..	13th
14th	..	..	..	*Kazan (East Russia) taken by Czecho-Slovak forces*	..	..	14th
15th	..	British Government protest against sand and gravel agreement between Germany and The Netherlands	..	..	..	..	15th
16th	..	..	..	..	*Field-Marshal Conrad von Hötzendorf* (*Commander-in-Chief Austro-Hungarian Armies*) *relieved of his command*	Ex-Tsar of Russia (*Nicholas II*), ex-Tsaritsa and family murdered at Ekaterinburg	16th
18th	..	..	..	Sir L. Worthington-Evans succeeds Lord Robert Cecil as British Minister for Blockade	..	..	18th
19th	..	..	Honduras declares war on Germany	..	..	..	19th
26th	*Coup d'état at Baku. Bolshevik Government replaced by Central Caspian Dictatorship*	British Government declare to M. Petrov that they have no intention of infringing the territorial integrity of Russia	..	*Troops of French Expeditionary Force join the North Russia Expeditionary Force at Murmansk*	..	..	26th

POLITICAL 1918.

Date.	EVENTS OF OUTSTANDING IMPORTANCE.			OTHER POLITICAL AND ECONOMIC EVENTS.			Date.
	General.	Diplomatic Correspondence.	Declarations, Treaties and Agreements.	Entente and Allies.	Central Powers.	Neutrals and Miscellaneous.	
1918. JULY 30th	..	..	..	..	Field-Marshal von Eichhorn (Commanding German Army in The Ukraine) assassinated in Kiev	..	1918. JULY 30th
AUG. 1st	*Entente Expeditionary Force attack and capture the defences of Archangel*	..	..	..	..	..	AUG. 1st
2nd	**Pro-Entente Revolution in Archangel** **Entente forces enter Archangel**			Japanese Government decide to land troops at Vladivostok. (*See* 11*th*)	..	..	2nd
3rd	*British ambulance transport " Warilda" sunk by submarine*	..	..	*British troops land at Vladivostok*	..	Samsam es Sultaneh, Persian Prime Minister, resigns	3rd
4th	*British force arrives at Baku* Bolshevik Committee at Enzeli arrested by British military authorities. (*See July 26th*)	..	..	..	..	..	4th
6th	..	..	British Government issue Declaration to Russian peoples stating that they have no intention of interfering in Russian politics	..	..	..	6th
7th	..	..	..	..	..	Vossuq ed Douleh appointed Persian Prime Minister	7th
9th	*Battle of Amiens begins*	British Government inform Finnish Government that they are in no way hostile to Finnish aspirations on the Murman Coast and in Karelia	..	..	..	..	8th
10th	..	..	..	..	..	Mushaver ul Mamalek, Persian Foreign Minister, resigns	10th
11th	..	..	..	*First Japanese contingents arrive at Vladivostok.* (*See 2nd*)	..	Mushaver ul Mamalek reappointed Persian Foreign Minister	11th
13th	..	..	**The Czecho-Slovaks declare war on Germany** **British Government recognise the Czecho-Slovaks as an allied nation**	..	Vice-Admiral von Behncke succeeds Admiral von Capelle as German Minister of Marine	..	13th
15th	..	..	..	*Last bombardment of Paris by German long-range gun.* (*See March 23rd*)		..	15th
17th	..	..	..	..	..	Slovene National Council meet at Ljubljara (*Laibach*)	17th

POLITICAL 1918.

Date.	EVENTS OF OUTSTANDING IMPORTANCE.			OTHER POLITICAL AND ECONOMIC EVENTS.			Date.
	General.	Diplomatic Correspondence.	Declarations, Treaties, and Agreements.	Entente and Allies.	Central Powers.	Neutrals and Miscellaneous.	
1918. AUG. 24th	Battle of Dukhovskaya (Eastern Siberia) (23rd/24th)	.. ..	.. ..	Coup d'état by General Horvat at Vladivostok. (See July 10th)	.. ..	.. ..	1918. AUG. 24th
27th	.. ..	.. ..	German and Russian Bolshevik Governments conclude complementary Treaty of Peace. (See March 3rd)	Krasnovodsk (Caspian) occupied by British force	.. ..	.. ..	27th
31st	Captain Cromie, R.N., British Naval Attaché murdered by Bolsheviki in British Embassy at Petrograd	.. ..	.. ..	.. ..	.. ..	.. ..	31st
SEPT. 2nd	.. ..	.. ..	.. ..	Italian contingent land at Murmansk to join Allied Expeditionary Force	.. ..	.. ..	SEPT. 2nd
3rd	.. ..	.. ..	United States Government recognise the Czecho-Slovaks as possessing a de facto Government	.. ..	.. ..	.. ..	3rd
4th	.. ..	.. ..	.. ..	United States contingent land at Murmansk to join Allied Expeditionary Force	.. ..	Hsu-Shih-Chang elected President of China	4th
14th 15th	British force evacuates Baku	.. ..	.. ..	.. ..	.. ..	.. ..	14th 15th
	Battle of the Dobropolje begins (15th/16th)	Austrian Government send Note to United States Government suggesting an "unofficial" peace conference **German Government make definite peace offer to Belgium**					
16th	.. ..	President Wilson sends reply to Austrian Peace Note rejecting suggestion for a peace conference	.. ..	.. ..	.. ..	.. ..	16th
19th	Battles of Megiddo (Palestine) begin	.. ..	.. ..	.. ..	.. ..	.. ..	19th
25th	.. ..	.. ..	Yugo-Slav State recognised as independent by Italy	.. ..	.. ..	.. ..	25th
27th	.. ..	**Bulgarian Government ask Entente Powers for an armistice**	.. ..	.. ..	.. ..	.. ..	27th
28th				Takashi Hara succeeds Count Terauchi as Japanese Prime Minister Count Yasuya Uchida succeeds Baron Goto as Japanese Foreign Minister Lieutenant-General Giichi Tanaka succeeds Lieutenant-General Kenichi Oshima as Japanese Minister for War	.. ..	.. ..	28th
30th*							30th*

* Continued next page.

POLITICAL 1918.

Date.	Events of Outstanding Importance.			Other Political and Economic Events.			Date.
	General.	Diplomatic Correspondence.	Declarations, Treaties and Agreements.	Entente and Allies.	Central Powers.	Neutrals and Miscellaneous.	
1918. SEPT. 30th (contd.)	Hostilities between Bulgaria and Entente Powers cease at 12 noon	..	Armistice between Bulgaria and Entente Powers signed	*Canadian contingent land at Archangel to join Allied Expeditionary Force*	Count Hertling and all German Secretaries of State resign	..	1918. SEPT 30th (contd.)
OCT 1st	..	..	..	*Damascus taken by British and Arab forces.* *Berat (Albania) retaken by Italian forces. (See August 26th)*	..	..	OCT. 1st
4th	..	German and Austro-Hungarian Governments send Notes to President Wilson proposing an armistice	..	*General Ironside takes over command of Allied forces at Archangel*	King Ferdinand of Bulgaria abdicates in favour of his son Prince Boris. Prince Max of Baden appointed German Imperial Chancellor and succeeds Admiral von Hintze as Foreign Minister	..	4th
5th	..	..	..	..	..	Yugo-Slav delegates meet at Agram and decide on the formation of a United National Council. (See 17th)	5th
6th	..	..	..	*Sidon (Syria) occupied by British forces*	..	..	6th
7th	..	..	..	*Beirut (Syria) occupied by French forces.* *Elbasan (Albania) taken by Italian forces.*	..	..	7th
8th	..	President Wilson replies to Note of German Government, and demands evacuation of occupied territories as first condition of armistice	..	..	..	..	8th
9th	..	..	..	..	General Scheuch succeeds General von Stein as German Minister for War	..	9th
10th	..	..	..	*Irish mail boat "Leinster" sunk by submarine*	..	..	10th
11th	..	..	..	..	..	Feng-Kuo-Chang, President of China, retires	11th
12th	..	German Government reply to President Wilson's Note accepting conditions	British Government recognise the Polish National Army as autonomous, allied, and co-belligerent	..	..	..	12th
13th	..	..	..	..	Izzet Pasha succeeds Talaat Pasha as Turkish Grand Vizier	..	13th

POLITICAL 1918.

Date.	Events of Outstanding Importance.			Other Political and Economic Events.			Date.
	General.	Diplomatic Correspondence.	Declarations, Treaties and Agreements.	Entente and Allies.	Central Powers.	Neutrals and Miscellaneous.	
1918. OCT. 14th	..	President Wilson replies to German Government attaching further military conditions to terms of armistice, and warning against further breaches of laws of war, and insists on dealing only with a democratic Government. Turkish Government Note to President Wilson re Armistice	..	Durazzo, Novi Bazar and Ipek retaken by Italian forces. British troops from Vladivostok reach Irkutsk (Siberia)	..	..	1918. OCT. 14th
16th	..	..	Austrian Emperor issues manifesto proclaiming a Federal State (excluding Hungary)	..	..	..	16th
18th	..	President Wilson replies to Austro-Hungarian Note of 4th. (See 27th)	..	..	..	..	18th
20th	Belgian coast completely reoccupied by Allied forces	German Government reply to President Wilson's Note of 14th accepting proposal contained therein	..	..	..	..	20th
21st	..	..	The Czecho-Slovaks declare independence	..	..	The Ban of Croatia refuses offer of Military Governor of Agram to suppress the Yugo-Slav National Council	21st
23rd	..	President Wilson sends reply to German Note of the 20th and agrees to submit the matter to the Allied and Associated Governments	..	..	..	..	23rd
24th	Battle of Vittorio Veneto begins	..	..	..	Dr. Wekerle, Hungarian Premier, resigns	..	24th
25th	..	..	..	..	Count Andrassy succeeds Baron Burian as Austro-Hungarian Foreign Minister	..	25th
26th	..	..	..	Aleppo taken by British forces	..	King of Montenegro issues manifesto in favour of a confederated Yugo-Slavia, with autonomous States	26th
27th	..	German Government acknowledge President Wilson's Note of 23rd. Austro-Hungarian Government send further Note to President Wilson. (See 4th and 18th) Austrian Government ask Italy for an armistice	..	..	General von Ludendorff resigns. (See August 29th, 1916)	..	27th

POLITICAL 1918.

Date	EVENTS OF OUTSTANDING IMPORTANCE.			OTHER POLITICAL AND ECONOMIC EVENTS.			Date
	General.	Diplomatic Correspondence.	Declarations, Treaties and Agreements.	Entente and Allies.	Central Powers.	Neutrals and Miscellaneous.	
1918. OCT. 29th	..	..	Yugo-Slav National Council at Agram repudiate Imperial policy and declare the independence of the Yugo-Slavs	..	..	..	**1918. OCT.** 29th
30th	Turkish army on the Tigris surrenders to the British forces	..	Armistice between Turkey and Entente Powers signed at Mudros / Croatian Congress ("*Sabor*") unanimously adhere to Yugo-Slav declaration of independence	..	..	"National Council of Fiume" proclaim the independence of the city and announce desire for union with Italy / Fiume surrendered to the Croats by the Hungarian authorities	30th
31st	Hostilities between the Entente and Turkey cease at 12 noon	..	..	*Scutari (Albania) retaken by Italian forces. (See January 23rd, 1916)*	Austrian Emperor makes over the Austro-Hungarian Fleet to the Yugo-Slav National Council / Count Tisza assassinated in Vienna. / Revolutions break out in Vienna and Budapest	..	31st
NOV. 1st	Belgrade retaken by Serbian forces	..	State of war begins between The Ukraine and Poland	..	Independent Hungarian Government formed, with Count Karolyi as Premier / Baron von Flotow succeeds Count Andrassy as Austro-Hungarian Foreign Minister / King Boris of Bulgaria abdicates	..	**NOV.** 1st
2nd	*Last British merchant vessels sunk by submarine**	..	..	..	..	Administration of Carniola taken over from the Austro-Hungarian authorities by Slovene leaders	2nd
3rd	Trieste occupied by Italian forces	Allied and Associated Governments agree to Armistice proposals submitted by President Wilson	Armistice between Austria-Hungary and the Entente signed	..	Mutiny breaks out in the German Fleet at Kiel	..	3rd
4th	Hostilities between Austria-Hungary and the Entente cease	..	..	*Mosul occupied by British forces* / *Antivari (Montenegro) occupied by Italian naval forces*	..	..	4th

* "Surada" and "Murcia."

POLITICAL
1918.

Date.	EVENTS OF OUTSTANDING IMPORTANCE.			OTHER POLITICAL AND ECONOMIC EVENTS.			Date.
	General.	Diplomatic Correspondence.	Declarations, Treaties and Agreements.	Entente and Allies.	Central Powers.	Neutrals and Miscellaneous.	
1918. NOV. 5th	Marshal Foch placed in supreme strategical direction of all forces operating against Germany on all fronts	President Wilson sends final Note to German Government forwarding Allies' acceptance of Armistice proposals	.. ..	.. ..	.. ..	Fiume (see October 30th) occupied by Italian naval forces	1918. NOV. 5th
6th	.. ..	.. ..	.. ..	King Peter of Serbia re-enters Belgrade	.. ..	.. ..	6th
7th	.. ..	.. ..	.. ..	.. ..	Bavaria proclaimed a Republic	Yugo-Slav Conference at Geneva decide to form a joint Yugo-Slav-Serbian Government to control military and foreign affairs	7th
8th	German armistice delegates reach Allied General Headquarters	.. ..	.. ..	M. Marghiloman, Rumanian Premier, and M. Arian, Rumanian Foreign Minister, resign	.. ..	.. ..	8th
9th	.. ..	.. ..	**Joint declaration by British and French Governments regarding future of Syria and Mesopotamia** Czech forces at Ekaterinenburg proclaim national independence	*Alexandretta (Syria) occupied by Allied naval forces*	**Revolution breaks out in Berlin** Imperial Chancellor (Prince Max of Baden) announces that the Kaiser has decided to abdicate Prince Max appointed Regent Herr Ebert appointed Imperial Chancellor	.. ..	9th
10th	Allied forces cross the Danube at Ruschuk and enter Rumania	.. ..	King of Rumania announces that the Rumanian nation have taken up arms again on the side of the Allies	.. ..	**The Kaiser crosses the frontier into Holland**	.. ..	10th
11th	**Hostilities on the Western front cease at 11 a.m.**	.. ..	**Armistice concluded between the Entente and Germany** British Government recognise Lettish Provisional Government as independent	.. ..	.. ..	New National Government formed in Estonia	11th
12th	Allied Fleet passes through the Dardanelles	.. ..	**German-Austrian Republic proclaimed**	.. ..	Emperor of Austria abdicates	.. ..	12th
13th	Allied Fleet arrives at Constantinople	.. ..	.. ..	.. ..	German force in East Africa receives news of Armistice	.. ..	13th

POLITICAL
1918.

Date.	EVENTS OF OUTSTANDING IMPORTANCE.			OTHER POLITICAL AND ECONOMIC EVENTS.			Date
	General.	Diplomatic Correspondence.	Declarations, Treaties and Agreements.	Entente and Allies.	Central Powers.	Neutrals and Miscellaneous.	
1918. NOV. 14th	Hostilities in East Africa cease	.. ..	.. ..	.. ..	.. ..	Professor Masaryk elected first President of the Czecho-Slovak Republic	1918. NOV. 14th
15th	German cruiser "Königsberg" with German naval delegates enters the Firth of Forth to arrange surrender of the German High Seas Fleet. (*See* 20th and 21st)	.. ..	Hungarian Government conclude separate armistice with General Officer Commanding Allied Army (*General Henry*) at Belgrade	.. ..	.. ..	General Petlyura commences revolt against the Ukrainian Government	15th
16th	Allied Armies begin march into Germany	.. ..	Polish Government (*M. Pilsudski*) issue declaration proclaiming Poland an independent and sovereign State Hungary declares independence	.. ..	.. ..	New National Government in Estonia order general mobilisation	16th
17th	.. ..	.. ..	.. ..	*Baku again occupied by British forces*	.. ..	M. Movaczewski appointed Polish Prime Minister Yugo-Slav National Council at Agram protest against the Italian occupation of Fiume	17th
18th	Brussels reoccupied by Belgian forces Last German troops recross French frontier	.. ..	.. ..	.. ..	.. ..	Counter-revolutionary *coup d'état* at Omsk. Russian Admiral Koltchak proclaimed "Dictator of all Russia" Italian troops reinforce naval forces in Fiume	18th
19th	*Metz occupied by French forces* *Antwerp reoccupied by Belgian forces*	.. ..	.. ..	.. ..	.. ..	.. ..	19th
20th	First contingent of German submarines surrender to the British Navy at Harwich Luxembourg frontier crossed by United States forces	.. ..	.. ..	General Manishevski appointed Governor-General and Commander-in-chief of Russian forces in Northern Russia (*Archangel*)	.. ..	.. ..	20th
21st	German High Seas Fleet arrives at Rosyth, *en route* for internment at Scapa Flow Belgian Government reinstated at Brussels French troops land in Constantinople	Greek, Serbian and Rumanian Governments issue circular memorandum announcing their decision to strengthen the union between the three countries by all available means	.. ..	M. Delacroix succeeds M. Cooreman as Belgian Prime Minister M. Masson succeeds General de Ceuninck as Belgian Minister for War	.. ..	.. ..	21st

POLITICAL 1918.

Date.	EVENTS OF OUTSTANDING IMPORTANCE.			OTHER POLITICAL AND ECONOMIC EVENTS.			Date.
	General.	Diplomatic Correspondance.	Declarations, Treaties and Agreements.	Entente and Allies.	Central Powers.	Neutrals and Miscellaneous.	
1918. NOV. 23rd	.. ..	.. ..	.. ..	.. ..	.. ..	Yugo-Slav National Council vote for union with Serbia and formation of a common State with Serbia and Montenegro	1918. NOV. 23rd
24th	*British and United States forces reach German frontier*	.. ..	.. ..	.. ..	.. ..	.. ..	24th
25th	Strasbourg occupied by French forces **German forces in East Africa surrender to the Allied Commander at Abercorn**	.. ..	.. ..	.. ..	.. ..	.. ..	25th
26th	Last German troops recross Belgian frontier French troops cross German frontier Allied Fleet arrives at Sevastopol and takes over remainder of the Russian Black Sea Fleet from the Germans	.. ..	.. ..	.. ..	.. ..	United States force enters Fiume	26th
28th	**Kaiser Wilhelm II signs abdication**	.. ..	.. ..	.. ..	.. ..	*Narva (Estonia) captured by Bolshevik forces* The General Congress of The Bukovina decide in favour of complete union with Rumania	28th
29th	.. ..	.. ..	.. ..	.. ..	.. ..	Montenegrin National Assembly (*Skupshtina*) meet at Podgoritza and vote for union with Serbia	29th
30th	**Rumanian Government re-established at Bukharest**	.. ..	.. ..	.. ..	.. ..	.. ..	30th
DEC. 1st	British and United States troops cross the German frontier *Trèves occupied by United States troops*	.. ..	**National Assembly of the Rumanians of Transylvania,** the Banat and other districts of Hungary, assembled at Alba-Julia (*Transylvania*), **decree their union with Rumania**	General Coanda appointed Rumanian Premier and Foreign Minister	.. ..	.. ..	DEC. 1st
3rd	Last Bulgarian troops evacuate the Dobrudja	.. ..	.. ..	.. ..	.. ..	.. ..	3rd

POLITICAL 1918.

Date.	EVENTS OF OUTSTANDING IMPORTANCE.			OTHER POLITICAL AND ECONOMIC EVENTS.			Date.
	General.	Diplomatic Correspondence.	Declarations, Treaties and Agreements.	Entente and Allies.	Central Powers.	Neutrals and Miscellaneous.	
1918. DEC. 4th	.. ..	.. ..	Yugo-Slav National Council at Agram proclaim the union of all Serbs, Croats, and Slovenes in one State	Demobilization of British Army begins	.. ..	.. ..	1918. DEC. 4th
6th	*Cologne entered by British forces*	.. ..	.. ..	.. ..	.. ..	.. ..	6th
7th	.. ..	.. ..		.. ..	.. ..	Deputation from the National Council of the Bukovina arrives at Jassy to inform Rumanian Government that National Council has voted for union with Rumania	7th
8th	*Coblenz occupied by United States troops*	.. ..	.. ..	*Naval action in the Caspian between British and Bolshevik vessels*	.. ..	.. ..	8th
9th	**Serbian Government reinstated at Belgrade**	.. ..	.. ..	.. ..	.. ..	.. ..	9th
10th	.. ..	.. ..	The Bessarabian National Council abrogate the stipulations for local autonomy and **declare the unconditional union of Bessarabia with Rumania**		.. ..	General Mannerheim elected Regent of Finland	10th
11th	.. ..	.. ..	.. ..	.. ..	.. ..	Odessa occupied by (*Petlyura's*) Ukrainian revolutionary forces	11th
12th	*British troops cross the Rhine at Cologne*	.. ..	.. ..	General Coanda, Rumanian Premier and Foreign Minister, resigns	.. ..	.. ..	12th
13th	.. ..	.. ..	.. ..	*Hodeida (South Arabia) taken by British forces*	.. ..	.. ..	13th
14th	.. ..	.. ..	Armistice on the Western front prolonged to January 17th, 1919	M. Bratianu appointed Rumanian Premier and Foreign Minister Dr. da Silva Paes, Portuguese President, assassinated	.. ..	.. ..	14th
15th	.. ..	.. ..	Poland severs diplomatic relations with Germany	.. ..	.. ..	.. ..	15th

POLITICAL
1918.

Date.	EVENTS OF OUTSTANDING IMPORTANCE.			OTHER POLITICAL AND ECONOMIC EVENTS.			Date.
	General.	Diplomatic Correspondence.	Declarations, Treaties and Agreements.	Entente and Allies.	Central Powers.	Neutrals and Miscellaneous.	
1918. DEC. 16th	**Marshal Mackensen and his force surrender to the Hungarians near Budapest**	.. ..	.. ..	Senhor Antunes appointed Portuguese President	First meeting of Imperial Conference of Soldiers and Workmen in Berlin Last German troops leave Finland	.. ..	1918. DEC. 16th
17th	.. ..	.. ..	.. ..	General Scheuch, German Minister for War, resigns	.. ..	.. ..	17th
20th	.. ..	.. ..	.. ..	M. Pasich, Premier of Serbia, resigns French troops land at Odessa	.. ..	Kiev occupied by (*Petlyura's*) Ukrainian revolutionary forces	20th
23rd	.. ..	.. ..	.. ..	Senhor J. T. de Souza Barboza, Portuguese Secretary of State for the Interior, appointed Prime Minister	.. ..	.. ..	23rd
24th	.. ..	.. ..	.. ..	.. ..	.. ..	*Perm* (*Eastern Russia*) *taken by Kolchak's forces*	24th
26th	.. ..	.. ..	Formation of West Ukraine Republic announced	.. ..	Dorpat (*Estonia*) evacuated by the German forces	.. ..	26th
27th	.. ..	.. ..	**King of Rumania issues Proclamation annexing the Rumanian Provinces of Austria Hungary**	Batum (*Georgia*) occupied by British force*	.. ..	.. ..	27th
29th	.. ..	.. ..	.. ..	M. Stoyan Protich appointed Prime Minister of the United Kingdom of the Serbs, Croats and Slovenes	.. ..	.. ..	29th

* This force, sent from Constantinople, subsequently occupied the whole of Georgia, with headquarters at Tiflis.

MILITARY OPERATIONS.
Main Theatres.
1914.

PART II.

SECTION II (A.).

MILITARY OPERATIONS: MAIN THEATRES OF WAR.

Western Theatre (France, Flanders, &c.) - from August 1914.
Italian Theatre - „ May 1915.
Balkan Theatre (excluding Rumania and Turkey) „ July 1914.
Eastern Theatre (Russia and Rumania) - „ August 1914.
Turkey { (Dardanelles, Egypt, Palestine, &c.) } „ October 1914.
{ (Caucasus, Persia, and Mesopotamia) }

NOTES.

1. In the column dealing with the Eastern Theatre, the German official names for battles have been adopted and, in view of the complexity of the German battle-names, an indication is given as to the higher formations engaged. This indication consists of small numbers or letters in brackets after the battle-names, thus: "Battle of Gawaiten-Gumbinnen (⁸)" means that this battle was fought by the German Eighth Army: "First Battle of Krasnik (ᵃ¹)" indicates that it was the Austrian First Army that was engaged.

These abbreviations are as follows:—

(¹), (²), &c.	German First, Second, &c., Armies.
(ᵃ¹), (ᵃ²), &c.	Austrian First, Second, &c., Armies.
(ᵇ)	"Bugarmee": ("Army of the Bug").
(ᵈ)	"Armeeabteilung D": ("Force D").
(ᵍ)	"Armeeabteilung Gallwitz": ("Gallwitz's Force").
(ʰ)	"Heeresgruppe Linsingen": ("Army Group of General Linsingen").
(ⁿ)	"Niemen armee": ("Army of the Niemen").
(ᵖ)	"Heeresgruppe Prinz Leopold": ("Army Group of Prince Leopold").
(ˢ)	"Südarmee": ("Southern Army").
(ʷ)	"Armeeabteilung Woyrsch": ("Woyrsch's Force").

The similar abbreviations for all the belligerent armies on the Western Front will be found in the Appendix.

2. In referring to events in the Western Theatre special attention is drawn to the Prefatory Note.

Date.	WESTERN THEATRE.	BALKAN THEATRE.	EASTERN THEATRE.	Date.
1914. JUNE 28th	.. .. ..	*The Archduke Franz Ferdinand assassinated at Sarajevo*	.. .. ..	1914 JUNE 28th
JULY 23rd	.. .. ..	*Austro-Hungarian Government send ultimatum to Serbia*	.. .. ..	JULY 23rd
25th	.. .. ..	*Serbian Government order mobilisation*	.. .. ..	25th
26th	.. .. ..	*Austro-Hungarian Government order partial mobilisation as against Serbia*	.. .. ..	26th
		Montenegrin Government order mobilisation		
28th	.. .. ..	*Austria-Hungary declares war on Serbia*	.. .. ..	28th
29th	.. .. ..	**Hostilities commence on the Serbian frontier.** Belgrade bombarded by Austrian artillery	*Russian Government order partial mobilisation, as against Austria*	29th
31st	*State of "Kriegsgefahr" proclaimed in Germany*	*Austro-Hungarian Government order general mobilisation*		31st
	Belgian Government order mobilisation		*State of "Kriegsgefahr" proclaimed in Germany*	
			Russian Government order general mobilisation	
AUG. 1st	*German Government order general mobilisation*	.. .. ..	*German Government order general mobilisation*	AUG. 1st
	French Government order general mobilisation		*Germany declares war on Russia*	
			Hostilities commence on Polish frontiers	
2nd	**Hostilities commence on French frontier.** German troops enter Luxembourg	.. .. ..	.. .. ..	2nd
	German Government send ultimatum to Belgium			
3rd	*Germany declares war on France*	.. .. ..	.. .. ..	3rd

MILITARY OPERATIONS.
Main Theatres.
1914.

Date.	WESTERN THEATRE.	BALKAN THEATRE.	EASTERN THEATRE.	Date.
1914. **AUG.** 4th	*Germany declares war on Belgium.* **Hostilities commence on Belgian frontier.** *German attack on Liége begins* *Great Britain declares war on Germany*	.. .. ..	.. .. ..	**1914.** **AUG.** 4th
5th	.. .. ..	*Montenegro declares war on Austria-Hungary*	.. .. ..	5th
6th	"**Battle of the Frontiers**"* begins	.. .. ..	*Austria-Hungary declares war on Russia*	6th
7th	City of Liége occupied by German forces *First units of British Expeditionary Force land in France*	.. .. ..	.. .. ..	7th
12th	.. .. ..	Austrian forces cross the Save and seize Shabatz	.. .. ..	12th
13th	.. .. ..	Austrian forces cross the Drina. **First Austrian invasion of Serbia begins**	.. .. ..	13th
14th	**Battles of Morhange and Sarrebourg begin**	.. .. ..	.. .. ..	14th
16th	*Landing of original British Expeditionary Force in France completed* Last forts of Liége taken by German forces	.. .. ..	.. .. ..	16th
17th	.. .. ..		.. .. ..	17th
18th	Battle of the Gette			18th
19th		Battle of the Tser and of the Jadar	Battle of Gawaiten-Gumbinnen (⁸) (*East Prussia*)	19th
20th	**Brussels occupied by German forces** **Battles of Morhange and Sarrebourg end**			20th
21st	German attack on Namur begins	Austrian forces retreat from the Jadar	.. .. ..	21st
22nd	Battles of Charleroi and of the Ardennes	.. .. ..	.. .. ..	22nd
23rd	Battle of Mons		**Battle of Tannenberg (⁸) begins**	23rd
24th	Retreat from Mons begins	.. .. ..	First battle of Krasnik (ᵃ¹)	24th
25th	Namur taken by German forces	Shabatz retaken by Serbian forces. Last Austrian forces recross the Drina. **End of First invasion of Serbia**		25th

* General term covering all operations of the French Armies up to the Battle of the Marne.

MILITARY OPERATIONS.
Main Theatres.
1914.

Date.	WESTERN THEATRE.	BALKAN THEATRE.	EASTERN THEATRE.	Date.
1914. AUG. 26th	Battle of Le Cateau		Battle of Zamosc-Komarow (a4) begins	1914. AUG. 26th
27th	Longwy capitulates to the German forces		1st Battle of Lemberg (a2 a3)	27th
29th	1st Battle of Guise			29th
30th				30th
31st			Battle of Tannenberg (8) ends	31st
SEPT. 1st	Soissons taken by German forces			SEPT. 1st
2nd			Battle of Zamosc-Komarow (a4) ends	2nd
3rd	Reims taken by German forces		Lemberg taken by Russian forces	3rd
4th	Battle of the Grand Couronné begins			4th
5th	End of the retreat from Mons; Battle of the Ourcq begins			5th
6th		Serbian passage of the Save: Serbian operations in Syrmia begin	Battle of the Masurian Lakes (8)	6th
7th	Maubeuge capitulates to German forces			7th
8th		Second Austrian passage of the Drina: **Second invasion of Serbia begins**	Battle of Tarnavka (a1)	8th
9th	Battle of the Marne			9th
			2nd Battle of Lemberg (a2 a3 a4)	
10th		Semlin (*Syrmia*) taken by Serbian forces		10th
11th		Serbian advance in Syrmia abandoned	Austrian forces in Galicia retreat	11th
12th	Battle of the Grand Couronné ends			12th
		Battle of the Drina		
15th	1st Battle of the Aisne		Czernowitz (*Bukovina*) taken by Russian forces	15th
17th		Serbian forces in Syrmia withdrawn; Semlin evacuated. Battle of the Drina ends*: Local actions on the Drina Heights begin		17th
21st			Jaroslaw taken by Russian forces	21st

* This is approximately the date on which the main force of the Austrian offensive had spent itself. But there was no definite end to this battle, which subsided into continuous sharp local actions for the heights south of the Drina. These did not terminate until the Serbian retreat in the first days of November.

MILITARY OPERATIONS.
Main Theatres.
1914.

Date.	WESTERN THEATRE.	BALKAN THEATRE.	EASTERN THEATRE.	Date.
1914. SEPT. 22nd			.. .. ..	1914. SEPT. 22nd
24th			Przemysl isolated by Russian forces	24th
	1st Battle of Picardy		Russian forces attack the Carpathian passes and begin first invasion of North Hungary	
25th				25th
26th	*First units of Indian Expeditionary Force "A" land at Marseilles*		Actions on the Niemen* ([8])	26th
27th	1st Battle of Artois begins			27th
29th				29th
OCT. 3rd			1st Siege of Przemysl	OCT. 3rd
			Maramaros-Sziget (*North Hungary*) taken by Russian forces	
			Austro-Hungarian retreat through Galicia ends	
4th		**Actions on the Drina Heights** (*continued*)	Austro-Hungarian counter offensive in Galicia begins ([a2 a3 a4 a1])	4th
	Siege of Antwerp		Battle of Opatow ([9])	
5th				5th
7th			Maramaros-Sziget retaken by Austrian forces	7th
8th			Russian forces evacuate North Hungary and retreat over the Carpathian passes	8th
9th			Przemysl relieved by Austrian forces	9th
			First German offensive against Warsaw. Battles of Warsaw ([9]) and Ivangorod ([9]) begin	
10th	Antwerp occupied by German forces		.. .. ..	10th
	Battle of La Bassée begins			
12th	1st Battle of Artois ends		.. .. ..	12th
	Ostend and Zeebrugge evacuated by the Belgian forces			
	Lille capitulates to German forces			

* This series of actions on the line of the Niemen, in which the Russian army stopped the victorious advance of the German 8th Army after the Battle of the Masurian Lakes, were of considerable strategic importance, and are referred to in contemporary Russian accounts as "the Battle of the Niemen." They appear, however, in the German list as "Gefechte am Njemen."

MILITARY OPERATIONS.
Main Theatres.
1914.

Date.	WESTERN THEATRE.	BALKAN THEATRE.	EASTERN THEATRE.	Dardanelles, Egypt, &c.	Caucasus, Persia, and Mesopotamia.	Date.
1914. OCT. 13th	..	..	..	..	..	1914. OCT. 13th
16th	Battle of the Yser begins	Actions on the Drina Heights (continued)	Battle of Chyrow (a2 a3) begins	..	..	16th
19th	Battles of Ypres, 1914, begin		Battle of Warsaw (9) ends	..	First units of I.E.F. "D" leave Bombay for the Persian Gulf	19th
20th			Battle of Ivangorod (Germ.) (9) ends	..	..	20th
22nd			Czernowitz (Bukovina) reoccupied by Austrian forces	..	..	22nd
23rd			Battle of Ivangorod (Aust.) (a1)	..	First units of I.E.F. "D" arrive at the Bahrein Islands (Persian Gulf)	23rd
27th				..	..	27th
28th		Serbian armies begin retreat from the Drina line	Czernowitz (Bukovina) retaken by Russian forces	..	..	28th
29th				..	Turkey commences hostilities against Russia	29th
30th				..	..	30th
31st	Battle of the Yser and Battles of Ypres, 1914		Battle of the Opatowka (a1)	..	..	31st
NOV. 1st			Battle of Chyrow (a2 a3) ends	Great Britain and France commence hostilities against Turkey		NOV. 1st
2nd			Austrian armies in Galicia retreat	..	Russia declares war on Turkey	2nd
3rd				Allied squadrons bombard forts at entrance of Dardanelles	..	3rd
4th					Russian forces cross Turkish frontier and advance on Erzerum	4th
5th		Serbian armies in retreat: rearguard action		Great Britain and France declare war on Turkey		5th
6th			Battle of Goritten (8)	..	Advanced troops of I.E.F. "D" effect landing at Fao (Mesopotamia) Keupri-Keui (Armenia) taken by Russian forces	6th
8th			2nd Siege of Przemysl begins Battle of Wloclawek Memel occupied by Russian forces*	Sheikh Said (Southern Arabia) stormed by British force	..	8th
10th	Battle of the Yser ends		Battle of the Kornintener Heide (8) begins		..	10th
11th				..	..	11th
13th				..	..	13th

* Approximate date.

MILITARY OPERATIONS.
Main Theatres.
1914.

Date.	WESTERN THEATRE.	BALKAN THEATRE.	EASTERN THEATRE.	Dardanelles, Egypt, &c.	TURKEY. Caucasus, Persia and Mesopotamia.	Date.
1914. NOV. 14th				..	Keupri-Keui (*Armenia*) retaken by Turkish forces	1914. NOV. 14th
15th	Battles of Ypres, 1914	Serbian armies in retreat; rear-guard actions	Battle of Kutno (⁹) Russian forces attack the Carpathian passes and begin Second Invasion of North Hungary Battle of Cracow (ᵃ¹ ᵃ⁴) begins	..	Affair of Saihan (*Mesopotamia*)	15th
16th			Battle of the Romintener Heide (⁸) ends Second German offensive against Warsaw; Battle of Lodz (⁹) begins	..	..	16th
17th				..	Affair of Sahil (*Mesopotamia*)	17th
22nd	Battles of Ypres, 1914, end		Battle of Cracow (ᵃ¹ ᵃ⁴) (*continued*)	..	Basra occupied by British forces Keupri-Keui (*Caucasus*) retaken by Russian forces	22nd
30th	..	Serbian forces evacuate Belgrade	Battle of Lowicz - Sanniki (⁹) begins	..		30th
DEC. 1st	..	..	Bartfa (*North Hungary*) taken by Russian forces	..	..	DEC. 1st
2nd	..	Belgrade occupied by Austrian forces		..	..	2nd
3rd	..	Battle of the Kolubara		..	..	3rd
4th	..		Battle of Limanova-Lapanow (ᵃ⁴)	..		4th
5th	..			..		5th
6th	..			..	1st Action of Qurna (*Mesopotamia*)	6th
7th	..		Austrian counter-offensive in North Hungary: Bartfa retaken	..		7th
8th	..			..		8th
9th	..	Austrian armies in retreat	Last Russian forces recross the Carpathian passes: Second Invasion of North Hungary ends	..	Qurna occupied by British forces	9th
10th	..			*Field-Marshal von der Goltz leaves Germany to take over control of the Turkish army*		10th
12th	..			..		12th
14th	Attack on Wytschaete			..		14th

168

MILITARY OPERATIONS.
Main Theatres.
1914-15.

Date	Western Front	Southern Front	Eastern Front			Other Theatres
15th		Belgrade reoccupied by Serbian forces	Battle of Lodz (⁹) ends	..	..	..
17th	Allied demonstrations on the Flanders front	Last Austrian forces evacuate Serbia: End of Second Invasion of Serbia	Battle of Lowicz-Sannik (⁹) ends	..	..	Turkish offensive against Kars begins: Keupri-Keui retaken
18th		..	Battle of the Rawka-Bzura (⁹) begins*	..	..	..
20th	1st Battle of Champagne begins	..	..	..	..	Turkish armies advancing towards Kars
21st	Defence of Givenchy, 1914	..	..	..	..	
26th	..	Italian force landed at Valona (*Albania*)	..	..	..	..
29th	..	..	..	..	..	..
1915. JAN. 2nd		..	..	..	..	Battle of Sarikamish
5th		..	..	..	..	Urmia evacuated by Russian forces
8th		..	..	..	..	Tabriz evacuated by Russian forces
13th	Battle of Soissons..	..	..	..	..	Tabriz occupied by Turkish forces; Battle of Kara Urgan
14th		..	..	..	..	
26th		..	..	..	..	..
29th		..	Battle of the Beskid Pass (⁴) begins	..	..	..
30th	1st Battle of Champagne (*continued*)	..	..	..	Turkish advance across Sinai	Tabriz reoccupied by Russian forces
31st		..	..	..		..
FEB. 2nd		..	Battle of Humin (⁹)	..		..

*See footnote in Part I.

MILITARY OPERATIONS.
Main Theatres.
1915.

Date.	WESTERN THEATRE.	BALKAN THEATRE.	EASTERN THEATRE.	TURKEY. Dardanelles, Egypt, &c.	TURKEY. Caucasus, Persia and Mesopotamia.	Date.
1915. FEB. 3rd				Turkish attack on the Suez Canal		1915. FEB. 3rd
4th			Battle of the Beskid Pass (⁸) ends			4th
5th			The Winter Battle in Masuria (¹⁰ ᵍ)	Turkish retreat across Sinai		5th
17th			Memel reoccupied by German forces (17th) Czernowitz (Bukovina) retaken by Austrian forces (17th)			17th
19th				Allied Naval attack on the Dardanelles forts commences		19th
20th						20th
22nd			1st Battle of Przasnysz (ᶠ)			22nd
23rd	1st Battle of Champagne (continued)			Lemnos occupied by British marines		23rd
27th						27th
MARCH 5th			Battle of Stolniki (⁹)			MARCH 5th
10th	Battle of Neuve Chapelle					10th
13th						13th
16th						16th
17th						17th
18th			Memel captured by Russian forces	Naval attack on the Dardanelles forts repulsed		18th
20th						20th
21st			Memel recaptured by German forces			21st
22nd			Capitulation of Przemysl			22nd

MILITARY OPERATIONS.
Main Theatres.
1915.

Date.	WESTERN THEATRE.	ITALIAN THEATRE.	BALKAN THEATRE.	EASTERN THEATRE.	TURKEY.		Date.
					Dardanelles, Egypt, &c.	Caucasus, Persia and Mesopotamia.	
1915. APRIL							**1915. APRIL**
2nd							2nd
8th						*Armenian massacres begin**	8th
12th				⎱ Battle of the Laborczatal			12th
13th				⎰		Battle of Shaiba	13th
14th							14th
16th						Urmia occupied by Turkish regular forces	16th
17th	⎱ Capture of Hill 60						17th
20th						Armenian revolt at Van	20th
22nd	⎰ The German gas attack				⎱ Allied forces effect landing at the Dardanelles		22nd
25th							25th
26th		Secret agreement signed between Italian Government and Entente Powers		German offensive into the Baltic Provinces begins (8)			26th
28th					1st Battle of Krithia	Armenian defence of Van	28th
MAY 1st	Battles of Ypres, 1915			⎱ Austro-German Spring offensive in Galicia begins with Battle of Gorlice-Tarnow(11 84)	⎱ Actions of Eski-Hissarlik	Battle of Dilman	**MAY 1st**
2nd		Italy denounces the Triple Alliance		⎰			2nd
4th							4th
5th							5th

* Approximate date.

MILITARY OPERATIONS.
Main Theatres.
1915.

Date.	WESTERN THEATRE.	ITALIAN THEATRE.	BALKAN THEATRE.	EASTERN THEATRE.	TURKEY.		Date.
					Dardanelles, Egypt, &c.	Caucasus, Persia and Mesopotamia.	
1915. MAY							1915. MAY
6th	Battles of Ypres, 1915 (continued)	..	..	..	..	..	6th
7th		..	..	..	2nd Battle of Krithia	..	7th
8th		..	..	Libau taken by German forces ([8])			8th
9th	Allied Spring offensive begins Battle of Aubers Ridge (9th) and	..	..		..	Armenian defence of Van (continued)	9th
11th		..	..	Battle of Sanok ([a2 a3]) and Rzeszow ([11 a4])	..		11th
14th	2nd Battle of Artois	..	..	Jaroslaw retaken by Austro-German forces	..		14th
15th		..	..		..		15th
16th	and	..	..		..		16th
18th		..	..		..		18th
19th	Battle of Festubert (15th–25th)	..	..	Battle of the San ([11 a4])	..	Armenian garrison of Van relieved by Russian force	19th
20th		..	..		The Defence of Anzac		20th
21st		Italy declares war against Austria-Hungary Hostilities commence on Italian frontier	..		..	Russian Expeditionary Force to West Persia lands at Enzeli	21st
23rd			..	Battles of Stryj ([8]) and Drohobycz ([8])	..		23rd
24th			..		..	Urmia re-taken by Russian forces	24th
25th	2nd Battle of Artois (continued)	..	Valona formally occupied by Italian forces. (See December 26th, 1914.)		..	..	25th
29th		..	..	Battle of Przemysl ([a2 11 a4]) Przemysl retaken by Austro-German forces	..	..	29th
31st		..	..		..	2nd action of Qurna	31st
JUNE 3rd		..	..		..	Pursuit to Amara	JUNE 3rd
4th		..	..		..	Amara taken by British forces	4th
5th	Anglo-French Conference at Calais	..	..		3rd Battle of Krithia	..	5th
6th		..	..	Battle of Zydaczow ([8]) begins	..	..	6th
10th		..	..		..	..	10th
11th		..	..		..	..	11th

MILITARY OPERATIONS.
Main Theatres.
1915.

Date	Western	Italian	Eastern	Gallipoli	Other
12th	2nd Battle of Artois (continued)				
15th					
17th			Battle of Mosciuska (a2) and Lubaczow (11 a4)		
18th			Battle of Zydaczow (b) (continued)		
22nd			3rd Battle of Lemberg (11 a2)		British advance up the Euphrates begins
27th			City recaptured by Austro-German forces		
28th					
29th			Battle of the Gnila-Lipa (s)		
JULY 1st		1st Battle of the Isonzo		Action of Gully Ravine	
2nd					
5th			2nd Battle of Krasnik (a4)		
7th					
13th			Great Austro-German Offensive— Battle of the Narew and Bobr (8) begins 2nd Battle of Przasnysz (g) begins Battles of Maslomencze (b) and Grabowiec (b) begin Battle of Schaulen (n) begins		
14th			Battle of Krasnostav (11) begins		
16th			Battle of Sienno (w) (one day) 2nd Battle of Przasnysz (g) ends		
17th			Battles of Maslomencze (b) and Grabowiec (b) end Battle of Krasnostav (11) ends		Actions for Nasiriya
18th			Battles of Hrubieszow (b) and Wojslawice (b) begin		
19th		2nd Battle of the Isonzo	2nd Battle of Ivangorod (w)		
20th					
21st			Battle of the Narew (g) begins		
23rd			Rozan and Pultusk stormed by German forces (f)		
24th			Battle of Schaulen (n) ends		
25th					Nasiriya taken by British forces

MILITARY OPERATIONS.
Main Theatres.
1915.

Date.	WESTERN THEATRE.	ITALIAN THEATRE.	BALKAN THEATRE.	EASTERN THEATRE.	TURKEY. Dardanelles, Egypt, &c.	TURKEY. Caucasus, Persia and Mesopotamia.
1915. JULY 26th	..		..	Battle of the Narew and Bobr [8] ends	..	..
29th	..		..		..	..
30th	..		..	Battle of Biskupice [11] .. Battles of Hruhieszow [b] and Wojslawice [b] end Battle of Kupischki [a] begins	..	..
31st	..		..	Battle of Strelcze [b] (one day)	..	..
AUG. 1st	..	2nd Battle of the Isonzo (continued)	..	Mitau taken by German forces [n] Battle of Cholm [b] .. Battle of the Narew [g] ends Ostrolenka captured by Austro-German forces [g]	..	..
3rd	..		..		..	Van evacuated by the Russian forces
4th	..		..		..	..
5th	..		..	Warsaw occupied by German forces	..	Van re-occupied by Turkish forces
6th	..		..	Battle of the Orz-Bach [g]	The Landing at Suvla ..	..
7th	..		..	Battle of Kupischki [a] ends Battle of the Ucherka [b] begins		..
8th	..		..	Siege of Kowno begins [10] ..	Battle of Sari Bair	..
9th	..		..	Battle of Ostrov [12]		..
10th	..		..			..
11th	..	..	..	Battle of Tschishew-Sambrow [12] Battle of the Ucherka [b] ends Battle of Schimanzy-Ponedeli [n] begins	The Battles of Suvla	..
12th	..	..	..			..
13th	..	..	..	Battle of Wlodawa [b]		..
17th	..	..	..			..
18th	..	..	..	Kowno stormed by the German forces [10]		..

MILITARY OPERATIONS.
Main Theatres.
1915.

175

Date		
19th		Battle of Schimanzy-Ponedeli (a) ends
20th		Battle of the Niemen (10) begins
21st		Battle of Bielst (12) begins
		Novo Georgievsk stormed by German forces
22nd	Battle of Scimitar Hill	Battle of the Pulwa-Nursec (p 9 w)
24th		Osoveta stormed by German forces (8)
25th		Battle of Bielst ends (12)
		Brest-Litovsk stormed by Austro-German forces (b)
26th		Bielostok taken by German forces
27th		Battle of the Zlota-Lipa (a) (one day)
31st		
SEPT. 1st		Battle of Horodec (b)
2nd		
3rd		Grodno stormed by German forces (8)
4th		Battle of Drohiczyn-Chomst (b) begins
5th		Tsar assumes supreme command of the Russian armies
6th		Battle of Drohiczyn-Chomst (b) ends
7th		Battle of Wolkowyszk (12)
8th		Battle of Tarnopol (a) begins
		Grand Duke Nicholas appointed Viceroy of the Caucasus
		Battle of the Niemen (10) ends
		Battle of the Zelwianka and the Niemen (12) begins
9th		Battle of Dvinsk (11) begins
		Battle of Vilna (10) begins
12th		Battle of Tarnopol (a)
		Battle of the Zelwianka and Niemen (12) ends
		Jelnia (12) begins
13th		Battle of Slonim (p 9 w) begins
16th		Battle of Tarnopol (a) ends
		Pinsk taken by Austro-German forces
17th		Battle of the Szczara and Jelnia (12) ends

MILITARY OPERATIONS.
Main Theatres.
1915.

Date.	WESTERN THEATRE.	ITALIAN THEATRE.	BALKAN THEATRE.	EASTERN THEATRE.	TURKEY. Dardanelles, Egypt, &c.	TURKEY. Caucasus, Persia and Mesopotamia.	Date.
1915. SEPT. 18th	..	..	..	Battle of Slonim ends (p 9 w) Vilna taken by Austro-German forces (10)	..	..	**1915. SEPT.** 18th
21st	..	..	*Bulgarian Government order partial mobilisation*		..	..	21st
22nd	..	..	*Bulgarian Government order general mobilisation for 25th*		..	..	22nd
23rd	..	..	*Greek Government order precautionary mobilisation*		..	..	23rd
25th	Allied Autumn offensive begins *including* Battle of Loos *and* 3rd Battle of Artois *and* 2nd Battle of Champagne	..	*Bulgarian mobilization begins*	Austro-German passage of the Styr (b)	..	..	25th
26th		..	..		..	..	26th
28th		..	..	Battle of Kormin and the Putilovka (h)	..	Battle of Kut, 1915	28th
OCT. 1st 2nd 4th		..	*Entente Powers send ultimatum to Bulgaria*	Battle of Vilna ends (10) Battle of Dvinsk (n) *(continued)*	..	..	**OCT.** 1st 2nd 4th
5th		..	French and British forces landed at Salonika		..	..	5th
6th	Battle of Loos *(continued)*	..	Final Austro-German invasion of Serbia begins		..	..	6th
7th		..	Austro-German Passage of the Save and Danube		..	..	7th
8th 9th		..	Belgrade taken by Austro-German forces Montenegro invaded by Austrian forces		..	..	8th 9th
11th		..	Semendria taken by Austro-German forces Hostilities commence between Bulgarian and Serbian forces		..	..	11th
13th		..	Hostilities commence between French and Bulgarian forces		..	..	13th

MILITARY OPERATIONS.
Main Theatres.
1915.

177

14th					
15th	End of 3rd Battle of Artois				
16th					
18th			1st Action of Strumitsa Station		
21st			Bulgaria and Serbia declare war on one another		
			Vranje taken by Bulgarian forces		
			Great Britain declares "*State of War*" with Bulgaria		
			France declares "*state of war*" with Bulgaria		
22nd			Dede Agach bombarded by Allied warships	Battle of Dvinsk (continued)	
			2nd Action of Strumitsa Station		
			Veles taken by Bulgarian forces		
			Shabatz taken by Austrian forces		
			Kumanovo and Üskub taken by Bulgarian forces		
24th			Negotin taken by Bulgarian forces		
27th			1st Action of Krivolak		
30th	2nd Battle of Champagne (continued)	3rd Battle of the Isonzo	2nd Action of Krivolak		
NOV. 1st			Capture of Kragujevatz by Austro-German forces		Kasvin (W. Persia) occupied by Russian forces (*see May 21st*)
2nd			1st Bulgarian attack on the Babuna pass	Battle of Dvinsk ends	
3rd				Battle of Siemikowce	
4th			3rd Action of Krivolak		
5th			**Nish taken by Bulgarian forces**		
6th	End of 2nd Battle of Champagne		**Battle of Kachanik**		
8th					

MILITARY OPERATIONS.
Main Theatres.
1915.

Date.	WESTERN THEATRE.	ITALIAN THEATRE.	BALKAN THEATRE.	EASTERN THEATRE.	TURKEY. Dardanelles, Egypt, &c.	TURKEY. Caucasus, Persia and Mesopotamia.	Date.
1915. NOV. 10th	..	⎫	..	..	..	..	1915. NOV. 10th
11th	..			Battle of Czartorysk (h)	..	First British advance on Baghdad begins	11th
13th	..			..	..		13th
16th	..		Babuna pass and Prilep taken by Bulgarian forces	..	..	British advance on Baghdad	16th
20th	..		Novi-Bazar taken by Austrian forces	..	..		20th
22nd	..		..	..	..		22nd
23rd	..		Pristina taken by Austro-German forces	..	Hostilities on western frontier of Egypt between British and Senussi begin	Battle of Ctesiphon	23rd
24th	..	4th Battle of the Isonzo	..	..	..	Field-Marshal von der Goltz takes command of Turkish forces in Mesopotamia	24th
25th	..		..	..	..		25th
30th	..		Serbian retreat through Albania begins	..	..		30th
DEC. 1st	..	⎭	Prizren taken by Bulgarian forces	..	..	British retreat from Ctesiphon to Kut	DEC. 1st
2nd	..		French retreat to Greek frontier begins: Krivolak evacuated	..	..		2nd
			Monastir taken by Bulgarians forces				
3rd	..		Headquarters of Serbian army reach Scutari	..	..		3rd

178

MILITARY OPERATIONS.
Main Theatres.
1915-16.

Date	Western Front	Eastern Front	Southern (Italian & Balkan)	Gallipoli & Egypt	Asiatic Theatres
5th	..	..	..	..	Defence of Kut begins*
6th	..	..	Action of Demir Kapu Durazzo bombarded by an Austrian squadron	..	..
7th	..	..	Ipek (*Montenegro*) taken by Austro-German forces 4th Battle of the Isonzo (*continued*)	..	..
8th	..	..	Actions of Kosturino Debra and Okhrida taken by Bulgarian forces	Evacuation of the Gallipoli Peninsula (Suvla and Anzac) ordered	..
10th	..	..	..	..	..
11th	..	..	Dorian and Gevgeli taken by Bulgarian forces	Affair of the Wadi Senab (*Western Egypt*)	..
13th	..	..	..	..	..
14th	..	..	..	..	Hamadan (*Western Persia*) occupied by Russian forces
15th	..	..	The last British and French forces in Macedonia withdrawn into Greek territory	..	Qasr-i-Shirin (*Western Persia*) occupied by Turkish forces
19th	..	..	*Bulgarian and Greek General Staffs conclude agreement establishing temporary neutral zone along Greek frontier*	Evacuation of the Gallipoli Peninsula begun Evacuation of Suvla and Anzac	..
20th	..	..	Durazzo occupied by Italian forces	..	..
25th	..	..	..	Affair of the Wadi Majid (*Western Egypt*)	..
30th	..	..	*Consuls of Central Powers at Salonika arrested and deported by French Commander*	..	Turkish Christmas Eve attack on Kut Kangavar occupied by Russian force (*Western Persia*)
1916. JAN. 4th	..	..	..	..	First Attempt to relieve Kut begins: Relieving force begins advance from 'Ali Gharbi
6th	..	..	..	..	..
7th	..	..	..	..	Action of Sheikh Sa'ad
8th	..	..	..	Evacuation of Helles Evacuation of the Gallipoli Peninsula completed	..
10th	..	..	Mount Lovchen (*Montenegro*) taken by Austrian forces	..	..
11th	..	..	Corfu occupied by French forces	..	Russian offensive towards Erzerum begins

* Date by which Kut had been placed in a state of defence; the investment was not actually complete until the 7th.

MILITARY OPERATIONS.
Main Theatres.
1916.

Date.	WESTERN THEATRE.	ITALIAN THEATRE.	BALKAN THEATRE.	EASTERN THEATRE.	TURKEY. Egypt, &c.	TURKEY. Caucasus, Persia and Mesopotamia.	Date.
1916. JAN. 12th	..	..	Armistice concluded between Montenegro and Austria. (*See* 20th)	..	..	..	**1916. JAN.** 12th
13th	..	..	Cetinje **occupied by Austrian forces**	..	..	Kirmanshah (*W. Persia*) occupied by Turkish force	13th
14th	..	..	..	..	..	Action of the Wadi (*near Kut*)	14th
15th	..	..	First Serbian troops land at Corfu. *Serbian Government transferred to Brindisi*	..	..	Russian advance on Keupri-Keui	15th
16th	..	..	*General Sarrail assumes command of all Allied forces at Salonika*	..	..	..	16th
17th	..	..	..	..	..	Keupri-Keui captured by Russian forces	17th
18th	..	..	..	..	..	..	18th
20th	..	..	Armistice between Montenegro and Austria ceases	..	..	1st Attack on Hanna repulsed **First Attempt to relieve Kut fails.** (*See March 8th*)	20th
21st	..	..	..	..	..	Russian advance on Erzerum	21st
22nd	..	..	Antivari occupied by Austrian forces	..	..	..	22nd
23rd	..	..	Scutari occupied by Austrian forces	..	..	..	23rd
25th	..	..	San Giovanni di Medua taken by Austrian forces	..	..	..	25th
FEB. 2nd	..	..	Elbasan (*Albania*) taken by Bulgarian force	..	..	..	**FEB.** 2nd
10th	..	..	Remnant of Serbian Army concentrated at Corfu	..	..	..	10th

MILITARY OPERATIONS.
Main Theatres.
1916.

Date	Western	Italian	Balkans	Eastern	Egypt	Turkey/Persia/Mesopotamia
12th	...	...	...	...	...	Russian attack on Erzerum
15th	...	...	...	...	...	Erzerum taken by Russian forces
16th	...	...	...	...	...	Control of operations in Mesopotamia taken over by the War Office
17th	...	...	Montenegrin forces land at Corfu	...	...	...
18th	...	...	...	...	...	Mush (*Armenia*) taken by Russian forces
21st	Battle of Verdun begins	...	Berat (*Albania*) occupied by Austrian forces	...	...	Kirmanshah (*Western Persia*) taken by Russian forces
26th						
27th		5th Battle of the Isonzo	Durazzo captured by Austrian forces	...	Action of Agagiya (*Western Egypt*)	...
MARCH						
2nd	...	...	...	...	...	Bitlis (*Armenia*) taken by Russian forces
4th	...	...	...	...	...	Russian force landed at Atna for attack on Trebizond
8th	...	...	...	...	...	Second Attempt to relieve Kut: Attack on Dujaila Redoubt repulsed
12th	...	...	...	...	...	Karind (*Western Persia*) occupied by Russian force
14th	Battle of Verdun	...	...	...	Sollum (*Western Egypt*) reoccupied by British forces	...
17th				Battles of Lake Naroch [10] and of Postawy [10] begin		
18th				Battle of Jacobstadt [8]		
19th	...	...	...	...	...	...
26th	...	...	...	Battle of Postawy [10] ends	...	...
27th	...	...	...	...	...	...
APRIL						
1st	...	...	...	...	...	Third Attempt to relieve Kut begins
4th	...	...	...	...	...	Action of Falahiya (*near Kut*)
5th	...	...	...	General Brusiloo appointed to command Russian Southern front	...	...
6th	...	...	...	...	...	1st Attack on Sanna-i-Yat
9th	...	...	...	Battle of Lake Naroch [10]	...	2nd Attack on Sanna-i-Yat Russian attack on Trebizond
15th	...	...	Serbian Army Head-quarters land at Salonika	...	...	...
17th	...	...	...	...	...	Trebizond taken by Russian forces
18th	...	...	...	...	...	Action of Bait Aissa (Mesopotamia)

MILITARY OPERATIONS.
Main Theatres.
1916.

Date.	WESTERN THEATRE.	ITALIAN THEATRE.	BALKAN THEATRE.	EASTERN THEATRE.	TURKEY. Egypt, Arabia, &c.	TURKEY. Caucasus, Persia and Mesopotamia.
1916. APRIL 19th						*Field-Marshal von der Goltz assassinated*
22nd				Battle of Lake Naroch (10) (continued)		3rd Attack on Sanna-i-Yat
23rd					Affair of Qatia	
24th						Final attempt to succour Kut: loss of H.M.S. "Julnar."
29th						Capitulation of Kut.
30th						
MAY 7th	Battle of Verdun (continued)	Austrian offensive in the Trentino begins				Qasr-i-Shirin (*Western Persia*) occupied by Russian force
14th						
15th		Austrian offensive in the Trentino				Khanaqin (*North-East of Baghdad*) taken by Russian force
18th						Rowanduz (*Northern Mesopotamia*) occupied by Russian force Detachment from Russian force in Western Persia effects junction with British army on the Tigris
19th	German attack on Vimy Ridge					Turkish army evacuates the As Sinn position and withdraws to position at Kut
21st						
24th						Mamakhatun (*Armenia*) taken by Russian force*
26th			Fort Rupel (*Greek Macedonia*) occupied by Bulgarian force			
31st						Mamakhatun retaken by Turkish forces*
JUNE 2nd						
3rd						

MILITARY OPERATIONS.
Main Theatres.
1916.

Date	Western Front	Salonika / Other	Eastern Front	Hejaz	Other (Persia/Armenia)
4th	Battle of Mount Sorrel		"Brusilov's Offensive" begins		
5th				Arab revolt in the Hejaz begins	Turkish offensive into West Persia begins*: Khanaqin evacuated by the Russian force
6th				Arab attack on Medina	
7th	Local counter-attacks on the Trentino front	"Pacific blockade" of Greece by Entente Powers begins	Battle of Wosuszka-Sereth(⁸)		
10th				Sherif of Mecca proclaims the independence of the Hejaz	
11th					
13th				Turkish garrison of Mecca surrenders to the Sherif	
16th					
17th			Czernovitz (Bukovino) again taken by Russian forces Battle of the Strypa(⁸)		
20th					Qasr-i-Shirin (Western Persia) taken by Turkish forces
22nd	Battle of Verdun (continued)	"Pacific blockade" of Greece suspended			
24th					
30th	Italian counter-offensive in the Trentino				
JULY 1st	Battles of the Somme, 1916, begin				
2nd					
7th					Kirmanshah (Western Persia) again taken by Turkish forces
9th			Battle of Baranovichi (ʷ)		
10th					
12th					Mamakhatun (Armenia) again taken by Russian forces*†
16th			Battle of Kekkau (⁶)		
19th				Turkish offensive from Ogh-ratina against the Suez Canal begins	
23rd		Reconstituted Serbian Army comes into action on the Salonika front	Battle of Gorodichi (ʷ) Battle of Baranovichi-		
25th					Erzinjan (Armenia) taken by Russian forces†

* Approximate date.   † Furthest points west reached by Russian forces.

MILITARY OPERATIONS.
Main Theatres.
1916.

Date.	WESTERN THEATRE. (France and Flanders.)	ITALIAN THEATRE.	BALKAN THEATRE. (Excluding Rumania and Turkey.)	EASTERN THEATRE. (Russia and Rumania.)	TURKEY. Egypt and Arabia.	TURKEY. Caucasus, Persia and Mesopotamia.	Date.
1916. JULY 27th	Battles of the Somme, 1916, *and* Battle of Verdun *(continued)*	..	..	..	..	..	1916. JULY 27th
28th		..	..	Battle of Chocimierez (ª³)	Yenbo (*Héjaz*) surrenders to Arab forces	..	28th
30th		..	Russian troops land at Salonika to join Allied force		Turkish offensive against the Suez Canal: advanced guard actions	..	30th
AUG. 2nd		..		Battle of Baranovichi-Gorodichi (ʷ) *(continued)*		..	AUG. 2nd
4th		..			Battle of Rumani	..	4th
5th		..				..	5th
6th		..		Battle of Kowel (ʰ) ..		..	6th
7th		..		Battle of Tlumacz (ª³)		..	7th
8th		Gorizia taken by Italian forces		Battle of Zalozce (ᵉ)	Turkish army in retreat: rearguard actions	..	8th
9th		6th Battle of the Isonzo	Battle of Doiran, 1916			..	9th
10th		..				Hamadan (*Western Persia*) taken by Turkish forces*	10th
12th		..	Bulgarian counter-offensive *including* Battle of Florina†			..	12th
15th		..				Mush and Bitlis (*Armenia*) retaken by Turkish forces	15th
17th		..		..	..	..	17th
18th		..	..	..	..	..	18th
19th		..	..	..	..	..	19th
21st		..	..	..	..	..	21st
23rd		..	..	..	..	Battle of Rayat (*Armenia*)	23rd
24th		..	..	..	..	Mush and Bitlis (*Armenia*) again taken by Russian forces	24th
27th		..	..	Rumanian Government order mobilisation and declare war on Austria-Hungary. Hostilities commence on Rumanian frontiers	..	..	27th
28th		..	..	Rumanian forces invade Transylvania	..	..	28th

MILITARY OPERATIONS.
Main Theatres.
1916.

Date	Western Front	Italian Front	Eastern Front / Balkans / Rumania
29th	Field-Marshal von Hindenburg succeeds General von Falkenhayn as Chief of German General Staff ‡		Field-Marshal von Hindenburg succeeds General von Falkenhayn as Chief of German General Staff ‡
30th			Brasov (*Transylvania*) occupied by Rumanian forces
31st	Defensive Battle of Verdun ends		Turkey declares war on Rumania
SEPT. 1st			Battle of Zborow (⁶)
6th			Bulgaria declares war on Rumania
8th			Sibiu (*Transylvania*) taken by Rumanian forces
9th			Battle of the Carpathians (*⁷) begins
10th	Battles of the Somme, 1916 (*continued*)		1st Battle of the Narajowka and the Zlota-Lipa (⁸)
12th			Tutrakan (*Dobrudja*) taken by Bulgarian forces §
14th		7th Battle of the Isonzo	Orsova (*Hungary*) occupied by Rumanian forces
15th	Battle of Flers-Courcelette (*Somme*) begins ‖		Silistra (*Dobrudja*) taken by Bulgarian forces §
16th			
18th			Battle of the Carpathians (*⁷)
19th			
26th			2nd Battle of the Narajowka and the Zlota-Lipa (⁸)
29th		Greek IVth Army Corps at Kavala surrenders voluntarily to the German forces	Battle of Sibiu (⁹) ** Sibiu retaken by Austro-Hungarian forces
30th		Battle of Kaimakchalan–Florina	
OCT. 1st			Battle of Brzezany (⁸)
2nd			
3rd			

* Approximate date. † German name and dates. ‡ With General von Ludendorff as Chief Quartermaster-General.
§ "Mackensen's Army."—composite army of Bulgarians, Germans and Turks, under Field-Marshal von Mackensen. ‖ Tanks in action for the first time.
** "Schlacht bei Hermannstadt."

MILITARY OPERATIONS.
Main Theatres.
1916.

Date.	WESTERN THEATRE. (France and Flanders.)	ITALIAN THEATRE.	BALKAN THEATRE. (Excluding Rumania and Turkey.)	EASTERN THEATRE. (Russia and Rumania.)	TURKEY. Egypt and Arabia.	TURKEY. Caucasus, Persia and Mesopotamia.
1916.						
OCT. 5th	Battles of the Somme, 1916 (*continued*)	⎱ 8th Battle of the Isonzo ⎰	⎱ Battle of the Cerna and Monastir‡ ⎰	⎱ Battle of the Geisterwalde (⁹) .. 3rd Battle of the Narajowka and the Zlota-Lipa (⁸) ⎰	..	..
6th					..	..
7th				Battle of Brasovt: city retaken by Austro-German forces (⁹)	..	..
9th					..	..
12th				⎱ Battle of the Lower Narajowka(⁸) Battle of Topraisar-Cobadinu (*Dobrudja*) ⎰	..	..
15th					..	..
19th					..	..
21st					..	..
22nd				Constanza (*Dobrudja*) captured by Bulgarian forces	..	..
24th					..	..
25th				Cernavoda (*Dobrudja*) captured by Bulgarian forces	..	..
28th					..	..
31st		⎱ 9th Battle of the Isonzo ⎰			..	..
NOV. 4th					..	..
10th	1st Offensive Battle of Verdun			Battle of Ozurduk (⁹)	..	..
11th					..	..
15th				Battle of Tărgu-Jiu (⁹) (*Rumania*)	British advance into Sinai begins	..
16th						..
17th	End of the Battles of the Somme, 1916					..
18th						..
19th			Monastir captured by Allied forces			..
21st				Craiova (*Rumania*) taken by German forces		..

MILITARY OPERATIONS.
Main Theatres. 1916.

Date	Western Front	Eastern Front (Rumania/Balkans)	Balkans/Greece	Other (Sinai/Mesopotamia)
22nd				
23rd		Orsova retaken by Austro-German forces		
27th		Passage of the Danube by Mackensen's army*	*Greek Provisional Government at Salonika declare war on Germany and Bulgaria*	
30th		Slatina (Rumania) taken by German forces	*Allied force landed at the Piraeus*	
DEC. 1st	1st Offensive Battle of Verdun (continued)		*Battle of the Cerna and Monastir (continued)*	British forces advancing into Sinai
5th		Battle of the Arges (m) (9) (Rumania)	*Allied force withdrawn from the Piraeus after fighting*	
6th		Bukharest capitulates to the German forces		
11th				
12th	General Nivelle succeeds General Joffre as French Commander-in-Chief			
13th			*Entente Powers send ultimatum to Greece; withdrawal of entire Greek Armies from Thessaly demanded*	British operations for the capture of Kut begin
14th				
15th			*Greek Government accept Allied ultimatum*	
18th				
21st				El Arish (Sinai) occupied by British forces
23rd				Affair of Magdhaba (Sinai)
25th				
26th	Anglo-French Conference in London to discuss the division of the Western Front	Battle of Rimnicul-Sarat (9) (Rumania)	*Anglo-French Conference in London to discuss the Balkan situation*	
27th		Austro-German offensive on the Trotus front (n1) (Moldavia)		

* At Islaz and Simnitza.
† "Schlacht bei Kronstadt."
‡ French title. The German name is "1st Battle of Monastir (October 3rd–November 27th)."
(m) Mackensen's Army Group (Germans and Bulgarians).

MILITARY OPERATIONS.
Main Theatres.
1917.

Date.	WESTERN THEATRE. (France and Flanders.)	ITALIAN THEATRE.	BALKAN THEATRE. (Excluding Rumania and Turkey.)	EASTERN THEATRE. (Russia and Rumania.)	TURKEY. Egypt and Arabia.	TURKEY. Caucasus, Persia and Mesopotamia.
1917. JAN. 4th	..	..	..	Austro-German offensive on the Trotus front (*Moldavia*) (*continued*)	..	..
5th	..	..	..	Braila (*Rumania*) taken by German forces	..	..
6th	..	..	..	Last Russian and Rumanian forces evacuate the Dobrudja	..	..
7th	..	..	..	Battle of the Putna (⁵)	..	..
8th	..	..	..		..	..
9th	..	..	..	Battle of the Aa* (⁶)	Action of Rafah (*Sinai*)	..
24th	..	..	..		Wejh (*Hejaz*) captured by Arab forces	..
FEB. 3rd	..	..	..	..	..	Battle of Kut, 1917
8th	..	..	..	..	Conclusion of British operations against the Senussi	
24th	..	..	..	..	..	
25th	..	..	..	..	..	
26th	Anglo-French Conference at Calais on the military situation†	..	..	..	..	The pursuit to Baghdad
27th		..	..	..	..	Hamadan (*Western Persia*) again taken by Russian forces
MARCH 2nd	..	..	..	..	..	
7th	..	..	..	..	..	
10th	..	..	..	..	..	Passage of the Diyala

MILITARY OPERATIONS.
Main Theatres.
1917.

Date.	WESTERN THEATRE. (France and Flanders.)	ITALIAN THEATRE.	BALKAN THEATRE. (Excluding Rumania and Turkey.)	EASTERN THEATRE. (Russia and Rumania.)	TURKEY. Palestine and Arabia.	TURKEY. Caucasus, Persia and Mesopotamia.	Date.
1917. MARCH 11th	.. ..	..	Allied offensive to free Monastir‡ including	..	..	Baghdad occupied by British forces	**1917. MARCH** 11th
12th	Anglo-French Conference in London on the military situation†	..		..	..	Kirmanshah (*Western Persia*) again taken by Russian forces	12th
13th		..	Battle of Lake Prespa	Russian Revolution begins	..	..	13th
14th		..	*and*	..	..	Action of Mushaidiya ..	14th
15th		..	Battle of Hill 1248	Provisional Government proclaimed	..	..	15th
17th	Capture of Bapaume	..		Tsar of Russia abdicates	..	Karind (*Western Persia*) again taken by Russian forces	17th
19th		..		..	..	..	19th
23rd		..		..	..	..	23rd
24th	German Retreat to the Hindenburg Line	..	..	..	British offensive into Palestine begins	..	24th
25th		..	..	..		Qasr-i-Shirin (*Western Persia*) again taken by Russian forces	25th
26th		..	..	..	1st Battle of Gaza	..	26th
27th		..	..	..		..	27th
APRIL 4th		..	..	..	..	Khanaqin (*North-East of Baghdad*) again taken by Russian forces	**APRIL** 4th
5th		..	..	..	..	..	5th
6th	United States of America declare war on Germany	..	..	..	..	..	6th
9th	Battle of Vimy Ridge and 1st Battle of the Scarpe, 1917, begins	..	..	..	..	..	9th
12th	Battle of Arras, 1917 ..	..	..	..	..	..	12th
16th	2nd Battle of the Aisne and "Battle of the Hills"§	..	..	..	..	..	16th
17th		..	..	..	2nd Battle of Gaza	..	17th
19th		..	..	..		..	19th
20th		..	..	..	..	..	20th

* "Winterschlacht an der Aa," divided in the German list into three phases. † For subjects discussed see Part I. These conferences initiated the idea of co-ordination of operations under French command.
‡ "Tentative pour dégager Monastir." The German name is "2nd Battle of Monastir" (11–26th March)." § "La Bataille des Monts" (in Champagne) otherwise called "3rd Battle of Champagne."

MILITARY OPERATIONS.
Main Theatres.
1917.

Date.	WESTERN THEATRE. (France and Flanders.)	ITALIAN THEATRE.	BALKAN THEATRE. (Excluding Rumania and Turkey.)	EASTERN THEATRE. (Russia and Rumania.)	TURKEY. Palestine and Arabia.	TURKEY. Caucasus, Persia and Mesopotamia.
1917. APRIL						
21st	Battles of Arras, 1917 (*continued*)					Action of Istabulat
22nd						
23rd			Battle of Doiran, 1917 (*1st phase*)			Samarra occupied by British forces
24th						
25th						
29th						Mush (*Armenia*) reoccupied by Turkish forces
30th						
MAY						
3rd						
4th	Battle of Bullecourt					
5th						
8th			Battle of the Var- dar* *including* Battle of Doiran (*2nd phase*) Battle of the Cerna Bend			
9th						
12th		10th Battle of the Isonzo				
17th						
19th						
22nd						
27th						
JUNE						
3rd			*Italy proclaims Protectorate over Albania*			
7th	Battle of Messines, 1917					
8th			*Janina (Greece) occupied by Italian forces*			
10th						
12th			*King Constantine of Greece abdicates*			
14th						

MILITARY OPERATIONS.
Main Theatres.
1917.

Date	Western Front		Eastern & Southern Fronts		Other Theatres	Date
17th	Portuguese troops in action on Western Front for the first time					17th
25th	First contingent of United States troops arrives in France					25th
27th						27th
28th			M. Venizelos assumes power at Athens. Declaration of war by Provisional Government against Germany and Bulgaria becomes effective for the whole of Greece		General Allenby succeeds General Murray as General Officer Commanding-in-Chief in Egypt	28th
29th						29th
30th						30th
JULY						**JULY**
3rd			Russian Summer Offensive, 1917, *including* Battles of Brzezany(*) and Koniuchy(*)			3rd
6th			Battle of Zloczow(*²)		Aqaba taken by Arab forces	6th
8th						8th
10th	German attack on Nieuport				Russian forces begin withdrawal from Western Persia: Qasr-i-Shirin evacuated	10th
11th						11th
14th					British attack on Ramadi	14th
18th			Battle of Dvinsk, 1917, begins(ᵈ)			18th
19th			Battle of Smorgon-Krevo begins(¹⁰)			19th
22nd			Battle of East Galicia(ᵃ²)			22nd
25th			Battle of Dvinsk, 1917, ends(ᵈ)			25th
27th			Battle of Smorgon-Krevo ends(¹⁰)			27th
28th						28th
31st	Battles of Ypres, 1917		Battle of Marasesti(⁹)(ᵃ¹)† (*Rumania*) (1st phase)			31st
AUG.						**AUG.**
1st			General Korniloff succeeds General Brusiloff as Russian Commander-in-Chief			1st
3rd			Czernowitz (*Bukovina*) again taken by Austro-German forces			3rd

* French official title.   † Rumanian name: German dates.

MILITARY OPERATIONS.
Main Theatres.
1917.

Date.	WESTERN THEATRE. (France and Flanders.)	ITALIAN THEATRE.	BALKAN THEATRE. (Excluding Rumania and Turkey.)	EASTERN THEATRE. (Russia and Rumania.)	TURKEY. Palestine and Arabia.	TURKEY. Caucasus, Persia and Mesopotamia.
1917. AUG. 6th						
15th	Battle of Hill 70					
17th						
20th				Battle of Marasesti (²) * (Rumania) (2nd phase)		
25th						
SEPT. 1st	Battles of Ypres, 1917 (continued)	11th Battle of the Isonzo				
3rd	2nd Offensive Battle of Verdun			Battle of Riga (³): city captured by German forces		
5th						
8th				General Kornilov heads revolt against Provisional Government and marches on Petrograd		
10th				*Provisional Government proclaim General Kornilov a traitor*		
12th						
13th				General Kornilov's revolt collapses		
14th				General Kornilov surrenders to the Provisional Government		
15th				*Russia declared a Republic*		
20th						Council of Trans-Caucasian People proclaim Trans-Caucasia a Federal Republic
21st				Jacobstadt stormed by German forces (³) (⁴)		
22nd						
28th						Ramadi captured by British forces
29th						

MILITARY OPERATIONS.
Main Theatres.
1917.

Date	Western Front	Italian Front	Russian / Baltic Front	Other Theatres
OCT. 11th	Battle of La Maison		German operations against the Baltic Islands begin	
16th	Battle of La Maison		German force captures Ösel Island	
17th	Battle of La Maison			
18th	Battle of La Maison		German force captures Moon Island and Dagö Island	
19th	Battle of La Maison			
20th	Battle of La Maison		German conquest of the Baltic Islands completed	
23rd	Battle of La Maison			
24th	Battles of Ypres, 1917 (continued)	Austro-German Offensive in the Julian Alps begins		
27th	Battles of Ypres, 1917 (continued)			
28th	Battles of Ypres, 1917 (continued)	Gorizia and Udine taken by Austro-German forces		
NOV. 1st	Battles of Ypres, 1917 (continued)	Austro-German Armies force passage of the Tagliamento		3rd Battle of Gaza
3rd	Battles of Ypres, 1917 (continued)	Arrival of French troops in Italy announced		3rd Battle of Gaza
4th	Battles of Ypres, 1917 (continued)	Arrival of British troops in Italy announced		3rd Battle of Gaza
6th	2nd Offensive Battle of Verdun (continued)	Allied Conference at Rapallo: Inception of Supreme War Council		Tikrit (*Mesopotamia*) occupied by British forces
7th	2nd Offensive Battle of Verdun (continued)	General Cadorna succeeded by General Diaz	Bolshevik *coup d'état* in Petrograd	3rd Battle of Gaza
8th		Vittorio Veneto captured by Austro-German forces		Turkish armies in retreat: Rearguard actions
9th	Battles of Ypres, 1917, end	12th Battle of the Isonzo		
10th	Battles of Ypres, 1917, end	12th Battle of the Isonzo		

* Rumanian name: German dates.

MILITARY OPERATIONS.
Main Theatres.
1917.

Date.	WESTERN THEATRE. (France and Flanders.)	ITALIAN THEATRE.	BALKAN THEATRE. (Excluding Rumania and Turkey.)	EASTERN THEATRE. (Russia and Rumania.)	TURKEY. Palestine and Arabia.	TURKEY. Caucasus, Persia and Mesopotamia.	Date.
1917. NOV. 11th		Austro-German forces reach the Piave	..	..	Turkish armies in retreat: Rearguard actions (*cont'd.*)	..	1917. NOV. 11th
12th			..	..		..	12th
13th			..	Kerenski's forces defeated by Bolsheviki near Petrograd	Action of El Mughar	..	13th
14th			..		Occupation of Junction Station	..	14th
16th			..	..	Jaffa taken by British forces	..	16th
17th			..	..		..	17th
18th	2nd Offensive Battle of Verdun (*continued*)		..	Ukrainian People's Republic proclaimed	Battle of Nebi Samwil	Death of General Maude at Baghdad	18th
20th			..	Bolshevik Government begin armistice pourparlers		..	20th
21st			..			..	21st
24th			..	..		..	24th
27th	Battle of Cambrai, 1917	12th Battle of the Isonzo (*continued*)	..	First meeting of Russian and German armistice delegates		..	27th
30th	The German counter-attacks at Cambrai	Fighting on the Asiago - Piave Line	..	..	..	..	30th
DEC. 1st			..	Hostilities suspended between Russian and Austro-German armies*	..	..	DEC. 1st
2nd			..		..	..	2nd
3rd			..	Hostilities suspended between forces of Central Powers and Rumania	..	..	3rd
6th			..	..	..	..	6th
7th			..	"*Truce of Focsani*" between Rumania and the Central Powers signed		..	7th
8th			..		Capture of Jerusalem	..	8th
9th			..	Hostilities between Rumania and the Central Powers cease		..	9th
10th			..		..	..	10th

MILITARY OPERATIONS.
Main Theatres.
1917-18.

Date			Event (Salonika/Western)	Event (Russia/Eastern)	Event (Palestine)	Event (Mesopotamia/Persia)
11th					General Allenby makes formal entry into Jerusalem	
15th				Armistice signed at Brest-Litovsk		
17th			General Guillaumat succeeds General Sarrail as Allied Commander-in-Chief at Salonika	Armistice between Russia and the Central Powers begins		
21st					Battle of Jaffa	
22nd				Peace negotiations between Bolshevik Government and Central Powers opened at Brest-Litovsk		
26th					Defence of Jerusalem	
30th						
1918. JAN. 1st						
4th				Independence of Finland recognised by the Bolshevik Government		
8th						Qasr-i-Shirin (West Persia) occupied by British forces
27th					Arab actions for Et Tafile	General Dunsterville's Mission leaves Baghdad for the Caspian
28th					Turkish Dead Sea flotilla seized by Arab camelry at El Mezraa	
FEB. 1st						
4th				Independence of The Ukraine recognised by the Central Powers		
6th				General Alexeiev, with Don Cossacks, moves towards Moscow against the Bolshevik forces		
9th				German Government send ultimatum to Rumania demanding peace negotiations within four days. Peace signed between Central Powers and Ukraine Rada		
10th				M. Trotski announces that state of war between Russia and Germany is ended, but that Russia will not sign formal peace treaty		
13th				General Alexeiev's forces defeated by the Bolsheviki		
17th				General Kaledin commits suicide		General Dunsterville's Mission arrives at Enzeli
18th				Hostilities resumed between Germany and Russia: German armies (8d 10 h) advance. Dvinsk seized by German forces (d)		

* See Note in Part I.

MILITARY OPERATIONS.
Main Theatres.
1918.

Date.	WESTERN THEATRE. (France and Flanders.)	ITALIAN THEATRE.	BALKAN THEATRE. (Excluding Rumania and Turkey.)	EASTERN THEATRE. (Russia and Rumania.)	TURKEY. Palestine and Arabia.	TURKEY. Caucasus, Persia and Mesopotamia.	Date.
1918. FEB.							**1918. FEB.**
19th	..	..	..	*Bolshevik Government notify willingness to sign peace treaty*	⎱ Capture of Jericho by British forces	..	19th
21st	..	..	..	..	⎰	..	21st
24th	..	..	..	*Dorpat taken by German forces*	..	Trebizond retaken by Turkish forces	24th
25th	..	..	..	*Pernau (⁸), Revul (⁸) and Pskov (ᵈ) taken by German forces*	..	Kirmanshah (*Western Persia*) occupied by British forces	25th
28th	..	..	..	*German force leaves Danzig for the Aaland Islands*	..	..	28th
MAR.							**MAR.**
1st	..	..	..	⎱ Capture of Kiev by German forces (ʰ)*	..	..	1st
3rd	..	..	..	*Peace signed between Bolshevik Government and Central Powers at Brest-Litovsk*	..	..	3rd
4th	..	..	..	*Narva occupied by German forces (⁸)*	..	..	4th
5th	..	..	..	*Preliminary treaty of peace between Rumania and Central Powers signed at Buftea*	..	..	5th
7th	..	..	..	*Peace signed between Finland and Germany*	..	..	7th
8th	..	..	..	..	⎱ Actions of Tel Asur	..	8th
9th	..	..	..	..	⎰	Hit (*Euphrates*) occupied by British forces	9th
12th	..	..	..	⎱ Capture of Odessa by German forces (ʰ)†	..	Erzerum retaken by Turkish forces	12th
14th	..	..	..	*Congress of Soviets meet at Moscow to ratify Peace Treaty*	..	..	14th
15th	..	..	..	*German Government proclaim protectorate over Kurland*	..	..	15th
16th	..	..	..	..	..	Hamadan (*Western Persia*) evacuated by Russian forces‡	16th

MILITARY OPERATIONS.
Main Theatres.
1918.

Date	Western Front	Eastern Front	Middle East / Other	Date
17th	..	..	..	17th
21st	**German offensive in Picardy begins** { Battle of St. Quentin	..	..	21st
23rd	Paris first shelled by long-range gun	..	..	23rd
24th	} 1st Battle of Bapaume	..	..	24th
25th		Nicolaiev captured by German forces	..	25th
26th	Doullens Conference: Decision taken to appoint General Foch to co-ordinate operations of French and British Armies		Passage of the Jordan by British forces	26th
27th		German forces advancing through The Ukraine		27th
28th	1st Battle of Arras, 1918		1st Action of Es Salt	28th
29th	1st Battles of the Somme, 1918 ("2nd Battle of Picardy")			29th
30th			1st Attack on Amman	30th
APRIL		Poltava captured by German forces		APRIL
1st		..	..	1st
3rd		German Expeditionary Force for Finland leaves Danzig	..	3rd
4th		German Expeditionary Force to Finland landed at Hangö	Enzeli (North-West Persia) evacuated by Russian forces‡	4th
5th		Ekaterinoslav taken by German forces	Sarikamish (Caucasus) taken by Turkish forces	5th
6th	German advance from Chauny to the Oise-Aisne Canal	..	Van (Armenia) retaken by Turkish forces	6th
8th		..	..	8th
9th	**German offensive in Flanders begins**	Kharkov captured by German forces	..	9th
11th	Sir D. Haig's "Backs to the wall" order	..	Turkish attack on the Jordan bridgeheads	11th
12th	General Foch appointed Commander-in-Chief of Allied armies in France§	..	..	12th
14th		Helsingfors captured by German forces	..	14th
15th	**Battles of the Lys**	..	Batum (Georgia) taken by Turkish forces	15th
19th		German forces enter the Crimea	..	19th

* City of Kiev actually taken on the 2nd March. † City of Odessa actually occupied on the 13th March.
‡ These dates refer only to the Russian regular forces. Irregular Russian forces and Cossacks in Persian pay remained in North-West Persia after the regular troops were withdrawn, and Enzeli was governed by a Bolshevik Committee till the 4th August.
§ The Belgian army was not included, but remained under the direction of the King of the Belgians, as Commander-in-Chief.

MILITARY OPERATIONS.
Main Theatres.
1918.

Date.	WESTERN THEATRE. (France and Flanders.)	ITALIAN THEATRE.	BALKAN THEATRE. (Excluding Rumania and Turkey.)	EASTERN THEATRE. (Russia and Rumania.)	TURKEY. Palestine and Arabia.	TURKEY. Caucasus, Persia and Mesopotamia.	Date.
1918. APRIL 23rd	*Blocking raid by British naval light forces on Ostend and Zeebrugge*	..	..	..	..	..	**1918. APRIL** 23rd
24th	⎫ *Actions of Villers Bre-*	..	..	..	..	..	24th
25th	⎬ *tonneux*	..	..	..	..	..	25th
27th	**Battles of the Lys** (*continued*)	..	..	..	..	Kars (*Georgia*) occupied by Turkish forces	27th
29th		..	..	German Government establish military dictatorship in The Ukraine with General Skoropadski as Hetman	..	Action of Tuz Khurmatli	29th
30th		..	..	Viborg (*Finland*) captured by Finnish White Guards and German forces	⎱ 2nd Action of Es Salt	..	30th
MAY 1st	..	..	..	**Capture of Sevastopol by German forces**	⎰	..	**MAY** 1st
4th	..	..	..		..	..	4th
7th	..	..	..	*Peace signed between Rumania and the Central Powers Frederickshamn (South Finland) captured by Finnish White Guards* **End of Finnish Civil War**	..	Kirkuk occupied by British forces	7th
8th	..	..	..	Rostov captured by German forces	..	..	8th
18th	..	..	..	..	..	Alexandropol (*Georgia*) occupied by Turkish forces	18th
24th	..	..	..	*General Poole arrives at Murmansk to organise the North Russian Expeditionary Force*	..	Kirkuk evacuated by British forces	24th
27th	⎫ **Battle of the Aisne, 1918**	..	..	..	..	..	27th
31st	⎬ ("*3rd Battle of the Aisne*")	..	Battle of the Skra di Legen	..	..	..	31st
JUNE 6th	⎭	..	..	..	..	..	**JUNE** 6th

MILITARY OPERATIONS.
Main Theatres.
1918.

Date	Western Front	Italian/Balkan	Russia/Eastern	Caucasus/Persia
8th				Georgian Government sign peace with Germany and Turkey
9th	⎫ Battle of the Matz			Armenian National Council sign peace with Turkey
12th	⎭			German Expeditionary Force to the Caucasus landed at Poti (Georgia)
14th				
15th		⎫ Battle of the Piave	British Expeditionary Force landed at Murmansk	Tiflis (Georgia) occupied by German force
23rd				Kurdamir (East Caucasus) occupied by Turkish forces
24th		⎭		Tabriz again occupied by Turkish forces
29th				
30th			⎫ Allied forces seize railway from Murmansk to Soroki	
JULY 6th			⎭	
10th				
15th	⎫ 4th Battle of Champagne			
18th	⎭			
20th		French and Italian forces begin offensive in Albania		British defence of Resht (Northern Persia)
26th	⎫ Battles of the Marne, 1918 ("2nd Battle of the Marne")	Berat (Albania) taken by Italian forces		"Coup d'État" at Baku. Bolshevik Government replaced by Central Caspian Dictatorship
30th	⎭		Field-Marshal von Eichhorn (commanding German Army in The Ukraine) assassinated in Kiev	
AUG. 1st			⎫ Archangel captured by Entente Expeditionary Force*	
2nd			⎭	
4th				British force landed at Baku
7th	⎫ Battle of Amiens and Battle of Montdidier			Bolshevik Committee at Enzeli arrested by British military authorities
8th				
11th	⎭			
15th				

* For subsequent events in North Russia, see Part II, Section II (B).

MILITARY OPERATIONS.
Main Theatres.
1918.

Date.	WESTERN THEATRE. (France and Flanders.)	ITALIAN THEATRE.	BALKAN THEATRE. (Excluding Rumania and Turkey.)	EASTERN THEATRE. (Russia and Rumania.)	TURKEY. Palestine and Arabia.	TURKEY. Caucasus, Persia and Mesopotamia.	Date.
1918. AUG. 17th		..	..	..	..	..	1918. AUG. 17th
21st	2nd Battle of Noyon	..	..	..	..	..	21st
22nd	2nd Battles of the Somme, 1918 *and* 2nd Battles of Arras, 1918	..	Austrian counter-offensive in Albania begins	..	..	..	22nd
26th		..	Berat (*Albania*) retaken by Austrian forces	..	..	..	26th
29th		..	..	..	..	..	29th
SEPT. 3rd		..	..	..	..	Defence of Baku	SEPT. 3rd
10th	Battle of Savy-Dallon	..	..	..	..		10th
12th	Battle of St. Mihiel	..	..	..	..		12th
13th		..	..	..	..		13th
14th	Battle of Vauxaillon	..	..	..	..	British force withdrawn from Baku (*night 14th/15th*)	14th
15th		..	Battle of the Dobropolje ("*Battle of the Moglenitza*")	..	..	Baku taken by Turkish forces	15th
16th		..		..	..		16th
18th	Battle of Epéhy (*one day*)	..	Battle of Doiran, 1918 (*British*)	..	British offensive in Palestine	..	18th
19th	Battles of the Hindenburg Line	..	Battle of Monastir-Doiran*	..	Battles of Megiddo	..	19th
20th		..		..		..	20th
22nd		..	Allied armies advancing into Bulgaria	..	Ma'an evacuated by the Turkish garrison	..	22nd
23rd		..		..	Haifa, Acre and Es Salt taken by British forces	..	23rd
24th		..	Ishtip and Veles taken by Serbian forces	..	Hejaz Railway cut by British cavalry at Amman	..	24th
25th		..		..		..	25th

MILITARY OPERATIONS.
Main Theatres.
1918.

Date	Western Front	Italian Front	Balkan Theatre	Turkish Theatres
26th	Battle of Champagne and Argonne begins; Battle of the Canal du Nord begins	..	..	..
27th		..	..	..
28th	Allied Offensive in Flanders begins; Battle of the St. Quentin Canal begins	..	*Bulgarian Government ask for armistice*	..
29th		..	*Allied armies advancing into Bulgaria (continued)*	Turkish Ma'an garrison surrenders near Amman
30th	Battle of Ypres, 1918; Battles of the Hindenburg Line (continued)	..	*Armistice between Bulgaria and Entente Powers signed* **Hostilities between Bulgaria and Entente Powers cease** (12 noon)	
OCT. 1st		..	Berat (*Albania*) retaken by Italian forces	Damascus taken by British and Arab forces
2nd		..		
5th	Battle of Champagne and Argonne	..	Vranje (*Serbia*) retaken by Allied forces	
6th		..		Sidon occupied by British forces
7th		..	Elbasan (*Albania*) taken by Italian forces	Beirut occupied by French naval forces
8th	Battle of Cambrai, 1918	..	Allied forces advancing through Serbia and Albania	
9th		..	Pristina (*Serbia*) retaken by French forces	The Pursuit through Syria
10th		..	Prizren and Nish (*Serbia*) retaken by Allied forces	
11th		..		
13th	Battle of Roulers (14th/15th) and Battle of Courtrai and Battle of Thourout - Thielt (14th/30th)	..	Durazzo, Novi Bazar and Ipek taken by Italian forces	Tripoli (*Syria*) occupied by Allied forces
14th		..		
15th		..		Homs (*Syria*) occupied by British cavalry
17th	Battle of the Selle	..		
19th		..		

* French official title, which includes the British Battle of Doiran.

MILITARY OPERATIONS.
Main Theatres.
1918.

Date	WESTERN THEATRE. (France and Flanders.)	ITALIAN THEATRE.	BALKAN THEATRE. (Excluding Rumania and Turkey.)	EASTERN THEATRE. (Russia and Rumania.)	TURKEY. Palestine and Arabia.	TURKEY. Caucasus, Persia and Mesopotamia.	Date
1918. OCT. 20th	Belgian coast reoccupied by Allied forces	..	..	..	..	..	**1918. OCT. 20th**
23rd	Battle of the Selle (*continued*)	..	..	..	The Pursuit through Syria (*continued*)	British forces begin advance on Mosul	23rd
24th		Final Italian Offensive begins		..		Advanced guard actions	24th
25th	Battle of the Serre	..	Allied forces advancing through Serbia and Albania (*continued*)	..			25th
26th		*Austrian Government ask for Armistice*		..	Aleppo occupied by Allied forces		26th
27th	*General von Ludendorff resigns*			..	Muslimiya Junction (*North of Aleppo*) occupied by British cavalry		27th
28th		Battle of Vittorio Veneto	San Giovanni di Medua occupied by Italian forces	..		Battle of Sharqat	28th
29th				..	*Armistice between Turkey and Entente Powers signed at Mudros*		29th
30th		*Revolution in Vienna*	Scutari taken by Italian forces *Revolution in Buda-Pest* Belgrade retaken by Serbian forces	..	**Hostilities between Turkey and Entente Powers cease** (12 noon)		30th
31st	Battle of the Lys (*Belgium*)			..	..	British forces advancing on Mosul *News of Armistice received*	31st
NOV. 1st	Battle of Valenciennes	Trieste occupied by Italian forces *Armistice between Austria - Hungary and Entente Powers signed*	Independent Hungarian Government formed in Buda-Pest	..	..		**NOV. 1st**
2nd	*Mutiny breaks out in the German Fleet at Kiel* Battle of Le Chesne and Buzancy		..	..	..	..	2nd
3rd			..	..	..	..	3rd
4th	Battle of the Sambre (*one day*) 2nd Battle of Guise	Hostilities on the Italian front cease	Antivari (*Montenegro*) occupied by Italian naval forces	..	..	Mosul occupied by British forces	4th
*5th	General advance of the Allied Armies	Fiume occupied by Italian naval forces	..	..	..	..	*5th

MILITARY OPERATIONS.
Main Theatres.
1918.

Date	Western Front	Italian Front / Central Europe	Balkans / Eastern	Mediterranean / Turkey	Other
6th	General advance of the Allied Armies (contd.)	..	King Peter of Serbia re-enters Belgrade	..	..
7th	Battle of Thiérache	..	..	..	..
8th	German Armistice delegates reach Allied Head-quarters	..	..	..	..
9th	Battle of Mézières / Revolution breaks out in Berlin	Emperor of Austria abdicates / German-Austrian Republic proclaimed	..	Alexandretta (Syria) occupied by Entente naval Forces	..
10th	Kaiser crosses the frontier into Holland	..	Allied forces cross Danube at Rus-chuk and enter Rumania	..	All Turkish troops withdrawn from the Mosul Vilayet
11th	Capture of Mons / Armistice concluded between Germany and Entente Powers / Hostilities on the Western Front cease (11 a.m.)	..	Rumania re-enters the war†	..	..
12th	..	..	..	Allied fleet passes through the Dardanelles	..
13th	..	Hungarian Government conclude separate Armistice with Allied commander at Belgrade / Hungary declares independence	..	Allied fleet arrives at Constantinople	..
15th	..	..	..	..	..
16th	Allied Armies begin march into Germany	..	Poland declares independence	..	Baku again occupied by British forces
17th	..	..	..	..	..
18th	Brussels reoccupied by Belgian forces / Last German troops recross French frontier	Italian military forces landed at Fiume	..	..	..
19th	Metz occupied by French forces / Antwerp reoccupied by Belgian forces	..	..	..	..
20th	Luxembourg frontier crossed by United States forces	..	..	..	..
21st	Namur occupied by British forces	..	..	French troops landed at Constantinople	..
24th	British and United States troops reach German frontier	..	..	..	..
25th	Strasbourg occupied by French forces	..	..	..	..
26th	Last German troops recross Belgian frontier	..	Sevastopol occupied by Allied naval forces	..	..
28th	French troops cross German frontier / Kaiser signs abdication	..	..	..	..

* On this day Marshal Foch was placed in supreme control of Allied forces on all Fronts.

† Announcement by King of Rumania that Rumania had again taken up arms on the side of her Allies.

MILITARY OPERATIONS.
Main Theatres.
1918.

Date.	WESTERN THEATRE. (France and Flanders.)	ITALIAN THEATRE.	BALKAN THEATRE. (Excluding Rumania and Turkey.)	EASTERN THEATRE. (Russia and Rumania.)	TURKEY.		Date.
					Palestine and Arabia.	Caucasus, Persia and Mesopotamia.	
1918. DEC. 1st	British and United States troops cross German frontier. Trèves occupied by United States forces	..	..	Bukharest re-occupied by Rumanian and Allied forces	..	..	1918. DEC. 1st
3rd	..	..	..	Last Bulgarian troops recross Rumanian (*Dobrudja*) frontier	..	..	3rd
4th	*Demobilization of the British Army begins*	..	..	..	..	..	4th
8th	Coblenz occupied by United States forces	..	..	..	..	..	8th
12th	British troops cross the Rhine at Cologne	..	..	..	..	..	12th
14th	*Armistice on the Western Front extended to January 17, 1919*	..	..	..	..	..	14th
16th	..	..	..	**Marshal Mackensen** and his force surrender to the Hungarians near Budapest	..	..	16th
20th	..	..	..	French force landed at Odessa	..	..	20th
27th	..	..	..	..	..	Batum (*Georgia*) occupied by British force*	27th

* This force subsequently occupied the whole of Georgia with headquarters at Tiflis.

MILITARY OPERATIONS.
Subsidiary Theatres.
1914.

PART II.

SECTION II (B).

MILITARY OPERATIONS: SUBSIDIARY THEATRES OF WAR.

    (i.) *South Africa* (including German South-West Africa) - up to July 1915.
   (ii.) *West Africa* - - - - - - - up to March 1916.
  (iii.) *East Africa* - - - - - - -
  (iv.) *Western Egypt and the Sudan* - - - - from November 1914 to March 1917.
   (v.) *Arabia* - - - - - - - - from November 1914 onwards.
  (vi.) *Asia* (excluding Turkish Empire) - - - up to March 1916.
       (a.) Central and Southern Asia ⎫
       (b.) Siberia and the Far East ⎬ - - from March 1916 onwards.
 (vii.) *North Russia* - - - - - - - from November 1917 onwards.

NOTE.—For events in the Pacific, including Australasia, see Section III (Naval).

Date.	SOUTH AFRICA. (Including German South-West Africa.)	WEST AFRICA.	EAST AFRICA.	ASIA. (Excluding Turkish Empire, West Persia, and the Caucasus.)	Date.
1914. AUG.					**1914. AUG.**
3rd	..	*Germany declares war on France*	..	..	3rd
4th	..	*Great Britain declares war on Germany*	..	..	4th
8th	..	British forces cross frontier of Togoland and occupy Lome	*Dar es Salaam bombarded by H.M.S. "Astræa."*	..	8th
13th	..	Allied advance on Kamina (*Togoland*) from Lome begins	..	..	13th
15th	..	..	Taveta occupied by German forces	*Japan sends ultimatum to Germany demanding the evacuation of Tsingtau*	15th
19th	..	..	First battalion of Indian Expeditionary Force* "C" leaves India for Mombasa	..	19th
21st	German force crosses the frontier of Cape Colony	..	..	..	21st
23rd	..	..	..	*Japan declares war on Germany*	23rd
25th	..	Nigerian frontier of the Cameroons crossed by British forces: Affair of Tepe *Chad frontier of the Cameroons crossed by French forces*	..	..	25th
26th	..	**German forces in Togoland capitulate to the Allied commander at Amuchu**	..	..	26th
27th	..	First attack on Mora (*Cameroons*)	..	..	27th
30th	..	First attack on Garua (*Cameroons*)	..	..	30th
31st	..	*Agreement concluded between French and British Governments defining provisional zones in Togoland*	..	..	31st

* Indian Expeditionary Force is abbreviated in later entries to I.E.F.

MILITARY OPERATIONS.
Subsidiary Theatres.
1914.

Date.	SOUTH AFRICA. (Including German South-West Africa.)	WEST AFRICA. (Cameroons).	EAST AFRICA.	WEST EGYPT AND SUDAN.	ARABIA.	ASIA. (Excluding Turkish Empire, West Persia, and the Caucasus.)	Date.
1914. SEPT.							**1914. SEPT.**
1st	.. ..	.. ..	First battalion of I.E.F. "C" arrives at Mombasa (*see August* 19*th*)	.. ..	.. ..	.. ..	1st
2nd	.. ..	.. ..	.. ..	.. ..	.. ..	Japanese forces land in Shantung to attack Tsingtau	2nd
5th	.. ..	.. ..	German force crosses frontier of Northern Rhodesia. Defence of Abercorn begins	.. ..	.. ..		5th
6th	.. ..	.. ..	Affair of Tsavo*	.. ..	.. ..		6th
7th	.. ..	Naval operations against Duala begin, in preparation for attack by Allied Expeditionary Force	.. ..	.. ..	.. ..		7th
9th	.. ..	.. ..	Affairs near Karonga (*Nyasaland*) Defence of Abercorn (*Rhodesia*) ends : German forces retreat	.. ..	.. ..		9th
15th	**Outbreak of rebellion in South Africa**	.. ..	.. ..	.. ..	.. ..		15th
19th	Lüderitzbucht (*German South-West Africa*) occupied by South African forces	.. ..	.. ..	.. ..	.. ..	Siege of Tsingtau	19th
20th	.. ..	.. ..	H.M.S. "Pegasus" sunk by German light cruiser "Königsberg" at Zanzibar	.. ..	.. ..		20th
23rd	.. ..	.. ..	.. ..	.. ..	.. ..	British force joins Japanese army before Tsingtau†	23rd
26th	.. ..	Duala taken by Allied forces	.. ..	.. ..	.. ..		26th
27th	.. ..		.. ..				27th
OCT.							**OCT.**
14th	.. ..	Yabasi taken by Allied forces	.. ..	.. ..	.. ..		14th
16th	.. ..	.. ..	First units of I.E.F. "B" leave India for Mombasa	.. ..	.. ..		16th
26th	.. ..	German forces begin an unprovoked invasion of Angola Edea (*Cameroons*) occupied by French forces	.. ..	.. ..	.. ..		26th
31st	.. ..	.. ..	First units of I.E.F. "B" arrive at Mombasa	.. ..	.. ..		31st

* This was the first engagement in the war in which Indian troops were engaged (the 29th Punjabis).
† Force landed 22nd; in action 24th.

MILITARY OPERATIONS.
Subsidiary Theatres.
1914-15.

Date.	SOUTH AFRICA. (Including German South-West Africa.)	WEST AFRICA (Cameroons).	EAST AFRICA.	WEST EGYPT AND SUDAN.	ARABIA.	ASIA. (Excluding Turkish Empire, West Persia, and the Caucasus.)	Date.
1914. NOV. 2nd	.. ..	.. ..		.. ..	.. ..		**1914 NOV.** 2nd
3rd	.. ..	.. ..	Affair of Longido **British attack on Tanga**	.. ..	.. ..		3rd
5th	.. ..	.. ..		*Great Britain and France declare war on Turkey*			5th
7th				.. ..	.. ..	Tsingtau capitulates to the Japanese forces	7th
10th	.. ..	.. ..	.. ..	.. ..	British force storms Sheikh Saïd (*South Arabia*) and destroys the defences	.. ..	10th
11th	.. ..	.. ..	.. ..	.. ..		.. ..	11th
14th	.. ..	.. ..	.. ..	*Sultan of Turkey as Khalif proclaims Jehad against those making war on Turkey or her Allies*	.. ..	.. ..	14th
20th	.. ..	*Allied Governments withdraw proposals for neutralisation of African free trade zone*		.. ..	.. ..	.. ..	20th
22nd	.. ..	.. ..	*War Office assume control of the East African operations*	.. ..	.. ..	.. ..	22nd
23rd	.. ..	*Portuguese Government announce prospective co-operation of Portugal with Great Britain*		.. ..	.. ..	.. ..	23rd
28th	.. ..	.. ..	.. ..	.. ..	.. ..	Affair of Miranshah (*North-West Frontier, India*)*	28th
29th	.. ..	.. ..	.. ..	.. ..	.. ..		29th
DEC. 1st	General De Wet captured by Union troops	.. ..	.. ..	.. ..	.. ..	.. ..	**DEC.** 1st
21st	.. ..	.. ..	Jasin occupied by British troops	.. ..	.. ..	.. ..	21st
28th	**End of organised rebellion in South Africa**	.. ..	.. ..	.. ..	.. ..	.. ..	28th
1915. JAN. 5th	.. ..	French defence of Edea	.. ..	.. ..	.. ..	.. ..	**1915. JAN.** 5th
10th	.. ..	.. ..	.. ..	.. ..	British defence of Muscat	.. ..	10th
11th	Last rebels in the Transvaal captured	.. ..	.. ..	.. ..		.. ..	11th
12th	.. ..	.. ..	Mafia Island seized by British force	.. ..	.. ..	.. ..	12th
14th	Swakopmund (*German South-West Africa*) occupied by South African forces	.. ..	.. ..	.. ..	.. ..	.. ..	14th

* First outbreak on North-West Frontier of India caused by German intrigue

MILITARY OPERATIONS.
Subsidiary Theatres.
1915.

Date.	SOUTH AFRICA. (Including German South-West Africa.)	WEST AFRICA.	EAST AFRICA.	WEST EGYPT AND SUDAN.	ARABIA.	ASIA. (Excluding Turkish Empire, West Persia, and the Caucasus.)	Date.
1915. JAN.							**1915. JAN.**
18th	..	..	} Affair of Jasin {	..	..	..	18th
19th	..	..		..	..	..	19th
23rd	} Defence of Upington {	..	..	..	..	..	23rd
24th		..	..	..	..	..	24th
31st	..	..	..	..	Arab forces (*Idrisi*) occupy Farasan Islands (*Red Sea*)	..	31st
FEB.							**FEB.**
15th	..	..	..	..	..	*Mutiny of the 5th Light Infantry (Indian Army) at Singapore*	15th
16th	..	Oyem (*Cameroons*) occupied by French forces	..	..	..	..	16th
22nd	South African Northern Force begins advance from Swakopmund on Windhuk	..	..	..	..	..	22nd
MAR.							**MAR.**
1st	..	..	*British blockade of German East Africa begins*	..	..	..	1st
20th	Actions of Jakalswater	..	..	..	..	..	20th
25th	..	..	..	..	..	} Action of Dardoni (North-West Frontier, India) {	25th
26th	..	..	..	..	..		26th
30th	Aus occupied by South African forces	..	..	..	..	..	30th
APR.							**APR.**
12th	..	First Advance on Yaunde begins	..	..	..	..	12th
18th	..	Operations of Allied force against Garua begin	..	..	..	1st affair of Hafiz Kor (North-West Frontier, India)	18th
23rd	..	*British blockade of the Cameroons begins*	..	..	..	..	23rd
25th	} Action of Gibeon {	..	..	..	..	..	25th
26th		..	..	..	..	..	26th
28th	..	..	..	..	British Government conclude treaty with the Idrisi	..	28th
MAY							**MAY**
7th	..	..	..	..	..	*Japan presents ultimatum to China demanding territorial concessions*	7th
9th	..	..	..	..	..	*Chinese Government yields to Japanese demands*	9th
13th	Windhuk occupied by South African Northern Force	..	..	..	..	..	13th

MILITARY OPERATIONS.
Subsidiary Theatres.
1915.

Date.	SOUTH AFRICA. (Including German South-West Africa.)	WEST AFRICA.	EAST AFRICA.	WEST EGYPT AND SUDAN.	ARABIA.	ASIA. (Excluding Turkish Empire, and the Caucasus.)	Date.
1915. MAY. 21st	..	..	..	..	..	Russian Expeditionary Force to West Persia lands at Enzeli	**1915. MAY.** 21st
25th	..	..	..	..	..	Formal treaty between Japan and China signed in Pekin	25th
30th	..	..	Affair of Sphinxhaven (Lake Nyassa)	..	..	..	30th
31st	..	Siege of Garua begins	..	..	..	..	31st
JUNE 7th	..	Allied Commander-in-Chief decides to abandon advance on Yaunde	..	..	..	..	**JUNE** 7th
10th	..	**Garua taken by Allied forces**	..	..	..	..	10th
14th	..	..	..	..	Turkish attack on Perim	..	14th
15th	..	..	..	..		..	15th
19th	South African forces begin advance on Otavifontein	..	..	..	..	..	19th
28th	..	Operations of the advance on Yaunde end. Ngaundere captured by the Allied Northern Force	..	..	..	..	28th
JULY 1st	Otavifontein captured by South African forces	..	..	..	..	..	**JULY** 1st
4th	..	..	..	..	Action of Lahej	..	4th
5th	..	..	..	..		..	5th
9th	**German South-West Africa capitulates to General Botha**	..	..	..	..	..	9th
11th		..	German cruiser "Königsberg" destroyed in Rufiji River by British monitors	..	..	..	11th
12th		..	..	..	..	British residency at Bushire attacked by Tangistani tribesmen	12th
20th		..	..	..	Affair of Sheikh 'Othman (Aden)	..	20th
22nd		..	Capture of Bukoba	..	..	..	22nd
23rd		..		..	..	..	23rd

MILITARY OPERATIONS.
Subsidiary Theatres.
1915.

Date.	WEST AFRICA.	EAST AFRICA.	WEST EGYPT AND SUDAN.	ARABIA.	ASIA. (Excluding Turkish Empire.)	Date.
1915.						**1915.**
JULY 29th	.. ..	.. ..	.. ..	.. ..	Establishment of East Persia cordon begun	**JULY** 29th
AUG. 8th	.. ..	.. ..	.. ..	.. ..	Bushire (*Persia*) occupied by British forces	**AUG.** 8th
12th	.. ..	.. ..	.. ..	.. ..	Destruction of Dilbar	12th
16th	.. ..	.. ..	.. ..	.. ..		16th
SEPT. 5th	.. ..	.. ..	.. ..	.. ..	Action of Hafiz Kor (*North-West Frontier of India*)	**SEPT.** 5th
8th	2nd attack on Mora	.. ..	.. ..	.. ..	.. ..	8th
9th		.. ..	.. ..	.. ..	.. ..	9th
22nd	Second advance on Yaunde begins	.. ..	.. ..	.. ..	.. ..	22nd
OCT. 7th	.. ..	.. ..	.. ..	.. ..	Birjand (*East Persia*) occupied by British forces	**OCT.** 7th
9th	.. ..	.. ..	.. ..	.. ..	2nd affair of Hafiz Kor	9th
30th		.. ..	.. ..	.. ..	.. ..	30th
NOV. 2nd	3rd attack on Mora	.. ..	.. ..	.. ..	Kasvin (*West Persia*) occupied by Russian force	**NOV.** 2nd
4th		.. ..	.. ..	.. ..	.. ..	4th
4th	Capture of Banyo	.. ..	.. ..	.. ..	.. ..	4th
6th		.. ..	Naval affair at Sollum*	.. ..	.. ..	6th
14th	.. ..	.. ..	Senussi commence hostilities against British by attacking Egyptian post at Sollum	.. ..	.. ..	14th
23rd	.. ..	.. ..	British operations against the Senussi begin	.. ..	.. ..	23rd
			Sollum post evacuated			
DEC. 11th	.. ..	.. ..	Affair of the Wadi Senab	.. ..	.. ..	**DEC.** 11th
13th	.. ..	.. ..		.. ..	.. ..	13th
14th	.. ..	.. ..	.. ..	.. ..	Hamadan (*West Persia*) occupied by Russian force	14th
15th	.. ..	.. ..	.. ..	.. ..	Qasr-i-Shirin (*West Persia*) occupied by Turkish force	15th

* Egyptian coastguard cruisers attacked by German submarine; "Abbas" sunk, "Nur el Bahr" disabled.

MILITARY OPERATIONS.
Subsidiary Theatres.
1915-16.

Date.	WEST AFRICA.	EAST AFRICA.	WEST EGYPT AND SUDAN.	ARABIA.	ASIA. (Excluding Turkish Empire.)	Date.
1915. DEC. 20th	..	..	..	..	Kum (*Persia*) occupied by a Russian force	**1915. DEC.** 20th
23rd	..	British naval operations on Lake Tanganyika begin	..	..	..	23rd
25th	..	..	Affair of the Wadi Majid	..	Kangavar (*West Persia*) occupied by a Russian force. Prince Firman Firma appointed Premier of Persia	25th
1916. JAN. 1st	Yaunde (*Cameroons*) taken by British forces	..	..	..	..	**1916. JAN.** 1st
13th	..	..	..	..	Kirmanshah (*West Persia*) occupied by a Turkish force	13th
FEB. 9th	..	British naval command of Lake Tanganyika secured	..	..	..	**FEB.** 9th
17th	Last German forces in South Cameroons cross border into Spanish territory	..	..	..	..	17th
18th	Mora surrenders to the British forces. **Conquest of the Cameroons by Allied forces completed**	..	..	..	..	18th
19th	..	*General Smuts assumes command of British forces in East Africa*	..	..	..	19th
26th	..	..	Action of Agagiya	..	Kirmanshah taken by Russian forces (*see January 13*)	26th
29th	*British blockade of the Cameroons raised*	..	..	..	..	29th
MAR. 1st	..	..	Hostilities between Sudan Government and Sultan of Darfur begin (*see March 16*)	..	..	**MAR.** 1st
3rd	*Agreement as to provisional administration of the Cameroons concluded between French and British Governments*	..	..	..	..	3rd
5th		British offensive towards Kilimanjaro begins	..	..	..	5th
9th		*Germany declares war on Portugal*	..	..	..	9th
10th		Taveta taken by British forces	..	..	..	10th

MILITARY OPERATIONS.
Subsidiary Theatres.
1916.

Date.	EAST AFRICA.	WEST EGYPT AND SUDAN.	ARABIA.	ASIA. Central and Southern Asia.	ASIA. Siberia and the Far East.	Date.
1916. MAR. 11th	Action of Latema Nek	..	..	..	..	**1916. MAR.** 11th
12th		..	..	Karind (*West Persia*) occupied by a Russian force	..	12th
13th	New Moshi taken by British forces	..	..	..	..	13th
14th	..	Sollum (*West Egypt*) reoccupied by British forces	..	..	..	14th
16th	..	Sudan force advances from Nahud into Darfur	..	..	..	16th
21st	Action of Kahe	..	..	..	..	21st
APRIL 11th	Kionga occupied by Portuguese forces			..		**APRIL** 11th
17th	Kondoa Irangi captured by British forces	..	..	..	..	17th
19th		..	..	..	..	19th
MAY 7th	..	..	..	Qasr-i-Shirin (*West Persia*) occupied by a Russian force	..	**MAY** 7th
11th	..	..	..	Kwash (*East Persia*) occupied by a British force	..	11th
15th	..	..	*Allied blockade of Hejaz coast begins*	Khanaqin and Rowanduz occupied by Russian forces	..	15th
18th	..	..	..	Cossack detachment from Russian force in West Persia joins British army on the Tigris	..	18th
22nd	..	Affair of Beringiya (*Darfur*)	..	..	..	22nd
23rd	..	El Fasher (*Darfur*) occupied by Sudan force	..	..	..	23rd
25th	British advance from Northern Rhodesia into German East Africa begins	..	..	..	..	25th
27th	Neu Langenburg occupied by British forces	..	..	..	..	27th
JUNE 5th	..	..	**Sherif of Mecca begins revolt against Turkish rule**	Turkish offensive into West Persia begins.* Russian forces evacuate Khanaqin	..	**JUNE** 5th
6th	..	..	*Arab attack on Medina repulsed*	..	..	6th
7th	..	..	*Sherif of Mecca proclaims the independence of the Hejaz*	..	..	7th
8th	Bismarckburg taken by British forces	..	..	..	..	8th

* Approximate date.

MILITARY OPERATIONS.
Subsidiary Theatres.
1916.

Date.	EAST AFRICA.	WEST EGYPT AND SUDAN.	ARABIA.	ASIA. Central and Southern Asia.	ASIA. Siberia and the Far East.	Date.
1916. JUNE. 9th	Action of Mkaramo	..	Jidda captured by Arab forces	..	..	**1916. JUNE.** 9th
10th	German attack on Kondoa Irangi	..	**Turkish garrison of Mecca surrenders to Arab forces**	..	..	10th
12th	..	..	..	Kerman (*Eastern Persia*) occupied by British forces	..	12th
13th	..	..	..	..	..	13th
19th	Handeni taken by British forces	..	..	..	..	19th
20th	..	..	..	Qasr-i-Shirin (*West Persia*) occupied by Turkish forces	..	20th
JULY 1st	..	..	..	Kirmanshah (*West Persia*) taken by Turkish forces	..	**JULY** 1st
7th	Tanga occupied by British forces	..	..	..	..	7th
14th	Mwanza taken by British forces	..	..	..	..	14th
27th	..	..	Yenbo taken by Arab forces	..	..	27th
31st	Kilmatinde taken by British forces	..	..	..	..	21st
AUG. 3rd	Ujiji (*Lake Tanganyika*) occupied by Belgian forces	..	..	..	..	**AUG.** 3rd
5th	British advance through the Nguru Hills begins	..	..	..	..	5th
10th	..	..	..	Hamadan (*West Persia*) taken by Turkish forces*	..	10th
11th	Mpwapwa occupied by British forces	..	..	..	..	11th
15th	Bagamoyo occupied by British forces†	..	..	..	..	15th
22nd	Kilosa taken by British forces	..	..	..	..	22nd
26th	Morogoro taken by British forces	..	..	..	..	26th
29th	Iringa taken by British forces	..	..	..	..	29th
SEPT. 4th	**Dar es Salaam surrenders to British forces**	..	..	..	..	**SEPT.** 4th
7th	Affair of Kisaki Kilwa occupied by British forces†	..	..	..	..	7th
16th	Lindi occupied by British forces†	..	..	..	..	16th
19th	Tabora occupied by Belgian forces	..	..	..	..	19th
22nd	..	..	Taif taken by Arab forces	..	..	22nd
OCT. 17th	..	Affairs in the Dakhla Oasis	..	..	..	**OCT.** 17th
22nd	..		..	..	..	22nd

* Approximate date. † Naval landing parties.

MILITARY OPERATIONS.
Subsidiary Theatres.
1916-17.

Date.	EAST AFRICA.	WEST EGYPT AND SUDAN.	ARABIA.	ASIA. Central and Southern Asia.	ASIA. Siberia and the Far East.	Date.
1916. NOV. 6th	.. ..	Affair of Gyuba (*Darfur*)*	.. ..	.. ..	.. ..	**1916. NOV.** 6th
12th	.. ..	.. ..	.. ..	Shiraz occupied by British forces	.. ..	12th
15th	.. ..	.. ..	.. ..	3rd affair of Hafiz Kor (*N.W. Frontier, India*)	.. ..	15th
DEC. 7th	.. ..	.. ..	Affair of Jabir (*Aden*)	.. ..	.. ..	**DEC.** 7th
31st	.. ..	End of the Darfur Campaign	.. ..	.. ..	.. ..	31st
1917. JAN. 3rd	⎱ Action of Beho-Beho	.. ..	.. ..	.. ..	.. ..	**1917. JAN.** 3rd
4th	⎰	.. ..	.. ..	.. ..	.. ..	4th
20th	*General Hoskins succeeds General Smuts in command of British forces in East Africa*	.. ..	.. ..	.. ..	.. ..	20th
24th	.. ..	.. ..	Wejh surrenders to Arab forces	.. ..	.. ..	24th
FEB. 3rd	.. ..	⎱ Affairs in the Siwa Oasis	.. ..	.. ..	.. ..	**FEB.** 3rd
5th	.. ..	⎰	.. ..	.. ..	.. ..	5th
8th	.. ..	End of British campaign against the Senussi	.. ..	.. ..	.. ..	8th
MAR. ..	.. ..		.. ..	.. ..	.. ..	**MAR.** ..
APRIL ..	.. ..		.. ..	.. ..	.. ..	**APRIL** ..
MAY 9th	.. ..		.. ..	⎱ Action of Kharkhwasta (*N.W. Frontier, India*)	.. ..	**MAY** 9th
10th	.. ..		.. ..	⎰	.. ..	10th
30th	*General van Deventer succeeds General Hoskins in command of British forces in East Africa*		.. ..	.. ..	.. ..	30th
JUNE 19th	.. ..		.. ..	⎱ Actions in the Shahur Valley (*N.W. Frontier, India*)	.. ..	**JUNE** 19th
24th	.. ..		.. ..	⎰	.. ..	24th
JULY 3rd	.. ..		Affair of Aba-el-Lissan	.. ..	.. ..	**JULY** 3rd
6th	.. ..		Aqaba taken by Arab forces	.. ..	.. ..	6th

* Ali Dinar (*ex-Sultan of Darfur*) defeated and killed.

MILITARY OPERATIONS.
Subsidiary Theatres.
1917-18.

Date.	EAST AFRICA.	ARABIA.	ASIA.		NORTH RUSSIA.	Date.
			Central and Southern Asia.	Siberia and the Far East.		
1917. JULY 19th	Action of Narungombe	..	..	..		**1917. JULY** 19th
AUG. ..	..	..	..	..		**AUG.** ..
SEPT. ..	..	..	..	..		**SEPT.** ..
OCT. 16th	⎧ Action of	..	..	..		**OCT.** 16th
19th	⎩ Nyangao	..	..	..		19th
21st	..	Turkish attack on Petra	..	..		21st
NOV. 8th	..	..	*Bolshevik coup d'état in Petrograd*			**NOV.** 8th
25th	German passage of the Rovuma at Ngomano. German operations in Portuguese East Africa begin	..	..	..		25th
28th	Tafel's force surrenders to British forces	..	..	..		28th
DEC. 1st	Last German forces driven out of German East Africa into Portuguese territory*	..	..	..		**DEC.** 1st
1918. JAN. 1st	..	..	..	..	..	**1918. JAN.** 1st
8th	..	⎫ Arab actions for Et Tafile	Qasr-i-Shirin (*West Persia*) occupied by British forces	..	..	8th
28th	..	⎭	..	..	..	28th
27th	..	..	General Dunsterville's Mission to North-West Persia leaves Baghdad	..	..	27th
FEB. 1st	..	..	Extension of British East Persia cordon into Khorasan begins†	..	..	**FEB.** 1st
17th	..	..	General Dunsterville's Mission reaches Enzeli	..	..	17th
MAR. 3rd	..	..	Meshed (*North-East Persia*) occupied by British forces*	..	..	**MAR.** 3rd
7th	..	..	..	..	*Peace signed between Germany and Finland*	7th
16th	..	..	Hamadan evacuated by Russian forces	..	..	16th
APRIL 3rd	..	..	..	..	German force lands in South Finland	**APRIL** 3rd
5th	..	..	..	Japanese and British marines land at Vladivostok	..	5th
13th	..	..	..	..	Helsingfors (*Finland*) taken by German forces	13th

* Approximate date.   † In relief of the Russian cordon, withdrawn by order of Bolshevik Government.

MILITARY OPERATIONS.
Subsidiary Theatres.
1918.

Date.	EAST AFRICA.	ARABIA.	ASIA. Central and Southern Asia.	ASIA. Siberia and the Far East.	NORTH RUSSIA.	Date.
1918. **MAY** 24th	..	..	..	..	General Poole arrives at Murmansk to organise the North Russia Expeditionary Force	**1918.** **MAY** 24th
JUNE 4th	..	..	..	..	British marines land at Pechenga	**JUNE** 4th
7th	..	..	..	Omsk occupied by Czecho-Slovak forces	..	7th
23rd	..	..	..	..	British Expeditionary Force to North Russia* arrives at Murmansk	23rd
29th	..	..	..	..	Allied forces seize the Murman Railway as far as Soroki	29th
30th	..	..	..	..		30th
JULY 1st	Affair of Nyamakura.†	..	..	..	..	**JULY** 1st
3rd		..	..	..	..	3rd
13th	..	..	..	Irkutsk occupied by Czecho-Slovak forces	..	13th
14th	..	..	..	Kazan (*East Russia*) taken by Czecho-Slovak forces	..	14th
19th	..	..	British operations in Trans-Caspia begin	..	..	19th
20th	..	..	British defence of Resht (*North-West Persia*).	..	..	20th
AUG. 1st	..	..	..	..	Archangel captured by Allied forces	**AUG.** 1st
2nd	..	..	..	..		2nd
3rd	..	..	..	British troops land at Vladivostok‡	..	3rd
4th	..	..	British force lands at Baku *Bolshevik Committee at Enzeli arrested by British military authorities*	..	..	4th
11th	..	..	..	First Japanese contingents land at Vladivostok	..	11th
13th	..	..	..	*Czecho-Slovaks declare war on Germany*	..	13th
15th	..	..	Action of Bairam Ali (*Trans-Caspia*).§	..	..	15th
18th	..	..	Merv taken by Bolshevik forces	..	..	18th
23rd	..	..	..	**Battle of Dukhovskaya**	..	23rd
24th	..	..	..	*Coup d'état by General Horvat at Vladivostok*	..	24th

* Forces previously designated "Syren" and "Elope."
† Near Quelimane; this was the most southerly point reached by the German force.
‡ 25th Battalion Middlesex Regiment.
§ Bolsheviki defeat Trans-Caspian Government forces.

MILITARY OPERATIONS
Subsidiary Theatres.
1918.

Date.	EAST AFRICA.	ARABIA.	ASIA. Central and Southern Asia.	ASIA. Siberia and the Far East.	NORTH RUSSIA.	Date.
1918. AUG. 26th	..	..	British defence of Baku begins	..	..	**1918. AUG.** 26th
27th	..	..	Krasnovodsk (*Caspian*) occupied by British forces	..	..	27th
28th	..	..	Affair near Kaakhka (*Trans-Caspia*)	..	..	28th
SEPT. 4th	..	..	Defence of Baku	..	Obozerskayá (*Archangel*) occupied by Allied forces. United States contingent lands at Murmansk	**SEPT.** 4th
5th	..	..		Khabarovsk (*East Siberia*) taken by Japanese forces	..	5th
11th	..	..		..	Ukhtinskaya (*Murman*) captured by Allied forces	11th
12th	..	..		..	Actions of Chamova (*Archangel*)	12th
14th	..	..	British Force evacuates Baku (14th/15th)	..	Actions of Chamova (*Archangel*)	14th
15th	..	..	**Baku taken by Turkish forces**	..	..	15th
18th	..	..	..	Blagovyeshchensk (*East Siberia*) occupied by Japanese forces	..	18th
19th	..	Battles of Megiddo begin	..	..	..	19th
23rd	..	Ma'an evacuated by the Turkish garrison	..	..	..	23rd
29th	German force recrosses the Rovuma and re-enters German territory	Turkish Ma'an garrison surrenders near Amman	..	..	..	29th
OCT. 3rd	..	..	..	..	Action near Pyavozero Lake (*Murman*)	**OCT.** 3rd
4th	..	..	..	..	General Ironside takes over command of Allied forces at Archangel	4th
12th	..	..	Action of Dushak	..	..	12th
14th	..	..	..	British troops from Vladivostok reach Irkutsk	..	14th

MILITARY OPERATIONS.
Subsidiary Theatres.
1918.

Date.	EAST AFRICA.	ARABIA.	ASIA.		NORTH RUSSIA.	Date.
			Central and Southern Asia.	Siberia and the Far East.		
1918. OCT. 18th	..	..	..	British troops from Vladivostok reach Omsk	..	**1918. OCT.** 18th
22nd	..	Affair of Imad (*Aden*)	..	..	..	22nd
30th	..	Armistice between Turkey and *Entente Powers* signed	..	..	..	30th
NOV. 1st	German force enters Rhodesia and attacks Fife	..	Merv reoccupied by Russian and British forces* (*see August 18th*)	..	..	**NOV.** 1st
9th	Kasama (*Rhodesia*) taken by German forces	..	..	Czech forces at Ekaterinburg declare national independence	..	9th
11th	Armistice between Germany and Entente Powers signed	..	..	..	..	11th
13th	German force reaches the Chambezi River. News of armistice received	..	..	..	..	13th
14th	**Hostilities in East Africa cease**	..	..	..	..	14th
18th	..	..	..	Counter-revolutionary coup d'etat at Omsk. Admiral Kolchak proclaimed "Dictator of all Russia"	..	18th
25th	German forces surrender at Abercorn	..	..	..	..	25th
DEC. 9th	..	Lahej reoccupied by British forces	..	..	..	**DEC.** 9th
13th	..	Hodeida taken by British forces	..	..	..	13th
24th	..	..	..	**Perm** (*East Russia*) taken by Kolchak's forces	..	24th
30th	..	..	..	Birsk (*East Russia*) taken by Kolchak's forces	Kadish taken by Allied forces	30th
31st	..	..	..	Ufa and Sterlitamak (*East Russia*) taken by Bolshevik forces	..	31st

* Approximate date.

PART II.

SECTION III.

NAVAL.

Date.	HOME WATERS.	BALTIC.	ATLANTIC.	MEDITERRANEAN AND BLACK SEA.	INDIAN OCEAN, RED SEA, AND PERSIAN GULF.	PACIFIC AND FAR EAST.	Date.
1914. JULY 23rd	.. ..	.. ..	.. ..	*Austro-Hungarian Government send ultimatum to Serbia*	.. ..	.. ..	1914. JULY 23rd
26th	British Admiralty countermand orders for dispersal of Fleets (see 28th)	.. ..	.. ..	.. ..	.. ..	.. ..	26th
27th	German High Seas Fleet recalled from Norway to war bases	.. ..	.. ..	.. ..	.. ..	.. ..	27th
28th	British Fleets ordered to their war bases (see 26th)	.. ..	.. ..	*Austria-Hungary declares war on Serbia*	.. ..	.. ..	28th
29th	British Admiralty send "Warning Telegram" to the Fleets	.. ..	.. ..	.. ..	.. ..	.. ..	29th
30th	.. ..	.. ..	.. ..	.. ..	.. ..	*Australian Government place Australian Navy at disposal of British Government*	30th
31st	.. ..	*German Government send ultimatum to Russia*	.. ..	.. ..	.. ..	.. ..	31st
AUG. 1st	British Government order naval mobilisation *French Government order general mobilisation*	*German Government order general mobilisation and declare war on Russia.* **Hostilities between Russia and Germany commence**	.. ..	.. ..	.. ..	.. ..	AUG. 1st
2nd	.. ..	Libau bombarded by German cruiser "Augsburg"	.. ..	.. ..	.. ..	.. ..	2nd
3rd	*Germany declares war on France.* **Hostilities between Germany and France commence** *British Government order general mobilisation* *British Government issue proclamation authorising requisitioning of shipping*	.. ..	.. ..	.. ..	.. ..	.. ..	3rd

NAVAL.
1914.

Date.	HOME WATERS.	BALTIC.	ATLANTIC.	MEDITERRANEAN AND BLACK SEA.	INDIAN OCEAN, RED SEA, AND PERSIAN GULF.	PACIFIC AND FAR EAST.	Date.
1914. AUG. 4th	*Germany declares war on Belgium* British Grand Fleet constituted under Admiral Sir John Jellicoe *Great Britain declares war on Germany.* **Hostilities between Great Britain and Germany commence** German armed merchant cruiser "Kaiser Wilhelm der Grosse" leaves Bremen	..	..	German warships "Goeben" and "Breslau" bombard Philippeville and Bona respectively (*Algeria*)	..	..	1914. AUG. 4th
5th	Minelaying in the open sea commenced by the Germans (East of Southwold (*See October 3rd*) German minelayer "Königin Luise" sunk off Yarmouth	..	..	..	..	..	5th
6th	H.M.S. "Amphion" sunk by mine off Yarmouth	..	Action between H.M.S. "Bristol" and German cruiser "Karlsruhe" in the West Indies	*Naval Convention concluded between Great Britain and France, giving control of operations in the Mediterranean to France*	..	Admiral von Spee's squadron leaves Ponape (*Caroline Islands*) German armed merchant cruiser "Prinz Eitel Friedrich" leaves Tsingtau	6th
7th	First units of British Expeditionary Force land in France	..	..	Action between H.M.S. "Gloucester" and the "Goeben" and "Breslau" off the coast of Greece	..	..	7th
8th	..	..	..	..	**Hostilities commence in East Africa** Dar es Salaam bombarded by H.M.S. "Astræa"	..	8th
9th	H.M.S. "Birmingham" sinks German submarine "U 15" in North Sea*	..	..	..	..	..	9th
10th	British aerial coast patrol established	..	..	..	..	..	10th
11th	..	..	..	"Goeben" and "Breslau" enter the Dardanelles	..	..	11th
12th	..	..	..	*Great Britain and France declare war on Austria-Hungary*	..	"Emden" joins Admiral von Spee and is detached	12th
15th	..	..	..	Junction of British and French squadrons affected at entrance to Adriatic	..	Japanese Government send ultimatum to Germany	15th
16th	Landing of original British Expeditionary Force in France completed†	..	..	Allied sweep in the Southern Adriatic: Austrian light cruiser "Zenta" sunk	..	..	16th

* First German submarine sunk.   † 4 divisions and 1 cavalry division.

NAVAL.
1914.

Date.	HOME WATERS.	BALTIC.	ATLANTIC.	MEDITERRA-NEAN AND BLACK SEA.	INDIAN OCEAN, RED SEA, AND PERSIAN GULF.	PACIFIC AND FAR EAST.	Date.
1914. AUG. 19th	..	..	..	..	First unit of Indian Expeditionary Force "C" leaves Karachi for Mombasa‡	..	1914. AUG. 19th
23rd	..	..	..	..	..	*Japan declares war on Germany*	23rd
24th	..	..	..	..	First units of I.E.F. "A" leave India* for France (in first place for Egypt)	..	24th
26th	..	Action off the Aaland Islands: German cruiser "Magdeburg" destroyed by Russian squadron	*German forces in Togoland capitulate to the Allied forces* Action between H.M.S. "Highflyer" and German armed merchant cruiser "Kaiser Wilhelm der Grosse"† off the Rio de Oro (*latter sunk*)	..	..	..	26th
27th	Force of British Marines landed at Ostend accompanied by R.N.A.S. unit	..	..	..	..	..	27th
28th	**Action off Heligoland.** (*German light cruisers "Köln," "Mainz," and "Ariadne" sunk*)	..	..	..	..	..	28th
30th	..	..	..	..	..	Samoa occupied by New Zealand Expeditionary Force	30th
SEPT. 1st	..	..	..	..	First unit of I.E.F. "C" arrives at Mombasa	..	SEPT. 1st
2nd	..	..	..	..	..	Japanese forces land in Shantung to attack Tsingtau	2nd
3rd	H.M.S. "Speedy" sunk by mine off the Humber	..	..	..	..	..	3rd
5th	H.M.S. "Pathfinder" sunk by submarine in the North Sea. (*The first British warship so destroyed*)	..	..	..	..	..	5th
7th	..	..	Naval operations against Duala (*Cameroons*) begin	..	..	..	7th
9th	..	..	..	..	First units of I.E.F. "A" arrive at Suez	..	9th
10th	..	..	..	..	German light cruiser "Emden" makes her first capture in the Indian Ocean (*Greek collier "Pontoporos."*)	..	10th

* Bombay.   † Left Bremen on August 4th.   ‡ Indian Expeditionary Force is abbreviated to I.E.F. in later entries.

NAVAL.
1914.

Date.	HOME WATERS.	BALTIC.	ATLANTIC.	MEDITERRANEAN AND BLACK SEA.	INDIAN OCEAN, RED SEA, AND PERSIAN GULF.	PACIFIC AND FAR EAST.	Date.
1914. **SEPT.** 11th	..	..	..	..	..	Australian Expeditionary Force lands on Bismarck Archipelago	**1914.** **SEPT.** 11th
14th	..	..	Action between British armed merchant cruiser "Carmania" and German armed merchant cruiser "Cap Trafalgar" in the South Atlantic (*latter sunk*)	..	..	..	14th
17th	..	..	..	*British Naval Mission leaves Turkey* Admiral Souchon (Imperial German Navy) assumes control of the Turkish Navy*	..	German New Guinea and surrounding colonies capitulate to Australian Expeditionary Force	17th
19th	Force of British Marines landed at Dunkirk	..	Lüderitzbucht (*German South-West Africa*) *occupied by South African forces*	Cattaro bombarded by French squadron First units of I.E.F. "A" leave Egypt for Marseilles	..	..	19th
20th	..	..	..	..	H.M.S. "Pegasus" sunk by German light cruiser "Königsberg" at Zanzibar	..	20th
21st	..	..	..	..	..	German armed forces in New Guinea surrender	21st
22nd	H.M.S. "Aboukir," "Cressy," and "Hogue" sunk by German submarine "U 9"	..	..	..	Madras bombarded by German light cruiser "Emden"	Papeete (*Tahiti*) bombarded by Von Spee's squadron. (*See August 6th*)	22nd
26th	..	..	Allied forces capture Duala (*Camerouns*)	First units of I.E.F. "A" land at Marseilles	..	..	26th
27th	..	..		..	..	..	27th
OCT. 3rd	Minelaying in the open sea (*between the Goodwins and Ostend*) commenced by the British. (*See August 5th*) First units of British Royal Naval Division (Marine Brigade) arrive at Antwerp	..	First units of Canadian Expeditionary Force leave Canada for England	..	..	..	**OCT.** 3rd
6th	Units of British 7th Division disembarked at Ostend and Zeebrugge	..	..	..	..	..	6th
7th	*Evacuation of Antwerp begun*	..	..	..	..	Yap Island occupied by a Japanese naval force	7th
10th	*Antwerp capitulates to the German forces*	..	..	..	..	..	10th

* Approximate date.

NAVAL. 1914.

Date.	HOME WATERS.	BALTIC.	ATLANTIC.	MEDITERRANEAN AND BLACK SEA.	INDIAN OCEAN, RED SEA, AND PERSIAN GULF.	PACIFIC AND FAR EAST.	Date.
1914. OCT. 11th	.. ..	Russian cruiser "Pallada" sunk by German submarine off Hangö	.. ..	.. ..	.. ..	German gunboat "Komet" captured by H.M.A.S. "Nusa" near Talassia (*Neu Pommern*)†	**1914. OCT.** 11th
13th	First appearance of a German submarine on the Southampton-Havre troop transport route (*see November 6th*)	.. ..	.. ..	.. ..	.. ..	.. ..	13th
15th	*Zeebrugge and Ostend occupied by German forces* H.M.S. "Hawke" sunk by German submarine in the North Sea First units of the Canadian Expeditionary Force land in England	.. ..	.. ..	.. ..	.. ..	.. ..	15th
16th	**Battle of the Yser begins***	.. ..	.. ..	.. ..	First units of I.E.F. "B" leave Bombay for Mombasa First units of I.E.F. "D" leave Bombay for the Persian Gulf	New Zealand Expeditionary Force leaves for France (*see December 1st*)	16th
17th	Action between H.M.S. "Undaunted" and destroyers and four German destroyers off the Dutch Coast (*latter all sunk*) German submarines attempt raid on Scapa Flow	First British submarines enter the Baltic ("*E 1*" and "*E 9*")	.. ..	.. ..	.. ..	First units of Australian Imperial Force leave for France	17th
18th	Grand Fleet withdraws from Scapa to the West of Scotland First bombardment of Ostend by British warships	.. ..	.. ..	.. ..	.. ..	Japanese light cruiser "Takachiho" sunk by German destroyer off Tsingtau	18th
20th	First merchant-vessel sunk by German submarine (*British s.s.* "*Glitra*")	.. ..	.. ..	.. ..	.. ..	.. ..	20th
23rd	.. ..	.. ..	.. ..	.. ..	Advanced troops of I.E.F. "D" arrive at the Bahrein Islands (*Persian Gulf*)	.. ..	23rd
27th	H.M.S. "Audacious" sunk by mine off the coast of Donegal	.. ..	.. ..	.. ..	.. ..	.. ..	27th

* Belgian date.   † Last episode in conquest of German Pacific possessions.

NAVAL. 1914.

Date.	HOME WATERS.	BALTIC.	ATLANTIC.	MEDITERRA- NEAN AND BLACK SEA.	INDIAN OCEAN, RED SEA, AND PERSIAN GULF.	PACIFIC AND FAR EAST.	Date.
1914. OCT. 28th	.. ..	.. ..	.. ..	.. ..	German light cruiser "Emden" raids Penang Roads and sinks Russian light cruiser "Zhemchug"	.. ..	**1914. OCT.** 28th
29th	*British Government issue Order in Council revising the list of contraband and modifying the Declaration of London* *Prince Louis of Battenberg, First Sea Lord, resigns*			**Turkey commences hostilities against Russia.** Odessa, Sevastopol and Theodosia bombarded by Turkish warships	.. ..	.. ..	29th
30th	British hospital ship "Rohilla" wrecked off Whitby *Lord Fisher appointed First Sea Lord*	.. ..	.. ..	.. ..	.. ..	.. ..	30th
31st	H.M.S. "Hermes" sunk by submarine in Straits of Dover	.. ..	.. ..	.. ..	German light cruiser "Königsborg" located in Rufiji River First units of I.E.F. "B" arrive at Mombasa	.. ..	31st
NOV. 1st	.. ..	.. ..	.. ..	**Britain commences hostilities against Turkey**		**Action off Coronel.** (*H.M.S. "Good Hope" and "Monmouth" sunk by Von Spee's squadron*)	**NOV.** 1st
2nd	British Admiralty declares the North Sea a military zone	.. ..	.. ..	*Russia declares war on Turkey*		Austrian cruiser "Kaiserin Elizabeth" sunk in Tsingtau Harbour	2nd
3rd	First German naval raid on British coast (near Gorleston) Grand Fleet ordered back to Scapa Flow	.. ..	.. ..	Allied squadrons bombard forts at entrance of the Dardanelles	British attack on Tanga (*German East Africa*)	.. ..	3rd
4th	British Admiralty orders two battle-cruisers from Grand Fleet to proceed to South Atlantic German cruiser "Yorck" sunk by mine off the German coast	.. ..	German light cruiser "Karlsruhe" sunk in the Atlantic (*by internal explosion*)	.. ..		.. ..	4th
5th	.. ..	.. ..	.. ..	*Britain and France formally declare war on Turkey*		.. ..	5th
6th	British Admiralty for the first time order troop transports from England to France to have direct destroyer escort (*see October 13th*) *French Government issue declaration modifying the Declaration of London*	.. ..	.. ..	British submarine "B 11" proceeds two miles up the Dardanelles*	I.E.F. "D" effects landing in Mesopotamia at Fao	.. ..	6th

* First warship to enter the Straits.

NAVAL.
1914.

Date.	HOME WATERS.	BALTIC.	ATLANTIC.	MEDITERRA-NEAN AND BLACK SEA.	INDIAN OCEAN, RED SEA, AND PERSIAN GULF.	PACIFIC AND FAR EAST.	Date.
1914. NOV. 7th	..	..	..	..	..	Tsingtau capitulates to the Japanese forces	**1914. NOV.** 7th
9th	*British and French Governments conclude convention as to naval "prizes"*	..	..	..	German light cruiser "Emden" destroyed by H.M.A.S. "Sydney" at the Cocos Islands	German gunboat "Geier" interned at Honolulu	9th
10th	..	..	..	..	British force storms Sheikh Saïd (S. Arabia) and destroys the defences	..	10th
11th	H.M.S. "Niger" sunk by German submarine off Deal	*Memel occupied by Russian forces**	..	..		..	11th
17th	..	Libau bombarded by German squadron (*see August 2nd*) German cruiser "Friedrich Carl" sunk by mine	..	Trebizond bombarded by Russian squadron	..	..	17th
18th	..	..	..	Indecisive action between Turkish and Russian fleets in the Black Sea	..	..	18th
22nd	..	..	..	..	Basra (Mesopotamia) occupied by British forces†	..	22nd
26th	H.M.S. "Bulwark" destroyed by internal explosion in Sheerness Harbour	..	..	..	..	..	26th
DEC. 1st	..	..	..	..	First units of Australian and New Zealand Expeditionary Forces arrive at Suez	..	**DEC** 1st
4th	..	..	..	..	1st Action of Qurna (Mesopotamia)	..	4th
8th	..	..	**Battle of the Falklands.** (*Von Spee's squadron destroyed.‡ "Dresden" escapes. (See March 14th, 1915)*)	..		..	8th
10th	..	..	..	Batum bombarded by "Goeben" and "Breslau"	..	..	10th
13th	..	..	..	Turkish battleship "Messoudieh" sunk by British submarine "B 11" in the Dardanelles	..	..	13th
14th	..	..	..	..	..	German armed merchant cruiser "Cormoran" interned at Guam	14th

* Approximate date. † This was the date of the surrender. The entry of the *troops* took place the following day.
‡ The following German cruisers were sunk: "Scharnhorst," "Gneisenau," "Leipzig," "Nürnberg."

NAVAL. 1914-1915.

Date.	HOME WATERS.	BALTIC.	ATLANTIC.	MEDITERRANEAN AND BLACK SEA.	INDIAN OCEAN, RED SEA, AND PERSIAN GULF.	PACIFIC AND FAR EAST.	Date.
1914. DEC.							**1914. DEC.**
16th	Scarborough and Hartlepool bombarded by German battle cruiser squadron	..	..	..	..	..	16th
25th	British seaplane raid on Cuxhaven	..	..	..	..	..	25th
26th	..	..	..	Italian force lands at Valona (see May 29th, 1915)	..	..	26th
1915. JAN.							**1915. JAN.**
1st	H.M.S. "Formidable" sunk by submarine in the English Channel	..	..	..	..	..	1st
12th	..	..	..	..	Mafia Island (German East Africa) seized by British force	..	12th
13th	..	..	..	British War Council resolve that Admiralty should prepare for a naval expedition in February against the Dardanelles	..	..	13th
14th	..	..	Swakopmund (German South-West Africa) occupied by South African forces	..	..	..	14th
24th	Action of the Dogger Bank. (German cruiser "Blücher" sunk)	..	..	..	..	..	24th
26th	..	..	..	Turkish advance through Sinai begins	..	..	26th
28th	..	..	United States s.v. "William P. Frye" sunk by German armed merchant cruiser "Prinz Eitel Friedrich"†	British Government definitely decide to make naval attack on the Dardanelles	..	..	28th
29th	Walney Island Battery (Barrow-in-Furness) shelled by German submarine*	..	..	..	..	..	29th
30th	British Admiralty warn British merchant vessels to fly neutral or no ensigns in vicinity of British Isles	..	..	..	..	..	30th

* First operation of a German submarine in the Irish Sea.   † First United States vessel sunk by belligerent warship.

NAVAL.
1915.

Date.	HOME WATERS.	BALTIC.	ATLANTIC.	MEDITERRA-NEAN AND BLACK SEA.	INDIAN OCEAN, RED SEA, AND PERSIAN GULF.	PACIFIC AND FAR EAST.	Date.
1915. JAN. 31st	.. ..	.. ..	.. ..	.. ..	*Arab forces (Idrisi) occupy Farasan Islands (Red Sea)*	.. ..	1915. JAN. 31st
FEB. 1st	*British Admiralty issue orders forbidding neutral fishing vessels to use British ports*	.. ..	.. ..	.. ..	.. ..	.. ..	FEB. 1st
3rd	.. ..	.. ..	.. ..	} Turkish attack on the Suez Canal {		.. ..	3rd
4th	*German Government announce that submarine blockade of Great Britain will begin on February 18th*	.. ..	.. ..			.. ..	4th
6th	*British ss. "Lusitania" arrives at Liverpool flying United States flag*	.. ..	.. ..	.. ..	.. ..	.. ..	6th
7th	*British Foreign Office issue statement justifying use of neutral flag at sea*	.. ..	.. ..	.. ..	.. ..	.. ..	7th
11th	*United States Government send Note to British Government deprecating use of neutral flag*	.. ..	.. ..	.. ..	.. ..	.. ..	11th
17th	.. ..	*Memel reoccupied by German forces*	.. ..	.. ..	.. ..	.. ..	17th
18th	**German submarine blockade of Great Britain begins**	.. ..	.. ..	.. ..	.. ..	.. ..	18th
19th	First neutral ship torpedoed without warning by German submarine* (*Norwegian ss. "Belridge"*)	.. ..	.. ..	**Allied Naval attack on the Dardanelles forts commences.** (First bombardment of the outer forts)	.. ..	.. ..	19th
22nd	Net barrage across the North Channel (*between Ireland and Scotland*) established	.. ..	.. ..	.. ..	.. ..	.. ..	22nd
23rd	. ..	.. ..	.. ..	Lemnos (*Ægean*) occupied by British marines	.. ..	.. ..	23rd
25th	.. ..	.. ..	.. ..	Bombardment of the Dardanelles resumed: outer forts partially destroyed	.. ..	.. ..	25th
26th	.. ..	.. ..	.. ..		.. ..	.. ..	26th

* German Government subsequently asserted that this ship was attacked in error.

NAVAL.
1915.

Date.	HOME WATERS.	BALTIC.	ATLANTIC.	MEDITERRANEAN AND BLACK SEA.	INDIAN OCEAN, RED SEA, AND PERSIAN GULF.	PACIFIC AND FAR EAST.	Date.
1915. MAR. 1st	..	..	..	Antivari bombarded by Austrian squadron	British blockade of German East Africa begins	..	1915. FEB. 1st
4th	First case of "indicator nets"* aiding in the destruction of a German submarine ("U. 8" in Straits of Dover)	..	..	Bombardment of the Dardanelles forts continued	..	..	4th
5th	..	..	..	Smyrna forts bombarded by British squadron	..	..	5th
9th	..	..	..		..	..	9th
11th	British Government issue the "Retaliatory Order in Council" (relating to detention of enemy goods) and Proclamation extending the list of "absolute" contraband	..	..	..	..	..	11th
12th	Dutch Government issue warning that foreign merchant ships using Dutch flag (see January 30th,) will be detained. French Government issue decrees similar to British Order in Council and Proclamation of March 11th	..	..	..	..	..	12th
13th	First neutral ship sunk without warning by German submarine (Swedish ss. "Hanna")	..	..	..	..	..	13th
14th	..	..	..	..	..	German light cruiser "Dresden" (the last German cruiser left at sea) sunk by British warships off Juan Fernandez	14th
15th	First merchant ship attacked by aircraft (ss. "Blonde")	..	..	British squadron blockading Smyrna withdrawn	..	..	15th
18th		Memel captured by Russian forces	..	**Allied Naval attack on the Narrows of the Dardanelles repulsed.** ("Bouvet," "Ocean" and "Irresistible" sunk)	..	..	18th
21st	..	Memel recaptured by German forces	..	..	..	..	21st
23rd	First kite-balloon ship commissioned (H.M.S. "Manica")	..	..	..	..	..	23rd

* First experiments with these nets were carried out in January 1915.

NAVAL.
1915.

Date.	HOME WATERS.	BALTIC.	ATLANTIC.	MEDITERRANEAN AND BLACK SEA.	INDIAN OCEAN, RED SEA, AND PERSIAN GULF.	PACIFIC AND FAR EAST.	Date.
1915. MAR. 25th	First neutral ship sunk by German submarine after visit and search (Dutch ss. "Medea")	.. ..	.. ..	.. ..	.. ..	.. ..	1915. MAR. 25th
27th	.. ..	.. ..	.. ..	Bosporus forts bombarded by Russian Black Sea Fleet	.. ..	.. ..	27th
28th	First passenger ship sunk by a German submarine (British ss. "Falaba")	.. ..	.. ..	.. ..	.. ..	.. ..	28th
APRIL 3rd	Dover Straits barrage completed	.. ..	.. ..	Indecisive action in Black Sea between the "Goeben" and the Russian Fleet. Turkish light cruiser "Medjidieh" sunk by mine off Odessa	.. ..	.. ..	APRIL 3rd
6th	.. ..	.. ..	.. ..	Smyrna bombarded by Allied squadron	.. ..	.. ..	6th
8th	.. ..	.. ..	German armed merchant cruiser "Prinz Eitel Friedrich" interned at Newport News, U.S.A.	.. ..	.. ..	.. ..	8th
17th	First instance of merchant vessel beating off submarine by gunfire (ss. "La Rosarina")	.. ..	.. ..	.. ..	.. ..	.. ..	17th
23rd	.. ..	.. ..	British blockade of the Cameroons begins	.. ..	.. ..	.. ..	23rd
25th	.. ..	.. ..	.. ..	**Allied forces effect landing at the Dardanelles.** Bosporus forts bombarded by Russian Black Sea Fleet	.. ..	.. ..	25th
26th	.. ..	.. ..	The last original German raider overseas interned (armed merchant cruiser "Kronprinz Wilhelm" at Newport News, U.S.A.)	French cruiser "Léor Gambetta" sunk by Austrian submarine in Straits of Otranto	.. ..	.. ..	26th
28th	.. ..	.. ..	.. ..	1st Battle of Krithia	.. ..	.. ..	28th
MAY. 1st	First United States ship torpedoed without warning by German submarine (ss. "Gulflight")	.. ..	.. ..	.. ..	.. ..	.. ..	MAY. 1st
6th	.. ..	.. ..	.. ..	⎫	.. ..	.. ..	6th
7th	Ss. "Lusitania" sunk by German submarine "U 20" (off Old Head of Kinsale)	Libau taken by German forces	.. ..	2nd Battle of Krithia ⎬	.. ..	.. ..	7th
8th	.. ..	.. ..	.. ..	⎭	.. ..	.. ..	8th

229

[8369]

NAVAL.
1915.

Date.	HOME WATERS.	BALTIC.	ATLANTIC.	MEDITERRANEAN AND BLACK SEA.	INDIAN OCEAN, RED SEA, AND PERSIAN GULF.	PACIFIC AND FAR EAST.	Date.
1915. MAY 10th	.. ..	.. ..	.. ..	Naval convention signed between Italy, France and Great Britain	.. ..	.. ..	**1915. MAY** 10th
13th	.. ..	.. ..	.. ..	H.M.S. "Goliath" sunk by Turkish destroyer in the Dardanelles	.. ..	.. ..	13th
15th	*Lord Fisher, First Sea Lord, tenders resignation*	.. ..	.. ..	.. ..	.. ..	.. ..	15th
23rd	.. ..	.. ..	.. ..	*Italy declares war on Austria-Hungary*	.. ..	.. ..	23rd
24th	.. ..	.. ..	.. ..	**Hostilities between Italy and Austria commence** (*midnight 24th/25th*)	.. ..	.. ..	24th
25th	.. ..	.. ..	.. ..	H.M.S. "Triumph" sunk by submarine off the Dardanelles	.. ..	.. ..	25th
26th	.. ..	.. ..	.. ..	*Italian Government announce blockade of the Austro-Hungarian coast* British battle squadron concentrates at Malta, prior to joining Italian Fleet in the Adriatic	.. ..	.. ..	26th
27th	British minelayer "Princess Irene" destroyed by internal explosion in harbour at Sheerness *Mr. Winston Churchill, First Lord of the Admiralty, resigns*	.. ..	.. ..	H.M.S. "Majestic" sunk by submarine off the Dardanelles British battle-squadron joins the Italian Fleet in the Adriatic	.. ..	.. ..	27th
28th	*New Admiralty chiefs appointed**	.. ..	.. ..	.. ..	.. ..	.. ..	28th
29th	.. ..	.. ..	.. ..	*Valona formally occupied by the Italians.* (*See December 26th, 1914*)	.. ..	.. ..	29th
31st	.. ..	.. ..	.. ..	.. ..	2nd action of Qurna (*Mesopotamia*)	.. ..	31st
JUNE 2nd	.. ..	.. ..	.. ..	*Blockade of coast of Asia Minor announced by British Government*	Pursuit to Amara (*Mesopotamia*)	.. ..	**JUNE** 2nd
3rd	.. ..	.. ..	.. ..	.. ..	Amara (*Mesopotamia*) occupied by British forces	.. ..	3rd
4th	.. ..	.. ..	.. ..	3rd Battle of Krithia	.. ..	.. ..	4th
JULY 2nd	.. ..	Action off Gottland between Russian and German squadrons (*German minelayer "Albatross" driven ashore*)	.. ..	.. ..	.. ..	.. ..	**JULY** 2nd

* Mr. Balfour, First Lord; Admiral Sir H. Jackson, First Sea Lord.

NAVAL.
1915.

Date	HOME WATERS.	BALTIC.	ATLANTIC.	MEDITERRANEAN AND BLACK SEA.	INDIAN OCEAN, RED SEA, AND PERSIAN GULF.	PACIFIC AND FAR EAST.	Date
1915. JULY 5th	.. ..	.. ..	.. ..	.. ..	1st action for Nasiriya (*Mesopotamia*)	.. ..	1915. JULY 5th
7th	.. ..	.. ..	.. ..	Italian cruiser "Amalfi" sunk by Austrian submarine in the Adriatic	.. ..	.. ..	7th
9th	.. ..	.. ..	*German South-West Africa capitulates to General Botha*	.. ..	.. ..	.. ..	9th
11th	.. ..	.. ..	.. ..	.. ..	German light cruiser "Königsberg" destroyed in Rufigi River by British monitors	.. ..	11th
13th	.. ..	.. ..	.. ..	.. ..	2nd action for Nasiriya (*Mesopotamia*)	.. ..	13th
14th	.. ..	.. ..	.. ..	.. ..		.. ..	14th
18th	.. ..		*Windau captured by German forces*	.. ..	Italian cruiser "Giuseppe Garibaldi" sunk by Austrian submarine in the Adriatic	.. ..	18th
24th	.. ..	.. ..	.. ..	.. ..	3rd action for Nasiriya (*Mesopotamia*)	.. ..	24th
25th	.. ..	.. ..	.. ..	.. ..	Nasiriya (*Mesopotamia*) taken by British forces	.. ..	25th
26th	.. ..	.. ..	.. ..	Pelagosa Island (*Adriatic*) seized by Italian forces	.. ..	.. ..	26th
AUG. 1st	.. ..	.. ..	.. ..	Constantinople harbour raided by British submarine	.. ..	.. ..	AUG. 1st
6th	.. ..	.. ..	.. ..	**Battle of Sari Bair and landing at Suvla begin**	.. ..	.. ..	6th
8th	.. ..		.. ..	Turkish battleship "Barbarousse-Hairedine" sunk by British submarine "E 11" in the Dardanelles	Bushire (*Persia*) occupied by British force	.. ..	8th
10th	.. ..		.. ..	**End of Battle of Sari Bair**	.. ..	.. ..	10th
12th	.. ..		.. ..	.. ..		.. ..	12th
13th	.. ..	German naval attack on Riga	.. ..	Transport "Royal Edward" sunk in Ægean by German submarine	Destruction of Dilbar (*South Persia*)	.. ..	13th
15th	.. ..		.. ..	**End of operations of the landing at Suvla**		.. ..	15th
16th	Lowca and Harrington, near Whitehaven (*Cumberland*) shelled by German submarine		.. ..	.. ..			6th
18th	.. ..		.. ..	.. ..	.. ..	.. ..	18th

NAVAL. 1915.

Date.	HOME WATERS.	BALTIC.	ATLANTIC.	MEDITERRANEAN AND BLACK SEA.	INDIAN OCEAN, RED SEA, AND PERSIAN GULF.	PACIFIC AND FAR EAST.	Date.
1915. AUG. 19th	British ss. "Arabic" sunk by German submarine. H.M.S. "Baralong" destroys German submarine "U. 27"	German battle-cruiser "Moltke" torpedoed by British submarine "E 1" in Gulf of Riga. German naval attack on Riga (contd.) British submarine "E 13" attacked by German warships while aground in Danish waters	..	..	..	..	**1915. AUG.** 19th
21st	First authenticated case of German submarine firing on a crew in boats (ss. "Ruel")	German naval attack on Riga abandoned	..	Italy declares war on Turkey	..	..	21st
SEPT. 1st	German Government inform United States Government that American demands for limitation of submarine activity are accepted	..	..	Ruad Island (off Syrian coast) occupied by French forces	..	..	**SEPT.** 1st
27th	..	..	..	Italian battleship "Benedetto Brin" destroyed by internal explosion in harbour at Brindisi	..	..	27th
28th	..	..	..	..	Battle of Kut, 1915 (Mesopotamia)	..	28th
OCT. 3rd	..	First German merchant vessel sunk by British submarine in the Baltic (ss. "Livonia")	..	..	..	..	**OCT.** 3rd
5th	..	..	..	Allied troops land at Salonika	..	..	5th
15th	..	..	..	Great Britain declares "state of war" with Bulgaria	..	..	15th
16th	..	..	..	France declares "state of war" with Bulgaria. Entente Governments proclaim blockade of Ægean coast of Bulgaria	..	..	16th
21st	..	..	..	Dede Agach bombarded by Allied squadron	..	..	21st
23rd	..	German cruiser "Prinz Adalbert" sunk by British submarine "E 8"	..	..	..	..	23rd
28th	H.M.S. "Argyll" wrecked on East Coast of Scotland	..	..	..	..	..	28th
NOV. 6th	..	..	..	Naval affair at Sollum (West Egypt)*	..	..	**NOV.** 6th
7th	..	German light cruiser "Undine" sunk by British submarine "E 19"	..	..	..	..	7th

* Egyptian coastguard cruisers attacked by German submarine: "Abbas" sunk, "Nur el Bahr" disabled

NAVAL. 1915-1916.

233

Date.	HOME WATERS.	BALTIC.	ATLANTIC.	MEDITERRA- NEAN AND BLACK SEA.	INDIAN OCEAN, RED SEA, AND PERSIAN GULF.	PACIFIC AND FAR EAST.	Date.
1915. NOV.							**1915. NOV.**
10th	British Order in Council issued authorising requisition of ships for carriage of foodstuffs	.. ..	.. ..	.. ..	.. ..	.. ..	10th
17th	British hospital ship "Anglia" sunk by mine off Dover	.. ..	.. ..	.. ..	.. .	.. ..	17th
22nd	.. ..	.. ..	.. ..	.. ..	Battle of Ctesiphon (Mesopotamia)	.. ..	22nd
24th	.. ..	.. ..	.. ..	.. ..		.. ..	24th
25th	.. ..	.. ..	.. ..	.. ..	Retreat to Kut (Mesopotamia)	.. ..	25th
DEC.							**DEC.**
3rd	.. ..	.. ..	.. ..	.. ..		.. ..	3rd
6th	.. ..	.. ..	.. ..	Durazzo bombarded by an Austrian squadron	.. ..	.. ..	6th
7th	.. ..	.. ..	.. ..	.. ..	Siege of Kut begins	.. ..	7th
17th	.. ..	German light cruiser "Bremen" sunk by British submarine	.. ..	.. ..	.. ..	.. ..	17th
19th	.. ..	.. ..	.. ..	Evacuation of Suvla and Auzac	.. ..	.. ..	9th
20th	.. ..	.. ..	.. ..	Durazzo occupied by Italian forces	.. ..	.. ..	20th
23rd	.. ..	.. ..	.. ..	.. ..	British naval operations on Lake Tanganyika (East Africa) begin	.. ..	23rd
26th	German raider "Moewe" leaves Germany on first cruise (see January 15th, 1916)	.. ..	.. ..	.. ..	German gunboat "Kingani" captured by H.M.S. "Mimi" and "Toutou" (Lake Tanganyika)	.. ..	26th
29th	.. ..	.. ..	.. ..	Durazzo raided by Austrian light forces: latter brought to action in Southern Adriatic	.. ..	.. ..	29th
30th	H.M.S. "Natal" destroyed by internal explosion in harbour in Cromarty Firth	.. ..	.. ..	.. ..	.. ..	.. ..	30th
1916. JAN.							**1916. JAN.**
4th	.. ..	.. ..	.. ..	.. ..	Operations for relief of Kut begin	.. ..	4th
6th	H.M.S. "King Edward VII" sunk by mine off North of Scotland	.. ..	.. ..	.. ..	.. ..	.. ..	6th
7th	.. ..	.. ..	.. ..	**Evacuation of the Gallipoli Peninsula completed**	.. ..	.. ..	7th
8th	.. ..	.. ..	.. ..		.. ..	.. ..	8th
11th	.. ..	.. ..	.. ..	Corfu occupied by French forces	.. ..	.. ..	11th
15th	.. ..	.. ..	British ss. "Appam" captured by German raider "Moewe" (see December 26th, 1915, and February 1st, 1916)	.. ..	.. ..	.. ..	15th

NAVAL.
1916.

Date.	HOME WATERS.	BALTIC.	ATLANTIC.	MEDITERRANEAN AND BLACK SEA.	INDIAN OCEAN, RED SEA, AND PERSIAN GULF.	PACIFIC AND FAR EAST.	Date.
1916. JAN. 22nd	.. ..	.. ..	.. ..	*Antivari (Montenegro) taken by Austrian forces*	.. ..	.. ..	**1916. JAN** 22nd
25th	.. ..	.. ..	.. ..	*San Giovanni di Medua (Albania) taken by Austrian forces*	.. ..	.. ..	25th
27th	*Shipping Control Committee formed by British Government*	.. ..	.. ..	.. ..	.. ..	.. ..	27th
FEB. 1st	.. ..	.. ..	*British ss. "Appam" brought to Norfolk (Va.) by German prize crew from raider "Moewe" (see January 15th)**	.. ..	.. ..	.. ..	**FEB.** 1st
8th	.. ..	.. ..	.. ..	*French cruiser "Amiral Charner" sunk by submarine off Syrian Coast*	.. ..	*British Government request naval assistance from Japan*	8th
9th	.. ..	.. ..	.. ..	.. ..	*German gunboat "Hedwig von Wissman" sunk by H.M.S. "Mimi" and "Fifi."† British command of Lake Tanganyika secured*	.. ..	9th
10th	.. ..	.. ..	*German Government inform United States Government that all defensively armed merchantmen will be treated as belligerents from March 1st onwards*	.. ..	.. ..	.. ..	10th
11th	*H.M.S. "Arethusa" sunk by mine in North Sea*	.. ..	.. ..	.. ..	.. ..	.. ..	11th
17th	.. ..	.. ..	.. ..	*Chios (Ægean) occupied by British forces*	.. ..	.. ..	17th
18th	.. ..	.. ..	*Conquest of the Cameroons by Entente forces completed*	.. ..	.. ..	.. ..	18th
21st	.. ..	.. ..	*German Government inform United States Government that defensively armed merchantmen will henceforth be regarded as cruisers*	.. ..	.. ..	.. ..	21st
23rd	*First Minister of Blockade, Great Britain, appointed (Lord Robert Cecil)*	.. ..	*German steamers in the Tagus seized by the Portuguese authorities*	.. ..	.. ..	.. ..	23rd
27th	.. ..	.. ..	.. ..	*Durazzo (Albania) taken by Austrian forces*	.. ..	.. ..	27th
29th	*Action in North Sea between German raider "Greif" and British auxiliary cruiser "Alcantara": both sunk*	.. ..	*British blockade of the Cameroons raised*	.. ..	.. ..	.. ..	29th

* First public intimation of operations of new German raiders.
† "Kingani" renamed, see *December 26th*, 1915.

NAVAL.
1916.

Date.	HOME WATERS.	BALTIC.	ATLANTIC.	MEDITERRA-NEAN AND BLACK SEA.	INDIAN OCEAN, RED SEA, AND PERSIAN GULF.	PACIFIC AND FAR EAST.	Date.
1916. MAR. 1st	German extended submarine campaign begins	..	..	..	..	..	1916. MAR. 1st
4th	German raider "Moewe" returns to Bremen from first cruise (see December 26th, 1915)	..	..	..	..	..	4th
14th	*Admiral von Capelle succeeds Admiral von Tirpitz as German Minister of Marine*	..	..	..	..	..	14th
15th		..	..	..	..	..	15th
24th	British ss. "Sussex" torpedoed by submarine in the English Channel	..	..	..	..	..	24th
30th	..	..	..	Russian hospital ship "Portugal" sunk by submarine in the Black Sea	..	..	30th
APRIL 17th	..	..	..	Trebizond (Asia Minor) taken by Russian forces (see February 24th, 1918)	..	..	APRIL 17th
20th	Disguised German transport "Aud" sinks herself after capture while trying to land arms on coast of Ireland	..	..	..	..	..	20th
24th	*Outbreak of rebellion in Ireland* Laying of Belgian coast barrage commenced	..	..	..	Final attempt to relieve Kut: Loss of H.M.S. "Julnar"	..	24th
25th	Lowestoft and Yarmouth raided by German battle cruiser squadron	..	..	..	..	..	25th
27th	..	..	..	H.M.S. "Russell" sunk by mine off Malta	..	..	27th
29th	..	..	..	..	*Capitulation of Kut*	..	29th
MAY 1st	*Collapse of Irish rebellion*	..	..	..	..	..	MAY 1st
15th	..	..	..	..	*Entente blockade of the Hejaz coast to assist revolt of the Sherif of Mecca commenced*	..	15th
31st	Battle of Jutland*	..	..	..	..	..	31st
JUNE 1st		..	..	..	..	..	JUNE 1st

* For names of ships sunk in this battle, see note at end of this section.

NAVAL.
1916.

Date.	HOME WATERS.	BALTIC.	ATLANTIC.	MEDITER-RANEAN AND BLACK SEA.	INDIAN OCEAN, RED SEA, AND PERSIAN GULF.	PACIFIC AND FAR EAST.	Date.
1916. JUNE.							**1916. JUNE.**
5th	H.M.S. "Hampshire" sunk by mine off the Orkneys. **Lord Kitchener and his Staff drowned**	..	..	..	Sherif of Mecca begins revolt against Turkish rule	..	5th
6th	..	..	..	"Pacific blockade" of Greece by Entente Powers begins	..	..	6th
7th	..	..	..	..	Sherif of Mecca proclaims independence of the Hejaz	..	7th
9th	..	..	..	..	Jidda taken by Arab forces	..	9th
22nd	..	..	..	"Pacific blockade" of Greece suspended	..	..	22nd
JULY 7th	British Government issue Order in Council rescinding the Declaration of London of 1909	..	..	..	Tanga (German East Africa) occupied by British forces	..	**JULY** 7th
10th	..	..	German commercial submarine "Deutschland" arrives at Norfolk (Va.)	Russian hospital ship "Vpered" sunk by submarine in the Black Sea	..	..	10th
11th	Seaham (Durham) shelled by German submarine	..	..	..	..	..	11th
27th	Captain Fryatt shot by order of a German court-martial in Belgium	..	..	..	Yenbo (port of Medina) taken by Arab forces	..	27th
AUG. 2nd	..	..	..	Italian Dreadnought "Leonardo da Vinci" sunk by internal explosion in harbour at Taranto	..	..	**AUG.** 2nd
15th	..	..	..	..	Bagamoyo (East Africa) captured by British naval landing parties	..	15th
19th	H.M.S. "Falmouth" and "Nottingham" sunk by submarine in North Sea	..	..	..	..	..	19th
23rd	..	..	German commercial submarine "Deutschland" returns to Germany*	..	..	..	23rd
27th	..	..	..	Rumania declares war on Austria-Hungary	..	..	27th
SEPT. 1st	..	..	..	Bulgaria declares war on Rumania	..	..	**SEPT.** 1st

* Approximate date.

NAVAL.
1916.

Date.	HOME WATERS.	BALTIC.	ATLANTIC.	MEDITERRA-NEAN AND BLACK SEA.	INDIAN OCEAN, RED SEA, AND PERSIAN GULF.	PACIFIC AND FAR EAST.	Date.
1916. SEPT. 2nd	..	..	..	German ships in Piræus Harbour seized by the Allies	..	..	**1916. SEPT.** 2nd
4th	..	..	..	..	Dar es Salaam (*German East Africa*) surrenders to the British forces	..	4th
7th	..	..	..	..	Kilwa (*German East Africa*) occupied by British forces	..	7th
16th	..	..	..	..	Lindi (*German East Africa*) occupied by British forces	..	16th
19th	..	..	..	Allies commence blockade of Greek Macedonian Coast from mouth of the Struma to mouth of the Mesto	..	..	19th
OCT. 8th	..	..	German submarine "U 53" captures and sinks five ships outside Newport (*Rhode island*)*	..	..	..	**OCT.** 8th
10th	..	..	..	Entente Governments send ultimatum to Greek Government demanding surrender of the Greek Fleet	..	..	10th
13th	Norwegian Government issue orders prohibiting belligerent submarines from using Norwegian territorial waters (*see February 1st, 1917*)	..	..	..	..	..	13th
20th	..	..	..	Russian battleship "Imperatritza Mariya" destroyed by internal explosion at Sevastopol	..	..	20th
22nd	..	..	..	Constanza (*Rumania*) taken by Bulgarian forces	..	..	22nd
26th	German destroyer raid in Dover Straits	..	..	..	..	..	26th
27th		..	..	..	..	..	27th
28th	British hospital ship "Galeka" sunk by mine off Havre	..	..	..	..	..	28th
NOV. 21st	..	..	..	British hospital ship "Britannic" sunk by mine in Ægean Sea	..	..	**NOV.** 21st
22nd	German raider "Seeadler" leaves Germany‡ (*see August 2nd, 1917*)	..	..	..	..	..	22nd
23rd	..	..	..	British hospital ship "Braemar Castle" mined† and beached in Ægean Sea	..	..	23rd

* Furthest west operations of German submarine. † Probably. ‡ Approximate date.

NAVAL. 1916-1917.

Date.	HOME WATERS.	BALTIC.	ATLANTIC.	MEDITERRA-NEAN AND BLACK SEA.	INDIAN OCEAN, RED SEA, AND PERSIAN GULF.	PACIFIC AND FAR EAST.	Date.
1916. NOV. 26th	Second German naval raid on Lowestoft German raider "Moewe" leaves Kiel on second cruise (see March 4, 1916, and March 22, 1917)	.. ..	French battleship "Suffren" sunk by submarine in the Bay of Biscay	.. ..	.. ..	.. ..	**1916. NOV.** 26th
29th	Admiral Sir David Beatty appointed Commander-in-Chief Grand Fleet	.. ..	.. ..	.. ..	.. ..	.. ..	29th
30th	.. ..	.. ..	.. ..	Allies land troops in Piræus. Greeks resist. Allied forces withdraw	.. ..	.. ..	30th
DEC. 1st	German raider "Wolff" leaves Germany* (see February 24th, 1918)	.. ..	.. ..	.. ..	.. ..	.. ..	**DEC.** 1st
3rd	Admiral Sir John Jellicoe succeeds Admiral Sir H. Jackson as First Sea Lord	.. ..	Funchal (Madeira) bombarded by German submarine	.. ..	.. ..	.. ..	3rd
4th		.. ..	.. ..	.. ..	.. ..	.. ..	4th
8th	.. ..	Murman Railway (from Murmansk to Petrograd) declared open	.. ..	Entente Powers begin blockade of Greece	.. ..	.. ..	8th
11th	.. ..	.. ..	.. ..	Italian battleship "Regina Margherita" sunk on Italian minefield	.. ..	.. ..	11th
12th	Sir Edward Carson succeeds Mr. Balfour as First Lord of the Admiralty	.. ..	.. ..	.. ..	.. ..	.. ..	12th
27th	.. ..	.. ..	.. ..	French battleship "Gaulois" sunk by submarine in the Mediterranean	.. ..	.. ..	27th
1917. JAN. 4th	.. ..	.. ..	.. ..	Russian battleship "Peresvyet" sunk by mine off Port Said	.. ..	.. ..	**1917. JAN.** 4th
5th	.. ..	.. ..	.. ..	Braila (Rumania) taken by German forces	.. ..	.. ..	5th
6th	"Inter-Allied Chartering Committee" established	.. ..	.. ..	.. ..	.. ..	.. ..	6th
9th	.. ..	.. ..	.. ..	H.M.S. "Cornwallis" sunk by submarine off Malta	Battle of Kut, 1917, begins	.. ..	9th
14th	.. ..	.. ..	.. ..	.. ..	.. ..	Japanese battle-cruiser "Tsukuba" sunk by internal explosion in harbour	14th
15th	.. ..	.. ..	.. ..	Italy accedes to Franco-British Convention as to naval "prizes" (see November 9, 1914)	.. ..	.. ..	15th
23rd	Harwich flotilla action with German 6th Torpedo-Boat Flotilla. (H.M.S. "Simoom" sunk)	.. ..	.. ..	.. ..	.. ..	.. ..	23rd

* Approximate date.

NAVAL.
1917.

Date.	HOME WATERS.	BALTIC.	ATLANTIC.	MEDITERRANEAN AND BLACK SEA.	INDIAN OCEAN, RED SEA, AND PERSIAN GULF.	PACIFIC AND FAR EAST.	Date.
1917. JAN. 24th	.. ..	.. ..	.. ..	Allied Naval Conference held in London as to policy in the Mediterranean	Wejh (Red Sea) taken by Arab forces	.. ..	1917. JAN. 24th
25th	German destroyer raid on Southwold and Wangford (Suffolk coast)	.. ..	.. ..	.. ..	.. ..	.. ..	25th
31st	German Government announce forthcoming "unrestricted submarine warfare," and threaten to sink hospital ships	.. ..	.. ..	.. ..	.. ..	.. ..	31st
FEB. 1st	German "unrestricted submarine warfare" begins *Norwegian Government issue orders forbidding all foreign submarines to use Norwegian territorial waters (see October 13th, 1916)*	.. ..	.. ..	.. ..	.. ..	.. ..	FEB. 1st
3rd	.. ..	.. ..	United States of America sever diplomatic relations with Germany	.. ..	.. ..	.. ..	3rd
13th	Scandinavian Governments publish joint protest against German submarine warfare	.. ..	.. ..	.. ..	.. ..	.. ..	13th
24th	.. ..	.. ..	.. ..	.. ..	Battle of Kut, 1917, ends	.. ..	24th
25th	British ss. "Laconia" sunk by submarine German destroyer raid on Margate and Broadstairs	.. ..	.. ..	.. ..	.. ..	.. ..	25th
26th	.. ..	.. ..	President Wilson in address to Congress asks for power to arm merchant ships	.. ..	Pursuit from Kut to Baghdad	.. ..	26th
MAR. 1st	British hospital ship "Glenart Castle" damaged by mine in English Channel	.. ..	.. ..	.. ..	.. ..	.. ..	MAR. 1st
11th	.. ..	.. ..	.. ..	.. ..	Baghdad occupied by British forces	.. ..	11th
12th	.. ..	Russian Revolution begins	United States Government announce arming of all merchant vessels in the war zone	Russian Revolution begins	.. ..	.. ..	12th
16th	German raider "Leopard" sunk by H.M.S. "Achilles" in North Sea	Mutiny breaks out in Russian fleet	.. ..	.. ..	.. ..	.. ..	16th
18th	German destroyer raid on Ramsgate and Broadstairs	.. ..	.. ..	.. ..	.. ..	.. ..	18th
19th	.. ..	.. ..	.. ..	French battleship "Danton" sunk by submarine in the Mediterranean	.. ..	.. ..	19th
21st	British hospital ship "Asturias" torpedoed by submarine off Start Point	.. ..	.. ..	.. ..	.. ..	.. ..	21st

NAVAL.
1917.

Date.	HOME WATERS.	BALTIC.	ATLANTIC.	MEDITERRA- NEAN AND BLACK SEA.	INDIAN OCEAN, RED SEA, AND PERSIAN GULF.	PACIFIC AND FAR EAST.	Date.
1917. **MAR.**							**1917.** **MAR.**
22nd	German raider "Moewe" returns to Kiel from second cruise (*see November* 26, 1916)	..	..	..	..	..	22nd
26th	..	..	..	} 1st Battle of Gaza	..	..	26th
27th	..	..	..		..	..	27th
30th	British hospital ship "Gloucester Castle" torpedoed in English Channel	..	..	..	..	..	30th
APRIL **3rd**	H.M.S. "Jason" sunk by mine off West Coast of Scotland	..	..	..	..	..	**APRIL** **3rd**
6th	..	..	United States of America declare war on Germany	..	..	..	6th
9th	*Admiral Sims, U.S.N., arrives in England*	..	..	..	..	..	9th
10th	British hospital ship "Salta" mined off Havre	..	..	..	..	..	10th
17th	British ambulance transports "Lanfranc" and "Donegal" sunk by submarine in English Channel	..	..	Two Japanese destroyer flotillas join Allied forces in Mediterranean. 2nd Battle of Gaza	..	..	17th
19th	..	..	..	..	..	..	19th
20th	Second German destroyer raid on Straits of Dover. (*Action by the "Swift" and "Broke"*)	..	..	..	..	..	20th
26th	} German destroyer raid on Ramsgate (*night* 26th/27th)	..	..	..	..	..	26th
27th		..	..	..	..	..	27th
MAY **2nd**	First United States destroyer flotilla arrives at Queenstown	..	..	..	..	..	**MAY** **2nd**
10th	..	..	Experimental convoy from Gibraltar to United Kingdom	..	..	..	10th
14th	German airship "L 22" destroyed by British warships in North Sea	..	..	..	..	..	14th
15th	..	..	..	Austrian naval raid in the Straits of Otranto: 14 British drifters sunk	..	..	15th
17th	*British Admiralty appoint Committee to draw up plan for convoy of merchant ships*	..	..	..	..	..	17th
24th	..	..	Experimental convoy sails from Newport News to United Kingdom	..	..	..	24th

NAVAL.
1917.

Date.	HOME WATERS.	BALTIC.	ATLANTIC.	MEDITERRA-NEAN AND BLACK SEA.	INDIAN OCEAN, RED SEA, AND PERSIAN GULF.	PACIFIC AND FAR EAST.	Date.
1917. MAY 26th	.. ..	.. ..	.. ..	British hospital ship "Dover Castle" sunk by submarine in the Mediterranean	.. ..	.. ..	1917. MAY. 26th
JUNE 12th	.. ..	.. ..	.. ..	Corinth and Larissa (*Greece*) occupied by Allied forces	.. ..	.. ..	JUNE 12th
14th	*British Admiralty approve scheme for convoy of merchant ships*	.. ..	.. ..	.. ..	.. ..	.. ..	14th
18th	*Admiral Sims, U.S.N., temporarily hoists flag at Queenstown*	.. ..	.. ..	.. ..	.. ..	.. ..	18th
21st	.. ..	.. ..	.. ..	Mutiny breaks out in the Russian Black Sea Fleet at Sevastopol	.. ..	.. ..	21st
25th	First contingent of United States troops arrives in France	.. ..	.. ..	.. ..	.. ..	.. ..	25th
27th	French cruiser "Kléber" sunk by submarine off Brest	.. ..	.. ..	Greece enters the war*	.. ..	.. ..	27th
JULY 2nd	.. ..	.. ..	First regular convoy of merchant ships sails from Hampton Roads (*Va.*)	.. ..	.. ..	.. ..	JULY 2nd
4th	.. ..	.. ..	Ponta Delgada (*Azores*) shelled by a German submarine Concerted attack by German submarines on United States transports defeated	.. ..	.. ..	.. ..	4th
6th	.. ..	.. ..	.. ..	.. ..	Aqaba (*Red Sea*) taken by Arab forces	.. ..	6th
9th	H.M.S. "Vanguard" sunk by internal explosion in harbour	.. ..	.. ..	.. ..	.. ..	.. ..	9th
19th	*Sir Edward Carson, First Lord of the Admiralty, resigns*	.. ..	.. ..	.. ..	.. ..	.. ..	19th
AUG. 2nd	.. ..				.. ..	German raider "Seeadler" wrecked on Mopelia Island (*see November 22nd, 1916*)	AUG. 2nd
3rd	Mutiny breaks out in German fleet at Wilhelmshaven	.. ..	.. ..	.. ..	.. ..	.. ..	3rd
4th	.. ..	.. ..	Liberia declares war on Germany	.. ..	.. ..	.. ..	4th
14th	.. ..	.. ..	.. ..	.. ..	.. ..	China declares war on Germany and Austria-Hungary	14th
SEPT. 1st	.. ..		.. ..	.. ..	.. ..	.. ..	SEPT. 1st
4th	German submarine raid on Scarborough	Battle of Riga: city captured by German forces	.. ..	.. ..	.. ..	.. ..	4th
5th	.. ..		.. ..	.. ..	.. ..	.. ..	5th

* See Part II, Section I.

NAVAL.
1917.

Date.	HOME WATERS.	BALTIC.	ATLANTIC.	MEDITERRA-NEAN AND BLACK SEA.	INDIAN OCEAN, RED SEA, AND PERSIAN GULF.	PACIFIC AND FAR EAST.	Date.
1917. **SEPT.** 6th	Sir Eric Geddes appointed First Lord of the Admiralty	.. ..	.. ..	.. ..	.. ..	.. ..	**1917.** **SEPT.** 6th
OCT. 2nd	H.M.S. "Drake" sunk by submarine in North Channel	.. ..	.. ..	.. ..	.. ..	.. ..	**OCT.** 2nd
5th	.. ..	.. ..	.. ..	.. ..	.. ..	Peru severs diplomatic relations with Germany	5th
10th	.. ..	.. ..	.. ..	British hospital ship "Goorkha" damaged by mine	.. ..	.. ..	10th
11th	.. ..	German operations against the Baltic Islands begin German force captures Ösel Island	.. ..	.. ..	.. ..	.. ..	11th
16th	.. ..	Naval action in Gulf of Riga (Russian battleship "Slava" sunk)	.. ..	.. ..	.. ..	.. ..	16th
17th	German cruisers raid British convoy in the North Sea. (H.M.S. "Strongbow" and "Mary Rose" sunk)	German force captures Moon Island and Dagö Island	.. ..	.. ..	.. ..	.. ..	17th
18th	.. ..		.. ..	.. ..	.. ..	.. ..	18th
20th	.. ..	German conquest of the Baltic Islands completed	.. ..	.. ..	.. ..	.. ..	20th
26th	.. ..	.. ..	Brazil declares war on Germany	.. ..	.. ..	.. ..	26th
27th	.. ..	.. ..	.. ..		.. ..	.. ..	27th
NOV. 2nd	Raid by British naval light forces in the Kattegat	.. ..	.. ..	3rd Battle of Gaza	.. ..	.. ..	**NOV.** 2nd
3rd	.. ..	.. ..	.. ..		.. ..	.. ..	3rd
7th	.. ..	.. ..	.. ..		.. ..	.. ..	7th
8th	.. ..	Bolshevik "coup d'état" in Petrograd	.. ..	.. ..	.. ..	.. ..	8th
15th	.. ..	.. ..	.. ..	.. ..	.. ..	Japanese Government unable to comply with request of British Government that two Japanese battle-cruisers should join the Grand Fleet	15th
16th	.. ..	.. ..	.. ..	Jaffa occupied by British forces	.. ..	.. ..	16th
17th	Light cruiser action off Heligoland	.. ..	.. ..	.. ..	.. ..	.. ..	17th
30th	Allied Naval Conference formed in London	.. ..	.. ..	.. ..	.. ..	.. ..	30th

NAVAL. 1917-1918.

Date.	HOME WATERS.	BALTIC.	ATLANTIC.	MEDITERRANEAN AND BLACK SEA.	INDIAN OCEAN, RED SEA, AND PERSIAN GULF.	PACIFIC AND FAR EAST.	Date
1917. DEC.							**1917. DEC.**
3rd	*Allied Conference in Paris decide to establish an Allied Maritime Transport Council*	.. ..	.. ..	.. ..	.. ..	.. ..	3rd
6th	U.S. Battleship Division joins Grand Fleet	.. ..	.. ..	.. ..	.. ..	.. ..	6th
10th		.. ..	.. ..	Italian naval raid on Trieste Harbour (*night 9th/10th*). (*Austrian battleship "Wien" sunk*)	.. ..	.. ..	10th
12th	German destroyers raid British convoy in the North Sea. (*H.M.S. "Partridge" sunk*)	.. ..	Funchal (*Madeira*) bombarded by German submarine	.. ..	.. ..	.. ..	12th
14th	.. ..	.. ..	.. ..	French cruiser "Château Renault" sunk by submarine	.. ..	.. ..	14th
17th	.. ..	**Armistice between Russia and Central Powers begins**	.. ..	**Armistice between Russia and Turkey begins**	.. ..	.. ..	17th
26th	Admiral Sir John Jellicoe, First Sea Lord, resigns, and is succeeded by Admiral Sir Rosslyn Wemyss	.. ..	.. ..	.. ..	.. ..	.. ..	26th
27th		.. ..	.. ..	.. ..	.. ..	.. ..	27th
1918. JAN.							**1918. JAN.**
4th	British hospital ship "Rewa" sunk by submarine in the Bristol Channel. *Allies formulate request for surrender of Dutch ships in Allied ports*	*Russian Government recognise the independence of Finland*	.. ..	.. ..	.. ..	.. ..	4th
13th	.. ..	*Estonian Government issue declaration of independence*	.. ..	.. ..	.. ..	.. ..	13th
14th	German destroyer raid on Yarmouth	.. ..	.. ..	.. ..	.. ..	.. ..	14th
20th	.. ..	.. ..	.. ..	Naval action outside the Dardanelles*	.. ..	.. ..	20th
27th	.. ..	.. ..	.. ..	"Goeben" refloated (*see 20th*). Turkish Dead Sea Flotilla seized by Arab camelry at El Mezraa'	.. ..	.. ..	27th
FEB.							**FEB.**
5th	Ss. "Tuscania" (*carrying United States troops*) sunk by submarine off the Irish coast	.. ..	.. ..	.. ..	.. ..	.. ..	5th
9th	.. ..	.. ..	.. ..	*Peace signed between Central Powers and the Ukraine Rada*	.. ..	.. ..	9th
15th	Third German destroyer raid in Straits of Dover (night 15th/16th). *Allied Governments arrange establishment of the Allied Maritime Transport Council (see Dec. 3rd, 1917)*	.. ..	.. ..	.. ..	.. ..	.. ..	15th
16th	Dover shelled by German submarine	.. ..	.. ..	.. ..	.. ..	.. ..	16th
18th		**Hostilities resumed by Germany against Russia**	.. ..	**Hostilities resumed by Central Powers against Russia**	.. ..	.. ..	18th

* "Breslau" and H.M.S. "Raglan" sunk. "Goeben" strikes mine and is beached.

NAVAL.
1918.

Date.	HOME WATERS.	BALTIC.	ATLANTIC.	MEDITERRA-NEAN AND BLACK SEA.	INDIAN OCEAN, RED SEA, AND PERSIAN GULF.	PACIFIC AND FAR EAST.	Date.
1918. FEB. 24th	German raider "Wolff" returns to Germany (see December 1st, 1916)	.. ..	.. ..	Trebizond retaken by Turkish forces (see April 17th, 1916)	.. ..	.. ..	**1918 FEB.** 24th
25th	.. ..	Reval and Pernau taken by German forces	.. ..	.. ..	.. ..	.. ..	25th
26th	British hospital ship "Glenart Castle" sunk by submarine in Bristol Channel	.. ..	.. ..	.. ..	.. ..	.. ..	26th
MAR. 2nd	.. ..	German force lands in the Aaland Islands	.. ..	.. ..	.. ..	.. ..	**MAR.** 2nd
3rd	.. ..	Peace signed between Russia and Central Powers at Brest-Litovsk	.. ..	.. ..	.. ..	.. ..	3rd
7th	.. ..	Peace signed between Finland and Germany	.. ..	.. ..	.. ..	.. ..	7th
10th	British hospital ship "Guildford Castle" torpedoed in Bristol Channel	.. ..	.. ..	.. ..	.. ..	.. ..	10th
11th	*First meeting of the Allied Maritime Transport Council (see February 15th)*	.. ..	.. ..	.. ..	.. ..	.. ..	11th
13th	.. ..	.. ..	.. ..	*Odessa occupied by German forces*	.. ..	.. ..	13th
17th	.. ..	.. ..	.. ..	*Nicolaiev occupied by German forces*	.. ..	.. ..	17th
20th	*Allied Blockade Committee formed*	.. ..	.. ..	.. ..	.. ..	.. ..	20th
21st	Destroyer action in the North Sea between Allied and German flotillas *Dutch ships in British ports requisitioned*	.. ..	*Dutch ships in United States ports requisitioned*	.. ..	.. ..	.. ..	21st
APRIL 3rd	.. ..	German force lands at Hangö (South Finland) British submarines destroyed at Helsingfors to avoid capture	.. ..	.. ..	.. ..	.. ..	**APRIL** 3rd
4th	.. ..	.. ..	.. ..	.. ..	.. ..	.. ..	4th
5th	.. ..	.. ..	.. ..	.. ..	.. ..	Japanese and British marines land at Vladivostok	5th
10th	.. ..	.. ..	Monrovia (*Liberia*) bombarded by German submarine (see August 4th, 1917)	.. ..	.. ..	.. ..	10th
13th	.. ..	Helsingfors captured by German forces	.. ..	.. ..	.. ..	.. ..	13th
15th	Raid by British naval light forces on the Kattegat	.. ..	.. ..	*Batum occupied by Turkish forces*	.. ..	.. ..	15th

NAVAL.
1918.

Date.	HOME WATERS.	BALTIC AND WHITE SEA.	ATLANTIC.	MEDITERRANEAN AND BLACK SEA.	INDIAN OCEAN, RED SEA, AND CASPIAN.	PACIFIC AND FAR EAST.	Date
1918. APRIL 22nd	Blocking raid by British naval light forces on Ostend and Zeebrugge	.. ..	.. ..	.. ..	.. ..	.. ..	1918. APRIL 22nd
23rd		.. ..	.. ..	.. ..	.. ..	.. ..	23rd
30th	.. ..	Viborg (*South Finland*) captured by German forces					30th
MAY 1st	.. ..	.. ..	.. ..	Sevastopol taken by German forces; part of Russian Black Sea Fleet seized	.. ..		MAY 1st
7th	.. ..	.. ..	.. ..	Peace signed between Rumania and the Central Powers	.. ..	.. ..	7th
9th	Blocking attack on Ostend (H.M.S. "Vindictive" sunk in the harbour)	.. ..			.. ..	.. ..	9th
10th		.. ..	.. ..	.. ..	.. ..	.. ..	10th
14th	.. ..	.. ..	.. ..	Italian naval raid on Pola Harbour	.. ..	.. ..	14th
15th	German submarine raid on St. Kilda	.. ..	.. ..	.. ..	.. ..	.. ..	15th
19th	.. ..	.. ..	.. ..		.. ..	Agreement signed between China and Japan for naval co-operation.	19th
24th	.. ..	General Poole lands at Murmansk	.. ..	.. ..	.. ..	.. ..	24th
JUNE 4th	.. ..	Force of British marines land at Pechenga	.. ..	.. ..	.. ..	.. ..	JUNE 4th
6th	Dutch hospital ship "Koningen Regentes" sunk	.. ..	.. ..	.. ..	.. ..	.. ..	6th
7th	.. ..	Kem (*North Russia*) occupied by Allied forces	.. ..	.. ..	.. ..	.. ..	7th
8th	.. ..	.. ..	.. ..	German troops land at Poti (*Georgia*)	.. ..	.. ..	8th
10th	.. ..	.. ..	.. ..	Naval action off Premuda Island (*Adriatic*). (Austrian battleship "Szent Istvan" sunk by Italian motor launch)	.. ..	.. ..	10th
18th	.. ..	.. ..	.. ..	Russian battleship "Svobodnaya Rossiya" destroyed in Black Sea (*to avoid surrender to the Germans*)	.. ..	.. ..	18th
23rd	.. ..	British Expeditionary Forces "Syren" and "Elope" land at Murmansk	.. ..	.. ..	.. ..	.. ..	23rd
27th	British hospital ship "Llandovery Castle" sunk by submarine off Irish coast	.. ..	.. ..	.. ..	.. ..	.. ..	27th

NAVAL.
1918.

Date.	HOME WATERS.	BALTIC AND WHITE SEA.	ATLANTIC.	MEDITERRANEAN AND BLACK SEA.	INDIAN OCEAN, RED SEA, AND CASPIAN.	PACIFIC AND FAR EAST.	Date.
1918. JUNE 29th	..	*Allied forces seize the railway from Murmansk to Soroki*	..	..	..	..	**1918. JUNE** 29th
30th	..		..	..	..	..	30th
JULY 12th	..	..	..	..	..	Japanese battleship "Kawachi" destroyed by internal explosion	**JULY** 12th
19th	..	..	United States cruiser "San Diego" sunk by mine off Fire Island	..	..	..	19th
AUG. 1st	..	Allied Expeditionary force attack and capture the defences of Archangel	..	..	..	..	**AUG.** 1st
2nd	..	Allied forces enter Archangel	..	..	..	..	2nd
3rd	British ambulance transport "Warilda" sunk by submarine	..	..	..	..	British troops land at Vladivostok	3rd
4th	..	..	..	..	British force arrives at Baku	..	4th
7th	..	..	French cruiser "Dupetit Thouars" sunk by submarine	..	..	..	7th
11th	..	..	..	..	..	First Japanese contingents arrive at Vladivostok	11th
13th	Vice-Admiral von Behnke succeeds Admiral von Capelle as German Minister of Marine	..	..	..	..	..	13th
15th		..	..	..	..	..	15th
26th	..	..	..	..	*Defence of Baku*	..	26th
SEPT. 15th	..				Baku taken by Turkish forces. (British force withdrawn 14th/15th)	..	**SEPT.** 15th
16th	H.M.S. "Glatton" sunk	..	..	..	..	..	16th
23rd	..	..	..	Haifa and Acre taken by British forces	..	..	23rd
30th	..	..	..	**Hostilities between Bulgaria and the Entente Powers cease**	..	..	30th
OCT. 1st	..	..	..	Allied net barrage across the Otranto Straits established	..	..	**OCT.** 1st
2nd	..	..	..	Durazzo bombarded by Allied squadron	..	..	2nd
7th	..	..	..	Beirut occupied by French forces	..	..	7th

NAVAL.
1918.

Date.	HOME WATERS	BALTIC AND WHITE SEA.	ATLANTIC.	MEDITERRANEAN AND BLACK SEA.	INDIAN OCEAN, RED SEA, AND CASPIAN.	PACIFIC AND FAR EAST.	Date.
1918.							**1918.**
OCT.							**OCT.**
10th	Irish mail-boat "Leinster" sunk by submarine	..	..	..	..	..	10th
13th	..	..	..	*Tripoli (Syria) occupied by Allied forces*	..	..	13th
14th	..	..	..	Durazzo retaken by Italian forces	..	..	14th
17th	Ostend retaken by Allied forces	..	..	..	..	..	17th
19th	Zeebrugge and Bruges retaken by Allied forces	..	..	..	..	..	19th
20th	Belgian coast completely occupied by Allied forces	..	..	..	..	..	20th
29th	..	..	..	*San Giovanni di Medua taken by Italian forces*	..	..	29th
31st	..	..	..	*Austrian Emperor makes over the Austro-Hungarian Fleet to the Yugo-Slav National Council* **Hostilities between Entente and Turkey cease**	..	..	31st
NOV.							**NOV.**
1st	..	..	..	Austrian battleship "Viribus Unitis" sunk in Pola Harbour	..	..	1st
2nd	..	..	..	Last British merchant vessels sunk by submarine*	..	..	2nd
3rd	Mutiny breaks out in the German Fleet at Kiel		..	Trieste occupied by Italian forces	..	..	3rd
4th	..	..	..	Antivari occupied by Italian naval forces **Hostilities between Austria-Hungary and the Entente cease**	..	..	4th
5th	H.M.S. "Campania" sunk by collision in the Firth of Forth	..	..	Fiume occupied by Italian naval forces	..	..	5th
7th	..	..	..	Last attack by submarine on British merchant vessel ("Sarpedon") unsuccessful	..	..	7th
9th	..	..	H.M.S. "Britannia" sunk by submarine off Cape Trafalgar	Alexandretta occupied by Entente naval forces	..	..	9th
11th	**Hostilities between Germany and the Entente cease**				..	..	11th

* "Surada" and "Murcia."

NAVAL. 1918.

Date.	HOME WATERS.	BALTIC AND WHITE SEA.	ATLANTIC.	MEDITERRANEAN AND BLACK SEA.	INDIAN OCEAN, RED SEA, AND CASPIAN.	PACIFIC AND FAR EAST.	Date.
1918. NOV.							1918. NOV.
12th	.. ..	.. ..	.. ..	Allied Fleet passes through the Dardanelles	.. ..	.. ..	12th
13th	.. ..	.. ..	.. ..	Allied Fleet arrives at Constantinople	.. ..	.. ..	13th
14th	H.M.S. "Cochrane" wrecked	.. ..	.. ..	.. ..	.. ..	.. ..	14th
15th	German cruiser "Königsberg," with German naval delegates, enters Firth of Forth to arrange surrender of the German Fleet. (*See 20th and 21st*)	.. ..	.. ..	.. ..	.. ..	.. ..	15th
17th	.. ..	.. ..	.. ..	.. ..	Baku (*Caspian*) re-occupied by a British force	.. ..	17th
18th	.. ..	.. ..	.. ..	*Italian troops arrive at Fiume* (*see 5th*)	.. ..	.. ..	18th
20th	First contingent of German submarines surrender to the British Navy at Harwich	.. ..	.. ..	.. ..	.. ..	.. ..	20th
21st	German High Seas Fleet arrives at Rosyth *en route* for internment at Scapa Flow.	.. ..	.. ..	*French troops land at Constantinople*	.. ..	.. ..	21st
26th	.. ..	.. ..	.. ..	Allied Fleet arrives at Sevastopol and takes over the Russian Black Sea Fleet from the Germans	.. ..	.. ..	26th
DEC. 4th	.. ..	H.M.S. "Cassandra" sunk by mine	.. ..	.. ..	.. ..	.. ..	DEC. 4th
8th	.. ..	.. ..	.. ..	.. ..	Naval action in the Caspian between British and Bolshevik vessels	.. ..	8th
11th	.. ..	.. ..	.. ..	*Odessa occupied by Petlyura's forces*	.. ..	.. ..	11th
13th	.. ..	.. ..	.. ..	.. ..	Hodeida (*Southern Arabia*) taken by British forces	.. ..	13th
20th	.. ..	.. ..	.. ..	*French troops land at Odessa*	.. ..	.. ..	20th
27th	.. ..	.. ..	.. ..	*Batum (Black Sea) occupied by British forces*	.. ..	.. ..	27th

Note.—In addition to the ships whose loss is recorded above, the following battleships and cruisers were sunk at the Battle of Jutland (May 31st/June 1st, 1916) :—

BRITISH.	GERMAN.
" Indefatigable."	" Pommern."
" Invincible."	" Lützow."
" Queen Mary."	" Wiesbaden."
" Black Prince."	" Rostock."
" Defence."	" Frauenlob."
" Warrior."	" Elbing."

PART II.

SECTION IV.

AIR.

Date.	WESTERN THEATRE OF WAR. (Including British Isles.)	OTHER THEATRES OF WAR.	Date.
1914. AUG. 4th	*Germany declares war on Belgium*		**1914. AUG.** 4th
	Two German airships pass over Brussels by night. **First hostile act in the Air**		
	Great Britain declares war on Germany		
9th	British aerial cross-Channel patrol (for protection of transports) instituted		9th
10th	British aerial coast patrol instituted		10th
13th 15th	Four squadrons Royal Flying Corps fly from Dover to France (*first units to cross by air*)		13th 15th
23rd	German airship "Z 8" shot down in Alsace		23rd
25th	*First use of aeroplanes for patrol purposes* (over retreating British armies)		25th
29th	.. ..	German airship "Z 5" brought down by gunfire at Mlawa (*Poland*)	29th
30th	First German aeroplane raid on Paris		30th
SEPT. 22nd	First British air raid on Germany (*Düsseldorf and Cologne*) (*to bomb airship sheds*)		**SEPT.** 22nd
	First use of wireless telegraphy from aeroplane to artillery (*by British Royal Flying Corps*)		
28th	*German aircraft adopt distinctive mark.* (*First definitely reported on this date*)		28th
OCT. 8th	Second British air raid on Germany. (*Düsseldorf and Cologne airship sheds attacked by British aeroplanes from Antwerp*)		**OCT.** 8th
NOV. 12th	*Orders issued for all British aeroplanes on Western Front to bear distinguishing mark*		**NOV.** 12th
21st	British air raid on Friedrichshaven (*by Royal Naval Air Service to attack Zeppelin hangars*)		21st
DEC. 15th	German airship sighted off East Coast of England. (*First appearance of hostile aircraft in vicinity of British Isles*)		**DEC.** 15th
21st	First aeroplane raid on England. Aeroplane drops bombs near Dover (*in the sea*)		21st
24th	Second aeroplane raid on England. (*First bomb dropped on English soil, near Dover*)		24th
25th	British seaplane raid on Cuxhaven		25th

AIR 1915

Date.	WESTERN THEATRE OF WAR. (Including British Isles.)	OTHER THEATRES OF WAR.	Date
1915. **JAN.** 19th	First German airship raid on England (*East Coast*)	.. ..	**1915.** **JAN** 19th
24th	.. ..	German airship "PL 19" brought down by rifle fire near Libau (Baltic)	24th
FEB. 17th	German airship "L 3" stranded and destroyed off Fanö and "L 4" destroyed near Blaavands Huk (*Denmark*)	.. ..	**FEB.** 17th
MAR. 15th	First merchant ship attacked by aircraft (*s.s. "Blonde"*)	.. ..	**MAR.** 15th
21st	First German airship raid on Paris	.. ..	21st
23rd	*First kite-balloon ship commissioned (H.M.S. "Manica")*	.. ..	23rd
APRIL ..	.. ..	.. ..	**APRIL** ..
MAY 31st	First German airship raid on London area ..	.. ..	**MAY** 31st
JUNE 7th	German airship "LZ 37" destroyed in mid-air by Lieutenant Warneford, near Ghent. (*First occasion of airship successfully attacked by aeroplane*)	.. ..	**JUNE** 7th
JULY ..	.. ..	.. ..	**JULY** ..
AUG. 10th	German airship "L 12" damaged by British aircraft off Ostend	.. ..	**AUG.** 10th
12th	.. ..	First enemy ship sunk by torpedo from British seaplane (*at the Dardanelles*)	12th
SEPT. ..	.. ..	.. ..	**SEPT.** ..
OCT. 1st	*Beginning of period in which the Germans obtained mastery in the air on the Western Front (due to the Fokker machine)**	.. ..	**OCT.** 1st
13th	East Coast of England, and London raided by airships. (*Heavy casualties, approximately 200, mostly civilian*)†	.. ..	13th
NOV. 5th	.. ..	German airship "LZ 39" destroyed near Grodno (Poland)	**NOV.** 5th
DEC. ..	.. ..	.. ..	**DEC.** ..

* Approximate date.　　　† This was the most severe airship raid on England.

Date.	WESTERN THEATRE OF WAR. (Including British Isles.)	OTHER THEATRES OF WAR.	Date.
1916. JAN. 29th	Last German airship raid on Paris	..	**1916. JAN.** 29th
31st	German airship raid on England. (*East Coast and industrial districts Midlands: furthest penetration westwards. Casualties 183, almost entirely civilian*)	..	31st
FEB. 2nd	German airship "L 19" founders in the North Sea	..	**FEB.** 2nd
16th	*The War Office take over from the Admiralty the anti-aircraft defence of London: also anti-aircraft defence throughout the kingdom*	..	16th
21st	German airship "LZ 77" brought down by French gunfire at Revigny (*night 21st/22nd*)	..	21st
28th	Nucleus formed of a British air squadron to bomb German industrial centres (*see June 5th, 1918*)	..	28th
MAR. 31st	German Airship raid on East Coast of England. (*Casualties 112, mostly military.*) German airship "L 15" brought down by gunfire near mouth of the Thames	..	**MAR.** 31st
APRIL 1st	*End of period of German mastery of the air on the Western Front* (see October 1st, 1915)*	..	**APRIL** 1st
14th	..	Constantinople and Adrianople bombed by British (*R.N.A.S.*) aeroplanes from Mudros	14th
MAY 3rd	German airship "L 20" returning from raid on Scotland wrecked at Stavanger (*Norway*)	..	**MAY** 3rd
4th	German airship "L 7" destroyed off the Slesvig coast	..	4th
5th	..	German airship "LZ 85" brought down by British gunfire at Salonika	5th
17th	*Air Board formed in Great Britain*	..	17th
31st	**Battle of Jutland:** First British aerial co-operation with fleet in action	..	31st
JUNE ..	..	..	**JUNE** ..
JULY 1st	**Battles of the Somme, 1916, begin:** Contact patrols first instituted	..	**JULY** 1st
30th	First aerial operations carried out by combined British and French air services on the French front	..	30th
AUG. ..	..	..	**AUG.** ..

* Approximate date.

AIR
1916–17

Date.	WESTERN THEATRE OF WAR. (Including British Isles.)	OTHER THEATRES OF WAR.	Date.
1916. **SEPT.** 2nd	German airship raid by fourteen airships (*greatest number to attack simultaneously*) on London, &c. German airship "SL 11" destroyed by aeroplane at Cuffley (*night 2nd/3rd*)	.. ..	**1916.** **SEPT.** 2nd
15th	Battle of Flers–Courcelette begins: First aerial co-operation with Tanks	.. ..	15th
23rd	German airship raid on East Coast of England and London involving serious casualties (170, *mostly civilian*). "L 32" destroyed by aeroplane at Billericay, "L 33" brought down by gunfire in Essex (*night 23rd/24th*)	.. ..	23rd
24th	Krupp works at Essen bombed by French aeroplanes	.. ..	24th
OCT. 1st	German airship "L 31" destroyed by aeroplane at Potter's Bar, near London (*night 1st/2nd*)	.. ..	**OCT.** 1st
NOV. 25th	German air force established as separate branch of the German army	.. ..	**NOV.** 25th
27th	German airship raid on East Coast of England. German airship "L 34" destroyed by aeroplane off Hartlepool, and "L 21" destroyed by aeroplane off Yarmouth (*night 27th/28th*)	.. ..	27th
28th	First German daylight aeroplane raid on London. (*Single aeroplane*)	.. ..	28th
DEC. ..	.. ..	.. ..	**DEC.** ..
1917. **JAN.** ..	.. ..	.. ..	**1917.** **JAN.** ..
FEB. ..	.. ..	.. ..	**FEB.** ..
MAR. 17th	German airship "L 39" returning from raid on England destroyed at Compiègne	.. ..	**MAR.** 17th
APRIL ..	.. ..	.. ..	**APRIL** ..
MAY 7th	First night aeroplane raid on London (*by moonlight by single aeroplane*)	.. ..	**MAY** 7th
14th	German airship "L 22" destroyed in North Sea by British warships	.. ..	14th
25th	First great aeroplane raid on England (*Kent and Folkestone*) to cause heavy casualties. (*Total approximately 290, over half of which civilian*)	.. ..	25th

Date.	WESTERN THEATRE OF WAR. (Including British Isles.)	OTHER THEATRES OF WAR.	Date.
1917. JUNE 5th	German daylight aeroplane raid on Sheerness and the naval establishments on the Medway	.. ..	1917. JUNE 5th
13th	**Great German aeroplane raid on London by daylight.** (*Total casualties approximately 590, nearly all civilian*)	.. ..	13th
14th	German airship "L 43" destroyed in the North Sea	.. ..	14th
17th	German airship "L 48" destroyed by aeroplane at Theberton (*Suffolk*)	.. ..	17th
JULY 7th	Severe aeroplane raid on England by daylight (*Margate and London*). (*Casualties 250, mostly civilian.*) (*Last raid on London by daylight*)	.. ..	JULY 7th
AUG. 21st	German airship "L 23" destroyed in North Sea ..	.. ..	AUG. 21st
22nd	Last German aeroplane raid on England by daylight (*on Kent coast*)	.. ..	22nd
SEPT. 2nd	First severe German aeroplane raid on England (Kent) by moonlight. (*Casualties about 250, mostly military*)	.. ..	SEPT. 2nd
3rd	Severe aeroplane raid on Kent by moonlight. (*Casualties approximately 230, mostly military*)	.. ..	3rd
4th	First German aeroplane raid on London by night in force	.. ..	4th
OCT. 19th	**Squadron of eleven German airships attack England.** (*Eight airships driven across to France by weather conditions.*) (*Last airship raid on London*)	.. ..	OCT. 19th
20th	Three German airships (*of the raiding squadron of 19th*) shot down in France*	.. ..	20th
21st	German airship "L 50" (*of the raiding squadron of 19th*) shot down in the Mediterranean	.. ..	21st
NOV. 21st	.. ..	German airship "L 59" leaves Yambol (*Bulgaria*) for East Africa†	NOV. 21st
23rd	.. ..	German airship "L 59" reaches East Africa but turns back without alighting†	23rd
25th	.. ..	German airship "L 59" returns to Yambol (*Bulgaria*) from flight to East Africa. (*Record flight up to date*)†	25th
29th	*Air Force (Constitution) Act, 1917, comes into operation in Great Britain*	.. ..	29th
DEC. 21st	*Order in Council issued instituting and defining duties of the Air Council (see November 29th)*	.. ..	DEC. 21st

* " L 44 " shot down at St. Clément.
" L 45 " „ „ Laragne.
" L 49 " „ „ Bourbonne-les-Bains.

† Evidence for this event is confined to unsubstantiated German statements.

AIR 1918

Date.	WESTERN THEATRE OF WAR. (Including British Isles.)	OTHER THEATRES OF WAR.	Date.
1918. **JAN.** 2nd	*Air Ministry formed in Great Britain*	..	**1918.** **JAN.** 2nd
3rd	*The Air Council (see December 21st, 1917) take over functions of the Air Board (see May 17th, 1916)*	..	3rd
FEB. ..	..	..	**FEB.** ..
MAR. 7th	First German aeroplane raid on London on a moonless night	..	**MAR.** 7th
25th	..	German airship raid on Naples from the Dalmatian coast	25th
APRIL 1st	**British Royal Flying Corps and Royal Naval Air Service amalgamated as the Royal Air Force**	..	**APRIL** 1st
12th	Last airship raid over England in which casualties were inflicted (27)	..	12th
MAY 18th	First British retaliatory raid on German towns (*Cologne bombed by day*)	..	**MAY** 18th
19th	Last German aeroplane raid on England in which casualties were inflicted. (*Kent, Essex, and London attacked by thirty-six aeroplanes. Seven brought down, three more crashed on return journey.*) (*Casualties 226, mostly civilian*) Severe German air raid on British camps and hospitals at Etaples	..	19th
JUNE 5th	**British Independent Air Force constituted in France** under tactical command of Major-General Sir H. M. Trenchard	..	**JUNE** 5th
JULY 20th	Last attempt to attack England with aeroplanes (*unsuccessful*)	..	**JULY** 20th
AUG. 5th	Last attempt to attack England with airships (*unsuccessful—"L 70" destroyed*)*	..	**AUG.** 5th
11th	German airship "L 53" destroyed off Frisian coast. (*Last German airship to be destroyed*)	..	11th
SEPT. 16th	Last German aeroplane raid on Paris	..	**SEPT.** 16th
OCT. ..	..	..	**OCT.** ..
NOV. 11th	Hostilities cease	..	**NOV.** 11th
DEC. ..	..	..	**DEC.** ..

* See footnote in Part I.

PART III.

ALPHABETICAL LIST.

A

AALAND ISLANDS—
    Naval action off (German cruiser "Magdeburg" destroyed) ... Aug. 26, 1914
    Occupied by German force ... Mar. 2, 1918
    German Government informs Swedish Government of the occupation of ... Mar. 3, 1918

ABBAS HILMI. See under "Khedive."

ABDICATION—
    Austria—Karl, *Emperor* ... signed Nov. 12, 1918
    Bulgaria—
        Ferdinand, *King* ... signed Oct. 4, 1918
        Boris, *King* ... signed Nov. 1, 1918
    Germany—Wilhelm II, *Kaiser* ... decision announced Nov. 9, 1918
        signed Nov. 28, 1918
    Greece—Constantine, *King* ... demanded by Entente Governments June 11, 1917
        signed June 12, 1917
    Russia—Nicholas II, *Tsar* ... signed Mar. 15, 1917

"ABOUKIR," H.M.S. (*Cruiser*)—
    Sunk ... Sept. 22, 1914

"ACHILLES," H.M.S. (*Cruiser*)—
    Action with German raider "Leopard" ... Mar. 16, 1917

ACRE (*Palestine*)—
    Occupied by British forces ... Sept. 23, 1918

ACTS—
    BRITISH PARLIAMENT—
        Air Force (Constitution), 1917 ... comes into operation Nov. 29, 1917
        Military Service—
            First ... passed by the Commons Jan. 24, 1916
            comes into operation Feb. 10, 1916
            Second ... passed by the Commons May 16, 1916
            becomes law May 25, 1916
            comes into operation June 8, 1916
            Third ... passed by the Commons Apr. 10, 1918
            comes into operation Apr. 18, 1918
        Munitions of War ... becomes law July 2, 1915
        Registration, National ... becomes law July 15, 1915
    CANADIAN PARLIAMENT—
        Conscription ... passed by the Commons July 6, 1917
        comes into operation Oct. 12, 1917
    NEW ZEALAND PARLIAMENT—
        Compulsory Service ... passed by the Commons June 10, 1916
        comes into operation Sept. 1, 1916

ADEN PROTECTORATE—
    Invaded by Turkish forces ... Feb. 2, 1915

ADMIRALTY, LORDS OF THE. See under "Britain—Ministers."

ABERCORN (North Rhodesia)—
    Defence of—
        Begins ... Sept. 5, 1914
        Ends ... Sept. 9, 1914
    German forces in East Africa surrender to Allied commander at ... Nov. 25, 1918

ADRIANOPLE—
    Raided by British aeroplanes (by R.N.A.S.) ... ... Apr. 14, 1916

ADRIATIC SEA—
    Italian Fleet commences operations in the ... ... May 25, 1915
    British Battle Squadron concentrates at Malta prior to joining Italian Fleet in the... May 26, 1915
    British Battle Squadron joins Italian Fleet in the ... ... May 27, 1915
    Action between Austrian and Allied light forces in the ... ... Dec. 29, 1915
    Action between Austrian and British light forces in the ... ... May 15, 1917

AERIAL CO-OPERATION—
    First British, instituted with Artillery ... ... Sept. 22, 1914
    First British, instituted with Fleet ... ... May 31, 1916
    First British, instituted with Infantry ... ... July 1, 1916
    First British, instituted with Tanks... ... ... Sept. 15, 1916

AERIAL SUPREMACY—
    Germans attain, on Western Front ... ... *Oct. 1, 1915
    British regain ... ... *Apr. 1, 1916

AERIAL PATROL (*British*)—
    Cross-Channel, instituted for the protection of transports conveying Expeditionary
        Force ... ... Aug. 9, 1914
    Of British coast established ... ... Aug. 10, 1914
    First used in France (over retreating British Armies) ... ... Aug. 25, 1914

AEROPLANES (marks, distinctive)—
    Adopted by Germans, first reported ... ... Sept. 28, 1914
    To be adopted, ordered by British ... ... Nov. 12, 1914

AFRICA—
  EAST—
    Hostilities—
      Begin† ... ... Aug. 8, 1914
      End—
        Allied Armistice terms delivered to German commander ... ... Nov. 14, 1918
        German forces surrender to Allied forces ... ... Nov. 25, 1918
    Frontier—
      Of British East Africa first crossed by German troops ... ... Aug. 15, 1914
      Of German East Africa—
        Northern—First crossed by British troops ... ... Nov. 3, 1914
    British Expeditionary Force—See under "Indian Expeditionary Forces 'B' and 'C.'"
    British Commander-in-Chief—
      1. General Stewart ... ... takes over command Sept. 1, 1914
                          relinquishes command Oct. 31, 1914
      2. General Aitken ... ... takes over command Oct. 31, 1914
                          recalled Dec. 4, 1914
      3. General Wapshare ... ... takes over command Dec. 4, 1914
                      transferred to Mesopotamia Apr. 16, 1915
      4. General Tighe ... ... takes over command Apr. 16, 1915
                          relinquishes command Feb. 19, 1916
      5. General Smith-Dorrien ... ... appointed‡ Nov. 22, 1915
                          resigns Jan. 31, 1916
      6. General Smuts ... takes over command from General Tighe Feb. 19, 1916
                          resigns Jan. 20, 1917
      7. General Hoskins ... ... takes over command Jan. 20, 1917
                          relinquishes command May 30, 1917
      8. General Van Deventer ... ... takes over command May 30, 1917
    Blockade of German East Africa—
      Begun ... ... Mar. 1, 1915
    Miscellaneous—
      War Office assume control of British operations in East Africa ... ... Nov. 22, 1914
      First aerial reconnaissance in East Africa ... ... Nov. 22, 1914
      German airship "L-59" reaches East Africa and turns back§ ... ... Nov. 23, 1917
  SOUTH—
    Hostilities—
      Begin (*German troops cross frontier of Cape Colony*) ... ... Aug. 21, 1914
      End (*German South-West Africa capitulates to General Botha*) ... ... July 9, 1915

    * Approximate date.
    † British naval forces bombard Dar es Salaam.
    ‡ Did not take over command owing to illness.
    § Evidence for this entry rests on unsubstantiated German statements. See also under
       "Airships, German."

AFRICA (continued)—
  SOUTH (continued)—
    Frontier—
      Of Cape Colony—Crossed by German troops... ... ... Aug. 21, 1914
      Of North Rhodesia—Crossed by German troops ... ... Sept. 5, 1914
      Of German South-West Africa—Crossed by Union troops ... ... Sept. 19, 1914
    Rebellion—
      Breaks out ... ... Sept. 15, 1914
      Ends* ... ... Dec. 28, 1914
      Last rebels in the Transvaal captured ... ... Jan. 11, 1915
  WEST—See under "Togoland," "Cameroons," &c.

AFRICAN FREE TRADE ZONE—
  Original Belgian proposal for neutralisation of—
    Formulated ... ... Aug. 9, 1914
    Germany agrees to proposal (made through Spanish Government) ... ... Aug. 22, 1914
    Withdrawn by British, Belgian and French Governments in view of altered
      situation ... ... Nov. 20, 1914

AGAGIYA (*Western Egypt*)—
  Action of ... ... Feb. 26, 1916

AGRAM (ZAGREB) (*Croatia*)—
  Yugo-Slav delegates meet at ... ... Oct. 5, 1918
  Yugo-Slav National Council (*q.v.*) meet at ... ... Oct. 29, 1918

AGREEMENTS. See under "Commitments" and "Sykes–Picot."

AHMED FUAD, *Prince*—
  Succeeds Hussein Kamel as Sultan of Egypt... ... ... Oct. 9, 1917

AIN ED DOULEH—
  Appointed Persian Premier ... ... Apr. 27, 1915
  Resigns ... ... Aug. 17, 1915
  Again appointed... ... ... Nov. 24, 1917
  Resigns ... ... Jan. 19, 1918

AIR BOARD (*Great Britain*)—
  Formed ... ... May 17, 1916

AIR COUNCIL (*Great Britain*)—
  Established by Air Force (Constitution) Act coming into operation ... ... Nov. 29, 1917
  Order in Council instituting, issued ... ... Dec. 21, 1917
  Takes over functions of Air Board ... ... Jan. 3, 1918

AIR DEFENCE (*Great Britain*)—
  Taken over by War Office from Admiralty for London, and established throughout
    the Kingdom ... ... Feb. 16, 1916

AIR FORCE, ROYAL—
  Royal Flying Corps and Royal Naval Air Service amalgamated to form a separate
    Service and designated the Royal Air Force ... ... Apr. 1, 1918
    (See also under "Flying Corps, Royal")

AIR FORCE, INDEPENDENT (*British*)—
  Nucleus first formed ... ... Feb. 28, 1916
  Constituted under Major-General Sir H. M. Trenchard ... ... June 5, 1918

* Organised rebellion ends on this date.

AIR MINISTRY (*Great Britain*)—

Formed ... Jan. 2, 1918

AIR RAIDS *—

British—
Aeroplane—
On Germany—
- First (on Düsseldorf and Cologne) ... Sept. 22, 1914
- Second ... Oct. 8, 1914
- On Friedrichshaven (by R.N.A.S.) ... Nov. 21, 1914
- First retaliatory, daylight ... May 18, 1918

On Turkey—
- Adrianople ... Apr. 14, 1916
- Constantinople ... Apr. 14, 1916

First aerial raid carried out by combined British and French Air Services ... July 30, 1916

Seaplane—
- On Cuxhaven ... Dec. 25, 1914

German—
Aeroplane—
On Great Britain—
- First ... Dec. 21, 1914
- First bombs dropped on English soil ... Dec. 24, 1914
- First important raid (Kent and Folkestone) to cause heavy casualties ... May 25, 1917
- Against Sheerness and naval establishments on the Medway ... June 5, 1917
- Last on England by daylight ... Aug. 22, 1917
- First by moonlight ... Sept. 2, 1917
- First undertaken on moonless night ... Mar. 7, 1918
- Last ... July 20, 1918

On London—
(1.) Daylight—
- First ... Nov. 28, 1916
- Largest ... June 13, 1917
- Last ... July 7, 1917

(2.) Night—
- First—By single aeroplane ... May 7, 1917
- For the first time by night in force ... Sept. 4, 1917
- Last in which casualties were inflicted ... May 19, 1918

On Paris—
- First ... Aug. 30, 1914
- Last ... Sept. 16, 1918

On Etaples hospitals ... May 19, 1918

Airships—
On England—
- First ... Jan. 19, 1915
- Most severe: on East coast and London ... Oct. 13, 1915
- Farthest penetration westwards ... Jan. 31, 1916
- Last in which casualties were inflicted ... Apr. 12, 1918
- Last ... Aug. 5, 1918

On London—
- First ... May 31, 1915
- By largest number (14) to attack simultaneously ... Sept. 2, 1916
- Last ... Oct. 19, 1917

On Naples ... Mar. 25, 1918

On Paris—
- First ... Mar. 21, 1915
- Last ... Jan. 29, 1916

AIRSHIPS, GERMAN—

- Pass over Brussels ... Aug. 4, 1914
- First sighted off East Coast of England ... Dec. 15, 1914
- "Z-8" shot down in Alsace ... Aug. 23, 1914
- "Z-5" brought down by gunfire at Mlawa ... Aug. 29, 1914
- "P.L-19" brought down by rifle fire near Libau ... Jan. 24, 1915
- "L-3" destroyed off Fanö ... Feb. 17, 1915
- "L-4" destroyed near Blaavands Huk ... Feb. 17, 1915
- "L.Z-37" destroyed by Lieut. Warneford near Ghent ... June 7, 1915
- "L-12" extensively damaged off Ostend ... Aug. 10, 1915
- "L.Z-39" destroyed near Grodno ... Nov. 5, 1915
- "L-19" founders in North Sea ... Feb. 2, 1916
- "L.Z-77" brought down at Revigny ... Feb. 21, 1916
- "L-15" brought down near mouth of the Thames ... Mar. 31, 1916
- "L-20" wrecked at Stavanger ... May 3, 1916
- "L-7" destroyed off Sleswig coast ... May 4, 1916
- "L.Z-85" brought down at Salonika ... May 5, 1916
- "S.L-11" destroyed by aeroplane at Cuffley ... Sept. 2, 1916

* Only the most important raids have been noted in Part III. See also Part II, Section IV.

AIRSHIPS, GERMAN (continued)—

"L-32" destroyed at Billericay	Sept. 23, 1916
"L-33" brought down in Essex	Sept. 23, 1916
"L-31" destroyed at Potter's Bar	Oct. 1, 1916
"L-21" destroyed off Yarmouth	Nov. 27, 1916
"L-34" destroyed off Hartlepool	Nov. 27, 1916
"L-39" destroyed at Compiègne	Mar. 17, 1917
"L-22" destroyed in North Sea	May 14, 1917
"L-43" destroyed in the North Sea	June 14, 1917
"L-48" destroyed at Theberton	June 17, 1917
"L-23" destroyed in North Sea	Aug. 21, 1917
"L-44" shot down at St. Clement	Oct. 20, 1917
"L-45" shot down at Laragne	Oct. 20, 1917
"L-49" shot down at Bourbonne-les-Bains	Oct. 20, 1917
"L-50" brought down in the Mediterranean	Oct. 21, 1917
"L-59"—	
Leaves Yambol for East Africa*	Nov. 21, 1917
Reaches East Africa and turns back*	Nov. 23, 1917
Returns to Yambol from East Africa*	Nov. 25, 1917
"L-70" destroyed near English coast	Aug. 5, 1918
"L-53" destroyed off Frisian coast	Aug. 11, 1918

(**Note.**—*This list is not exhaustive, as no mention is made of Airships destroyed in their sheds by bombing raids, &c.*)

AISNE, River (*France*)—

Battle of the, 1914 (*First battle of the†*)—

Begins	Sept. 12, 1914
Ends	Sept. 15, 1914

Transfer of British Army from the, to Flanders—

Begins	Oct. 3, 1914
Completed	Oct. 19, 1914

Second Battle of the†—

Begins	Apr. 16, 1917
Ends	Apr. 20, 1917

Battle of the, 1918 (*Third battle of the†*)—

Begins	May 27, 1918
Ends	June 6, 1918

AITKEN, *Major-General* A. E.—

Takes over command of British forces in East Africa	Oct. 31, 1914
Recalled	Dec. 4, 1914

ALA ES SULTANEH—

Appointed Persian Premier	Jan. 11, 1913
Resigns and takes office as Foreign Minister	Aug. 19, 1914
Resigns	Feb. 20, 1915
Again appointed Premier and Foreign Minister	June 6, 1917
Resigns	Nov. 24, 1917

ALBANIA—

(1.) **Government**—

Prince William of Wied leaves Albania	Sept. 3, 1914

Provisional Government of Essad Pasha—

Set up at Durazzo	Oct. 4, 1914
Leaves Durazzo	Feb. 24, 1916
Set up at Naples	Feb. 28, 1916
Set up at Salonika	Sept. 20, 1916

(2.) **Protectorate by Italy**—

Proclaimed	June 3, 1917

(3.) **Frontier** (crossed)—

By Serbian troops (*in retreat to Corfu*)	Nov. 30, 1915

(4.) **Miscellaneous**—

Entente Governments send communication to Greek, Serbian, and Montenegrin Governments deprecating their intervention in Albania	Feb. 2, 1915
Entente Governments warn Montenegrin Government that they will not recognise Montenegrin occupation of Albanian territory	July 29, 1915
French and Italian offensive in, begins	July 6, 1918
Allied offensive in, checked	July 22, 1918

"ALBATROSS" (*German Minelayer*)—

Driven ashore on coast of Gottland	July 2, 1915

* Evidence for this event rests on unsubstantiated German statements.
† French official name.

ALBERT (*France*)—
  Battle of, 1916—
    Begins ... July 1, 1916
    Ends ... July 13, 1916
  Captured by German forces ... Mar. 26, 1918
  Battle of, 1918 ... Aug. 21–23, 1918
  Recaptured by British forces ... Aug. 22, 1918

"ALCANTARA," H.M.S. (*Auxiliary Cruiser*)—
  Action with German raider "Greif" (*both sunk*) ... Feb. 29, 1916

ALEPPO (*Syria*)—
  Taken by British forces ... Oct. 26, 1918

ALEXANDER, Prince—
  Succeeds King Constantine as King of Greece ... June 12, 1917

ALEXANDRETTA (*Syria*)—
  Occupied by Entente naval forces ... Nov. 9, 1918

ALEXANDROPOL (*Georgia*)—
  Occupied by Turkish forces ... May 18, 1918

ALEXEIEV, General—
  Appointed Chief of Staff to the Russian armies under the Tsar as Commander-in-Chief ... Sept. 5, 1915
  Officiates as Commander-in-Chief on abdication of the Tsar ... Mar. 15, 1917
  Removed by Provisional Government ... June 4, 1917
  Commences operations against Bolsheviki ... Feb. 4, 1918
  Defeated by Bolsheviki ... Feb. 13, 1918

ALI DINAR (*Sultan of Darfur*)—
  Killed in action ... Nov. 6, 1916

'ALI GHARBI (*Mesopotamia*)—
  Kut relief force begins advance from ... Jan. 4, 1916
  Cossacks from Baratov's force join British army at ... May 18, 1916

ALLENBY, General Sir Edmund—
  Takes over command of Egyptian Expeditionary Force ... June 28, 1917
  Makes formal entry into Jerusalem ... Dec. 11, 1917

ALLIANCES. See under "Commitments."

ALMEIDA, Dr. A. José da.
  Appointed Portuguese Premier ... Mar. 15, 1916
  Resigns ... Apr. 25, 1917

ALSACE—
  French troops cross frontier of ... Aug. 7, 1914
  British Government give pledge as to restitution of ... Feb. 15, 1917
  British Government reiterate pledge as to restitution of ... Nov. 15, 1917
  Finally occupied by French forces ... *Nov. 26, 1918

"AMALFI" (*Italian Cruiser*)—
  Sunk ... July 7, 1915

AMARA (*Mesopotamia*)—
  Taken by British forces ... June 3, 1915

* Approximate date.

AMERICA, UNITED STATES OF—
    RELATIONS (severed)—
        With Germany ... Feb. 3, 1917
        By Austria-Hungary ... April 8, 1917
        By Bulgaria ... April 10, 1917
        By Turkey ... April 20, 1917
    WAR (declared)—
        On Germany ... Apr. 6, 1917
        On Austria-Hungary ... Dec. 7, 1917
    MINISTERS—
        I.—**Secretary of State**—
            (1.) Bryan, *Mr.*—Resigns ... June 24, 1915
            (2.) Lansing, *Mr.*—Appointed ... June 24, 1915
        II.—**Secretary for War**—
            (1.) Garrison, *Mr.*—Resigns ... Feb. 10, 1916
            (2.) Baker, *Mr.*—Appointed ... Mar. 6, 1916
        III.—**Secretary of the Navy**—
            Daniels, *Mr.*—Appointed ... Mar. 5, 1913
    ARMY—
        Expeditionary Forces—
            (i.) Government decide to send a division to France ... May 19, 1917
            (ii.) To France—First contingents land in France ... June 25, 1917
            (iii.) To Italy—First contingents arrive in Italy ... June 30, 1918
            (iv.) To North Russia—First contingents land at Murmansk ... Sept. 4, 1918
        Expansion of the Army—
            Congress passes Bill for an army of 500,000 men ... Apr. 28, 1917
            Compulsory service becomes law ... May 18, 1917
    NAVY—
        United States flotilla arrives at Queenstown ... May 2, 1917
        Flag of United States Admiral hoisted at Queenstown ... June 18, 1917
        United States squadron joins the Grand Fleet ... Dec. 6, 1917
    PEACE NEGOTIATIONS. See under "Peace" and "Wilson."
    TREATIES, &c. See under "Commitments."

AMIENS (*France*)—
    Taken by German forces ... Aug. 31, 1914
    Reoccupied by French forces ... Sept. 13, 1914
    Battle of ... Aug. 8–11, 1918

"AMIRAL CHARNER" (*French Cruiser*)—
    Sunk ... Feb. 8, 1916

AMMAN (*Palestine*)—
    First British attack on ... Mar. 27–30, 1918
    British cavalry cut Hejaz Railway at ... Sept. 25, 1918
    Turkish garrison of Ma'an (Hejaz Railway) surrender near ... Sept. 29, 1918

"AMPHION," H.M.S. (*Light Cruiser*)—
    Sunk ... Aug. 6, 1914

AMUCHU. See under "Togoland."

ANA (*Mesopotamia*)—
    Occupied by British forces ... Mar 28, 1918

"ANCONA," S.S. (*Italian*)—
    Sunk ... Nov 7, 1915

ANCRE HEIGHTS (*France*)—
    Battle of ... Oct. 1–Nov. 11, 1916

ANCRE, River (*France*)—
    Battle of the, 1916 ... Nov. 13–18, 1916
    Battle of the, 1918 ... Apr. 5, 1918

ANDRASSY, *Count*—
    Appointed Austro-Hungarian Foreign Minister ... Oct. 25, 1918
    Resigns ... Nov. 1, 1918

ANGOLA (*Portuguese West Africa*)—
    German forces begin unprovoked invasion of ... Oct. 26, 1914
    Portuguese Expeditionary Force leaves Lisbon for ... Dec. 4, 1914

ANTIVARI (*Montenegro*)—
    Bombarded by Austrian squadron ... ... Mar. 1, 1915
    Occupied by Austrian forces ... ... Jan. 22, 1916
    Occupied by Italian forces ... ... Nov. 4, 1918

ANTUNES, *Senhor* J. C. C. S.—
    Appointed Acting President of Portugal ... ... Dec. 16, 1918

ANTWERP (*Belgium*)—
    Belgian Government transferred from Brussels to ... ... Aug. 17, 1914
    Belgian Government transferred to Ostend from ... ... Oct. 7, 1914
    Siege of. Events in—
        Begins ... ... Sept. 27, 1914
        Marine Brigade, Royal Naval Division, arrives to aid in ... ... Oct. 3, 1914
        Evacuation begins ... ... Oct. 7, 1914
        Last forts taken by the Germans ... ... Oct. 9, 1914
        City capitulates to the Germans ... ... Oct. 10, 1914
    Reoccupied by the Belgians ... ... Nov. 19, 1918

ANZAC (*Gallipoli*)—
    Landing at ... ... Apr. 25, 1915
    Evacuation—
        Ordered ... ... Dec. 8, 1915
        Completed ... ... Dec. 20, 1915
        (See also under "Sari Bair.")

"APPAM," S.S. (*British*)—
    Captured by German raider "Moewe" ... ... Jan. 15, 1916
    Brought to Norfolk (*Va.*) by German prize crew ... ... Feb. 1, 1916

AQABA (*Arabia*)—
    Taken by Arab forces ... ... July 6, 1917

"ARABIC," S.S. (*British*)—
    Sunk ... ... Aug. 19, 1915

ARABS—
    1. **Independence**—
        Lord Kitchener transmits guarantee of ... ... Oct. 31, 1914
        Guaranteed by British Government ... ... Dec. 17, 1917
        British Government reaffirm pledges ... ... Feb. 4, 1918
    2. **Boundaries** of future Arab State defined by British Government ... ... Oct. 24, 1915
    3. "**King of the Arabs**"—
        Sherif of Mecca (*q.v.*)—
            Proclaimed as ... ... Oct. 29, 1916
            Coronation as ... ... Nov. 4, 1916
            Recognised by British Government as "King of the Hejaz" (*q.v.*) ... Dec. 15, 1916
    4. **Treaties, &c.** See under "Commitments."

ARCHANGEL. See under "Russia, North."

ARCHDUKE FRANZ FERDINAND—
    Assassinated at Sarajevo ... ... June 28, 1914

ARDENNES, Forest (*France*)—
    Battle of the* ... ... Aug. 22-24, 1914

"ARETHUSA," H.M.S. (*Light Cruiser*)—
    Sunk ... ... Feb. 11, 1916

ARGES (*Rumania*)—
    Battle of ... ... Dec. 1-5, 1916

ARGONNE (*France*). See under "Champagne and Argonne."

"ARGYLL," H.M.S. (*Cruiser*)—
    Sunk ... ... Oct. 28, 1915

* French official name.

"ARIADNE" (*German Light Cruiser*)—
    Sunk ... ... Aug. 28, 1914

ARIAN, *M.* Constantine—
    Appointed Rumanian Minister for Foreign Affairs ... ... Mar. 21, 1918
    Resigns ... ... Nov. 8, 1918

ARLEUX (*France*)—
    Battle of .. .. Apr. 28–29, 1917

ARMENIA—
    Massacre of Armenians commences ... ... *Apr. 8, 1915
    Entente Powers declare that they will hold Turkish Ministers personally
        responsible for ... ... May 24, 1915
    National Council—
        Assume charge of Armenian affairs ... ... May 26, 1918
        Turco-German Peace Delegates arrive at Batum ... ... May 6, 1918
        Sign peace with Turkey ... ... June 8, 1918
        (See also under "Trans-Caucasia.)

ARMENTIERES (*France*)—
    Battle of ... ... Oct. 13—Nov. 2, 1914
    Occupied by German forces ... ... Oct. 9, 1914
    Taken by Allied forces ... ... Oct. 17, 1914
    Taken by German forces ... ... Apr. 11, 1918
    Retaken by British forces ... ... Oct. 3, 1918

ARMISTICE—
    Central Powers and—
        Montenegro—
            Concluded ... ... Jan. 12, 1916
            Ceases ... ... Jan. 20, 1916
        Rumania—("Truce of Focsani")—Concluded ... ... Dec. 9, 1917
        Russia—Russian Provisional Government refuse German proposals for ... June 9, 1917
            1. Temporary—Concluded ... ... Dec. 6, 1917
            2. Final—
                Concluded ... ... Dec. 15, 1917
                Comes into effect ... ... Dec. 17, 1917

    Entente Powers and—
        Austria-Hungary—
            Proposals for an armistice sent to President Wilson by ... ... Oct. 4, 1918
            President Wilson replies to proposals of October 4th ... ... Oct. 18, 1918
            Further note to President Wilson asking for immediate armistice ... Oct. 27, 1918
            Austria-Hungary asks Italy for ... ... Oct. 27, 1918
            Concluded ... ... Nov. 3, 1918
        Bulgaria—
            Bulgaria asks for ... ... Sept. 27, 1918
            Concluded ... ... Sept. 30, 1918
        Germany—
            German armistice proposals sent to President Wilson... ... ... Oct. 4, 1918
            President Wilson replies stating primary conditions ... ... Oct. 8, 1918
            German Government accept the primary conditions ... ... Oct. 12, 1918
            President states further conditions ... ... Oct. 14, 1918
            German Government accept the further conditions ... ... Oct. 20, 1918
            President Wilson agrees to submit armistice proposals to Allied and
                Associated Powers ... ... Oct. 23, 1918
            President Wilson's note of October 23rd acknowledged ... ... Oct. 27, 1918
            Allied Governments agree to President Wilson's proposals ... ... Nov. 3, 1918
            President Wilson sends final note to German Government ... ... Nov. 5, 1918
            German armistice delegates reach Allied headquarters ... ... Nov. 8, 1918
            Armistice concluded ... ... Nov. 11, 1918
            News of armistice received by German East African Force ... ... Nov. 13, 1918
            Armistice prolonged to January 17, 1919 ... ... Dec. 14, 1918
        Hungary—(Separate)—Concluded ... ... Nov. 15, 1918
        Turkey—Concluded... ... ... Oct. 30, 1918

    Russia and—
        The Ukraine (German-Ukrainian command) concluded at Korenevo ... May 4, 1918
        The Ukraine, concluded at Kiev ... ... June 12, 1918
        (For dates of actual cessation of hostilities see under "Hostilities";
            see also under "Peace.")

* Approximate date.

ARRAS (*France*)—

Evacuated by French forces	Aug. 29, 1914
Reoccupied by French forces	Sept. 30, 1914
Battles of, 1917	Apr. 9—May 4, 1917
First Battle of, 1918	Mar. 28, 1918
Second Battles of, 1918	Aug. 26—Sept. 3, 1918

ARRIAGA, Dr. Manoel—

Elected Portuguese President	Aug. 24, 1911
Resigns	May 29, 1915

ARTOIS—

Battles of (*French*)—

First	Sept. 27—Oct. 12, 1914
Second	May 9—June 18, 1915
Third	Sept. 25—Oct. 15, 1915

AS SINN Position (*Mesopotamia*). See under "Kut al Amara."

ASIA MINOR—

BLOCKADE OF—Announced by British Government... June 2, 1915

PARTITION OF. See under "Commitments."

"SYKES-PICOT" AGREEMENTS, regarding. See under "Sykes-Picot Agreements."

ASQUITH, Mr. H. H.—

Appointed Prime Minister, Great Britain	April 8, 1908
Appointed Secretary of State for War, Great Britain	Mar. 31, 1914
Resigns as Secretary of State for War	Aug. 6, 1914
Forms Coalition Government	May 25, 1915
Resigns as Prime Minister	Dec. 4, 1916

ASSASSINATION—

Franz Ferdinand, *Archduke*	June 28, 1914
Goltz, *Field-Marshal* von der	Apr. 19, 1916
Stürgkh, *Count* Karl	Oct. 21, 1916
Mirbach, *Count*	July 6, 1918
Nicholas II, ex-Tsar of Russia	July 16, 1918
Ex-Tsaritsa and Family	July 16, 1918
Eichhorn, *Field-Marshal* von	July 30, 1918
Tisza, *Count* Stephen	Oct. 31, 1918
Paes, *Dr.*, ex-President of Portugal	Dec. 14, 1918

ASSURANCES. See under "Guarantees."

ATHENS (*Greece*)—

Massacre of Venizelists in ... Dec. 6, 1916

(See also under "Piræus.")

"AUD" (*German Transport*)—

Sinks herself off coast of Ireland ... Apr. 20, 1916

"AUDACIOUS," H.M.S. (*Battleship*)—

Sunk ... Oct. 27, 1914

AUBERS RIDGE (*France*)—

Battle of ... May 9, 1915

AUS (*German South-West Africa*)—

Occupied by South African forces ... Mar. 30, 1915

AUSTRALIA—
  1. AUSTRALIAN IMPERIAL FORCE—
    First units of—
      Embark for France ... Oct. 17, 1914
      Disembark in Egypt ... Dec. 1, 1914
      Ordered to the Dardanelles ... Feb. 20, 1915
  2. AUSTRALIAN NAVY—Placed at disposal of British Government ... July 30, 1914
  3. AUSTRALIAN PARLIAMENT—War Government formed... Feb. 17, 1917

AUSTRIA-HUNGARY—
  COUNCIL OF MINISTERS—
    Decide on action against Serbia ... July 14, 1914
    Approve draft ultimatum to Serbia ... July 19, 1914
  ULTIMATUM (presented)—
    To Serbia ... July 23, 1914
  MOBILISATION—
    Partial ... July 26, 1914
    General ... July 31, 1914
  RELATIONS (severed)—
    With Serbia ... July 25, 1914
    By France ... Aug. 10, 1914
    With Japan ... Aug. 24, 1914
    With Portugal ... Mar. 15, 1916
    With United States of America ... Apr. 8, 1917
    By Greece ... June 27, 1917
  WAR (declared)—
    On Serbia ... July 28, 1914
    By Montenegro ... Aug. 5, 1914
    On Russia ... Aug. 6, 1914
    By Britain ... Aug. 12, 1914
    By France ... Aug. 12, 1914
    On Belgium... Aug. 22, 1914
    By Japan* ... Aug. 25, 1914
    By Italy ... May 23, 1915
    By San Marino ... June 3, 1915
    On Portugal ... Mar. 15, 1916
    By Rumania ... Aug. 27, 1916
    By Greece* ... June 27, 1917
    By Siam ... July 22, 1917
    By China ... Aug. 14, 1917
    By United States of America ... Dec. 7, 1917
    By Panama ... Dec. 10, 1917
    By Cuba ... Dec. 16, 1917
    By Nicaragua ... May 8, 1918
  HOSTILITIES—
    Begin—
      With Serbia ... July 29, 1914
      In other cases, date of Declaration of War.
    Cessation of—
      With Montenegro ... Jan. 12, 1916
        " " resumed ... Jan 20, 1916
      With Russia ... Dec. 17, 1917
      With Entente (on Italian front) ... Nov. 4, 1918
      " " (on Western front) ... Nov. 11, 1918
  ARMISTICE—
    With Montenegro—
      Concluded ... Jan. 12, 1916
      Ceases ... Jan. 20, 1916
    With Rumania—Concluded ... Dec. 6, 1917
    With Russia—Concluded ... Dec. 17, 1917
    With Entente Powers—Concluded ... Nov. 3, 1918
      (See also under " Armistice " and " Brest-Litovsk.")
  PEACE—
    With The Ukraine—Signed ... Feb. 9, 1918
    With Bolshevik Russia—Signed ... Mar. 3, 1918
    With Rumania—Preliminary Treaty—Signed ... Mar. 5, 1918
    With Rumania—Signed ... May 7, 1918
    With Finland—Signed ... May 29, 1918
  PEACE NEGOTIATIONS. See under " Peace " and " Wilson.'
  EMPEROR—
    Francis Joseph dies ... Nov. 21, 1916
    Karl—
      Succeeds to the throne ... Nov. 21, 1916
      Makes peace overtures to French President ... Mar. 31, 1917
      Proclaims a Federal State on principle of nationality ... Oct. 16, 1918
      Makes over the Austro-Hungarian Fleet to the Yugo-Slav National Council Oct. 31, 1918
      Abdicates ... Nov. 12, 1918

* State of war proclaimed to exist.

AUSTRIA-HUNGARY (*continued*)—
    MINISTERS—
        (A.) AUSTRO-HUNGARIAN FOREIGN MINISTER—
            1. Berchtold, *Count*—
                Appointed ... ... Feb. 19, 1912
                Resigns ... ... Jan. 13, 1915
            2. Burian, *Baron*—
                Appointed ... ... Jan. 13, 1915
                Resigns ... ... Dec. 22, 1916
            3. Czernin, *Count*—
                Appointed ... ... Dec. 22, 1916
                Resigns ... ... Apr. 15, 1918
            4. Burian, *Baron*—
                Appointed ... ... Apr. 17, 1918
                Resigns ... ... Oct. 25, 1918
            5. Andrassy, *Count*—
                Appointed ... ... Oct. 25, 1918
                Resigns ... ... Nov. 1, 1918
            6. Flotow, *Baron* von—
                Appointed provisionally ... ... Nov. 1, 1918
        (B.) AUSTRIAN PREMIER—
            1. Stürgkh, *Count*—
                Appointed ... ... Nov. 3, 1911
                Assassinated ... ... Oct. 21, 1916
            2. Körber, *Dr.* von—
                Appointed ... ... Oct. 28, 1916
                Resigns ... ... Dec. 14, 1916
            3. Clam-Martinitz, *Count*—
                Appointed ... ... Dec. 21, 1916
                Resigns ... ... June 18, 1917
            4. Seidler, *Dr.* von—
                Appointed ... ... June 23, 1917
                Resigns ... ... June 21, 1918
                (For Hungarian Ministers, see under "Hungary.")
    FLEET—
        Austrian Emperor makes over the Austro-Hungarian Fleet to the Yugo-Slav National Council... ... ... Oct. 31, 1918
    MISCELLANEOUS—
        Austro-Hungarian Minister to Serbia leaves Belgrade ... ... July 25, 1914
    TREATIES, &c. See under "Commitments."

AVERESCU, *General*—
    Succeeds M. Bratianu as Premier of Rumania ... ... Feb. 9, 1918
    Resigns ... ... Mar. 12, 1918

AVRE, River (*France*)—
    Battle of ... ... Apr. 4, 1918

AZERBAIJAN—
    Republic proclaimed ... ... May 26, 1918
                (See also under "Trans-Caucasia.")

B

"B 11" (*British Submarine*)—
    Enters the Dardanelles ... ... Nov. 6, 1914
    Sinks Turkish battleship "Messoudieh" ... ... Dec. 13, 1914

BABUNA PASS (*South Serbia*)—
    Taken by Bulgarian forces ... ... Nov. 16, 1915

BADEN, *Prince* Max of. See "Max of Baden, Prince."

BAGAMOYO (*German East Africa*)—
    Occupied by British forces ... ... Aug. 15, 1916

BAGHDAD (*Mesopotamia*)—
    First advance on, begins ... Nov. 11, 1915
    Entered by British forces ... Mar. 11, 1917

BAHREIN ISLANDS (*Persian Gulf*).
    Advanced troops of Indian Expeditionary Force "D" arrive at ... Oct. 23, 1914

BAILLEUL (*France*)—
    Occupied by German forces ... Oct. 4, 1914
    Taken by British forces ... Oct. 14, 1914
    Battle of ... Apr. 13–15, 1918
    Taken by German forces ... Apr. 15, 1918
    Retaken by British forces ... Aug. 30, 1918

BAIRAM ALI (*Trans-Caspia*)—
    Action of ... Aug. 15, 1918

BAIT AISSA (*Mesopotamia*)—
    Action of ... Apr. 17–18, 1916

BAKHTIARI—
    Agreement between British Government and Chieftains of the—Concluded ... Feb. 15, 1916

BAKU (*Caspian Sea*)—
    Coup d'état in ... July 26, 1918
    British force arrives at ... Aug. 4, 1918
    Turkish attack on, begins ... Aug. 26, 1918
    British evacuation of, begins ... Sept. 14, 1918
    Captured by the Turks. British force finally withdrawn from ... Sept. 15, 1918
    Reoccupied by British troops ... Nov. 17, 1918

BALFOUR, Mr. A. J.—
    Appointed First Lord of the Admiralty, Great Britain ... May 28, 1915
    Resigns ... Dec. 11, 1916
    Appointed Minister for Foreign Affairs ... Dec. 11, 1916

BALTIC ISLANDS—
    German operations against ... Oct. 11–20, 1917
    (See also under "Ösel Island," "Moon Island" and "Dagö Island.")

BALTIC PROVINCES—
    United Diets of, request German Government to form them into a separate State in the German Empire ... Apr. 13, 1918
    (See also "Kurland," "Estonia," "Latvia," "Livonia.")

BAN OF CROATIA. See under "Croatia."

BANAT, The—
    Vote for union with Rumania ... Dec. 1, 1918

BANYO (*Cameroons*)—
    Captured by Allied force ... Nov. 6, 1915

BAPAUME (*France*)—
    Occupied by German forces ... Sept. 26, 1914
    Occupied by British forces ... Mar. 17, 1917
    Retaken by German forces ... Mar. 24, 1918
    Retaken by British forces ... Aug. 29, 1918
    First Battle of ... Mar. 24–25, 1918
    Second Battle of ... Aug. 31—Sept. 3, 1918

BAR. See under "Antivari."

"BARALONG," H.M.S. (Special Service Ship)—
    Destroys German submarine "U-27" ... Aug. 19, 1915

BARANOVICHI (West Russia)—
    Battle of ... July 2-9, 1916

"BARBAROUSSE-HAIREDINE" (Turkish Battleship)—
    Sunk ... Aug. 8, 1915

BARBOZA, Senhor J. T. de Sousa—
    Appointed Portuguese Secretary for the Interior ... May 16, 1918
    Resigns ... Dec. 22, 1918
    Appointed Portuguese Prime Minister ... Dec. 23 1918

BARRAGE, NET—
    Of Dover Straits—Completed ... Apr. 3, 1915
    Of North Channel—Established ... Feb. 22, 1915
    Of Straits of Otranto—Established ... Oct. 1, 1918
    Of Belgian Coast—Commenced ... Apr. 24, 1916

BARRETT, Lieut.-General Sir A. A.—
    Appointed commander designate of Indian Expeditionary Force "D" ... Sept. 28, 1914
    Takes over command in Mesopotamia ... Nov. 13, 1914
    Relieved ... Apr. 9, 1915

BARROW (Lancashire)—
    Walney Island Battery shelled by German submarine ... Jan. 29, 1915

BARTHOU, M.—
    Appointed French Foreign Minister ... Oct. 23, 1917
    Resigns ... Nov. 14, 1917

BASRA (Mesopotamia)—
    Occupied by British forces ... Nov. 22, 1914

BASSÉE, LA (France)—
    Battle of—
        Begins ... Oct. 10, 1914
        Ends ... Nov. 2, 1914

BATTENBERG, Prince Louis of—
    Appointed First Sea Lord, Great Britain ... Dec. 9, 1912
    Resigns ... Oct. 29, 1914

BATUM (Georgia)—
    Bombarded by German cruisers "Goeben" and "Breslau" ... Dec. 10, 1914
    Taken by Turkish forces ... Apr. 15, 1918
    Turco-German peace delegates arrive at ... May 6, 1918
    Occupied by British forces ... Dec. 27, 1918

BAVARIA—
    Proclaimed a Republic ... Nov. 7, 1918

BAZENTIN RIDGE (France)—
    Battle of ... July 14-17, 1916

BEATTY, *Admiral Sir* David—
    Succeeds Admiral Sir John Jellicoe as Commander-in-Chief, Grand Fleet ... Nov. 29, 1916

BEAUMONT HAMEL (*France*)—
    Stormed by British forces ... ... Nov. 13, 1916

BEAUREVOIR LINE (*France*)—
    Battle of ... ... Oct. 3-5, 1918

BEHNKE, *Admiral* von—
    Appointed German Minister of Marine ... ... Aug. 15, 1918

BEHO-BEHO (*German East Africa*)—
    Action of ... ... Jan. 3-4, 1917

BEIRUT (*Palestine*)—
    Occupied by French forces... ... ... Oct. 7, 1918

BEISAN (*Palestine*)—
    Occupied by British cavalry ... ... Sept. 20, 1918

BELGIUM—
    MOBILISATION—Ordered ... ... July 31, 1914
    ULTIMATUM (presented)—
        By Germany ... ... Aug. 2, 1914
        Belgium refuses German demands ... ... Aug. 3, 1914
    RELATIONS (severed)—
        With Germany ... ... Aug. 4, 1914
        By Turkey ... ... Nov. 6, 1914
    WAR (declared)—
        By Germany ... ... Aug. 4, 1914
        By Austria-Hungary ... ... Aug. 22, 1914
        Austrian Declaration received ... ... Aug. 28, 1914
    FRONTIER—
        First German troops cross ... ... Aug. 4, 1914
        Last German troops recross ... ... Nov. 26, 1918
    COAST LINE—
        Reached by German forces ... ... Oct. 15, 1914
        Completely reoccupied by Allied forces ... ... Oct. 20, 1918
    GOVERNMENT—
        Transferred from Brussels to Antwerp ... ... Aug. 17, 1914
        Transferred from Antwerp to Ostend ... ... Oct. 7, 1914
        Set up at Havre ... ... Oct. 13, 1914
        Reinstated at Brussels ... ... Nov. 21, 1918
    MINISTERS—
        Prime Minister*—
            1. de Broqueville, *Baron*—
                Appointed ... ... —, 1911
                Resigns ... ... May 31, 1918
            2. Cooreman, *M.* -
                Appointed ... ... May 31, 1918
                Resigns ... ... Nov. 21, 1918
            3. Delacroix, *M.*—
                Appointed ... ... Nov. 21, 1918

* Baron de Broqueville and M. Cooreman presided over the Cabinet without holding the title of Prime Minister. This title was instituted first with M. Delacroix's Cabinet.

BELGIUM (*continued*)—
   MINISTERS (*continued*)—
      Minister for Foreign Affairs—
         1. Davignon, *M.**—

Appointed	Feb. 28, 1914
Resigns	Jan. 18, 1916

         2. Beyens, *Baron**—

Appointed	Jan. 18, 1916
Resigns	Aug. 4, 1917

         3. de Broqueville, *Baron*—

Appointed	Aug. 4, 1917
Resigns	Jan. 1, 1918

         4. Hymans, *M.*—

Appointed	Jan. 1, 1918

      Minister for War—
         1. de Broqueville, *Baron*—

Appointed	Feb. 28, 1914
Resigns	Aug. 4, 1917

         2. de Ceuninck, *Lieut.-General*—

Appointed	Aug. 4, 1917
Resigns	Nov. 21, 1918

         3. Masson, *M.*—

Appointed	Nov. 21, 1918

   COLONIES—

Integrity guaranteed by British Government	Sept. 19, 1914

   PEACE OFFER—

By Germany	Sept. 15, 1918

   MISCELLANEOUS—

Government declare Belgium will uphold her neutrality "whatever the consequences"	July 24, 1914
Entente Governments make declaration guaranteeing to Belgium eventual independence and indemnification	Feb. 14, 1916

   TREATIES, &c. See under "Commitments."

BELGRADE (*Serbia*)—

Austrian Minister leaves	July 25, 1914
Serbian Government transferred to Nish from	July 25, 1914
Bombarded by Austrian artillery	July 29, 1914
Evacuated by Serbian forces	Nov. 30, 1914
Occupied by Austrian forces	Dec. 2, 1914
Reoccupied by Serbian forces	Dec. 15, 1914
Again taken by Austrian forces	Oct. 9, 1915
Reoccupied by Serbian forces	Nov. 1, 1918
Government reinstated at	Dec. 9, 1918

BELLEWAERDE RIDGE (*Ypres*)—

Battle of	May 24–25, 1915

"BELRIDGE," S.S. (*Norwegian*)—

First neutral ship torpedoed without warning	Feb. 19, 1915

"BENEDETTO BRIN" (*Italian Battleship*)—

Sunk	Sept. 27, 1915

BENEDICT XV, *Pope*. See under "Pope."

BERAT (*Albania*)—

Taken by Austrian forces	Feb. 17, 1916
Taken by Italian forces	July 10, 1918
Retaken by Austrian forces	Aug. 26, 1918
Again taken by Italian forces	Oct. 1, 1918

---

* M. Davignon was obliged to take leave, owing to ill-health, from 26th July, 1915, to 18th January, 1916. During this period Baron Beyens officiated as Minister for Foreign Affairs.

BERCHTOLD, Count—
    Appointed Austro-Hungarian Foreign Minister ... Feb. 19, 1912
    Resigns ... Jan. 13, 1915

BERINGIYA (Darfur)—
    Action of ... May 22, 1916

BERLIN—
    Revolution breaks out in ... Nov. 9, 1918

BERNSTORFF, Count—
    Correspondence re intrigues published ... Sept. 21, 1917

BESSARABIA—
    INDEPENDENCE—
        Proclaimed (as "the Moldavian Republic") ... Dec. 23, 1917
    UNION WITH RUMANIA—
        Articles of, signed at Kishinev, with stipulation for local autonomy... Apr. 9, 1918
        Protests against the union—
            (i.) By Ukraine Government ... Apr. 16, 1918
            (ii.) By Russian Bolshevik Government ... Apr. 23, 1918
        Unconditional union declared ... Dec. 10, 1918

BETHMANN-HOLLWEG, Herr von—
    Appointed German Imperial Chancellor ... July 14, 1909
    Resigns ... July 14, 1917

BETHUNE (France)—
    Battle of ... April 18, 1918

BEYENS, Baron—
    Appointed Belgian Minister for Foreign Affairs ... Jan. 18, 1916
    Resigns ... Aug. 4, 1917

BILLERICAY (Essex)—
    German airship "L-32" destroyed at ... Sept. 23, 1916

BILLS (Parliamentary). **See under "Act."**

BIRDWOOD, General Sir William—
    Assumes temporary command, Mediterranean Expeditionary Force ... Oct. 17, 1915
    Hands over command to Sir Charles Monro ... Oct. 28, 1915
    Appointed to command M.E.F. ... Nov. 4, 1915
    Appointed G.O.C. Dardanelles Army (in reconstituted M.E.F.) ... Nov. 25, 1915
    *Vacates appointment ... Jan. 9, 1916

BIRJAND (East Persia)—
    Occupied by British forces ... Oct. 7, 1915

"BIRMINGHAM," H.M.S. (Cruiser)—
    Sinks German submarine "U. 15" in the North Sea ... Aug. 9, 1914

BISMARCK ARCHIPELAGO—
    Australian Expeditionary Force lands in ... Sept. 11, 1914
        (See also under New Guinea.)

* Afterwards temporarily commanded successively the Fourth Army in France and the Australian Corps till he took over permanent command of the Fifth Army on May 23, 1918.

BISMARCKBURG (*German East Africa*)—
    Taken by British forces ... ... June 8, 1916

BITLIS (*Armenia*)—
    Taken by Russian forces ... ... Mar. 2, 1916
    Retaken by Turkish forces ... ... Aug. 15, 1916
    Again taken by Russian forces ... ... Aug. 24, 1916

"BLACK PRINCE," H.M.S. (*Cruiser*)—
    Sunk ... ... May 31, 1916

BLAAVANDS HUK (*Denmark*)—
    German airship " L-4 " destroyed near ... ... Feb. 17, 1915

BLAGOVYESHCHENSK (*Siberia*)—
    Occupied by Japanese forces ... ... Sept. 18, 1918

BLISS, *General* (*U.S.A.*)—
    Appointed to Supreme War Council ... ... Nov. 27, 1917

BLOCKADE—
    OF AUSTRIA-HUNGARY—Proclaimed by Italian Government ... ... May 26, 1915
    OF BULGARIA—(*Ægean Coast*)—Proclaimed by Entente Governments ... Oct. 16, 1915
    OF GREECE—
        British Government put economic pressure on Greece by making " Export
            Restrictions " apply to the country... ... ... Dec. 6, 1915
        British Government order partial relaxation of economic pressure on Greece ... Dec. 13, 1915
        " Pacific Blockade "—
            Begins ... ... June 6, 1916
            Suspended ... ... June 22, 1916
        Of Greek Macedonian Coast—Begins ... ... Sept. 19, 1916
        Coercive blockade—
            Announced ... ... Dec. 7, 1916
            Begins ... ... Dec. 8, 1916
    OF GREAT BRITAIN (*Submarine*)—
        Announced by Germany ... ... Feb. 4, 1915
        Begins ... ... Feb. 18, 1915
        "Extended Campaign"—Begins ... ... Mar. 1, 1916
        "Unrestricted Submarine Warfare"—
            Announced ... ... Jan. 31, 1917
            Begins ... ... Feb. 1, 1917
    OF GERMANY—
        British Government issue Order in Council modifying the Declaration of London Oct. 29, 1914
        British Government send note to United States Government in defence of
            British policy ... ... Dec. 29, 1914
        Great Britain and France sign Declaration prohibiting trade by or with
            Germany ... ... Mar. 1, 1915
        British Government issue the " retaliatory " Order in Council ... ... Mar. 11, 1915
        Dutch Government protest against British Blockade policy... ... ... Mar. 19, 1915
        " Trading with the Enemy (Extension of Powers) Act, 1915 " (beginning of
            " Black List " policy), comes into force in Great Britain ... ... Dec. 23, 1915
        United States Government protest against British " Black List " policy ... Jan. 26, 1916, and
            July 28, 1916
        Italy issues Decree prohibiting trade with Germany ... ... Apr. 17, 1916
        (See also under " Contraband " and " Poland, vii.")

    OF GERMAN COLONIES—
        Cameroons—
            Begins... ... ... Apr. 23, 1915
            Raised ... ... Feb. 29, 1916
        German East Africa—
            Begins ... ... Mar. 1, 1915
    OF TURKEY—
        Asia Minor—Announced by Great Britain ... ... June 2, 1915
        The Hejaz—Commenced, in aid of rebellion ... ... May 15, 1916
        (See also under " Contraband " and " Declaration of London.")

BLOCKADE COMMITTEE, ALLIED—
    First meeting in London ...   Mar. 20, 1918

BLOCKADE MINISTERS. See under "Britain" and "France."

"BLONDE," *S.S.*—
    First merchant ship attacked by aircraft ...   Mar. 15, 1915

"BLÜCHER" (*German Cruiser*)—
    Sunk ...   Jan. 24, 1915

BOLIVIA—
    Severs diplomatic relations with Germany ...   Apr. 13, 1917

BOLSHEVIKI—
    I. Bolshevik coup d'état—
        In Petrograd (*MM. Lenin and Trotski assume power*) ...   Nov. 8, 1917
    II. Bolshevik Government. See under "Brest-Litovsk" and "Russia."

BONA (*Algeria*)—
    Bombarded by German cruiser "Breslau" ...   Aug. 4, 1914

BORDEAUX—
    French Government transferred from Paris to ...   Sept. 2, 1914
    French Government returns to Paris from ...   Nov. 18, 1914

BORDEN, Sir Robert (*Prime Minister of Canada*)—
    Attends meeting of British Cabinet...   July 14, 1915

BORIS, *Prince*—
    Succeeds his father, King Ferdinand, as King of Bulgaria ...   Oct. 4, 1918
    Abdicates ...   Nov. 1, 1918

BOSELLI, *Signor*—
    Appointed Italian Premier ...   June 15, 1916
    Resigns ...   Oct. 25, 1917

BOSNIA—
    British Foreign Minister gives pledge to Serbian Government as to eventual conditional cession of ...   May 7, 1915
    British Foreign Minister gives guarantee as to eventual freedom and self-determination of ...   Aug. 30, 1915

BOSPORUS FORTS—
    Bombarded by Russian Black Sea Fleet ...   Mar. 27, 1915
    Apr. 25, 1915

BOURBONNE-LES-BAINS (*France*)—
    German airship "L-49" shot down at ...   Oct. 20, 1917

"BOUVET" (*French Battleship*)—
    Sunk ...   Mar. 18, 1915

BOY-ED, *Captain (German Military Attaché)*—
    United States Government request the recall of ... ... Dec. 4, 1915
    Recalled from United States by German Government... ... ... Dec. 10, 1915

"BRAEMAR CASTLE" *(British Hospital Ship)*—
    Beached after explosion—probably mined ... ... Nov. 23, 1916

BRAGA, *Dr. J. T.*—
    Elected President of Portugal ... ... May 28, 1915
    Resigns ... ... Oct. 5, 1915

BRAILA *(Rumania)*—
    Taken by German forces ... ... Jan. 5, 1917

BRASOV (KRONSTADT) *(Transylvania)*—
    Occupied by Rumanian forces ... ... Aug. 29, 1916
    Battle of: City retaken by Austro-German forces ... ... Oct. 7–9, 1916

BRATIANU, *M. J. J. C.*—
    Appointed Rumanian Premier and Foreign Minister ... ... Jan. 14, 1914
    Resigns ... ... Feb. 6, 1918
    Again appointed Premier and Foreign Minister ... ... Dec. 14, 1918

BRAZIL—
    Severs diplomatic relations with Germany ... ... Apr. 11, 1917
    Declares war on Germany ... ... Oct. 26, 1917

"BREMEN" *(German Light Cruiser)*—
    Sunk ... ... Dec. 17, 1915

"BRESLAU" *(German Light Cruiser)*—
    Bombards Bona ... ... Aug. 4, 1914
    Action with H.M.S. "Gloucester" off Greek coast ... ... Aug. 7, 1914
    Enters the Dardanelles ... ... Aug. 11, 1914
    Bombards Batum ... ... Dec. 10, 1914
    Sunk ... ... Jan. 20, 1918

BREST-LITOVSK *(Poland)*—
    Taken by German forces ... ... Aug. 25–26, 1915
    Negotiations at—
        Russian Bolshevik Government suggest an armistice to Germany and her allies   Nov. 21, 1917
        Germany agrees to negotiate ... ... Nov. 29, 1917
        Austria-Hungary agrees to negotiate ... ... Nov. 30, 1917
        First session of armistice delegates—Russian Bolshevik Government, Central
            Powers, Bulgaria and Turkey ... ... Dec. 3, 1917
        Temporary armistice concluded (7th to 17th December) and negotiations
            suspended ... ... Dec. 6, 1917
        Negotiations resumed ... ... Dec. 13, 1917
        Armistice concluded ... ... Dec. 15, 1917
        Definitive armistice comes into effect ... ... Dec. 17, 1917
        Peace negotiations opened ... ... Dec. 22, 1917
        Ukrainian Delegation arrives ... ... Jan. 3, 1918
        Bolshevik Government demand transfer of negotiations to Stockholm;
            negotiations suspended ... ... Jan. 5, 1918
        Negotiations resumed (Bolsheviki having withdrawn demand for transfer) ... Jan. 8, 1918
        Bolshevik Government accuse Central Powers of falsification of reports of
            proceedings ... ... Jan. 22, 1918
        Negotiations suspended ... ... Jan. 23, 1918
        Negotiations resumed ... ... Jan. 30, 1918
        Bolshevik Government announce end of state of war with Central Powers and
            their allies, but refuse to sign an annexationist peace ... ... Feb. 10, 1918
        Armistice terminates; Germany resumes hostilities ... ... Feb. 18, 1918
        Bolshevik Government surrender to German terms ... ... Feb. 19, 1918
        Negotiations resumed ... ... Feb. 28, 1918
        Peace Treaty signed between Russian Bolshevik Government and Central
            Powers, Bulgaria and Turkey. Russian Delegation protest against German
            terms ... ... Mar. 3 1918

BRIAND, M.—
    Succeeds M. Viviani as French Premier and Foreign Minister ... ... Oct. 30, 1915
    Confirmed in office on reorganisation of Ministry ... ... Dec. 12, 1916
    Resigns ... ... Mar. 17, 1917

BRINDISI—
    Serbian Government transferred to, from Scutari ... ... Jan. 15, 1916

"BRISTOL," H.M.S. (*Light Cruiser*)—
    Action with German cruiser "Karlsruhe" in the West Indies ... ... Aug. 6, 1914

BRITAIN, GREAT—
    Mobilisation—
        Naval, ordered ... ... Aug. 1, 1914
        General, ordered ... ... Aug. 3, 1914
    Ultimatum (presented)—To Germany ... ... Aug. 4, 1914
    Relations—(severed)—
        With **Turkey** ... ... Oct. 30, 1914
        With **Bulgaria** ... ... Oct. 13, 1915
    War (declared)—
        On **Germany** ... ... Aug. 4, 1914
        On **Austria-Hungary** ... ... Aug. 12, 1914
        On **Turkey**... ... ... Nov. 5, 1914
        By **Turkey** (Jehad) ... ... Nov. 14, 1914
        On **Bulgaria*** ... ... Oct. 15, 1915
    Hostilities with—
        Austria-Hungary—
            Begin ... ... Aug. 12, 1914
            Cease ... ... Nov. 4, 1918
        Bulgaria—
            Begin ... ... Oct. 15, 1915
            Cease ... ... Sept. 30, 1918
        Germany—
            Begin ... ... Aug. 4, 1914
            Cease ... ... Nov. 11, 1918
        Turkey—
            Begin ... ... Nov. 1, 1914
            Cease ... ... Oct. 31, 1918
    Armistice—Concluded—
        With Bulgaria ... ... Sept. 30, 1918
        With Turkey ... ... Oct. 30, 1918
        With Austria-Hungary ... ... Nov. 3, 1918
        With Germany ... ... Nov. 11, 1918
        With Independent Government of Hungary ... ... Nov. 15, 1918
    Cabinet—
        (*a.*) War Council—
            First meeting ... ... Aug. 5, 1914
            Last meeting ... ... May 14, 1915
        (*b.*) Dardanelles Committee—
            First meeting ... ... June 7, 1915
            Last meeting ... ... Oct. 30, 1915
        (*c.*) War Committee—
            First meeting ... ... Nov. 3, 1915
            Last meeting ... ... Dec. 1, 1916
        (*d.*) War Cabinet—First meeting ... ... Dec. 9, 1916
    Ministers—
        I. Prime Minister—
            1. Asquith, *Mr.*—
                Appointed ... ... Apr. 8, 1908
                Resigns ... ... Dec. 4, 1916
            2. Lloyd George, *Mr.*—Appointed ... ... Dec. 7, 1916
        II. Secretary for Foreign Affairs—
            1. Grey, *Sir* Edward—
                Appointed ... ... Dec. 11, 1905
                Resigns ... ... Dec. 11, 1916
            2. Balfour, *Mr.*—Appointed ... ... Dec. 11, 1916
        III. Secretary for War—
            1. Asquith, *Mr.*—
                Appointed ... ... Mar. 31, 1914
                Resigns ... ... Aug. 6, 1914
            2. Kitchener, *Earl*—
                Appointed ... ... Aug. 6, 1914
                Lost at sea ... ... June 5, 1916
            3. Lloyd George, *Mr.*—
                Appointed ... ... July 7, 1916
                Resigns ... ... Dec. 11, 1916
            4. Derby, *Earl* of—
                Appointed ... ... Dec. 11, 1916
                Resigns ... ... Apr. 20, 1918
            5. Milner, *Viscount*—
                Appointed ... ... Apr. 20, 1918

* State of war proclaimed as existing.

BRITAIN, GREAT (continued)—
   Ministers (continued)—
      IV. ADMIRALTY—
         (A.) **First Lord**—
            1. Churchill, *Mr.* Winston—
               Appointed ... Oct. 24, 1911
               Resigns ... May 27, 1915
            2. Balfour, *Mr.* Arthur—
               Appointed ... May 28, 1915
               Resigns ... Dec. 11, 1916
            3. Carson, *Sir* Edward—
               Appointed ... Dec. 12, 1916
               Tenders resignation ... July 19, 1917
            4. Geddes, *Sir* Eric—
               Appointed ... Sept. 6, 1917
         (B.) **First Sea Lord**—
            1. Battenberg, *Prince* Louis of—
               Appointed ... Dec. 9, 1912
               Resigns ... Oct. 29, 1914
            2. Fisher, *Lord*—
               Appointed ... Oct. 30, 1914
               Tenders resignation ... May 15, 1915
            3. Jackson, *Sir* Henry—
               Appointed ... May 28, 1915
               Resigns ... Dec. 3, 1916
            4. Jellicoe, *Sir* John—
               Appointed ... Dec. 4, 1916
               Resigns ... Dec. 26, 1917
            5. Wemyss, *Sir* Rosslyn—Appointed ... Dec. 27, 1917
      V. MINISTER OF BLOCKADE—
         1. Cecil, *Lord* Robert—
            Appointed ... Feb. 23, 1916
            Resigns ... July 18, 1918
         2. Worthington-Evans, *Sir* L.—Appointed ... July 18, 1918
MINISTRY, COALITION—Formed—
   First (Mr. Asquith) ... May 25, 1915
   Second (Mr. Lloyd George) ... Dec. 11, 1916
MINISTRIES, NEW—Formed—
   Air ... Jan. 2, 1918
   Blockade ... Feb. 23, 1916
   Food ... Dec. 22, 1916
   Information ... Feb. 21, 1918
   Labour ... Dec. 11, 1916
   Munitions ... July 2, 1915
   National Service ... Nov. 1, 1917
   Pensions ... Dec. 22, 1916
   Reconstruction ... Aug. 21, 1917
   Shipping ... Dec. 22, 1916
ARMY—
   (I.) EXPEDITIONARY FORCES—
      (A.) To **France**—
         First units land in France ... Aug. 7, 1914
         Landing of original Expeditionary Force completed ... Aug. 16, 1914
         Commander-in-Chief—
            1. French, *Sir* John, Field-Marshal—
               Appointed ... Aug. 4, 1914
               Resigns ... Dec. 15, 1915
            2. Haig, *Sir* Douglas, General—
               Appointed ... Dec. 15, 1915
               Takes over command ... Dec. 19, 1915
         Chief of General Staff—
            1. Lieut.-General *Sir* A. J. Murray—
               Appointed ... Aug. 4, 1914
               Resigns ... Jan. 24, 1915
            2. Lieut.-General *Sir* W. R. Robertson—
               Appointed ... Jan. 25, 1915
               Resigns ... Dec. 22, 1915
            3. Lieut.-General *Sir* L. E. Kiggell—
               Appointed ... Dec. 22, 1915
               Resigns ... Jan. 27, 1918
            4. Lieut.-General *The Hon. Sir* H. A. Lawrence—
               *Appointed ... Jan. 24, 1918
         Adjutant-General—
            1. Lieut.-General *Sir* C. F. N. Macready—
               Appointed ... Aug. 4, 1914
               Resigns ... Feb. 21, 1916
            2. Lieut.-General *Sir* G. H. Fowke—Appointed ... Feb. 22, 1916

* Took up appointment in France on January 27th.

BRITAIN, GREAT (*continued*)—
ARMY (*continued*)—
I. EXPEDITIONARY FORCES (*continued*) –
(A.) **To France** (*continued*)—
Quartermaster-General—
1. Lieut.-General *Sir* W. R. Robertson—
Appointed	Aug. 4, 1914
Resigns	Jan. 24, 1915

2. Lieut.-General *Sir* R. C. Maxwell—
Appointed	Jan. 27, 1915
Resigns	Dec. 22, 1917

3. Lieut.-General *Sir* Travers E. Clarke—Appointed ... Dec. 23, 1917

(B.) For other Expeditionary Forces see under "Dardanelles," "Africa—East," "Egypt," "Italy," "Mesopotamia," "Russia—North" "Salonika."

(II.) NEW ARMIES—
First New Army—Formation authorised	Aug. 21, 1914
Second " " "	Sept. 11, 1914
Third " " "	Sept. 13, 1914
First "New Army" Division leaves England for France	May 9, 1915

(See also "Territorial Force" and "Compulsory Service.")

(III.) HOME FORCES—
Commander-in-Chief—
1. Field-Marshal *Sir* John French—
Appointed	Dec. 19, 1915
Resigns	May 8, 1918

2. General *Sir* W. R. Robertson—
Appointed	May 30, 1918

Chief of Imperial General Staff—
1. General *Sir* C. W. H. Douglas—
Appointed	Apr. 6, 1914
Dies	Oct. 25, 1914

2. Lieut.-General *Sir* J. Wolfe Murray—
Appointed	Oct. 26, 1914
Resigns	Sept. 25, 1915

3. Lieut.-General *Sir* A. J. Murray—
Appointed	Sept. 26, 1915
Resigns	Dec. 22, 1915

4. General *Sir* W. R. Robertson—
Appointed	Dec. 23, 1915
Resigns	Feb. 18, 1918

5. General *Sir* H. H. Wilson—Appointed ... Feb. 19, 1918

Adjutant-General—
1. Lieut.-General *Sir* H. C. Sclater—
Appointed	Apr. 9, 1914
Resigns	Feb. 21, 1916

2. Lieut.-General *Sir* C. F. N. Macready—
Appointed	Feb. 22, 1916
Resigns	Aug. 30, 1918

3. Lieut.-General *Sir* G. W. M. Macdonogh—Appointed ... Sept. 11, 1918

Quartermaster-General—
Lieut.-General *Sir* J. S. Cowans—
Appointed	June 3, 1912

(Holding same appointment at end of war.)

(IV.) DEMOBILISATION—Begins ... Dec. 4, 1918

FLEET—
Orders for dispersal countermanded	July 26, 1914
Ordered to war bases	July 28, 1914
"Warning Telegram" sent to Fleets by the Admiralty	July 29, 1914
Mobilisation ordered	Aug. 1, 1914
First aerial co-operation with, in action	May 31, 1916

Grand Fleet—
Constituted	Aug. 4, 1914

Commander-in-Chief—
(i.) Jellicoe, Admiral Sir John—
Appointed	Aug. 4, 1914
Resigns	Nov. 29, 1916

(ii.) Beatty, Admiral Sir David—Appointed ... Nov. 29, 1916
Joined by United States Battleship Division	Dec. 6, 1917
German High Seas Fleet surrender to	Nov. 21, 1918

ROYAL AIR FORCE—Formed as separate Service ... Apr. 1, 1918

MILITARY SERVICE ACTS. See under "Acts."

NATIONAL REGISTRATION—
Act becomes law	July 15, 1915
Register taken	Aug. 15, 1915

BRITAIN, GREAT (continued)—
    NATIONAL SERVICE—
        Government decide to institute ... ... Dec. 19, 1916
        Ministry of, formed ... ... Nov. 1, 1917
    ROYAL HOUSE (Name of)—Changed to Windsor ... ... July 17, 1917
    SHIPPING—
        Requisition of, authorised ... ... Aug. 3, 1914
        Port and Transit Executive Committee appointed ... ... Nov. 3, 1915
        Ship Licensing Committee appointed: foreign traffic restricted ... ... Nov. 10, 1915
        Requisitioning (Carriage of Foodstuffs) Committee appointed ... ... Nov. 10, 1915
        Control Committee of, appointed ... ... Jan. 27, 1916
        Order in Council extends powers of Ship Licensing Committee to all voyages Feb. 15, 1916
        (See also under "Britain—Ministries," "Convoys," "Merchant Vessels" and "Shipping.")
    TREATIES, &c. See under "Commitments."

"BRITANNIC" (British Hospital Ship)—
    Sunk by mine ... ... Nov. 21, 1916

"BRITANNIA," H.M.S. (Battleship)—
    Sunk ... ... Nov. 9, 1918

BROADSTAIRS (Kent)—
    German destroyer raids on ... ... { Feb. 25, 1917
                                                          { Mar. 18, 1917

"BROKE," H.M.S. (Destroyer)—
    Action in Dover Straits ... ... Apr. 20, 1917

BROODSEINDE (Flanders)—
    Battle of ... ... Oct. 4, 1917

BROQUEVILLE, Baron de—
    Appointed Belgian Prime Minister* ... ... ——, 1911
    Appointed Minister for War ad interim ... ... Feb. 28, 1914
    Resigns as Minister for War ... ... Aug. 4, 1917
    Appointed Minister for Foreign Affairs ... ... Aug. 4, 1917
    Resigns as Minister for Foreign Affairs ... ... Jan. 1, 1918
    Resigns as Prime Minister ... ... May 31, 1918

BRUGES (Belgium)—
    Occupied by German forces ... ... Oct. 14, 1914
    Reoccupied by Belgian forces ... ... Oct. 19, 1918

BRUSILOV, General—
    Appointed to command Russian South-Western front ... ... Apr. 4, 1916
    Succeeds General Alexeiev as Russian Commander-in-Chief ... ... June 4, 1917
    Succeeded by General Kornilov as Russian Commander-in-Chief ... ... Aug. 1, 1917

BRUSSELS (Belgium)—
    Two German airships pass over (first hostile act in the air) ... ... Aug. 4, 1914
    Belgian Government transferred to Antwerp from ... ... Aug. 17, 1914
    Occupied by German forces ... ... Aug. 20, 1914
    Reoccupied by Belgian forces ... ... Nov. 18, 1918
    Belgian Government reinstated at ... ... Nov. 21, 1918

BRYAN, Mr.—
    Succeeded by Mr. Lansing as United States Secretary of State ... ... June 24, 1915

BUDAPEST (Hungary)—
    Revolution in.—Breaks out ... ... Oct. 31, 1918

* Presided over the Cabinet but without holding the title of Prime Minister. This title was first instituted with M. Delacroix's Cabinet.

BUFTEA (*Rumania*)—
    Preliminary treaty of peace between Rumania and Central Powers signed at ... Mar. 5, 1918

BUKHAREST (*Rumania*)—
    Rumanian Government transferred to Jassy from ... Dec. 1, 1916
    Capitulates to German forces ... Dec. 6, 1916
    Peace negotiations begin at ... Feb. 25, 1918
    Rumanian Government re-established at ... Nov. 30, 1918

BUKHAREST, TREATY OF—
    Peace between Rumania and the Central Powers, Bulgaria and Turkey, signed ... May 7, 1918

BUKOBA (*on Victoria Nyanza*)—
    Attack on, and capture of, by British force ... July 22–23, 1915

BUKOVINA, The—
    Austrian forces driven out of ... June 24, 1916
    General Congress of, decide in favour of union with Rumania ... Nov. 28, 1918
    National Council of, send deputation to Jassy to announce desire for union with Rumania ... Dec. 7, 1918

BULGARIA—
    MOBILISATION (ordered)—
        Partial ... Sept. 21, 1915
        General (for 25th) ... Sept. 22, 1915
    ULTIMATUM (presented)—By Entente Powers ... Oct. 4, 1915
    RELATIONS (severed)—
        By Russia ... Oct. 5, 1915
        By Britain ... Oct. 13, 1915
        By Rumania ... Aug 30, 1916
        With United States of America ... Apr. 10, 1917
    WAR (declared)—
        On Serbia ... Oct. 14, 1915
        By Serbia ... Oct. 14, 1915
        By Britain ... Oct. 15, 1915
        By France ... Oct. 16, 1915
        By Italy ... Oct. 19, 1915
        By Russia ... Oct. 19, 1915
        On Rumania ... Sept. 1, 1916
        By Greek Provisional Government ... Nov. 23, 1916
        By Greece ... June 27, 1917
    HOSTILITIES—
        With Serbia—Commence ... Oct. 11, 1915
        With other Entente countries—Commence ... Date of declaration of war
        With Entente and Allies—Cease ... Sept. 30, 1918
    BLOCKADE—Of Bulgarian Ægean coast by the Entente Powers—Proclaimed ... Oct. 16, 1915
    KING (TSAR)—
        1. **Ferdinand**—Abdicates ... Oct. 4, 1918
        2. **Boris**—
            Succeeds ... Oct. 4, 1918
            Abdicates ... Nov. 1, 1918
    MINISTER—PREMIER—
        1. **Radoslavov, M.**—
            Appointed ... July 20, 1913
            Resigns ... June 18, 1918
        2. **Malinov, M.**—Appointed ... June 18, 1918
    LOAN—
        With German Government (£3,000,000)—Concluded ... Feb. 3, 1915
        With Austro-German banks (400,000,000 fr.)—Concluded ... Aug. 6, 1915
    ARMISTICE—
        With Entente Powers—
            Asked for ... Sept. 27, 1918
            Concluded ... Sept. 30, 1918

BULGARIA (continued)—
   PEACE—Signed—
      With Bolshevik Russia ... Mar. 3, 1918
      With Rumania (preliminary) ... Mar. 5, 1918
      With Rumania (final) ... May 7, 1918
        (For Peace negotiations see under "Peace.")

   TREATIES, &c. See under "Commitments."

BULLECOURT (*France*)—
   Battle of ... May 3–17, 1917

"BULWARK," H.M.S. (*Battleship*)—
   Blown up in harbour ... Nov 26, 1914

BURIAN, *Baron*—
   Appointed Austro-Hungarian Foreign Minister ... Jan. 13, 1915
   Resigns ... Dec. 22, 1916
   Again appointed ... Apr. 17, 1918
   Again resigns ... Oct. 25, 1918

BUSHIRE (*South Persia*)—
   British Residency attacked by Tangistani tribesmen ... July 12, 1915
   Occupied by British forces ... Aug. 8, 1915
   Again attacked by tribesmen ... Sept. 9, 1915

BYELOSTOK (*Poland*)
   Taken by German forces ... Aug. 26, 1915

BYELYAEV, *General*—
   Appointed Russian Minister for War ... Jan. 17, 1917
   Superseded by Revolutionary Government ... Mar. 13, 1917

C

CABINET. See under "Britain."

CADORNA, *General*—
   Appointed Italian Commander-in-Chief* ... May 23, 1915
   Relieved of his command ... Nov. 7, 1917
   Appointed to Supreme War Council, Versailles ... Nov. 27, 1917

†CAMBRAI (*France*)—
   City occupied by German forces ... Aug. 26, 1914
   Battle of, 1917—
      Begins ... Nov. 20, 1917
      German counter-attacks begin ... Nov. 30, 1917
      Ends ... Dec. 3, 1917
   Battle of, 1918 ... Oct. 8–9, 1918
   City captured by British forces ... Oct. 9, 1918

CAMEROONS—
   Blockade—
      Begins ... Apr. 23, 1915
      Raised ... Feb. 29, 1916
   Frontier—
      (*a.*) Nigerian—
         Crossed by British troops ... Aug. 25, 1914
      (*b.*) Chad—
         Crossed by French troops ... Aug. 25, 1914
      (*c.*) Spanish—
         Crossed by last German troops‡ ... Feb. 17, 1916
   Conquest of, completed (*garrison of Mora surrenders*) ... Feb. 18, 1916
   Agreement as to administration between French and British Governments concluded ... Mar. 3, 1916

      * Officially designated "Chief of Staff."
      † See also under "Hindenburg Line."
      ‡ Crossing into Spanish Muni for internment.

"CAMPANIA," *H.M.S.* (*Aircraft Carrier*)—
    Sunk by collision ... Nov. 5, 1918

CANADA—
    I. **Compulsory Service**—
        Passed by Canadian House of Commons ... July 6, 1917
        Comes into operation ... Oct. 12, 1917
    II. **Canadian Expeditionary Force**—
        First units sail from Canada for England ... Oct. 3, 1914
        First units land in England ... Oct. 15, 1914
        First division embarks for France ... Feb. 9, 1915
        General Currie appointed to command of ... June 19, 1917
    III. **Parliament**—
        War Cabinet formed ... Oct. 12, 1917

CANAL DU NORD (*France*)—
    Battle of ... Sept. 27—Oct. 1, 1918

"CAP TRAFALGAR" (*German Armed Merchant Cruiser*)—
    Sunk in action with H.M.S. "Carmania" ... Sept. 14, 1914

CAPE HELLES (*Gallipoli*)—
    Allied forces effect landing at ... Apr. 25–26, 1915
    Evacuated ... Jan. 7–8, 1916

CAPELLE, *Admiral* Edouard von—
    Appointed German Minister of Marine ... Mar. 15, 1916
    Resigns ... Aug. 13, 1918

"CAPITULATIONS, THE"—
    Turkish Government announces abolition of ... Sept. 9, 1914

CAPORETTO* (*Italy*)—
    Battle of—See under "Twelfth Battle of the Isonzo."

"CARMANIA," *H.M.S.* (*Armed Merchant Cruiser*)—
    Sinks German armed merchant cruiser "Cap Trafalgar" ... Sept. 14, 1914

CARNIOLA (*Austria*)—
    Administration taken over from the Austro-Hungarian authorities by the Slovene leaders ... Nov. 2, 1918

CAROLINE ISLANDS—
    Admiral von Spee's squadron leaves ... Aug. 6, 1914

CARSON, *Sir* Edward—
    Appointed First Lord of the Admiralty, Great Britain ... Dec. 12, 1916
    Tenders resignation ... July 19, 1917

CASEMENT, Roger—
    Lands in Ireland and is arrested ... Apr. 20, 1916
    Executed ... Aug. 3, 1916

CASPIAN SEA—
    Naval action between British and Bolshevik vessels in the ... Dec. 8, 1918

* This name for the battle in question is unofficial, and is unpopular in Italy.

"CASSANDRA," H.M.S. (*Light Cruiser*)—
    Sunk ... ... Dec. 4, 1918

CASTELNAU, *General*—
    Appointed Chief of Staff to General Joffre ... ... Dec. 9, 1915

CASTRO, *Dr.* José de—
    Appointed Portuguese Prime Minister ... ... June 19, 1915
    Resigns ... ... Nov. 29, 1915

CASTRO, *General* Pimenta da—
    Appointed Portuguese Prime Minister ... ... Jan. 25, 1915
    Resigns ... ... May 14, 1915

CATEAU, LE (*France*)—
    Battle of ... ... Aug. 26, 1914

CATTARO (*Montenegro*)—
    Bombarded by French squadron ... ... Sept. 19, 1914

CAUCASIAN REPUBLIC. See under "Trans-Caucasia."

CAUCASUS, VICEROY OF THE—
    Grand Duke Nicholas appointed ... ... Sept. 8, 1915

CAVELL, *Miss* Edith—
    Shot ... ... Oct. 12, 1915

CECIL, *Lord* Robert—
    Appointed Minister of Blockade, Great Britain ... ... Feb. 23, 1916
    Resigns ... ... July 18, 1918

CENTRAL POWERS. See under "Germany," "Austria-Hungary," "Bulgaria," "Turkey," and "Commitments."

CERNA AND MONASTIR (*Serbia*)—
    Battle of ... ... Oct. 5—Dec. 11, 1916

CERNAVODA (*Dobrudja*)—
    Taken by Bulgarian forces ... ... Oct. 25, 1916

CETINJE (*Montenegro*)—
    Occupied by Austrian forces ... ... Jan. 13, 1916

CEUNINCK, *Lieut.-General* A. de—
    Appointed Belgian Minister for War ... ... Aug. 4, 1917
    Resigns ... ... Nov. 21, 1918

CHAGAS, *Senhor*, J. Pinheiro—
    Appointed Portuguese Prime Minister ... ... May 15, 1915
    Resigns ... ... June 19, 1915

CHAMBEZI RIVER (*East Africa*)—
    German force reaches the ... ... Nov. 13, 1918

CHAMOVA (*North Russia*)—
    Actions of ... ... Sept. 12–14, 1918

CHAMPAGNE (*France*)—
    First Battle of ... ... Dec. 20, 1914—Mar. 17, 1915
    Second Battle of ... ... Sept. 25—Nov. 6, 1915
    *****Third Battle of** ... ... Apr. 17–20, 1917
    Fourth Battle of ... ... July 15–18, 1918

CHAMPAGNE AND ARGONNE (*France*)—
    Battle of ... ... Sept. 26—Oct. 15, 1918

CHARLEROI (*France*)—
    Battle of ... ...†Aug. 21–24, 1914

CHARLES, *King of Rumania*—
    Dies ... ... Oct. 10, 1914

"CHÂTEAU RENAULT" (*French Cruiser*)—
    Sunk ... ... Dec. 14, 1917

CHATEAU THIERRY (*France*)—
    Taken by German forces ... ... May 31, 1918
    Retaken by Allied forces ... ... July 21, 1918

CHAUNY (*France*)—
    Taken by German forces ... ... Mar. 24, 1918

CHICHÉRIN, *M.*—
    Appointed Russian (Bolshevik) Minister for Foreign Affairs ... ... Mar. 8, 1918

CHINA—
    I. RELATIONS WITH JAPAN—
        Japanese ultimatum—
            Formulated ... ... May 7, 1915
            Accepted ... ... May 9, 1915
    II. RELATIONS WITH CENTRAL POWERS—
        (*a.*) Diplomatic relations with Germany severed ... ... Mar. 14, 1917
        (*b.*) War declared—
            On Austria-Hungary ... ... Aug. 14, 1917
            On Germany ... ... Aug. 14, 1917
    III. EMPEROR—
        1. **Yuan-Shih-Kai**—
            Accepts the throne ... ... Dec. 11, 1915
            Relinquishes the throne ... ... Mar. 22, 1916
        2. **Manchu Emperor** (Hsuan-Fung)—
            Restored to the throne ... ... July 1, 1917
            Abdicates ... ... July 7, 1917
    IV. PRESIDENT—
        1. **Yuan-Shih-Kai**—
            (Elected ... ... Oct. 6, 1913)
            Dies ... ... June 6, 1916
        2. **Li Yuan-Hung**—
            Succeeds ... ... June 6, 1916
            Resigns ... ... July 6, 1917
        3. **Feng-Kuo-Chang**‡—
            Succeeds ... ... July 6, 1917
            Term expires ... ... Oct. 11, 1918
        4. **Hsu-Shih-Chang**—Elected ... ... Sept. 4, 1918
    V. MISCELLANEOUS—
        Agreement between Chinese and British Governments as to employment of Chinese labour in France—Concluded ... ... Dec. 30, 1916
    VI. TREATIES, &c. See under "Commitments."

* Otherwise called "La Bataille des Monts."   † French official dates.
‡ Acting President; not recognised by the South.

CHIOS (*Ægean*)— ...
    Occupied by British forces ... Feb. 17, 1916

CHURCHILL, *Mr.* Winston S.—
    Appointed First Lord of Admiralty, Great Britain ... Oct. 24, 1911
    Resigns ... May 27, 1915

CHYROW (*Galicia*)—
    Battle of ... Oct. 13—Nov. 2, 1914

CILICIA (*Asia Minor*)—
    French claim to, lodged with British Government ... Mar. 17, 1915

CLAM-MARTINITZ, *Count* Heinrich—
    Appointed Austrian Premier ... Dec. 21, 1916
    Resigns ... June 18, 1917

CLARKE, *Lieut.-General Sir* T. E.—
    Appointed Quartermaster-General, B.E.F., France ... Dec. 23, 1917

CLAYE (*France*)—
    Occupied by German forces. (Nearest point to Paris reached during the war) ... Sept. 5, 1914

CLÉMENCEAU, *M.*
    Appointed French Premier and Minister for War ... Nov. 16, 1917

COBLENZ (*Germany*)—
    Occupied by United States troops ... Dec. 8, 1918

COCHIN, *M. D.*—
    Appointed French Under-Secretary of State for Blockade ... Mar. 20, 1916
    Resigns ... Aug. 17, 1917

"COCHRANE," H.M.S. (*Cruiser*)—
    Wrecked ... Nov. 14, 1918

COLOGNE (*Germany*)—
    First British air raid on ... Sept. 22, 1914
    Second British air raid on ... Oct. 8, 1914
    British retaliatory air raid on ... May 18, 1918
    British troops enter ... Dec. 6, 1918
    British troops cross the Rhine at ... Dec. 12, 1918

COMMANDER-IN-CHIEF of Allied Armies—
    General Foch—
        Appointed to supreme control in France ... Mar. 26, 1918
        Given title of Commander-in-Chief in France ... Apr. 14, 1918
        Given supreme control on all Fronts ... Nov. 5, 1918

    (For other Commanders-in-Chief, military and naval, see under the respective countries.)

COMMERCE DESTROYERS, GERMAN (other than regular cruisers)—
    I. **Raiders overseas on Declaration of War**—
        "**Cap Trafalgar**"—
            Sunk ... Sept. 14, 1914
        "**Kaiser Wilhelm der Grosse**"*—
            Sunk ... Aug. 26, 1914
        "**Kronprinz Wilhelm**"†—
            Interned ... Apr. 26, 1915
        "**Prinz Eitel Friedrich**"—
            Leaves Tsingtau ... Aug. 6, 1914
            Interned ... Apr. 8, 1915
        (See also "Dresden," "Emden," "Karlsruhe," "Königsberg," &c.)

* Strictly speaking, this vessel was not "overseas" on declaration of war, as she sailed from Bremen on 4th August.
† Last survivor of the original German commerce destroyers.

285

COMMERCE DESTROYERS, GERMAN (continued)—
  II. Subsequent Raiders—
    "Greif"—
      Sunk ... ... Feb. 29, 1916
    "Leopard"—
      Sunk ... ... Mar. 16, 1917
    "Moewe"—
      First cruise—
        Sails from Bremen ... ... Dec. 26, 1915
        Sends British s.s. "Appam" with prize crew to Norfolk (Va.) ... Feb. 1, 1916
        Returns to Bremen ... ... Mar. 4, 1916
      Second cruise—
        Sails from Kiel ... ... Nov. 26, 1916
        Returns to Kiel ... ... Mar. 22, 1917
    "Seeadler"—
      Leaves Germany ... ... *Nov. 22, 1916
      Wrecked ... ... Aug. 2, 1917
    "Wolff"—
      Leaves Germany ... ... *Dec. 1, 1916
      Returns to Germany ... ... Feb. 24, 1918

COMMITMENTS†—
  AMERICA, UNITED STATES OF—**Panama**—Protocol. Use of Panama Canal
    by ships of belligerents ... ... Oct. 10, 1914

  AUSTRIA-HUNGARY. See under "Germany."

  BAKHTIARI CHIEFTAINS. See under "Britain."

  BELGIUM—
    Declaration to maintain neutrality "whatever the consequences" ... ... July 24, 1914
      See also under "Britain," "France," and "Entente."

  BESSARABIA. See under "Rumania."

  BRITAIN, GREAT. See also under "Entente" and "Italy."
    American cotton interests—Agreement. Cotton to be contraband ... Mar. 18, 1915
    American rubber interests—Agreement. Export of rubber to Britain only Mar. 29, 1915
    Bakhtiari chieftains—Agreement. For military aid ... ... Feb. 15, 1916
    Belgium—
      Agreement. Armed support should Germany violate Belgian neutrality... Aug. 3, 1914
      Agreement. Integrity of Belgian colonies ... ... Sept. 19, 1914
      Agreement. Delimitation of Uganda-Congo boundary ... ... Feb. 3, 1915
    Denmark—Agreement (Danish merchants). To restrict supplies to Germany Nov. 24, 1915
    France—
      Guarantee. Of British naval protection of French coasts against German
        naval attack ... ... Aug. 2, 1914
      Naval Convention agreed to, defining co-operation and allocating areas of
        control ... ... Aug. 6, 1914
      Convention. Defining respective zones of Togoland (see 27th December,
        1916) ... ... Aug. 31, 1914
      Convention—Prizes captured during the war ... ... Nov. 9, 1914
      Adherence to Franco-Moorish Treaty of 1912—Announced ... Dec. 19, 1914
      Agreement. Maritime prizes; supplementing agreement of 9th November,
        1914 ... ... Feb. 15, 1915
      Joint declaration. Prevention of trade by or with Germany ... Mar. 1, 1915
      Agreement. Administration of the Cameroons ... ... Mar. 3, 1916
      Agreement. Partition of Asia-Minor ("Sykes-Picot Agreement") (see
        "France—Russia" and "Britain—Russia") ... ... May 9, 1916
      Agreement. Respecting claims in Turkey ... ... May 16, 1916
      Agreement. Administration of Togoland (see 31st August, 1914) ... Dec. 27, 1916
      Agreement. To appoint General Foch to co-ordinate efforts of British
        and French armies (Doullens Agreement) ... ... Mar. 26, 1918
      Joint declaration. Policy in Syria and Mesopotamia ... Nov. 9, 1918
    Greece—
      Offer of territorial concessions in return for help to Serbia ... Jan. 24, 1915
      Offer declined ... ... Jan. 29, 1915
      Guarantee. Eventual cession of Lemnos by Turkey to Greece ... Mar. 20, 1915
      Guarantee. Eventual cession of Mitylene by Turkey to Greece ... July 25, 1915
    Hejaz—
      Guarantee. Arabian independence to Sherif of Mecca ... Oct. 31, 1914
      Guarantee. Future independence of Arab peoples ... ... Dec. 17, 1917
      Reaffirmed ... ... Feb. 4, 1918
    Ibn Sa'ud—Agreement of co-operation ... ... Dec. 26, 1915
    Idrisi—Agreement of co-operation ... ... Apr. 28, 1915

* Approximate date.
† If the commitment involves more than two countries, see sub-heading under "Entente" or "Central Powers."

COMMITMENTS (continued)—
  BRITAIN, GREAT (continued)—
    Netherlands—

Agreement with Netherlands Overseas Trust for rationing Holland	Nov. 23, 1915
Further agreement with Netherlands Overseas Trust for rationing Holland	June 30, 1916
Protest against agreement between Germany and the Netherlands regarding sand and gravel	July 15, 1918

    Russia—

Recognition of Franco-Russian "Sykes-Picot Agreement" of 26th April, 1916 (q.v.)	May 23, 1916
Agreement. Partition of Asia-Minor ("Sykes-Picot Agreement") (see entry next above and "Britain—France")	Sept. 1, 1916
Declaration. No intention of infringing territorial integrity of Russia	July 26, 1918
Declaration to Russian peoples. No intention of interfering in Russian politics	Aug. 6, 1918
Serbia—Conditional guarantee. As to territorial expansion. See under "Entente"	May 7, 1915
Yugo-Slavs—Guarantee. As to eventual freedom and self-determination of Yugo-Slav lands	Aug. 30, 1915

  BULGARIA—
    Greece—Convention. Neutral zone defined   Dec. 14, 1915
    Turkey—

Frontier Convention	Sept. 9, 1915
(Dede Agatch Agreement)	Sept. 22, 1915

CAMEROONS. See under "Britain—France."

CENTRAL POWERS—**Bulgaria and Turkey**—Alliance. Cession of Albania to Bulgaria for intervention in war   July 17, 1915

CHINA. See under "Japan."

DENMARK. See under "Britain."

ENTENTE POWERS. See also under respective countries—
  Britain, France and Russia—

Pact of London. Signatories guarantee not to conclude a separate peace. (For adherence of other members of the "Entente" see under "Pact of London")	Sept. 5, 1914
Rumania refuses suggestion of, to aid Serbia	Jan. 25, 1915
Agreement. To pool financial resources	Feb. 5, 1915

  Britain and France—

Offer Smyrna to Greece in return for action against Turkey	Apr. 12, 1915
Offer rejected	Apr. 14, 1915
Britain, France and Italy—Naval Convention	May 10, 1915
Britain, France and Russia—Joint declaration. To hold Turkish Ministers personally responsible for Armenian massacres	May 24, 1915
Britain and France—Conditional offer of territorial concessions to Serbia	Aug. 15, 1915
Britain, France and Russia—Guarantee. Eventual independence and indemnification to Belgium	Feb. 14, 1916
Belgium, Britain, France, Italy, Japan, Portugal, Russia and Serbia—Declaration of Unity: Regarding military, economic and diplomatic affairs	Mar. 28, 1916
Britain, France, Italy, Japan and Russia—Guarantee. Territorial integrity of Belgian Congo (The Havre Declaration)	Apr. 29, 1916

  Britain, France, Rumania and Russia—

Secret Treaty. Rumania's intervention in the war	Aug. 17, 1916
Military convention	Aug. 17, 1916
Britain, France and Italy—Provisional arrangement as to future policy in Asia Minor	Aug. 18, 1917
Britain, China, France, Japan and Russia—Agreement: Prevention of German penetration in Far East	May 15, 1918
Britain, France and Italy—Support national aspirations of Czecho-Slovaks, Poles and Yugo-Slavs	June 3, 1918
Britain, France and United States of America—Agreement: With Murman Sovdep concerning Allied expedition to Murman coast	July 7, 1918

FRANCE. See also under "Britain" and "Entente"—

Belgium—Arrangement suspending Convention of 30th July, 1891 (Military Service Laws)	Mar. 13, 1915
Netherlands—Agreement with Netherlands Overseas Trust for rationing Holland concluded	Dec. 7, 1915
Italy—Agreement. Zones in Asia Minor	July 27, 1917
Russia—Agreement. Partition of Asia-Minor, (First of "Sykes-Picot" Agreements.) (See also "Britain—France" and "Britain—Russia")	Apr. 26, 1916

GERMANY—
  Austria-Hungary—Military treaty ("Waffenbund"). Signed   May 12, 1918
  Japan and Mexico—Projected alliance against U.S.A.—

Instructions sent by German Government	Jan. 19, 1917
Instructions published in United States press	Feb. 28, 1917

COMMITMENTS (*continued*)—
  GERMANY (*continued*)—
    Netherlands—Agreement. Sand and gravel ... ... May 2, 1918
    Poland—Military Convention ... ... Feb. 25, 1918
    Russia. See under "Russia."
    Turkey—
      Treaty of Alliance, signed ... ... Aug. 4, 1914
      Settlement Treaty—
        Signed ... ... Jan. 11, 1917
        Ratified ... ... Apr. 10, 1918
  GREECE. See under "Britain, Rumania and Serbia."
  HEJAZ. See under "Britain."
  HOLLAND. See under "Britain, France and Germany."
  IBN SA'UD. See under "Britain."
  IDRISI. See under "Britain."
  ITALY. See also under "Entente," "France" and "Pact of London"—
    Renounces Triple Alliance ... ... May 4, 1915
    Accession of, to Franco-British "Prize Treaty" (see "Britain—France,"
      9th November, 1914) ... ... Jan. 15, 1917
    Czecho-Slovakia—Treaty. Recognition of Czecho-Slovak Council ... June 30, 1918
    Rumania—Existence of secret agreement announced ... ... Jan. 15, 1915
    Yugo-Slavs—Agreement ... ... Apr. 10, 1918
  JAPAN. See also under "Pact of London"—
    Britain—Declaration. Not to withdraw from occupied German islands ... Dec. 16, 1914
    China—
      Agreement. Future policy in Manchuria ... ... Mar. 23, 1915
      Treaty. South Manchuria and Eastern Inner Mongolia ... ... May 25, 1915
      Treaty. Shantung Province ... ... May 25, 1915
      Agreement. Tsingtau customs ... ... Aug. 6, 1915
      Agreement. Military co-operation for protection against German and
        Bolshevik aggression ... ... May 16, 1918
      Agreement. Naval co-operation ... ... May 19, 1918
  MANCHURIA. See under "Japan."
  MONGOLIA. See under "Japan."
  NETHERLANDS. See under "Britain, France and Germany."
  PANAMA. See under "America, United States of."
  POLAND. See under "Germany."
  RUMANIA. See also under "Italy" and "Russia"—
    Declaration. Refusal to support Greece against Germany ... ... Dec. 6, 1914
    Bessarabia—Articles of Union with ... ... Apr. 9, 1918
    Greece and Serbia—Declaration. To cement union between ... ... Nov. 21, 1918
    Serbia—Refuses to aid Serbia ... ... Oct. 15, 1915
  RUSSIA. See also under "Brest-Litovsk."
    Declaration. Repudiating separate peace ... ... May 19, 1917
    China—Agreement concerning Mongolia ... ... June 7, 1915
    Germany—Secret Convention concerning Poland ... ... Dec. 22, 1917
    Japan—Agreement. Alliance for maintenance of peace in the Far East ... July 3, 1916
    Rumania—Secret agreement for mutual support ... ... Sept. 19, 1914
  SERBIA. See also under "Greece" and "Rumania."
    Declaration. Not to conclude peace without Allies' consent ... ... Dec. 5, 1914
    Greece—
      Guarantee by Serbia to cede Doiran and Gevgeli eventually to Greece,
        and waive claim to Strumitza ... ... Sept. 25, 1915
      Claim for Greek help under Serbo-Greek Treaty of 1912 rejected by
        Greek Government ... ... Oct. 10, 1915
  TOGOLAND. See under "Britain—France."
  TURKEY. See under "Bulgaria," "Britain—France" and "Germany."

COMPULSORY SERVICE—
  I. In the British Empire—
    (A.) Great Britain—
      1. First Compulsory Service Act—
        Passed by the Commons ... ... Jan. 24, 1916
        Comes into operation ... ... Feb. 10, 1916
      2. Second Act—
        Passed by the Commons ... ... May 16, 1916
        Comes into operation ... ... June 8, 1916
      3. Third Act—
        *Passed by the Commons ... ... Apr. 10 1918
        Comes into operation ... ... Apr. 18, 1918

* Age limit raised to 50 years and conscription extended to Ireland.

COMPULSORY SERVICE (continued)—
   I. **In the British Empire** (continued)—
     (B.) **Canada**—
       Compulsory Service Act—
         Passed by the Canadian Commons ... ... July 6, 1917
         Comes into operation ... ... Oct. 12, 1917
     (C.) **New Zealand**—
       Compulsory Service Act—
         Passed by New Zealand Commons ... ... June 10, 1916
         Comes into operation ... ... Sept. 1, 1916
   II. **In United States of America**—
       Comes into operation ... ... May 18, 1917

CONFERENCE*—
   I. **International Conference to avert War**—
     Proposals by British Foreign Minister—
       Formulated ... ... July 24, 1914
       Accepted by French and Italian Governments ... ... July 27, 1914
       Rejected by German Government ... ... July 28, 1914
   II. **Inter-Allied Conferences** during the War—
     Economic—
       Allied Conference on Economic War—
         Opens in Paris (see "Finance") ... ... June 3, 1915
         Reassembles in Paris ... ... June 14, 1916
         Recommendations ratified... ... ... June 27, 1916
       Inter-Allied on Finance, at London ... ... July 14–15, 1916
       Anglo-French on Finance, at Calais ... ... Aug. 24, 1916
     Military and Political—
       First Anglo-French Conference at Calais ... ... June 5, 1915
       Anglo-French at Paris ... ... Nov. 17, 1915
       Allied Military Conference at Chantilly... ... ... Mar. 12, 1916
       Inter-Allied at Paris ... ... Mar. 26–28, 1916
       Anglo-French at Boulogne ... ... Oct. 20, 1916
       Inter-Allied at Paris ... ... Nov. 15–16, 1916
       Anglo-French at London ... ... Dec. 26–28, 1916
       Inter-Allied at Rome... ... ... Jan. 5–7, 1917
       Inter-Allied "Commission de Ravitaillement" at Petrograd Jan. 17—Feb. 20, 1917
       Anglo-French at Calais ... ... Feb. 26–27, 1917
       Anglo-French at London ... ... March 12–13, 1917
       Anglo-French at London ... ... May 28–29, 1917
       Inter-Allied at Paris ... ... July 25–26, 1917
       Anglo-French at London ... ... Sept. 4, 1917
       Anglo-French at Boulogne ... ... Sept. 25, 1917
       Allied at Rapallo ... ... Nov. 7, 1917
     War Aims—
       Great Inter-Allied Conference. First meeting of, in Paris ... ... Nov. 29, 1917
     Naval—
       Allied, in London, re Mediterranean policy ... ... Jan. 24, 1917
       Allied Naval Council formed ... ... Nov. 30, 1917
   III. **Inter-Belligerent Conferences** during the War—
     Prisoners of War Conference—
       First meeting (at the Hague) ... ... June 9, 1918
   IV. **British Empire**—
     Imperial War Conference—
       British Government decide to initiate... ... ... Dec. 19, 1916
       First meeting ... ... Mar. 20, 1917
   V. **Other Conferences**—
     Labour Conference, see under "Labour."
     Yugo-Slav Conference, see under "Yugo-Slav."

CONSCRIPTION. See under "Compulsory Service."

CONSTANTINOPLE—
   Passports demanded by Entente Ambassadors at ... ... Oct. 30, 1914
   Russian claim to—
     Formulated by Russian Government ... ... Mar. 4, 1915
     Accepted by British Government ... ... Mar. 12, 1915
     Accepted by French Government ... ... Apr. 12, 1915
     Russian Premier announces Allied acceptance of ... ... Dec. 2, 1916
   Harbour of, raided by British submarine ... ... Aug. 1, 1915
   British air raid on ... ... Apr. 14, 1916
   Allied Fleet arrives at ... ... Nov. 13, 1918
   French troops land at ... ... Nov. 21, 1918

CONSTANZA (*Rumania*)—
   Captured by German and Bulgarian forces ... ... Oct. 22, 1916

* For details of subjects discussed see Part I.

CONTRABAND—
<table>
<tr><td>British proclamation issued specifying articles to be treated as contraband</td><td>Aug. 4, 1914</td></tr>
<tr><td>French Government issue first list of contraband articles</td><td>Aug. 11, 1914</td></tr>
<tr><td>French Government issue new decree defining contraband</td><td>Aug. 25, 1914</td></tr>
<tr><td>British proclamation issued adding to list of contraband</td><td>Sept. 21, 1914</td></tr>
<tr><td>British Order in Council issued modifying Declaration of London, and revising list of contraband</td><td>Oct. 29, 1914</td></tr>
<tr><td>French Government issue revised list of contraband</td><td>Nov. 6, 1914</td></tr>
<tr><td>British Government issue proclamation containing further revised list of contraband</td><td>Dec. 23, 1914</td></tr>
<tr><td>French Government issue further revised list of contraband</td><td>Jan. 3, 1915</td></tr>
<tr><td>British proclamation issued extending prohibition of "trading with the enemy" to territories in British, enemy or friendly occupation</td><td>Feb. 16, 1915</td></tr>
<tr><td>Declaration signed between Great Britain and France prohibiting trade by or with Germany</td><td>Mar 1, 1915</td></tr>
<tr><td>British proclamation issued extending list of "absolute" contraband, and regarding detention of enemy goods ("Retaliatory Order in Council")</td><td>Mar. 11, 1915</td></tr>
<tr><td>Italian decrees issued prohibiting trading with Germany</td><td>Apr. 17, 1916</td></tr>
</table>
(See also under "Commitments—Britain" and "Declaration of London.")

CONVENTION. See under "Commitments."

CONVOYS—
<table>
<tr><td>British convoys in the North Sea—German raids on</td><td>{ Oct. 17, 1917
Dec. 12, 1917</td></tr>
<tr><td>British plan to convoy merchant ships formulated</td><td>May 17, 1917</td></tr>
<tr><td>British convoy scheme formally approved</td><td>June 14, 1917</td></tr>
<tr><td>First regular convoy sails from Hampton Roads (U.S.A.)</td><td>July 2, 1917</td></tr>
</table>

COOREMAN, M. G.—
<table>
<tr><td>Appointed Belgian Prime Minister*</td><td>May 31, 1918</td></tr>
<tr><td>Resigns</td><td>Nov. 21, 1918</td></tr>
</table>

CORFU, Island of (Ægean)—
I. **Occupation by the French**—
<table>
<tr><td>Entente Governments notify Greek Government of proposed occupation of</td><td>Jan. 10, 1916</td></tr>
<tr><td>Occupied by French force</td><td>Jan. 11, 1916</td></tr>
<tr><td>Greek Government refuse consent to the occupation of</td><td>Jan. 13, 1916</td></tr>
</table>
II. **Occupation by the Italians**—
<table>
<tr><td>Italian detachment reaches</td><td>Feb. 11, 1916</td></tr>
</table>
III. **Serbian retreat to**—
<table>
<tr><td>Forthcoming transfer of Serbian Army to, notified to Greek Government</td><td>Jan. 10, 1916</td></tr>
<tr><td>First Serbian troops land at</td><td>Jan. 15. 1916</td></tr>
<tr><td>Serbian Army concentrated at</td><td>Feb. 10, 1916</td></tr>
<tr><td>Greek Government refuses overland transport route for Serbian Army to Salonika from</td><td>Apr. 3, 1916</td></tr>
<tr><td>Serbian Army Headquarters land at Salonika from</td><td>Apr. 15, 1916</td></tr>
</table>
IV. **Serbian Government**—
<table>
<tr><td>Arrive at</td><td>Feb. 9, 1916</td></tr>
<tr><td>Leave for Salonika</td><td>May 20, 1917</td></tr>
</table>
V. **Montenegrin retreat to**—
<table>
<tr><td>Entente Governments notify Greek Government of forthcoming transfer of Montenegrin Army to</td><td>Feb. 13, 1916</td></tr>
<tr><td>Remnants of Montenegrin Army land at</td><td>Feb. 16, 1916</td></tr>
</table>

CORINTH (Greece)—
<table>
<tr><td>Occupied by Entente forces</td><td>June 12, 1917</td></tr>
</table>

"CORMORAN" (German Armed Merchant Cruiser)—
<table>
<tr><td>Interned at Guam</td><td>Dec. 14, 1914</td></tr>
</table>

"CORNWALLIS," H.M.S. (Battleship)—
<table>
<tr><td>Sunk</td><td>Jan. 9, 1917</td></tr>
</table>

CORONEL (Chili)—
<table>
<tr><td>Naval action off</td><td>Nov. 1, 1914</td></tr>
</table>

* Presided over the Cabinet without the title of Prime Minister. This title was instituted first with M. Delacroix's Cabinet.

COSSACKS—
   I. DON COSSACKS—
      Move on Moscow (under General Alexeiev) ... Feb. 4, 1918
      Defeated by the Bolsheviki ... Feb. 13, 1918
      Declare independence ... June 4, 1918
   II. MISCELLANEOUS—Cossack detachment reaches British Army at 'Ali-Gharbi, Mesopotamia ... May 18, 1916

COSTA, Dr. Affonzo—
   Appointed Portuguese Premier ... Nov. 29, 1915
   Resigns ... Mar. 15, 1916

COSTA RICA—
   Severs diplomatic relations with Germany ... Sept. 21, 1917
   Declares war on Germany... ... May 23, 1918

COUNCIL—
   I. NATIONAL COUNCIL. See under respective countries.
   II. WAR COUNCIL—
      Inter-Allied Council of War—
         Project approved in principle ... Nov. 17, 1915
         Agreement regarding, reached... Dec. 29, 1915
      Allied Supreme War Council—
         Inaugurated ... Dec. 1, 1917
         Enlargement of powers (*announced by British Government*)... Feb. 3, 1918
         (See also under "Britain—Cabinet.")

COURCELETTE (*France*)—
   Battle of ("Flers-Courcelette") ... Sept. 15–22, 1916

COURLAND. See under "Kurland."

COURONNÉ DE NANCY. See under "Grand Couronné."

COUTINHO, *Senhor* V. H. d'Azevedo—
   Appointed Portuguese Prime Minister ... Dec. 12, 1914
   Resigns ... Jan. 25, 1915

COURTRAI (*Flanders*)—
   Battle of ... Oct. 14–19, 1918

COWANS, *Lieut.-General Sir* J. S.—
   Appointed Quartermaster-General, Home Forces, Great Britain ... June 3, 1912

CRACOW (*Galicia*)—
   Battle of ... Nov. 15—Dec. 2, 1914

CRAIOVA (*Rumania*)—
   Taken by German forces ... Nov. 21, 1916

CRAONNE (*France*)—
   Occupied by German forces ... Sept. 1, 1914
   Taken by French forces ... May 4, 1917
   Again taken by German forces ... May 27, 1918
   Again retaken by French forces ... Oct. 12, 1918

"CRESSY," H.M.S. (*Cruiser*)—
   Sunk ... Sept. 22, 1914

CRETE, Island of—
    Formation of Greek Provisional Government in, announced ... ... Sept. 29, 1916

CRIMEA, The—
    German forces enter ... ... Apr. 19 1918

CROATIA—
    British give guarantee as to eventual freedom and self-determination of ... Aug. 30, 1915
    Ban of Croatia refuses offer of Agram to suppress Yugo-Slav National Council ... Oct. 21, 1918
    Croatian "Sabor" unanimously adhere to Yugo-Slav declaration of independence... Oct. 30, 1918
        (See also under "Agram.")

CROMIE, Captain F. N. A. (British Naval Attaché)—
    Murdered by the Bolsheviki at Petrograd ... ... Aug. 31, 1918

CTESIPHON (Mesopotamia)—
    Battle of ... ... Nov. 22–24, 1915
    British forces retreat from ... ... Nov. 25, 1915

CUBA—
    Declares war on Germany ... ... Apr. 7, 1917
    Declares war on Austria-Hungary ... ... Dec. 16, 1917

CUFFLEY (Essex)—
    German airship "SL–11" destroyed at ... ... Sept 2, 1916

CURRIE, Major-General A. W.—
    Appointed to command Canadian troops in France ... ... June 19, 1917

CUXHAVEN (Germany)—
    British seaplane raid on ... ... Dec. 25, 1914

CYPRUS (Mediterranean)—
    Annexed by Great Britain... ... ... Nov. 5, 1914
    Offer by British Government to Greece—
        Formulated ... ... Oct. 16, 1915
        Rejected ... ... Oct. 20, 1915

CZECHO-SLOVAKS—
    British, French and Italian Governments make declaration supporting national
        aspirations of ... ... June 3, 1918
    Declare war on Germany ... ... Aug. 13, 1918
    Recognised as an Allied nation by Great Britain ... ... Aug. 13, 1918
    Recognised by the United States as possessing a *de facto* Government ... Sept. 3, 1918
    Declare independence ... ... Oct. 21, 1918
    Czech forces at Ekaterinenburg proclaim national independence ... ... Nov. 9, 1918
    Professor Masaryk elected First President of the ... ... Nov. 14, 1918

CZERNIN, Count Ottokar—
    Appointed Austro-Hungarian Foreign Minister ... ... Dec. 22, 1916
    Replies to statements on War Aims by President Wilson and Mr. Lloyd George ... Jan. 24, 1918
    Resigns... ... ... Apr. 15, 1918

CZERNOWITZ (Bukovina)—
    Taken by Russian forces ... ... Sept. 15, 1914
    Reoccupied by Austrian forces ... ... Oct. 22, 1914
    Reoccupied by Russian forces ... ... Oct. 28, 1914
    Retaken by Austrian forces ... ... Feb. 17, 1915
    Reoccupied by Russian forces ... ... June 17, 1916
    Retaken by Austro-German forces ... ... Aug. 3, 1917

D

"DACIA" (*German S.S.*)—
    Sold to Mr. Breitung (a United States citizen) ... Jan. 6, 1915
    Sails for Bremen from United States of America with cargo of cotton ... Feb. 11, 1915
    Seized by French warships ... Feb. 27, 1915
    French Prize Court declares seizure valid ... Mar. 22, 1915

DAGHESTAN. See under "Trans-Caucasia."

DAGÖ ISLAND (*Baltic*)—
    Captured by German forces ... Oct. 18, 1917

DAKHLA OASIS (*West Egypt*)—
    Affairs in—
        Begin ... Oct. 17, 1916
        End ... Oct. 22, 1916

DALMATIA, SOUTH—
    British Foreign Minister gives guarantee of eventual freedom and self-determination of ... Aug. 30, 1915

DAMASCUS (*Syria*)—
    Capitulates to British and Arab forces ... Oct. 1, 1918

"DANTON" (*French Battleship*)—
    Sunk ... Mar. 19, 1917

DARDANELLES, The—
    Entered by the "Goeben" and "Breslau" ... Aug. 11, 1914
    Forts bombarded by Allied squadrons ... Nov. 3, 1914
    Straits first entered by British submarine ... Nov. 6, 1914
    Expedition to the Dardanelles—
        Grand Duke Nicholas suggests British expedition against the Turks to ease the situation in the Caucasus ... Dec. 30, 1914
        British Admiralty ordered to prepare for a naval expedition against the Dardanelles ... Jan. 13, 1915
        British Government definitely decide to make naval attack ... Jan. 28, 1915
        British Government decide to send a division to the Dardanelles ... Feb. 16, 1915
        British Government issue orders for Australian and New Zealand troops in Egypt to proceed to the Dardanelles ... Feb. 20, 1915
        Naval Attack—
            Commenced ... Feb. 19, 1915
            Repulsed ... Mar. 18, 1915
        French Government decide to send expeditionary force to the Dardanelles ... Mar. 4, 1915
        M. Venizelos proffers Greek fleet and troops to the Entente for attack on the Dardanelles ... Mar. 5, 1915
        Landing—
            (i.) Helles, Anzac and Gulf of Xeros ... Apr. 25, 1915
            (ii.) Suvla ... Aug. 6, 1915
        Lord Kitchener—
            Leaves England ... Nov. 4, 1915
            Arrives at the Dardanelles ... Nov. 10, 1915
        Evacuation—
            (i.) Of Suvla and Anzac—
                Ordered ... Dec. 8, 1915
                Completed ... Dec. 20, 1915
            (ii.) Of Helles—
                Ordered ... Dec. 28, 1915
                Begins ... Jan. 7, 1915
                Completed ... Jan. 8, 1916
    Commander-in-Chief, Mediterranean Expeditionary Force—
        1. Hamilton, Sir Ian—
            Appointed ... Mar. 12, 1915
            Takes over command ... Mar. 17, 1915
            Recalled ... Oct. 15, 1915

DARDANELLES, The (*continued*)—
   Expedition to the Dardanelles (*continued*)—
      Commander-in-Chief, Mediterranean Expeditionary Force (*continued*)—
         *2. Monro, Sir Charles—
            Appointed ... Oct. 15, 1915
            Vacates appointment ... Jan. 9, 1916
         *3. Birdwood, Sir William—
            (Appointed G.O.C. Dardanelles Army) ... Nov. 4, 1915
            Appointed ... Nov. 25, 1915
      Naval action outside the Straits ("Raglan" and "Breslau" sunk) ... Jan. 20, 1918
      Allied fleets pass through the Straits ... Nov. 12, 1918
         (See also "Helles," "Krithia," "Sari Bair," "Suvla," &c.)

DARDONI (*North-West Frontier of India*)—
   Action of ... Mar. 25–26, 1915

DAR ES SALAAM (*German East Africa*)—
   Bombarded by British warship ... Aug. 8, 1914
   Surrenders to British forces ... Sept. 4, 1916

DARFUR—
   Hostilities between, and Sudan Government begin ... Mar. 1, 1916
   Sudan force advances into ... Mar. 16, 1916
   Forces defeated at Beringiya ... May 22, 1916
   Sudan force occupy El Fasher ... May 23, 1916
   Sultan of, killed at Affair of Gyuba ... Nov. 6, 1916
   Campaign against, ends ... Dec. 31, 1916

DAVIGNON, M. J.—
   Appointed Belgian Minister for Foreign Affairs ... Feb. 28, 1914
   Resigns ... Jan. 18, 1916

DEBRA (*Serbia*)—
   Taken by Bulgarian forces ... Dec. 8, 1915

DECLARATIONS—
   "DECLARATION OF LONDON"—
      British Order in Council revises ... Aug. 20, 1914
      French Government inform United States that they will observe "Declaration of London" subject to certain modifications ... Sept. 3, 1914
      German Government agree to observe "Declaration of London" if other belligerents conform thereto, and issue their list of contraband ... Sept. 4, 1914
      British Order in Council modifies ... Oct. 29, 1914
      French Government issue declaration modifying ... Nov. 6, 1914
      Dutch Government protest against modification of ... Nov. 13, 1914
      British Order in Council rescinds ... July 7, 1916
      French Government issue Order rescinding ... July 7, 1916
         (See also under "Commitments—Britain" and "Contraband.")

   DECLARATIONS OF INDEPENDENCE. See under "Independence."

   DECLARATIONS OF WAR. See under "War."

   OTHER POLITICAL DECLARATIONS. See under "Commitments."

DEDE AGATCH (*Bulgaria*)—
   Bombarded by Allied squadron ... Oct. 21, 1915

DEDE AGATCH AGREEMENT—
   Between Turkey and Bulgaria—Concluded ... Sept. 22, 1915

---

* From 4th to 25th November General Monro was officially commanding the Salonika Force and General Birdwood commanding the M.E.F. On 25th November General Monro assumed supreme command of the reconstituted M.E.F., including both the Dardanelles and Salonika Armies.

"DEFENCE," H.M.S. (*Cruiser*)—
    Sunk ... ... May 31, 1916

DELACROIX, *M*. Léon—
    Appointed Belgian Prime Minister*... ... ... Nov. 21, 1918

DELCASSÉ, *M.*—
    Appointed French Foreign Minister ... ... Aug. 26, 1914
    Resigns ... ... Oct. 13, 1915

DELVILLE WOOD (*Somme*)—
    Battle of ... ... July 15– Sept. 3, 1916

DEMIR KAPU (*Serbia*)—
    Action of ... ... Dec. 5, 1915

DEMOBILISATION—
    Of British Army begins ... ... Dec. 4, 1918

DENMARK. See under "Commitments."

DERBY, *Earl of*—
    Assumes control of recruiting in Great Britain ... ... Sept. 30, 1915
    Appointed Minister for War, Great Britain ... ... Dec. 11, 1916
    Resigns ... ... Apr. 20, 1918

"DEUTSCHLAND" (*German Commercial Submarine*)—
    Arrives at Norfolk (*Va.*) ... ... July 10, 1916
    Returns to Germany ... ... Aug. 23, 1916

DEVENTER, *General* van—
    Succeeds General Hoskins in command of British forces, East Africa ... ... May 30, 1917

DEVONPORT, *Lord*—
    Appointed Food Controller, Great Britain ... ... Dec. 26, 1916

DE WET, *General* (*South African rebel*)—
    Captured ... ... Dec. 1, 1914

DIAZ, *General*—
    Succeeds General Cadorna as Italian Commander-in-Chief† ... ... Nov. 7, 1917

DILBAR (*South Persia*)—
    Attack on, by British forces from Bushire—
        Begins ... ... Aug. 12, 1915
        Ends: destruction completed ... ... Aug. 16, 1915

DILMAN (*North Persia*)—
    Battle of ... ... May 1, 1915

DIMOTIKA—
    Turco-Bulgarian Convention signed at ... ... Sept. 9, 1915

        * The first Minister to hold the title of Prime Minister.
        † Nominally Chief of Staff to the King.

DIPLOMATIC RELATIONS (severed)—
    By **Austria-Hungary** with **Serbia** ... July 25, 1914
    By **Belgium** with **Germany** ... Aug. 4, 1914
    By **Montenegro** with **Germany** ... Aug. 8, 1914
    By **France** with **Austria-Hungary** ... Aug. 10, 1914
    By **Germany** with **Japan** ... Aug. 23, 1914
    By **Austria-Hungary** with **Japan** ... Aug. 24, 1914
    By **Japan** with **Austria-Hungary** ... Aug. 25, 1914
    By **Great Britain** with **Turkey** ... Oct. 30, 1914
    By **France** with **Turkey** ... Oct. 30, 1914
    By **Russia** with **Turkey** ... Oct. 30, 1914
    By **Turkey** with **Belgium** ... Nov. 6, 1914
    *By **Germany** with **Italy** ... May 24, 1915
    By **Russia** with **Bulgaria** ... Oct. 5, 1915
    By **Great Britain** with **Bulgaria** ... Oct. 13, 1915
    By **Austria-Hungary** with **Portugal** ... Mar. 15, 1916
    By **Rumania** with **Bulgaria** ... Aug. 30, 1916
    By **United States of America** with **Germany** ... Feb. 3, 1917
    By **China** with **Germany** ... Mar. 14, 1917
    By **Austria-Hungary** with **United States of America** ... Apr. 8, 1917
    By **Bulgaria** with **United States of America** ... Apr. 10, 1917
    By **Brazil** with **Germany** ... Apr. 11, 1917
    By **Bolivia** with **Germany** ... Apr. 13, 1917
    By **Turkey** with **United States of America** ... Apr. 20, 1917
    By **Guatemala** with **Germany** ... Apr. 27, 1917
    By **Liberia** with **Germany** ... May 5, 1917
    By **Honduras** with **Germany** ... May 17, 1917
    By **Nicaragua** with **Germany** ... May 18, 1917
    By **Santo Domingo** with **Germany** ... June 11, 1917
    By **Haiti** with **Germany** ... June 16, 1917
    By **Greece** with **Germany** ... June 27, 917
    By **Greece** with **Austria-Hungary** ... June 27, 1917
    By **Greece** with **Turkey** ... June 27, 1917
    By **Costa Rica** with **Germany** ... Sept. 21, 1917
    By **Peru** with **Germany** ... Oct. 5, 1917
    By **Uruguay** with **Germany** ... Oct. 7, 1917
    By **Ecuador** with **Germany** ... Dec. 7, 1917
    By **Russia (Bolshevik)** with **Rumania** ... Jan. 28, 1918
    By **Poland** with **Germany** ... Dec. 15, 1918

DIXMUDE (*Belgium*)—
    Stormed by German forces ... Nov. 10, 1914
    Retaken by Belgian forces ... Sept. 29, 1918

DIYALA, River (*Mesopotamia*)—
    Passage of the ... Mar. 7–10, 1917

DOBELL, *Brig.-General* C. M.—
    Appointed to command Allied land forces, Cameroons ... Aug. 23, 1914
    Duala surrenders to ... Sept. 27, 1914

DOBROPOLJE (*Macedonia*)—
    Battle of the ... Sept. 15–16, 1918

DOBRUDJA, The—
    Entered by Russian forces ... Aug. 25, 1916
    Invaded by German and Bulgarian forces ... Sept. 2, 1916
    Evacuated by Russian and Rumanian forces ... Jan. 6, 1917
    Evacuated by the last Bulgarian troops ... Dec. 3, 1918
        (See also " Cernavoda," " Constanza," " Silistra," " Tutrakan.")

DOGGER BANK, The (*North Sea*)—
    Action of ... Jan. 24, 1915

* See footnote in Part I.

DOIRAN (*South Serbia*)—
- Taken by Bulgarian forces ... Dec. 11, 1915
- **Battle of, 1916**—
  - Begins ... Aug. 2, 1916
  - Ends ... Aug. 21, 1916
- **Battle of, 1917**—
  - Begins ... Apr. 24, 1917
  - Ends ... May 9, 1917
- **Battle of, 1918**—
  - Begins ... Sept. 18, 1918
  - Ends ... Sept. 19, 1918
- Recaptured by British forces ... Sept. 22, 1918

(See also under "Monastir-Doiran.")

DOMINIONS, British—
- Secretary for Colonies states that Dominions will be consulted as to peace terms ... Apr. 14, 1915
- A Dominion Premier for first time attends meeting of British Cabinet* ... July 14, 1915

DON COSSACKS. See under "Cossacks."

"DONEGAL" (*British Ambulance Transport*)—
- Sunk ... Apr. 17, 1917

DORMANS (*France*)—
- Captured by German forces ... May 31, 1918
- Retaken by French forces ... July 22, 1918

DORPAT (*Estonia*)—
- Occupied by German forces ... Feb. 24, 1918
- Evacuated by German forces ... Dec. 26, 1918

DOUAI (*France*)—
- Occupied by German forces ... Aug. 26, 1914
- Retaken by Allied forces ... Oct. 17, 1918

DOUAUMONT, FORT (*Verdun*)—
- Stormed by German forces ... Feb. 25, 1916
- Recaptured by French forces ... Oct. 24, 1916

DOUGLAS, *General Sir* C. W. H.—
- Appointed Chief of the Imperial General Staff ... Apr. 6, 1914
- Dies ... Oct. 25, 1914

DOULLENS AGREEMENT. See under "Commitments—Britain, France."

DOUMERGUE, M.—
- Appointed French Foreign Minister ... Aug. 3, 1914
- Resigns ... Aug. 26, 1914

DOVER (*Kent*)—
- First attempted air raid on ... Dec. 21, 1914
- Second air raid on (first bomb dropped near) ... Dec. 24, 1914
- Shelled by German submarine ... Feb. 16, 1918

"DOVER CASTLE" (*British Hospital Ship*)—
- Sunk ... May 26, 1917

DOVER STRAITS—
- I. **Barrage**—Established ... Apr. 3, 1915
- II. **German destroyer raids**—
  - First ... Oct. 26-27, 1916
  - Second (action by "Swift" and "Broke") ... Apr. 20, 1917
  - Third ... Feb. 15, 1918

"DRAKE," H.M.S. (*Cruiser*)—
- Sunk ... Oct. 2, 1917

* Sir Robert Borden, Canadian Premier.

"DRESDEN" (*German Cruiser*)—
    Joins Admiral von Spee at Easter Island ... Oct. 12, 1914
    Escapes from Battle of the Falklands ... Dec. 8, 1914
    Sunk (*off Juan Fernandez*)... Mar. 14, 1915

DRINA, River (*Serbia*)—
    Austrian forces cross the ... Aug. 13, 1914
    Austrians driven back over the ... Aug. 25, 1914
    Austrian troops again cross the ... Sept. 8, 1914
    Battle of the ... Sept. 8–17,* 1914

DROCOURT-QUÉANT LINE (*France*)—
    Battle of ... Sept. 2–3, 1918

DUALA (*Cameroons*)—
    Naval operations against, begin ... Sept. 7, 1914
    Captured by Allied forces ... Sept. 26–27, 1914

DUJAILA REDOUBT (*Mesopotamia*)—
    Kut Relief Force repulsed at ... Mar. 8, 1916

DUKHOVSKAYA (*Eastern Siberia*)—
    Battle of ... Aug. 24, 1918

DUMBA, Dr.—
    (Appointed Austro-Hungarian Ambassador to the United States ... Mar. —, 1913)
    Recall requested by United States Government ... Sept. 9, 1915
    Recalled from the United States ... Sept. 28, 1915

"DUNDEE," H.M.S. (*Boarding Steamer*)—
    Action with German raider "Leopard" ... Mar. 16, 1917
        (See also under "Achilles.")

DUNSTERVILLE, *Major-General* L. C.—
    Mission of—
        Leaves Baghdad for North-West Persia ... Jan. 27, 1918
        Arrives at Enzeli ... Feb. 17, 1918
        (See also under "Baku.")

"DUPETIT THOUARS" (*French Cruiser*)—
    Sunk ... Aug. 7, 1918

DURAZZO (*Albania*)—
    Provisional Government of Essad Pasha set up at ... Oct. 4, 1914
    Occupied by Serbian forces ... July 4, 1915
    Evacuated by the Serbians (*at request of Italian Government*) ... July 17, 1915
    Reoccupied by Serbian forces ... Aug. 31, 1915
    Bombarded by Austrian warships ... Dec. 6, 1915
    Occupied by Italian forces ... Dec. 20, 1915
    Raided by Austrian naval light forces ... Dec. 29, 1915
    Provisional Government of Essad Pasha leaves ... Feb. 24, 1916
    Captured by Austrian forces ... Feb. 27, 1916
    Bombarded by Italian and British warships ... Oct. 2, 1918
    Retaken by Italian forces ... Oct. 14, 1918

DUSHAK (*Trans-Caspia*)—
    Action of ... Oct. 12, 1918

DÜSSELDORF (*Germany*)—
    First British air raid on airship sheds at ... Sept. 22, 1914
    Second British air raid on airship sheds at ... Oct. 8, 1914

DUTCH SHIPS (*in Entente ports*). See under "Netherlands."

DVINSK (*Poland*)—
    Battle of ... Sept. 9–Nov. 1, 1915
    Taken by German forces ... Feb. 18, 1918

* See footnote in Part II.

E

"E 1" (*British Submarine*)—
 Enters the Baltic .... Oct. 17, 1914
 Torpedoes German battle cruiser "Moltke" .... Aug. 19, 1915

"E 8" (*British Submarine*)—
 Sinks German cruiser "Prinz Adalbert" .... Oct. 23, 1915

"E 9" (*British Submarine*)—
 Enters the Baltic .... Oct. 17, 1914

"E 11" (*British Submarine*)—
 Sinks Turkish battleship "Barbarousse-Hairedine" .. Aug. 8, 1915

"E 13" (*British Submarine*)—
 Attacked by German warships while aground in Danish waters .. Aug. 19, 1915

"E 19" (*British Submarine*)—
 Sinks German cruiser "Undine" .... Nov. 7, 1915

EAST AFRICA. See under "Africa, East."

EAST GALICIA—
 Battle of .... July 18-28, 1917

EAST PERSIA CORDON (*Anglo-Russian*)—
 Establishment of, begins .... July 29, 1915
 Birjand occupied by British force .... Oct. 7, 1915
 Kwash occupied by British force .... May 11, 1916
 Extension into Khorasan begins .... Feb. 1, 1918
 Meshed occupied by British force .... Mar. 3, 1918

EBERT, *Herr*—
 Succeeds Prince Max of Baden as German Imperial Chancellor ... Nov. 9, 1918

ECKHARDT, von. See under "Mexico."

ECONOMIC CONFERENCE, ALLIED. See under "Conference."

ECUADOR—
 Severs diplomatic relations with Germany .... Dec. 7, 1917

EDEA (*Cameroons*)—
 Occupied by French forces .... Oct. 26, 1914
 French repulse German attack on .... Jan. 5, 1915

EGYPT—
 I. POLITICAL CHANGES, &c.—
  German and Austrian representatives expelled from Egypt ... Sept. 10, 1914
  Martial law proclaimed .... Nov. 1, 1914
  British protectorate proclaimed .... Dec. 18, 1914
  Khedive Abbas Hilmi declared deposed .... Dec. 19, 1914
  Prince Hussein Kamel—
   Proclaimed Sultan .... Dec. 19, 1914
   Dies .... Oct. 9, 1917
  Prince Ahmed Fuad proclaimed Sultan .... Oct. 9, 1917
 II. FRONTIER (*Eastern*)—
  Last Turkish troops driven back over* .... Jan. 9, 1917
 III. BRITISH COMMANDER-IN-CHIEF—
  1. Maxwell, *Sir* John—
   Takes over command .... Sept. 8, 1914
   Resigns .... Mar. 19, 1916
  2. Murray, *Sir* Archibald—
   Takes over command .... Mar. 19, 1916
   Resigns .... June 28, 1917
  3. Allenby, *Sir* Edmund—Takes over command ... June 28, 1917

 * Turkish troops had crossed the frontier a few weeks after outbreak of war.

EICHHORN, von, *Field-Marshal* (Commanding German troops at Kiev)—
    Assassinated ... ... July 30, 1918

EKATERINBURG (*East Russia*)—
    Ex-Tsar and family murdered at ... ... July 16, 1918

EKATERINOSLAV (*South Russia*)—
    Taken by German forces ... ... Apr. 3, 1918

EL ARISH (*Sinai*)—
    Occupied by British forces ... ... Dec. 21, 1916

EL FASHER (*Capital of Darfur*)—
    Occupied by Sudan force ... . May 23, 1916

ELBASAN (*Albania*)—
    Taken by Bulgarian forces ... ... Feb. 2, 1916
    Occupied by Italian forces ... ... Oct. 7, 1918

"ELBING" (*German Light Cruiser*)—
    Sunk ... ... May 31, 1916

EL HANNA. See under "Umm al Hanna."

EL MEZRAA' (*Dead Sea*)—
    Turkish Dead Sea flotilla seized by Arab camelry at ... ... Jan. 27, 1918

EL MUGHAR (*Palestine*)—
    Action of ... ... Nov. 13, 1917

"ELOPE" (*British Expeditionary Force*)—
    Disembarks at Murmansk ... ... June 23, 1918

"EMDEN" (*German Light Cruiser*)—
    Joins Admiral von Spee at Pagan Island and is detached ... ... Aug. 12, 1914
    Begins raid on Bay of Bengal (*by capture of Greek collier "Pontoporos"*) ... Sept. 10, 1914
    Bombards Madras ... ... Sept 22, 1914
    Raids Penang Roads and sinks Russian Light Cruiser "Zhemchug" ... ... Oct. 28, 1914
    Destroyed by H.M.A.S. "Sydney" ... ... Nov. 9, 1914

ENSIGNS. See under "Flags."

ENTENTE POWERS. See under "Commitments."

ENZELI (*Persia*)—
    Russian Expeditionary Force to West Persia lands at ... ... May 21, 1915
    Reached by General Dunsterville's Mission ... ... Feb. 17, 1918
    Evacuated by the Russian regular forces ... ... Apr. 1, 1918
    Bolshevik leaders arrested at ... ... Aug. 4, 1918

EPÉHY (*France*)—
    Battle of ... ... Sept. 18, 1918

ERZERUM (*Asia Minor*)—
    Attack on begins ... ... Feb. 12, 1916
    Taken by Russian forces ... ... Feb. 16, 1916
    Retaken by Turkish forces ... ... Mar. 12, 1918

*ERZINJAN (*Armenia*)—
    Taken by Russian forces ... July 25, 1916

ES SALT (*Palestine*)—
    First action of ... Mar. 24–25, 1918
    Second action of ... Apr. 30–May 4, 1918
    Occupied by British forces ... Sept. 23, 1918

ESSAD PASHA. See under "Albania."

ESSEN (*Germany*)—
    French air raid on Krupp Works at ... Sept. 24, 1916

ESTAIRES (*France*)—
    Taken by German forces ... Oct. 9, 1914
    Recaptured by British forces ... Oct. 10, 1914
    Battle of ... Apr. 9–11, 1918
    Again taken by German forces ... Apr. 10, 1918
    Retaken by British forces ... Aug. 20, 1918

ESTERHAZY, *Count*—
    Appointed Hungarian Premier ... June 15, 1917
    Resigns office ... Aug. 9, 1917

ESTONIA—
    I. INDEPENDENCE—
        Declared by local Diet ... Nov. 28, 1917
        Declaration of, published ... Jan. 13, 1918
        Recognised by British Government ... Feb. 25, 1918
    II. MOBILISATION—Ordered ... Nov. 16, 1918
    (And see "Baltic Provinces.")

ETAPLES (*France*)—
    German air raid on hospitals and camps at ... May 19, 1918

ET TAFILE (*Arabia*)—
    Actions for, by Arab forces ... Jan. 1–28, 1918

EXPEDITIONARY FORCE. See under respective countries.

F

"FALABA," S.S. (*British*)—
    Sunk ... Mar. 28, 1915

FALAHIYA (*Mesopotamia*)—
    Action of ... Apr. 5, 1916

FALKENHAYN, *General* von—
    Appointed German Minister for War ... —, 1906
    Succeeds General von Moltke as Chief of the General Staff of the German Field Armies (*remains Minister for War*) ... Sept. 14, 1914
    Succeeded as Minister for War by General Wild von Hohenborn (*remains Chief of Staff*) ... Jan. 21, 1915
    Dismissed as Chief of General Staff of the Field Armies ... Aug. 29, 1916

FALKLANDS, THE—
    Battle of ... Dec. 8, 1914

* See Part I.

"FALMOUTH," H.M.S. (*Light Cruiser*)—
    Sunk ... ... Aug. 19, 1916

FANÖ (*Denmark*)—
    German airship "L–3" destroyed off ... Feb. 17, 1915

FAO (*Mesopotamia*)—
    Captured by British forces ... Nov. 6, 1914

FARASAN ISLANDS (*Red Sea*)—
    Occupied by Arabs (Idrisi) ... Jan. 31, 1915

FENG-KUO-CHANG—
    Succeeds to Acting Presidency of China ... July 6, 1917
    Resigns on expiration of term ... Oct. 11, 1918

FERDINAND, *King of Bulgaria*—
    Abdicates ... Oct. 4, 1918

FERDINAND, *King of Rumania*—
    Succeeds to the throne ... Oct. 10, 1914
    Announces that Rumania has taken up arms again on the side of the Allies ... Nov. 10, 1918

FERE, LA (*France*)—
    Taken by German forces ... Aug. 30, 1914
    Retaken by French forces... ... Oct. 13, 1918

FÈRE-EN-TARDENOIS (*France*)—
    Taken by German forces ... May 30, 1918
    Retaken by Allied forces ... July 28, 1918

FESTUBERT (*France*)—
    Battle of—
        Begins ... May 15, 1915
        Ends ... May 25, 1915

FIFE (*Rhodesia*)—
    Attacked by German force... ... Nov. 1, 1918

FINANCE—
    Great Britain, France, and Russia agree to pool their financial resources ... Feb. 5, 1915
    (And see "Economic Conference.")

FINLAND—
    I. INDEPENDENCE—
        Declared ... Dec. 6, 1917
        Recognised by—
            Russian Bolshevik Government ... Jan. 4, 1918
            French and Swedish Government ... Jan. 4, 918
            Danish and Norwegian Governments ... Jan. 10, 1918
    II. REGENT—
        General Mannerheim elected ... Dec. 11, 1918
    III. PEACE (signed)—
        With Russian Bolshevik Government ... Mar. 1, 1918
        With Germany ... Mar. 7, 1918
        With Turkey ... May 11, 1918
        With Austria-Hungary ... May 29, 1918
    IV. MISCELLANEOUS—
        German force leaves Danzig for ... Apr. 1, 1918
        German force lands in South Finland* ... Apr. 3, 1918
        Last German troops leave... ... Dec. 16, 1918
        End of Finnish Civil War† ... May 7, 1918

* See Part I, April 13, 1918.
† See Part I, note to May 7, 1918.

FIRMAN FIRMA, *Prince*—
    Appointed Persian Premier ... Dec. 25, 1915
    Resigns ... Mar. 5, 1916

FISHER, *Admiral of the Fleet Lord*—
    Appointed First Sea Lord, Great Britain ... Oct. 30, 1914
    Tenders resignation ... May 15, 1915

FISHING VESSELS, NEUTRAL—
    British Admiralty forbid, to use British ports ... Feb. 1, 1915

FIUME (*Croatia*)—
    Surrendered to the Croats by the Hungarian authorities ... Oct. 30, 1918
    "National Council of," announce independence and desire for union with Italy ... Oct. 30, 1918
    Occupied by Italian Naval Division ... Nov. 5, 1918
    Yugo-Slav National Council protest against Italian occupation of ... Nov. 17, 1918
    Italian troops reinforce Naval Division in ... Nov. 18, 1918
    United States troops enter... ... Nov. 26, 1918

FLAG, NEUTRAL—
    British Admiralty warn British merchant vessels to fly either neutral ensigns or no ensigns in the vicinity of the British Isles ... Jan. 30, 1915
    British s.s. "Lusitania" arrives at Liverpool flying United States flag ... Feb. 6, 1915
    British Foreign Office issue statement justifying use of ... Feb. 7, 1915
    United States Government send note deprecating use of ... Feb. 11, 1915
    Dutch Government issue warning that foreign ships using the Dutch flag will be detained ... Mar. 12, 1915

FLANDERS RIDGES—
    Battle of ... *Sept. 28–Oct. 10, 1918

FLERS (*France*)—
    Battle of ("Flers-Courcelette") ... Sept. 15–22, 1916

FLEURY (*France*)—
    Stormed by German forces ... June 24, 1916

FLOTOW, *Baron von*—
    Appointed Austro-Hungarian Foreign Minister ... Nov. 1, 1918

FLYING CORPS, ROYAL—
    First squadrons of, fly from Dover to France ... Aug. 13, 1914
    (See also under "Air Force, Royal" and "Air Force, Independent.")

FOCH, Ferdinand, *Marshal*—
    Appointed to command Allied Armies (less Belgians) defending the coast ... Oct. 8, 1914
    Succeeds General Pétain as Chief of General Staff at French Ministry of War ... May 15, 1917
    Appointed to Supreme Council ... Nov. 27, 1917
    Appointed to supreme control of Allied Armies in France ... Mar. 26, 1918
    Appointed titular Commander-in-Chief of Allied Armies in France (less Belgians)... Apr. 14, 1918
    Created Marshal of France ... Aug. 6, 1918
    Given supreme strategical direction of all forces operating against Germany ... Nov. 5, 1918

FOCSANI (*Rumania*)—
    Taken by German forces ... Jan. 3, 1917
    "Truce of Focsani"—between Rumania and Central Powers—concluded ... Dec. 9, 1917

FOREIGN MINISTERS. See under respective countries and under individual names.

* French official dates.

"FORMIDABLE," H.M.S. (*Battleship*)—
    Sunk ... ... Jan. 1, 1915

"FOURTEEN POINTS, THE." See under "Points, the Fourteen."

FOWKE, *Lieut.-General Sir* G. H.—
    Appointed Adjutant-General, B.E.F., France ... ... Feb. 22, 1916

FRANCE—
    MOBILISATION—Ordered ... ... Aug. 1, 1914
    RELATIONS (severed)—
        With Austria-Hungary ... ... Aug. 10, 1914
        With Turkey ... ... Oct. 30, 1914
    WAR (declared)—
        By **Germany** ... ... Aug. 3, 1914
        On **Austria-Hungary** ... ... Aug. 12, 1914
        On **Turkey** ... ... Nov. 5, 1914
        By Turkey (Jehad) ... ... Nov. 14, 1914
        On **Bulgaria*** ... ... Oct. 16, 1915
    FRONTIER—
        Recrossed by last German troops ... ... Nov. 18, 1918
    GOVERNMENT—
        Transferred from Paris to Bordeaux ... ... Sept. 2, 1914
        Retransferred to Paris from Bordeaux ... ... Nov. 18, 1914
        Reorganisation of : War Cabinet formed ... ... Dec. 12, 1916
    MINISTERS—
        I. **Premier**—
            1. Viviani, *M.*—
                Appointed ... ... June 14, 1914
                Resigns ... ... Oct. 29, 1915
            2. Briand, *M.*—
                Appointed ... ... Oct. 30, 1915
                Resigns ... ... Mar. 17, 1917
            3. Ribot, *M.*—
                Appointed ... ... Mar. 20, 1917
                Resigns ... ... Sept. 9, 1917
            4. Painlevé, *M.*—
                Appointed ... ... Sept. 12, 1917
                Resigns ... ... Nov. 14, 1917
            5. Clémenceau, *M.*—
                Appointed ... ... Nov. 16, 1917
        II. **Minister for Foreign Affairs**—
            1. Doumergue, *M.*—
                Appointed ... ... Aug. 3, 1914
                Resigns ... ... Aug. 26, 1914
            2. Delcassé, *M.*—
                Appointed ... ... Aug. 26, 1914
                Resigns ... ... Oct. 13, 1915
            3. Viviani, *M.*—
                Acting ... ... Oct. 13, 1915
                Resigns ... ... Oct. 29, 1915
            4. Briand, *M.*—
                Appointed ... ... Oct. 30, 1915
                Resigns ... ... Mar. 17, 1917
            5. Ribot, *M.*—
                Appointed ... ... Mar. 20, 1917
                Resigns ... ... Sept. 9, 1917
            6. Ribot, *M.*—
                Reappointed ... ... Sept. 12, 1917
                Resigns ... ... Oct. 23, 1917
            7. Barthou, *M.*—
                Appointed ... ... Oct. 23, 1917
                Resigns ... ... Nov. 14, 1917
            8. Pichon, Stephen, *M.*—
                Appointed ... ... Nov. 16, 1917
        III. **Minister for War**—
            1. Messimy, *M.*—
                Appointed ... ... June 14, 1914
                Resigns ... ... Aug. 26, 1914
            2. Millerand, *M.*—
                Appointed ... ... Aug. 27, 1914
                Resigns ... ... Oct. 29, 1915

* "State of War" proclaimed to exist.

FRANCE (continued)—
  MINISTERS (continued)—
    III. **Minister for War** (continued)—
      3. Galliéni, *General*—
        Appointed ... Oct. 30, 1915
        Resigns ... Mar. 16, 1916
      4. Roques, *General*—
        Appointed ... Mar. 16, 1916
        Resigns ... Mar. 17, 1917
      5. Painlevé, *M.*—
        Appointed ... Mar. 20, 1917
        Resigns ... Nov. 14, 1917
      6. Clémenceau, *M.*—
        Appointed ... Nov. 16, 1917
    IV. **Minister for Blockade**—
      (*a.*) Under-Secretary of State for—
        1. Cochin, *M.**—
          Appointed ... Mar. 20, 1916
          Resigns ... Aug. 17, 1917
        2. Métin, *M.**—
          Appointed ... Aug. 17, 1917
          Resigns ... Nov. 16, 1917
      (*b.*) Minister for—
        1. Jonnart, *M.*†—
          Appointed ... Nov. 16, 1917
          Resigns ... Nov. 23, 1917
        2. Lebrun, *M.*—
          Appointed ... Nov. 23, 1917
  ARMY—
    I. **Commander-in-Chief**—
      1. Joffre, *General*—
        Appointed ... Dec. 3, 1915
        Resigns ... Dec. 12, 1916
      2. Nivelle, *General*—
        Appointed ... Dec. 12, 1916
        Resigns ... May 15, 1917
      3. Pétain, *General*—
        Appointed ... May 15, 1917
    II. **Chief of General Staff** –
      1. Joffre, *General*—
        Appointed ... July 28, 1911
        Vacates appointment‡ ... Dec. 3, 1915
      2. Pétain, *General*—
        Appointed ... Apr. 29, 1917
        Vacates appointment ... May 15, 1917
      3. Foch, *General*—
        Appointed ... May 15, 1917
        Vacates appointment ... Apr. 14, 1918
    III. **Expeditionary Forces**—
      1. To the **Dardanelles**—French Government decide to send ... Mar. 4, 1915
        (And see under "Dardanelles.")
      2. To **Salonika**—First units land ... Oct 3, 1915
      3. To **Italy**—Arrival of first units announced ... Nov. 3, 1917
      4. To **North Russia**—First units land ... July 26, 1918
  FLEET—
    Naval Convention concluded with Great Britain, regarding co-operation in general and French command in the Mediterranean ... Aug. 6, 1914
  TREATIES, &c. See under "Commitments."

FRANCHET D'ESPEREY, *General*—
  Takes over command as Allied Commander-in-Chief, Salonika ... June 18, 1918

FRANCIS JOSEPH, *Emperor of Austria*—
  Dies ... Nov. 21, 1916

FRANZ FERDINAND, *Archduke*—
  Assassinated at Sarajevo ... June 28, 1914

* *MM.* Cochin and Métin were Under-Secretaries of State for Foreign Affairs and combined Blockade with their office.
  † *M.* Jonnart was the first Minister of the new Department for "Blockade and Liberated Territories."
  ‡ Appointment lapsed till April 29, 1917.

"FRAUENLOB" (*German Light Cruiser*)—
    Sunk ... ... May 31, 1916

FREDERICKSHAMN (*Finland*)—
    Captured by Finnish White Guards ... ... May 7, 1918

FREE TRADE ZONE, African. See under "African Free Trade Zone."

FRENCH, *Field-Marshal Sir* John—
    Appointed to command British Expeditionary Force, France ... ... Aug. 4, 1914
    Resigns ... ... Dec. 15, 1915
    Appointed Field-Marshal Commanding-in-Chief, Home Forces ... ... Dec. 19, 1915
    Appointed Lord-Lieutenant of Ireland ... ... May 5, 1918

FREZENBERG RIDGE (*Ypres*)—
    Battle of ... ... May 8–13, 1915

"FRIEDRICH KARL" (*German Cruiser*)—
    Sunk ... ... Nov. 17, 1914

FRIEDRICHSHAVEN (*Germany*)—
    British naval air raid on ... ... Nov. 21, 1914

FRONTIER. See under respective countries.

"FRONTIERS, BATTLE OF THE" (*France*) ... ... Aug. 6—Sept. 5, 1914

FRYATT, *Captain* Charles A.
    Shot ... ... July 27, 1916

FUNCHAL (*Madeira*)—
    Bombarded by German submarine ... ... {Dec. 3, 1916 / Dec. 12, 1917}

G

GALLIÉNI, *General*—
    Appointed Military Governor of Paris ... ... Aug. 26, 1914
    Appointed French Minister for War ... ... Oct. 30, 1915

GALLIPOLI PENINSULA. For Allied Landings and Evacuations see under "Dardanelles."

GARUA (*Cameroons*)—
    First attack on ... ... Aug. 30, 1914
    Operations of Allied force against, begin ... ... Apr. 18, 1915
    Siege of—
        Begins ... ... May 31, 1915
        Ends ... ... June 10, 1915

GAS, POISON—
    Germans accuse French of using ... ... Apr. 14, 1915
    Germans use, for first time ... ... Apr. 22, 1915

"GAULOIS" (*French Battleship*)—
   Sunk ... ... Dec. 27, 1916

GAWAITEN-GUMBINNEN (*East Prussia*)—
   Battle of ... ... Aug. 19–20, 1914

GAZA (*Palestine*)—
   First Battle of—
      Begins ... ... Mar. 26, 1917
      Ends ... ... Mar. 27, 1917
   Second Battle of—
      Begins ... ... Apr. 17, 1917
      Ends ... ... Apr. 19, 1917
   Third Battle of—
      Begins ... ... Oct. 27, 1917
      Ends ... ... Nov. 7, 1917

GEDDES, *Sir* Eric—
   Appointed First Lord of the Admiralty, Great Britain ... ... Sept. 6, 1917

"GEIER" (*German Gunboat*)—
   Interned at Honolulu ... ... Nov. 9, 1914

GENERAL STAFF, CHIEFS OF. See under respective countries.

GEORGIA (*Trans-Caucasia*)—
   I. INDEPENDENCE—Declared ... ... May 26, 1918
   II. PEACE—
      1. Turco-German Peace Delegates arrive at Batum ... ... May 6, 1918
      2. With Germany and Turkey, signed ... ... June 8, 1918
   III. MISCELLANEOUS—
      German troops land at Poti ... ... June 8, 1918
      German troops occupy Tiflis ... ... June 12, 1918
      British troops occupy Batum ... ... Dec. 27, 1918
      (See also under "Trans-Caucasia.")

GERMANY—
   MOBILISATION—
      State of "Kriegsgefahr"—Proclaimed ... ... July 31, 1914
      General mobilisation—Ordered ... ... Aug. 1, 1914
   ULTIMATUM (presented)—
      To Russia (midnight 31st/1st) ... ... July 31, 1914
      To Belgium ... ... Aug. 2, 1914
      By Britain ... ... Aug. 4, 1914
      By Japan ... ... Aug. 15, 1914
      To Rumania ... ... Feb. 6, 1918
   RELATIONS (severed)—
      By Belgium ... ... Aug. 4, 1914
      By Montenegro ... ... Aug. 8, 1914
      With Japan ... ... Aug. 23, 1914
      With Italy ... ... *May 24, 1915
      By United States of America ... ... Feb. 3, 1917
      By China ... ... Mar. 14, 1917
      By Brazil ... ... Apr. 11, 1917
      By Bolivia ... ... Apr. 13, 1917
      By Guatemala ... ... Apr. 27, 1917
      By Liberia ... ... May 5, 1917
      By Honduras ... ... May 17, 1917
      By Nicaragua ... ... May 18, 1917
      By Santo Domingo ... ... June 11, 1917
      By Haiti ... ... June 16, 1917
      By Greece ... ... June 27, 1917
      By Costa Rica ... ... Sept. 21, 1917

* See footnote in Part I.

GERMANY (*continued*)—
    RELATIONS (severed)—(*continued*)—

By Peru	Oct. 5, 1917
By Uruguay	Oct. 7, 1917
By Ecuador	Dec. 7, 1917
By Poland	Dec. 15, 1918

    WAR (declared)—

On **Russia**	Aug. 1, 1914
On **France**	Aug. 3, 1914
On **Belgium**	Aug. 4, 1914
By **Britain**	Aug. 4, 1914
By **Serbia**	Aug. 6, 1914
By **Montenegro**	Aug. 8, 1914
By **Japan**	Aug. 23, 1914
On **Portugal**	Mar. 9, 1916
On **Rumania**	Aug. 28, 1916
By **Italy**	Aug. 28, 1916
By **Greece**—Provisional Government of	Nov. 23, 1916
By **United States of America**	Apr. 6, 1917
By **Cuba**	Apr. 7, 1917
By **Panama**	Apr. 7, 1917
By **Greece**—Alexander's Government of	June 27, 1917
By **Siam**	July 22, 1917
By **Liberia**	Aug. 4, 1917
By **China**	Aug. 14, 1917
By **Brazil**	Oct. 26, 1917
By **Nicaragua**	May 8, 1918
By **Costa Rica**	May 23, 1918
By **Haiti**	July 12, 1918
By **Honduras**	July 19, 1918
By **Czecho-Slovaks**	Aug. 13, 1918

    HOSTILITIES—

Against **France**, commence	Aug. 2, 1914
Against **Japan**, commence	Sept. 2, 1914
Against **Russia**—	
Commence	Aug. 1, 1914
Suspended	*Dec. 2, 1917
Resumed	Feb. 18, 1918
Cease	Feb. 28, 1918
Against **Rumania**, cease	Dec. 6, 1917

(Hostilities against other countries began on date of Declaration of War (see above) and ended on date of signing of Armistice (see below).)

    ARMISTICE (concluded)—

With **Rumania**	Dec. 9, 1917
With **Russia**	Dec. 15, 1917
With **Entente**	Nov. 11, 1918

(For details see "Armistice" and "Brest-Litovsk.")

    PEACE (signed)—

With **The Ukraine**	Feb. 9, 1918
With **Russia**	Mar. 3, 1918
With **Rumania**—Preliminary Treaty	Mar. 5, 1918
With **Finland**	Mar. 7, 1918
With **Rumania**—Final Treaty	May 7, 1918
With **Georgia**	June 8, 1918

(For details of negotiations, see under "Brest-Litovsk" and "Peace.")

    EMPEROR—

Returns from the Baltic to Berlin	July 26, 1914
Crosses frontier into Holland	Nov. 10, 1918
Signs abdication	Nov. 28, 1918

    REGENT—Prince Max of Baden—appointed   Nov. 9, 1918

    MINISTERS—
        I. Imperial Chancellor—

1. Bethmann-Hollweg, *Herr* von—	
Appointed	July 14, 1909
Resigns	July 14, 1917
2. Michaelis, *Dr.*—	
Appointed	July 14, 1917
Resigns	Oct. 30, 1917
3. Hertling, *Count* von—	
Appointed	Oct. 30, 1917
Resigns	Sept. 30, 1918
4. Max of Baden, *Prince*—	
Appointed	Oct. 4, 1918
Resigns	Nov. 9, 1918
5. Ebert, *Herr*—Appointed	Nov. 9, 1918

* See footnote in Part I.

GERMANY (*continued*)—

MINISTERS (*continued*)—

II. Foreign Minister—
1. Jagow, *Herr* von—
   - Appointed ... Jan. 1913
   - Resigns ... Nov. 20, 1916
2. Zimmermann, *Dr.*—
   - Appointed ... Nov. 21, 1916
   - Resigns ... July 15, 1917
3. Kuhlmann, *Herr* von—
   - Appointed ... Aug. 5, 1917
   - Resigns ... July 9, 1918
4. Hintze, *Admiral* von—
   - Appointed ... July 9, 1918
   - Resigns ... Oct. 4, 1918

III. Army—

(A.) **Minister for War**—
1. Falkenhayn, *Lieutenant-General* von—
   - (Appointed ... ——, 1913)
   - Resigns ... Jan. 21, 1915
2. Hohenborn, *Lieutenant-General* von—
   - Appointed ... Jan. 21, 1915
   - Resigns ... Oct. 30, 1916
3. Stein, *Lieutenant-General* von—
   - Appointed ... Oct. 30, 1916
   - Resigns ... Oct. 9, 1918
4. Scheuch, *Major-General*—
   - Appointed ... Oct. 9, 1918
   - Resigns ... Dec. 17, 1918

(B.) **Chief of the General Staff of the Field Armies**—
1. Moltke, *General* von*—
   - Appointed ... Aug. 2, 1914
   - Resigns ... Sept. 14, 1914
2. Falkenhayn, *General* von—
   - Appointed (temporary till November 3, 1914) ... Sept. 14, 1914
   - Dismissed ... Aug. 29, 1916
3. Hindenburg, *Field-Marshal* von—Appointed ... Aug. 29, 1916

(C.) **Chief Quartermaster-General**—
Ludendorff, *General* von—
   - Appointed ... Aug. 29, 1916
   - Resigns ... Oct. 27, 1918

IV. Minister of Marine—
1. Tirpitz, *Admiral* von—
   - (Appointed ... ——, 1897)
   - Resigns ... Mar. 14, 1916
2. Capelle, *Admiral* von—
   - Appointed ... Mar. 15, 1916
   - Resigns ... Aug. 13, 1918
3. Behnke, *Vice-Admiral*—Appointed ... Aug. 15, 1918

NAVY—

I. **High Seas Fleet**—
   - Recalled from Norway to war bases ... July 27, 1914
   - Battle of Jutland ... May 31, 1916
   - Mutiny in—
     - First ... Aug. 3, 1917
     - Second ... Nov. 3, 1918
   - Surrender to the Grand Fleet—
     - Delegates arrive at Rosyth ... Nov. 15, 1918
     - Fleet surrenders ... Nov. 21, 1918
II. **Submarines**—First contingent surrender at Harwich ... Nov. 20, 1918
   (And see under "Submarines.")

AIR FORCE—Established as separate branch of the army ... Nov. 25, 1916

COLONIES. See under "Africa, East," "Africa, South-West," "Cameroons," "Islands, Pacific," "New Guinea," "Samoa," "Togoland."

MISCELLANEOUS—
- The Kaiser promises support to Austria ... July 5, 1914
- Government submit note to Entente Governments approving Austrian ultimatum to Serbia ... July 24, 1914
- Government reject British proposal for a conference to avert war ... July 28, 1914
- Proposal made to secure British neutrality ... July 29, 1914
- Government inform neutral Governments that defensively armed merchantmen will be regarded as belligerents ... Feb. 10, 1915
- The "Reichstag Resolution" ... July 19, 1917
- Allied troops begin march into Germany ... Nov. 16, 1918
- First meeting of Imperial Conference of soldiers and workmen in Berlin ... Dec. 16, 1918

TREATIES, &c. See under "Commitments."

---

* Was Chief of the Great General Staff from 1906 to August 2, 1914.

GETTE, River (*Belgium*)—
    Battle of the ... ... Aug. 18–19, 1914

GEVGELI (*South Serbia*)—
    Serbian Government give undertaking to Greek Government of the eventual cession
        of, to Greece ... ... Sept. 25, 1915
    Taken by Bulgarian forces ... ... Dec. 11, 1915

GHELUVELT (*Ypres*)—
    Battle of ... ... Oct. 29–31, 1914

GHENT (*Belgium*)—
    Occupied by German forces ... ... Oct. 12, 1914
    Reoccupied by Allied forces ... ... Nov. 10, 1918

GIBEON (*German South-West Africa*)—
    Action of ... ... Apr. 25–26, 1915

GINCHY (*Somme*)—
    Battle of ... ... Sept. 9, 1916

" GIUSEPPE GARIBALDI " (*Italian Cruiser*) –
    Sunk ... ... July 18, 1915

GIVENCHY (*France*)—
    British defence of ... ... Dec. 20–21, 1914

"GLATTON," H.M.S. (*Coast Defence Ship*)—
    Sunk by explosion ... ... Sept. 16, 1918

" GLENART CASTLE " (*British Hospital Ship*)—
    Damaged by mine in English Channel ... ... Mar. 1, 1917
    Sunk ... ... Feb. 26, 1918

"GLITRA," S.S. (*British*)—
    First merchant vessel sunk by German submarine ... ... Oct. 20, 1914

" GLOUCESTER," H.M.S. (*Light Cruiser*)—
    Action with German cruisers "Goeben" and "Breslau" off Greek coast .. Aug. 7, 1914

"GLOUCESTER CASTLE" (*British Hospital Ship*)—
    Torpedoed, but towed in ... ... Mar. 30, 1917

" GNEISENAU " (*German Cruiser*)—
    Sunk ... ... Dec. 8, 1914

" GOEBEN " (*German Battle Cruiser*)—
    Bombards Philippeville ... ... Aug. 4, 1914
    Action off Greek coast with H.M.S. "Gloucester" ... ... Aug. 7, 1914
    Enters Dardanelles ... ... Aug. 11, 1914
    Bombards Sevastopol ... ... Oct. 29, 1914
    Bombards Batum ... ... Dec. 10, 1914
    Action in Black Sea with Russian fleet ... ... Apr. 3, 1915
    Mined in action outside Dardanelles, but beached ... ... Jan. 20, 1918
    Refloated ... ... Jan. 27, 1918

"GOLIATH," H.M.S. (*Battleship*)—
    Sunk ... ... May 13, 1915

GOLITSIN, *Prince*—
    Appointed Premier of Russia ... ... Jan. 8, 1917
    Removed from office ... ... Mar. 13, 1917

GOLTZ, Field-Marshal von der—
    Leaves Germany to take over control of Turkish Army   Dec. 10, 1914
    Takes command of Turkish forces in Mesopotamia   Nov. 24, 1915
    Assassinated   Apr. 19, 1916

" GOOD HOPE," H.M.S. (Cruiser)—
    Sunk   Nov. 1, 1914

"GOORKHA" (British Hospital Ship)—
    Damaged by mine   Oct. 10, 1917

GOREMIKIN. M.—
    Appointed Premier of Russia   Jan. 30, 1914
    Resigns   Feb. 1, 1916

GORIZIA (Italy)—
    Battle of (*Sixth Battle of the Isonzo*)—
        Begins   Aug. 6, 1916
        Town taken by Italian forces   Aug. 9, 1916
        Ends   Aug. 17, 1916
    Retaken by Austro-German forces   Oct. 28, 1917

GORLESTON (Suffolk)—
    German naval raid on British coast near   Nov. 3, 1914

GORLICE–TARNOW (Galicia)—
    Battle of   May 1–5, 1915

GOTTLAND, Island of—
    Naval action off   July 2, 1915

GOTO, Baron—
    Appointed Japanese Minister for Foreign Affairs   Apr. 22, 1918
    Resigns   Sept. 28, 1918

GOUNARIS, M.—
    Appointed Premier of Greece   Mar. 9, 1915
    Resigns   Aug. 22, 1915

GOVERNMENT. See under respective countries.

GRAND COURONNE (DE NANCY)—
    Battle of   Sept. 4–12, 1914

GRAND FLEET. See under " Britain, Fleet."

GRAVENSTAFEL RIDGE (Ypres)—
    Battle of   Apr. 22–23, 1915

GREAT BRITAIN. See under " Britain, Great."

GREECE—
    I. MOBILISATION—
        Precautionary, ordered   Sept. 23, 1915
    II. RELATIONS (severed)—
        With Austria-Hungary   ⎫
        With Germany   ⎬ June 27, 1917
        With Turkey   ⎭

GREECE (continued)—
  III. WAR (declared)—
    By **Provisional Government**—
      On **Bulgaria** .. .. Nov. 23, 1916
      On **Germany** .. .. Nov. 23, 1916
    By whole State—
      On **Austria-Hungary*** .. .. June 27, 1917
      On **Bulgaria**† .. .. June 27, 1917
      On **Germany**† .. .. June 27, 1917
      On **Turkey*** .. .. June 27, 1917
  IV. HOSTILITIES—Commence—Date of "Declarations of War."
  V. NOTES (by Entente Powers)—
    First (*demanding demobilisation*)—
      Presented.. .. .. June 21, 1916
      Accepted .. .. June 21, 1916
      Greek Government issue orders .. .. June 27, 1916
    Second (*demanding surrender of Greek fleet*)—
      Presented .. .. Oct. 10, 1916
      Accepted.. .. .. Oct. 11, 1916
    Third (*demanding dismissal of Ministers of Central Powers and surrender of Greek military material*)—
      Presented .. .. Nov. 19, 1916
      Refused .. .. Dec. 1, 1916
    Fourth (*demanding complete demobilisation*)—
      Presented .. .. Dec. 11, 1916
    Fifth (*demanding withdrawal of Greek army from Thessaly*)‡—
      Presented .. .. Dec. 14, 1916
      Accepted.. .. .. Dec. 15, 1916
    Sixth (*demanding the abdication of King Constantine*) —
      Presented .. .. June 11, 1917
      Accepted .. .. June 12, 1917
  VI. BLOCKADE (by Entente Powers)—
    British Government put economic pressure on Greece by making "export restrictions" apply to the country .. .. .. Dec. 6, 1915
    British Government order partial relaxation of the economic pressure on Greece .. .. Dec. 13, 1915
    "**Pacific Blockade**"—
      Begins .. .. June 6, 1916
      Suspended .. .. June 22, 1916
    Blockade of Greek Macedonian coast—Begins .. .. Sept. 19, 1916
    Coercive blockade—
      Announced .. .. Dec. 7, 1916
      Begins .. .. Dec. 8, 1916
  VII. FRONTIER—Of Greek Macedonia—Crossed by German and Bulgarian troops May 26, 1916
  VIII. KING—
    1. **Constantine**—
      Abdication—Demanded by Entente Powers .. .. June 11, 1917
      Signed .. .. June 12, 1917
    2. **Alexander**—Succeeds .. .. June 12, 1917
  IX. PREMIER—
    1. Venizelos, *M.*—
      Appointed .. .. Oct. 19, 1910
      Resigns .. .. Mar. 6, 1915
    2. Gounaris, *M.*—
      Succeeds .. .. Mar. 9, 1915
      Resigns .. .. Aug. 22, 1915
    3. Venizelos, *M.*—
      Succeeds .. .. Aug. 22, 1915
      Resigns .. .. Oct. 5, 1915
    4. Zaimis, *M.*—
      Succeeds .. .. Oct 6, 1915
      Resigns .. .. Nov. 5, 1915
    5. Skouloudhis, *M.*—
      Succeeds .. .. Nov. 6, 1915
      Resigns .. .. June 21, 1916
    6. Zaimis, *M.*—
      Succeeds .. .. June 21, 1916
      Resigns .. .. Sept. 11, 1916
    7. Kalogeropoulos, *M.*—
      Succeeds .. .. Sept. 16, 1916
      Resigns .. .. Oct. 3, 1916
    8. Lambros, *Prof.*—
      Succeeds .. .. Oct. 10, 1916
      Resigns .. .. May 3, 1917

* State of war proclaimed to exist.
† Declaration of war by Provisional Government becomes effective for the whole of Greece.
‡ This was delivered in the form of an Ultimatum.

GREECE (continued)—
    IX. PREMIER (continued)—
        9. Zaimis, M.—
            Succeeds .. May 3, 1917
            Resigns .. June 24, 1917
        10. Venizelos, M.—Succeeds .. June 26, 1917
    X. PROVISIONAL GOVERNMENT—
        Set up in Crete .. Sept. 29, 1916
        Declare war on Germany and Bulgaria .. Nov. 23, 1916
        Recognised by British Government .. Dec. 19, 1916
    XI. FLEET—
        Proffered to Entente by M. Venizelos for attack on Dardanelles .. Mar. 5, 1915
        Surrender to Entente—
            Demanded by Entente .. Oct. 10, 1916
            Agreed to by Greek Government .. Oct. 11, 1916
    XII. LOAN—With Entente Governments—
        First (1,600,000*l*.)—Concluded .. Nov. 8, 1915
        Second (800,000*l*.)—Concluded .. July 20, 1916
    XIII. MISCELLANEOUS—
        (i.) King Constantine's assurance of neutrality announced .. Oct. 6, 1915
        (ii.) Policy of armed neutrality announced .. Oct. 8, 1915
        (iii.) Entente Powers send Note to Greek Government demanding non-interference with Allied troops and guaranteeing eventual restoration of occupied Greek territory .. Nov. 23, 1915
        (iv.) Venizelist revolt in Salonika begins .. Aug. 30, 1916
        (v.) Allied withdrawal from the Piræus marked by conflicts with Greeks .. Dec. 1, 1916
        (vi.) Massacre of Venizelist partisans in Athens .. Dec. 6, 1916
        (vii) Greek Government apologise for disturbances of December 1, 1916 .. Jan. 24, 1917
    XIV. TREATIES, &c. See under "Commitments."
        (See also under "Venizelos.")

"GREIF" (*German Raider*)—
    Action in North Sea with British armed merchant cruiser "Alcantara" (*both sunk*) .. Feb. 29, 1916

GREY, *Sir* Edward (created Viscount in July 1916)—
    (Appointed Secretary of State for Foreign Affairs, Great Britain .. Dec. 11, 1905)
    Initiates proposals for international conference .. July 24, 1914
    Resigns .. Dec. 11, 1916

GRODNO (*Lithuania*)—
    Stormed by German forces .. Sept. 2-3, 1915

GUARANTEES (POLITICAL). See under "Commitments."

GUATEMALA—
    Severs diplomatic relations with Germany .. Apr. 27, 1917
    Declares war on Germany .. Apr. 23, 1918

GUCHKOV, *General*—
    Appointed Russian Minister for War .. Mar. 15, 1917
    Resigns .. May 16, 1917

"GUILDFORD CASTLE" (*British Hospital Ship*)—
    Torpedoed, but reaches port .. Mar. 10, 1918

GULLY RAVINE (*Dardanelles*)—
    Action of .. June 28—July 2, 1915

GUILLAUMAT, *General*—
    Succeeds General Sarrail as Allied Commander-in-Chief at Salonika .. Dec. 22, 1917
    Recalled .. June 6, 1918
    Appointed Governor of Paris .. June 15, 1918

GUILLEMONT (*Somme*)—
    Battle of .. .. Sept. 3-6, 1916

GUIMARÃES, *Dr.* Bernardino Machado—
    Appointed Portuguese Premier .. .. June 23, 1914
    Vacates .. .. Dec. 11, 1914
    Elected President .. .. Aug. 6, 1915
    Takes office .. .. Oct. 5, 1915
    Deposed .. .. Dec. 11, 1917

GUINEA (*Muni*), Spanish—
    German forces evacuate South Cameroons and cross border for internment in .. Feb. 17, 1916

GUISE (*France*)—
    First Battle of.. .. .. Aug. 29-30, 1914
    Second Battle of .. .. Nov. 4-5, 1918

"GULFLIGHT," S.S. (*United States*)—
    First United States ship attacked by German submarine .. .. .. May 1, 1915

GUMBINNEN (*East Prussia*)—
    Battle of. See under "Gawaiten-Gumbinnen."

GYUBA (*Darfur*)—
    Affair of .. .. Nov. 6, 1916

H

HAFIZ KOR (*North-West Frontier of India*)—
    First affair of .. .. Apr. 18, 1915
    Action of .. .. Sept. 5, 1915
    Second affair of .. .. Oct. 9, 1915
    Third affair of .. .. Nov. 15, 1916

HAGUE, The (*Holland*)—
    First meeting of Anglo-German Conference on Prisoners of War at .. .. June 9, 1918

HAIFA (*Palestine*)—
    Occupied by British forces .. .. Sept. 23, 1918

HAIG, *Field-Marshal Sir* Douglas—
    Appointed Commander-in-Chief of British Armies in France .. .. .. Dec. 19, 1915
    Promoted Field-Marshal .. .. Jan. 1, 1917
    Issues Order of the Day to the British Army in France *re* serious situation .. Apr. 12, 1918

HAITI, Republic of—
    Severs diplomatic relations with Germany .. .. June 16, 1917
    Declares war on Germany.. .. .. July 12, 1918

HAMADAN (*Western Persia*)—
    Occupied by Russian forces .. .. Dec. 14, 1915
    Taken by Turkish forces .. .. Aug. 10, 1916
    Recaptured by Russian forces .. .. Mar. 2, 1917
    Evacuated by Russian regular forces .. .. Mar. 16, 1918

HAMILTON, *General Sir* Ian—
    Appointed to command Mediterranean Expeditionary Force .. .. .. Mar. 12, 1915
    Recalled .. .. Oct. 15, 1915
    Relinquishes command .. .. Oct. 17, 1915

"HAMPSHIRE," H.M.S. (*Cruiser*)—
    Sunk .. .. June 5, 1916

HANDENI (*East Africa*)—
    Taken by British forces .. .. June 19, 1916

HANGÖ (*Finland*)—
    Russian cruiser "Pallada" sunk off .. .. Oct. 11, 1914
    German Expeditionary Force lands at .. .. Apr. 3, 1918

HANNA Position (*Mesopotamia*)—
    British attack on .. .. Jan. 21, 1916

"HANNA," S.S. (*Swedish*)—
    First neutral ship sunk by German submarine .. .. Mar. 13, 1915

HARA, TAKASHI—
    Appointed Japanese Prime Minister .. .. Sept. 29, 1918

HARRINGTON (*Cumberland*)—
    Shelled by German submarine .. .. Aug. 16, 1915

HARTLEPOOL (*Durham*)—
    Bombarded .. .. Dec. 16, 1914

HARWICH (*Essex*)—
    First contingent of German submarines surrender at .. .. Nov. 20, 1918

HAVRE, LE (*France*)—
    Belgian Government set up at .. .. Oct. 13, 1914

HAVRINCOURT (*France*)—
    Battle of .. .. Sept. 12, 1918

"HAWKE," H.M.S. (*Cruiser*)
    Sunk .. .. Oct. 15, 1914

HAZEBROUCK (*France*)—
    Taken by German forces .. .. Oct. 9, 1914
    Retaken by British forces .. .. Oct. 10, 1914
    Battle of .. .. Apr. 12-15, 1918

HEJAZ, The—
    I. BLOCKADE—
        By Entente, in support of revolution in—Begins .. .. .. May 15, 1916
    II. REVOLT—
        Under Sherif of Mecca—Begins .. .. June 5, 1916
    III. INDEPENDENCE—
        Declared .. .. June 7, 1916
    IV. KING—
        Sherif of Mecca—
            Proclaimed "King of the Arabs" .. .. Oct. 29, 1916
            Coronation .. .. Nov. 4, 1916
            Recognised by British Government as "King of the Hejaz" .. Dec. 15, 1916
        (See also under "Arabs" and "Mecca, Sherif of.")

    V. TREATIES, &c. See under "Commitments."

HEJAZ RAILWAY. See under "Ma'an."

HELLES, CAPE (*Gallipoli*)—
    Landing at—
        Begins .. .. Apr. 25, 1915
        Completed .. .. Apr. 26, 1915
    Evacuation of—
        Begins .. .. Jan. 7, 1916
        Completed .. .. Jan. 8, 1916

HELIGOLAND—
    Naval actions off .. .. { Aug. 28, 1914
                                                                                                                            Nov. 17, 1917

HELSINGFORS (*Finland*)—
    British submarines at, destroyed to avoid capture .. .. April 3-4, 1918
    Captured by German force .. .. Apr. 13, 1918

HENRY, *General* (*G.O.C. Allied Forces in Serbia*)—
    Concludes Armistice with Hungarian Government .. .. Nov. 15, 1918

HERBERTSHÖHE (*German New Guinea*)—
    Affair of .. .. Sept. 12, 1914

"HERMES," *H.M.S.* (*Cruiser*)—
    Sunk .. .. Oct. 31, 1914

HERTLING, *Count*—
    Succeeds Dr. Michaelis as German Imperial Chancellor .. .. .. Oct. 30, 1917
    Outlines German War Aims .. .. Jan. 24, 1918

HERZEGOVINA—
    British Foreign Minister gives pledge to Serbian Government as to eventual
        conditional cession of .. .. May 7, 1915
    British Foreign Minister gives guarantee as to eventual freedom and self-deter-
        mination of .. .. Aug. 30, 1915

"HIGHFLYER," *H.M.S.* (*Cruiser*)—
    Sinks German armed merchant cruiser "Kaiser Wilhelm der Grosse" .. .. Aug. 26, 1914

HILL 60 (*Ypres*)—
    Capture of .. .. Apr. 17-22, 1915

HILL 70 (*Lens*)—
    Battle of .. .. Aug. 15-25, 1917

"HILLS, BATTLE OF THE" (*Champagne*) .. .. Apr. 17-20, 1917
                (See also under "Champagne.")

HINDENBURG, *Field-Marshal* von—
    Appointed to command of German Eighth Army .. .. .. Aug. 23, 1914
    Appointed Commander-in-Chief of German Armies in Eastern Theatre .. Sept. 18, 1914
    Promoted Field-Marshal .. .. Nov. 27, 1914
    Succeeds General von Falkenhayn as Chief of the General Staff of the German
        Field Armies .. .. Aug. 29, 1916

HINDENBURG LINE, The—
    Battles of the—
        Begin .. .. Sept. 12, 1918
        End .. .. Oct. 9, 1918
        (See also under "Retreats.")

HINTZE, *Admiral* von—
    Appointed German Foreign Minister .. .. July 9, 1918
    Resigns .. .. Oct. 4, 1918

HIT (*Mesopotamia*)—
    Occupied by British forces .. .. Mar. 9, 1918

HODEIDA (*South Arabia*)—
    Taken by British forces .. .. Dec. 13, 1918

"HOGUE," *H.M.S.* (*Cruiser*)—
    Sunk .. .. Sept. 22, 1914

HOHENBORN, *General Count* Wild von—
    Appointed German Minister for War .. .. Jan. 21, 1915
    Resigns .. .. Oct. 30, 1916

HOLLAND. See under "Netherlands."

HOLY PLACES, MUSSULMAN—
    Government of India announce immunity of, during war .. .. .. Nov. 2, 1914

HOMS (*Syria*)—
    Occupied by British cavalry .. .. Oct. 15, 1918

HONDURAS—
    Severs diplomatic relations with Germany .. . . May 17, 1917
    Declares war on Germany .. .. July 19, 1918

HORVAT, *General*—
    Forms new Government at Vladivostok .. .. July 10, 1918
    Carries out *coup d'état* at Vladivostok .. .. Aug. 24, 1918

HOSKINS, *Major-General* A. R.—
    Succeeds General Smuts in command of British forces, East Africa .. .. Jan. 20, 1917
    Succeeded by General van Deventer .. .. May 30, 1917

HOSPITAL SHIPS—
    "Rohilla"—Wrecked .. .. Oct. 30, 1914
    "Anglia"—Sunk by mine .. .. Nov. 17, 1915
    "Galeka"—Damaged by mine, total wreck .. .. Oct. 28, 1916
    "Britannic"—Sunk by mine .. .. Nov. 21, 1916
    "Braemar Castle"—Damaged (possibly mined) and beached .. .. .. Nov. 23, 1916
    "Glenart Castle"—Damaged by mine .. .. Mar. 1, 1917
    "Salta"—Sunk by mine .. .. Apr. 10, 1917
    "Goorkha"—Damaged by mine .. .. Oct. 10, 1917
    "Koningin Regentes" (**Dutch**)—Sunk by mine or torpedo .. .. .. June 6, 1918
    German Government threaten to sink, by submarine .. .. Jan. 31, 1917
    Ships attacked—
        British—
            "Asturias"—Torpedoed and beached .. .. Mar. 21, 1917
            "Gloucester Castle"—Damaged by torpedo .. .. Mar. 30, 1917
            "Lanfranc" (Ambulance Transport)—Sunk .. .. Apr. 17, 1917
            "Donegal" (Ambulance Transport)—Sunk .. .. Apr. 17, 1917
            "Dover Castle"—Sunk .. .. May 26, 1917
            "Rewa"—Sunk .. .. Jan. 4, 1918
            "Glenart Castle"—Sunk .. .. Feb. 26, 1918
            "Guildford Castle"—Torpedoed, but reaches port .. .. .. Mar. 10, 1918
            "Llandovery Castle"—Sunk . .. . June 27, 1918
            "Warilda" (Ambulance Transport)—Sunk .. .. Aug. 3, 1918
        Russian—
            "Portugal"—Sunk .. .. Mar. 30, 1916
            "Vpered"—Sunk .. .. July 10, 1916

HOSTILITIES. See under respective countries.

HÖTZENDORFF, *Field-Marshal* Conrad von (*C.-in-C. Austro-Hungarian Armies*)—
    Relieved of his command .. .. July 16, 1918

HOWARD, *Sir* Henry—
    Appointed British Envoy to the Vatican .. .. Dec. 7, 1914

HSUAN-FUNG (*Manchu Emperor*)—
    Restored to the throne .. .. July 1, 1917
    Abdicates .. .. July 7, 1917

HSU-SHIH-CHANG—
    Elected President of China .. .. Sept. 4, 1918

HUNGARY—
    INVASIONS of North, by Russian forces—
        First—
            Begins .. .. Sept. 24, 1914
            Ends .. .. Oct. 8, 1914
        Second—
            Begins .. .. Nov. 15, 1914
            Ends .. .. Dec. 12, 1914
    ARMISTICE—With Entente Powers—
        Concluded by Austria-Hungary .. .. Nov. 3, 1918
        Concluded at Belgrade by Hungarian Government separately .. .. Nov. 15, 1918
    REVOLUTION—Begins in Budapest .. .. Oct. 31, 1918
    INDEPENDENT GOVERNMENT—Formed .. .. Nov. 1, 1918
    INDEPENDENCE—Declared .. .. Nov. 16, 1918
    RUMANIANS of—Declare their union with Rumania .. .. .. Dec. 1, 1918
    MINISTERS—
        I. PREMIER—
            (A.) UNDER JOINT MONARCHY—
                1. **Tisza,** *Count*—
                    Appointed .. .. June 10, 1913
                    Resigns .. .. May 23, 1917
                2. **Esterhazy,** *Count*—
                    Appointed .. .. June 15, 1917
                    Resigns .. .. Aug. 9, 1917
                3. **Wekerle,** *Dr.*—
                    Appointed .. .. Aug. 21, 1917
                    Resigns .. .. Apr. 17, 1918
                    Again appointed .. .. Apr. 27, 1918
                    Resigns .. .. Oct. 24, 1918
            (B.) INDEPENDENT GOVERNMENT—
                Karolyi, *Count*—Appointed .. .. Nov. 1, 1918

HUSSEIN KAMEL, *Prince*—
    Proclaimed Sultan of Egypt .. .. Dec. 19, 1914
    Dies .. .. Oct. 9, 1917

HYMANS, *M.* P.—
    Appointed Belgian Minister for Foreign Affairs .. .. Jan. 1, 1918

I

IBN SA'UD. See under "Nejd, Emir of."

IDRISI (*Arabs*)—
    Farasan Islands occupied by the .. .. Jan. 31, 1915
    British Government conclude Treaty with the .. .. Apr. 28, 1915

IMAD (*Aden*)—
    Affair of .. .. Oct. 22, 1918

"IMPERATRITSA MARIYA" (*Russian Battleship*)—
    Blown up .. .. Oct. 20, 1916

IMPERIAL WAR CONFERENCE. See under "Conference."

"INDEFATIGABLE," H.M.S. (*Battle Cruiser*)—
    Sunk .. .. May 31, 1916

INDEPENDENCE, DECLARATIONS OF—*
    Azerbaijan .. .. May 26, 1918
    Bessarabia .. .. Dec. 23, 1917
    Czecho-Slovaks .. .. Oct. 21, 1918
    Don Cossacks .. .. June 4, 1918
    Estonia .. .. Jan. 13, 1918
    Finland .. .. Dec. 6, 1917
    Fiume .. .. Oct. 30, 1918
    Georgia .. .. May 26, 1918
    Hejaz .. .. June 7, 1916
    Hungary .. .. Nov. 16, 1918
    Latvia .. .. Jan. 12, 1918
    Poland .. .. Nov. 16, 1918
    †Siberia .. .. July 4, 1918
    Trans-Caucasia .. .. Apr. 22, 1918
    Ukraine, The .. .. Nov. 20, 1917
    Yugo-Slavs .. .. Oct. 29, 1918

INDIA—
    INDIAN EXPEDITIONARY FORCES—
        I.E.F. "A"—
            First units—
                Leave India .. .. Aug. 24, 1914
                Arrive at Suez .. .. Sept. 9, 1914
                Leave Egypt for France .. .. Sept. 19, 1914
                Land at Marseilles .. .. Sept. 26, 1914
                Reach Flanders front .. .. Oct. 19, 1914
                Leave France for Mesopotamia .. .. .. Nov. 10, 1915
        I.E.F. "B"—
            First units—
                Leave India .. .. Oct. 16, 1914
                Arrive at Mombasa .. .. Oct. 31, 1914
        I.E.F. "C"—
            First unit—
                Leaves India .. .. Aug. 19, 1914
                Arrives at Mombasa .. .. Sept. 1, 1914
                Amalgamation with I.E.F. "B" ordered‡ .. .. Dec. 31, 1914
        I.E.F. "D"—
            First units—
                Leave India .. .. Oct. 16, 1914
                Reach Bahrein Islands .. .. Oct. 23, 1914
                Land in Mesopotamia .. .. Nov. 6, 1914
        I.E.F. "E"§—
            First units—Formed in Egypt from details of I.E.F. "A" .. .. Oct. 2, 1914
        I.E.F. "F"§—
            First units—
                Leave India .. .. Nov. 2, 1914
                Land in Egypt .. .. Nov. 16, 1914
                Amalgamated with I.E.F. "E" .. .. .. Mar. 25, 1915
        I.E.F. "G"—
            First Indian units—Leave Egypt .. .. Apr. 7, 1915
            Last units leave Gallipoli to amalgamate with I.E.F. "E" .. Dec. 29, 1915

"INDICATOR" NETS—
    First submarine destroyed by aid of .. .. Mar. 4, 1915

* Iceland also declared independence, but is not included, as Denmark was a neutral country.
† Declaration cancelled on 6th November, 1918.
‡ Combined force designated I.E.F. "B."
§ These two forces were not officially designated in this manner by the Government of India until the 4th December, 1914.

INTERNATIONAL CONFERENCE. See under "Conference, International."

"INVINCIBLE," H.M.S. (Battle Cruiser)—
    Sunk .. .. May 31, 1916

IPEK (Montenegro)—
    Taken by Austrian forces.. .. .. Dec. 6, 1915
    Retaken by Italian forces.. .. .. Oct. 14, 1918

IRELAND—
    Roger Casement lands in, and is arrested .. .. Apr. 20, 1916
    Rebellion breaks out in .. .. Apr. 24, 1916
    Martial Law proclaimed in Dublin and county .. .. Apr. 27, 1916
    Rebellion in, collapses .. .. May 1, 1916
    Leaders of rebellion executed .. .. May 3, 1916
    Conscription extended to .. .. Apr. 10, 1918
    Lord French appointed Lord-Lieutenant of .. .. May 5, 1918
    Sinn Fein leaders arrested and interned .. .. May 17, 1918
    Account of Irish-German plots in, published by British Government .. .. May 25, 1918

IRINGA (German East Africa)—
    Occupied by British forces .. .. Aug. 29, 1916

IRISH SEA—
    First operations of German submarine in .. .. Jan. 29, 1915

IRKUTSK (Siberia)—
    Occupied by Czecho-Slovak forces .. .. July 13, 1918
    British troops from Vladivostok reach .. .. Oct. 14, 1918

IRONSIDE, Major-General W. E.—
    Takes over command at Archangel.. .. .. Oct. 4, 1918

"IRRESISTIBLE," H.M.S. (Battleship)—
    Sunk .. .. Mar. 18, 1915

ISHII, Viscount—
    Appointed Japanese Minister for Foreign Affairs .. .. Sept. 21, 1915
    Resigns .. .. Oct. 9, 1916

ISHTIP (Serbia)—
    Taken by Bulgarian forces .. .. Oct. 19, 1915
    Retaken by Serbian forces .. .. Sept. 25, 1918

ISLANDS, PACIFIC, GERMAN (North of Equator)—
    British Government agree to Japanese request that Australia should not occupy .. Dec. 3, 1914
    Japanese Government declare Japan will not give up .. .. Dec. 16, 1914
    British Government gives conditional promise of support to Japanese claim to .. Feb. 14, 1917

ISLAZ (Rumania)—
    Austro-German army crosses Danube at .. .. Nov. 23, 1916

ISONZO, River (Italy)—
    First Battle of the .. .. June 29—July 7, 1915
    Second   „ .. .. July 18—Aug. 10, 1915
    Third   „ .. .. Oct. 18—Nov. 3, 1915
    Fourth   „ .. .. Nov. 10—Dec. 10, 1915
    Fifth   „ .. .. Feb. 15—Mar. 17, 1916
    Sixth   „ .. .. Aug. 6-17, 1916
    Seventh   „ .. .. Sept. 14-18, 1916
    Eighth   „ .. .. Oct. 9-12, 1916
    Ninth   „ .. .. Oct. 31—Nov. 4, 1916
    Tenth   „ .. .. May 12—June 8, 1917
    Eleventh   „ .. .. Aug. 17—Sept. 12, 1917
    Twelfth   „ .. .. Oct. 24—Dec. 26, 1917

ISTABULAT (*Mesopotamia*)—
    Action of .. .. Apr. 21–22, 1917

ITALY—

NEUTRALITY—Declares .. .. Aug. 3, 1914
DENOUNCES THE TRIPLE ALLIANCE .. .. May 4, 1915
MOBILISATION—
    Ordered .. .. May 23, 1915
RELATIONS (severed)—
    By Germany .. .. *May 24, 1915
WAR (declared) on—
    Austria-Hungary .. .. May 23, 1915
    Turkey .. .. Aug. 21, 1915
    Bulgaria .. .. Oct. 19, 1915
    Germany .. .. Aug. 28, 1916
MINISTERS—
  I. PREMIER—
    1. Salandra, *Signor*—
      Appointed .. .. Mar. 24, 1914
      Remains Premier on reconstitution of Cabinet .. .. Oct. 30, 1914
      Proffers resignation .. .. May 13, 1915
      Remains Premier on reconstitution of Cabinet .. .. May 16, 1915
      Resigns .. .. June 11, 1916
    2. Boselli, *Signor*—
      Appointed .. .. June 15, 1916
      Resigns .. .. Oct. 25, 1917
    3. Orlando, *Signor*—Appointed .. .. Oct. 29, 1917
  II. FOREIGN MINISTER—
    1. San Giuliano, *Marquis* di—
      Appointed .. .. Mar. 24, 1914
      Dies .. .. Oct. 16, 1914
    2. Sonnino, *Baron*—
      Appointed .. .. Nov. 3, 1914
      Resigns .. .. May 13, 1915
      Reappointed .. .. May 16, 1915
ARMY—
  I. COMMANDER-IN-CHIEF†—
    1. Cadorna, *General*—
      Appointed .. .. May 23, 1915
      Relieved .. .. Nov. 7, 1917
    2. Diaz, *General*—Appointed .. .. Nov. 7, 1917
  II. ITALIAN EXPEDITIONARY FORCES—
    To **Valona** (Albania)—
      First troops land .. .. Dec. 26, 1914
      Formally occupied .. .. May 29, 1915
    To **Salonika**—First units land .. .. Aug. 12, 1916
    To **Corfu**—Troops land .. .. Feb. 11, 1916
    To **France**—Troops arrive‡ .. .. Apr. 27, 1918
    To **North Russia**—First units land .. .. Sept. 2, 1918
  ITALIAN LEGION IN FRANCE (Garibaldi's volunteers)—
    In action for first time .. .. Dec. 26, 1914
ALLIED EXPEDITIONARY FORCES TO ITALY—
  Arrival announced—
    French .. .. Nov. 3, 1917
    British .. .. Nov. 4, 1917
    United States .. .. June 30, 1918
FLEET—
  Commences operations in the Adriatic .. .. May 25 1915
  Joined by British Battle Squadron .. .. May 27, 1915

TREATIES, &c.—
  Secret agreement concluded with Entente for military co-operation .. .. Apr. 26, 1915
    See also under "Commitments."

IVANGOROD (*Poland*)—

Battle of (*German*) .. .. Oct. 9–20, 1914
Invested by Austro-German forces .. .. July 21, 1915
Taken by Austro-German forces .. .. Aug. 5, 1915

IZZET, *Pasha*—

Appointed Grand Vizier of Turkey .. .. Oct. 13, 1918

    * See footnote, Part 1.
    † Officially "Chief of Staff," the King being "Commander-in-Chief."
    ‡ Approximate date.

J

JACKSON, *Admiral Sir* Henry—
    Appointed First Sea Lord, Great Britain .. .. May 28, 1915
    Resigns .. .. Dec. 3, 1916

JADAR, River *(Serbia)*—
    Battle of the ("Battle of the Tser and the Jadar").. .. .. .. Aug. 17–21, 1914

JAGOW, *Herr* von—
    Appointed German Foreign Minister .. .. Jan. —, 1913
    Resigns .. .. Nov. 20, 1916

JAFFA *(Palestine)*—
    Occupied by British forces .. .. Nov. 16, 1917
    Battle of .. .. Dec. 21–22, 1917

JAKALSWATER *(German South-West Africa)*—
    Action of .. .. Mar. 20, 1915

JAKOBSTADT *(Baltic Provinces)*—
    Taken by German forces .. .. Sept. 21–22, 1917

JANINA *(Greece)*—
    Occupied by Italian forces .. .. June 8, 1917

JAPAN—
  ULTIMATUM—
    To China—
      Presented .. .. May 7, 1915
      Accepted .. .. May 9, 1915
      To Germany—Presented .. .. Aug. 15, 1914
  RELATIONS (severed)—
    By Germany .. .. Aug. 23, 1914
    By Austria-Hungary .. .. Aug. 24, 1914
  WAR (declared)—
    On Germany .. .. Aug. 23, 1914
    On Austria-Hungary .. .. Aug. 25, 1914
  HOSTILITIES—With Central Powers—Commenced .. .. Sept. 2, 1914
  PEACE PROPOSALS—
    Japanese Government inform British Government of German overtures for a
      separate peace .. .. Apr. 14, 1915
  MINISTERS—
    Prime Minister—
      1. Marquis Okuma—
        Appointed .. .. April 16, 1914
        Resigns .. .. Oct. 9, 1916
      2. Count Terauchi—
        Appointed .. .. Oct. 9, 1916
        Resigns .. .. Sept. 29, 1918
      3. Hara, Takashi—
        Appointed .. .. Sept. 29, 1918
    Minister for Foreign Affairs—
      1. Viscount Kato—
        Appointed .. .. April 16, 1914
        Resigns .. .. Aug. 9, 1915
      2. Marquis Okuma—
        Appointed (*ad interim*) .. .. Aug. 10, 1915
        Resigns .. .. Sept. 21, 1915
      3. Viscount Ishii—
        Appointed .. .. Sept. 21, 1915
        Resigns .. .. Oct. 9, 1916
      4. Count Terauchi—
        Appointed (*ad interim*) .. .. Oct. 9, 1916
        Resigns .. .. Nov. 20, 1916

JAPAN (continued)—
    MINISTERS (continued)—
        Minister for Foreign Affairs (continued)—
          5. Viscount Motono—
            Appointed .. .. Nov. 21, 1916
            Resigns .. .. April 21, 1918
          6. Baron Goto—
            Appointed .. .. April 22, 1918
            Resigns .. .. Sept. 28, 1918
          7. Count Yasuya Uchida—
            Appointed .. .. Sept. 29, 1918
        Minister for War—
          1. Lieutenant-General Oka—
            Appointed .. .. April 16, 1914
            Resigns .. .. Mar. 29, 1916
          2. Lieutenant-General Kenichi Oshima—
            Appointed .. .. Mar. 30, 1916
            Resigns .. .. Sept. 29, 1918
          3. Lieutenant-General Baron Giichi Tanaka—
            Appointed .. .. Sept. 30, 1918
    ARMY—Japanese Cabinet decide not to send troops to Europe .. .. Nov. 14, 1914
    NAVY—
        Japanese Cabinet decide not to send warships to Europe .. .. .. Nov. 14, 1914
        British request for Japanese naval assistance—Formulated .. .. Feb. 8, 1916
        Japanese Flotilla arrives in the Mediterranean .. .. Apr. 17, 1917
        British request that Japan should send two battle cruisers to join the Grand
          Fleet in the North Sea—Unable to comply .. .. Nov. 15, 1917
    TREATIES, &c. See under "Commitments."

JAROSLAW (Galicia)—
    Taken by Russian forces .. .. Sept. 21, 1914
    Retaken by Austro-German forces .. .. May 14, 1915

JASIN (East Africa)—
    Captured by British forces .. .. Dec. 21, 1914
    Recaptured by German forces .. .. Jan. 19, 1915

"JASON," H.M.S. (Torpedo Gunboat)—
    Sunk by mine .. .. Apr. 3, 1917

JASSY (Rumania)—
    Rumanian Government transferred from Bukharest to .. .. .. Dec. 1, 1916
    Deputation from National Council of the Bukovina (q.v.) arrive at .. Dec. 7, 1918

"JEHAD"—
    Sheikh ul Islam issues Fatwa, declaring against Entente .. .. Nov. 11, 1914
    Proclaimed by Sultan of Turkey .. .. Nov. 14, 1914

JELLICOE, Admiral Sir John—
    Assumes command of the Grand Fleet .. .. Aug. 4, 1914
    Resigns .. .. Nov. 29, 1916
    Appointed First Sea Lord, Great Britain .. .. Dec. 4, 1916
    Resigns .. .. Dec. 26, 1917

JERICHO (Palestine)—
    Taken by British forces .. .. Feb. 21, 1918

JERUSALEM—
    Surrenders to British forces .. .. Dec. 9, 1917
    General Allenby makes formal entry into .. .. Dec. 11, 1917
    British defence of .. .. Dec. 26-30, 1917

JIDDA (Arabia)—
    Captured by Arab forces .. .. June 9, 1916

JIU, TÂRGA. See under "Târga Jiu."

JOFFRE, *Marshal* Joseph—
    Appointed Chief of French General Staff .. .. July 28, 1911
    Appointed Commander-in-Chief French Armies .. .. Dec. 3, 1915
    Vacates appointment and becomes Technical Military Adviser to French War
        Cabinet .. .. Dec. 12, 1916
    Created Marshal of France .. .. Dec. 26, 1916

JONNART, *M.*—
    Appointed French Minister for Blockade .. .. Nov. 16, 1917
    Resigns .. .. Nov. 23, 1917

JORDAN, River (*Palestine*)—
    Passage of, by British forces .. .. Mar. 21-23, 1918

"JULNAR," H.M.S. (*River Gunboat*)—
    Destroyed on the Tigris .. .. Apr. 24, 1916

JUTLAND—
    Battle of—
        Begins .. .. May 31, 1916
        Ends .. .. June 1, 1916

K

KAAKIIKA (*Trans-Caspia*)—
    Affair near .. .. Aug. 28, 1918

KACHANIK PASS (*Serbia*)—
    Battle of .. .. Nov. 5-8, 1915

KADISH (*North Russia*)—
    Taken by Allied forces .. .. Dec. 30, 1918

KAHE (*German East Africa*)—
    Action of .. .. Mar. 21, 1916

KAISER WILHELM II—
    Promises support to Austria and leaves for cruise .. .. July 5, 1914
    Returns from the Baltic to Berlin .. .. July 26, 1914
    Crosses frontier into Holland .. .. Nov. 10, 1918
    Signs abdication.. .. .. Nov. 28, 1918

"KAISER WILHELM DER GROSSE" (*German Armed Merchant Cruiser*)—
    Leaves Bremen .. .. Aug. 4, 1914
    Sunk by H.M.S. "Highflyer" .. .. Aug. 26, 1914

"KAISERIN ELISABETH" (*Austrian Cruiser*)—
    Sunk .. .. Nov. 2, 1914

KALEDIN, *General* (*Russia*)—
    Commits suicide . .. . Feb. 13, 1918

KALOGEROPOULOS, *Professor*—
    Appointed Greek Premier .. .. Sept. 16, 1916
    Resigns .. .. Oct. 3, 1916

KAMEL, HUSSEIN, *Prince*—
    Proclaimed Sultan of Egypt .. .. Dec. 19, 1914
    Dies .. .. Oct. 9, 1917

KAMINA (*Togoland*)—
    Allied advance on, from Lome begins .. .. Aug. 13, 1914
    Surrenders to Allied forces .. .. Aug. 26, 1914

KANGEVAR (*West Persia*)—
    Occupied by a Russian force .. .. Dec. 25, 1915

KARA URGAN (*Caucasus*)—
    Battle of .. .. Jan 8–13, 1915

KARELIA—
    British Government inform Finnish Government that they are not hostile to Finnish
        aspirations in .. .. Aug. 8, 1918

KARIND (*West Persia*)—
    Occupied by a Russian force (later withdrawn) .. .. Mar. 12, 1916
    Again occupied by a Russian force.. .. .. Mar. 17, 1917

KARL, *Emperor*—
    Succeeds Francis Joseph as Emperor of Austria .. .. Nov. 21, 1916
    Proclaims a Federal State on principle of nationality .. .. Oct. 16, 1918
    Makes over Austro-Hungarian fleet to Yugo-Slav National Council .. .. Oct. 31, 1918
    Abdicates .. .. Nov. 12, 1918

" KARLSRUHE " (*German Cruiser*)—
    Action with the British light cruiser " Bristol " in West Indies.. .. .. Aug. 6, 1914
    Sunk by internal explosion .. .. Nov. 4, 1914

KAROLYI, *Count*—
    Appointed Hungarian Premier . .. . Nov. 1, 1918

KARONGA (*Nyasaland*)—
    Affair near .. .. Sept. 9, 1914

KARS (*Georgia*)—
    Occupied by Turkish forces .. .. Apr. 27, 1918

KASAMA (*Rhodesia*)—
    Taken by German forces .. .. Nov. 9, 1918

KASVIN (*West Persia*)—
    Occupied by a Russian force .. .. Nov. 2, 1915

KATO, *Viscount*—
    Appointed Japanese Minister for Foreign Affairs .. .. Apr. 16, 1914
    Resigns .. .. Aug. 9, 1915

KATTEGAT, The—
    British naval raids on—
        First .. .. Nov. 2, 1917
        Second .. .. Apr. 15, 1918

KAVALA (*Greece*)—
 Greek IVth Army Corps surrenders to the Germans at..   Sept. 18, 1916

KAWACHI " (*Japanese Battleship*)—
 Sunk by internal explosion   July 12, 1918

KAZAN (*East Russia*)—
 Taken by Czecho-Slovak force   July 14, 1918

KEM (*North Russia*)—
 Occupied by Allied forces..   June 7, 1918

KEMMEL RIDGE (*Flanders*)—
 First Battle of..   Apr. 17–19, 1918
 Second Battle of   Apr. 25–26, 1918
 Evacuated by German forces   Aug. 31, 1918

KERENSKI, M.—
 Appointed Russian War Minister   May 16, 1917
 Succeeds Prince Lvov as Premier of Russia—
  1. Temporarily   July 19, 1917
  2. Definitely   Aug. 6, 1917
 Assumes Dictatorship   Sept. 10, 1917
 Bolshevik *coup d'état* deposes   Nov. 8, 1917
 Forces of, defeated near Petrograd..   Nov. 13, 1917
 Flight of   Nov. 15, 1917

KEUPRI-KEUI (*Armenia*) —
 Taken by Russian forces ..   Nov. 6, 1914
 Retaken by Turkish forces   Nov. 14, 1914
 Again taken by Russian forces   Nov. 22, 1914
 Again retaken by Turkish forces   Dec. 17, 1914
 Again taken by Russian forces   Jan. 17, 1916
 Reoccupied by Turkish forces   *Apr. 1, 1918

KHABAROVSK (*Siberia*)—
 Taken by Japanese forces..   Sept. 5, 1918

KHANAQIN (*North-East of Baghdad*)—
 Taken by Russian forces ..   May 15, 1916
 Evacuated by Russian forces   June 5, 1916
 Again occupied by Russian forces ..   Apr. 4, 1917

KHAN BAGHDADI (*Mesopotamia*)—
 Action of ..   Mar. 26–27, 1918

KHARKOV (*South Russia*)—
 Captured by German forces   Apr. 8, 1918

KHEDIVE OF EGYPT (*Abbas Hilmi*)—
 Deposed   Dec. 19, 1914

KHORASAN (*Persia*)—
 Extension of British East Persia cordon to, begins   Feb. 1, 1918

* Approximate date.

KIEL—
    Mutiny in the German fleet at .. .. Aug. 3, 1917
    Mutiny in the German fleet at .. . . Nov. 3, 1918

KIEV (*The Ukraine*)—
    Occupied by German forces .. .. Mar. 2, 1918
    Occupied by (*Petlyura's*) Ukrainian revolutionary forces .. .. .. Dec. 20, 1918

KIGGELL, *Lieut.-General Sir L. E.*—
    Appointed Chief of the General Staff, B.E.F., France .. . . Dec. 22, 1915
    Resigns .. .. Jan. 27, 1918

KILIMANJARO (*East Africa*)—
    Operations for conquest of—
        Begin .. .. Mar. 5, 1916
        End .. .. Mar. 21, 1916

KILIMATINDE (*East Africa*)—
    Taken by British forces .. .. July 31, 1916

KILOSA (*East Africa*)—
    Taken by British forces .. .. Aug. 22, 1916

KILWA (*German East Africa*)—
    Occupied by British Naval forces .. .. Sept. 7, 1916

"KING EDWARD VII," H.M.S. (*Battleship*)—
    Sunk .. .. Jan. 6, 1916

"KINGANI" (*German Gunboat*)—
    Captured on Lake Tanganyika .. . . Dec. 26, 1915

KIONGA (*German East Africa*)—
    Occupied by Portuguese forces .. .. Apr. 11, 1916

KIRKUK (*Mesopotamia*)—
    Taken by British forces .. .. May 7, 1918
    Evacuated by British forces .. .. May 24, 1918
    Again taken by British forces .. .. Oct. 25, 1918

KIRMAN (*East Africa*)—
    Occupied by British forces .. .. June 12, 1916

KIRMANSHAH (*Persia*)—
    Occupied by Turkish forces .. .. Jan. 13, 1916
    Occupied by Russian forces .. .. Feb. 26, 1916
    Retaken by Turkish forces .. .. July 1, 1916
    Again taken by Russian forces .. .. Mar. 11, 1917
    Occupied by British forces .. .. Feb. 25, 1918

KISAKI (*German East Africa*)—
    Affair of .. .. Sept. 7, 1916

KISHINEV (*Bessarabia*)—
    Moldavian Republic proclaimed at .. .. Dec. 23, 1917

KITCHENER, *Field-Marshal Earl*—
    Appointed Minister for War, Great Britain .. .. Aug. 6, 1914
    Visits France to confer with Sir John French .. .. Sept. 1, 1914
    Leaves England for the Dardanelles .. .. Nov. 4, 1915
    Arrives in the Dardanelles .. .. Nov. 10, 1915
    Lost at sea .. .. June 5, 1916

"KLÉBER" (*French Cruiser*)—
    Sunk .. .. June 27, 1917

KOLCHAK, *Admiral*—
    Proclaimed dictator of all Russia after counter-revolutionary *coup d'état*.. .. Nov. 18, 1918

"KÖLN" (*German Light Cruiser*)—
    Sunk .. .. Aug. 28, 1914

KOLUBARA, River (*Serbia*)—
    Battle of the .. .. Dec. 3-6, 1914

"KOMET" (*German Gunboat*)—
    Captured by H.M.A.S. "Nusa" .. .. Oct. 11, 1914

KONDOA IRANGI (*East Africa*)—
    British attack on, begins .. .. Apr. 17, 1916
    Occupied by British forces .. .. Apr. 19, 1916
    German attack on—
        Begins .. .. June 9, 1916
        Repulsed .. .. June 10, 1916

"KÖNIGSBERG" (*German Cruiser*)—
    (First)—
        Sinks H.M.S. "Pegasus" at Zanzibar .. .. Sept. 20, 1914
        Located in Rufiji River .. .. Oct. 31, 1914
        Destroyed in Rufiji river by British monitors .. .. .. July 11, 1915
    (Second)—With German naval delegates enters Firth of Forth to arrange surrender
        of German fleet .. .. Nov. 15, 1918

"KÖNIGIN LUISE" (*German Minelayer*)—
    Sunk .. .. Aug. 5, 1914

"KONINGIN REGENTES" (*Dutch Hospital Ship*)—
    Sunk .. .. June 6, 1918

KÖRBER, *Dr.* Ernst von—
    Appointed Austrian Premier .. .. Oct. 28, 1916
    Resigns .. .. Dec. 14, 1916

KORNILOV, *General*—
    Succeeds General Brusilov as Russian Commander-in-Chief .. .. Aug. 1, 1917
    Leads revolt against Provisional Government and marches on Petrograd .. Sept. 8, 1917
    Revolt of, collapses .. .. Sept. 13, 1917
    Surrenders to Provisional Government .. .. Sept. 14, 1917

KOSTURINO (*Bulgaria*)—
    Actions of .. .. Dec. 7-8, 1915

KOWNO (*Lithuania*)—
    Stormed by German forces .. .. Aug. 17-18, 1915

KRAGUJEVATZ (*Serbia*)—
    Taken by Austrian forces.. .. .. Nov. 1, 1915

KRASNIK (*Poland*)—
    First Battle of .. .. Aug. 23-25, 1914
    Second Battle of .. .. July 1-19, 1915

KRASNOVODSK (*Caspian Sea*)—
    Occupied by British forces .. .. Aug. 27, 1918

"KRIEGSGEFAHR," State of—
    Proclaimed in Germany .. .. July 31, 1914

KRITHIA (*Gallipoli*)—
    First Battle of .. .. Apl. 28, 1915
    Second Battle of—
        Begins .. .. May 6, 1915
        Ends . .. . May 8, 1915
    Third Battle of .. .. June 4, 1915

KRIVOLAK (*Macedonia*)—
    First action of .. .. Oct. 24, 1915
    Second action of.. .. .. Oct. 30, 1915
    Third action of .. .. Nov. 3-5, 1915
    Evacuated by French forces .. .. Dec. 2, 1915

"KRONPRINZ WILHELM" (*German Armed Merchant Cruiser*)—
    Interned at Newport News, U.S.A... .. .. Apr. 26, 1915

KRONSTADT (*Transylvania*). See under "Brasov."

KRUPP WORKS (*Essen*)—
    French air raid on .. .. Sept. 24, 1916

KUHLMANN, *Dr.* Richard—
    Appointed German Foreign Minister .. .. Aug. 5, 1917
    Resigns .. .. July 9, 1918

KUMANOVO (*Serbia*)—
    Taken by Bulgarian forces .. .. Oct. 22, 1915

KURDAMIR (*East Caucasus*)—
    Occupied by Turkish forces .. .. June 12, 1918

KURLAND—
    German protectorate over, proclaimed .. .. Mar. 15, 1918
        (See also under "Baltic Provinces.")

KUT AL AMARA (*Mesopotamia*)—
    Battle of, 1915 .. .. Sept. 28, 1915
    British Army retreating from Ctesiphon reaches .. .. Dec. 3, 1915
    Siege of—Begins .. .. Dec. 7, 1915
    Turkish Christmas Eve attack on .. .. Dec. 24-25, 1915

KUT AL AMARA (*Mesopotamia*) (*continued*)—
    *Relief operations—
        First attempt—
            Relieving force begins advance from 'Ali Gharbi   Jan. 4, 1916
            Attempt fails   Jan. 21, 1916
        Second attempt—Relieving force repulsed   Mar. 8, 1916
        Third attempt—
            Begins   Apr. 1, 1916
            Fails   Apr. 22, 1916
        Garrison capitulates to the Turks   Apr. 29, 1916
        Turks evacuate As Sinn position and withdraw to   May 19, 1916
        British offensive for capture of, begins   Dec. 13, 1916
    Battle of, 1917:—
        Begins   Jan. 9, 1917
        Town reoccupied by the British   Feb. 23, 1917
        Ends   Feb. 24, 1917

KWASH (*East Persia*)—
    Occupied by British forces   May 11, 1916

L

LA BASSÉE. See under "Bassée, La."

LA MALMAISON. See under "Malmaison, La."

LABOUR CONFERENCE—
    I. International Conference at Stockholm—
        British Labour Party decide to send Delegates to   Aug. 10, 1917
        British Government refuse passports for Delegates to   Aug. 13, 1917
    II. Inter-Allied Conference in London—
        Passes resolution as to War Aims   Feb. 23, 1918

"LACONIA," S.S. (*British*)—
    Sunk by submarine   Feb. 25, 1917
    Statement by President Wilson as to sinking of   Feb. 27, 1917

LAHEJ (*South Arabia*)—
    Taken by Turkish forces   July 4–5, 1915
    Reoccupied by British forces   Dec. 9, 1918

LAIBACH. See under "Ljubljana."

LAKE, *Lieut.-General Sir Percy*—
    Appointed Commander-in-Chief in Mesopotamia   Jan. 14, 1916
    Takes over command   Jan. 19, 1916
    Resigns   Aug. 28, 1916

LANGEMARCK (*Flanders*)—
    Battles of, 1914   Oct. 21–24, 1914
    Battle of, 1917   Aug. 16–18, 1917

"LANFRANC" (*British Ambulance Transport*)—
    Sunk   Apr. 17, 1917

LANSING, Mr.—
    Succeeds Mr. Bryan as United States Secretary of State   June 24, 1915

LAON (*France*)—
    Occupied by German forces   Aug. 30, 1914
    Retaken by French forces   Oct. 13, 1918

* For detail of actions in these operations see Part II.

LARAGNE (*France*)—
    German airship "L. 45" shot down at .. .. Oct. 20, 1917

LARISSA (*Greece*)—
    Occupied by Entente forces .. .. June 12, 1917

LATEMA NEK (*East Africa*)—
    Action of .. .. Mar. 11–12, 1916

LATVIA—
    I. Independence of, declared .. .. Jan. 12, 1918
    II. Provisional Government—
        Recognised by British Government as an Independent Government.. .. Nov. 11, 1918

LAWRENCE, *Lieut.-General the Hon. Sir H. A.*—
    Appointed Chief of the General Staff, B.E.F., France .. .. Jan. 24, 1918

LE CATEAU. See under "Cateau, Le."

LEBRUN, *M.*—
    Appointed French Minister of Blockade .. .. Nov. 23, 1917

"LEINSTER," *S.S.* (*Irish Mail Boat*)—
    Sunk .. .. Oct. 10, 1918

"LEIPZIG" (*German Light Cruiser*)—
    Joins Admiral von Spee at Easter Island .. .. Oct. 14, 1914
    Sunk .. .. Dec. 8, 1914

LEMBERG (*Galicia*)—
    First Battle of .. .. Aug. 26–30, 1914
        City captured by the Russian forces .. .. Sept. 3, 1914
    Second Battle of .. .. Sept. 8–11, 1914
    Third Battle of .. .. June 17–22, 1915
        City recaptured by the Austro-German forces .. .. .. June 22, 1915
        Taken by Polish forces .. .. Nov. 23, 1918

LEMNOS ISLAND (*Ægean*)—
    Occupied by British marines .. .. Feb. 23, 1915
    Greek Government request explanation as to occupation of .. .. Mar. 7, 1915
    British Government send reply as to occupation of .. .. .. Mar. 9, 1915
    British Government guarantee eventual cession by Turkey of, to Greece.. .. Mar. 20, 1915

LENIN, *M.* Vladimir Ilich Ulianov—
    Assumes power in Petrograd .. .. Nov. 8, 1917

LENS (*France*)—
    Occupied by German forces .. .. Oct. 4, 1914
    Captured by British forces .. .. Sept. 3, 1918

"LÉON GAMBETTA" (*French Cruiser*)—
    Sunk .. .. Apr. 26, 1915

"LEONARDO DA VINCI" (*Italian Battleship*)—
    Sunk by internal explosion .. .. Aug. 2, 1916

"LEOPARD" (*German Raider*)—
    Sunk in action with H.M.S. "Achilles" and boarding steamer "Dundee" .. Mar. 16, 1917

LETTLAND. See under "Latvia."

LIBAU (*Baltic Provinces*)—
    Bombarded by German cruiser "Augsburg" .. .. Aug. 2, 1914
    Bombarded by German squadron .. .. Nov. 17, 1914
    German airship "P.L. 19" brought down near .. .. Jan. 24, 1915
    Taken by German forces .. .. May 7, 1915

LIBERIA—
    Severs diplomatic relations with Germany .. .. May 5, 1917
    Declares war on Germany .. .. Aug. 4, 1917
                      (See also "Monrovia.")

LIÉGE (*Belgium*)—
    Attacked by German forces .. .. Aug. 4, 1914
    City occupied by German forces .. .. Aug. 7, 1914
    Last forts captured by German forces .. .. Aug. 16–17, 1914

LI-YUAN-HUNG—
    Succeeds Yuan-Shih-Kai as President of China .. .. June 6, 1916
    Resigns .. .. July 6, 1917

LILLE (*France*)—
    Occupied by German cavalry .. .. Aug. 27, 1914
    Evacuated by the German forces .. .. Sept. 5, 1914
    Capitulates to German forces .. .. Oct. 12, 1914
    Retaken by Allied forces .. .. Oct. 17, 1918

LIQUID FIRE—
    First used by the Germans .. .. Feb. 26, 1915

LIMANOVA-LAPANOV (*Galicia*)—
    Battle of .. .. Dec. 1–17, 1914

LINDI (*East Africa*)—
    Occupied by British naval forces .. .. Sept. 17, 1916

LIVONIA. See under "Baltic Provinces."

"LIVONIA," *S.S.*—
    First German merchant vessel sunk by British submarine .. .. .. Oct. 3, 1915

LJUBLJANA (*Carniola*)—
    Slovene National Council meet at .. .. Aug. 17, 1918

"LLANDOVERY CASTLE" (*British Hospital Ship*)—
    Sunk .. .. June 27, 1918

LLOYD GEORGE, *Mr.* D.—
    Appointed Secretary of State for War, Great Britain .. .. .. July 7, 1916
    Resigns .. .. Dec. 11, 1916
    Appointed Prime Minister .. .. Dec. 7, 1916
    Forms Coalition Government .. .. Dec. 11, 1916

LOAN—
    Bulgarian—
        Concluded with Germany (3,000,000*l.*) .. .. Feb. 3, 1915
        Concluded with Austro-German banks (400,000,000 fr.) .. .. Aug. 6, 1915
    Greek—
        First, concluded with Entente (1,600,000*l.*) .. .. .. Nov. 8, 1915
        Second, concluded with Entente (800,000*l.*) .. .. .. July 20, 1916
    Rumanian—Concluded in Great Britain (5,000,000*l.*) .. .. Jan. 11, 1915

LODZ (*Poland*)—
  Battle of—
    Begins .. .. Nov. 16, 1914
    Ends .. .. Dec. 15, 1914

LOME (*Togoland*)—
  Occupied by British forces .. .. Aug. 8, 1914

LONDON, DECLARATION OF. See under " Declaration of London."

LONDON, German Air Raids on. See under " Air Raids, German."

LONDON, PACT OF. See under " Pact of London."

LONDON STOCK EXCHANGE. See under " Stock Exchange."

LONGIDO (*German East Africa*)—
  Affair of .. .. Nov. 3, 1914

LONGWY (*France*)—
  Siege of, begins .. .. Aug. 20, 1914
  Capitulates to German forces .. .. Aug. 26, 1914

LOOS (*France*)—
  Battle of—
    Begins .. .. Sept. 25, 1915
    Ends .. .. Oct. 8, 1915

LORRAINE. See under " War Aims."

LOUVAIN (*Belgium*)—
  Sack of .. .. Aug. 26, 1914

LOVCHEN, Mount (*Montenegro*)—
  Taken by the Austrian forces .. .. Jan. 10, 1916

LOWCA (*Cumberland*)—
  Shelled by German submarine .. .. Aug. 16, 1915

LOWESTOFT (*Suffolk*)—
  German naval raids on—
    First .. .. Apr. 25, 1916
    Second .. .. Nov. 26, 1916

LOWICZ-SANNIKI (*Poland*)—
  Battle of .. .. Nov. 30—Dec. 17, 1914

LUDENDORFF, *General* von—
  Appointed Chief Quartermaster General, German General Staff .. .. .. Aug. 29, 1916
  Resigns .. .. Oct. 27, 1918

LÜDERITZBUCHT (*German South-West Africa*)—
  Occupied by South African forces .. .. Sept. 19, 1914

"LUSITANIA," S.S.—
    Arrives at Liverpool flying United States flag .... Feb. 6, 1915
    Sunk .... May 7, 1915

"LUTZOW" (*German Battle Cruiser*)—
    Sunk .... May 31, 1916

LUXEMBOURG—
    German troops cross frontier of .... Aug. 2, 1914
    United States troops enter .... Nov. 20, 1918

LVOV, *Prince* George—
    Appointed Premier of Russia .... Mar. 15, 1917
    Resigns .... July 19, 1917

LYS, River (*Flanders*)—
    Battles of the*—
        Begin .... Apr. 9, 1918
        End .... Apr. 29, 1918

M

MA'AN (*on Hejaz Railway*)—
    Evacuated by Turkish garrison .... Sept. 23, 1918
    Turkish garrison of, surrenders near Amman (Palestine) .... Sept. 29, 1918

MACEDONIA—
    Retreat of Allied forces from, into Greek territory—
        Begins .... Dec. 2, 1915
        Completed .... Dec. 15, 1915
    Blockade of coast by Allies—Commences .... Sept. 19, 1916

MACDONOGH, *Lieut.-General Sir* G. M. W.—
    Appointed Adjutant-General, Home Forces, Great Britain .... Sept. 11, 1918

MACKENSEN, *Field-Marshal* von—
    Surrenders to the Hungarians near Budapest .... Dec. 16, 1918

MACREADY, *Lieut.-General Sir* C. F. N.—
    Appointed Adjutant-General, B.E.F., France .... Aug. 4, 1914
    Resigns .... Feb. 21, 1916
    Appointed Adjutant-General, Home Forces, Great Britain .... Feb. 22, 1916
    Resigns .... Aug. 30, 1918

MADRAS (*India*)—
    Bombarded by German cruiser "Emden" .... Sept. 22, 1914

MAFIA ISLAND (*German East Africa*)—
    Seized by a British force .... Jan. 12, 1915

"MAGDEBURG" (*German Light Cruiser*)—
    Destroyed by Russian squadron off the Aaland Islands .... Aug. 26, 1914

---

* British title and dates. For other battles bearing the same name in the French and German lists, see Appendix.

MAGDHABA (*Sinai*)—
    Affair of .. .. Dec. 23, 1916

MAHON, *Lieut.-General Sir* Bryan—
    Appointed British Commander-in-Chief, Salonika .. .. Oct. 28, 1915
    Resigns .. .. May 9, 1916

MAILS. See under "Note."

"MAINZ" (*German Light Cruiser*)—
    Sunk .. .. Aug. 28, 1914

"MAJESTIC," H.M.S. (*Battleship*)—
    Sunk .. .. May 27, 1915

MALINES (*Belgium*)—
    Battle of .. .. Aug. 25–27, 1914
    Taken by German forces .. .. Sept. 28, 1914

MALINOV, M.—
    Appointed Bulgarian Premier and Foreign Minister .. .. June 18, 1918

MALMAISON, LA (*France*)—
    Battle of .. .. Oct. 23—Nov. 1, 1917

MALMÖ (*Sweden*)—
    Scandinavian Kings meet at .. .. Dec. 18 1914

MAMAKHATUN (*Armenia*)—
    Taken by Russian forces .. .. May 24, 1916
    Retaken by Turkish forces .. .. May 31, 1916
    Again taken by Russian forces .. .. July 12, 1916

"MANICA," H.M.S.—
    First kite balloon ship commissioned .. .. Mar. 23, 1915

MANCHU EMPEROR—
    Restored to Throne .. .. July 1, 1917
    Abdicates .. .. July 7, 1917

MANCHURIA. See under "Commitments."

MANNERHEIM, *General*—
    Elected Regent of Finland .. .. Dec. 11, 1918

MARASESTI (*Rumania*)—
    Battle of—
        First phase* .. .. July 22—Aug. 1, 1917
        Second phase* .. .. Aug. 6—Sept. 3, 1917

MARAMAROS—SZIGET (*North Hungary*)—
    Taken by Russian forces .. .. Oct. 3, 1914
    Retaken by Austrian forces .. .. Oct. 7, 1914

MARGATE—
    German destroyer raid on .. .. Feb. 25, 1917

* German dates.

MARGHILOMAN, *M. Alexandre*—
    Appointed Premier of Rumania .... Mar. 21, 1918
    Resigns .... Nov. 8, 1918

MARNE, River (*France*)—
    Battle of the—
        Begins* .... Sept. 6, 1914
        Ends† .... Sept. 10, 1914
        Again reached by German forces .... May 31, 1918
    Second Battle of the—‡
        Begins* .... July 18, 1918
        Ends* .... Aug. 7, 1918

MARSHALS OF FRANCE (created)—
    Joffre, Joseph .... Dec. 26, 1916
    Foch, Ferdinand .... Aug. 6, 1918
    Pétain, Philippe .... Nov. 19, 1918

MARSHALL, *Lieut.-General Sir W. R.*—
    Takes over command of Mesopotamia Expeditionary Force .... Nov. 18, 1917

MARTIAL LAW—
    Proclaimed in Egypt .... Nov. 1, 1914
    Proclaimed in parts of Ireland .... Apr. 27, 1916
    Proclaimed in Salonika .... June 3, 1916

MARTINITZ. See under "Clam-Martinitz."

MARTINPUICH (*France*)—
    Captured by British forces .... Sept. 15, 1916

MARUSHEVSKI, *General*—
    Becomes Governor-General and Commander-in-Chief of Russian forces in North Russia (Archangel) .... Nov. 20, 1918

"MARY ROSE," H.M.S. (*Destroyer*)—
    Sunk .... Oct. 17, 1917

MASARYK, *Professor*—
    Elected First President of the Czecho-Slovak Republic .... Nov. 14, 1918

MASSON, *M. E.*—
    Appointed Belgian Minister for War .... Nov. 21, 1918

MASURIA (*East Prussia*)—
    The Winter Battle in .... Feb. 4–22, 1915

MASURIAN LAKES (*East Prussia*)—
    Battle of .... Sept. 5–15, 1914

MATZ, River (*France*)—
    Battle of the .... June 9–14, 1918

* French date. For the various dates given for the beginning and ending of this battle, see Appendix.
† British date.   ,,   ,,   ,,   ,,   ,,   ,,
‡ French title.

MAUBEUGE (*France*)—
    Invested by German forces .. .. Aug. 25, 1914
    Capitulates to German forces .. .. Sept. 7, 1914
    Recaptured by British forces .. .. Nov. 8, 1918

MAUDE, *Lieut.-General Sir* Stanley—
    Appointed Commander-in-Chief in Mesopotamia .. .. Aug. 28, 1916
    Takes over command .. .. Aug. 28, 1916
    Dies .. .. Nov. 18, 1917

MAX OF BADEN, *Prince*—
    Appointed German Imperial Chancellor .. .. Oct. 4, 1918
    Resigns .. .. Nov. 9, 1918
    Becomes Regent on abdication of Kaiser .. .. Nov. 9, 1918

MAXWELL, *General Sir* John—
    Takes over command of British forces in Egypt .. .. Sept. 8, 1914
    Resigns .. .. Mar. 19, 1916

MAXWELL, *Lieut.-General Sir* R. C.—
    Appointed Quartermaster-General, B.E.F., France .. .. Jan. 27, 1915
    Resigns .. .. Dec. 22, 1917

MECCA—
    Turkish garrison of, surrenders to the Sherif .. .. June 10, 1916

MECCA, Sherif of—
    Lord Kitchener sends conditional guarantee of independence to .. .. Oct. 31, 1914
    Opens negotiations with British Government .. .. .. July 14, 1915
    British Government send letter to, defining territorial limits of proposed Arab State   Oct. 24, 1915
    Begins revolt against Turkish rule .. .. June 5, 1916
    Issues proclamation denouncing the Committee of Union and Progress, and proclaiming the independence of the Hejaz .. .. June 7, 1916
    Proclaimed "King of the Arabs" .. .. Oct. 29, 1916
    Crowned as "King of the Arabs" .. .. Nov. 4, 1916
    Recognised by British Government as "King of the Hejaz" .. .. Dec. 16, 1916
    (See also under "Arabs" and "Hejaz.")

"MEDEA" *S.S.* (*Dutch*)—
    First neutral ship sunk by German submarine after search .. .. Mar. 25, 1915

MEDINA (*Arabia*)—
    Attack on, by revolting Arabs .. .. June 6, 1916

"MEDJIDIEH" (*Turkish Cruiser*)—
    Sunk .. .. Apr. 3, 1915

MEDUA, SAN GIOVANNI DI (*Albania*)—
    Occupied by Montenegrin forces .. .. June 26, 1915
    Occupied by Austrian forces .. .. Jan. 25, 1916
    Occupied by Italian forces .. .. Oct. 29, 1918

MEGIDDO (*Palestine*)—
    Battles of (Sharon and Nablus) .. .. Sept. 19–25, 1918

MEMEL (*East Prussia*)—
    Occupied by Russian forces .. .. *Nov. 11, 1914
    Reoccupied by German forces .. .. Feb. 17, 1915
    Again captured by Russian forces .. .. Mar. 18, 1915
    Finally recaptured by German forces .. .. Mar. 21, 1915

* Approximate date

MEMORANDUM (DIPLOMATIC). See under "Notes."

MENIN (*Belgium*)—
    Occupied by German forces   *Oct. 9, 1914
    Captured by Allied forces..   Oct. 15, 1918

MENIN ROAD RIDGE (*Flanders*)—
    Battle of   Sept. 20-25, 1917

MERCHANT VESSELS—
    British Admiralty warns British vessels to fly neutral ensigns   Jan. 30, 1915
    Defensively armed—
        German Government announce intention to treat as belligerents   Feb. 10, 1916
        German Government announce intention to treat as cruisers   Feb. 21, 1916
        President Wilson asks United States Congress for power to arm   Feb. 26, 1917
        Arming of all American, in war zone announced by United States Government   Mar. 12, 1917
        (See also under "Britain—Shipping," "Convoys" and "Shipping.")

MERSA MATRUH. See under "Wadi Senaab"

MERV (*Trans-Caspia*)—
    Taken by the Bolsheviki ..   *Aug. 18, 1918
    Retaken by Menshevik and British forces   *Nov. 1, 1918

MERVILLE (*France*)—
    Taken by German forces ..   Oct. 9, 1914
    Retaken by British forces   Oct. 11, 1914
    Again taken by German forces   Apr. 11, 1918
    Again retaken by British forces   Aug. 19, 1918

MESHED (*North-East Persia*)—
    Occupied by troops of the British East Persia cordon ..   *Mar. 3, 1918

MESSIMY, *M.*—
    Appointed French Minister for War   June 14, 1914
    Resigns   Aug. 26, 1914

MESSINES (*Flanders*)—
    Battle of, 1914   Oct. 12—Nov. 2, 1914
        Taken by German forces   Nov. 1, 1914
    Battle of, 1917 (taken by British forces)   June 7-14, 1917
    Battle of, 1918   Apr. 10-11, 1918
        Taken by German forces   Apr. 10, 1918
        Retaken by British forces..   Sept. 28, 1918

MESOPOTAMIA—
    British Expeditionary Force. See under "Indian Expeditionary Force 'D.'"
    Commanders-in-Chief—
        1. †**Barrett**, *Lieut.-General Sir A. A.*—
            Designated as Commander   Sept. 28, 1914
            Takes over command ..   Nov. 13, 1914
            Resigns   Apr. 9, 1915
        2. **Nixon**, *General Sir J. E.*—
            Appointed   Mar. 18, 1915
            Takes over command   Apr. 9, 1915
            Resigns   Jan. 19, 1916
        3. **Lake**, *Lieut.-General Sir P.*—
            Appointed   Jan. 14, 1916
            Takes over command   Jan. 19, 1916
            Resigns   Aug. 28, 1916
        4. **Maude**, *Lieut.-General Sir S.*—
            Appointed   Aug. 28, 1916
            Takes over command   Aug. 28, 1916
            Dies ..   Nov. 18, 1917
        5. **Marshall**, *Lieut.-General Sir W. R.*—Takes over command   Nov. 18, 1917
    Control of operations in, taken over by the War Office from the India Office   Feb. 16, 1916

* Approximate date.
† Proceeded to Mesopotamia in command of 6th Indian Division, which constituted original Indian Expeditionary Force "D."

"MESSOUDIEH" (*Turkish Battleship*)—
    Sunk .. .. Dec. 13, 1914

MÉTIN, *M.*—
    Appointed French Under-Secretary of State for Blockade .. .. .. Aug. 17, 1917
    Resigns .. .. Nov. 16, 1917

METZ (*Lorraine*)—
    Occupied by French forces .. .. Nov. 19, 1918

MEUSE, River—
    Battle of .. ..*Aug. 25–28, 1914

MEXICO, GERMAN MINISTER IN (*von Eckhardt*)—
    Receives instructions to negotiate alliance with Japan against the United States .. Jan. 19, 1917
    Instructions sent by German Government to, published in New York press .. Feb. 28, 1917

MÉZIÈRES (*France*)—
    Occupied by German forces .. .. Aug. 27, 1914
    Retaken by French forces .. .. Nov. 10, 1918

MICHAELIS, *Dr.*—
    Succeeds Herr von Bethmann-Hollweg as German Imperial Chancellor .. .. July 14, 1917
    Resigns .. .. Oct. 30, 1917

MIHIEL, St. (*France*). See under "St. Mihiel."

MILITARY SERVICE ACTS (*Great Britain*). See under "Acts."

MILLERAND, *M.*—
    Appointed French Minister for War .. .. Aug. 27, 1914
    Resigns .. .. Oct. 29, 1915

MILNE, *Lieutenant-General Sir G. F.*—
    Takes over command as British Commander-in-Chief, Salonika .. .. .. May 9, 1916

MILNER, *Viscount*—
    Appointed Minister for War, Great Britain .. .. Apr. 20, 1918

MILYUKOV, *M.* Paul—
    Appointed Russian Foreign Minister .. .. Mar. 15, 1917
    Resigns .. .. May 16, 1917

MINISTERS and MINISTRIES. See under respective countries.

MINELAYING IN OPEN SEA—
    Commenced by the Germans .. .. Aug. 5, 1914
    Commenced by the British .. .. Oct. 3, 1914

MIRANSHAH (*North-West Frontier of India*)—
    Affair of .. .. Nov. 28–29, 1914

* French official dates.

MIRBACH, *Count*—
    Appointed German Ambassador at Moscow ..   Apr. 9, 1918
    Murdered ..   July 6, 1918

MISSION, BRITISH NAVAL. See under "Naval Mission."

MITROVITZA (*Serbia*)—
    Taken by Austro-German forces ..   Nov. 23, 1915

MITYLENE (*Ægean*)—
    British Government guarantee to Greece cession of, by Turkey..   July 25, 1915

MKARAMO (*German East Africa*)—
    Action of ..   June 9, 1916

MOBILISATION—
    Ordered by—
        Austria-Hungary—
            Partial ..   July 26, 1914
            General ..   July 31, 1914
        Belgium ..   July, 31, 1914
        Britain, Great—
            Naval ..   Aug. 1. 1914
            General ..   Aug. 3, 1914
        Bulgaria—
            Partial..   Sept. 21, 1915
            General ..   Sept. 25, 1915
        Estonia ..   Nov. 16, 1918
        France ..   Aug. 1, 1914
        Germany—General..   Aug. 1, 1914
        Greece—Precautionary   Sept. 23. 1915
        Italy ..   May 23, 1915
        Montenegro ..   July 26, 1914
        Rumania ..   Aug. 27, 1916
        Russia—
            Partial..   July 29. 1914
            General ..   July 31, 1914
        Serbia ..   July 25, 1914
        Switzerland ..   Aug. 8, 1914
        Turkey ..   July 31, 1914

"MOEWE" (*German Raider*)—
    First cruise—
        Sails from Bremen ..   Dec. 26, 1915
        Sends British s.s. "Appam" with prize crew to Norfolk (*Va.*)   Feb. 1, 1916
        Returns to Bremen ..   Mar. 4, 1916
    Second cruise—
        Sails from Kiel   Nov. 26, 1916
        Returns to Kiel   Mar. 22, 1917

MOHAMMED V (*Sultan of Turkey*)—
    Dies ..   July 3, 1918

MOHAMMED VI (*Sultan of Turkey*)—
    Succeeds to the throne ..   July 3, 1918

MOHAMMEDAN HOLY PLACES. See under "Mussulman."

MOHTASHEM ED DOULEH—
    Appointed Persian Foreign Minister ..   Apr. 27, 1915
    Resigns ..   Mar. 5, 1916

"MOLDAVIAN REPUBLIC" (BESSARABIA)—
    Establishment of the, proclaimed ..   Dec. 23, 1917
    (For subsequent union with Rumania see under "Bessarabia.")

MOLTKE, *General* von—
    Appointed Chief of German Great General Staff   ——, 1906
    Appointed Chief of the General Staff of the Field Armies   Aug. 2, 1914
    Resigns   Sept. 14, 1914

"MOLTKE" (*German Battle Cruiser*)—
    Torpedoed by British submarine   Aug. 19 1915

MONASTIR (*Serbia*)—
    Taken by Bulgarian forces   Dec. 2, 1915
    Captured by Allied forces   Nov. 19, 1916

MONASTIR-DOIRAN—
    Battle of   Sept. 18-24, 1918
        (And see Part II for two compound battle-names.)

MONFALCONE (*Isonzo*)—
    Taken by Italian forces   June 9, 1915

MONGOLIA. See under "Commitments."

"MONMOUTH," H.M.S. (*Cruiser*)—
    Sunk   Nov. 1, 1914

MONRO, *General Sir* Charles—
    Appointed Commander-in-Chief, Mediterranean Expeditionary Force   Oct. 15, 1915
    Assumes command   Oct. 28, 1915
    Appointed Commander-in-Chief, Salonika Force   Nov. 4, 1915
    Appointed to and assumes command of reconstituted Mediterranean Expeditionary Force   Nov. 25, 1915
    Vacates command of Mediterranean Expeditionary Force*   Jan. 9, 1916

MONROVIA (*Liberia*)—
    Bombarded by a German submarine   Apr. 10, 1918

MONS (*Belgium*)—
    Battle of   Aug. 23-24, 1914
    Retreat from
        Begins   Aug. 24, 1914
        Ends   Sept. 5, 1914
    Retaken by British forces   Nov. 11, 1918

MONTDIDIER (*France*)—
    Taken by German forces   Mar. 27, 1918
    Battle of   Aug. 8-15, 1918
    Retaken by Allied forces   Aug. 10, 1918

MONTENEGRO—
    MOBILISATION—Ordered   July 26, 1914
    RELATIONS (severed)—
        With Germany   Aug. 8, 1914
    WAR (declared)—
        On **Austria-Hungary**   Aug. 5, 1914
        On **Germany**†   Aug. 8, 1914
        On **Bulgaria**†   Oct. 15, 1915
    ARMISTICE—With Austria—
        Concluded   Jan. 12, 1916
        Ceases   Jan. 20, 1916

    * Later appointed Commander-in-Chief in India.
    † "State of War" proclaimed to exist.

MONTENEGRO (continued)—
   ARMY—
      Entente Governments notify Greek Government of forthcoming transfer of
         Montenegrin army to Corfu .. .. Feb. 13, 1916
      Lands in Corfu .. .. Feb. 16, 1916
   MISCELLANEOUS—
      King Nicholas issues manifesto in favour of a confederated Yugo-Slavia .. Oct. 26, 1918
      Skupshtina vote for union with Serbia .. .. Nov. 29, 1918

"MONTS, LA BATAILLE DES." See under "Champagne."

MOON ISLAND (*Baltic*)—
   Captured by German forces .. .. Oct. 18, 1917

MORA (*Cameroons*)—
   First Allied attack on .. .. Aug. 27, 1914
   Second Allied attack on .. .. Sept. 8-9, 1915
   Third Allied attack on .. . . Oct. 30—Nov. 4, 1915
   Surrenders to British forces .. .. Feb. 18, 1916

MORACZEWSKI, *M.*—
   Appointed Prime Minister of Poland .. .. Nov. 17, 1918

MORATORIUM—
   In Great Britain—
      Proclaimed .. .. Aug. 2, 1914
      Ends .. .. Nov. 4, 1914

MORHANGE (*Lorraine*)—
   Battle of .. .. Aug. 14-20, 1914

MOROGORO (*East Africa*)—
   Taken by British forces .. .. Aug. 26, 1916

MORTAGNE, River (*Vosges*)—
   Battle of the—
      Begins .. .. Aug. 25, 1914
      Ends .. .. Sept. 3, 1914

MORVAL (*Somme*)—
   Battle of .. .. Sept. 25-28, 1916

MOSHI, NEW (*East Africa*)—
   Taken by British forces .. .. Mar. 13, 1916

MOSUL (*Mesopotamia*)—
   British advance on, begins .. .. Oct. 23, 1918
   Occupied by British forces .. .. Nov. 4, 1918

MOTONO, *Viscount*—
   Appointed Japanese Minister for Foreign Affairs .. .. Nov. 21, 1916
   Resigns .. .. Apr. 21, 1918

MOUNT SORREL (*Ypres*)—
   Battle of .. .. June 2-13, 1916

MPWAPWA (*German East Africa*)—
    Occupied by British forces . . . . Aug. 11, 1916

MUAVIN ED DOULEH—
    Appointed Persian Foreign Minister . . . . Feb. 20, 1915
    Resigns . . . . Apr. 26, 1915

MUDROS (*Ægean*)—
    Armistice between Turkey and the Entente signed at . . . . . . Oct. 30, 1918

MULHOUSE (*Alsace*)—
    Occupied by French forces . . . . Aug. 8, 1914
    Retaken by German forces . . . . Aug. 11, 1914
    Again taken by French forces . . . . Aug. 19, 1914
    Again retaken by German forces . . . . Aug. 25, 1914
    Occupied by French forces . . . . Nov. 17, 1918

MUNITIONS—
    Munitions of War Act becomes law in Great Britain . . . . . . } July 2, 1915
    Ministry of Munitions formed in Great Britain . . . . . .
    M. Albert Thomas announces completion of inter-allied organisation for munitions   Nov. 25, 1915

MURMAN COAST—
    British Government inform Finnish Government that Great Britain is not hostile to
        Finnish aspirations on the . . . . Aug. 8, 1918
        (See also under " Russia—North " and " Commitments.")

MURMAN RAILWAY—
    Declared open . . . . Dec. 8, 1916
    Seized by Allied forces (from Murmansk to Soroki) . . . . . . June 30, 1918

MURMAN SOVDEP (*Soviet*)—
    Decide to support Entente against Bolsheviki . . . . June 30, 1918
    Agreement signed between Britain, France and United States of America with . . July 7, 1918

MURMANSK. See under " Russia—North."

MURRAY, *General Sir* Archibald—
    Appointed Chief of the General Staff, B.E.F., France . . . . . . Aug. 4, 1914
    Resigns . . . . Jan. 24, 1915
    Appointed Chief of the Imperial General Staff . . . . . . Sept. 26, 1915
    Resigns . . . . Dec. 22, 1915
    Takes over command of Mediterranean Expeditionary Force . . . . Jan. 10, 1916
    Takes over whole command in Egypt . . . . Mar. 19, 1916
    Resigns . . . . June 28, 1917

MURRAY, *Lieut.-General Sir* J. Wolfe—
    Appointed Chief of the Imperial General Staff . . . . . . Oct. 26, 1914
    Resigns . . . . Sept. 25, 1915

MUSCAT (*Western Arabia*)—
    British defence of . . . . Jan 10–11, 1915

MUSH (*Turkish Armenia*)—
    Captured by Russian forces . . . . Feb. 18, 1916
    Recaptured by Turkish forces . . . . Aug. 15, 1916
    Again taken by Russian forces . . . . Aug. 24, 1916
    Reoccupied by Turkish forces . . . . Apr. 30, 1917

MUSHAIDIYA (*Mesopotamia*)—
    Action of .. .. Mar. 14, 1917

MUSHAVER UL MAMALEK—
    Appointed Persian Foreign Minister .. .. Jan. 19, 1918
    Resigns .. .. Aug. 10, 1918
    Reappointed .. .. Aug. 11, 1918

MUSHIR ED DOULEH—
    Appointed Persian Premier .. .. Mar. 14, 1915
    Resigns .. .. Apr. 26, 1915

MUSLIMIYA JUNCTION (*Syria*)—
    Occupied by British cavalry .. .. Oct. 28, 1918

MUSSULMAN HOLY PLACES—
    Government of India announce immunity of, during war .. .. .. Nov. 2, 1914

MUSTAUFI UL MAMALEK—
    Appointed Persian Premier .. .. Aug. 19, 1914
    Resigns .. .. Mar. 14, 1915
    Again appointed .. .. Aug. 18, 1915
    Again resigns .. .. Dec. 24, 1915
    Again appointed .. .. Jan. 19, 1918
    Again resigns .. .. May 3, 1918

MUTINY—
    Of 5th Light Infantry (Indian Army) at Singapore .. .. Feb. 15, 1915
    In Russian navy in the Baltic .. .. Mar. 16, 1917
    In Russian navy at Sevastopol .. .. June 21, 1917
    In German navy at Kiel .. .. {Aug. 3, 1917
                                                                                                         {Nov. 3, 1918

MWANZA (*on Victoria Nyanza*)—
    Taken by British forces .. .. July 14, 1916

MWITI VALLEY (*German East Africa*)—
    German force surrenders to British in .. .. Nov. 28, 1917

N

NABLUS (*Palestine*)—
    Battle of .. .. Sept. 19-25, 1918

NAGYSZEBN (*Transylvania*). See under "Sibiu."

NAMUR (*Belgium*)—
    Attacked by German forces .. .. Aug. 21, 1914
    Captured by German forces .. .. Aug. 25, 1914
    Occupied by British forces .. .. Nov. 21, 1918

NAPLES—
    Essad Pasha's Provisional Government set up at .. .. .. Feb. 28, 1916
    German airship raid on (*from Dalmatian coast*) .. .. .. Mar. 25, 1918

NAROCH, LAKE (*White Russia*)—
    Battle of—
        Begins .. .. Mar. 18, 1916
        Ends .. .. Apr. 30, 1916

NARUNGOMBE (*German East Africa*)—
    Action of   July 19, 1917

NARVA (*Estonia*)—
    Occupied by German forces   Mar. 4, 1918
    Captured by Bolshevik forces   Nov. 28, 1918

NASIRIYA (*Mesopotamia*)—
    Taken by British forces   July 25, 1915

"NATAL," H.M.S. (*Cruiser*)—
    Sunk by internal explosion   Dec. 30, 1915

NATIONAL REGISTER (GREAT BRITAIN). See under "Britain."

NATIONAL SERVICE (GREAT BRITAIN). See under "Britain."

NAVAL MISSION, BRITISH—
    Leaves Turkey   Sept. 17, 1914

NAZARETH (*Palestine*)—
    Occupied by British cavalry   Sept. 20, 1918

NEBI SAMWIL (*Palestine*)—
    Battle of   Nov. 17–24, 1917

NEGOTIN (*North Serbia*)—
    Taken by Bulgarian forces   Oct. 24, 1915

NEJD, EMIR OF (*Ibn Sa'ud*)—
    Concludes treaty with British Government   Dec. 26, 1915
    Treaty ratified   July 18, 1916

NETHERLANDS, Kingdom of The—
    MISCELLANEOUS—
        Joint Trade Committee of Entente Powers formed in the Netherlands   May 9, 1918
        Kaiser crosses frontier into   Nov. 10, 1918
        Dutch ships in Entente ports—
            Allied request for use of—
                Formulated..   Jan. 4, 1918
                Final Allied Note despatched ..   Mar. 7, 1918
                Accepted by Dutch Government   Mar. 18, 1918
                Requisitioned by British and United States Governments   Mar. 21, 1918
    TREATIES, &c. See under "Commitments."

NETHERLANDS OVERSEAS TRUST—
    Formed   Nov. 23, 1914
    Act passed in British Parliament regarding exports to Holland to be consigned to..   June 3, 1915
    Agreement concluded between French Government and   Dec. 7, 1915
        (See also under "Commitments—Great Britain, Netherlands.")

NETS, ANTI-SUBMARINE. See under "'Indicator' Nets" and "Barrage."

NEU LANGENBURG (*German East Africa*)—
    Occupied by British forces   May 27, 1916

NEUTRAL FISHING VESSELS. See under "Fishing Vessels."

NEUTRAL FLAG. See under "Flag."

NEUTRALITY—
    NOTE.—For countries which became belligerents at various dates see under "Declarations of War," and for those which broke off relations with any belligerent see under "Diplomatic Relations." Owing to the large number of entries which would be necessary to indicate the various declarations of neutrality by non-belligerents these entries have not been included in Parts I and II. The following are the countries which remained officially neutral throughout the war:—

    Abyssinia.
    Afghanistan.
    Argentine Republic.
    Chile.
    Colombia.
    Denmark.
    Luxembourg.
    Mexico.
    Netherlands, The.
    Norway.
    Paraguay.
    Persia.
    Salvador.
    Spain.
    Sweden.
    Switzerland.
    Venezuela.

NEUVE CHAPELLE (*France*)—
    Battle of—
        Begins; village taken by British forces   Mar. 10, 1915
        Ends   Mar. 13, 1915
        Retaken by German forces   Apr. 9, 1918
        Reoccupied by British forces   Sept. 1, 1918

NEW ARMIES. See under "Britain, Army."

NEW GUINEA, German—
    Australian Expeditionary Force lands in   Sept. 11, 1914
    Capitulates to Australian Expeditionary Force   Sept. 17, 1914
    German forces in, surrender   Sept. 21, 1914

NEW ZEALAND—
    I. EXPEDITIONARY FORCE—
        First units sail from New Zealand   Oct. 16, 1914
        First units arrive in Egypt   Dec. 1, 1914
        First units land in Gallipoli   Apr. 25, 1915
    II. COMPULSORY SERVICE—
        Passed by New Zealand Parliament   June 10, 1916
        Comes into operation   Sept. 1, 1916

NEWFOUNDLAND—
    EXPEDITIONARY FORCE—
        Leaves Newfoundland   Oct. 3, 1914
        Lands in Great Britain   Oct. 15, 1914

NEWPORT (*Rhode Island*)—
    German submarine "U. 53" captures and destroys five ships outside   Oct. 8, 1916

NEWPORT NEWS (*Va.*)—
    German raider "Kronprinz Wilhelm" interned at   Apr. 26, 1915
    German raider "Prinz Eitel Friedrich" interned at   Apr. 8, 1915

NGAUNDERE (*Cameroons*)—
    Captured by British forces   June 28, 1915

NGOMANO (*Portuguese East Africa*)
    Affair of   Nov. 25, 1917

NGURU HILLS (*German East Africa*)—
    British advance through, begins   Aug. 5, 1916

NICARAGUA—
    Severs diplomatic relations with Germany   May 18, 1917
    Declares war on Germany and Austria-Hungary   May 8, 1918

NICHOLAS II. See under "Tsar."

NICHOLAS, *Grand Duke*—
    Appointed Russian Commander-in-Chief   Aug. 3, 1914
    Issues proclamation promising autonomy to Poland   Aug. 14, 1914
    Suggests a British expedition against Turks to ease situation in the Caucasus   Dec. 30, 1914
    Superseded as Commander-in-Chief by the Tsar   Sept. 5, 1915
    Appointed Viceroy of the Caucasus   Sept. 8, 1915

NICHOLAS, *King of Montenegro*—
    Issues manifesto in favour of a confederated Yugo-Slavia with autonomous states..   Oct. 26, 1918

NICOLAIEV (*South Russia*)—
    Captured by German forces   Mar. 17, 1918

NIEMEN, River (*Poland*)—
    Actions on the ..   Sept. 25–29, 1914

"NIGER," H.M.S. (*Torpedo Gunboat*)—
    Sunk off Deal   Nov. 11, 1914

NISH (*Serbia*)—
    Serbian Government transferred from Belgrade to   July 25, 1914
    Serbian Government leaves   Nov. 3, 1915
    Taken by Bulgarian forces   Nov. 5, 1915
    Reoccupied by Serbian forces   Oct. 11, 1918

NIVELLE, *General*—
    Appointed French Commander-in-Chief   Dec. 12, 1916
    Resigns   May 15, 1917

NIXON, *General Sir J. E.*—
    Appointed Commander-in-Chief in Mesopotamia   Mar. 18, 1915
    Takes over command   Apr. 9, 1915
    Resigns   Jan. 19, 1916

NONNE BOSSCHEN (*Ypres*)—
    Battle of   Nov. 11, 1914

NORFOLK (*Va.*)—
    British steamship "Appam" brought by German prize crew to   Feb. 1, 1916
    German commercial submarine "Deutschland" arrives at   July 10, 1916

NORTH CHANNEL (*Ireland and Scotland*)—
    Net barrage across, established   Feb. 22, 1915

NORTH RUSSIA. See under "Russia—North."

NORTH RUSSIA EXPEDITIONARY FORCE. See under "Russia—North."

NORTH SEA—
 Actions between German and Allied light forces in   { Oct. 17, 1914
  Mar. 21, 1918
 Declared a military zone by the British Admiralty   Nov. 2, 1914
 Harwich flotilla action with German 6th T.B. flotilla   Jan. 23, 1917
 German cruiser raids on British convoys in   { Oct. 17, 1917
  Dec. 12, 1917
  (See also under "Raids—Naval.")

NORWAY—
 Issues orders prohibiting belligerent submarines from entering her territorial waters   Oct. 13, 1916
 Forbids all foreign submarines to use her territorial waters   Feb. 1, 1917

NOTES (MEMORANDA, &c.) to and from UNITED STATES GOVERNMENT—
 I. BY BRITISH GOVERNMENT—
  To United States Government in defence of British blockade policy   Dec. 29, 1914
 II. BY GERMAN GOVERNMENT—
  To United States Government accepting United States demands for limitation of submarine activity   Sept. 1, 1915
  To United States Government stating that defensively armed merchantmen will henceforth be treated as belligerents   Feb. 10, 1916
  To United States Government stating that defensively armed merchantmen will henceforth be treated as cruisers   Feb. 21, 1916
  To United States Government stating that it is not intended to postpone the extended submarine campaign   Feb. 29, 1916
  To United States Government rejecting British offer to permit passage of foodstuffs to Poland   July 29, 1916
  To United States Government in reply to United States note of the 18th (see below)   Dec. 26, 1916
 III. BY UNITED STATES GOVERNMENT—
  Circular—To belligerent Governments stating that United States Government will insist on existing rules of international law   Oct. 22, 1914
  To British Government deprecating use of neutral flag (q.v.)   Feb. 11, 1915
  To German Government on the "Sussex" case, and on submarine policy in general   Apr. 18, 1916
  To British Government respecting search of mails   May 26, 1916
  To British Government—Formal protest against "Black List" policy   July 28, 1916
  Circular—Suggesting negotiations for peace   Dec. 18, 1916
  (See also under "Armistice," "Peace" and "Wilson.")

"NOTTINGHAM," H.M.S. (Light Cruiser)—
 Sunk   Aug. 19, 1916

NOVI BAZAR (Serbia)—
 Taken by Austrian forces   Nov. 20, 1915
 Occupied by Allied forces   Oct. 14, 1918

NOVO-GEORGIEVSK (Poland)—
 Stormed by German forces   Aug. 20, 1915

NOYON (France)—
 Taken by German forces   Aug. 26, 1914
 Retaken by French forces   Sept. 21, 1914
 Retaken by German forces   Sept. 25, 1914
 Occupied by French forces   Mar. 18, 1917
 Again taken by German forces   Mar. 25, 1918
 Retaken by French forces   Aug. 29, 1918
 First Battle of   Mar. 21–Apr. 9, 1918
 Second Battle of   Aug. 17–29, 1918

"NÜRNBERG" (German Cruiser)—
 Joins Admiral von Spee   Aug. 6, 1914
 Sunk   Dec. 8, 1914

NYAMAKURA (Portuguese East Africa)—
 Affair of   July 1–3, 1918

NYANAGAO (*East Africa*)—
    Action of .. .. Oct. 16–19, 1917

NYASSALAND—
    British advance against German East Africa commences from .. .. .. May 25, 1916

O

"OBJECTS OF THE WAR." See under "War Aims."

OBOZERSKAYA (*North Russia*)—
    Occupied by Allied forces .. .. Sept. 4, 1918

"OCEAN," H.M.S. (*Battleship*)—
    Sunk .. .. Mar. 18, 1915

ODESSA (*Russia*)—
    Bombarded by Turkish warships .. .. Oct. 29, 1914
    Occupied by German forces .. .. Mar. 13, 1918
    Occupied by Ukrainian revolutionary forces (*Petlyura's*) .. .. .. Dec. 11, 1918
    French troops land at .. .. Dec. 20, 1918

OFFENSIVES. See Part II.

OKA, *Lieut.-General*—
    Appointed Japanese Minister for War .. .. Apr. 16, 1914
    Resigns .. .. Mar. 29, 1916

OKHRIDA (*Serbia*)—
    Taken by Bulgarian forces .. .. Dec. 8, 1915

OKUMA, *Marquis* Shigenobu—
    Appointed Japanese Prime Minister .. .. Apr. 16, 1914
    Appointed Acting Minister for Foreign Affairs .. .. Aug. 10, 1915
    Relinquishes office of Foreign Minister .. .. Sept. 21, 1915
    Resigns office of Prime Minister .. .. Oct. 9, 1916

OMSK (*Siberia*)—
    Occupied by Czecho-Slovak forces .. .. June 7, 1918
    British troops from Vladivostok reach .. .. Oct. 18, 1918
    Counter-revolutionary *coup d'état* at .. .. Nov. 18, 1918

ORLANDO, *Signor*—
    Succeeds Signor Boselli as Italian Premier .. .. Oct. 29, 1917

ORSOVA (*Serbia*)—
    Occupied by Rumanian forces .. .. Sept. 8, 1916
    Recaptured by Austro-German forces .. .. Nov. 22, 1916

ÖSEL ISLAND (*Baltic*)—
    Occupied by German forces .. .. Oct. 12, 1917

OSHIMA, *Lieut.-General* Kenichi—
    Appointed Japanese Minister for War .. .. Mar. 30, 1916
    Resigns .. .. Sept. 29, 1918

OSOVETS (North Poland)—
Stormed by German forces ... Aug. 22, 1915

OSTEND (Belgium)—
British Marines landed, and R.N.A.S. unit established at ... Aug. 27, 1914
British 7th Division disembarked at ... Oct. 6, 1914
Belgian Government established at ... Oct. 7, 1914
Evacuated by the Belgian forces ... Oct. 12, 1914
Occupied by German forces ... Oct. 15, 1914
First bombarded by British warships ... Oct. 18, 1914
British naval blocking raids—
   First ... Apr. 23, 1918
   Second (H.M.S. "Vindictive" sunk in the harbour) ... May 9, 1918
Reoccupied by Allied forces ... Oct. 17, 1918

OTAVIFONTEIN (German South-West Africa)—
Advance on, by South African forces—
   Begins ... June 19, 1915
   Captured ... July 1, 1915

OTRANTO, STRAITS OF—
Allied blockade of, begins ... Aug. 15, 1914
French cruiser "Léon Gambetta" sunk in ... Apr. 26, 1915
Austrian naval raid on ... May 15, 1917
Net barrage established across ... Oct. 1, 1918

OURCQ, River (France)—
Battle of ... Sept. 5–10, 1914

OUTTERSTEENE RIDGE (Flanders)—
Action of ... Aug. 18, 1918

OYEM (Cameroons)—
Occupied by French forces ... Feb. 16, 1915

P

PACIFIC ISLANDS, GERMAN. See under "Islands."

PACT OF LONDON—
British, French, and Russian Governments sign the, not to conclude a separate Peace ... Sept. 5, 1914
Entente Governments agree to hold applicable to Turkey, the ... Jan. 26, 1915
Secret declaration signed in London by which Italy adheres to the ... Apr. 26, 1915
Japan declares adherence to the ... Oct. 19, 1915
Formal signature of the, by Great Britain, France, Russia, Japan, and Italy ... Nov. 30, 1915
Italy announces adherence to the ... Dec. 1, 1915

PAES, Dr. S. B. C. da Silva—
Appointed Premier of Portugal ... Dec. 10, 1917
Resigns ... May 15, 1918
Appointed Acting President ... Dec. 28, 1917
Elected President ... May 9, 1918
Assassinated ... Dec. 14, 1918

PAINLEVÉ, M.—
Appointed French Minister for War ... Mar. 20, 1917
Succeeds M. Ribot as French Premier (remains Minister for War) ... Sept. 12, 1917
Resigns ... Nov. 14, 1917

"PALLADA" (*Russian Cruiser*)—
    Sunk ... Oct. 11, 1914

PALESTINE—
    British invasion of—Begins ... Mar. 24, 1917
    British Government, in message to King of the Hejaz, declare intentions with regard to the future of ... Jan. 4, 1918

PANAMA—
    Signs Agreement with United States of America allowing ships of belligerents use of Canal ... Oct. 10, 1914
    Declares war on—
        Germany ... Apr. 7, 1917
        Austria-Hungary ... Dec. 10, 1917

PAPEETE (*Tahiti*)—
    Bombarded by Admiral von Spee's squadron ... Sept. 22, 1914

PAPEN, *Captain* von (*German Military Attaché in U.S.A.*)—
    United States Government request recall of ... Dec. 4, 1915
    Recalled by German Government ... Dec. 10, 1915
    Papers of, published in United States ... Jan. 15, 1916

PARIS—
    I. GERMAN ADVANCE ON—Nearest point to Paris (*Claye*) reached . ... Sept. 5, 1914
    II. FRENCH GOVERNMENT—
        Transferred to Bordeaux ... Sept. 2, 1914
        Retransferred from Bordeaux ... Nov. 18, 1914
    III. GERMAN AIR RAIDS ON—
        First { Aeroplane ... Aug. 30, 1914
               { Airship.. ... Mar. 21, 1915
        Last { Aeroplane ... Sept. 16, 1918
              { Airship ... Jan. 29, 1916
    IV. BOMBARDMENT by long-range gun—
        First ... Mar. 23, 1918
        Last ... Aug. 15, 1918

PARTITION OF ASIA MINOR. See under "Commitments."

"PARTRIDGE," H.M.S. (*Destroyer*)—
    Sunk ... Dec. 12, 1917

PASICH, *M.*—
    Appointed Premier of Serbia ... ——, 1912
    Resigns ... Dec. 20, 1918

PASSCHENDAELE (*Belgium*)—
    Captured by British forces ... Nov. 6, 1917
    Reoccupied by German forces ... Apr. 16, 1918
    Recaptured by Allied forces ... Sept. 29, 1918
    First Battle of ... Oct. 12, 1917
    Second Battle of ... Oct. 26—Nov. 10, 1917

PASSENGER SHIP. See under "Submarines" and under names of ships.

"PATHFINDER," H.M.S. (*Light Cruiser*)—
    Sunk ... Sept. 5, 1914

PEACE. See also under "Commitments" and "Armistice."

I. PEACE PROPOSALS—
   By Central Powers—
      Identic note submitted by Governments of Austria-Hungary, Bulgaria,
         Germany and Turkey suggesting peace negotiations .. .. Dec. 12, 1916
      Rejected by Entente Governments .. .. .. Dec. 30, 1916
      Austro-Hungarian and German Governments repudiate responsibility
         for continuance of war .. .. Jan. 11, 1917
      Austrian Emperor makes peace proposal to French President .. Mar. 31, 1917
      Austrian peace proposal published by French Government .. .. Apr. 11, 1918
      German Government makes offer of peace to Belgium .. .. Sept. 15, 1918
      Austro-Hungarian Government submit note to President Wilson
         suggesting a peace conference .. .. Sept. 15, 1918
      Rejected by President Wilson .. .. Sept. 16, 1918
   By the Pope—
      To belligerent Governments .. .. { July 30, 1915
                                                                                                          Aug. 1, 1917
   By President Wilson—
      Note suggesting negotiations issued .. .. .. Dec. 18, 1916
      Austro-Hungarian, German and Turkish Governments send reply to .. Dec. 26, 1916
      Bulgarian Government accept note .. .. Dec. 30, 1916
      Belgian Government send reply to .. .. .. Jan. 10, 1917
      Entente Governments send joint reply to .. .. .. Jan. 10, 1917

   MISCELLANEOUS—
      Japanese Government inform British Government of German overtures
         for a separate peace .. .. Apr. 14, 1915
      Russian Government issue declaration repudiating the idea of a separate
         peace . .. . May 19, 1917
      Serbian Government declares Serbia will never make peace without
         Allies' consent .. .. Dec. 5, 1914

II. PEACE TERMS—British Secretary for Colonies states that the Dominions
     will be consulted as to Peace Terms .. .. Apr. 14, 1915
                 (See also under "War Aims.")

III. PEACE TREATY—
   Between CENTRAL POWERS and BOLSHEVIK RUSSIA—
      Beginning of negotiations (at Brest-Litovsk) for .. .. .. Dec. 22, 1917
      Signed .. .. Mar. 3, 1918
      Ratified by Congress of Soviets .. .. Mar. 14, 1918
      Entente Governments refuse to recognise .. .. .. Mar. 18, 1918
      Complementary Treaty—Concluded .. .. .. Aug. 27, 1918
                 (See also under "Brest-Litovsk.")

   Between GERMANY and GEORGIA—
      Turco-German Peace Delegates arrive at Batum .. .. May 6, 1918
      Treaty signed .. .. June 8, 1918

   Between CENTRAL POWERS and RUMANIA—
      Negotiations for—
         Demanded by German Government .. .. Feb. 6, 1918
         Begin (at Bukharest) .. .. Feb. 25, 1918
      Preliminary Treaty—Signed at Buftea .. .. .. Mar. 5, 1918
      Final Treaty—Signed at Bukharest .. .. .. May 7, 1918

   Between CENTRAL POWERS and THE UKRAINE—
      Signed, together with supplementary Treaties .. .. Feb. 9, 1918
      British Government inform Polish National Committee that Great
         Britain does not accept the Treaty .. .. .. Feb. 20, 1918

   Between FINLAND and BOLSHEVIK RUSSIA—Signed .. Mar. 1, 1918
   Between FINLAND and GERMANY—Signed .. .. .. Mar. 7, 1918
   Between FINLAND and TURKEY—Signed .. .. .. May 11, 1918
   Between FINLAND and AUSTRIA-HUNGARY—Signed .. May 29, 1918
   Between TURKEY and ARMENIA and GEORGIA—Signed .. June 8, 1918
   Between BOLSHEVIK RUSSIA and RUMANIA—Signed .. Mar. 9, 1918

"PEGASUS," H.M.S. (*Light Cruiser*)—
   Sunk .. .. Sept. 20, 1914

PELAGOSA ISLAND (*Adriatic*)—
   Occupied by Italian force .. .. July 26, 1915

PENANG ROADS—
   Action in (*raid by German cruiser "Emden"*) .. .. .. Oct. 28, 1914

"PERESVYET" (*Russian Battleship*)—
   Sunk .. .. Jan. 4, 1917

PERIM (*Red Sea*)—
    Turkish attack on .. .. June 14–15, 1915

PERM (*East Russia*)—
    Taken by Kolchak's forces .. .. Dec. 24, 1918

PERNAU (*Gulf of Riga*)—
    Taken by German forces .. .. Feb. 25, 1918

PÉRONNE (*France*)—
    Taken by German forces .. .. Sept. 24, 1914
    Occupied by Allied forces .. .. Mar. 18, 1917
    Again taken by German forces .. .. Mar. 24, 1918
    Retaken by British forces .. .. Sept. 1, 1918

PERSHING, *Major-General* John—
    Appointed to command U.S.A. Expeditionary Force .. .. May 10, 1917
    Arrives in England .. .. June 8, 1917
    Arrives in France .. .. June 13, 1917
    Promoted to General .. .. Oct. 6, 1917

PERSIA—
    MINISTERS—
        (A.) PREMIER—
            1. Ala es Sultaneh—
                Appointed .. .. Jan. 11, 1913
                Resigns .. .. Aug. 19, 1914
            2. Mustaufi ul Mamalek—
                Appointed .. .. Aug. 19, 1914
                Resigns .. .. Mar. 14, 1915
            3. Mushir ed Douleh—
                Appointed .. .. Mar. 14, 1915
                Resigns .. .. Apr. 26, 1915
            4. Ain ed Douleh—
                Appointed .. .. Apr. 27, 1915
                Resigns .. .. Aug. 17, 1915
            5. Mustaufi ul Mamalek—
                Appointed .. .. Aug. 18, 1915
                Resigns .. .. Dec. 24, 1915
            6. Firman Firma—
                Appointed . .. . Dec. 25, 1915
                Resigns .. .. Mar. 5, 1916
            7. Sipahsalar A'zam—
                Appointed .. .. Mar. 6, 1916
                Resigns .. .. Aug. 29, 1916
            8. Vossuq ed Douleh—
                Appointed .. .. Aug. 29, 1916
                Resigns .. .. May 29, 1917
            9. Ala es Sultaneh—
                Appointed .. .. June 6, 1917
                Resigns .. .. Nov. 24, 1917
            10. Ain ed Douleh—
                Appointed .. .. Nov. 24, 1917
                Resigns .. .. Jan. 19, 1918
            11. Mustaufi ul Mamalek—
                Appointed .. .. Jan. 19, 1918
                Resigns .. .. May 3, 1918
            12. Samsam es Sultaneh—
                Appointed .. .. May 3, 1918
                Resigns .. .. May 31, 1918
                Reappointed .. .. June 20, 1918
                Resigns .. .. Aug. 3, 1918
            13. Vossuq ed Douleh—Appointed .. .. Aug. 7, 1918

        (B.) FOREIGN MINISTER—
            1. Vossuq ed Douleh—
                Appointed .. .. Jan. 11, 1913
                Resigns .. .. Aug. 18, 1914
            2. Ala es Sultaneh—
                Appointed .. .. Aug. 19, 1914
                Resigns .. .. Feb. 20, 1915

PERSIA (continued)—
    MINISTERS (continued)—
        (B.) FOREIGN MINISTER (continued)—
            3. Muavin ed Douleh—
                Appointed .. .. Feb. 20, 1915
                Resigns .. .. Apr. 26, 1915
            4. Mohtashem ed Douleh—
                Appointed .. .. Apr. 27, 1915
                Resigns .. .. Mar. 5, 1916
            5. Sarim ed Douleh—
                Appointed .. .. Mar. 6, 1916
                Resigns .. .. Aug. 29, 1916
            6. Vossuq ed Douleh—
                Appointed .. .. Aug. 29, 1916
                Resigns .. .. May 29, 1917
            7. Ala es Sultaneh—
                Appointed .. .. June 6, 1917
                Resigns .. .. Jan. 19, 1918
            8. Mushaver ul Mamalek—
                Appointed .. .. Jan. 19, 1918
                Resigns .. .. Aug. 10, 1918
                Reappointed .. .. Aug. 11, 1918
    MISCELLANEOUS—
        British and Russian Governments agree to monthly subvention to Persian
            Government .. .. Sept. 28, 1915

PERSIA CORDON, EAST. See under "East Persia Cordon."

PERU—
    Severs diplomatic relations with Germany .. .. Oct 5, 1917

PÉTAIN, *General* Philippe—
    Appointed Chief of French General Staff .. .. Apr. 29, 1917
    Succeeds General Nivelle as French Commander-in-Chief .. .. May 15, 1917
    Created Marshal of France .. .. Nov. 19, 1918

PETER, *King of Serbia.* See under "Serbia."

PETLYURA, *General*—
    Commences revolt against The Ukraine Government .. .. Nov. 15, 1918
    Takes Odessa .. .. Dec. 11, 1918
    Takes Kiev .. .. Dec. 20, 1918

PETRA (*Arabia*)—
    Turkish attack on Arab stronghold at, repulsed .. .. Oct. 21, 1917

PETROGRAD—
    Revolution in, begins .. .. Mar. 12, 1917
    Provisional Government proclaimed at .. .. Mar. 14, 1917
    Bolshevik *coup d'état* at .. .. Nov. 8, 1917

PHILIPPEVILLE (*Algeria*)—
    Bombarded by German cruiser "Goeben" .. .. Aug. 4, 1914

PIAVE, River (*Italy*)—
    Austro-German forces reach the .. .. Nov. 11, 1917
    Battle of the .. .. June 15–24, 1918

PICARDY (*France*)—
    First Battle of .. .. Sept. 22–26, 1914
    Second Battle of* .. .. Mar. 21—Apr. 9, 1918

* Corresponds to the "First Battles of the Somme, 1918."

PICHON, *M.* Stephen—
    Appointed French Foreign Minister   Nov. 16, 1917

PILCKEM RIDGE (*Flanders*)—
    Battle of   July 31—Aug. 2, 1917

PINSK (*Poland*)—
    Occupied by German forces   Sept. 16, 1915

PIRÆUS (*Greece*)—
    German ships in, seized by the Allies   Sept. 2, 1916
    Allied forces land at the ..   Nov. 30, 1916
    Allied forces withdrawn from the ..   Dec. 1, 1916

PIUS X, *Pope.* See under "Pope."

PLEDGES (*Political*). See under "Commitments."

PODGORITSA (*Montenegro*)—
    Occupied by the Austrian forces ..   Jan. 23, 1916
    Montenegrin National Assembly meet at   Nov. 29, 1918

POELCAPPELLE (*Flanders*)—
    Battle of   Oct. 9, 1917

"POINTS, THE FOURTEEN"—
    Laid down by President Wilson in message to Congress   Jan. 8, 1918
    FOUR ADDITIONAL—
        Laid down by President Wilson in message to Congress   Feb. 11, 1918

POKROVSKI—
    Appointed Russian Foreign Minister   Dec. 12, 1916
    Resigns   Jan. 27, 1917

POLA Harbour—
    Italian naval raid on   May 14, 1918

POLAND—
    I. AUTONOMY—
        Proclamation promising autonomy by Russian Commander-in-Chief (Grand Duke Nicholas)—Issued   Aug. 14, 1914
        Russian Imperial Ukase granting municipal self-government to Poland—Issued   Apr. 3, 1915
        Proclamation by Central Powers announcing the formation of an "Independent State of Poland"—Issued   Nov. 5, 1916
        Proclamation by Russian Provisional Government acknowledging the independence of Poland—   Mar. 30, 1917
        British Government inform Russian Provisional Government of their adherence to the principle of an independent and united Poland ..   Apr. 5, 1917
        Grant by Central Powers of temporary Constitution to Poland—Announced ..   Sept. 12, 1917
        Regency Council appointed   Oct. 15, 1917
        British Government assure Bolshevik Government of their support in creation of an independent Poland   Jan. 10, 1918
        British Foreign Minister (Mr. Balfour) informs Polish National Committee that Great Britain does not accept the Treaty between The Ukraine and Central Powers   Feb. 20, 1918
        Declaration by British, French, and Italian Governments in support of national aspirations of the Polish people—Issued   June 3, 1918
        Polish National Army recognised by Great Britain as autonomous, allied, and co-belligerent ..   Oct. 12, 1918
    II. INDEPENDENCE—Declared   Nov. 16, 1918
    III. PREMIER (AND FOREIGN MINISTER)—
        Moraczewski, *M.*—Appointed under Regency Council   Nov. 17, 1918

POLAND (*continued*)—
    IV. RELATIONS (severed)—
        With Germany .. .. Dec. 15, 1918
    V. WAR—
        "State of War" with The Ukraine, proclaimed .. .. .. Nov. 1, 1918
    VI. MISCELLANEOUS—
        Offer by British Government to send foodstuffs to Poland—Rejected by German Government .. .. July 29, 1916
    VII. TREATIES, &c. See under "Commitments."

POLIVANOV, *General*—
    Appointed Russian Minister for War .. .. June 26, 1915
    Resigns .. .. Mar. 29, 1916

POLTAVA (*South Russia*)—
    Captured by German forces .. .. Mar. 29, 1918

POLYGON WOOD (*Ypres*)—
    Battle of .. .. Sept. 26—Oct. 3, 1917

"POMMERN" (*German Battleship*)—
    Sunk .. .. May 31, 1916

APE (*Caroline Islands*)—
    Admiral von Spee's squadron leaves .. .. Aug. 6, 1914

PONTA DELGADA (*Azores*)—
    Shelled by German submarine .. .. July 4, 1917

"PONTOPOROS" (*Greek Collier*)—
    Captured by German cruiser "Emden" .. .. Sept. 10, 1914

POOLE, *Major-General* F. C.—
    Lands at Murmansk to organise North Russia Expeditionary Force .. .. May 24, 1918

POPE—
    Pius X—Dies .. .. Aug. 20, 1914
    Benedict XV—
        Elected .. .. Sept. 3, 1914
        Belgian Government reject mediation of .. .. Nov. 5, 1914
        Sends appeal for peace to belligerent Governments .. .. .. July 30, 1915
        Sends peace proposals to belligerent Governments .. .. .. Aug. 1, 1917

PORTUGAL—
    I. ENTRY INTO THE WAR—
        German forces begin unprovoked invasion of Angola .. .. .. Oct. 26, 1914
        Government announce forthcoming co-operation with Great Britain .. Nov. 23, 1914
        Expeditionary force leaves for Angola .. .. Dec. 4, 1914
        Government seize German steamers in the Tagus .. .. .. Feb. 23, 1916
        Government decide to extend Portuguese military co-operation to Europe Aug. 8, 1916
        Relations (severed)—By Austria-Hungary .. .. Mar. 15, 1916
        War declared—
            By Germany .. .. Mar. 9, 1916
            By Austria-Hungary .. .. Mar. 15, 1916
        Expeditionary Force—
            To Angola—Leaves Lisbon .. .. Dec. 4, 1914
            To France—
                Advanced troops land in France .. .. .. Jan. 3, 1917
                First units come into action .. .. June 17, 1917

PORTUGAL (continued)—
  II. PRESIDENT—
    1. Arriaga, *Dr.* de—
      Elected .. .. Aug. 24, 1911
      Resigns .. .. May 29, 1915
    2. Braga, *Dr.*—
      Elected .. .. May 28, 1915
      Resigns .. .. Oct. 5, 1915
    3. Guimarães, *Dr.* Machado—
      Elected .. .. Aug. 6, 1915
      Takes office .. .. Oct. 5, 1915
      Deposed*.. .. .. Dec. 11, 1917
    4. Paes, *Dr.* da Silva—
      Appointed† .. .. Dec. 28, 1917
      Elected .. .. May 9, 1918
      Assassinated .. .. Dec. 14, 1918
    5. Antunes, *Senhor* Silva—
      Appointed† .. .. Dec. 16, 1918

  III. PREMIER—
    1. Guimarães, *Dr.* Machado—
      Appointed .. .. June 23, 1914
      Vacates appointment .. .. Dec. 11, 1914
    2. Coutinho, *Senhor* d'Azevedo
      Appointed .. .. Dec. 12, 1914
      Resigns .. .. Jan. 25, 1915
    3. Castro, *General* da—
      Appointed .. .. Jan. 25, 1915
      Resigns .. .. May 14, 1915
    4. Chagas, *Senhor* Pinheiro—
      Appointed .. .. May 15, 1915
      Resigns.. .. .. June 19, 1915
    5. Castro, *Dr.* de—
      Appointed .. .. June 19, 1915
      Resigns .. .. Nov. 29, 1915
    6. Costa, *Dr.* da—
      Appointed .. .. Nov. 29, 1915
      Resigns .. .. Mar. 15, 1916
    7. d'Almeida, *Dr.* José—
      Appointed .. .. Mar. 15, 1916
      Resigns .. .. Apr. 25, 1917
    8. Costa, *Dr.* da—
      Appointed .. .. Apr. 25, 1917
      Resigns .. .. Dec. 10, 1917
    9. Paes, *Dr.* da Silva—
      Appointed .. .. Dec. 10, 1917
      Resigns .. .. May 15, 1918
    10. Barboza, *Senhor* de Sousa‡—
      Appointed Premier and Minister of Interior .. .. .. Dec. 23, 1918

  IV. REVOLUTION—
    Breaks out in Lisbon .. .. Dec. 11, 1917

  V. TREATIES, &c. See under "Commitments."

"PORTUGAL," S.S. (*Russian Hospital Ship*)—
  Sunk .. .. Mar. 30, 1916

POTI (*Georgia*)—
  German troops landed at .. .. June 8, 1918

POTSDAM—
  Kaiser receives Austrian envoy and promises support to Austria .. .. July 5, 1914

POZIÈRES RIDGE (*Somme*)—
  Battle of .. .. July 23–Sept. 3, 1916

PREMUDA ISLAND (*Adriatic*)—
  Naval action off (*Austrian battleship* "*Szent Istvan*" *sunk*) .. .. .. June 10, 1918

---

* Revolution.   † Temporary Acting President.
‡ Between May 16th and December 23rd the office of Premier lapsed, but Senhor Barboza acted as Secretary of the Interior.

PRILEP (*South Serbia*)—
    Taken by Bulgarian forces   Nov. 16, 1915
    Retaken by French forces   Sept. 23, 1918

PRIME MINISTER. See under respective countries.

"PRINCESS IRENE" (*British Minelayer*)—
    Sunk by internal explosion   May 27, 1915

"PRINZ ADALBERT" (*German Cruiser*)—
    Sunk   Oct. 23, 1915

"PRINZ EITEL FRIEDRICH" (*German Armed Merchant Cruiser*)—
    Leaves Tsingtau   Aug. 6, 1914
    Sinks United States s.v. "William P. Frye"   Jan. 28, 1915
    Interned at Newport News (Va.)   Apr. 8, 1915

PRISONERS OF WAR—
    I. TRANSFER OF DISABLED PRISONERS TO SWITZERLAND—
        Proposal by British Government agreed to by German Government   April 26, 1916
        Ratified in London   May 13, 1916
        First British party reaches England   Sept. 11, 1917
    II. EMPLOYMENT OF—
        Anglo-German Agreement, regarding—
            Signed at Berlin   May 10, 1916
            Signed at London   May 29, 1916
    III. AGREEMENT—Signed at The Hague for the exchange of combatant and civilian British and German prisoners of war   July 2, 1917
    IV. ANGLO-GERMAN CONFERENCE, regarding (at The Hague)—First meeting   June 9, 1918

PRISTINA (*Serbia*)—
    Taken by Austro-German forces   Nov. 23, 1915
    Retaken by French forces   Oct. 10, 1918

PRIZES. See under "Commitments."

PRIZREN (*Serbia*)—
    Serbian Government leave, for Scutari   Nov. 23, 1915
    Taken by Bulgarian forces   Dec. 1, 1915
    Retaken by French forces   Oct. 11, 1918

PROTECTORATE—
    Over—
        Egypt—Proclaimed by Great Britain   Dec. 18, 1914
        Albania—Proclaimed by Italy   June 3, 1917
        Kurland—Proclaimed by Germany   Mar. 15, 1918

PROTICH, *M.* Stoyan—
    Appointed Prime Minister of United Serbia, Croatia and the Slovenes   Dec. 29, 1918

PROVISIONAL GOVERNMENT. See under "Albania," "Greece," and "Russia."

PRZASNYSZ (*North Poland*)—
    First Battle of   Feb. 22–27, 1915
    Second Battle of   July 13–17, 1915

PRZEMYSL (*Galicia*)—
    First siege of, by Russian forces—
        Begins .. .. Sept. 24, 1914
        Ends .. .. Oct. 9, 1914
    Second siege of, by Russian forces—
        Begins .. .. Nov. 10, 1914
        Ends: Fortress capitulates .. .. Mar. 22, 1915
    Battle of .. .. May 24—June 11, 1915
    City retaken by Austro-German forces .. .. June 3, 1915

PSKOV (*Baltic Provinces*)—
    Taken by German forces .. .. Feb. 25, 1918

PULTUSK (*North Poland*)—
    Stormed by German forces .. .. July 24, 1915

PYAVOZERO LAKE (*Murman Front*)—
    Action near .. .. Oct. 3, 1918

Q

QASR-I-SHIRIN (*Western Persia*)—
    Occupied by Turkish forces .. .. Dec. 15, 1915
    Occupied by Russian forces .. .. May 7, 1916
    Taken by Turkish forces .. .. June 20, 1916
    Again taken by Russian forces .. .. Mar. 25, 1917
    Evacuated by Russian forces .. .. July 8, 1917
    Occupied by British forces .. .. Jan. 8, 1918

"QUEEN MARY," H.M.S. (*Battle Cruiser*)—
    Sunk .. .. May 31, 1916

QUEENSTOWN (*Ireland*)—
    First Division United States Destroyer Flotilla arrives at .. .. .. May 2, 1917
    Flag of United States Admiral (acting Commander-in-Chief, Irish Command)
        hoisted at .. .. June 18, 1917

QUENTIN, ST. See under "St. Quentin."

QURNA (*Mesopotamia*)—
    First action of .. .. Dec. 4–8, 1914
    Occupied by British forces .. .. Dec. 9, 1914
    Second action of .. .. May 31, 1915

R

RADOSLAVOV, M.—
    Appointed Bulgarian Premier .. .. July 20, 1913
    Resigns .. .. June 18, 1918

RADAUTZ (*Bukovina*)—
    Taken by Russian forces .. .. June 21, 1916

RAFAH (*Sinai*)—
    Action of .. .. Jan. 9, 1917

"RAGLAN," H.M.S. Monitor)—
    Sunk .. .. Jan. 20, 1918

RAIDERS, GERMAN. See under " Commerce Destroyers."

RAIDS, AIR. See under " Air Raids."

RAIDS, NAVAL—
    British—
        On the Kattegat .. .. Nov. 2, 1917
        On the Kattegat .. .. Apr. 15, 1918
    British Blocking—
        On Ostend and Zeebrugge .. .. Apr. 22, 1918
        On Ostend .. .. May 9, 1918
    German Cruiser—
        First on British coast (near Gorleston) .. .. Nov. 3, 1914
        On Scarborough and Hartlepool .. .. Dec. 16, 1914
        On Lowestoft and Yarmouth .. .. Apr. 25, 1916
        On Lowestoft .. .. Nov. 26, 1916
        On British convoy in North Sea .. .. Oct. 17, 1917
    German Destroyer—
        On Dover Straits .. .. Oct. 26-27, 1916
        On Southwold and Wangford (Suffolk) .. .. Jan. 25, 1917
        On Margate and Broadstairs .. .. Feb. 25, 1917
        On Ramsgate and Broadstairs .. .. Mar. 18, 1917
        On Dover Straits: action by H.M.S. " Swift" and " Broke" .. Apr. 20-21, 1917
        On Ramsgate .. .. Apr. 26-27, 1917
        On British convoy in North Sea .. .. Dec. 12, 1917
        On Yarmouth .. .. Jan. 14, 1918
    German Submarine—
        On Scapa Flow .. .. Oct. 17, 1914
        On Walney Island Barracks (Barrow) .. .. Jan. 29, 1915
        On Whitehaven (Cumberland) .. .. Aug. 16, 1915
        On Seaham (Durham) .. .. July 11, 1916
        On Funchal (Madeira) .. .. Dec. 3, 1916
        On Ponta Delgada (Azores) .. .. July 4, 1917
        On Scarborough (Yorkshire) .. .. Sept. 4, 1917
        On Funchal (Madeira) .. .. Dec. 12, 1917
        On Dover .. .. Feb. 16, 1918
        On Monrovia (Liberia) .. .. Apr. 10, 1918
        On St. Kilda (Hebrides) .. .. May 15, 1918
    Italian—
        On Trieste Harbour .. .. Dec. 9-10, 1917
        On Pola Harbour .. .. May 14, 1918

RAMADI (*Mesopotamia*)—
    Action of .. .. Sept. 28-29, 1917

RAMSGATE (*Kent*)—
    German destroyer raid on—
        First .. .. Mar. 18, 1917
        Second .. .. Apr. 26, 1917

RAPALLO (*Italy*)—
    Allied Conference at .. .. Nov. 7, 1917

RASPUTIN—
    Murdered .. .. Dec. 31, 1916

RAWKA-BZURA (*Poland*)—
    Battle of, begins* .. .. Dec. 18, 1914

RAYAT (*Armenia*)—
    Battle of .. .. Aug. 23, 1916

* See footnote, Part I.

REBELLION—
  IRISH—
    Begins .. .. Apr. 24, 1916
    Ends .. .. May 1, 1916
    Leaders of, executed .. .. May 3, 1916
  SOUTH AFRICAN—
    Begins .. .. Sept. 15, 1914
    General De Wet captured .. .. Dec. 1, 1914
    Ends .. .. Dec. 28, 1914
    Last rebels in the Transvaal captured .. .. Jan. 11, 1915
        (See also under " Revolution.")

"REGINA MARGHERITA" (*Italian Battleship*)—
  Sunk .. .. Dec. 11, 1916

REGISTER, NATIONAL, in Great Britain. See under "Britain."

REIMS (*France*)—
  1. **City**—
    Taken by German forces .. .. Sept. 5, 1914
    Evacuated by German forces .. .. Sept. 14, 1914
  2. **Cathedral**—First bombarded by German artillery.. .. .. .. Sept. 19, 1914

RELATIONS, DIPLOMATIC. See under "Diplomatic Relations."

RESHT (*North-West Persia*)—
  British defence of .. .. July 20, 1918

RETHEL (*France*)—
  Taken by French forces .. .. Nov. 6, 1918

RETREATS—
  (A.) WESTERN THEATRE—
    1. From Mons (British)—
      Begins .. .. Aug. 24, 1914
      Ends .. .. Sept. 5, 1914
    2. From the Somme to Hindenburg Line (German)—
      Begins .. .. Mar. 14, 1917
      Ends .. .. April 5, 1917
    3. From the Isonzo to the Piave (Italian)—
      Begins .. .. Oct. 24, 1917
      Ends .. .. Nov. 11, 1917
  (B.) BALKAN THEATRE—
    1. Through Albania (Serbian)—
      Begins .. .. Nov. 30, 1915
      First Serbian troops reach Corfu .. .. .. Jan. 15, 1916
      Serbian forces concentrated at Corfu .. .. .. Feb. 10, 1916
    2. From Macedonia to Greek Frontier (Allied Forces)—
      Begins .. .. Dec. 2, 1915
      Ends .. .. Dec. 15, 1915
  (C.) THE DARDANELLES—
    Evacuation by British—
      Ordered .. .. Dec. 8, 1915
      Completed .. .. Jan. 8, 1916
  (D.) MESOPOTAMIA—
    From Ctesiphon to Kut al Amara (British)—
      Begins .. .. Nov. 25, 1915
      Ends .. .. Dec. 3, 1915

REVAL (*Russia*)—
  Taken by German forces .. .. Feb. 25, 1918

REVIGNY (*France*)—
  German airship "L.Z. 77" brought down near .. .. .. Feb. 21, 1916

REVOLUTION in—
   1. **Austria** (Vienna)—
      Begins .. .. Oct. 31, 1918
      Emperor abdicates.. .. .. Nov. 12, 1918
   2. **Germany** (Berlin)—
      Begins .. .. Nov. 9, 1918
      Kaiser crosses frontier into Holland .. .. Nov. 10, 1918
   3. **Hungary** (Budapest)—
      Begins .. .. Oct. 31, 1918
      Independent Government formed .. .. Nov. 1, 1918
   4. **Portugal** (Lisbon)—
      Begins .. .. Dec. 11, 1917
   5. **Russia** (Petrograd)
      1. Begins.. .. .. Mar. 12, 1917
        Tsar abdicates .. .. Mar. 15, 1917
      2. (*Bolshevik*)—Begins .. .. Nov. 8, 1917

" REWA " (*British Hospital Ship*)—
   Sunk .. .. Jan. 4, 1918

RHINE, River (*Germany*)—
   Crossed by British troops at Cologne .. .. Dec. 12, 1918

RHODESIA—
   Defence of Abercorn .. .. Sept. 5–9, 1914
   British advance against German East Africa commences from .. .. .. May 25, 1916
   German force enters, and attacks Fife .. .. Nov. 1, 1918
   Kasama captured by German force.. .. .. Nov. 9, 1918
   German forces in East Africa surrender to Allies at Abercorn .. .. .. Nov. 25, 1918

RIBOT, *M.*—
   Appointed French Premier and Foreign Minister .. .. Mar. 20, 1917
   Resigns .. .. Sept. 9, 1917
   Reappointed Foreign Minister .. .. Sept. 12, 1917
   Resigns .. .. Oct. 23, 1917

RIGA (*Baltic Provinces*)—
   I. **City**—Captured by the Germans .. .. Sept. 3, 1917
   II. **Gulf of Riga**—German naval operations in—
      First .. .. *Aug. 8–21, 1915
      Second.. .. .. Oct. 16, 1917
   III. **Battle of** .. .. Sept. 1–5, 1917

ROBERTS, *Field-Marshal Earl*—
   Dies in France .. .. Nov. 14, 1914

ROBERTSON, *General Sir* William—
   Appointed Quartermaster-General B.E.F., France .. .. .. Aug. 4, 1914
   Resigns .. .. Jan. 24, 1915
   Appointed Chief of the General Staff, B.E.F., France .. .. .. Jan. 25, 1915
   Resigns .. .. Dec. 22, 1915
   Appointed Chief of the Imperial General Staff .. .. .. Dec. 23, 1915
   Resigns .. .. Feb. 18, 1918
   General Officer Commanding-in-Chief, Great Britain .. .. .. May 30, 1918

RODMAN, *Rear-Admiral* (*U.S.N.*)—
   Joins Grand Fleet with United States Battleship Division .. .. Dec. 6, 1917

" ROHILLA " (*British Hospital Ship*)—
   Wrecked off Whitby .. .. Oct. 30, 1914

ROQUES, *General*—
   Appointed French Minister for War.. .. .. Mar. 16, 1916
   Resigns .. .. Mar. 17, 1917

* Approximate dates.

ROSIÈRES (*Somme*)—
 Battle of .. .. Mar. 26–27, 1918

" ROSTOCK " (*German Light Cruiser*)—
 Sunk .. .. May 31, 1916

ROSTOV (*South Russia*)—
 Captured by German forces .. .. May 8, 1918

ROSYTH—
 German delegates arrive at, to arrange surrender of fleet .. .. .. Nov. 15, 1918
 German High Seas Fleet arrives at, for internment in Scapa Flow .. .. Nov. 21, 1918

ROULERS (*Belgium*)—
 Taken by German forces .. .. Oct. 18, 1914
 Recaptured by Allied forces .. .. Oct. 14, 1918

ROVERETO (*Trentino*)—
 Taken by Italian forces .. .. Nov. 23, 1915

ROVUMA, River (*East Africa*)—
 German forces cross the, into Portuguese territory .. .. Nov. 25, 1917
 German forces recross the, into German territory .. .. Sept. 29, 1918

ROWANDUZ (*Northern Mesopotamia*)—
 Occupied by Russian forces .. .. May 15, 1916

"ROYAL EDWARD" (*British Transport*)—
 Torpedoed and sunk .. .. Aug. 13, 1915

ROYAL FLYING CORPS. See "Flying Corps."

ROYE (*France*)—
 Occupied by German forces .. .. Aug. 30, 1914
 Occupied by French forces .. .. Mar. 17, 1917
 Captured by German forces .. .. Mar. 26, 1918
 Recaptured by British forces .. .. Aug. 27, 1918

ROZAN (*North Poland*)—
 Stormed by German forces .. .. July 24, 1915

RUAD ISLAND (*off Syrian Coast*)—
 Occupied by a French force .. .. Sept. 1, 1915

"RUEL," S.S. (*British*)—
 Sunk .. .. Aug. 21, 1915

RUFIJI, River (*German East Africa*)—
 German light cruiser "Königsberg"—
  Located in .. .. Oct. 31, 1914
  Destroyed in .. .. July 11, 1915

RUMANI (*Sinai*)—
 Battle of .. .. Aug. 4–5, 1916

RUMANIA—
- **INTERVENTION—**
  - Negotiations with Russia for military assistance begin .. Jan. 22, 1916
  - Agreement with Entente Powers concluded .. Aug. 17, 1916
- **MOBILISATION**—Ordered .. Aug. 27, 1916
- **DIPLOMATIC RELATIONS (severed)—**
  - With Bulgaria .. Aug. 30, 1916
  - By Russian Bolshevik Government .. Jan. 28, 1918
- **WAR (declared)—**
  - On **Austria-Hungary** .. Aug 27, 1916
  - By **Germany** .. Aug. 28, 1916
  - By **Turkey** .. Aug. 30, 1916
  - By **Bulgaria** .. Sept. 1, 1916
- **HOSTILITIES**—With Central Powers—
  - Commence .. On dates of declarations of war
  - Suspended .. Dec. 6, 1917
  - Cease .. Dec. 10, 1917
  - Resumed .. Nov. 10, 1918
- **FRONTIER—**
  - Of **Transylvania**—Crossed by Rumanian troops .. Aug. 28, 1916
  - Of **Dobrudja**—Crossed by Bulgarian troops .. Sept. 2, 1916
  - Of **Transylvania**—Crossed by German troops .. Oct. 14, 1916
- **ARMISTICE**—With Central Powers—Concluded ("Truce of Focsani") .. Dec. 9, 1917
- **PEACE**—(Signed)—
  - Preliminary, with Austria-Hungary, Bulgaria, Germany, and Turkey .. Mar. 5, 1918
  - With Russian Bolshevik Government .. Mar. 9, 1918
  - Final, with Austria-Hungary, Bulgaria, Germany and Turkey ("Treaty of Bukharest") .. May 7, 1918
- **GOVERNMENT—**
  - Removed from Bukharest to Jassy .. Dec. 1, 1916
  - Re-established at Bukharest .. Nov. 30, 1918
- **UNION WITH OTHER NATIONALS.** See under "Banat," "Bessarabia," "Bukovina," "Hungary" and "Transylvania."
  - Proclamation issued annexing Rumanian parts of Austria-Hungary .. Dec. 27, 1918
- **KING—**
  - **Charles**—Dies .. Oct. 10, 1914
  - **Ferdinand**—Succeeds .. Oct. 10, 1914
- **MINISTERS—**
  - (A.) PREMIER—
    1. Bratianu, *M.*—
       - Appointed .. Jan, 14, 1914
       - Resigns .. Feb. 6, 1918
    2. Averescu, *General*—
       - Appointed .. Feb. 9, 1918
       - Resigns .. Mar. 12, 1918
    3. Marghiloman, *M.*—
       - Appointed .. Mar. 21, 1918
       - Resigns .. Nov. 8, 1918
    4. Coanda, *General*—
       - Appointed .. Dec. 1, 1918
       - Resigns .. Dec. 12, 1918
    5. Bratianu, *M.*—Appointed .. Dec. 14, 1918
  - (B.) FOREIGN MINISTER—
    1. Bratianu, *M.*—
       - Appointed .. Jan. 14, 1914
       - Resigns .. Feb. 6, 1918
    2. Averescu, *General*—
       - Appointed .. Feb. 9, 1918
       - Resigns .. Mar. 12, 1918
    3. Arian, *M.*—
       - Appointed .. Mar. 21, 1918
       - Resigns .. Nov. 8, 1918
    4. Coanda, *General*—
       - Appointed .. Dec. 1, 1918
       - Resigns .. Dec. 12, 1918
    5. Bratianu, *M.*—Appointed .. Dec. 14, 1918
- **LOAN**—With Great Britain (£5,000,000)—Concluded .. Jan. 11, 1915
- **TREATIES, &c.** See under "Commitments."

RUPEL, Fort (*Greek Macedonia*)—
- Occupied by a Bulgarian and German force .. May 26, 1916
- Entente Governments protest to Greece against occupation of .. May 31, 1916

RUSCHUK (*Bulgaria*)—
    Allied forces cross Danube at   Nov. 10, 1918

RUSSIA—
  MOBILISATION (ordered)—
    Partial   July 29, 1914
    General   July 31, 1914
  ULTIMATUM (presented)—By Germany   July 31, 1914 (midnight)
  RELATIONS (severed)—
    With Turkey   Oct. 30, 1914
    With Bulgaria   Oct. 5, 1915
    With Rumania   Jan. 28, 1918
  WAR (declared)—
    By **Germany**   Aug. 1, 1914
    By **Austria-Hungary**   Aug. 6, 1914
    On **Turkey**   Nov. 2, 1914
    By **Turkey** (*Je ad*)   Nov. 14, 1914
    On **Bulgaria**   Oct 19, 1915
  HOSTILITIES—
    With **Turkey**—Commence   Oct. 29, 1914
    With other Central Powers—Commence   Date of declaration of war.
    Truce arranged with Central Powers   Dec. 6, 1917
    Hostilities suspended   Dec. 7, 1917
    Hostilities resumed   Feb. 18, 1918
    Hostilities cease   Feb. 28, 1918
  ARMISTICE—With Bulgaria, Central Powers and Turkey—Concluded   Dec. 15, 1917
    With The Ukraine (German-Ukrainian command)   May 4, 1918
    With The Ukraine, whole State of   June 12, 1918
    (For details of negotiations, &c., see under "Brest-Litovsk.")
  PEACE (signed)—
    With Finland   Mar. 1, 1918
    With Bulgaria, Central Powers and Turkey (see also under "Brest-Litovsk")   Mar. 3, 1918
    With Rumania   Mar. 9, 1918
  EMPEROR (TSAR)—**Nicholas II**—
    Signs order for mobilisation of Russian army   July 30, 1914
    Assumes appointment of Commander-in-Chief Russian armies   Sept. 5, 1915
    Abdicates   Mar. 15, 1917
    Murdered   July 16, 1918
  REVOLUTION—begins   Mar. 12, 1917
  PROVISIONAL GOVERNMENT—
    Proclaimed   Mar. 14, 1917
    Recognised by Great Britain, France, Italy, United States of America, Rumania and Switzerland   Mar. 22, 1917
    Dictatorship of, assumed by Kerenski   Sept. 10, 1917
    Overthrown by Bolshevik *coup d'état*   Nov. 8, 1917
    Kerenski's forces defeated by the Bolsheviki   Nov. 13, 1917
  REPUBLIC—declared   Sept. 15, 1917
  CONSTITUENT ASSEMBLY—
    Meet in Petrograd   Dec. 11, 1917
    Dispersed by the Bolsheviki   Dec. 13, 1917
    Again meet in Petrograd   Jan. 18, 1918
    Again dispersed by the Bolsheviki   Jan. 19, 1918
  SOVIETS, CONGRESS OF (at Moscow)—
    Decide to ratify Treaty of Peace with Central Powers   Mar. 14, 1918
  MINISTERS—
    PREMIER—
      1. Goremikin, *M.*—
        Appointed   Jan. 30, 1914
        Resigns   Feb. 1, 1916
      2. Stürmer, *M.*—
        Appointed   Feb. 1, 1916
        Resigns   Nov. 24, 1916
      3. Trepov, *M.*—
        Appointed   Nov. 24, 1916
        Resigns   Jan. 8, 1917
      4. Golitsin, *Prince*—
        Appointed   Jan. 8, 1917
        Removed from office   Mar. 13, 1917
      5. Lvov, *Prince*—
        Appointed   Mar. 15, 1917
        Resigns   July 19, 1917
      6. Kerenski, *M.*—Takes office   Aug. 6, 1917
      7. Lenin, *M.*—Assumes office   Nov. 8, 1917

RUSSIA (continued)—
  MINISTERS (continued)—
    MINISTER FOR FOREIGN AFFAIRS—
      1. Sazonov, M.—
        (Appointed .... —, 1910)
        Resigns .... July 22, 1916
      2. Stürmer, M.—
        Appointed .... July 22, 1916
        Resigns .... Nov. 24, 1916
      3. Pokrovski—
        Appointed .... Dec. 12, 1916
        Resigns .... Jan. 27, 1917
      4. Milyukov, M.—
        Appointed .... Mar. 15, 1917
        Resigns .... May 16, 1917
      5. Tereshchenko, M.—
        Appointed .... May 16, 1917
        Superseded .... Nov. 8, 1917
      6. Trotski, M.—
        Takes office .... Nov. 8, 1917
        Resigns .... Mar. 8, 1918
      7. Chichérin, M.—Appointed .... Mar. 8, 1918

    MINISTER FOR WAR—
      1. Sukhomlinov, General—
        (Appointed .... —, 1909)
        Resigns .... June 26, 1915
      2. Polivanov, General—
        Appointed .... June 26, 1915
        Resigns .... Mar. 29, 1916
      3. Shuvaev, General—
        Appointed .... Mar. 29, 1916
        Resigns .... Jan. 17, 1917
      4. Byelyaev, General—
        Appointed .... Jan. 17, 1917
        Superseded .... Mar. 13, 1917
      5. Guchkov, General—
        Appointed .... Mar. 15, 1917
        Resigns .... May 16, 1917
      6. Kerenski, M.—
        Appointed .... May 16, 1917
        Deposed .... Nov. 8, 1917
      7. Trotski, M.—Assumes office .... Mar. 8, 1918

  ARMY—
    I. COMMANDER-IN-CHIEF—
      1. Nicholas, Grand Duke—
        Appointed .... Aug. 3, 1914
        Resigns .... Sept. 5, 1915
      2. The Tsar—
        Appointed* .... Sept. 5, 1915
        Resigns on abdication .... Mar. 15, 1917
      3. Alexeiev, General*—
        Appointed .... Sept. 5, 1915
        Resigns .... June 4, 1917
      4. Brusilov, General—
        Appointed .... June 4, 1917
        Resigns .... Aug. 1, 1917
      5. Kornilov, General—
        Appointed .... Aug. 1, 1917
        Heads revolt against Government .. Sept. 8, 1917

    II. EXPEDITIONARY FORCES—
      To France—First units land at Marseilles .... Apr. 20, 1916
      To Salonika—First units land from Marseilles .... July 30, 1916

  FLEET—
    Black Sea fleet bombards Bosporus forts .... { Mar 27, 1915
                                                          Apr. 25, 1915
    Mutiny in Baltic fleet .... Mar. 16, 1917
    Mutiny in Black Sea fleet .... June 21, 1917
    Part of Black Sea fleet surrenders to the Germans .... May 1, 1918
    Battleship "Svobodnaya Rossiya" destroyed in Black Sea to avoid surrender.. June 18, 1918
    Black Sea portion of fleet taken over by the Allies .... Nov. 26, 1918
    (See also under "Riga.")

---

* General Alexeiev was Chief of Staff to the Tsar from September 5, 1915, to March 15, 1917, and as such was virtual, though not nominal, Commander-in-Chief. He continued to direct the armies until superseded by General Brusilov.

RUSSIA (continued)—
  NORTH—
    I. **Expeditionary Force, Allied**—
      (a.) Murmansk—

General Poole lands at, to organise the Expeditionary Force	May 24, 1918
British marines land at Pechenga	June 4, 1918

        Allied contingents—

(i.) British Expeditionary Forces " Syren " and " Elope " land at	June 23, 1918
(ii.) Bulk of French contingent land at	July 26, 1918
(iii.) Italian contingent land at	Sept. 2, 1918
(iv.) United States contingent land at	Sept. 4, 1918

      (b.) Archangel—

Defences of, attacked and captured by Allies	Aug. 1, 1918
Allied forces enter	Aug. 2, 1918
Canadian contingent arrive at	Sept. 30, 1918
General Ironside takes over command at	Oct. 4, 1918

    II. **Political, &c.**—

Expeditionary Force ordered to leave Russia by Bolshevik Government	June 8, 1918
Murman Sovdep decide to support the Allies against the Bolsheviki	June 30, 1918
Pro-Ally Revolution in Archangel	Aug. 2, 1918
General Marushevski appointed Governor-General of North Russia	Nov. 20, 1918

  TREATIES, &c. See under " Commitments."

" RUSSELL," H.M.S. (*Battleship*)—

Sunk	Apr. 27, 1916

S

SA'ID HALIM, *Pasha*—

Appointed Grand Vizier of Turkey	June , 1913
Resigns	Feb. 4, 1917

ST. CLEMENT (*France*)—

German airship " L. 44 " shot down at	Oct. 20, 1917

ST. JULIEN (*Ypres*)—

Battle of	Apr. 24—May 4, 1915

ST. KILDA (*Hebrides*)—

Bombarded by German submarine	May 15, 1918

ST. MIHIEL (*France*)—

Battle of	Sept. 12–13, 1918

ST. QUENTIN (*France*)—

Battle of*	Mar. 21–23, 1918
Town retaken by French forces	Oct. 1, 1918

ST. QUENTIN CANAL—

Battle of the	Sept. 29— Oct. 2, 1918

SAHIL (*Mesopotamia*)—

Affair of	Nov. 17, 1914

SAIHAN (*Mesopotamia*)—

Affair of	Nov. 15, 1914

  * British title and dates. For other battles bearing the same name in the French and German lists, see Appendix.

SALONIKA (*Greece*)—
  1. **Landing of Allied troops at**—
    Requested by Greek Premier (*M. Venizelos*) .. .. Oct. 2, 1915
    Arrive .. .. Oct. 3, 1915
    British and French troops land .. .. Oct. 5, 1915
    Italian troops land . .. . Aug. 12, 1916
    Russian troops land .. .. July 30, 1916
  2. **Withdrawal of Greek troops from**—
    Demanded by General Sarrail .. .. Dec. 9, 1915
    Refused by Greek Government .. .. Dec. 11, 1915
  3. **Governments set up at**—
    1. Albanian (Essad Pasha) .. .. Sept. 20, 1916
    2. Serbian .. .. May 7, 1916
  4. **Allied Commander-in-Chief**—
    1. Sarrail, *General*—
      Assumes command .. .. Jan. 16, 1916
      Recalled .. .. Dec. 14, 1917
    2. Guillaumat, *General*—
      Assumes command .. .. Dec. 22, 1917
      Recalled .. .. June 6, 1918
    3. Franchet d'Esperey, *General*—
      Appointed .. .. June 18, 1918
  5. **British Commander**—
    1. Mahon, *Lieutenant-General Sir* Bryan—
      Appointed .. .. Oct. 28, 1915
      Resigns .. .. May 9, 1916
    2. Milne, *Lieutenant-General Sir* G. F.—
      Takes over command .. .. May 9, 1916
  6. **Miscellaneous**—
    Consuls of Central Powers arrested and deported by order of General Sarrail Dec. 30, 1915
    German airship "L.Z. 85" shot down.. .. .. May 5, 1916
    Martial law proclaimed by General Sarrail .. .. June 3, 1916
    Venizelist revolution—Breaks out .. .. Aug. 30, 1916

SALT. See under "Es Salt."

"SALTA" (*British Hospital Ship*)—
  Sunk by mine .. .. Apr. 10, 1917

SAMARRA (*Mesopotamia*)—
  Taken by British forces .. .. Apr. 23–24, 1917

SAMBRE, River (*France*)—
  Battle of the .. .. Nov. 4, 1918

SAMOA (*Pacific*)—
  Occupied by New Zealand Expeditionary Force .. .. Aug. 30, 1914

SAMSAM ES SULTANEH—
  Appointed Persian Premier .. .. May 3, 1918
  Resigns .. .. May 31, 1918
  Reappointed .. .. June 20, 1918
  Resigns .. .. Aug. 3, 1918

SAN, River (*Galicia*)—
  Battle of the .. .. May 16–23, 1915

SANDERS, *General* Liman von—
  Appointed Commander of Turkish Dardanelles Army .. .. .. Mar. 25, 1915

"SAN DIEGO" (*United States Cruiser*)—
  Sunk by mine .. .. July 19, 1918

SAN GIOVANNI DI MEDUA. See under "Medua."

SAN MARINO—
Declares war on Austria-Hungary . . . . June 3, 1915

SANNA-I-YAT (*Mesopotamia*)—
First attack on . . . . Apr. 6, 1916
Second attack on . . . . Apr. 9, 1916
Third attack on . . . . Apr. 22, 1916
Capture of . . . . Feb. 17–24, 1917

SANTO DOMINGO—
Severs diplomatic relations with Germany . . . . June 11, 1917

SARAJEVO (*Bosnia*)—
Archduke Franz Ferdinand assassinated at . . . . June 28, 1914

SARRAIL, General (*G.O.C. French Forces at Salonika*)—
Demands withdrawal of Greek troops from Salonika . . . . . . Dec. 9, 1915
Causes arrest and deportation of consuls of Central Powers at Salonika . . Dec. 30, 1915
Assumes command of Allied troops at Salonika . . . . . . Jan. 16, 1916
Recalled to France . . . . Dec. 14, 1917

SARI BAIR (*Gallipoli*)—
Battle of—
Begins . . . . Aug. 6, 1915
Decisive day of . . . . Aug. 9, 1915
Ends . . . . Aug 10, 1915

SARIM ED DOULEH—
Appointed Persian Foreign Minister . . . . Mar. 6, 1916
Resigns . . . . Aug. 29, 1916

SARIKAMISH (*Caucasus*)—
Battle of—
Begins . . . . Dec. 29, 1914
Ends . . . . Jan. 2, 1915
Occupied by Turkish forces . . . . Apr. 4, 1918

SARREBOURG (*Lorraine*)—
Battle of . . . . Aug. 14–20, 1914

SAVE, River (*Serbia*)—
First crossed by Austro-German forces . . . . Aug. 12, 1914

SA'UD. See under " Nejd, Emir of."

SAZONOV, M.—
Appointed Russian Foreign Minister . . . . —— 1910
Resigns . . . . July 22, 1916

SCANDINAVIA—
Kings of Scandinavian States meet at Malmö . . . . . . Dec. 18, 1914
Governments' joint protest against German submarine warfare published . . Feb. 13, 1917

SCAPA FLOW—
German submarine raid on . . . . Oct. 17, 1914
Grand Fleet—
Withdraws from . . . . Oct. 18, 1914
Ordered back to . . . . Nov. 3, 1914
German High Seas Fleet arrives at Rosyth, for internment in . . . . Nov. 21, 1918

SCARBOROUGH (*Yorkshire*)—
    Bombarded .. .. Dec. 16, 1914
    Submarine raid on .. .. Sept. 4, 1917

SCARPE, River (*France*)—
    First Battle of, 1917 .. .. Apr. 9–14, 1917
    Second Battle of, 1917 .. .. Apr 23–24, 1917
    Third Battle of, 1917 .. .. May 3–4, 1917
    Battle of, 1918 .. .. Aug. 26–30, 1917

"SCHARNHORST" (*German Cruiser*)—
    Sunk .. .. Dec. 8, 1914

SCHERPENBERG, The (*France*)—
    Battle of .. .. Apr. 29, 1918

SCHEUCH, *Major-General*—
    Appointed German Minister for War .. . . Oct. 9, 1918
    Resigns .. .. Dec. 17, 1918

SCIMITAR HILL (*Suvla*)—
    Battle of .. .. Aug. 21, 1915

SCLATER, *Lieut.-General Sir* H. C.—
    Appointed Adjutant-General, Home Forces, Great Britain .. .. .. Apr. 9, 1914
    Resigns .. .. Feb. 21, 1916

SCUTARI (*Albania*)—
    Serbian Government leaves Prizren for .. .. Nov. 23, 1915
    Serbian Government set up at .. .. Dec. 3, 1915
    Occupied by Austrian forces .. .. Jan. 23, 1916
    Taken by Italian forces .. .. Oct. 31, 1918

SEAHAM (*Durham*)—
    Shelled by German submarine .. .. July 11, 1916

SEAPLANE (*British*)—
    First enemy ship sunk by torpedo from (*in Dardanelles*) .. .. .. Aug. 12, 1915

SEDAN (*France*)—
    Taken by German forces .. .. Aug. 29, 1914
    Taken by United States forces .. .. Nov. 6, 1918

"SEEADLER" (*German Raider*)—
    Leaves Germany .. .. Nov. 22, 1916
    Wrecked on Mopelia Island .. .. Aug. 2, 1917

SEIDLER, *Dr.* Ernst Ritter von—
    Appointed Austrian Premier .. .. June 23, 1917
    Resigns .. .. June 21, 1918

SELLE, River (*France*)—
    Battle of the .. .. Oct. 17–25, 1918

SEMENDRIA (*Serbia*)—
    Taken by Austrian forces .. .. Oct. 11, 1915

SEMLIN (*Hungary*)—
    Occupied by Serbian forces .. .. Sept. 10, 1914
    Evacuated by Serbian forces .. .. Sept. 17, 1914

SENUSSI—
    Commence hostilities against the British .. .. Nov. 14, 1915
    Operations against—
        Begin .. .. Nov. 23, 1915
        End .. .. Feb. 8, 1917
    (See also under " Agagiya," " Siwa," " Sollum," " Wadi Majid," and " Wadi Senaab.")

SERBIA—
    I. ULTIMATUM (presented)—
        By Austria-Hungary .. .. July 23, 1914

    II. MOBILISATION—Ordered .. .. July 25, 1914

    III. RELATIONS (severed)—
        By Austria-Hungary .. .. July 25, 1914

    IV. WAR (declared)—
        By **Austria-Hungary** .. .. July 28, 1914
        On **Germany** .. .. Aug. 6, 1914
        On **Turkey** .. .. Nov. 2, 1914
        By **Turkey** (*Jehad*) .. .. Nov. 14, 1914
        On **Bulgaria** .. .. Oct. 14, 1915
        By **Bulgaria** .. .. Oct. 14, 1915

    V. INVASIONS (by Austrian and German forces)—
        First—
            Begins .. .. Aug. 13, 1914
            Ends .. .. Aug. 25, 1914
        Second—
            Begins .. .. Sept. 8, 1914
            Ends .. .. Dec. 15, 1914
        Final—Begins .. .. Oct. 6, 1915

    VI. KING—
        Peter—
            Arrives at Salonika .. .. Jan. 1, 1916
            Leaves Salonika .. .. Jan. 15, 1916
            Arrives at Edypsos .. .. Jan. 17, 1916
            Re-enters Belgrade .. .. Nov. 6, 1918

    VII. MINISTERS—PREMIER—
        (A.) Of SERBIA—
            Pasich, *M.*—
                (Appointed .. .. ——, 1912)
                Resigns .. .. Dec. 20, 1918
        (B.) Of UNITED KINGDOM OF SERBS, CROATS AND SLOVENES—
            Protich, *M.*—Appointed .. .. Dec. 29, 1918

    VIII. GOVERNMENT—
        Transferred from Belgrade to Nish .. .. July 25, 1914
        Leave Nish .. .. Nov. 3, 1915
        Leave Prizren for Scutari .. .. Nov. 23, 1915
        Set up at Scutari .. .. Dec. 3, 1915
        Set up at Brindisi .. .. Jan. 15, 1916
        Set up at Corfu .. .. Feb. 9, 1916
        Set up at Salonika .. .. May 7, 1916
        Re-established at Belgrade .. .. Dec. 9, 1918

    IX. ARMY—
        1. **Retreat through Albania**—Begins .. .. Nov. 30, 1915
        2. **Concentration at Corfu**—
            Entente Governments inform Greek Government of proposed
                transport of Serbian Army to Corfu .. .. .. Jan. 10, 1916
            First Serbian troops land in Corfu .. .. .. Jan. 15, 1916
            Serbian Army concentrated at Corfu .. .. .. Feb. 10, 1916
        3. **Transfer from Corfu to Salonika**—
            Greek Government refuse overland route .. .. .. Apr. 3, 1916
            First units land at Salonika from Corfu .. .. April 15, 1916
            First units come into action on the Salonika front .. July 25, 1916

    X. MISCELLANEOUS—
        Entente *démarche* in Athens, Sofia and Bukharest to secure help for .. Dec. 5, 1914

    XI. TREATIES, &c. See under " Commitments."

SEVASTOPOL (*South Russia*) —
    Bombarded by the "Goeben" .. .. Oct. 29, 1914
    Russian battleship "Imperatritsa Mariya" blown up at .. .. .. Oct. 20, 1916
    Naval mutiny at.. .. .. June 21, 1917
    Taken by German forces .. .. May 1, 1918
    Allied Fleet arrives at .. .. Nov. 26, 1918

SHABATZ (*Serbia*)—
    Captured by Austrian forces .. .. Aug. 12, 1914
    Recaptured by Serbian forces .. .. Aug. 25, 1914
    Again captured by Austro-German forces .. .. Oct. 22, 1915

SHAIBA (*Mesopotamia*)—
    Battle of .. .. Apr. 12–14, 1915

SHANTUNG (*China*)—
    Japanese forces land in .. .. Sept. 2, 1914

SHARON (*Palestine*)—
    Battle of .. .. Sept. 19–25, 1918

SHARQAT (*Mesopotamia*)—
    Battle of—
        Begins .. .. Oct. 28, 1918
        Ends (*Turkish Army on the Tigris surrenders*) .. .. Oct. 30, 1918

SHATT AL ARAB, River (*Mesopotamia*)—
    British forces effect landing at mouth of .. .. Nov. 6, 1914

SHAVLI (*Baltic Provinces*)—
    Occupied by German forces .. .. Apr. 30, 1915
    Evacuated by German forces .. .. May 11, 1915

SHEIKH SA'AD (*Mesopotamia*)—
    Action of .. . . Jan. 6–8, 1916

SHEIKH SAÏD (*South Arabia*)—
    Stormed by British force .. .. Nov. 10, 1914
    Defences destroyed .. .. Nov 11, 1914

SHEIKH UL ISLAM. See under "Jehad."

SHERIF OF MECCA. See under "**Mecca, Sherif of.**"

SHIPPING—
    The "Clémentel Agreement" concluded between British and French Governments   Dec. 3, 1916
    Inter-Allied Chartering Committee established .. .. Jan. 6, 1917
    Agreement concluded between British, French and Italian Governments for tonnage
        for Allied foodstuffs .. .. Nov. 3, 1917
    Decision taken to form Allied Maritime Transport Council .. .. .. Dec. 3, 1917
    Establishment of Allied Maritime Transport Council agreed upon .. .. Feb. 15, 1918
    First meeting of Allied Maritime Transport Council .. .. Mar. 11, 1918
        (See also under "Britain—Shipping," "Convoys" and "Merchant Vessels.")

SHIRAZ (*South Persia*)—
    Occupied by British forces .. .. Nov. 12, 1916

SHKODRA. See under "Scutari."

SHUVAEV, *General*—
    Appointed Russian Minister for War   Mar. 29, 1916
    Resigns   Jan. 17, 1917

SIAM—
    Declares war on Germany and Austria-Hungary   July 22, 1917

SIBERIA—
    Independence declared by Council of   July 4, 1918
    Declaration of Independence cancelled   July 6, 1918

SIBIU (HERMANNSTADT) (*Transylvania*)—
    Taken by Rumanian forces   Sept. 1, 1916
    Battle of   Sept. 26–29, 1916
    Retaken by Austro-German forces   Sept. 29, 1916

SIDON (*Syria*)—
    Occupied by British forces   Oct. 6, 1918

SILISTRA (*Dobrudja*)—
    Taken by Bulgarian forces   Sept. 10, 1916

SIMS, *Admiral* (*U.S.N.*)—
    Arrives in England   Apr. 9, 1917
    Hoists his flag at Queenstown as Acting Commander-in-Chief, Irish Command   June 18, 1917

SIMNITZA (*Rumania*)—
    Austro-German army crosses Danube at   Nov. 23, 1916

"SIMOOM," H.M.S. (*Destroyer*)—
    Sunk in action   Jan. 23, 1917

SINGAPORE (*Malay States*)—
    Mutiny of the 5th Light Infantry (Indian Army) at   Feb. 15, 1915

SINN, AS, POSITION (*Mesopotamia*). See under "Kut al Amara."

SINN FEIN. See under "Ireland."

SIPAHSALAR A'ZAM—
    Appointed Persian Premier   Mar. 6, 1916
    Resigns   Aug. 29, 1916

SIWA OASIS (*Western Egypt*)—
    Affairs in   Feb. 3–5, 1917

SIXTE OF BOURBON, *Prince*—
    Communicates Austrian Emperor's peace proposal to French President   Mar. 31, 1917

SKOROPADSKI, *General*—
    Appointed "Hetman" of The Ukraine (*under German Military Dictatorship*)   Apr. 29, 1918

SKOULOUDHIS, *M.*
    Appointed Premier of Greece   Nov. 6, 1915
    Resigns   June 21, 1916

SKRA DI LEGEN (*Macedonia*)—
    Battle of .. .. May 31, 1918

SKUPSHTINA, MONTENEGRIN—
    Votes for union with Serbia .. .. Nov. 29, 1918

SLAV RACES—
    United States Government announce their views in favour of the ultimate freedom of all branches of the .. .. June 29, 1918
        (See under " Poles," " Czecho-Slovaks," " Yugo-Slavs," &c.)

" SLAVA " (*Russian Battleship*)—
    Sunk .. .. Oct. 16, 1917

SLAVONIA—
    British Foreign Minister gives guarantee as to eventual freedom and self-determination of .. .. Aug. 30, 1915

SLOVAKS. See under " Czecho-Slovaks."

SLOVENES—
    National Council of, meet at Lyubliana .. .. Aug. 17, 1918
    National leaders of, take over administration of Carniola from Austrian authorities.. Nov. 2, 1918

SMITH-DORRIEN, *General Sir* H.—
    Appointed to command of British forces, East Africa .. .. Nov. 22, 1915
    *Resigns.. .. .. Jan. 31, 1916

SMUTS, *General* J. C.—
    Takes command of British forces in East Africa .. .. Feb. 19, 1916
    Resigns .. .. Jan. 20, 1917

SMYRNA (*Asia Minor*)—
    Bombarded by British squadron .. .. Mar. 5-9, 1915
    Entente offer to Greece of—
        Made .. .. Apr. 12, 1915
        Rejected .. .. Apr. 14, 1915

SOISSONS (*France*)—
    Taken by German forces .. .. Sept. 1, 1914
    Retaken by French forces .. .. Sept. 13, 1914
    Battle of .. .. Jan. 8-14, 1915
    Again taken by German forces .. .. May 29, 1918
    Retaken by Allied forces .. .. Aug. 2, 1918

SOISSONNAIS AND OURCQ (*France*)—
    Battle of† .. .. July 23—Aug. 2, 1918

SOLLUM (*Western Egypt*)—
    Bombarded by German submarine .. .. Nov. 6, 1915
    Attacked by Senussi .. .. Nov. 14, 1915
    Evacuated by British (*Egyptian*) force .. .. Nov. 23, 1915
    Reoccupied by British forces .. .. Mar. 14, 1916

SOMME, River (*France*)—
    Battles of the, 1916 .. .. July 1—Nov. 18, 1916
    German retreat from, 1917 .. .. Mar. 14—Apr. 5, 1917
    First Battles of the, 1918 .. .. Mar. 21—Apr. 5, 1918
    Second Battles of the, 1918 .. .. Aug. 21—Sept. 3, 1918

        * Did not take over command owing to illness.
        † British dates.

SONNINO, *Baron* Sidney—
    Appointed Italian Foreign Minister .. .. Nov 3, 1914
    Resigns .. .. May 13, 1915
    Reappointed .. .. May 16, 1915

SOROKI (*Murman Railway*)—
    Allied forces seize Railway from Murmansk to .. .. June 30, 1918

SORREL, Mount. See under "Mount Sorrel."

SOUCHON, *Admiral*—
    Assumes control of Turkish navy .. .. Sept. 17, 1914

SOUTH AFRICA. See under "Africa, South."

SOUTH-WEST AFRICA. See under "Africa, South-West."

SOUTHWOLD (*Suffolk*)—
    Shelled by German destroyers .. .. Jan. 25, 1917

SOVDEP (*Murman Soviet*)—
    Decide to support the Entente against the Bolshevik Government .. .. June 30 1918

SOVIETS, CONGRESS OF. See under "Russia."

SPEE, *Admiral Count* von (*commanding German Pacific Squadron*)—
    Leaves Ponape (Caroline Islands) .. .. Aug. 6, 1914
    Bombards Papeete . .. . Sept. 22, 1914
    Defeats British Squadron in action off Coronel .. .. Nov. 1, 1914
    Lost with his ship at Battle of the Falklands .. .. Dec. 8, 1914

"SPEEDY," H.M.S. (*Torpedo Gunboat*)—
    Sunk by mine off the Humber .. .. Sept. 3, 1914

SPHINXHAVEN (*Lake Nyassa*)—
    Affair of .. .. May 30, 1915

STAFF, GENERAL, CHIEFS OF. See under the respective countries.

STANISLAU (*Galicia*)—
    Taken by Russian forces .. .. Oct. 30, 1914
    Recaptured by Austrian forces .. .. Feb. 19, 1915
    Retaken by Russian forces .. .. Mar. 4, 1915
    Recaptured by Austro-German forces .. .. June 8, 1915
    Again taken by Russian forces .. .. Aug. 10, 1916
    Again recaptured by Austrian forces .. .. July 24, 1917

STATE OF WAR. See under "War, Declarations of."

STEIN, *Lieut.-General* von—
    Appointed German Minister for War .. .. Oct. 30, 1916
    Resigns .. .. Oct. 9, 1918

STERLITAMAK (*East Russia*)—
    Taken by Bolshevik forces .. .. Dec. 31, 1918

STEWART, *Brig.-General* J. M.—
    Takes over command of British forces in East Africa .. .. Sept. 1, 1914
    Relinquishes command .. .. Oct. 31, 1914

STOCK EXCHANGE (*London*)—
    Closed .. .. July 31, 1914
    Reopened .. .. Jan. 4, 1915

STOCKHOLM—
    Labour Conference at. British London Party decide to send delegates to .. Aug. 10, 1917
    British Government refuse passports for delegates to .. .. Aug. 13, 1917

STRASBOURG (*Alsace*)—
    Occupied by French forces .. .. Nov. 25, 1918

"STRONGBOW," H.M.S. (*Destroyer*)—
    Sunk .. .. Oct. 17, 1917

STRYJ (*Galicia*)—
    Battle of .. .. May 24—June 11, 1915

STRUMITSA (*Bulgaria*)—
    Serbian Government give Greek Government undertaking not to claim .. .. Sept. 25, 1915
    First Action of Strumitsa Station .. .. Oct. 14, 1915
    Second Action of Strumitsa Station.. .. .. Oct. 21, 1915

STRYPA, River (*Galicia*)—
    Battle of .. .. June 11–30, 1916

STÜRGKH, *Count*—
    (Appointed Austrian Premier .. .. Nov. 3, 1911)
    Assassinated .. .. Oct. 21, 1916

STÜRMER, *M.*—
    Appointed Premier of Russia .. .. Feb. 1, 1916
    Takes office also as Foreign Minister .. .. July 22, 1916
    Resigns both offices .. .. Nov. 24, 1916

SUBMARINES—
    (A.) INDIVIDUAL SUBMARINES—
        1. **British**—
            "E. 1" and "E. 9"—First submarines to enter Baltic .. .. Oct. 17, 1914
            "B. 11"—
                First submarine to enter Dardanelles .. .. .. Nov. 6, 1914
                Sinks Turkish battleship "Messoudieh" in Dardanelles .. Dec. 13, 1914
            "E. 11"—Sinks Turkish battleship "Barbarousse-Hairedine" .. Aug. 8, 1915
            "E. 1"—Torpedoes German battle cruiser "Moltke" .. .. Aug. 19, 1915
            "E. 8"—Sinks German cruiser "Prinz Adalbert" .. .. Oct. 23, 1915
            "E. 13"—Destroyed in Danish waters .. .. .. Aug. 19, 1915
            "E. 19"—Sinks German cruiser "Undine" .. .. .. Nov. 7, 1915
        2. **German**—
            "U. 15"—Sunk by H.M.S. "Birmingham" in the North Sea (first
                sunk) .. .. Aug. 9, 1914
            "U. 9"—Sinks H.M.S. "Aboukir," "Cressy," and "Hogue" .. Sept. 22, 1914
            "U. 20"—Sinks s.s. "Lusitania" .. .. May 7, 1915
            "U. 27"—Destroyed by H.M.S. "Baralong" .. .. .. Aug. 19, 1915
            "U. 53"—Captures and destroys five ships outside Newport
                (Rhode Island) .. .. Oct. 8, 1916
            "Deutschland" ("commercial submarine")—
                Arrives at Norfolk (Va.) .. .. July 10, 1916
                Returns to Germany .. .. Aug. 23, 1916

SUBMARINES (continued)—
  (B.) SHIPS SUNK BY SUBMARINES—
    1. **British**—
      (a.) **Warships** (excluding destroyers and other light craft)—

"Aboukir"	Sept. 22, 1914
"Britannia"	Nov. 9, 1918
"Cornwallis"	Jan. 9, 1917
"Cressy"	Sept. 22, 1914
"Drake"	Oct. 2, 1917
"Falmouth"	Aug. 19, 1916
"Formidable"	Jan. 1, 1915
"Hawke"	Oct. 15, 1914
"Hermes"	Oct. 31, 1914
"Hogue"	Sept. 22, 1914
"Majestic"	May 27, 1915
"Niger"	Nov. 11, 1914
"Nottingham"	Aug. 19, 1916
"Pathfinder"*	Sept. 5, 1914
"Triumph"	May 25, 1915

      (b.) **Hospital Ships**—

"Donegal" (Ambulance Transport)	Apr. 17, 1917
"Dover Castle"	May 26, 1917
"Glenart Castle"	Feb. 26, 1918
"Lanfranc" (Ambulance Transport)	Apr. 17, 1917
"Llandovery Castle"	June 27, 1918
"Rewa"	Jan. 4, 1918
"Warilda" (Ambulance Transport)	Aug. 3, 1918

        (N.B.—Torpedoed but not sunk—"Asturias," Mar. 21, 1917; "Gloucester Castle," Mar. 30, 1917; and "Guildford Castle," Mar. 10, 1918.)

      (c.) **Merchant Ships, &c.** (of outstanding importance)—

"Arabic"	Aug. 19, 1915
"Falaba"	Mar. 28, 1915
"Laconia"	Feb. 25, 1917
"Leinster"	Oct. 10, 1918
"Lusitania"	May 7, 1915
"Ruel"	Aug. 21, 1915
"Surada"†	Nov. 2, 1918
"Tuscania"	Feb. 5, 1918

        (N.B.—Torpedoed but not sunk—"Sussex," Mar. 24, 1916.)

      (d.) **Transport**—

"Royal Edward"‡	Aug. 13, 1915

    2. **French Warships**—

"Amiral Charner"	Feb. 8, 1916
"Château Renault"	Dec. 14, 1917
"Danton"	Mar. 19, 1917
"Dupetit Thouars"	Aug. 7, 1918
"Gaulois"	Dec. 27, 1916
"Kléber"	June 27, 1917
"Léon Gambetta"	Apr. 26, 1915
"Suffren"	Nov. 26, 1916

    3. (a.) **German Warships**—

"Prinz Adalbert"	Oct. 23, 1915
"Undine"	Nov. 7, 1915
"Bremen"	Dec. 17, 1915

      (b.) **German Merchant Ship**—

"Livonia"	Oct. 3, 1915

    4. **Italian Warships**—

"Amalfi"	July 7, 1915
"Giuseppe Garibaldi"	July 18, 1915

    5. **Italian Merchant Ship**—

"Ancona"	Nov. 7, 1915

    6. **Russian**—
      (a.) **Warship**—

"Pallada"	Oct. 11, 1914

      (b.) **Hospital Ships**—

"Portugal"	Mar. 30, 1916
"Vpered"	July 10, 1916

    7. **Turkish Warships**—

"Barbarousse Hairedine"	Aug. 8, 1915
"Messoudieh"	Dec. 13, 1914

(C.) LOCALITIES RAIDED—

    1. BY BRITISH SUBMARINES—Constantinople   Aug. 1, 1915

---

* First British warship to be sunk by submarine.
† Last merchant vessel sunk by submarine.
‡ First transport sunk.

SUBMARINES (*continued*)—
   (C.) LOCALITIES RAIDED (*continued*)—
     2. BY GERMAN SUBMARINES—

Scapa Flow	Oct. 17, 1914
Barrow (Walney Island)	Jan. 29, 1915
Whitehaven (Cumberland)	Aug. 16, 1915
Sollum (West Egypt)	Nov. 6, 1915
Seaham (Durham)	July 11, 1916
Funchal (Madeira)	Dec. 3, 1916
Ponta Delgada (Azores)	July 4, 1917
Scarborough	Sept. 4, 1917
Funchal (Madeira)	Dec. 12, 1917
Dover	Feb. 16, 1918
Monrovia (Liberia)	Apr. 10, 1918
St. Kilda (Hebrides)	May 15, 1918

   (D) GERMAN SUBMARINE BLOCKADE OF GREAT BRITAIN.—

Announced	Feb. 4, 1915
Begins	Feb. 18, 1915
American demand for limitation of German submarine warfare accepted by German Government	Sept. 1, 1915
German Government send Note to United States Government stating that it is not intended to postpone extended submarine campaign	Feb. 29, 1916
(See also under "Notes.")	
"Extended campaign"—Begins	Mar. 1, 1916
"Unrestricted submarine warfare"—Begins	Feb. 1, 1917

   (E.) ANTI-SUBMARINE NETS—
     1. "Indicator" Nets—

First submarine ("U. 8") destroyed by aid of	Mar. 4, 1915

     2. Net Barrage—

Of Dover Straits—Boom established	Apr. 3, 1915
„ North Channel—Established	Feb. 22, 1915
„ Otranto Straits—Established	Oct. 1, 1918
„ Belgian Coast—Begun	Apr. 24, 1916

   (F.) STAGES OF GERMAN SUBMARINE WARFARE—

First British warship sunk (H.M S. "Pathfinder")	Sept. 5, 1914
First British merchant vessel sunk (s.s. "Glitra")	Oct. 20, 1914
First neutral ship torpedoed without warning (Norwegian s.s. "Belridge")	Feb. 19, 1915
First neutral ship sunk without warning (Swedish s.s. "Hanna")	Mar. 13, 1915
First neutral ship sunk after visit and search (Dutch s.s. "Medea")	Mar. 25, 1915
First passenger ship sunk (s.s. "Falaba")	Mar. 28, 1915
First instance of merchant vessel beating off submarine by gunfire (s.s. "La Rosarina")	Apr. 17, 1915
First United States ship torpedoed without warning (s.s. "Gulflight")	May 1, 1915
First British transport sunk ("Royal Edward")	Aug. 13, 1915
First authenticated case of German submarine firing on a crew in boats (s.s. "Ruel")	Aug. 21, 1915
First British hospital ship torpedoed ("Asturias")	Mar. 21, 1917
First British hospital ship sunk ("Dover Castle")	May 26, 1917
First contingent of German submarines surrender at Harwich	Nov. 20, 1918

(For other details, see Part II (Naval).)

SUEZ CANAL—

First Turkish offensive against	Jan. 26–Feb. 17, 1915
Actions on the	Feb. 3–4, 1915
Second Turkish offensive against	July 19–Aug. 12, 1916
Battle of Rumani	Aug. 4–5, 1916

"SUFFREN" (*French Battleship*)—

Sunk	Nov. 26, 1916

SUKHOMLINOV, *General*—

Appointed Russian Minister for War	1909
Resigns	June 26, 1915

"SUSSEX," S.S. (*British*)—

Torpedoed	Mar. 24, 1916

SUVLA (*Gallipoli*)—
  Landing at, operations of—
    Begin   Aug. 6, 1915
    End   Aug. 15, 1915
  Evacuation of—
    Ordered   Dec. 8, 1915
    Completed   Dec. 20, 1915

"SVOBODNAYA ROSSIYA" (*Russian Battleship*)—
  Destroyed in Black Sea   June 18, 1918

SWAKOPMUND (*German South-West Africa*)—
  Occupied by South African forces   Jan. 14, 1915

"SWIFT," H.M.S. (*Destroyer*)—
  Action in Dover Straits   Apr. 20, 1917

SWITZERLAND—
  Orders mobilisation   Aug. 8, 1914

"SYDNEY," H.M.A.S. (*Light Cruiser*)—
  Destroys German cruiser "Emden"   Nov. 9, 1914

"SYKES-PICOT" AGREEMENTS—
  1. Between French and Russian Governments as to eventual partition of Asia Minor—
    Concluded   Apr. 26, 1916
    British Government notify Russian Government of their recognition of   May 23, 1916
  2. Between British and French Governments as to eventual partition of Asia Minor, &c.   May 9, 1916
  3. Between Russian and British Governments as to eventual partition of Asia Minor   Sept. 1, 1916

"SYREN" (*British Expeditionary Force*)—
  Disembarks at Murmansk   June 23, 1918

SYRIA—
  French claim to, lodged with British Government   Mar. 17, 1915

"SZENT-ISTVAN" (*Austrian Battleship*)—
  Sunk   June 10, 1918

T

TABORA (*East Africa*)—
  Occupied by Belgian forces   Sept. 19, 1916

TABRIZ (*North Persia*)—
  Evacuated by Russian forces*   Jan. 5, 1915
  Occupied by Turkish forces   Jan. 8, 1915
  Reoccupied by Russian forces   Jan. 30, 1915
  Again occupied by Turkish forces   June 14, 1918

TAGUS RIVER—
  German ships in, seized by the Portuguese   Feb. 23, 1916

* Was occupied before declaration of war.

TAIF (*Hejaz*)—
    Surrenders to the Sherif of Mecca..   Sept. 22, 1916

"TAKACHIHO" (*Japanese Cruiser*)—
    Sunk   Oct. 18, 1914

TALAAT *Pasha*—
    Appointed Grand Vizier of Turkey..   Feb. 4, 1917
    Resigns   Oct. 13, 1918

TANAKA, *Lieut.-General* Giichi—
    Appointed Japanese Minister for War   Sept. 30, 1918

TANGA (*German East Africa*)—
    British attack on repulsed   Nov. 2–5, 1914
    Occupied by British forces   July 7, 1916

TANGANYIKA, LAKE (*Central Africa*)—
    British naval operations on, begin   Dec. 23, 1915
    * Naval action on   Dec. 26, 1915
    * Naval action on   Feb. 9, 1916

TANGISTANI Tribesmen—
    Attack British Residency at Bushire   July 12, 1915
     Sept. 9, 1915

TANKS (*British*)—
    In action for first time   Sept. 15, 1916
    Aerial co-operation instituted with..   Sept. 15, 1916
    Corps formed   July 28, 1917

TANNENBERG (*East Prussia*)—
    Battle of   Aug. 23–31, 1914

TARDENOIS (*France*)—
    Battle of †   July 29–Aug. 7, 1918

TÂRGA JIU (*Rumania*)—
    Battle of   Nov. 16–17, 1916

TARNAVKA (*Galicia*)—
    Battle of   Sept. 7–9, 1914

TARNOPOL (*Galicia*)—
    Battle of   Sept. 7–16, 1915
    Captured by Austro-German forces   July 24, 1917

TATAR NATIONAL COUNCIL—
    Proclaims establishment of Republic of Azerbaijan   May 26, 1918
        (See also under "Trans-Caucasia.")

    * For vessels engaged, see Part I.
    † French dates.

TAVETA (*East Africa*)—
    Occupied by a German force .. .. Aug. 15, 1914
    Taken by British forces .. .. Mar. 10, 1916

TEHERAN (*North Persia*)—
    Representatives of Central Powers leave .. .. Nov. 15, 1915

TEKRIT (*Mesopotamia*). See "Tikrit."

"TELEGRAM, WARNING." See under "Warning Telegram."

TEPE (*Cameroons*)—
    Affair of .. .. Aug. 25, 1914

TERAUCHI, *Count*—
    Appointed Japanese Prime Minister .. .. Oct. 9, 1916
    Appointed acting Minister for Foreign Affairs .. .. Oct. 9, 1916
    Relinquishes Acting appointment .. .. Nov. 20, 1916
    Resigns office as Prime Minister .. .. Sept. 29, 1918

TERESHCHENKO, *M.*—
    Appointed Russian Foreign Minister .. .. May 16, 1917
    Superseded .. .. Nov. 8, 1917

TERRITORIAL FORCE (*British*)—
    First division of, leaves for France.. .. .. Feb. 24, 1915

TERMONDE (*Belgium*)—
    Taken by German forces .. .. Oct. 2, 1914

THEBERTON (*Suffolk*)—
    German airship "L-48" destroyed at .. .. June 17, 1917

THEODOSIA (*Crimea*)—
    Bombarded by Turkish warships .. .. Oct. 29, 1914

THESSALY (*Greece*)—
    Entente Powers demand entire withdrawal of Greek armies from .. .. Dec. 14, 1916

THIAUMONT, Fort (*Verdun*)—
    Stormed by German forces .. .. June 23, 1916
    Retaken by French forces .. .. June 30, 1916

THIEPVAL RIDGE (*France*)—
    Battle of .. .. Sept. 26–28, 1916

THOMAS, *M.* Albert—
    Announces arrangement completed for inter-Allied organisation of munitions .. Nov. 25, 1915

TIFLIS (*Georgia*)—
    Occupied by German forces .. .. June 12, 1918

TIGHE, *Major-General M.*—
    Takes over command of British forces in East Africa .. .. Apr. 16, 1915
    Succeeded by General Smuts .. .. Feb. 19, 1916

TIKRIT (*Mesopotamia*)—
    Action of .. .. Nov. 5, 1917
    Occupied by British forces .. .. Nov. 6, 1917

TIRPITZ, *Admiral* von—
    Appointed German Minister of Marine .. .. —, 1897
    Resigns .. .. Mar. 14, 1916

TISZA, *Count* Stephan—
    Appointed Hungarian Prime Minister (*under Joint Monarchy*) .. .. .. June 10, 1913
    Resigns .. .. May 23, 1917
    Assassinated in Vienna .. .. Oct. 31, 1918

TOGOLAND—
    British forces cross frontier of .. .. Aug. 8, 1914
    Allied advance on Kamina from Lome begins .. .. Aug. 13, 1914
    Capitulates to Allied commander at Amuchu .. .. Aug. 26, 1914
    Franco-British agreement concluded defining respective zones of .. .. Aug. 31, 1914
    Agreement concluded *re* administration of .. .. Dec. 27, 1916

TRADE COMMITTEE, JOINT (*of Entente Powers*)—
    Formed in Holland .. .. May 9, 1918

"TRADING WITH THE ENEMY." See under "Contraband."

TRANS-CASPIA—
    British operations in, begin .. .. July 19, 1918
    Affair near Kaakhka .. .. Aug. 28, 1918
    Action of Dushak .. .. Oct. 12, 1918

TRANS-CAUCASIA—
    Federal Republic of Armenia, Georgia, Azerbaijan and Daghestan—Proclaimed .. Sept. 20, 1917
    Independence—Declared .. .. Apr. 22, 1918
    Dissolution of Federal Republic announced .. .. May 26, 1918
    (See also under "Armenia," "Azerbaijan" and "Georgia.")

TRANSLOY RIDGES (*Somme*)—
    Battle of .. .. Oct. 1–18, 1916

TRANSVAAL. See under "Africa, South."

TRANSYLVANIA—
    Invaded by Rumanian forces .. .. Aug. 28, 1916
    National Council of, vote for union with Rumania .. .. Dec. 1, 1918

TREATIES. See under "Commitments."

TREBIZOND (*Asia Minor*)—
    Bombarded by Russian squadron .. .. Nov. 17, 1914
    Russian forces begin attack on .. .. Apr. 6, 1916
    Taken by Russian forces .. .. Apr. 17, 1916
    Retaken by Turkish forces .. .. Feb. 24, 1918

TRENCHARD, *Major-General Sir* H. M.—
    Takes over tactical command of the Independent Air Force in France .. .. June 5, 1918

TRENTINO, THE—
    Frontier of, crossed by Italian troops .. May 24, 1915
    Austrian offensive in—
        Begins .. May 14, 1916
        Ends .. June 3, 1916
    Italian counter-offensive in—
        Begins .. June 16, 1916
        Ends .. July 7, 1916

TREPOV, *M.*—
    Appointed Premier of Russia .. Nov. 24, 1916
    Resigns .. Jan. 8, 1917

TRÈVES (*Germany*)—
    Occupied by United States troops .. Dec. 1, 1918

TRIESTE (*Austria*)—
    Italian naval raid on .. Dec. 9, 1917
    Occupied by Italian forces.. Nov. 3, 1918

TRIPLE ALLIANCE, THE—
    Italy denounces.. May 4, 1915

TRIPOLI (*Syria*)—
    Occupied by Allied forces.. Oct. 13, 1918

" TRIUMPH," H.M.S. (*Battleship*)—
    Sunk .. May 25, 1915

TROTSKI, *M.* Leo—
    Assumes power in Petrograd .. Nov. 8, 1917
    Appointed People's Commissary for Foreign Affairs .. Nov. 8, 1917
    Announces cessation of hostilities on Russian front and opening of negotiations for separate peace with Germany .. Nov. 29, 1917
    Agrees to German demand to continue negotiations at Brest-Litovsk .. Jan. 8, 1918
    Issues Circular Note complaining of German peace terms .. Jan. 23, 1918
    Announces end of war between Russia and Central Powers .. Feb. 10, 1918
    Vacates office and becomes Minister for War .. Mar. 8, 1918

TSAR (*Nicholas II*)—
    Signs order for mobilisation of Russian army .. July 30, 1914
    Assumes supreme command of the Russian armies .. Sept. 5, 1915
    Abdicates .. Mar. 15, 1917
    Murdered at Ekaterinburg .. July 16, 1918

TSARITSA (and family)—
    Murdered at Ekaterinburg .. July 16, 1918

TSAVO (*East Africa*)—
    Affair of .. Sept. 6, 1914

TSER AND JADAR (*Serbia*)—
    Battle of the .. Aug. 17–21, 1914

TSINGTAU (*China*)—
    Japan sends ultimatum to Germany demanding evacuation of .. Aug. 15, 1914
    Japanese forces land in Shantung to attack .. Sept. 2, 1914
    British force joins Japanese besieging .. Sept. 23, 1914
    Capitulates to the Japanese forces .. Nov. 7 1914
    Agreement concluded between Japan and China as to Customs of .. Aug. 6, 1915

"TSUKUBA" (*Japanese Battle Cruiser*)—
    Sunk by internal explosion .. .. Jan. 14, 1917

TURKEY—
    MOBILISATION—Ordered .. .. July 31, 1914
    HOSTILITIES (commenced)—
        Against Russia .. .. Oct. 29, 1914
        By Britain .. .. Nov. 1, 1914
    I. ULTIMATUM (presented)—By Allies.. .. .. .. Oct. 30, 1914
    II. RELATIONS (severed)—
        By Britain ⎫
        By France ⎬ .. .. Oct. 30, 1914
        By Russia ⎭
        With Belgium .. .. Nov. 6, 1914
        With United States of America .. .. Apr. 20, 1917
        By Greece .. .. June 27, 1917
    III. WAR (declared)—
        By **Russia** .. .. Nov. 2, 1914
        By **Serbia** .. .. Nov. 2, 1914
        By **Britain** .. .. Nov. 5, 1914
        On all Entente Powers (Holy War).. .. .. .. Nov. 14, 1914
        By **France** .. .. Nov. 5, 1914
        By **Italy** .. .. Aug. 21, 1915
        On **Rumania** .. .. Aug. 30, 1916
        By **Greece** .. .. June 27, 1917
    IV. PEACE (signed)—
        With Russian Bolshevik Government .. .. .. Mar. 3, 1918
        With Rumania—preliminary Treaty .. .. .. Mar. 5, 1918
        With Rumania—final Treaty .. .. May 7,
        With Finland .. .. May 11, 1918
        With Georgia ⎱
        With Armenia ⎰ .. .. June 8, 1918
    V. TREATY WITH BULGARIA—
        (*a.*) Frontier Convention with Bulgaria signed .. .. Sept. 9, 1915
        (*b.*) "**Dede Agatch Agreement**" concluded .. .. Sept. 22, 1915
    VI. SULTAN—
        1. **Mohammed V**—
            Proclaims Jehad.. .. .. Nov. 14, 1914
            Dies .. .. July 3, 1918
        2. **Mohammed VI**—Succeeds .. .. July 3, 1918
    VII. MINISTERS—
        Grand Vizier—
            1. **Sa'id Halim** *Pasha*—
                Appointed .. .. June 1913
                Resigns .. .. Feb. 4, 1917
            2. **Talaat** *Pasha*—
                Appointed .. .. Feb. 4, 1917
                Resigns .. .. Oct. 13, 1918
            3. **Izzet** *Pasha* .. .. Oct. 13, 1918
    VIII. TREATIES, &c. See under "Commitments."

"TUSCANIA," *S.S.* (*British*)—
    Sunk .. .. Feb 5 1918

TUTRAKAN (*Dobrudja*)—
    Captured by Bulgarian forces .. .. Sept. 6, 1916

U

"**U-BOATS**." See under "Submarines."

UCHIDA, *Count* Yasuya—
    Appointed Japanese Minister for Foreign Affairs .. .. .. Sept. 29, 1918

UDINE (*Venetia*)—
    Captured by Austro-German forces.. .. .. Oct. 28, 1917
    Recaptured by Italian forces .. .. Nov. 3, 1918

UFA (*East Prussia*)—
 Captured by Bolshevik forces .. .. Dec. 31, 1918

UGANDA (*Africa*)—
 Agreement concluded between Great Britain and Belgium *re* delimitation of Uganda-Congo boundary .. .. Feb. 3, 1915

UJIJI (*German East Africa*)—
 Occupied by Belgian forces .. .. Aug. 3, 1916

UKHTINSKAYA (*Murman Front*)—
 Captured by Allied forces .. .. Sept. 11, 1918

UKRAINE, THE—
 REPUBLIC—
  Declared .. .. Nov. 20, 1917
  Recognised by Central Powers .. .. Feb. 1, 1918
 DICTATORSHIP—Germany establishes .. .. Apr. 29, 1918
 PRESIDENT—Ustemovich, *M.*—Proclaimed .. .. May 9, 1918
 HETMAN—Skoropadski, *General*—Proclaimed .. .. Apr. 29, 1918
 ARMISTICE—
  With Bolshevik Russia, concluded (*by German-Ukrainian Command*) .. May 4, 1918
  With Bolshevik Russia (*by whole State of*) .. .. .. June 12, 1918
 PEACE—
  With Bulgaria, Central Powers and Turkey signed, together with supplementary Treaties with Germany and Austria-Hungary .. .. .. Feb. 9, 1918
  British Foreign Minister informs Polish National Committee that Great Britain does not accept the Treaty between The Ukraine and Central Powers .. Feb. 20, 1918
 WAR—
  "State of War" with Poland—Begins .. .. Nov. 1, 1918
  Revolt of General Petlyura—Begins .. .. Nov. 15, 1918
 WEST—Republic formed .. .. Dec. 26, 1918

ULTIMATUM—
 1. **Austria-Hungary** to **Serbia**—Presented .. .. July 23, 1914
 2. **Britain** to **Germany**—Presented .. .. Aug. 4, 1914
 3. **Entente Powers** to—
  (1.) **Bulgaria**—Presented .. .. Oct. 4, 1915
  (2.) **Greece**—*
   First (demanding demobilisation)—
    Presented .. .. June 21, 1916
    Accepted .. .. June 21, 1916
   Second (demanding surrender of the Greek Fleet)—
    Presented .. .. Oct. 10, 1916
    Accepted .. .. Oct. 11, 1916
   Third (demanding dismissal of Ministers of Central Powers and surrender of Greek military material)—
    Presented .. .. Nov. 19, 1916
    Refused .. .. Dec. 1, 1916
   Fourth (demanding withdrawal of Greek armies from Thessaly)—
    Presented .. .. Dec. 14, 1916
    Accepted .. .. Dec. 15, 1916
   Fifth (demanding the abdication of King Constantine)—
    Presented .. .. June 11, 1917
    Accepted .. .. June 12, 1917
 4. **Germany** to—
  Belgium .. .. Aug. 2, 1914
  Rumania (demanding peace) .. .. Feb. 6, 1918
  Russia .. .. July 31, 1914
 5. **Japan** to—
  China—
   Presented .. .. May 7, 1915
   Accepted .. .. May 9, 1915
  Germany—Presented .. .. Aug. 15, 1914

M M AL HANNA (*Mesopotamia*)—
 Kut relieving force repulsed at (*Action of Hanna*) .. .. .. Jan. 21, 1916
 Captured by British forces (*Action of Falahiya*) .. .. .. Apr. 5, 1916

* Only the fourth of these was officially described as an "Ultimatum."

"UNDAUNTED," H.M.S. (*Light Cruiser*)—
    Action with German destroyers off Dutch Coast .. .. Oct 17, 1914

UNDERTAKINGS (Political). See under "Commitments."

"UNDINE" (*German Light Cruiser*)—
    Sunk .. .. Nov 7, 1915

UPINGTON (*South Africa*)—
    Defence of .. .. Jan. 23–24, 1915

URMIA (*Persian Armenia*)—
    Evacuated by Russian forces* .. .. Jan. 2, 1915
    Occupied by Turkish regular forces .. .. Apr. 16, 1915
    Retaken by Russian forces .. .. May 24, 1915

URUGUAY—
    Severs diplomatic relations with Germany .. .. Oct. 7, 1917

ÜSKÜB (*Serbia*)—
    Taken by Bulgarian forces .. .. Oct. 22, 1915

USTEMOVICH, M.—
    Proclaimed President of The Ukraine .. .. May 9, 1918

V

VALENCIENNES (*France*)—
    Taken by German forces .. .. Aug 25, 1914
    Battle of .. .. Nov. 1–2, 1918
    Entered by British forces .. .. Nov. 3, 1918

VALONA (*Albania*)—
    Italian force landed at .. .. Dec. 26, 1914
    Italian Government notify Austrian Government of provisional occupation of .. Dec. 26, 1914
    Formally occupied by Italian forces .. .. May 29, 1915

VAN (*Turkish Armenia*)—
    Armenian revolt at .. .. Apr. 20, 1915
    Armenian defence of .. .. Apr. 20—May 19, 1915
    Occupied by Russian forces .. .. May 19, 1915
    Evacuated by Russian forces .. .. Aug. 3, 1915
    Reoccupied by Turkish forces .. .. Aug. 5, 1915

"VANGUARD," H.M.S. (*Battleship*)—
    Sunk by internal explosion .. .. July 9, 1917

VARDAR, River (*Macedonia*)—
    Battle of the .. .. May 5–22, 1917

VATICAN, The—
    British Envoy appointed to .. .. Dec. 7, 1914

VAUX, Fort (*Verdun*)—
    Stormed by German forces .. .. June 2, 1916
    Recaptured by French forces .. .. Nov. 1, 1916
    (See also under "Verdun.")

* Urmia was occupied by Russian forces before the outbreak of the war.

VELES (*South Serbia*)—

Taken by Bulgarian forces	Oct. 21, 1915
Retaken by Serbian forces	Sept. 25, 1918

VENIZELIST PARTY—

Venizelist revolt in Salonika—Begins	Aug. 30, 1916
Massacre of Venizelist partisans in Athens	Dec. 6, 1916

VENIZELOS, M. E. K.—

Appointed Premier of Greece	Oct. 19, 1910
Proffers Greek Fleet and troops to Entente for attack on Gallipoli	Mar. 5, 1915
King of Greece refuses assent to the policy	Mar. 6, 1915
Resigns office	Mar. 6, 1915
Again appointed Premier	Aug. 22, 1915
Request for guarantee of Allied support in event of Greek intervention—	
Formulated	Sept. 21, 1915
Guarantee given	Sept. 24, 1915
Obtains secret consent of King to proposed Salonika expedition	Sept. 27, 1915
Requests Entente Governments to land troops at Salonika	Oct. 2, 1915
King refuses to support policy of	Oct. 5, 1915
Resigns office	Oct. 5, 1915
Withdraws from Athens	Sept. 25, 1916
Announces formation of Greek Provisional Government in Crete	Sept. 29, 1916
Lands at Salonika	Oct. 9, 1916
Warrant for arrest issued by Greek Government	Dec. 17, 1916
Government of, recognised by Great Britain	Dec. 19, 1916
Again appointed Premier of Greece	June 26, 1917

(See also "Greece: Provisional Government.")

VERDUN (*France*)—

Battle of (*the Defensive Battle*)*—

German offensive begins	Feb. 21, 1916
Fort Douaumont stormed by German forces	Feb. 25, 1916
Fort Vaux stormed by German forces	June 2, 1916
Fort Thiaumont stormed by German forces	June 23, 1916
Fort Thiaumont retaken by French forces	June 30, 1916
German offensive ends	Aug. 31, 1916

First Offensive Battle of—*

Begins	Oct. 24, 1916
Fort Douaumont recaptured	Oct. 24, 1916
Fort Vaux recaptured	Nov. 1, 1916
Ends	Dec. 18, 1916

Second Offensive Battle of—*

Begins	Aug. 20, 1917
Ends	Dec. 15, 1917

VERSAILLES—

Supreme War Council of, inaugurated	Dec. 1, 1917
Powers of Supreme War Council of, enlarged	Feb. 3, 1918

(See under "Council, War.")

VIBORG (*Finland*)—

Captured by German force and Finnish White Guards	Apr. 30, 1918

VIENNA—

Revolution in—Breaks out	Oct. 31, 1918

VILLERS-BRETONNEUX (*Somme*)—

Actions of	Apr. 24–25, 1918

VILNA (*Lithuania*)—

Battle of	Sept. 9—Oct. 2, 1915
Taken by German forces	Sept. 18, 1915

* French official titles

VIMY RIDGE (*Arras, France*)—
    Battle of .... Apr. 9–14, 1917

"VINDICTIVE," H.M.S. (*Light Cruiser*)—
    In blocking raid on Zeebrugge .... Apr. 22, 1918
    Sunk to block Ostend Harbour .... May 9, 1918

"VIRIBUS UNITIS" (*Austrian Battleship*)—
    Sunk .... Nov. 1, 1918

VITTORIO VENETO (*Italy*)—
    Battle of—
        Begins .... Oct. 24, 1918
        Ends .... Nov. 4, 1918

VIVIANI, M.—
    Appointed French Premier .... June 14, 1914
    Appointed Acting Foreign Minister in addition .... Oct. 13, 1915
    Resigns .... Oct. 29, 1915

VLADIVOSTOK (*Siberia*)—
    Japanese and British marines land at .... Apr. 5, 1918
    General Horvat forms Siberian Government at .... July 10, 1918
    Japanese Government decide to land troops at .... Aug. 2, 1918
    British troops land at .... Aug. 3, 1918
    First Japanese contingents land at .... Aug. 11, 1918
    Coup d'état by General Horvat at .... Aug. 24, 1918
    British troops from, reach Omsk .... Oct. 18, 1918

VOSSUQ ED DOULEH—
    Appointed Persian Foreign Minister .... Jan. 11, 1913
    Resigns .... Aug. 18, 1914
    Appointed Persian Premier and Foreign Minister .... Aug. 29, 1916
    Resigns .... May 29, 1917
    Again appointed Persian Premier .... Aug. 7, 1918

VPERED" (*Russian Hospital Ship*)—
    Sunk .... July 10, 1916

VRANJE (*Serbia*)—
    Taken by Bulgarian forces .... Oct. 15, 1915
    Retaken by Serbian forces .... Oct. 5, 1918

W

WADI, The (*Mesopotamia*)—
    Action of .... Jan. 13–14, 1916

WADI MAJID (*Western Egypt*)—
    Affair of .... Dec. 25, 1915

WADI SENAB (*Western Egypt*)—
    Affair of .... Dec. 11–13, 1915

WALNEY ISLAND BATTERY (*Barrow*)—
    Shelled by German submarine .... Jan. 29, 1915

WANGFORD (*Suffolk*)—
    Shelled by German destroyers .... Jan. 25, 1917

WAPSHARE, Major-General R.—
    Takes over command of British forces in East Africa .. .. Dec. 4, 1914
    Succeeded by General Tighe .. .. Apr. 16, 1915

WAR AIMS, STATEMENTS AS TO. See also under "Commitments."
    Entente—
        Entente Governments outline Allied terms of peace .. .. .. Jan. 10, 1917
    British—
        British Premier declares Serbian independence to be an essential object of the war .. .. Nov. 2, 1915
        British Government give pledges that restitution of Alsace-Lorraine is an object of the war .. .. { Feb. 15, 1917 / Nov. 15, 1917
        British Premier outlines British war aims .. .. Jan. 5, 1918
    French—French Foreign Minister outlines French war aims .. .. .. Dec. 28, 1917
    German—
        Reichstag passes resolution as to German war aims .. .. .. July 19, 1917
        Count Hertling and Count Czernin make public replies to Entente statements of war aims .. .. Jan. 24, 1918
    Labour—Inter-Allied Labour and Socialist Conference in London pass resolution as to war aims .. .. Feb. 23, 1918
    Russia—Provisional Government declare in favour of self-determination of peoples Apr. 9, 1917

WAR CABINET. See under "Britain—Cabinet."

WAR COMMITTEE. See under "Britain—Cabinet."

WAR COUNCIL. See under "Council" and under "Britain—Cabinet."

WAR, DECLARATIONS OF—
    Austria-Hungary on—
        Serbia .. .. July 28, 1914
        Russia .. .. Aug. 6, 1914
        Belgium .. .. Aug. 22, 1914
        Portugal .. .. Mar. 15, 1916
    Brazil on—**Germany** .. .. Oct. 26, 1917
    Britain on—
        Germany (11 P.M., Greenwich Mean Time, or midnight, 4th-5th Central European Time).. .. .. Aug. 4, 1914
        Austria-Hungary .. .. Aug. 12, 1914
        Turkey .. .. Nov. 5, 1914
        Bulgaria* .. .. Oct. 15, 1915
    Bulgaria on—
        Serbia .. .. Oct. 14, 1915
        Rumania .. .. Sept. 1, 1916
    China on—
        Austria-Hungary .. .. Aug. 14, 1917
        Germany .. .. Aug. 14, 1917
    Costa Rica on—**Germany** .. .. May 23, 1918
    Cuba on—
        Germany .. .. Apr. 7, 1917
        Austria-Hungary .. .. Dec. 16, 1917
    Czecho-Slovaks on—**Germany** .. .. †Aug. 13, 1918
    France on—
        Austria-Hungary .. .. Aug. 12, 1914
        Turkey .. .. Nov. 5, 1914
        Bulgaria* .. .. Oct. 16, 1915
    Germany on—
        Russia .. .. Aug. 1, 1914
        France .. .. Aug. 3, 1914
        Belgium .. .. Aug. 4, 1914
        Portugal .. .. Mar. 9, 1916
        Rumania .. .. Aug. 28, 1916
    Greece (*Provisional Government of*) on—
        Bulgaria .. .. Nov. 23, 1916
        Germany .. .. Nov. 23, 1916
    Greece (*King Alexander's Government*) on—
        Austria-Hungary* .. .. June 27, 1917
        Bulgaria .. .. June 27, 1917
        Germany .. .. June 27, 1917
        Turkey* .. .. June 27, 1917

* "State of War" proclaimed to exist.
† October 28 is officially accepted as the date of entry into the war of Czecho-Slovakia as a belligerent nation. This was the date of the declaration of independence at Prague. On August 13 the declaration was made in the name of the Czecho-Slovaks as a people.

WAR, DECLARATIONS OF (continued)—

Guatemala on—Germany	Apr. 23, 1918
Haiti on—Germany	July 12, 1918
Honduras on—Germany	July 19, 1918
Italy on—	
Austria-Hungary	May 23, 1915
Turkey	Aug. 21, 1915
Bulgaria	Oct. 19, 1915
Germany	Aug. 28, 1916
Japan on—	
Germany	Aug. 23, 1914
Austria-Hungary*	Aug. 25, 1914
Liberia on—Germany	Aug. 4, 1917
Montenegro on—	
Austria-Hungary	Aug. 5, 1914
Germany*	Aug. 8, 1914
Bulgaria*	Oct. 15, 1915
Nicaragua on—	
Austria-Hungary	May 8, 1918
Germany	May 8, 1918
Panama on—	
Germany	Apr. 7, 1917
Austria-Hungary	Dec. 10, 1917
Rumania on—Austria-Hungary	Aug. 27, 1916
Russia on—	
Turkey	Nov. 2, 1914
Bulgaria	Oct. 19, 1915
San Marino on—Austria-Hungary	June 3, 1915
Siam on—	
Austria-Hungary	July 22, 1917
Germany	July 22, 1917
Serbia on—	
Germany	Aug. 6, 1914
Turkey*	Nov. 2, 1914
Bulgaria	Oct. 14, 1915
Turkey on—	
All Entente Powers (Holy War) (see also under "Jehad")	Nov. 14, 1914
Rumania	Aug. 30, 1916
Ukraine, The, on—Poland*	Nov. 1, 1918
United States of America on—	
Germany	Apr. 6, 1917
Austria-Hungary	Dec. 7, 1917

WAR MINISTERS. See under respective countries.

"WARILDA," S.S. (British Ambulance Transport)—
Sunk .. Aug. 3, 1918

WARNEFORD, Flight Sub-Lieutenant R. A. J., R.N.A.S.—
Destroys German airship "L.Z. 37" near Ghent .. June 7, 1915

"WARNING TELEGRAM"—
By British Admiralty to fleet .. July 29, 1914
By War Office, ordering "Precautionary Period" .. July 29, 1914

"WARRIOR," H.M.S. (Cruiser)—
Sunk .. June 1, 1916

WARSAW (Poland)—
Battle of .. Oct. 9–19, 1914
City occupied by German forces .. Aug. 5, 1915

WEJH (Arabia)—
Captured by Arab forces .. Jan. 24, 1917

* "State of War" proclaimed to exist.

WEKERLE, Dr.—
    Appointed Hungarian Premier ... Aug. 21, 1917
    Resigns ... Apr. 17, 1918
    Again appointed.. ... Apr. 27, 1918
    Resigns ... Oct. 24, 1918

WEMYSS, *Admiral Sir* Rosslyn—
    Appointed First Sea Lord, Great Britain ... Dec. 27, 1917

WHITEHAVEN (*Cumberland*)—
    Coast near, shelled by German submarine ... Aug. 16, 1915

WIED, *Prince* William of—
    Leaves Albania ... Sept. 3, 1914

" WIEN " (*Austrian Battleship*)—
    Sunk ... Dec. 9, 1917

" WIESBADEN " (*German Light Cruiser*)—
    Sunk ... May 31, 1916

WILLIAM II. *German Emperor.* See under " Kaiser."

WILLIAM OF WIED, *Prince.* See under " Wied."

" WILLIAM P. FRYE " S.V. (*United States*)—
    Sunk by " Prince Eitel Friedrich " ... Jan. 28, 1915

WILSON, *General Sir* H. H.—
    Appointed to Supreme War Council ... Nov. 27, 1917
    Appointed Chief of the Imperial General Staff ... Feb. 19, 1918

WILSON, *President*—
    Speech re " Lusitania " ... May 9, 1915
    Re-elected ... Nov. 7, 1916
    Asks for power to arm merchant ships ... Feb. 26, 1917
    States views with regard to the sinking of the " Laconia " ... Feb. 27, 1917
    Delivers message to Congress laying down the " Fourteen Points " ... Jan. 8, 1918
    In further message to Congress lays down four additional " Points " ... Feb. 11, 1918
    Peace negotiations—
        Issues Circular Peace Note ... Dec. 18, 1916
        Austro-Hungarian, German and Turkish Governments reply to Note ... Dec. 26, 1916
        Bulgarian Government reply to Note ... Dec. 30, 1916
        Belgian Government reply to Note ... Jan. 10, 1917
        Entente Governments send joint reply to Note ... Jan. 10, 1917
        Austro-Hungarian Note to, suggesting peace conference ... Sept 15, 1918
        Reply sent by, to Austro-Hungarian Note ... Sept. 16, 1918
        Austro-Hungarian Note to, proposing an armistice ⎱ Oct. 4, 1918
        German Note to, proposing an armistice ⎰
        (For further Notes, see under " Armistice.")

WINDHUK (*German South-West Africa*)—
    South African (Northern) force begins advance on ... Feb. 22, 1915
    Occupied by South African force ... May 13, 1915

WINDSOR—
    Proclamation issued changing name of British Royal House to ... July 17, 1917

"WOLFF" (*German Raider*)—
    Leaves Germany .. .. *Dec. 1, 1916
    Returns to Germany .. .. Feb. 24, 1918

WORTHINGTON-EVANS, *Sir* Laming—
    Appointed Minister for Blockade, Great Britain .. .. July 18, 1918

WYTSCHAETE (*Flanders*)†—
    Allied attack on .. .. Dec. 14, 1914

X

XEROS, Gulf of. See under "Dardanelles, Expedition to."

Y

YABASI (*Cameroons*)—
    Captured by British forces .. .. Oct. 14, 1914

YAMBOL (*Bulgaria*)—
    German Airship "L. 59" leaves, for East Africa‡ .. .. Nov. 21, 1917
    German Airship "L. 59" returns to, from East Africa‡ .. .. .. Nov. 25, 1917

YAP ISLAND (*Pacific*)—
    Occupied by Japanese naval forces.. .. .. Oct. 7, 1914

YARMOUTH (*Norfolk*)—
    Bombarded by German battle cruiser squadron .. .. { Nov. 3, 1914
                                                                                                                                                                                      { Apr. 25, 1916
    Bombarded by German destroyers .. .. Jan. 14, 1918

YAROSLAV. See under "Jaroslaw."

YAUNDE (*Cameroons*)—
    First Allied advance on—
        Begins .. .. Apr. 12, 1915
        Abandoned .. .. June 7, 1915
        Operations concluded.. .. .. June 28, 1915
    Second Allied advance on, begins .. .. Sept. 22, 1915
    Taken by the Allied forces .. .. Jan. 1, 1916

YENBO (*Arabia*)—
    Taken by Arab forces .. .. July 27, 1916

"YORCK" (*German Cruiser*)—
    Sunk .. .. Nov. 4, 1914

YPRES (*Belgium*)—
    Occupied by German cavalry .. .. Oct. 3, 1914
    Reoccupied by Allied forces .. .. Oct. 13, 1914
    Battles of, 1914—
        Begin .. .. Oct. 19, 1914
        Critical day in .. .. Oct. 31, 1914
        Critical day in .. .. Nov. 11, 1914
        End .. .. Nov. 22, 1914

* Approximate date.
† Subsequent captures and recaptures formed part of the Battles of Messines, 1917 and 1918.
‡ Evidence for this statement rests on unsubstantiated German statements.

YPRES (*Belgium*) (*continued*)—

Battles of, 1915—
Begin .. Apr. 22, 1915
End .. May 25, 1915

Battles of, 1917—
Begin .. July 31, 1917
End .. Nov. 10, 1917

Battle of, 1918—
Begins .. Sept. 28, 1918
Ends .. Oct. 2, 1918

YSER, River (*Belgium*)—

Battle of the—
Begins .. *Oct. 16, 1914
Ends .. †Nov. 10, 1914

YUAN-SHIH-KAI—

Elected President of China .. Oct. 6, 1913
Accepts throne of China .. Dec. 11, 1915
Relinquishes throne of China .. Mar. 22, 1916
Dies .. June 6, 1916

YUGO-SLAVS—

Agreement reached between Italy and the .. Apr. 10, 1918
British, French, and Italian Governments make declarations supporting the national aspirations of the .. June 3, 1918
Recognised as independent by Italy .. Sept. 25, 1918
Delegates meet at Agram.. .. Oct. 5, 1918
Austrian Emperor grants autonomy to the Yugo-Slavs of Austria .. Oct. 16, 1918
King of Montenegro declares for a confederated Yugo-Slav State .. Oct. 26, 1918

National Council of the Yugo-Slavs—
Meet at Agram and declare independence .. Oct. 29, 1918
Austrian Emperor makes over the Austro-Hungarian fleet to the .. Oct. 31, 1918
Conference at Geneva decides to form a joint Yugo-Slav-Serbian Government .. Nov. 7, 1918
Protest against Italian occupation of Fiume .. Nov. 17, 1918
Vote for union with Serbia, and formation of a common State with Serbia and Montenegro .. Nov. 23, 1918
Proclaim union of all Serbs, Croats, and Slovenes in one State .. Dec. 4, 1918
M. Stoyan Protich appointed Premier of the United Kingdom of Serbs, Croats and Slovenes .. Dec. 29, 1918

TREATIES, &c. See under "Commitments."

Z

ZAGREB. See "Agram."

ZAIMIS, M.—

Appointed Greek Premier.. .. Oct. 6, 1915
Resigns .. Nov. 5, 1915
Again appointed Premier .. June 21, 1916
Resigns .. Sept. 11, 1916
Again appointed Premier .. May 3, 1917
Resigns .. June 24, 1917

ZALESZCZYKI (*Galicia*)—

Taken by Russian forces .. June 12, 1916
Retaken by Austro-German forces .. July 30, 1917

ZAMOSC–KOMAROW (*South Poland*)—

Battle of .. Aug. 26—Sept. 2, 1914

ZANZIBAR—

H.M.S. "Pegasus" sunk by German cruiser "Königsberg" off.. .. Sept. 20, 1914

* Belgian date. † French date.

ZEEBRUGGE (*Belgium*)—

British 7th Division disembark at	Oct. 6, 1914
Evacuated by Belgian forces	Oct. 12, 1914
Occupied by German forces	Oct. 15, 1914
Blocking raid by British naval force on	Apr. 23, 1918
Reoccupied by Belgian forces	Oct. 19, 1918

"ZENTA" (*Austrian Light Cruiser*)—

Sunk	Aug. 16, 1914

ZEPPELIN, *Count*—

Dies	Mar. 8, 1917

ZEPPELINS. See "Airships, German."

"ZHEMCHUG" (*Russian Cruiser*)—

Sunk	Oct. 28, 1914

ZIMMERMANN, *Dr.* Artur—

Appointed German Foreign Minister	Nov. 21, 1916
Resigns	July 15, 1917

HISTORY OF THE GREAT WAR
BASED ON OFFICIAL DOCUMENTS.

The following histories are in course of preparation :—

NAVAL OPERATIONS. Sir Julian S. Corbett.
(London : Longmans, Green and Co.)

SEABORNE TRADE. C. Ernest Fayle.
(London : John Murray.)

THE MERCHANT NAVY. Archibald Hurd.
(London : John Murray.)

MILITARY OPERATIONS:

(Western Theatre) Brigadier-General J. E. Edmonds.
(London : Macmillan and Co., Ltd.)

(Gallipoli) Professor G. S. Gordon.

(Mesopotamia) Brigadier-General F. J. Moberly.
(London : His Majesty's Stationery Office.)

THE WAR IN THE AIR. Sir Walter Raleigh.
(Oxford : The Clarendon Press.)

MEDICAL SERVICES. Major-Gen. Sir W. G. Macpherson.
(London : His Majesty's Stationery Office.)

PRINCIPAL EVENTS 1914-1918.

APPENDIX TO PART II—SECTION II (A).

COMPARATIVE LIST OF THE OFFICIAL NAMES AND DATES OF BATTLES, &c., IN FRANCE AND FLANDERS.

EXPLANATORY NOTES.

1. The list which follows is rendered necessary by the fact that each of the belligerents in the Western Theatre of War has produced an official list giving the names of the engagements in which their forces took part, with dates.

It was at first hoped to combine these into one general list, indicating the discrepancies by footnotes. These discrepancies, however, proved on examination to be so numerous and so marked that it is felt that a comparative list, such as follows, is essential.

It is assumed that the names officially adopted and here shown will be used by historians in the future; at the same time a variety of unofficial names of battles, differing from those detailed below, have been employed in popular histories and accounts.

2. The following are the official lists published by the various belligerents:—

British.—"The Official Names of the Battles and Actions . . . . during the Great War, 1914–1919" (Report of the Battles Nomenclature Committee as approved by the Army Council) published March 1921.

French.—"Tableau indiquant les Dénominations des Batailles auxquelles ont pris part les Armées françaises sur le Front français," issued to the French press, and received officially by the Historical Section from the French Military Mission, January 1920.

Belgian.—"Nomenclature for the Battles and Actions throughout the War officially adopted and approved by His Majesty the King of the Belgians," communicated to the Historical Section by the Belgian Military Attaché, August 1920.

German.—"Die Schlachten und Gefechte des Grossen Krieges 1914–1918 . . . . zusammengestellt vom Grossen Generalstab" ("The Battles and Actions of the Great War, 1914–1918 . . . . compiled by the Great General Staff"), published 1919.

United States of America.—No specific list of Battles of the United States Forces has been published. But Battle-clasps have been authorised for the "Victory Medal" and the names authorised for these clasps have been ordered to be borne on the Colours of the Regiments engaged. These names are generally in accord with the British and French names. A few exceptions are referred to in the body of the list.

3. The marked discrepancies between both the names and the dates given in the different lists are due for the most part to different treatment of the following points:—

(1.) The subdivision of the major operations.
(2.) The classification of certain engagements.
(3.) The names for particular engagements.
(4.) The system adopted in determining the chronological limits of engagements.

Taking these in turn—

(1.) An outstanding feature of the fighting in the Western Theatre of War was the unprecedented size and duration of many of the "Battles." In many cases such "Battles" lasted for longer than a month, in as many cases they extended over a front of over 20 miles. Such great "Battles" were frequently made up of a series of successive attacks with intervening pauses, while the forces engaged have often included on each side two or more "Armies," operating side by side, but more or less independently, under the orders of the Higher Command.

In such cases there are obviously three methods of nomenclature:—

(i.) The whole great operation may be called one "Battle."
(ii.) A subdivision may be made chronologically into "phases," each successive attack being denominated a separate "Battle."
(iii.) A subdivision may be made, so to speak, "laterally," the front covered being broken up and the operations of each individual "Army" engaged being styled a separate "Battle."

Broadly speaking it may be said of these three methods of nomenclature the first is the simplest, the second the most accurate, while the third would appeal most to the troops engaged, who would naturally tend to remember the name of the locality in their immediate vicinity.

Again, of the two methods of subdivision, the second system is obviously the more suitable in the case of struggles of long duration on a comparatively narrow front*; on the other hand, where the fighting has been of no great duration but the front covered has been wide and the formations engaged simultaneously have been numerous the third or "lateral" subdivision may be necessary.†

In many cases a combination of both methods of subdivision is possible.

Cases of the use of each one of these three methods of nomenclature are to be found in the names included in each one of the lists here given. In general, however, it may be said that the French tendency has been towards the simplicity of the first method, while the compilers of the British and German lists have, on the contrary, felt the necessity for subdivision. Of these latter the British have, for the most part, adopted the second method and have subdivided the great "Offensives" into "Battles" representing their successive phases, while the German Staff have, in many cases, followed the contrary ("lateral") method and have entitled the operations of each one of their "Armies" during a given period a separate "Battle."

In cases in which such subdivision has been made, the British practice has been to call the whole major operation a "Group of Battles," with a distinctive name. The French plan has been somewhat similar, such major operations being entitled "Batailles d'ensemble" with or without subordinate "Batailles." The Germans have in general used the same term "Battle" ("Schlacht") both for the major operation and also for its subdivisions. In some cases, however, the separate "Battles" of the individual "Armies" engaged in one of the "major operations" are shown separately with no indication that they form part of a greater whole.

Thus, for instance, the German offensive in the Lys Valley in April 1918 appears in the British list as a "Group of Battles"—"The Battles of the Lys"—subdivided into eight "Battles" which represent the outstanding phases of the German advance. The French list, on the other hand, shows the whole operation simply as one "Battle"—"The 3rd Battle of Flanders"—without any attempt at subdivision. The German presentment, however, is influenced by the fact that the offensive was carried out by two separate "Armies," working in concert but with differing objectives, and it appears consequently in the form of two separate "Battles" ("Battle of Armentières" for the VIth Army, "Battle of Kemmel" for the IVth Army) named respectively after the most important locality which the Army concerned was successful in taking.

It must be remembered that it is much easier for the attacker than for the defender to define the "phases" of a prolonged "Offensive." The latter is not in a position easily to differentiate between the main, the subsidiary and the feint attacks made upon him, and is not at the time able to realize what effect the success or failure of each attack has had on the enemy's plan. It is probably due to the consciousness of this difficulty that the German list, otherwise so detailed, makes no attempt to subdivide the majority of the Allied "Offensives."§

(2.) Certain points of difference in regard to the *classification* adopted are also to be noted. In several cases an engagement appears in the one list as a "Battle," but in the opponent's list as a minor action or group of minor actions.

Notable examples of this are to be found in the treatment by the two opposing sides of "The Battle of the Gette" (August 18th–19th, 1914), "The December Battle in French Flanders" (December 14th–24th, 1914), "The 1st Offensive Battle of Verdun" (October 24th–December 18th, 1916) and "The Battle of la Malmaison" (October 23rd–November 1st, 1917).

These differences in classification may in most cases be ascribed to a desire to conceal failure or to magnify success, but in some instances they may be due to a genuine misconception: thus it is quite conceivable that a number of simultaneous minor attacks and demonstrations over a wide front may give the defender the impression that he is repulsing a definite and serious "Offensive."‡ In the same way an enveloping attack against the flanks of an extended position may appear to the attackers, who are conscious of the unity of plan, as one great battle. To the defenders, however, the same operation may mean no more than the comparatively unimportant fighting round the widely separated localities on either flank, whereof the loss causes the abandonment of the defended line.‖

(3.) The preceding paragraphs have indicated the principal causes of discrepancy; but also there are to be found, as in most preceding wars, many cases of differing names being used by the opposing sides to denote the same engagement. Thus the counter-attack of the French Vth Army against the pursuing German IInd Army (August 29th–30th, 1914) is called by the French the "Battle of Guise," but by the Germans the "Battle of St. Quentin": many other similar instances are also to be noted.

(4.) Considerable discrepancies in the dates recorded follow naturally on the differences in subdivision and classification explained above. But two particular points appear to call for some explanation:—

(i.) The opening of the great offensive Battles was, as a rule, preceded by a "preparatory period" of minor attacks and bombardments gradually increasing in intensity up to the moment when, at "zero," the infantry of the attacking side "went over the top." The British Committee decided that "owing to the varying length of the preparatory action, and the difficulty of fixing its actual commencement, this period should not be included, but . . . . 'zero day' should be taken as the first day"* of each battle. The French practice would appear to be the same. In the German list, however, the "preparatory period" has in several cases been included in the dates given for the battles.† ‡

(ii.) The date for the termination of the offensive Battles is a matter of still greater discrepancy. After each of the great attacks there followed a period of "consolidation" and "exploitation," including local attacks and counter-attacks by either side.

The British Committee have laid it down that this period of "consolidation . . . . should, as a general rule, be included" in the battle.* The contrary view would appear to be held by the French Staff, as witness their terminal date (April 20th) for the Aisne-Champagne Offensive of 1917 as opposed to that shown in the German list (May 27th). The German view is not clear, but in general it may be taken that the success or failure of such minor operations, as also their influence on the plans of the Higher Command, must naturally have influenced the decision as to their inclusion in the major battle.

4. Two peculiarly difficult instances of different nomenclature, caused by differing methods of subdivision (see above, paragraph 2), would appear to demand more explanation than can be given in footnotes to the pages§:—

(i.) The operations in Flanders, October 10th–November 30th, 1914. The confusing names and dates adopted for these operations can best be understood if the campaign is regarded in succession from the point of view of each of the four belligerents—

(A.) *German.*—

(*a.*) The German VIth Army, engaged since October 1st in the "*Battle of Arras,*" extended its right flank to the north-west in order to cut off and seize Lille. Allied forces advancing from Hazebrouck to prevent this development were intercepted and held at La Bassée‖ and Festubert‖ (October 11th) and Lille was occupied on the 12th. The Allied forces were reinforced and pressed their efforts to regain the city. To meet this offensive the fighting at Arras was allowed to die down into trench warfare, the bulk of the VIth Army was moved up to the Lille area, and a definite battle to cover the city ensued (*Battle of Lille, October 15th–28th*).¶

(*b.*) Meanwhile the German IVth Army, advancing past the right flank of the VIth Army, had struck at the Allied forces on the Yser and to the north of Ypres. The struggle which ensued, round Dixmude and on the northern face

* *E.g.*, The Allied Offensive in Flanders in 1917.
† *E.g.*, The Marne in 1914.
‡ *E.g.*, "The December Battle in French Flanders."
§ Notably "The Battle of the Somme (1916)."
‖ *E.g.*, "The Battle of the Gette."

* *Report of the Battles Nomenclature Committee.*
† The practice of the Italian General Staff is similar.
‡ Where this is undoubtedly so, a footnote to this effect has been added, but there are a few doubtful cases.
§ A third period of great complexity of names is that of the Allied Offensive in Picardy, August 8th–September 3rd, 1918; but it is felt that more explanation than is given in the footnotes would here be unnecessary.
‖ The "Battle of Arras" is shown as terminating on October 13th and these engagements consequently appear as "tactical incidents" in that battle.
¶ On a front extending to the north as far as Gheluve.

of the Ypres Salient,* lasted till the end of November (*Battle of the Yser, October 18th–November 30th*).

(c.) At the end of October it was decided that Lille was safe and that the reduction of the Ypres Salient was of the first importance. The main energy of the VIth Army (see above, paragraph (a)) was turned northward and devoted to a great effort towards breaking in the southern face of the Ypres Salient (*Battle of Ypres, October 30th–November 24th*).†

(B.) *Belgian.—*

The whole of the Belgian forces were throughout engaged to the north of Ypres, the main centre of their fighting line being Dixmude. The majority of the Belgian troops had been relieved by their Allies before the end of October. To them, therefore, the whole period is represented by "*The Battle of the Yser*" (*October 16th–31st*).

(C.) *British.—*

The British Army came into the Flanders campaign piecemeal, the four Corps each becoming engaged independently with between each considerable intervals, which were filled for the most part by French reinforcements. Thus to the British the fighting presented the appearance of four separate struggles—centering respectively on La Bassée (IInd Corps), Armentières (IIIrd Corps), Messines

* The left flank of this Army was about Gheluvelt.
† On a front from Gheluvelt to Ploegsteert (inclusive).

(Cavalry Corps), and Ypres (Ist Corps). Each of these operations has been denominated a separate "Battle" with the exception of that at Ypres, which, in view of the length and severity of the fighting, has been subdivided into its three successive "phases," and presented as a "Group of Battles" (*see above, paragraph 3 (1)*).

(D.) *French.*

The French forces in the Flanders struggle did not form any strategic unit, but were thrown in by individual corps and divisions to reinforce threatened points of the line and to fill gaps. The names shown in their list—the "*Little of the Yser*" and the "*Battle of Ypres*"—follow the accepted Belgian and British nomenclature, but with dates to cover the operations of the French troops engaged.

(ii.) The final offensive of the Allied Armies in Flanders grouped under the command of King Albert has been treated differently by each of the belligerents.

Broadly speaking the offensive comprised four successive main "phases"—each initiated by an Allied attack which was more or less general along the whole front of the Allied Armies. The initial days of these four successive attacks were respectively September 28th, October 14th, October 25th, and October 31st.*

* A fresh general attack was planned for November 11th, but did not materialise. Had it eventuated it would, according to the Belgian official list, have been denominated "Battle of the Escaut and the Terneuzen Canal."

The method in which these phases have been named differently in each of the four lists—can best be shown in tabular form:—

Allied attack commencing on	Belgian.	British.	French.	German.
Sept. 28th	Battle of the Flanders Ridge	Battle of Ypres, 1918	Battle of the Flanders Ridges	Defensive Battle of Flanders, 1918.
Oct. 14th	Battle of Thourout-Thielt	Battle of Courtrai	Battle of Roulers	
Oct. 25th		Action of Ooteghem	Action of the Lys and the Escaut	
Oct. 31st	Battle of the Lys	Action of Tieghem		Battle of the Lys.

The concluding date for each one of the engagements named varies, naturally, in accordance with the conclusion of fighting by the Army concerned.

EXPLANATION OF ABBREVIATIONS, &c.

1. The entries in the different lists which represent the same engagement are connected by a dotted line.

2. The significance of the varieties of type employed is as follows:—

(A.) **Heavy Type.**

(i.) In the British official list two sizes of type are used in the roll of battles, the heavier type being employed only for the names of the "Groups of battles"* and for three individual battles of outstanding importance.† This distinction in type has here been preserved.

(ii.) In the French list the distinction officially drawn between the "Batailles d'ensemble"* and the lesser "Batailles" has here been indicated by printing the former in the heavier type.‡

(iii.) No distinction either in title or in type is made in the German list between greater and lesser battles.§ Here, however, in order to assist comparison with the lists of the Allies, these battles have been put into the heavier type which corresponds in scale, more or less, to the British "Groups of Batailles d'ensemble" or to the French "Groups of Battles."

(B.) **Italics.**

Certain events which are not given in the official lists of battles, but of which the inclusion in this list is considered desirable, are entered in italics.

3. With a view to facilitating the recognition of the localities and areas after which the engagements are named, the entries have been placed 'en échelon,' the position of the point in question on the line of the Western Front being indicated, more or less, by the position of the initial letter‖ of the entry in the column, the northernmost entries being placed on the left and the remainder in geographical succession to the right.

Thus the southernmost fighting (nearest the Swiss frontier) is entered with the initial letter of the entry (the "B" in "Battle of Alsace") next to the vertical line over which is placed the letter "S" in the column heading, while the northernmost entry is placed with the initial letter (the "G" of "German Attack on Nieuport") against the left-hand

* (See "Notes," above, paragraph 3 (i)).
† Loos; Messines, 1917; Amiens.
‡ In the actual French official list the distinction between "Batailles d'ensemble" and "Batailles," is indicated not by variety of type but by an arrangement in different columns.
§ See below, paragraph 8.
‖ Prefixed numbers in brackets (see next paragraph) do not affect the position of the initial letter, by which alone the area should be located.

line of the column under the letter "N." All other entries are placed proportionately between these limits.

4. The fact that a given battle itself forms part of a greater battle or of a "Group of Battles" is shown* by a prefixed number in brackets, which indicates its relative position as a subdivision of the major operation.

5. Square brackets round an entry indicate that it is a "tactical incident" in a battle.

6. To assist the identification of the different battles, the "Armies" engaged have been indicated in the majority of cases. This has been effected by small numbers superimposed to the name of the battle in question,† the numbers in the French list referring to French Armies, those in the German list to the German Armies, &c.

7. In cases in which the name of a locality has alternative spellings, French and German, the French form has been adopted, even in translating the German list.

Thus, for example, "Schlacht bei Saarburg" appears in the list as "Battle of Sarrebourg," while "Mülhausen" has been rendered into its French form "Mulhouse."

8. (a.) The terms for the various classes of engagement used in the French and German official lists have throughout been translated into those officially adopted by the Battles Nomenclature Committee as follows:—

French.	German.	British.
Bataille d'ensemble	Schlacht	Battle.†
Bataille		
Combat	Kämpfe§	Action.
	Gefecht	Affair.
	Erstürmung	Storming.
Prise	Eroberung	Capture.
	Einnahme	
	Besetzung	Occupation.

* Except in a few cases in which only one subordinate engagement is indicated within the greater battle.
† Footnotes are indicated not by numbers but by signs or letters.
‡ As explained above, the French "Bataille d'ensemble" corresponds in many cases to the British "(group of) Battles."
§ Almost invariably used in the plural, as shown, and has occasionally been translated "Fighting at . . . ." where this rendering appeared appropriate.

(b.) The following additional French and German terms, not to be found in the British official list, have been rendered as follows:—

French.	German.	Translation.
Bataille défensive	Abwehrschlacht	Defensive Battle.
Bataille offensive	Angriffsschlacht	Offensive Battle.
	Durchbruchschlacht	Battle. (*With footnote stating the literal translation*).*
	Frühjahrsschlacht	Spring Battle.
	Sommerschlacht	Summer "
	Herbstschlacht	Autumn "
	Winterschlacht also	Winter "
	Dezemberschlacht &c.	December Battle,† &c.
	Tankschlacht	Tank Battle.

* Literally should be—" Break-through-battle."
† And similarly for other names of months.

9. Reference is made in some cases to "semi-official" names for engagements. By these are meant names which, though not included in the actual official list from which this list has been compiled, have nevertheless been used in other official publications of the country concerned.

H. FITZ M. STACKE,
Captain, The Worcestershire Regiment.

OFFICIAL NAMES AND DATES OF BATTLES, &c., IN THE WESTERN THEATRE OF WAR.

Date.	BRITISH.	FRENCH (AND BELGIAN).	GERMAN.	Date.
1914. AUG. 1		General Mobilisation ordered (France and Belgium).	General Mobilisation ordered.[a]	1914. AUG. 1
3	General Mobilisation ordered.		Germany declares War on France.	3
4	Great Britain declares War on Germany.[a]		Germany declares War on Belgium.	4
6		Defence of Liège begins (Belg.).	Attack on Liège begins.	6
7	British Expeditionary Force begins to land in France.	Battle of Alsace[d] begins (see 24th).		7
8		Mulhouse taken by French forces.		8
9			1st Battle of Mulhouse[d] { begins.	9
10		"BATTLE OF THE FRONTIERS"[c] BEGINS.	{ ends.	10
11			Mulhouse reoccupied by German forces.	11
14		Battle of Lorraine begins including (1.) Battle of Morhange[e] begins. (2.) Battle of Sarrebourg[f] begins.		14
16	landing of original British Expeditionary Force completed.[b]	Defence of Liège ends (Belg.).	Last forts of Liège captured.	16
18		Actions of Grimde and of Hauteau Ste. Marguerite (Belg.).	Battle of the Gette[g] begins. { begins	18
19		Action of Aerschot (Belg.). Mulhouse again taken by French forces.	Battle of the Gette[g] ends. Action at Sarrebourg[f] { ends. 2nd Battle of Mulhouse (one day)	19
20		(1.) Battle of Morhange[e] ends. (2.) Battle of Sarrebourg[f] ends.	Brussels occupied by German forces. Siege of Longwy begins. Battle of Lorraine begins[7] including Battle of Sarrebourg (one day) Battle of the Central Vosges[i] begins.[7]	20

[a] 11 P.M. (Midnight 4th/5th by Central European time).   [b] Four Divisions and one Cavalry Division.   [c] General heading, covering all operations of the French Armies up to the Battle of the Marne.
[d] The German "1st and 2nd Battles of Mulhouse" correspond respectively to the two principal phases of the French "Battle of Alsace."
[e] On August 2nd General von Moltke was officially appointed "Chief of the General Staffs of the Field Armies."
[f] Included under the general heading of "Actions for the protection of the Lorraine frontier." ("Grenzschutzgefechte in Lothringen") from August 8th to 19th
[g] Alternative official title is "Battle of Tirlemont."   [h] Alternative official title is "Battle between Metz and the Vosges."   [i] "Schlacht in den mittleren Vogesen."

Date.	BRITISH.	FRENCH (AND BELGIAN).	GERMAN.	Date.
1914. AUG.				1914. AUG.
21				21
22		**Battle of Belgium begins** *including* (i.) Battle of Charleroi begins.[5]	Attack on Namur begins.[b] Battle of Neufchâteau begins.[4] Battle of Longwy-Longuyon begins.[5 c] Battle of Lorraine ends.[6 7 d] Battle for Nancy-Epinal begins.[6 7] Battle of the Central Vosges ends.	22
23	Battle of Mons begins	(ii.) Battle of the Ardennes begins[3 4]	Battle of Mons begins.[1] Battle of Charleroi begins.[2 c] Battle of Dinant begins.[3] Battle of Neufchâteau ends.[4]	23
24	Battle of Mons ends. *Retreat from Mons begins.*[a]	(i.) Battle of Charleroi ends[5] (ii.) Battle of the Ardennes ends[3 4] and **Battle of Belgium ends.** Battle of Alsace ends. (*See Ger.*, "*Mulhouse*"—19th.)	Battle of Charleroi ends.[2 c] Battle of Dinant ends.[3] Battle of the Meuse begins.[4 d] *Mulhouse retaken by German forces.*	24
25	Rearguard Action of Solesmes	{ Actions of Weerde and of Hofstade-Schiplaeken begin (*Belg.*).}[b] Defence of Namur ends (*Belg.*).[b] Battle of the Meuse begins.[4] (3) Battle of the Mortagne begins.[f]	Battle of Malines begins. Battle of Solesmes-le Cateau begins.[1] Capture of Namur. Siege of Maubeuge begins.	25
26	Battle of le Cateau	{ Actions of Weerde and of Hofstade-Schiplaeken e d (*Belg.*). Action of Haecht (*Belg.*).	*Sack of Louvain.* Battle of Solesmes-le Cateau ends.[1] Capitulation of Longwy.	26
27			Battle of Malines ends. Battle of Longwy-Longuyon ends.[5 c]	27

[a] In the British list the "Retreat from Mons" includes the Battle and is therefore shown as commencing on the 23rd. [b] The Belgian list begins the Defence of Namur on August 4th.
[c] Schlacht bei Longwy-Longuyon und am Othain-Abschnitt. [d] Alternative official title is "Battle between Metz and the Vosges." [e] Alternative official title is "Battle of Namur."
[f] This is the date for the commencement of this battle by the German IVth Army. The battle was extended to the right by the German IIIrd Army on the 27th and to the left by the right wing of the Vth Army on the 28th.
[g] A subdivision of the Battle of Lorraine (see page 5).

Date.	BRITISH.	FRENCH (AND BELGIAN).	GERMAN.	Date.
1914. AUG.				1914. AUG.
28		Battle of the Meuse ends[a]		28
29		Battle of Guise begins[5]	Battle of St. Quentin begins.[2]	29
30		Battle of Guise ends[5]	Battle of St. Quentin ends.[2]	30
31			Battle of the Aisne begins.[3]	31
SEPT. 1			Battle of the Aisne ends.[3] [*Noisons tabra by the Germans.*] Battle of the Meuse ends [5] [b]	SEPT. 1
2			1st Battle of Varennes { begins ends.	2
3		(3.) Battle of the Mortagne[a] ends.[1]		3
4		(4.) Battle of the Grand Couronné[c] begins.[2]		4
5	Retreat from Mons ends.	"BATTLE OF THE FRONTIERS" ENDS. Battle of the Ourcq begins.[d]	**Battles of the Marne begin** *including* (i.) Battle of the Ourcq begins.[1]	5
6		**Battle of the Marne[e] begins** *including:—* (ii.) Battle of the two Morins[d] begins[2]. (iii.) Battle of the Marshes of St. Gond begins[3]. (iv.) Battle of Vitry begins[4]. (v.) Battle of Revigny begins[5].	(ii.) Battle of the Petit Morin begins.[2] (iii.) Battle of Fère-Champenoise begins.[3] (iv.) Battle of the Marne begins.[4] (v.) Battle of Vaudecourt–Fleury begins.[5]	6
7	Battle of the Marne, 1914, begins		Capitulation of Maubeuge.	7

[a] In the French list the Battle of the Ourcq is included within the Battle of the Marne, although the respective dates are as shown.
[b] This is the date for the ending of this battle on the front of the German Vth Army. On the IIIrd Army front it is shown as ending on August 30th and on the IVth Army front on August 29th.
[c] Alternative official title—"Battle of Varennes–Montfaucon"
[d] The "Bataille des deux Morins" is shown in the French list as a "Bataille d'ensemble" and, as such, should, strictly, be in heavier type, the general heading, " Battle of the Marne," being still heavier.
[e] Subdivisions of the Battle of Lorraine (see pp. 5, 6 and 8).

[8369]

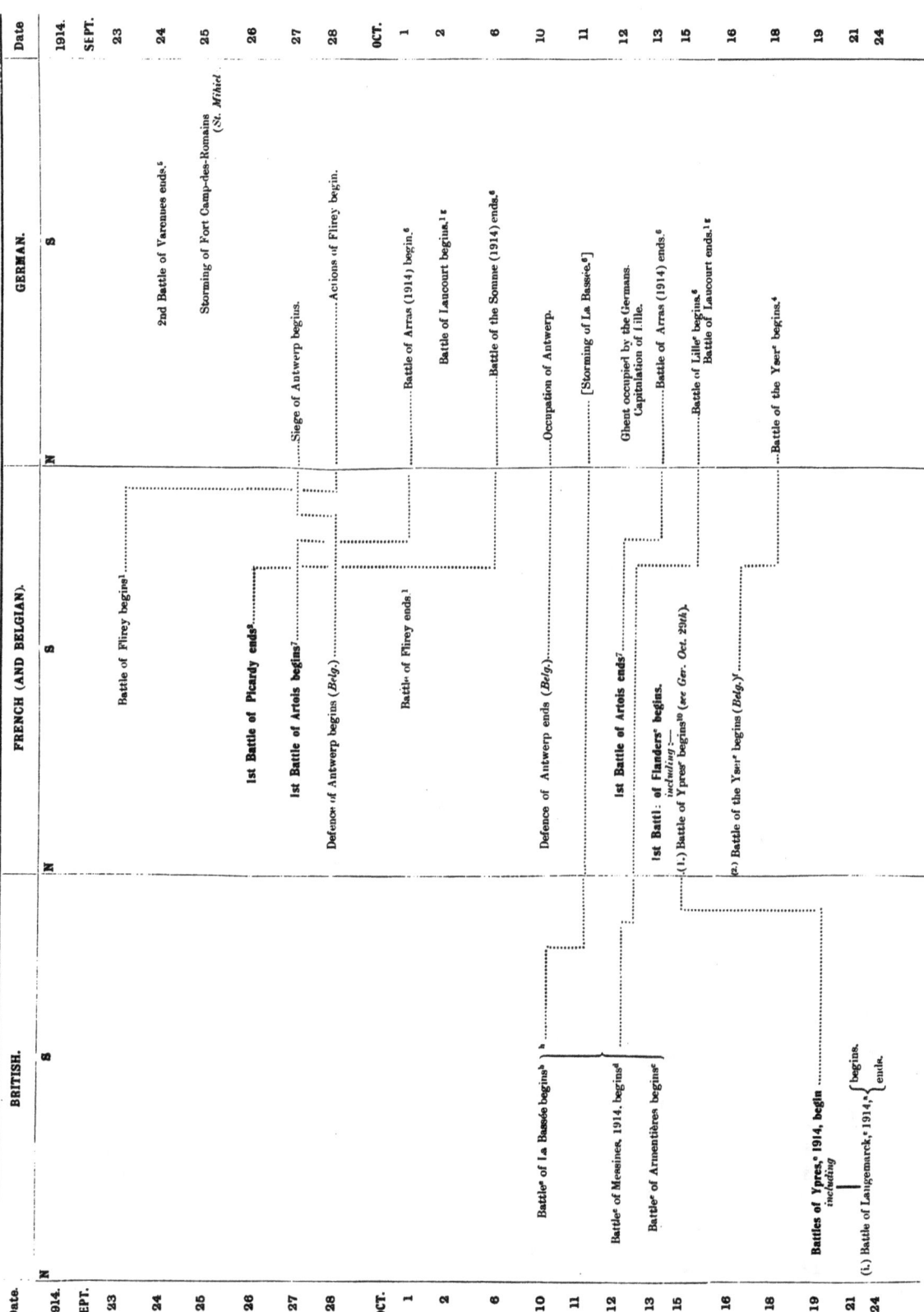

Date.	BRITISH.		FRENCH (AND BELGIAN).		GERMAN.		Date.
	N	S	N	S	N	S	
1914. OCT.							1914. OCT.
28					Battle of Lille ends.[c]		28
29	{begins.........						29
30	(ii.) Battle of Gheluvelt				Battle of Ypres begins[d] (see Br. 19th and Fr. 13th).		30
31	} ends.		Battle of the Yser ends (Belg.)				31
NOV.							NOV.
2		Battle of Messines, 1914,[a] ends[d] Battle of Armentières ends[c] Battle of La Bassée ends[b]					2
6							6
10			(2.)Battle of the Yser ends (Fr.)		[Dixmude stormed by German forces.[d]]		10
11	(iii.) Battle of Nonne Boschen[a] (one day)						11
13			(1.) Battle of Ypres ends[10] and 1st Battle of Flanders ends.				13
22	**Battles of Ypres, 1914, end**						22
24					Battle of Ypres ends.[d]		24
27							27
30					Battle of the Yser ends.[d]		30

[a] British Ist Corps.   [b] British IInd Corps.   [c] British IIIrd Corps.   [d] British Cavalry Corps.

[e] Up to October 28th the British "Battle of Messines," 1914, corresponds to the northern portion of the German "Battle of Lille." After that date the fighting round the Messines Ridge is considered by the Germans as the southern portion of the "Battle of Ypres."

11

Date.	BRITISH.	FRENCH (AND BELGIAN).	GERMAN.	Date.
1914. DEC.				1914. DEC.
14	Attack on Wytschaete.		The December Battle in French Flanders begins.[e]	14
20	Defence of Givenchy, 1914, {begins.	1st Battle of Champagne begins[d]. (See March 17th, 1915.)	1st Battle of Perthes begins.[a,3]	20
21	ends.			21
24			The December Battle in French Flanders ends.[e]	24
30			*1st Battle of Perthes ends.[3]	30
1915. JAN.				1915. JAN.
8		Actions of Crouy begin[d]	Battle of Soissons begins.[1] *2nd Battle of Perthes begins.[b,3]	8
13			*2nd Battle of Perthes ends.[3]	13
14		Actions of Crouy end[d]	Battle of Soissons ends.[1]	14
25	1st Action of Givenchy, 1915.		Affair at Givenchy.	25
FEB.				FEB.
1			*3rd Battle of Perthes begins.[c,3]	1
5			*3rd Battle of Perthes ends.[3]	5
16			*4th Battle of Perthes begins.[b,3]	16
17		1st Action of Vauquois (one day)†. 1st Action of les Eparges begins†	Action at Vauquois. Actions at Combres begin (see March 28th).	17
19			*4th Battle of Perthes ends.[3] 1st Battle of Münster begins.	19
21		1st Action of les Eparges ends‡ (see March 18th).	*The Winter Battle in Champagne begins.[3]	21
28		2nd Action of Vauquois begins‡ (see March 6th).	Actions at Vauquois begin (see April 16th).	28

[a] Alternative official title—" Battle of Souain, Perthes-les-Hurlus and Beausejour."
[b] Alternative official title—" Battle of Perthes-les-Hurlus and Beausejour."
[c] Alternative official title—" Battle of Perthes-les-Hurlus and Massiges."   [d] Alternative unofficial title—" Affair at Soissons.
* These five Battles together correspond to the French " 1st Battle of Champagne."
† Semi-official.   ‡ The names of these actions are semi-official, but the dates are from unofficial sources.

[8369]

Date	BRITISH	FRENCH (AND BELGIAN)	GERMAN	Date
1915. MARCH.				1915. MARCH.
6		2nd Action of Vauquois ends‡ (see Ger. April 16th)		6
10	Battle of Neuve Chapelle begins[1]		Battle of Neuve Chapelle begins.	10
13	Battle of Neuve Chapelle ends[1]			13
14			Battle of Neuve Chapelle ends.	14
17		1st Battle of Champagne ends[4] (See Dec. 20th, 1914.)		17
18		2nd Action of les Éparges begins‡ (see Feb. 21st.)		18
20			The Winter Battle in Champagne ends.[3] 1st Battle of Münster ends.	20
27		2nd Action of les Éparges ends‡		27
28			Actions at Combres end (see Feb. 17th).	28
APRIL.				APRIL.
3		1st Battle of the Woevre begins		3
5		3rd Action of les Éparges begins‡	The April Actions at Flirey begin. Actions at Combres begin.	5
9			Actions at Combres end.	9
12		3rd Action of les Éparges ends‡		12
16			Actions at Vauquois end (see Fr. Mar. 6th).	16
17	Capture of Hill 60[2]—fighting begins		Actions of Hill 60 begin.	17
20			The April Actions at Flirey end.	20
21			Actions of Hill 60 end.	21
22	Capture of Hill 60[2]—fighting ends. Battles of Ypres, 1915, begin[3] including { begins[a]	Actions of Steenstraet begin (Belg.)	Fighting at Ypres[b] begins.[a] including Battle of Pilkem–Langemarck[a] begins.[a]	22
23	(i.) Battle of Gravenstafel Ridge[3] { ends	1st Battle of the Woevre ends	Battle of Pilkem–Langemarck[a] ends.	23

[a] The first gas attack.
[b] The full official title of this battle is "The Great Break-through over Pilkem–Langemarck and the heights north of Ypres." ("Grosser Durchbruch über Pilkem–Langemarck bis zu den Höhen nördlich Ypern"). "Kämpfe um Ypern."
‡ The names of these actions are semi-official, but the dates are from unofficial sources.

Date.	BRITISH.	FRENCH (AND BELGIAN).	GERMAN.	Date.
1915. APRIL.				1915. APRIL.
24	(ii.) Battle of St. Julien[a] { begins.		Actions at les Eparges begin.[d]	24
MAY.				MAY.
4	} ends.			4
5		Actions of Steenstraet end (Belg.).		5
7			Actions at les Eparges end.[d]	7
8	(iii.) Battle of Frezenberg Ridge begins.[a]			8
9	*Battle of Aubers Ridge (one day)	*2nd Battle of Artois begins[b]	.......The Spring Battle of La Bassée and Arras begin.[c] [e]	9
13	(iii.) Battle of Frezenberg Ridge ends.[a]			13
15	*Battle of Festubert begins.[1]			15
24	(iv.) Battle of Bellewaerde Ridge begins.[a]			24
25	(iv.) Battle of Bellewaerde Ridge ends.[a] *and* Battles of Ypres, 1915, end[a]. *Battle of Festubert ends.[1]			25
JUNE.				JUNE.
15	*2nd Action of Givenchy, 1915,[1] { begins.		Fighting at Ypres ends.[a]	15
16	} ends.			16
18		*2nd Battle of Artois ends[b]		18
JULY.				JULY.
19	1st Action of Hooge.[a]			19
20		Actions of the Lingekopf begin.‡	.......2nd Battle of Münster begins. (See Oct. 14th.)	20
23			.......The Spring Battle of La Bassée and Arras ends.[c] [e]	23
30	2nd Action of Hooge.[a] †			30
AUG.				AUG.
9	3rd Action of Hooge		.......Affair at Hooge.	9
22		Actions of the Lingekopf end.‡ (See Ger. Oct. 14th.)		22

[a] The German entry covering these two actions is:—"Fighting at Hooge, May 26th–Sept. 30th. The action of August 9th is, however, mentioned separately. [c] Alternative official title—"Battle of the Loreto Height."
[d] These actions were German counter-attacks against the positions lost in the three French attacks (see previous page). † The first liquid fire attack.
[e] These engagements together correspond to the German "Spring Battle of La Bassée and Arras." ‡ This name is semi-official, but the dates are from unofficial sources.

[8369] B 3

Date.	BRITISH.	FRENCH (AND BELGIAN).	GERMAN.	Date.
1915.				1915.
SEPT.				SEPT.
22			The Autumn Battle in Champagne begins.[7]	22
25	Battle of Loos begins[1]	2nd Battle of Champagne begins. 3rd Battle of Artois begins[10]	The Autumn Battle of La Bassée and Arras begins.[a,6]	25
OCT.				OCT.
8	Battle of Loos ends[1]			8
13			The Autumn Battle of La Bassée and Arras ends.[a,6]	13
14			2nd Battle of Münster ends. (See July 20th and Fr. Aug 22nd.)	14
15		3rd Battle of Artois ends[10]		15
NOV.				NOV.
3			The Autumn Battle in Champagne ends.[3]	3
6		2nd Battle of Champagne ends		6
DEC.				DEC.
1916.				1916.
JAN.				JAN.
FEB.				FEB.
21		Battle of Verdun begins. including (1.) The Defensive Battle of Verdun begins.	Battle of Verdun begins.[5]	21
25			[Storming of Fort Douaumont.]	25
26				26
MAR.				MAR.
APRIL.				APRIL.
MAY.				MAY.
21	German Attack on Vimy Ridge		Actions of Givenchy-en-Gohelle begin.	21
JUNE.				JUNE.
2[b]			Actions of Givenchy-en-Gohelle end.	2[b]

[a] Alternative official title—" Battle of Loos and Hulluch." [b] And see next page.

Date	BRITISH.	FRENCH (AND BELGIAN).	GERMAN.	Date
1916.				1916.
JUNE.				JUNE.
2	Battle of Mount Sorrel begins[a]		Actions of Double-Hill 60 and Hooge begin. [Storming of Fort Vaux.]	2
3			Actions of Double-Hill 60 and Hooge end.[b]	3
13	Battle of Mount Sorrel ends[a]			13
24		Battle of the Somme begins[c]	Battle of the Somme begins.[c 1 2]	24
JULY.				JULY.
1	Battles of the Somme, 1916, begin *including*			1
	(i.) Battle of Albert, 1916, begins.[4]			
13	(i.) Battle of Albert, 1916, ends.[4]			13
14	(ii.) Battle of Bazentin Ridge begins.[4]			14
15	(iii.) Battle of Delville Wood begins.[4]			15
17	(ii.) Battle of Bazentin Ridge ends.[4]			17
23	(iv.) Battle of Pozières Ridge begins.[5]			23
AUG.				AUG.
29			(Field-Marshal von Hindenburg succeeds General von Falkenhayn as Chief of the General Staff of the Field Armies.)	29
31		(1.) The Defensive Battle of Verdun ends		31
SEPT.				SEPT.
3	(v.) Battle of Guillemont begins.[4] (iii.) Battle of Delville Wood ends.[4] (iv.) Battle of Pozières Ridge ends.[5]			3
6	(v.) Battle of Guillemont ends.[4]			6
9	(vi.) Battle of Ginchy (*one day*).[4]		Battle of Verdun ends.[5]	9
15	(vii.) Battle of Flers–Courcelette begins.[4 5]			15
22	(vii.) Battle of Flers–Courcelette ends.[4 5]			22

[a] Canadian Corps. [b] This date in the German list may possibly be a misprint for "13." [c] Includes the "preparatory period." This battle-front was held originally by the German IInd Army. The front was subdivided and the southern portion allotted to the 1st Army on July 19th

[8369]

Date.	BRITISH.		FRENCH (AND BELGIAN).		GERMAN.		Date.
	N	S	N	S	N	S	
1916.							1916.
SEPT.							SEPT.
25		(viii.) Battle of Morval begins.⁴					25
26		(ix.) Battle of Thiepval Ridge begins.⁵					26
28		(ix.) Battle of Thiepval Ridge ends.⁵ (viii.) Battle of Morval ends.⁴					28
OCT.							OCT.
1		(x.) Battle of the Transloy Ridges begins.⁴ (xi.) Battle of the Ancre Heights begins⁵					1
18		(x.) Battle of the Transloy Ridges ends.⁴					18
24			1st Offensive Battle of Verdun begins		Actions of Douaumont and Fort Vaux (one day).		24
NOV.							NOV.
11		(xi.) Battle of the Ancre Heights ends.⁵					11
13		(xii.) Battle of the Ancre, 1916, begins.⁵					13
18		(xii.) Battle of the Ancre, 1916, ends⁵ *and* Battles of the Somme, 1916, end⁵		Battle of the Somme ends⁵				18
26						Battle of the Somme ends.¹ ²	26
DEC.							DEC.
12			(*General Nivelle succeeds General Joffre as French Commander-in-Chief.*)				12
15						Actions of Louvemont and Bezonvaux {begin.	15
16			1st Offensive Battle of Verdun ends		{end.		16
18							18

¹ The French official dates for the "Battle of the Somme" are "1ᵉʳ juillet à la mi-novembre."

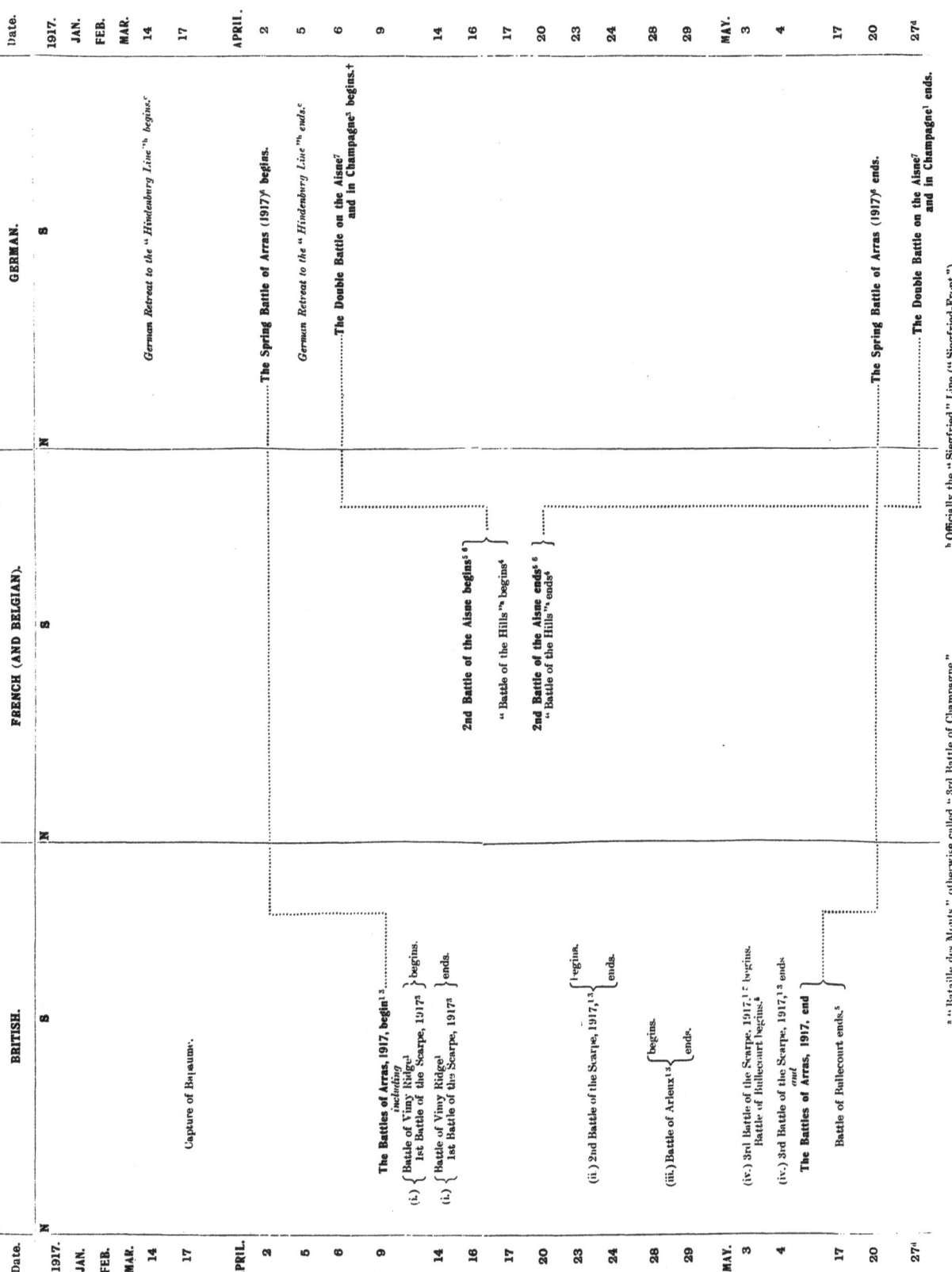

Date.	BRITISH.	FRENCH (AND BELGIAN).	GERMAN.	Date.
1917.	N S	N S	N S	1917.
MAY.				MAY.
27[a]			Battle of Flanders (1917) (first phase[b]) begins.[4]	27[a]
JUNE.				JUNE.
7	Battle of Messines, 1917, begins[2]		Battle of Wyschaete and Messines (*one day*).[4] Battle of Hooge (*one day*).	7
14	Battle of Messines, 1917, ends[2]			14
JULY.				JULY.
9				9
10	German Attack on Nieuport (*one day*)		Storming of the Bridgehead at the Yser Mouth { begins.	10
11			{ ends.	11
21			(First phase of the Battle of Flanders (1917)[b] ends.)	21
22			The Summer Battle of Flanders (1917)[c] begins.[c,4]	22
31	The Battles of Ypres, 1917, begins[5] *including* (i.) Battle of Pilckem Ridge begins.	2nd Battle of Flanders begins[1]	*	31
AUG.				AUG.
2	(i.) Battle of Pilckem Ridge, ends.			2
12			...The Defensive Battle of Verdun begins.[5]	12
15	Battle of Hill 70 begins[1]		Actions at Lens begin.[6]	15
16	(ii.) Battle of Langemarck, 1917[5,9] { begins. { ends.		*	16
18				18
20		2nd Offensive Battle of Verdun begins[5]		20
25	Battle of Hill 70 ends[1]			25
27			Actions at Lens end.[6]	27
SEPT.				SEPT.
17			The Summer Battle of Flanders (1917)[c] ends.[4]	17
18			The Autumn Battle of Flanders (1917)[d] begins.[c,4]	18
20	(iii.) Battle of the Menin Road Ridge[5,9] { begins. { ends.		*	20
25				25
26	(iv.) Battle of Polygon Wood begins.[5,9]		*	26

[a] *And see previous page.*
[b] This "first phase" includes the actions in the "preparatory period" before the Messines battle.
[d] Officially considered the "third phase" of the "Battle of Flanders."
[e] Includes the "preparatory period."
[f] Officially noted as "days of heavy fighting" ("Grosskampftage") in the Flanders battle.
[c] Officially considered the "second phase" of the "Battle of Flanders."
[f] After the Battle of Pilckem Ridge the British Second Army co-operated in these battles. Other dates so noted are—10th, 22nd and 27th August.

Date.	BRITISH.	FRENCH (AND BELGIAN).	GERMAN.	Date.
1917.	N S	N S	S	1917.
OCT. 3	(iv.) Battle of Polygon Wood ends.[5] [2]			OCT. 3
4	(v.) Battle of Broodseinde (one day).[5] [2]			4
9	(vi.) Battle of Poelcapelle (one day).[5] [2]	2nd Battle of Flanders ends[1]	The Defensive Battle of Verdun ends.[5]	9
12	(vii.) 1st Battle of Passchendaele (one day).[5] [2]		*	12
23		Battle of la Malmaison begins[6]	Affair of Chavignon (one day).[7]	23
24			Actions on the Ailette begin.[7]	24
26	(viii.) 2nd Battle of Passchendaele begins [5] [2]			26
NOV. 1		Battle of la Malmaison ends[6]		NOV. 1
2			Actions on the Ailette end.[7]	2
7	Decision to create Allied Supreme War Council.†			7
10	(viii.) 2nd Battle of Passchendaele ends[5] [2] and The Battles of Ypres, 1917, end[5] [2]			10
20	Battle of Cambrai, 1917, begins[3]		The Tank Battle of Cambrai begins.[b] [2]	20
29			The Tank Battle of Cambrai ends.[b] [2]	29
30	[The German Counter-Attacks at Cambrai begin]		The Offensive Battle of Cambrai begins.[b] [2]	30
DEC. 1	Allied Supreme War Council inaugurated.			DEC. 1
3	Battle of Cambrai, 1917, ends[3]		The Autumn Battle of Flanders (1917) ends[4] and The Battle of Flanders (1917) ends.[4]	3
7			The Offensive Battle of Cambrai ends.[b] [2]	7
15		2nd Offensive Battle of Verdun ends[5]		15

* Officially "Actions on and South of the Ailette." • Officially noted as "days of heavy fighting" ("Grosskampftage") in the Flanders battle.
† See de Italian Theatre of War in Part II (A).

[a] Alternative official titles.—[3] Actions from Fontaine-les-Croisilles to Bellicourt." [b] Alternative official titles. Other dates so noted are the 22nd and 30th October and the 6th November.

Date.	BRITISH.		FRENCH (AND BELGIAN).		GERMAN.		Date.
	N	S	N	S	N	S	
1918.							1918.
JAN.							JAN.
FEB.							FEB.
MAR.							MAR.
21		1st Battles of the Somme, 1918, begin[3] [5]...........		..........2nd Battle of Picardy begins...........		..........."The Great Battle in France"[a] begins[c]	21
		including		*including*		*including*	
		(i.) Battle of St. Quentin begins.[3] [5].		(i.) 1st Battle of Noyon begins[3].		(i a.) Battle[d] of Mouchy–Cambrai begins.[17]	
						(i b.) Battle[d] of Gouzeaucourt–Vermand[e] begins.[2]	
22						(i c.) Battle[d] of St. Quentin–La Fère begins.[18]	22
23		(i.) Battle of St. Quentin ends[3] [5].				(i c.) Battle[d] of St. Quentin–La Fère ends.[18]	23
						{ (i a.) Battle[d] of Mouchy–Cambrai ends.[17]	
						{ (i b.) Battle[d] of Gouzeaucourt–Vermand[e] ends.[2]	
24		(ii.) 1st Battle of Bapaume begins[3].				(ii.) Battle of Bapaume begins.[17]	24
25		(ii.) 1st Battle of Bapaume ends[3].				(ii.) Battle of Bapaume ends.[17]	25
26		(iii.) Battle of Rosieres begins[3] [7]		...........(ii.) Battle of the Avre begins[1]		[Capture of Albert.][18]	26
		(The Doullens Conference.—French and British Governments appoint General Foch to co-ordinate Allied forces.[b]*)*					
27		(iii.) Battle of Rosieres ends[a] [5]				[Seizure of Warfusée–Abancourt.][a] [18]	27
28		(iv.) 1st Battle of Arras, 1918,[3] *(one day)*...........				(iii.) Offensive on the Scarpe *(one day)*.[17]	28
31						(iv.) Battle of Hamel[f] begins.[2]	31
APRIL.						........Actions on the Avre at Moreuil begin.[2]	APRIL.
4		(v.) Battle of the Avre[a] *(one day)*...........				(iv.) Battle of Hamel[f] ends.[2]	4
5		(vi.) Battle of the Ancre, 1918,[3] *(one day)*...........				........Action at Serre.[17]	5
		and				........Actions on the Avre at Moreuil end.[2]	
		1st Battles of the Somme, 1918, end[3] [5].					
6						(v.) { Storming of the Amigny Heights } *(one day)*[f]	6
						{ Passage of the Oise at Chauny }	
						and	
						..........."The Great Battle in France"[a] ends[c]	
8				(ii.) Battle of the Avre ends[1]		........Storming of Coucy-le-Château.[7]	8
				(i.) 1st Battle of Noyon ends[3]			
9*				...........2nd Battle of Picardy ends...........		........(?)	9*

* The whole of the fighting from this date to the Armistice is often referred to, in semi-official and unofficial French accounts as "The Battle of France."
[a] In the German list no direct reference is made to this fighting. The German seizure of Warfusée–Abancourt which compelled the withdrawal from the Rosières line was effected by troops who had crossed the Somme at Chipilly and had taken no part in the Fifth Army battle of the 26th and 27th.
[b] "Grosses Schlacht in Frankreich."   [c] The numbers here given to the phases of this battle are not official.   [d] "Break-through battle" ("Durchbruchschlacht").
[e] "The Break-through between Gouzeaucourt and Vermand."   } Apparently classed as "Battles."   [g] *And see next page.*
[f] "The Break-through through the Hamel position east of Amiens."   }   [h] *See April 14th.*
[j] "The Great Battle in France" is shown as ending on the 6th, as far as the operations of the German XVIIth, IInd and XVIIIth Armies are concerned; but for the German VIIth Army, the terminal date is extended to the 9th, to cover the storming of Coucy-le-Château and the advance to the Oise-Aisne Canal.

Date.	BRITISH.	FRENCH (AND BELGIAN).	GERMAN.	Date.
1918. APRIL.				1918. APRIL.
9	The Battles of the Lys begin[1] *including* (i.) Battle of Estaires begins[a]	3rd Battle of Flanders begins	Battle of Armentières begins.[c 6]	9†
10	(ii.) Battle of Messines, 1918, begins[b] (i.) Battle of Estaires ends[a]		Battle of Kemmel begins.[d 4]	10
11	(ii.) Battle of Messines, 1918, ends.[b]			11
12	(iii.) Battle of Hazebrouck begins[a]			12
13	(iv.) Battle of Bailleul begins.[b]			13
14	*General Foch appointed Commander-in-Chief of Allied Armies[e] in France and Flanders.[g]*			14
15	(iii.) Battle of Hazebrouck ends.[a] (iv.) Battle of Bailleul ends.[b]			15
17	(v.) 1st Battle of Kemmel Ridge begins.[b]			17
18	(vi.) Battle of Béthune (*one day*)[a]	Battle of Merckem (*one day*) (*Belg.*).‡	Battle of Armentières ends.[c 6]	18
19	(v.) 1st Battle of Kemmel Ridge ends.[b]			19
24	Actions of Villers-Bretonneux begin		Battle of Villers-Bretonneux, &c.[e] begins.[2]	24
25	(vii.) 2nd Battle of Kemmel Ridge begins.[b] Actions of Villers-Bretonneux end			25
26	(vii.) 2nd Battle of Kemmel Ridge ends.[b]		Battle of Villers-Bretonneux, &c., ends.[3]	26
29	(viii.) Battle of the Scherpenberg (*one day*)[b] *and* Battles of the Lys end[1]		Battle of Kemmel ends.[d 4]	29
30		3rd Battle of Flanders ends		30
MAY.				MAY.
27	Battle of the Aisne, 1918, begins[h]	3rd Battle of the Aisne begins[f 5]	Battle of Soissons and Reims begins.[1 7]	27

† *And see previous page.* ‡ No direct reference is made in the German list to this battle.
[a] These battles together correspond to the German "Battle of Kemmel." [e] These battles together correspond to the German "Battle of Armentières."
[b] These battles together correspond to the German "Battle of Kemmel." [c] Corresponds to (i), (iii) and (vi) of the British list. [d] Corresponds to (ii), (iv), (v), (vii) and (viii) of the British list.
[e] Excluding the Belgian Army. [f] Battle of Villers-Bretonneux, of the Luce and of the Avre. [g] *See March 26th.* [h] British IXth Corps.

[8369]

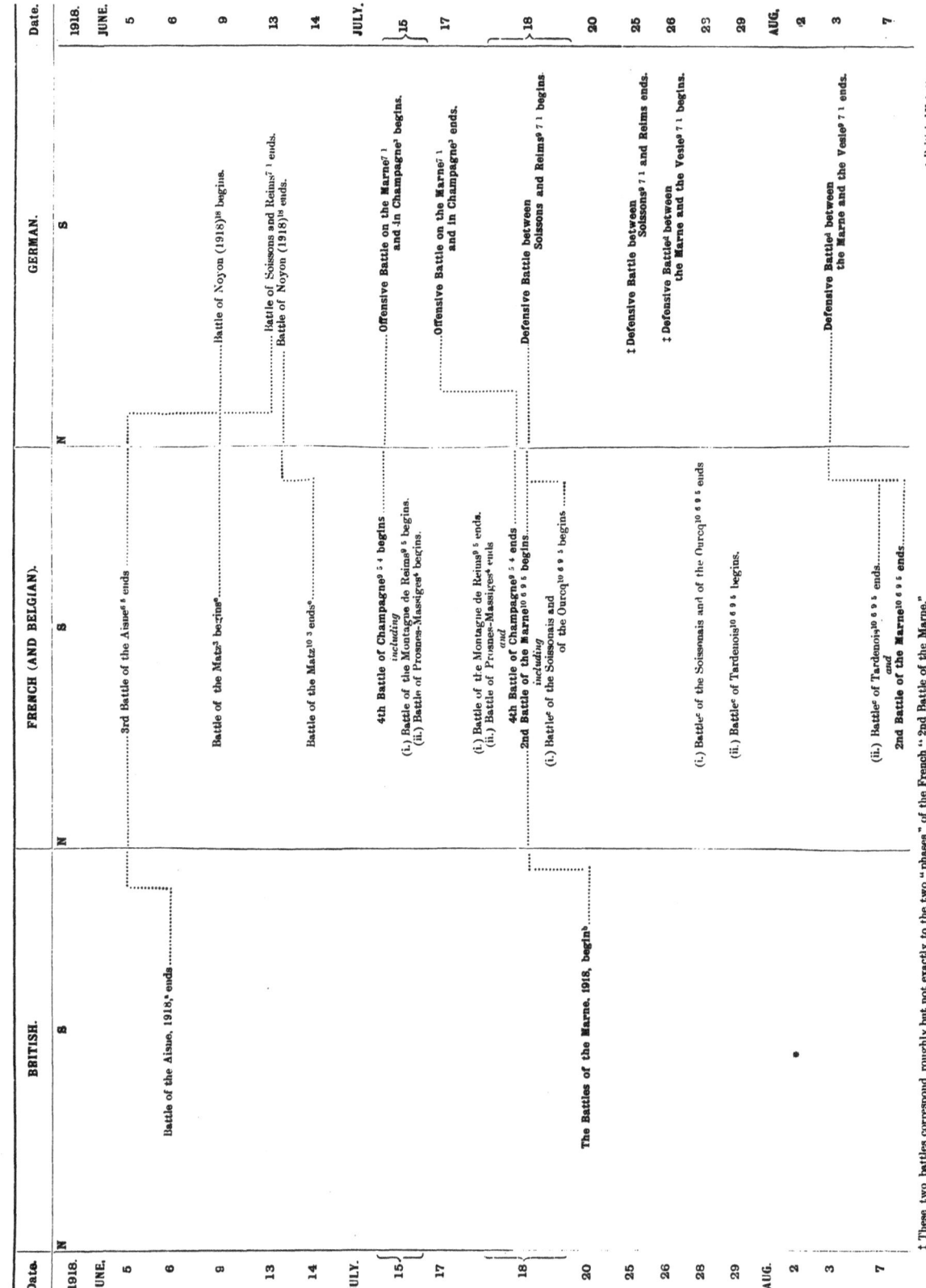

Date.	BRITISH.	FRENCH (AND BELGIAN).	GERMAN.	Date.
1918.				1918.
JUNE.				JUNE.
5		3rd Battle of the Aisne[6] ends		5
6	Battle of the Aisne, 1918,[a] ends			6
9		Battle of the Matz[3] begins	Battle of Noyon (1918)[18] begins.	9
13			Battle of Soissons and Reims[7] ends.	13
14		Battle of the Matz[10 3] ends	Battle of Noyon (1918)[18] ends.	14
JULY.				JULY.
15		4th Battle of Champagne[9 5 4] begins *including* (i.) Battle of the Montagne de Reims[9 5] begins. (ii.) Battle of Prosnes-Massiges[4] begins.	Offensive Battle on the Marne[6 7 1] and in Champagne[6] begins.	15
17			Offensive Battle on the Marne[7 1] and in Champagne[5] ends.	17
18		(i.) Battle of the Montagne de Reims[9 5] ends. (ii.) Battle of Prosnes-Massiges[4] ends *and* 4th Battle of Champagne[9 5 4] ends 2nd Battle of the Marne[10 6 9 5] begins *including* (i.) Battle of the Soissonais and of the Ourcq[10 6 9 5] begins	Defensive Battle between Soissons and Reims[9 7 1] begins.	18
20	The Battles of the Marne, 1918, begin[b]			20
25			†Defensive Battle between Soissons[9 7 1] and Reims ends.	25
26			†Defensive Battle[4] between the Marne and the Vesle[9 7 1] begins.	26
28		(i.) Battle of the Soissonais and of the Ourcq[10 6 9 5] ends		28
29		(ii.) Battle of Tardenois[10 6 9 5] begins.		29
AUG.				AUG.
2	*			2
3		(ii.) Battle of Tardenois[10 6 9 5] ends *and* 2nd Battle of the Marne[10 6 9 5] ends	Defensive Battle[4] between the Marne and the Vesle[9 7 1] ends.	3
7				7

† These two battles correspond roughly but not exactly to the two "phases" of the French "2nd Battle of the Marne."
‡ British XXnd Corps. This date is that of the first engagement of British troops. In the British list this "Group of Battles" is shown as subdivided into the same two battles as in the French list, but with dates, to cover the engagements of the British forces, as follows :—(i.) Battle of the Soissonais and of the Ourcq—July 23rd–August 2nd (*British 15th and 34th Divisions*); (ii.) Battle of Tardenois—July 20th–31st (*British 51st and 62nd Divisions*).

[a] British IXth Corps.
[b] Date British troops were withdrawn from the Marne battles.
[c] These battles represent the two successive phases of the "2nd Battle of the Marne," and, in spite of the distinctive names, each of these two battles covers the whole battle area between Soissons and Reims.
[d] "Die bewegliche Abwehrschlacht"—literally "The Retreating Defensive Battle."
[e] This battle began on June 9th by the offensive of the German XVIIIth Army against the French IIIrd Army. On the 11th the French Xth Army came into the battle with a counter-attack against the right flank of the German advance

Date.	BRITISH.	FRENCH (AND BELGIAN).	GERMAN.	Date.
1918. AUG.				AUG. 1918.
8	Battle of Amiens¹ begins.	3rd Battle of Picardy begins *including* (1.) Battle of Montdidier¹ begins.ᵇ	Defensive Battle between the Somme and the Avreᵃ begins *including* (i.) The Tank-Battle between the Ancre and the Avreᵃ begins. † Defensive Battle between the Somme and the Oiseᵇ begins.	8
9			*including* (1.) Battle of Roye and Lassigny¹⁸ begins. The Tank Battle between the Ancre and the Avreᵃ ends.	9
10			(ii.) Battle of the Roman Roadᵇ begins.	10
11	Battle of Amiens¹ ends.			11
12			(ii.) Battle of the Roman Road ends.	12
15	Actions round Damery begin.ᵇ	(1.) Battle of Montdidier¹ ⁸ ends.ᵇ		15
17	Actions round Damery end.ᵇ⁴	(2.) 2nd Battle of Noyon¹⁰ ᶜ begins. (See Ger. Aug. 28th.)	† Defensive Battle between the Oise and the Aisneᶜ begins.	17
18	Action of Outtersteene Ridge (*one day*).ᵉ			18
20			Defensive Battle between the Somme and the Avreᵃ ends.	20
21	2nd Battles of the Somme, 1918, begin⁵ ⁺ ‡ *including* (i.) Battle of Albert, 1918, begins¹ (*1st phase*)		† Defensive Battle between the Scarpe and the Somme¹⁷ ² begins *including* (i.) Battle of Monchy-Bapaume¹⁷ begins.	21
22	[*2nd phase of Battle of Albert, 1918,⁴ begins.*]		(ii.) Battle of Albert-Péronneᵈ begins.	22
23	(i.) Battle of Albert, 1918, ends.³ ⁴			23
26	2nd Battles of Arras, 1918,¹ begin‡ *including* (1.) Battle of the Scarpe, 1918,¹ begins.			26

† These two battles together correspond to the French "3rd Battle of Picardy."
‡ The British "2nd Battles of the Somme (1918)" and "2nd Battles of Arras (1918)" together correspond to the German "Defensive Battle between the Scarpe and Somme." Their respective subdivisions, however, do not correspond, being arranged to cover the operations of the various armies.
ᵃ No direct reference is made in the German list to this action, which forced the evacuation of the Lys salient. It is covered by the general heading—" Actions on the Ypres-La Bassée front, August 5th–September 6th
ᵇ Offensive by French 1st Army (August 8th) and French IIIrd Army (August 10th).
ᶜ Offensive by British IIIrd Army on 21st, IVth Army on 22nd, and by both IIIrd and IVth Armies on 23rd.
ᵈ Alternative official title—"Battle of the Oise and the Aillette"
ᵉ Includes the offensive of the French Xth Army between the Oise and Aisne and also the operations of the French Ist and IIIrd Armies north of the Oise and thus corresponds to both the German "Defensive Battle between the Oise and the Aisne" and also the "Battle of Roye and Lassigny."

[8369]   D 2

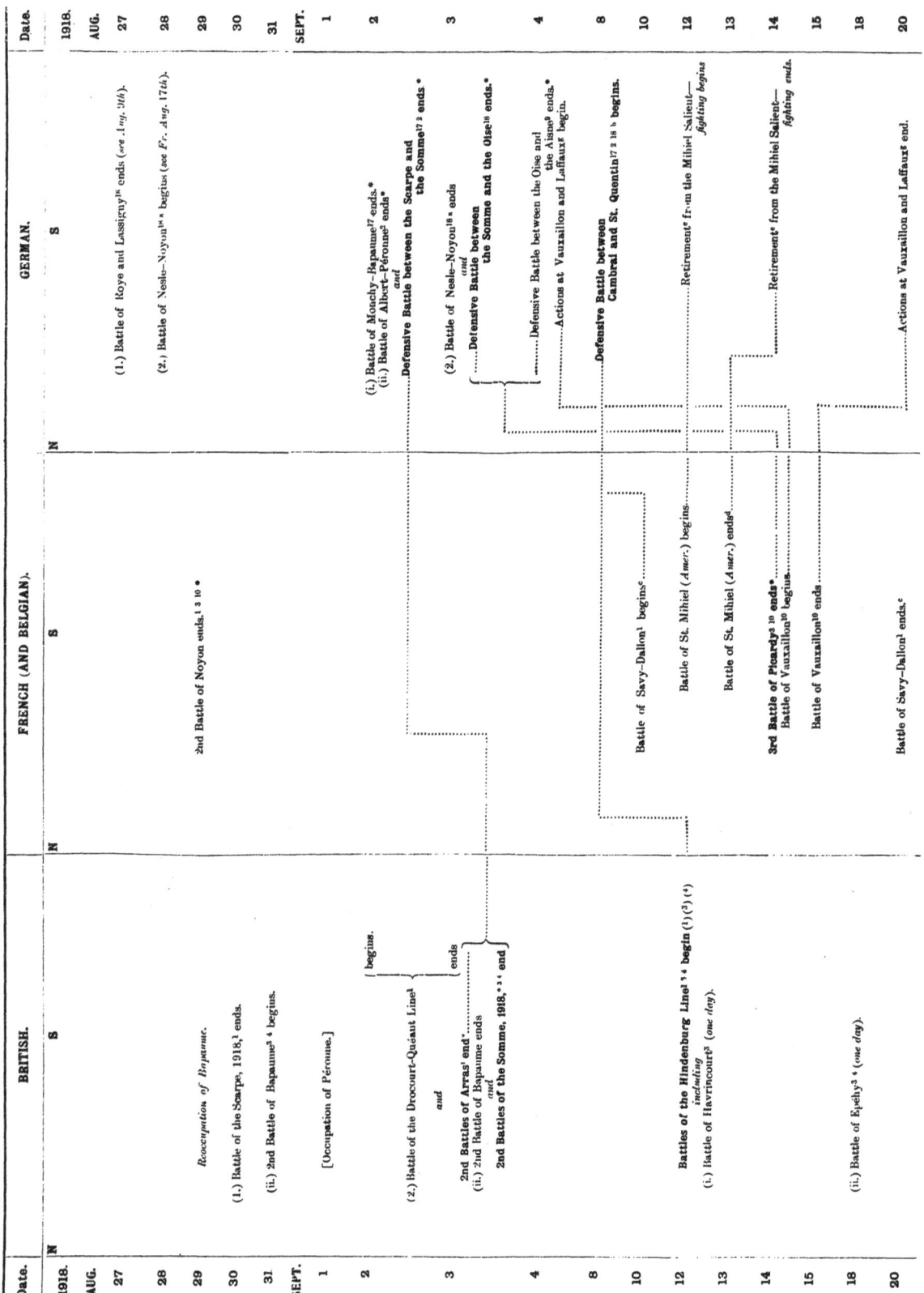

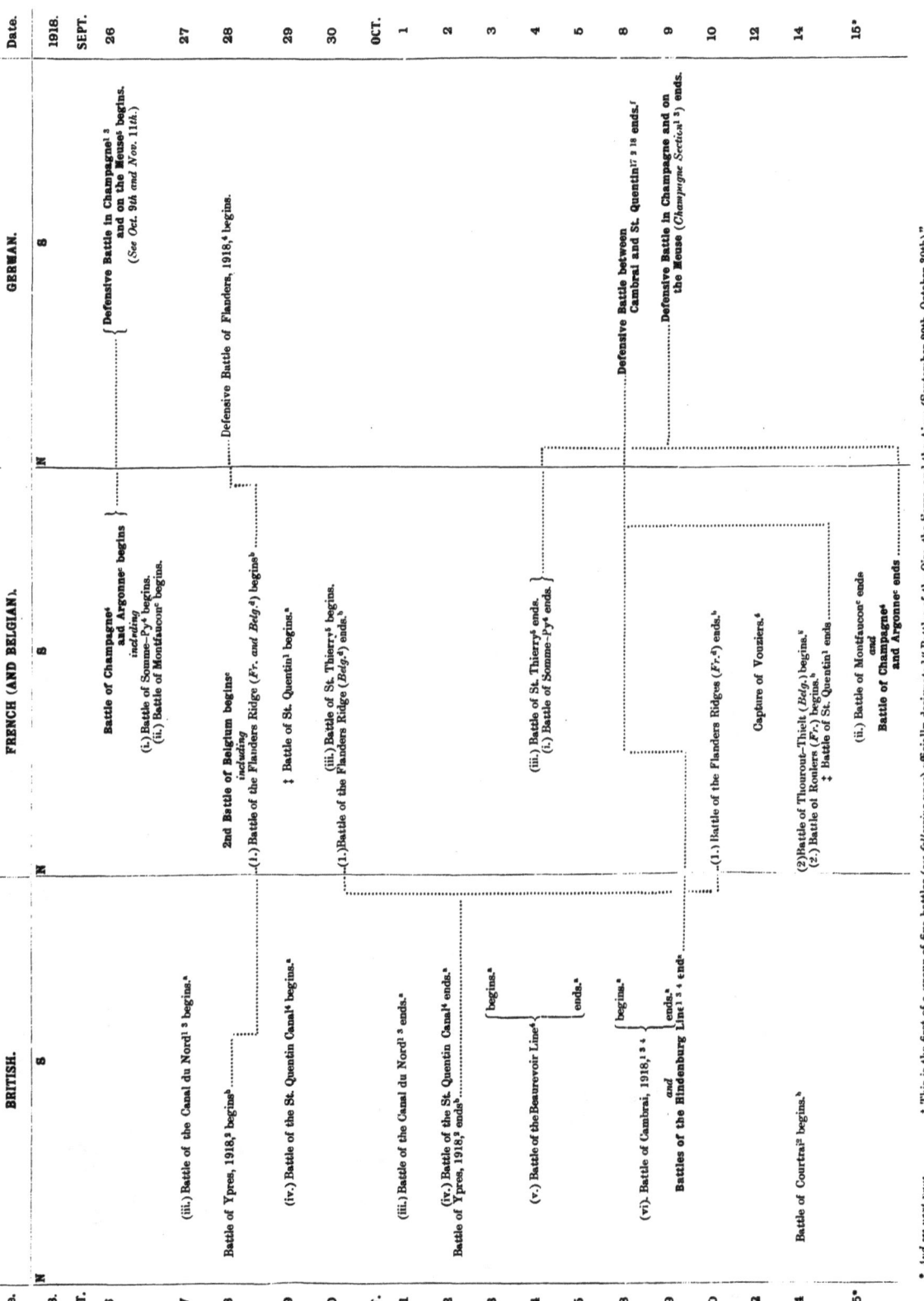

Date.	BRITISH.	FRENCH (AND BELGIAN).	GERMAN.	Date.
1918. SEPT.				1918. SEPT.
26		Battle of Champagne and Argonne begins *including* (i.) Battle of Somme-Py begins. (ii.) Battle of Montfaucon begins.	Defensive Battle in Champagne and on the Meuse begins. (*See Oct. 9th and Nov. 11th.*)	26
27	(iii.) Battle of the Canal du Nord begins.			27
28	Battle of Ypres, 1918, begins.	2nd Battle of Belgium begins including (1.) Battle of the Flanders Ridge (*Fr. and Belg.*) begins.	Defensive Battle of Flanders, 1918, begins.	28
29	(iv.) Battle of the St. Quentin Canal begins.	‡ Battle of St. Quentin begins.		29
30		(iii.) Battle of St. Thierry begins. (i.) Battle of the Flanders Ridge (*Belg.*) ends.		30
OCT.				OCT.
1	(iii.) Battle of the Canal du Nord ends.			1
2	(iv.) Battle of the St. Quentin Canal ends. Battle of Ypres, 1918, ends.			2
3	{ begins.			3
4	(v.) Battle of the Beaurevoir Line { ends.	(iii.) Battle of St. Thierry ends. (i.) Battle of Somme-Py ends.		4
5	{ begins.			5
8	(vi.) Battle of Cambrai, 1918, and { ends. Battles of the Hindenburg Line ends.		Defensive Battle between Cambrai and St. Quentin ends.	8
9		(1.) Battle of the Flanders Ridges (*Fr.*) ends.	Defensive Battle in Champagne and on the Meuse (*Champagne Section*) ends.	9
10		Capture of Vouziers.		10
12				12
14	Battle of Courtrai begins.	(2) Battle of Thourout–Thielt (*Belg.*) begins. (2.) Battle of Roulers (*Fr.*) begins. ‡ Battle of St. Quentin ends.		14
15*		(ii.) Battle of Montfaucon ends *and* Battle of Champagne and Argonne ends		15*

* *And see next page.* ‡ This is the first of a group of five battles (*see following page*) officially designated "Battles of the Oise, the Serre, and the Aisne (September 29th–October 30th)."

a These battles together correspond to the German "Defensive Battle between Cambrai and St. Quentin." b These battles together correspond to the German "Defensive Battle of Flanders, 1918."

c The "Battle of Champagne and Argonne" is the French name for the offensive carried out in concert by the French IVth Army and the American 1st Army. The Americans captured Montfaucon on the first day and their share of the "Bataille d'ensemble" (*up to October 15th*) is called in the French list the "Battle of Montfaucon." The name does not appear in the United States Clasp list: the American Clasp covering this operation is "Meuse-Argonne, September 26th–November 11th."

d "Bataille de la Crête des Flandres" (*Belg.*); "Battle des Crêtes des Flandres" (*Fr.*).

e This is the French general title to cover all the operations of the Group of Armies under the orders of King Albert. The Belgian list uses the equivalent general heading "Offensive des Flandres, 28 septembre–11 novembre 1918," with numbered subdivisions as shown. (See Explanatory Note 4 (ii), page 3.)

f Date extended to the 9th in the case of the XVIIIth Army.

[8369]

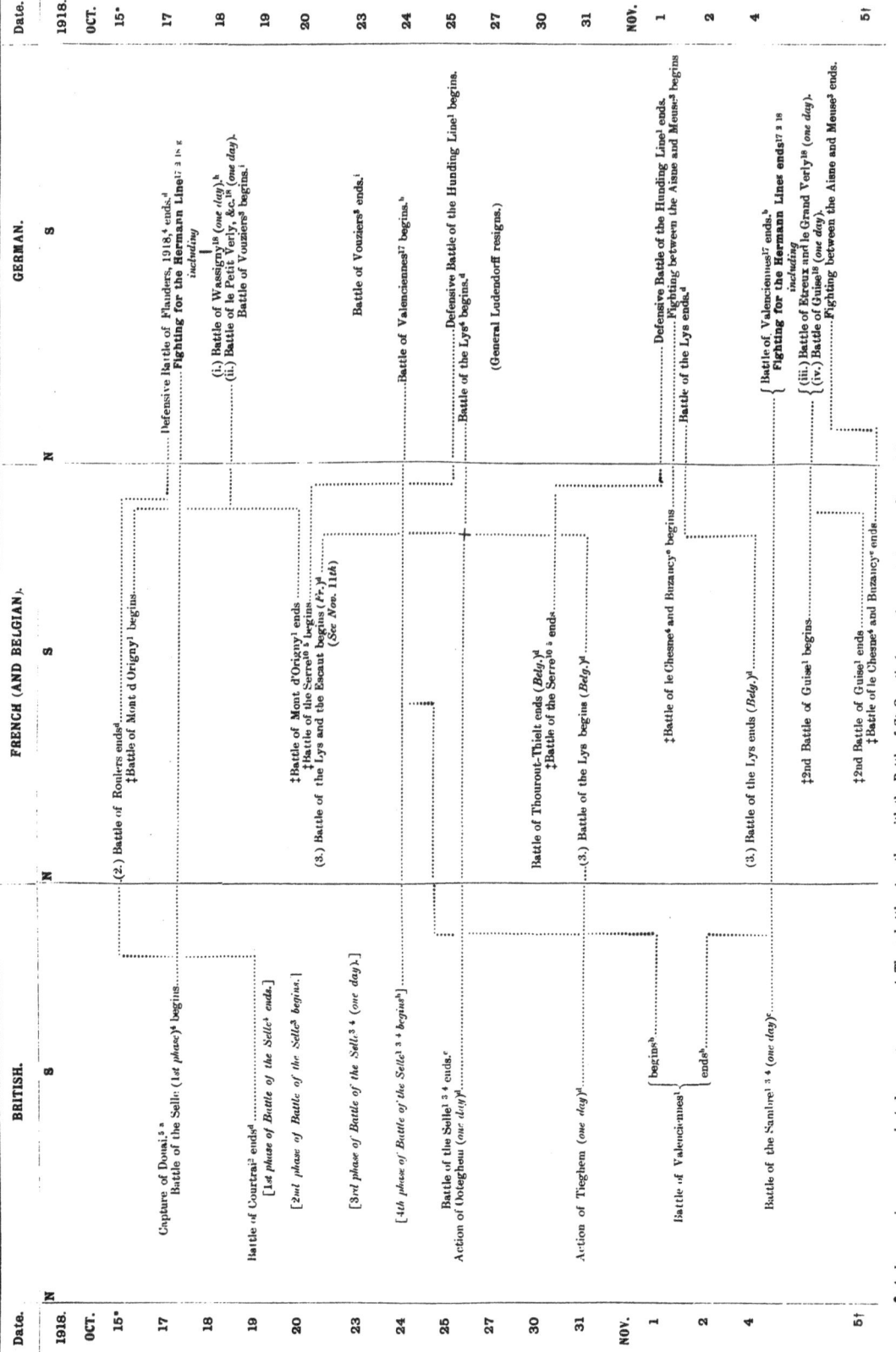

Date.	BRITISH.	FRENCH (AND BELGIAN).	GERMAN.	Date.
1918. NOV. 5†			Fighting to cover the retreat to the Antwerp-Meuse Line[b] begins.	1918. NOV. 5†
6	Capture of Maubeuge.	Battle of Thiérache[1] begins.		6
8		Battle of Mézières[1] begins.	(German Armistice Delegates reach Allied Headquarters.)	8
9			(Revolution breaks out in Berlin.)	9
10			(Kaiser crosses the frontier into Holland.)	10
11	Capture of Mons[1].	(3.) Battle of the Lys and the Escaut ends. *and* 2nd Battle of Belgium ends. Battle of Thiérache[1] ends. Battle of Mézières[1] ends. Meuse-Argonne[a] Offensive (Amer.) ends.	Fighting to cover the retreat to the Antwerp-Meuse Line[b] ends. Defensive Battle in Champagne and on the Meuse (*Meuse Section*[5]) ends. (*See Oct. 9th.*)	11

† *And see previous page.*
[a] "This is the name on the United States Clasp list covering the operations from September 26th to November 11th (*see footnote* [a] *of page 22 and footnote* [c] *of page 21*).
[b] "Rückzugskämpfe vor der Antwerpen-Maas Stellung"—*literally* "*Retreating Actions for the Antwerp-Meuse Position*"). This heading covers the operations of all the German Armies west of the Meuse, viz (from north to south), IV, VI, XVII, II, XVIII, VII, I, III.
[c] *See Note* [a] *to September 26th.*

www.ingramcontent.com/pod-product-compliance
Lightning Source LLC
Chambersburg PA
CBHW080835010526
44114CB00017B/2312